Industrial Engineering Methods and Controls

Industrial Engineering Methods and Controls

Donald R. Herzog

Reston Publishing Company, Inc.
A Prentice-Hall Company
Reston, Virginia

Library of Congress Cataloging in Publication Data

Herzog, Donald R.
Industrial engineering methods and controls.

1. Industrial engineering. 2. Production control.
T56.H376 1985 658.5 83-3343
ISBN 0-8359-3069-6

10 9 8 7 6 5 4 3 2 1

Printed in the United States of America

Contents

Preface

Industrial engineering plays an important role in our national economy and in world economics. Although the industrial engineering function exists in virtually every organization, it is particularly evident in manufacturing and servicing organizations.

This book provides the most comprehensive treatment of the field of industrial engineering methods and controls that is practical in a single volume, with content appropriate for courses in industrial engineering, production, or operations management. An instructor's manual provides answers to questions at the end of each chapter and objective-type examinations for the chapters.

The study of industrial engineering methods and controls may be a basis for future industrial engineering and management studies. It is designed for students of engineering, management engineering, business administration, operations research, and production management, and it provides fundamentals for students majoring in the sciences and managerial economics as well. This book is also intended as a study and reference for executives in all functional areas. The only prerequisites are a knowledge of basic statistics and the ability to think quantitatively.

Many undergraduate and graduate students in business and engineering have never had a course in industrial engineering, production, or operations management, and they need to learn about the production function in an industrial context. Since this book emphasizes methods and controls rather than rigorous theories, it is particularly well suited for introducing the subject.

Because the students who will study this book come from a variety of backgrounds, it begins with industrial engineering and builds from there. Whether used in a technical school, a school of management, a college of engineering, or university, this textbook will adequately serve the student who wants the basic background knowledge as a foundation upon which more advanced industrial engineering courses may be based.

The sequence of topics in this book is as follows: Part I, "Introduction to Industrial Engineering," contains one chapter on industrial engineering in a production environment. Part II, "Quantitative Methods," contains three chapters on statistics, operations research, and engineering economics for industrial engineers. The techniques employed here have been carefully selected so as not to exceed the mathematical capability of an undergraduate university student.

Part III, "Production and Operations Activities," is concerned with the production of goods. It brings together the related components of the industrial engineer as a manager, production engineering, value engineering, materials handling, and plant layout.

Part IV, "Work Methods," contains two chapters, one on work scheduling and one on work measurement. These two chapters are to acquaint the student with a subject that has been slighted in recent textbooks on industrial engineering. Work methods, along with capital investments, are the greatest sources of increasing industrial productivity in America.

Part V, "Operations Control," is an attempt to gather together the types of controls in an industrial production system—production control, statistical quality control, and inventory control.

Part VI, "Safety Engineering," contains two chapters to acquaint the student with industrial safety, industrial hygiene, and environmental engineering. Much legislation on safety has been passed at both the federal and state levels since 1970.

Human factors and safety engineering are very closely entwined, so Part VII, "Human Factors," covers three chapters on this subject. These chapters are concerned with understanding humans as an important part of the man-machine system. Industrial engineers must have an understanding of the physical and mental capabilities and limitations of humans in order to plan and design a production system.

This book contains more material than is required for a three-semester-hour course. It can be used in a three-semester-hour course by assigning selected chapters. The subject matter of Chapters 3 and 4 may be omitted for students in undergraduate business administration degree programs who are less inclined toward quantitative studies.

The book can also be lengthened to a four-semester-hour course by including topics of special interest to the instructor or by assigning special report topics to the student. A student field trip to a manufacturing plant is recommended to gain a better understanding of industrial operations.

Many people have assisted in the preparation of this book. Particular thanks go to Dr. Emil Albert, Associate Professor of Finance, Indiana University at South Bend, for writing Chapter 11, and to Dr. Phillip Freedman, Associate Professor of Psychology, University of Illinois at Chicago, for writing Chapter 17. Special thanks go to Dr. James H. Greene, Emeritus Professor of Industrial Engineering, Purdue University, for his help in refining and improving the first rough manuscript. I also want to acknowledge Professor Fayette Brown, P.E., Emeritus Professor of Mechanical Engineering, California State University at Chico, for review and evaluation of the first revised manuscript. I am indebted to the Department of Defense for using some of their instructional material and to former employers in the aerospace, defense, and electronic industries.

I wish to thank my son, Darwin, for his patience and understanding in foregoing social activities and other events during weekends for many years while this book was under preparation and development. I would also like to thank my secretaries, Mrs. Vivian Sherman, who typed some of the additions and corrections in the first rough manuscript, and Mrs. Carolyn Brochu, for her many hours of contribution. To all individuals at Reston Publishing Company who were assigned to this book, I express my appreciation for their contribution and assistance.

Donald R. Herzog

Industrial Engineering Methods and Controls

Part I
Introduction

Chapter 1

Introduction to Industrial Engineering

CHARACTERISTICS OF INDUSTRIAL ENGINEERING POSITIONS

Two factors, in combination, characterize industrial engineering and serve to differentiate it from other occupations: (1) the kind of work performed; and (2) the qualifications required for the work.

Industrial engineering positions are characterized by the application of scientific and mathematical methods to evaluate or predict the resources needed to produce a product or render a service. This concern with scientific methods forms the basis for the classification of positions in industrial engineering. It should be noted, however, that many industrial engineering positions involve related functions and responsibilities.

For the purposes of this definition, integrated systems of men, materials, and equipment may be found in almost all commercial and government installations engaged in fabrication, assembly, repair, overhaul, or storage: in warehousing or operations involving mechanized materials-handling equipment and related processes required in receipt, packing, storing, and shipping; in managerial, clerical, data processing, or other types of office activities; or in other service functions.

The nature of the function performed is such that the industrial engineer must have broad and intensive knowledge—theoretical and practical—of the characteristics, potentials, and limitations of: (1) the components of the system (men, materials and equipment); and (2) the processes, methods, techniques, and procedures applied in the planning, design, analysis, improvement, and installation of such systems.

The basic means of preparing an individual for professional work in industrial engineering is through completion of a full four- or five-year accredited curriculum in industrial engineering. The curricula vary to some extent, depending upon the fields of industrial engineering that a college or university emphasizes. However, industrial engineering curricula accredited by the Accreditation Board for Engineering and Technology require: (1) courses common to all branches of engineering, including physics, chemistry, mathematics through differential equations, and engineering sciences such as statics, dynamics, strength of materials, thermodynamics, and fluid mechanics; (2) social studies; and (3) specialized subjects characteristic of industrial engineering, such as organization planning, safety engineering, work measurement, facilities planning and layout, materials handling, production planning and control, principles of administration, human engineering, cost accounting, engineering economy, systems and procedures analysis, computer sciences, quality control, operations research, and applied statistics.

While industrial engineering emphasizes the social sciences and industrial management, it shares a large core of knowledge with all branches of engineering. The work of the industrial engineer typically differs from that of other engineers in the relative intensity of application of basic knowledge of those physical and engineering sciences that are common to all branches of engineering; it does not differ in terms of required basic knowledge and understanding of such sciences.

For example, industrial engineering may involve the utilization of professional engineering knowledge in establishing performance requirements, and in reviewing and analyzing the designs of engineers in specialized fields of engineering, with a view toward the successful incorporation of these designs into an integrated system. The industrial engineer, in establishing requirements and analyzing the designs of engineers in other specialized fields of engineering, applies professional knowledge of engineering fundamentals and practice.

Some examples of industrial engineering objectives, and the use of various mathematical disciplines and engineering techniques in the solution of problems are:

1. Developing programs for the optimum utilization of resources by evaluating, specifying, and integrating the processes and the adjuncts to the processes through the use of human engineering systems analyses, mathematical interpretations, statistical analyses, and other specialized techniques.
2. Providing management with the information required to make decisions by designing, evaluating, and improving management information systems and by conducting engineering economy and value analysis studies of alternative courses of action.
3. Improving the efficiency and effectiveness of the organization by various approaches, such as developing organizational, administrative, operating, and production procedures; designing tools, equipment, work processes and methods; developing performance standards, work measurement systems, and other management controls; and designing long-range planning programs, as may be appropriate to the organization served.

INDUSTRIAL ENGINEERING FUNCTIONS

Management and Operations

This broad group of functions covers work performed by industrial engineers in planning and advising management and production officials on the most effective type and form of organization, and on basic standards, methods, and systems and procedures to be used within these organizations. Generally, industrial engineers propose improvements in the form of alternatives and predictions of the results that can be expected from different courses of action. Economy and effectiveness of operations are prime considerations.

Since industrial engineers work with the total system, they are necessarily responsible for the integration of the worker into that system. Industrial engineers are concerned with factors that govern work performance to a greater extent than are most other engineers. Typically, they are required to be familiar with and to apply modern analytical methods in industrial management and industrial psychology.

Industrial engineers advise management on matters such as establishing organizational patterns and systems and procedures, planning flow of work, establishing work controls, planning and controlling quality of a process or product, establishing cost and budgetary controls, and measuring the overall effectiveness of the organization, methods, systems, and procedures. They identify the need for changes in the organization and procedures, and develop plans for the reorganization of facilities. They investigate and evaluate factors affecting performance of men, materials, equipment, and integrated systems. They make or review the results of work measurement and work simplification studies, and they analyze factors leading to fatigue, or affecting safety.

Because of their broad understanding of the basic activities of management and their engineering approach to management problems, industrial engineers are frequently used as staff advisors to top management on nonengineering problems of a high management level, as well as on problems that are characteristic of industrial engineering per se.

Facilities Layout

Facilities layout involves planning or improving the arrangement of machines, equipment, processes, and service areas into a system for achieving the most efficient and economical operation. In making a facilities or office layout, industrial engineers may plan the arrangement or rearrangement of systems of machinery, office equipment, and processes within an individual department or unit, or they may plan for several departments or units comprising an entire operating facility with auxiliary administrative offices.

A facility layout project may involve an investigation and analysis of one process—such as the receipt and storage of incoming materials; methods of packing completed materials; or manufacturing operations, such as metal casting, forging, machining, and the like. Office layout may involve physical placement of personnel and office equipment for optimum space utilization and proper flow to improve office operation effectiveness. On the other hand, the project may require an analysis of all processes carried out in the facility to produce one or more end items or to provide a service.

Plant Design and Location

Plant design involves the functional design of new buildings or the alteration of existing buildings to provide for the introduction of new processes or functions, or improvements of existing processes or functions. Typically, plant design is performed by industrial engineers in conjunction with facility layout work and it may be considered a part of the facility layout phase.

Plant design requirements are generally based on a facility layout developed for an article to be produced or service to be rendered and for the activity or volume of production that is anticipated. The request for a design may originate when a need is recognized as a result of an industrial engineer's analysis of existing production facilities.

Preliminary to plant design, industrial engineers may perform location work for plants or offices. In evaluating proposed sites for plants or offices, industrial engineers generally analyze factors such as available labor supply, available facilities for transportation, accessibility of fuel power and water supply, availability of sanitary and waste disposal facilities, fire protection facilities, topographic features of the site, relative cost of land and buildings, and defense or security considerations.

Industrial Production Planning

This activity involves investigating and evaluating current or future requirements for items to be produced, evaluating and advising on production capability of contractors, and planning production. The production requirements may call for large quantities of products, or for single or small quantities of unique and complex products such as prototype components, developmental models, or test facilities or devices. This activity is comparable to the facility layout phases in that these activities require similar professional knowledge of production systems, machinery, equipment, products, work methods, and procedures. For example, a knowledge of industrial engineering comparable to that employed in facility layout work may be required to make a decision on the capability of a prospective contractor to produce the required item.

DISTINCTIONS BETWEEN INDUSTRIAL ENGINEERING AND RELATED FIELDS

Management Analysis

Management analysts study entire systems or any broad aspect of organizations and operations concerned with management problems but not involving the application of engineering principles and practice. The work requires analytical ability combined with a comprehensive knowledge of: (a) the functions, processes, and principles of management; and (b) the methods used to gather, analyze, and evaluate information concerning the management process.

In nonindustrial and other organizations where primarily knowledge and skill in the principles and techniques of management analysis are important, but professional engineering competence is not a basic requirement, the work of the management analyst and the industrial engineer overlap to a great extent. Distinguishing between the two on the basis of tasks performed during any given assignment may not be feasible in that:

- Both occupations use many of the same analytical tools and fact-finding techniques, including mathematical and statistical methodology.
- Both occupations may exist in the same organization and be concerned with the same general range of management problems.
- Both occupations involve a similar range of levels of difficulty and responsibility extending from training levels to top levels in the system.

In staffing organizations that have as their objective the improvement of management effectiveness, firms may elect to fill their positions with management analysts, industrial engineers, or both. Thus, such positions may be classified as industrial engineers or as management analysts on the basis of the qualifications required by recruitment sources, career ladders, and staffing patterns established by management rather than on the basis of tasks performed or the work environment.

Mechanical Engineering

Industrial engineering is a very dynamic field covering an area of engineering activity that is constantly growing and changing in emphasis.

Most industrial engineering curricula were developed initially as options in mechanical engineering curricula. Thus a close relationship exists between industrial and mechanical engineering, and many positions involve mixtures of activities from these two fields.

Industrial engineers sometimes perform essentially mechanical engineering tasks in the analysis of product design in order to determine how the components may be produced and assembled most efficiently and economically. Recommendations may be specified in terms of minimum standards for health, safety, and comfort, the plans being made by mechanical engineers in another organization, or the recommendations may be in the form of preliminary plans and specifications.

Industrial engineers specializing in the application of materials-handling equipment, for example, may make preliminary plans and develop detailed specifications for an industrial facility. They investigate and furnish advice to production officials on materials-handling procedures, methods, and systems. The recommendations of industrial engineers are based on their study of the facilities where the materials-handling equipment will be installed. Findings typically include an analysis of the methods and organization for handling materials (the human factors) as well as an analysis of the mechanical features of the equipment. The industrial engineers determine the optimum characteristics of the materials-handling equipment, prepare cost analyses and justifications, select and adapt commercial equipment, and prepare plans and specifications for procurement or local manufacture; they may also design simple items of equipment not available commercially (detailed designs are generally made by mechanical or electrical engineers from performance requirements specified by the industrial engineer).

Chemical Engineering

Professional positions involving the design or layout of chemical processing plants, chemical processing equipment, chemical production processes, work methods, and procedures are classifiable under chemical engineering when such design or layout work is based predominantly on a professional knowledge of the chemical reactions occurring in the materials being produced.

Operations Research

Industrial engineers utilize the mathematical techniques of operations research—for example, linear programming—to ensure the most efficient use of resources. However, the work performed by industrial engineers differs from that of operations research analysts in that industrial engineers are required to use professional engineering knowledge and techniques as well as mathematical techniques in planning production processes, work methods, and procedures.

Technician Positions

Certain techniques used by industrial engineers in analyzing organizations, work methods, and procedures are similar to those used in other fields. For example, technicians in industrial engineering undertake work measurement studies and work simplification studies similar to those carried out by industrial engineers. Therefore, a position cannot be identified as a professional industrial engineering position solely on the basis of techniques applied in analyzing organizations, work methods, and procedures. These techniques may be likened to some of the tools that industrial engineers and others use in completing a total analysis.

The similar nonprofessional positions differ from those of industrial engineers in that work performed by the former is based upon a limited and specialized knowledge of production, organization, processes, or facilities. This knowledge is normally of the type obtained by work experience, in contrast to the complete knowledge of the industrial engineer, which includes not only practical work experience but also basic and specialized theories and principles in the mathematical, physical, engineering, and social sciences.

Some technician positions in industrial engineering can be distinguished from industrial engineering positions on the basis of responsibility—that is, the former involve responsibility for only one or a limited number of phases of work present in professional industrial engineering positions. Typical positions in this category involve work measurement studies of production jobs; estimating costs of specific production processes according to standardized techniques; phases of production control such as scheduling and expediting production; and machine layouts or machine utilization studies using standardized procedures or instructions furnished by an industrial engineer.

MANAGEMENT

Two titles are common for positions in industrial engineering: industrial engineer, and manager of industrial engineering. The title of manager should be used for industrial engineering positions involving managerial duties and responsibilities that require managerial qualifications. These titles do not pertain to specializations in subject matter or function.

All positions above the entrance level require application of varying degrees of specialized knowledge relating to the specific work performed. However, the specialized knowledge is typically subordinate to knowledge applied in performing the industrial engineering work that characterized this entry level. When knowing the characteristics of a particular product becomes more important than applying the knowledge in order to adapt the product to production, the position is considered to be outside of industrial engineering.

The qualifications required for all industrial engineering positions are discussed under "Characteristics of Industrial Engineering Positions" at the beginning of this chapter. Additional qualifications required for the work at grade levels are not discussed separately but can be determined from the nature and variety of work, and other pertinent factors.

The Functions of Management

INTRODUCTION

Industrial management encompasses the functions of management performed by and within an organization at its various levels of line and staff. This section deals with management from the organizational point of view.

The five functions of management are:

1. Planning
2. Organizing
3. Directing
4. Coordinating
5. Controlling

Collectively, the functions of management make up the managerial action of the organization. These functions are interwoven and the management process is an ever changing and evolving pattern. It is a cycle of functions; it is rare for management to have only one function at a time; but when viewed sequentially, management logically begins with planning. Table 1–1 lists the various tasks associated with these functions of management.

PLANNING

Planning is the designing of a course of action to meet future needs. Some definitions of planning are:

1. Projecting a course of action.
2. Determining a forward program for governing the future.
3. Proposing a scheme to carry out a decision or project. Planning means providing an orderly step-by-step transition from one situation to another, from one environment to another, or from operating under one set of rules to operating under another set.

Planning is the management tool that recognizes where we are and that delineates where we should go, how and when we should arrive, and the resources we are willing to expend. When the general aspects of a plan are converted into schedules, the time phasing and the means allotted for attainment of specific objectives constitute a program. It is a major device for coordinating the acquisition and utilization of the resources available to the manager.

TABLE 1-1
The Functions of Management

Management efficiency employs men, money, and material, and facilitates the accomplishment of the mission. The functions of management, performed throughout an organization, are described below. They overlap and interlock to produce a total effort.

Planning	*Organizing*	*Directing*	*Coordinating*	*Controlling*
1. Study decision and situation in detail, including limitations.	1. Determine functions required to accomplish the task.	1. Determine the extent of direction necessary by considering the type of operation, the type of organization, the experience and competence of executives, and the policies of top management in relation to the assigned task.	1. Promote intelligent cooperation and mutual understanding.	1. Determine extent, types, and methods of controls necessary to keep all actions oriented toward accomplishing the task.
2. Make reasonable assumptions.	2. Subdivide broad functions into management tasks and group-related functions.	2. Issue timely instructions including when, where, and by whom each task is to be completed; and ensure these instructions are properly understood.	2. Cross-train supervisors and keep them well informed as to overall goals and objectives.	2. Collect, analyze, and evaluate pertinent management information.
3. Develop an initial detailed plan.	3. Establish organizational relationships; use optimum span of control.	3. Supervise execution of the instructions. Be available for consultation and guidance.	3. Encourage lateral and vertical communication throughout the organization.	3. Establish a norm for measuring results.
4. Determine time and resource requirements to support this plan.	4. Select and assign appropriate personnel and other resources to accomplish the task.		4. Synchronize as required with external activities involved.	4. Establish acceptable variances from this norm.
5. Check available resources against requirements of initial plan.	5. Allow for change in mission or resources.		5. Use SOPs and administrative instructions to promote coordination.	5. Take corrective action promptly when acceptable variances are exceeded.
6. If required, adjust initial plan in areas that will least affect the overall task, to balance requirements against available resources.	6. Assign duties and responsibilities with commensurate authority.			6. Make controlling both constant and repetitive.
7. Develop alternate plans.	7. Emphasize essentiality, balance, cohesion, flexibility, and efficiency.			
8. Outline policies and procedures under which the plan will be implemented.				

Concurrent and Continuous Planning

All aspects of planning must be carried on concurrently and continuously. There is no end to planning. Before one phase has been accomplished, plans for successive phases must be prepared. After a phase has become operational, plans must be made for its refinement and improvement. Planning is the responsibility of every level of management.

Planning often includes speculation in areas where many variables occur. Conclusions must be subject to amendment. As implementation unfolds, continual modification and adoption of better courses of action are required. Planning is a continuous process.

Forecasting as a Part of Planning

Forecasting is required in advance of planning. Forecasting means taking a reasoned look into the future to consider the range of possibilities resulting from a projection of current forces and trends. A well-reasoned forecast results in an estimate of the future. This estimate is a basis for planning.

Forecasting is an estimate of anticipated results established from previous experience. Forecasts are influenced by such circumstances as:

1. Proposed or approved budgets.
2. Probable task changes.
3. Limitations of physical plant.
4. Trend of government spending.
5. Known production or work capabilities.
6. Probable availability of manpower.
7. Amount of overtime necessary.

After all the pertinent factors have been considered, the initial groundwork is laid for developing a forecast. It is at this point that the line between forecasting and planning becomes less clear.

The development of a forecast is almost exclusively a matter of forward thinking and decision. The amount of detail will depend largely on whether it is a short-range, mid-range, or long-range forecast; the amount of detail decreases as the range increases.

Often the final result of the forecast will be the probable number of units to be produced or handled during specific time phases, such as trucks to be loaded per week, sales orders to be filled per day, or klystron tubes to be produced per month. A forecast should be stated in simple terms. All of its pertinent elements must be carefully weighed, as plans for future operations will be phased in relation to the forecast.

It is essential that all assumptions used in the forecast be carefully, clearly, and fully stated so that if changes occur during the time covered by the forecast, modifications can be made to keep planning current.

Forecasting is not an exact science. Long-range predictions of five, ten, or fifteen years into the future always involve guesswork to some extent. The payoff results from being able to differentiate between a rational appraisal of the range of possibilities and a guess that is simply a gamble.

Preparing a Plan

After the forecast has been considered, as described above, one is ready to prepare the plan itself. Here again the distinction dims between a forecast and a plan. Preliminary parts of the plan may have been formed mentally, or in writing, during the forecasting. If so, these parts may now become the beginning of the plan. The forecast and the plan will probably overlap in terms of what is to be done to accomplish the mission. As the plan develops, the actions to be taken will become more specific and detailed than they were in the forecast.

The following five steps are guides in preparing a plan. They are not necessarily all-inclusive, nor are they arranged in a particular sequence. The individual planner will make adaptions to fit his particular circumstances.

1. Analyze the Situation to Determine What Is To Be Accomplished. Study in detail the mission, the situation, and the decision. Include in the study all inherent limitations and restrictions that may be imposed. Determine and define in specific detail precisely what is to be accomplished to reach the objective. Make each step an orderly progression from the preceding one. Subdivide the whole problem into manageable segments. Make reasonable assumptions where necessary.

Such an analysis requires the collection of all available information concerning the objective to be attained. Here the planner must determine the purpose of the task assigned. He must visualize the need that created the objective and develop a basic concept of what the objective really is, what service or function it is intended to perform, or what problem it is intended to solve.

2. Determine Time and Resource Requirements. It is essential that the manager know what total resources will be required to accomplish the task assigned to him. A demand to fill these requirements must be placed in the appropriate channels. If the total resources required are not to be made available to him, then it is equally essential that he know what the shortfall is and determine whether or not the task, as originally stated, can be supported.

The manager should consider the requirements for and the consumption rate of manpower, money, material, facilities, and time.

Specific consideration must often be given to the strategic, tactical, legal, political, and economic impacts of the plan. All the above information and requirements must be converted into a detailed and attainable pattern of actions, with alternative actions to meet any logical eventuality.

3. Outline Policies and Procedures within Which the Plan Will Be Implemented. It is necessary to delineate the general policies and procedures within which the plan will be implemented. Appropriate policy statements should be formulated as to the availability and limitations of resources, the time factors, and the character and type of service to be performed for others. Additional policy statements may apply to the manner of execution. Several policies require implementation by:

a. Bold or cautious operation.
b. Commercial contract.
c. Local purchase, or use of inventory.
d. Use of commercial or other facilities.

Procedures are somewhat more specific than policies. They provide more definite guidance on how to accomplish particular portions of the total task. A standard operating procedure (SOP) is often specified for use in accomplishing a repetitive task.

4. Establish Measurable Checkpoints for Direction and Control. Goals provide the basis for control of the plan. Whether a plan is for a short period, such as a day, a week, or longer, it must include checkpoints that provide measurements of the rate of progress toward completion. Checkpoints may be established in relation to:

a. Time.
b. Quantity, in terms of items produced, received, purchased, and used.
c. Quality, which may include work completed to specified standards or attainment of a specified level of performance by persons, organizations, or units; and attainment of qualitative goals through

research, such as reliability of control devices.

Combinations of time, quantity, and quality make it possible to review and to analyze the whole plan in periodic progress reports. Whatever the objective of the plan, deliberate effort should be directed toward reporting its progress. Thus, the checkpoints mentioned above might be combined so that the manager can be kept fully informed.

5. Time-phase the Plan; Make It a Program. Objectives must be subdivided into intermediate goals, or phases, to facilitate control. In view of the continual shortage of resources, the planner must determine the degree of urgency or priority associated with attainment of each goal. A time frame should be set for each phase or goal.

If, for example, a decision is made to close a factory ten months from now, but the factory is required to operate for the next seven months, the analysis of the situation might indicate the need for a plan in two phases. Phase I might cover the period prior to the close of active operations, while Phase II might cover the closedown.

Plan Review

After a plan has been prepared, it should be checked to make sure it includes as many of the following factors as are necessary for its success: resources to be used, outside cooperation or assistance needed, clearly stated assumptions, progress reports to be rendered, time phasing of progress, anticipated trouble areas, final objective to be obtained, and priorities.

Plans for short periods of time are generally better defined than longer range plans. Whether a short-term or long-term plan has been prepared, a decision must be made as to whether it is to serve as a general guide or as a rigid directive.

Special Elements of Planning

In drawing up plans that directly affect employees—for example, plans on work, safety, welfare, working hours, and so on—many organizations now use employees' associations or representation boards to assist in such planning. This procedure is helpful in developing an atmosphere of understanding and acceptance.

One element of planning that is frequently overlooked is personnel relations. What will be the reaction of the people who must carry out the plan? Normally some selling in advance of announcement of the plan is in order, particularly if the plan is contrary to the normal or accepted procedure. The degree of acceptance of the plan by those who must implement it will usually be in direct proportion to the extent that they participated in the preparation of it.

Most people tend to support their own work. If they have had an active part in preparing a plan of action, they feel morally obligated to accept and to support that plan to the best of their ability. That attitude is the manager's reward for encouraging maximum participation of his subordinates throughout the planning process.

Management by crisis or management by drives is normally a sign of confusion and a lack of clear objectives. For example, during an economy drive certain clerks and typists are likely to be released, and key personnel will be forced to do a clerk's job. Such management is an indication of incompetence and a sign that management does not know how to plan.

Alternate Plans

Normally a manager will consider several alternate courses of action before he makes his final decision. Once his decision is made and published, subordinates forecast and plan to implement that decision. Any implementing plans that they may prepare will be limited within the framework of the decision.

This limitation, however, does not preclude the preparation of alternate plans, within that framework, to meet unforeseen contingencies. Alternate plans may be essential to assure accomplishment of the task, and normally no operation should be undertaken without one or more alternate plans. No person can foresee all circumstances, or be assured that circumstances will remain favorable to any single plan that may be prepared. For this reason, alternate plans to provide for varying circumstances are indispensable tools for the astute manager.

Limitations of Planning

Planning is not the panacea for every problem or situation, nor can there be a plan for every possible contingency. Many problems, situations, and contingencies can be handled satisfactorily with a knowledge of the facts, general policies of the organization, and the availability of resources. Several factors that should be evaluated prior to directing the preparation of a plan are:

1. *Time.* Time is expensive. All phases of a plan, its development, coordination, and maintenance, are time-consuming.
2. *Money.* The cost of salaries in developing a plan that is never used is a loss. It must be determined whether the situation warrants this potential loss of productive effort.
3. *Accuracy.* The accuracy of forecasts varies. Experience in forecasting may prove to be unreliable to such a degree that reasonable plans cannot be made.
4. *Margin of error.* In most operations, some margin of error should be tolerated. It is possible to operate without formal plans up to a certain level. Errors may be accepted up to the point where they become more costly than the time and expense of preparing the plans.
5. *Effect on the organization.* Plans cause people to operate in a groove—the groove of the plan. To the extent that they help a manager with limited knowledge, skill, or initiative to conduct an operation in a satisfactory manner, they are good. To the extent that they cause a knowledgeable and skillful manager with a high degree of initiative to operate under severe restrictions, they are bad. Plans permitting great freedom of action may be excellent for one organization but poor for another because of the different capabilities of their managers. Therefore, when possible, consider the need to prepare the plan in terms of the character of the manager who is to execute it.
6. *Changing situations.* When situations change, plans may have to vary. One or more of the following actions may be helpful in reducing work and minimizing the impact of these changes on the morale of the organization:
   a. Provide all who would normally receive the plan with current statements of facts and policies as a general guide for action, rather than making a formal plan.
   b. Prepare a general but basic plan, and arrange for a simplified system of making changes.
   c. Shift the planning to a different level in the organization.

ORGANIZING

Organizing covers far more than merely drawing lines and boxes. Organization must be concerned with results rather than with functions as ends in themselves.

Organizing means dividing and grouping work to be done into separate and manageable tasks, and assigning resources to be used to accomplish the desired results. Clear definitions of responsibility, authority, and duties, and their relationships are essential. Organizing means determining and establishing the structure, the procedures, and the resource requirements appropriate to the course of action selected. Organizing is a means of simplifying the task of the manager through logical arrangement of the work and the personnel who will do it.

The Organizing Process

Organizing entails the following:

1. Determining the essential functions and work to be done in order to accomplish all tasks.
2. Grouping related functions to facilitate efficiency of operations and use of resources.
3. Defining and establishing organizational relationships.
4. Assigning responsibilities and prescribing commensurate authority and appropriate relationships.
5. Establishing the structure, that is, forming the design for repetitive operations. The organizatonal structure establishes a common set of suppositions and calculated anticipations; it prescribes which element and members of the organization are responsible for which decisions and actions. The structure itself delineates the subgoals for the various parts of the organization and specifically outlines responsibilities at each level. It further describes the pattern for communication and other relationships between and among elements.
6. Assigning personnel and other resources. At this point, arrangement for ideal achievement must be tempered by realism. If adequate resources are not available, the organizational structure may have to be reconsidered or modified, and it may be necessary to ask higher echelons for additional means or alteration of missions.
7. Developing optimum span of control.

The Importance of Organization

Proper arrangement of work and of personnel into logical groupings promotes effectiveness of the organization. The manager, therefore, should give high priority to organization if his efforts and the efforts of others are to attain maximum effectiveness.

Basic Principles of Organization

The following ten basic principles of organization are widely accepted and may be used to evaluate organizational soundness:

Clear objective. The organization should have a clearly stated objective and every segment of the organization should understand its purpose.

Well-defined responsibility. The responsibilities assigned to all segments and to all members of the organization should be specific and understandable.

Decentralization. Authority to act should be delegated to the lowest level practicable, and should be sufficient to allow that level to carry out the responsibilities assigned to it.

Unitary command. Every member of the organization should report to one, and only one, superior.

Limited span of control. The number of individuals reporting directly to a supervisor should not exceed the number that can be effectively coordinated and directed.

Clear channels of communication. Every member of an organization should know to whom he should report and who should report to him. Established channels should be used for all official action.

Functional organization. Each necessary function of the organization should be assigned to a single segment of the organization. Related functions should be grouped and unrelated functions separated.

Defined staff relationship. Staff personnel should act only within the scope of their responsibilities. The more the top manager considers it important for managers to attend to a specific responsibility—such as public relations, safety, planning, and executive development—the more likely it is that the staff position will report to the top manager.

Consistency of organization. To the maximum extent practicable, consistent patterns of organization should be used at all levels.

Management by exception. Delegation refers to the entrustment of responsibility and authority to another and the creation of accountability for performance. Once this has been accomplished, the manager is in a position to invoke the management-by-exception principle whereby he can devote his time and efforts to problems that are exceptional. Success depends on first developing a smoothly operating organization within the range of recognized and acceptable tolerances, thereby establishing the norm from which the exceptions can be determined.

Types of Organizations

No one organizational structure is best. Some believe that personalities should not be a factor, and that organizing is an impersonal application of engineering techniques. Others consider the organization a framework into which people must be fitted, or permitted to fit themselves. The ideal probably lies somewhere between these two extremes. Organization forms usually follow one of four patterns for communications: line, functional, line and staff, or directorate.

Line organization is the vertical type of organization in which authority is transmitted directly to subordinates. The line organization provides excellent control, but in large organizations management tends to suffer from lack of staff assistance for specialized and diversified requirements. In simple line organizations for industry, a supervisor supervises his workers, the manager leads his department, and the director directs his division. Figure 1–1 illustrates this kind of organization.

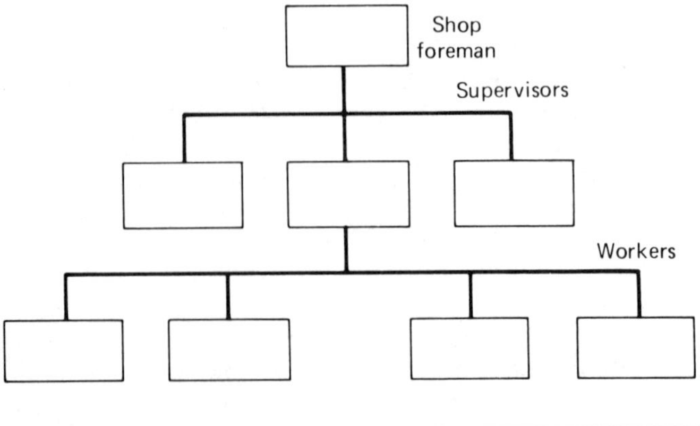

FIGURE 1–2. Line Organization.

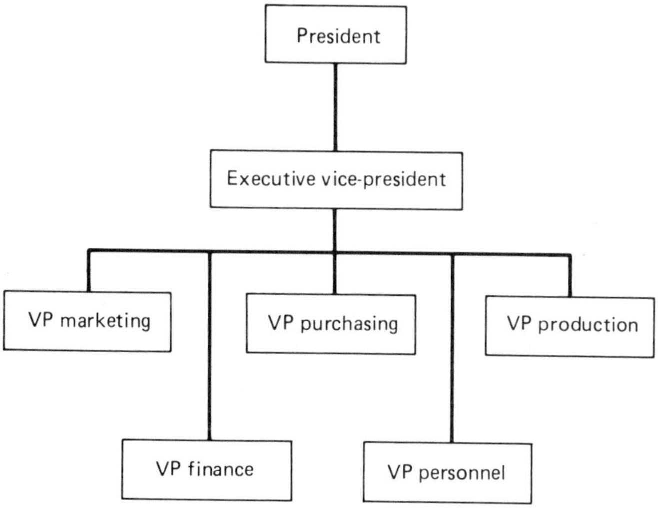

FIGURE 1–2. Functional Organization.

The *functional organization* is the horizontal organization in which each specialist or specialist group is responsible for a function throughout the organization. This scheme provides full use of specialists but may cause poor coordination and control. Many activities lend themselves to grouping by function. Finance and accounting offices are examples of functional organizations. Figure 1–2 shows an example of this type organization.

A modified version of the functional organization has been proposed.[1] It is called the *functional-teamwork* concept. The author of this system postulates that a practical organizational system requires a natural division of responsibilities. Thus the system demands that each function cooperate with every other function in a team effort aimed at achieving the total corporate objectives.

The functional teamwork concept reduces all activities of an organization to the following three:

1. *Process functions.* These are research, purchasing, manufacturing, distribution—anything that must be accomplished by means of repetition.
2. *Resources control.* This is the control of any resource that must be acquired, husbanded, and disposed of, such as: money from stockholders, banks, or higher headquarters; skills of people; facilities, patents, and inventions.
3. *Relations function.* This function embraces the organization's communications effort as it affects the behavior of people inside and outside of it. The function includes timing, effectiveness, and cohesion of the organization's communications as they create an image of the organization in the eyes of customers, government, labor, the community, stockholders, the general public, and the organization's own employees. This function concerns itself not with what is to be communicated, but with how and when it is communicated. It constantly evaluates the effect that communications will have on recipients. Figure 1–3 shows how a commercial organization may be arranged under the functional-teamwork concept.

[1]Fisch, Gerald G., "Line-Staff is Obsolete," *Harvard Business Review,* Vol. 39, No. 5. September–October 1961, pp. 67–86.

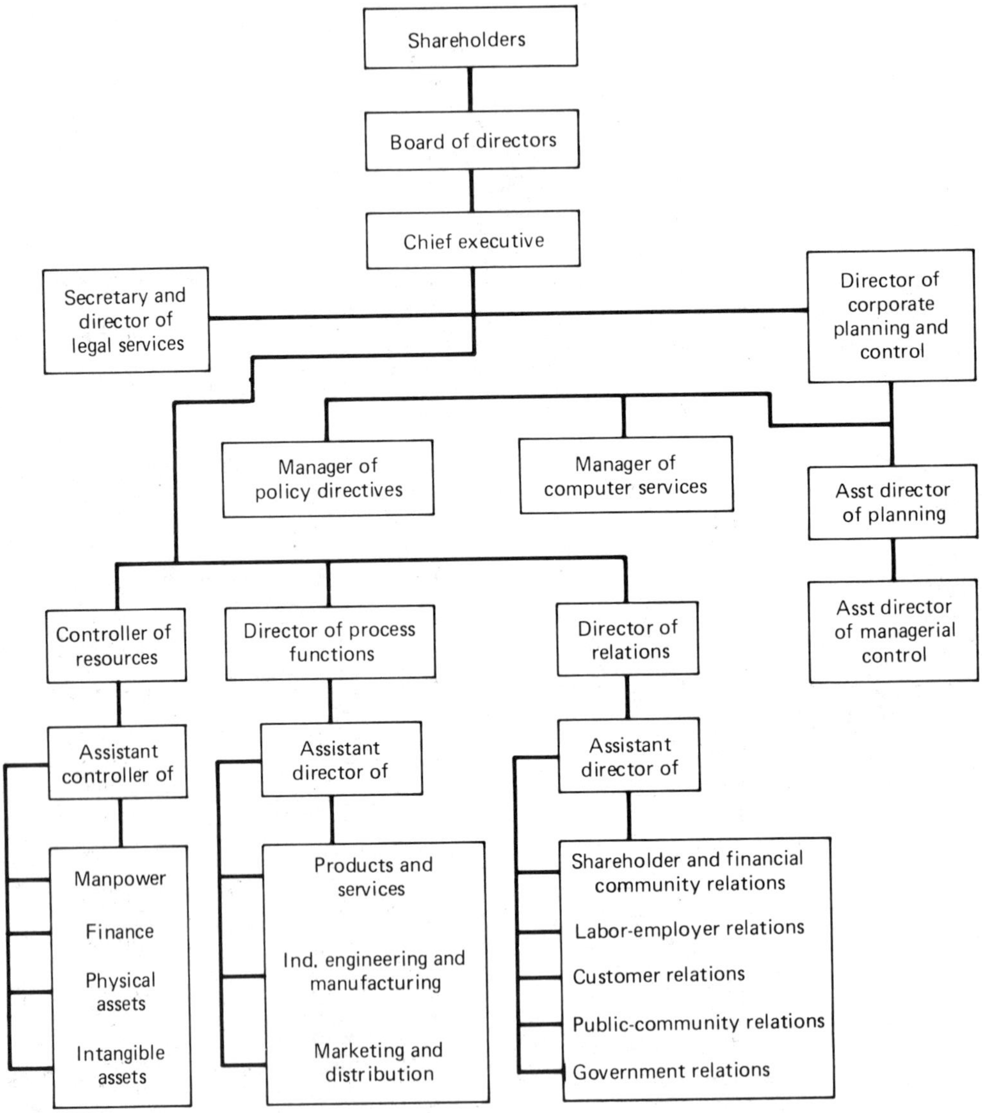

FIGURE 1–3. Functional-Teamwork Concept of Organization.

The line-and-staff organization is a combination of the line-and-functional types. The line has command and operating responsibility; the staff advises on functions, and thus cuts across the entire organization.

The staff is normally a group of specialists. Centralizing such specialized and technical talent into a staff creates certain advantages:

1. Standardizing and coordinating operating practices.
2. Furnishing centralized services for financing, marketing research, person-

nel operations, public relations, legal services, and transportation services.

A directorate type of organization follows either a line, or a line-and-staff pattern, to which much authority has been delegated from above. Depending upon the authority actually invested in an individual such as director of, deputy for, or assistant is used as his title.

The functional arrangement of two organizations may be comparable, but the heads of the respective organizations may have different titles.

There are many variations and combinations of the line, functional, line-and-staff, and directorate organizations described above. Some organizations follow one pattern at one level, and a different pattern at another level. Depending upon such factors as size and complexity, this can be either desirable or undesirable. The type of organization needed to accomplish a job depends almost entirely upon the personal characteristics of the leader and the situation. The functioning of each person and the coordinated effort of the group are both more important than the type organization selected.

Essentials of Organization

While there are many essentials of organization, the following are representative:

1. *Essentiality.* Every activity must contribute to the main objective.
2. *Balance.* Each activity must be effective in doing its part, and its size must conform to the difficulty of the task.
3. *Cohesion.* The structure must facilitate adequate and timely communication and appropriate coordination.
4. *Flexibility.* The organization must permit either expansion or contraction, without disruption.
5. *Efficiency.* Each individual must use all resources economically and to the fullest capacity.

To apply these essentials in the light of functions to be performed requires three basic steps:

1. Breaking the functions down into specific areas of action.
2. Determining the relative importance of each area of action.
3. Setting time schedules for each area of action.

After the above steps have taken place, each area of action is weighed against the appropriate segment of the existing organization to determine if the above five essentials apply. If any one of the five cannot be applied, a trouble area is likely to develop. Either the task or the organization will have to be modified.

Use of Committees

A recent trend has been to make committees an integral part of organizations. Committees provide a wide range of experience and brains to assist top executives in reaching decisions, but care must be exercised that they do not degenerate into general discussion groups that do not produce recommended decisions or the means of implementing them.

The following points are useful in getting the most out of committees:

1. *Size.* If possible, no more than three to seven persons.
2. *Selection.* Persons most directly affected by the problems and the possible solutions.
3. *Advance notice.* Agenda distributed in time to study.
4. *Responsibility.* Normally, purely advisory.

5. *Subject matter.* Must be appropriate to committee composition.

Formal and Informal Organizations

The organization chart is a static picture of the desired formal organization. It shows lines of authority and may indicate lines of staff supervision. It is the framework for allocating work and it often shows the title of the organizational segment, the name of the chief incumbent, and, sometimes, a short statement of the duties. Its main use as far as management is concerned is to prevent an overlapping of responsibilities, to show formal communications channels, and to show how coordination is to be achieved. A chart is static and lifeless; it's the people occupying the boxes on the chart who get the work accomplished. Hanging an organizational chart on the wall will not roll a lift truck off the end of the assembly line.

As an explanation of, and supplementary to the organization chart, an organization and functions manual may be prepared. It usually lists each job shown on the chart and it includes duties, limits of authority, and so on.

Every formal organization also has an informal organization. This informal organization is an unofficial grouping of people, or the unofficial lines of communication based on the day-to-day relationships of individuals and groups within the formal organization. These may be friendship, hobby, or church groups that carry over from outside activities and tend to affect the internal workings of the formal organization. Some contend that the informal organization really accomplishes, or fails to accomplish, the day-to-day mission of the entire organization. It has also been said that the smoothest running organization is one in which the formal and informal organizations are nearly identical. Since it is most difficult, if not impossible, to make major changes in the informal organization, some thought should be given to changing the formal organization when the way things actually happen varies greatly from the way the organization chart indicates they are supposed to be accomplished.

The Leader's Relationship to the Organization

There is considerable discussion in industry concerning the leader's relationship to his organization. The following may assist in analyzing this relationship.

If the purpose of an organization is to produce new ideas, or ideas that will stimulate and persuade others, then it would seem that the dominant frame of reference should be internal, and the organization should be group-oriented rather than leader-oriented. Each member of such a group must be subject to the loosest direction so that he can assert his own ideas, which, interacting freely with the ideas of others, will produce constructive synthesis. Actually this kind of organization is typical of professional groups such as college faculties, scientific research divisions, and law partnerships.

If, on the other hand, the purpose of an organization is to produce something efficiently, it must be leader-oriented, and the management must generally adopt an external frame of reference. Similarly, if the group functions in a highly competitive environment, the leader orientation tends to dominate, for only in this way can the group organize efficiently to meet whatever threat or need exists at any given moment.

The organization should be the eyes and ears of the manager. It should be an extension of his capabilities, multiply these capabilities, and mirror his philosophy. Each office, division, branch, section, and individual must execute its particular task within the framework of the whole organization.

Changing the Organization

Some factors that may cause changes in an organization are:

1. *Changes in tasks.* As tasks are changed, added, or deleted, the elastic structure of an organization can accept and handle them up to a point; but if the expansion of tasks is too great, new operating units and possibly special services will be required. A considerable contraction of tasks may result in subtraction of units and services, and some functions may have to be combined to maintain a reasonable span of control.
2. *Changes in resources.* Changes in men, money, material, time, or facilities may necessitate organizational changes.
   a. *Manpower.* The addition of manpower may add a requirement for additional personal services, training, and logistical support, and for more maintenance in terms of repairs and utilities. Thus, change in this area alone may cause a chain reaction in the operating functions of the organization. Expansion can lead to the creation of new supervisory units in order to retain management efficiency.
   b. *Money.* The availability of a greater or lesser number of dollars may result in the expansion of facilities on one hand, or the practice of retrenchment on the other. Either a considerable increase or decrease in funds may require reorganization.
   c. *Material.* Requirements for care and maintenance of additional quantities of highly specialized equipment or material may require a change in the organization. This is particularly true in the case of introduction of new products or change in design and manufacture of existing products.
   d. *Time.* The time schedule for the completion of a project is frequently changed. Time schedules are usually shortened; seldom are they lengthened. A reduced time schedule may be accomplished by the existing organization within limits, depending upon the capacity of the group. Beyond these limits, the organization must be enlarged, must increase its output, or resort to overtime. This eventuality must be provided for in organizing.
   e. *Facilities.* Buildings, grounds, and laboratories for research, communications, or power generation place heavy demands on an organization. This is particularly true when changes take place in a facility. When a facility is added or subtracted from the major manufacturing plant, organizational changes are often required.
3. *Changes in management.* A shift in the top management structure results in reorganization at different levels within the total organization in terms of either functions or the degree of functions. The establishment of a company headquarters is an example of a change in the management structure. This may result in the elimination of functions at one level and their introduction at another. Substantial staffing changes must be anticipated in such instances.

An additional cause for change may be found in the personality of a new president. He may see reasons for doing things differently and for changing his organization to accommodate innovations. The wise manager will study the situation thoroughly prior to acting to avoid a crisis where none is warranted. Change for the sake of change can destroy the efficiency of the organization.

Centralized and Decentralized Organizations

In popular usage, the meaning of the term *decentralized* varies widely. It may be used to describe delegation of decisionmaking, the reorganization of large units into smaller ones, and geographical dispersion.

Decentralization is often used interchangeably with delegation. An organization is sometimes said to be decentralized if the point of decisionmaking has been pushed down, preferably to the lowest practical level. The location of responsibility and authority is the key to this concept, and the extent of decentralization is measured by the number and importance of decisions made at any given level.

To some degree, decentralization combines the advantages of a small organization's efficiency with the strength and specialization inherent in a large organization. It does so by establishing small integrated units and providing them with specialized services and consultation from headquarters.

DIRECTING

Directing is the act of propelling and focusing operations on target. It refers to the initiating and supervising action used to guide the execution of plans. Furthermore, directing consists of issuing instructions and otherwise indicating to subordinates and lower echelons what is to be done. Directing is the managerial function that gives life to the operations of the organization and constitutes the initiation of actions and day-to-day supervision. Directing provides guidance that keeps the organization producing. Directing keeps the organization in balance with the demands made upon it, and controls the rate of utilization of the organization's resources in fulfilling these demands. With proper direction, the organization becomes an active, living thing, capable of attaining its objectives.

Without proper direction, the unit or enterprise may stagger along. The act of directing ranges from issuing broad mission-type instructions to the other extreme of providing minute details. Experience, the nature of the operation, time, and the size and complexity of the organization will determine the optimum procedure.

The process of directing consists of:

1. Determining the extent of guidance necessary.
2. Selecting the best means of communicating.
3. Motivating individuals or groups to assure the actions desired.
4. Issuing timely short- and long-range instructions that state the tasks and when, where, and by whom they are to be accomplished. These instructions include specific enunciation and amplification of the policies and procedures outlined in the plan.
5. Supervising execution of the decision and keeping abreast of pertinent aspects of the situation. Management must be flexible, and be prepared to react to developments by issuing more, modified, or corrective guidance.

Executing the Decision

The ultimate end of directing is executing the decision. This means implementing action. In this phase, the industrial manager must frequently promote acceptance of his decision by higher authority, and must always motivate subordinate echelons toward enthusiastic compliance with his desires. As mentioned earlier, managerial action consists of a cycle of functions, and at this point the manager must apply with creative imagination all of his personal actions toward ensuring appropriate and willing implementation.

His decision in itself has not changed anything. He must now prescribe actions in sufficient detail and supervise compliance that will change existing circumstances into the situation desired. Frequently only his capacity and experience can assist him; results will be the measure of his success or failure.

Extent of Direction Necessary

The extent of direction necessary depends upon such factors as:

1. *Type of operation.* A stable or continuing type of operation requires less direction than a changing operation. An industrial type of operation turning out the same product repetitively is a vastly different situation than a training activity having varying inputs and frequently changing requirements.

2. *Degree of organization.* Generally a greater directing effort is required in the more complex organizations. It can be expected that greater effort in direction will be required for an organization of several geographically dispersed units than for one in a single location. Usually the directive effort expended will be less in the organization in which the executives practice delegation.

3. *Level of experience.* Whether the entire enterprise or only a portion of it is being contemplated, the requirement for directive effort decreases as the members of the organization develop operating experience. Many matters that initially require considerable problem solving and much directive effort soon become commonplace, and SOPs replace much of the individual supervisory effort.

4. *Competence of executives.* One of the primary reasons for seeking executives and supervisors of demonstrated competence is to reduce the directive effort required at each level of operation. This factor is closely allied with delegation, since there is a greater willingness to delegate if competent executives are present. The authority to take action should be placed at the lowest possible organizational level capable of taking proper action. This leaves the higher executive levels with the greatest p[illegible]ble freedom for major policy directio[illegible]

5. *Management policies.* Managers in an industrial firm are particularly responsive to the will of the president. If the manager personally involves himself in the direction of minor matters that are often the proper responsibilities of subordinates, the result will often be that all executives throughout the organization will follow the same general pattern. This leads the organization to adopt a policy of overdirecting at each organizational level. This is commonly referred to as diluting or usurping the authority of subordinates, or unnecessarily meddling in their business.

Determining the extent of the direction is a matter requiring careful study. In a new organization, considerable direction may be essential. If so, it should be provided but progressively adjusted downward as experience is gained and less direction is necessary.

Communication can make the difference between success and failure. If the manager fails to make known in an understandable manner the exact nature of his requirement, he must be willing to accept the responsibility for possible failure. When comparing face-to-face versus telephone communication, face-to-face communication should always be used unless time, distance, or some other consideration makes it impossible. Even this approach is not infallible, and frequently it is wise to have the receiver repeat the instruction to the originator.

A properly written memorandum or note not only provides a record of the communication for both the originator and the receiver, but it also enhances the chance of accuracy. Writing a requirement and then discussing it orally will usually permit good communication. The manager may know exactly what he wants, but this does not help the members of his organization

... understand him. The ...unication is proper im... ...ould be practiced in an ...nsure that its members ... other and are able to hand... ...ies accurately when they occur.

Directing by Motivating Actions

Every organization has some *esprit de corps.* It may be manifested in the way its members conduct themselves, do their work, engage in social activities, react to orders, or feel about their superiors. Through motivation it is possible to adjust or alter the willingness of an organization to respond to direction. Whenever possible, motivation should be directed toward the individual.

Not everyone is motivated by the same incentives. The members of an organization are likely to be motivated by a number of factors, such as nature of work, working conditions, fair treatment, opportunity for advancement, financial income, and security.

COORDINATING

Coordinating refers to the combining of money, talents, and facilities into a unified effort toward a predetermined and accepted objective. It unifies the efforts of each organizational element into the total effort and unifies balanced execution of collective responsibilities. Proper coordinating practice involves relationships and cross functioning in all directions. Proper coordinating is but an extension of the fundamental principle of unity of effort, and frequently results in discovery of the need for realignment and redirection.

Through coordination the efforts of all members of an organization are directed toward a common purpose. The various functional elements of the organization accomplish their individual portions of the total mission in harmony with all the other elements. Coordination is a management function of such importance that the industrial manager must frequently check the efforts of his organization for both internal and external coordination.

Staff studies, reports, and electronic feedback were never intended to supplant management's responsibility to achieve unification of effort. Coordination becomes even more vital with an increase in automation. The more extended the effort, the more complex the organization, and the greater the need for coordination. Nothing can be more destructive to the attempt to attain organizational goals than the situation in which each element operates without maintaining a cooperative effort with all other elements.

Coordination is the responsibility of every member of an organization, and should be provided for by every manager. It is the thread that ties the whole organization together at every level of activity. It extends down to the individual operator who works in close contact with other operators.

Coordinating must be practiced throughout the management process before, during, and after the planning phase. Frequently it is essential that requirements for coordination be written into each plan. Coordination must be planned and directed, but is more effective when it is spontaneous, automatic, and voluntary. Plans must be prepared, compared, and checked to insure that the degree of balance, which generates further plans and policies, is in harmony with the objectives.

One of the prerequisites is an appreciation and knowledge of goals and objectives, how they are to be reached, and how each unit and element fits into the total scheme. Goals and objectives, assessed and reassessed, must be clearly established. Programs and policies must be clearly enunciated, and authority and responsibility subject to minimum misinterpretation.

Although sometimes necessary, hasty expedients and erratic shifting of emphasis frequently result in confusion and lowered morale. Intelligent cooperation and mutual understanding are required.

Communications and Coordination

Like directing, coordinating is intimately associated with the manager's personal function of communicating. There must be an adequate oral and written communication system throughout the organization.

The manager must be provided with information so he may be assured that good coordination exists within his organization. In order to have at hand information concerning the interrelationships of separate activities, a system of reports should be established on a periodic basis. The simplest indicators should be sought that will provide the information needed. SOPs, extra routing of essential papers, and periodic, but not too frequent, staff meetings are also excellent means of providing lateral and vertical communication.

Another prerequisite for good coordination is an understanding of the various categories of the coordinative effort. Internal coordination aims at unified effort throughout the organization itself. External coordination involves achieving smoothness and reconciliation of efforts with those of higher, lower, and lateral activities not under the jurisdiction of the management. It frequently necessitates clearances, approvals, and authorizations.

Type of Organization

Another distinct influence on coordination is the type of organization. While primarily a matter of the organizing function, overfunctionalization, or excessive specialization, complicates coordination. It generates parochialism and begets disputes; it fosters separate empires and unhealthy competition. In brief, this organization defect simply aggravates management's coordinating task.

Management must be able to recognize the presence of proper coordination, as well as its absence, typified by slowdowns and shortfalls, poor morale, and disruption. Also, it must make itself aware of the coordinative capacity of subordinate management. Abuse of the function, or overcoordination, causes unnecessary confusion, delays, and weak compromises. Results obtained by the organization will be less than the optimum if coordination is not executed appropriately by successive management levels.

Promoting Mutual Understanding

Coordination is intended to generate in all members of the organization a knowledge and appreciation of the organizational objective, how it is to be accomplished, and how each individual or unit fits into the total scheme of the operations. Every opportunity should be exploited to further this effort. Periodic bulletins, newsletters, and similar communications are excellent media. They provide readers with otherwise unobtainable information on what the organization is doing in its own and related fields of activity. This approach helps to build coordination through the promotion of intelligent cooperation and mutual understanding.

The promotion of voluntary coordination through contacts between executives helps each become aware of the total objectives of the organization. Each executive must see his operation in terms of its support of the total operation, and must be prepared to adjust his performance and that of his unit as necessary to achieve integrated action toward a common goal. Coordination must become a voluntary matter that is looked upon as part of the job. A fellow executive may find a weakness or a factor that should be strengthened. It is better for all concerned that the coordinating action reveal this weakness.

CONTROLLING

Controlling refers to the systematic collection, analysis, and evaluation of management information for timely decisionmaking to support continuing or corrective action. Control is concerned with a special relationship between plans and operations. The manager uses controls to learn whether his operation is proceeding according to plan and on schedule. Managerial control means to ensure that each step is carried out as planned, by the person to whom it was assigned, within the time limit allowed, and at the least possible cost for the desired quality.

Controlling provides information on variances from planned actions or established standards that may constitute the basis for corrective action. It includes analysis and appraisal of performance versus established goals and objectives. Controlling is dependent upon the process of planning, organizing, directing, and coordinating. The more efficiently these functions are executed, the easier it will be to control the operation. Some believe that controlling negates delegation of authority and decentralization of operations. Others argue that controlling is such an integral part of the other four functions that it is undesirable to consider controlling separately. It is safe to state that controlling is closely related to the other management functions.

Often the difference between a successful and an unsuccessful operation is a matter of delicate balance. The manager must keep his organization operating at an acceptable standard to meet the demands placed upon it. If the balance swings too far one way, the missions will not be accomplished, and Herculean efforts will be required to restore the operation to a satisfactory position. Conversely, if the balance swings too far the other way, an overpotential is generated and resources are wasted.

Steps in Controlling

The four essential steps in controlling are:

1. To establish a basis for measuring performance in accord with the progress and checkpoint requirements of the plan.
2. To collect necessary data.
3. To review and analyze the data and pertinent related information.
4. To determine need for action, if any.

Each plan or program should include finite and measurable goals and periodic checkpoints. Required data must be collected and at appropriate intervals management must review and analyze progress. This is simply appraisal and measurement of performance. Examples are monthly, quarterly, or semiannual reviews where accomplishments and failures can be measured in terms of deviation from valid goals and realistic standards. In some cases, standards may be prescribed by corporate headquarters; in others, it may be necessary to design either theoretical or engineered standards.

Extent of Controls Required

The extent of controlling required is determined by the:

1. Complexity of missions and tasks.
2. Size and structure of the organization.
3. External controls and restrictions imposed.
4. Amount of delegation and the degree of decentralization practiced.

5. Characteristics of management at all levels.

The more the delegation of authority and decentralization of operations are practiced, the greater is the need for adequate controls. Still, reports required should be limited to the essentials for continuing decisions in pursuit of the task under changing conditions.

The problem of control is one is devising methods that will detect deviations from an approved standard so they can be corrected at the earliest possible time. This correction must be made in order to maintain a balance between the progress of the program and the consumption rates of resources.

Systems of control usually involve performance measurements and reporting in terms of quantity, quality, and the use of men, money, material, time, and facilities. When incorporated into the operating procedures of the organization, they are referred to as built-in controls.

Other Factors in Controlling

Controlling must be constant and repetitive, and management must correct and adjust imbalances. Under new or changing conditions, performance must be measured, reevaluated, and corrected if necessary. Like execution of the other management functions, controlling must receive management's continuous attention.

Most activities of management, if properly carried out, tend to assist in establishing and maintaining control. Probably the most important control, however, is the organization itself. It is the responsibility of each organizational level to control a specific function or segment of the operation. If the organization is operating properly, tasks flow downward, becoming more detailed as they go down through the levels of the organization. Reports flow up, in a form to indicate progress, such as units produced, orders received, quantity shipped, and so on. Reports normally become less detailed as they flow upward.

Developing Standards

Control is implemented through standards against which performance can be measured. Standards afford a yardstick with which to measure efficiency and progress. Additionally, they provide goals of attainment. Standards must be representative of the task being performed and must be capable of measurement. Planning determines standards and goals of an organization. These goals are the intermediate and strategic points at which progress should be measured. Standards of performance should be set up for these points and used as a basis for comparing the actual performance against expected performance.

Standards must also be related to individual responsibility and should be expressed in terms of a manager's assigned tasks. Standards may be determined by: (1) time and motion study, predetermined time standards, and standard data, and (2) sampling, frequency analysis, and similar methods of treatment (based on accomplishments and experience).

Essential Data

The manager should collect only the data that are required to establish and maintain control. He must ensure that plans are being followed and that the task is being accomplished. To do this he must collect information he considers essential to control:

1. Direction of effort of the personnel.
2. Property, buildings, equipment, and finances.
3. Costs.

4. Quality.
5. Quantity.

Once the manager has assembled the data required from personnel reports, engineering data, manufacturing reports, accounting and progress reports, for example, he must interpret the fact in order to evaluate the information and compare it with established standards. Only after this has been accomplished is he in a position to select a course of action and implement it. The manager will seldom, if ever, have all the information he would like to have concerning a given situation, but his job of making decisions will be easier and more fruitful if he is selective in the types of information required.

Collecting Data

Having determined the standards against which performance is to be measured and the points at which these measurements are to be made, the next step is to determine how to collect the necessary data. The manager is concerned with finding how often he needs information for control purposes. Some managers desire to feel the pulse of the organization continuously, while others are satisfied with doing so occasionally. Many managers use both formal and informal sources to obtain data and information. They also use various experience factors to keep them posted on performance.

Most of the data collected reflect status or trends. Information that shows the current situation is known as status data. Information that compares the current situation with that previously set forth in the program is also status data. Such data can be used to evaluate progress. Deviations from the program are indicators on which the manager may take corrective action. Trends are often of vital significance but are frequently overlooked because they are in a status report and do not stand out.

Internal control information and data can be acquired by the industrial manager for purposes of controlling through:

1. Periodic staff meetings.
2. Briefings concerning particular activities.
3. Committee reports concerning special activities.
4. Statistical compilations.
5. Regular and special reports.
6. Periodic program review and analysis.

Control Data

To exercise control, the industrial manager must be informed about significant deviations in performance relative to the:

1. *Satisfaction of task requirements.* Some of the areas involved are services furnished to specific standards, and use of manpower.
2. *Use of funds.* Data on job accomplishment, reimbursement for services, and contractual services apply in this area.
3. *Use of material.* The use of material in production, transportation services, and so on.
4. *Use of facilities.* Date in terms of the facilities used for manufacturing or for support functions.

Time permitting, there is no substitute for personal visits and inspections. By this means the industrial manager assures himself that he is familiar with the steps being taken to accomplish the work. Control through statistical examination, reports, and personal inspection is also desirable, since it combines the analytical efforts of the organization and visual inspection by the manager.

Performance ratios are a useful type control that can be used in a number of areas.

Some examples are:

Use of equipment	$\frac{\text{actual producing machine hours}}{\text{machine hours capacity}}$
Labor	$\frac{\text{annual sales in dollars}}{\text{total annual payroll dollars}}$
Quality of output	$\frac{\text{goods passing inspection}}{\text{total goods produced}}$
Budget performance	$\frac{\text{actual performance}}{\text{estimated performance}}$

Other control techniques are also useful. At least as a starting point, your particular operations can be compared with established industrial averages. For example, compare the number of inspectors in a production unit with Table 1–2.

TABLE 1-2

Industry	*Ratio of Inspectors to Workers*
Ball bearing manufacturing	1 to 4 or 5
Small and very precise interchangeable parts	1 to 8 or 10
Automotive high grade close work	1 to 10 up to 1 in 20
Simple automotive work	1 to 20 up to 1 in 40
Machine tool work	1 to 15 up to 1 in 40
Foundry and general machine shop	1 to 50

Elements of Controlling

The following elements are involved in the process of controlling:

Coordination. Relates all the factors of the plan in point of time and place.

Standards. These are essential to control; they form the comparison yardstick.

Exception principle. Only meaningful deviations from routine should require the special attention of the manager.

Statistical methods. These can enable the manager to utilize the results of analysis of complex data.

Graphic presentation. This element facilitates comparison of performance.

Control Feedback

In a management cycle, the link between review and new planning is often called feedback. It means channeling back into the planning state the lessons learned from experience and includes recommendations on how future plans can be improved. This information, to be effective, must pass to the individual who can act on it and who can make a decision. Feedback provides data on which decisions are made to compensate for variances from the original plan. It is the link that closes the management cycle.

Feedback may be accomplished in a number of ways. Since it is largely a communication problem, any or all communications techniques may be useful for taking corrective action. These techniques include reports, conferences, lectures, staff meetings, charts, and personal inspections. Charts are especially useful in presenting these data in an understandable form, since the information usually concerns variation from an established norm. Charts or graphs may be of many types, such as bar charts, line charts, pie charts, and so on. By gathering, evaluating, and plowing this information back into further planning, the management cycle becomes continuous, and steady progress toward the desired objective is facilitated.

Review and Analysis

Many manufacturing divisions and subsidiaries conduct program reviews and analysis activities on a monthly or quarterly basis in compliance with corporate headquarters' directives. The terms *review* and *analysis,* when not used in connection with the work program, refer to the general process of examining, analyzing, and evaluating any type of data or information.

Essentially, the process of control consists of appraisal. The intermediate goals established during planning may become standards of the control process. Program review and analysis refer to an appraisal of performance against the goals set forth in the program.

Raw data may or may not be in usable form when received. All evaluation is relative to something. Raw data are often compared with past data or standards to determine their true meaning. Existing deviations must be considered in the light of their significance. If deviations are expressed as percentages, then the magnitude of their base (100%) must be examined. For example, a deviation of 10% in a $100 program is only $10, but is $100,000 in a $1,000,000 program. Having determined the significance, the manager must decide what impact it will cause on operations, and take the necessary action to correct the situation.

If an analysis of a single area of operations is desired, a staff study may prove adequate. In a comprehensive appraisal of the performance of the major production division or subsidiary, the quarterly review and analysis procedure as outlined by the corporate information system should be employed.

Policies in Controlling

Policies are another potent control medium. A policy is essentially a principle or group of related principles with their consequent rules of action that condition and govern the successful achievement of certain objectives toward which they are directed. The following are characteristics and requirements of a sound policy:

1. It is based on a careful analysis of the organization's objectives.
2. It should make possible the determination of effective, economical relationships between functions, physical factors, and personnel on the one hand, and organization objectives on the other.
3. It must conform to the accepted standards of conduct.
4. It should be defined in clear terms.
5. It should have stability and flexibility.
6. It should have sufficient breadth to make it comprehensive.
7. It should be complementary or supplementary to other policies already established.

Corrective Action

The manager, having been informed of deviations in performance that indicate a need for adjustments in the operating program of the organization, must initiate corrective action. There are several ways that such action may be communicated to the organization:

1. A formal written directive may be used. Such action may be a directive prepared by a program coordinator and forwarded to the major activity director concerned.
2. A less formal memorandum may be used, in which the manager includes his views and any guidance that he may have for the recipient.
3. The manager may directly inform his subordinates of the corrective action desired. During a briefing, a staff meeting, or a personal inspection, he may inform the responsible individual of his wishes.
4. An announcement in the weekly bulletin is another method of starting corrective action. The house organ or a neighboring community paper may also be a valid and adequate medium for initiating corrective action concerning routing of traffic, parking, care of buildings and grounds, or safety measures.
5. Speeches, on formal or semiformal occasions, afford an opportunity for the

manager to explain his operation and his philosophy for accomplishment, to those having responsibility for implementation. Speeches to the members of the management team on special occasions, such as anniversaries, permit the expression of appreciation for work well done, and furnishing additional guidance as an aid to even better performance.

Corrective action should be directly related to the operation. Any directive that initiates corrective action should be processed through the program coordinator or other responsible individuals so that a formal program change order can be published, and the change properly recorded.

Taking corrective action without recording the action involving the organization is a principal cause of confusion in the orderly process of operations management. A positive mechanism for rapidly processing corrective actions through the organization is required in order to assure internal coordination and the availability of an up-to-date program.

Summary

This chapter has defined the duties of some industrial engineering positions and the functions of management from the organization point of view. Although the five functions of management have been treated individually, the manager must be aware that one or more of the functions is present at all times. The management cycle consists of these five functions with or without reference to each other, and the manager may be actively involved in all five functions concurrently. Feedback from subordinates should keep the manager informed as to the success or failure of the management functions active within the organization at any given time. The functions of planning, organizing, directing, coordinating, and controlling of organizational activities are prerequisites to the successful attainment of assigned objectives.

Planning constitutes the basis for the operations of the organization and assists the manager in determining what has to be accomplished and how much time and resources are necessary for the successful attainment of recognized goals.

Organizing provides for the building of a suitable structure with which to carry out the task of the manager. The organization must support the manager and enable him to get things done efficiently through the organization by promoting efficiency, morale, and production by the group.

Directing keeps the organization on its plotted course and enables it to continue on this course in pursuit of the mission. Motivation, as an essential element of direction, is the spirit that directs men toward desirable actions.

Coordinating is an essential function that allows an organization to attain the assigned goals through balance and cohesive efforts from all resources available. Timely and imaginative coordination promotes acceptance of organizational objectives and harmonizes the programs and policies that will integrate all actions required to promote intellectual cooperation and mutual understanding.

Controlling is actually dependent on the other four functions. It is the one function requiring continual attention, for otherwise the manager cannot be assured that the goals assigned are being attained in accordance with his wishes. This control may be personal or impersonal, but in either case the manager must ensure that he is periodically informed of the imbalances in the execution of the program as viewed against the acceptable standards.

Questions

1. What factors, in combination, distinguish industrial engineering from other related occupations?
2. What are the basic means of preparing an individual for professional work in industrial engineering?
3. List four broad groups of functions performed by industrial engineers.
4. From what major engineering discipline did industrial engineering evolve?
5. How does an industrial engineering technician differ in training and duties from a professional industrial engineer?
6. What are the five functions of management? Briefly explain each.
7. Suppose you were the plant manager in charge of a high technology product firm and you wanted to encourage planning and start preparing a plan for the future. What steps would you probably take?
8. What endogenous and exogenous factors influence forecasting for an industrial firm?
9. What does the organizing process entail?
10. What basic principles of organization may be used to evaluate organizational soundness?
11. Differentiate between line, staff, and functional types of organizations.
12. Select an organization with which you are familiar. Make an organization chart for it. What is the primary form of departmentalization? Is the organization centralized or decentralized? What evidence did you consider?
13. What are some factors that may bring about changes in an organization?
14. What does the process of directing consist of?
15. Define coordinating. Is coordination necessary in a small organization? Why is it necessary in a large manufacturing company?
16. What is the relationship between planning and control?
17. What does an industrial executive do when he is controlling? What steps does an executive take to maintain control?
18. After one implements standards to measure performance, collects the data, and makes a comparison with standards, what must be done next?
19. What are some of the elements involved in the process of controlling?
20. What ways does an executive initiate corrective action?

Bibliography

Ackoff, L. R. *A Concept of Corporate Planning*. New York: John Wiley and Sons, 1970.

Andrews, K. *The Concept of Corporate Strategy*. Homewood, Ill.: Richard D. Irwin, 1971.

Ansoff, H. I., Declerck, R. P., and Hays, R. L., eds. *From Strategic Planning to*

Strategic Management. New York: John Wiley and Sons, 1976.

Bierman, H., and Smidt, S. *The Capital Budgeting Decision.* New York: Macmillan, 1966.

Bowers, D. *Systems of Organization.* Ann Arbor: University of Michigan Press, 1976.

Brigham, E. F. *Financial Management: Theory and Practice.* Hinsdale, Ill.: Dryden Press, 1979.

Brown, A. *Organization of Industry.* Englewood Cliffs, N.J.: Prentice-Hall, 1947.

Chandler, A. D. *Strategy and Structure.* Cambridge, Mass.: MIT Press, 1962.

Christensen, C. R., Berg, N. A., and Salter, M. S. *Policy Formulation and Administration.* Homewood, Ill.: Richard D. Irwin, 1976.

Chruden, H. J., and Sherman, A. W. *Personnel Management: The Utilization of Human Resources.* Cincinnati: South-Western, 1980.

Dale, E. *Organization.* New York: American Management Association, 1967.

———. *Planning and Developing the Company Organization Structure.* New York: American Management Association, 1952.

Dale, E., and Urwick, L. F. *Staff in Organization.* New York: McGraw-Hill, 1960.

Davis, R. C. *The Fundamentals of Top Management.* New York: Harper and Brothers, 1951.

Dew, R. B., and Gee, K. P. *Management Control and Information.* New York: Macmillan, 1973.

Downs, A. *Inside Bureaucracy.* Boston: Little, Brown, 1967.

Drucker, P. F. *The Effective Executive.* New York: Harper and Row, 1977.

Ewing, D. W. *The Human Side of Planning.* New York: The Macmillan Co., 1969.

Famularo, J. J. *Organizational Planning Manual.* New York: American Management Association, 1970.

Fisch, George G. "Line-Staff is Obsolete," *Harvard Business Review,* (September-December, 1961).

Fournies, F. F. *Coaching for Improved Work Performance.* New York: Van Nostrand Reinhold, 1978.

Fox, W. J. *The Management Process.* Homewood, Ill.: Richard D. Irwin, 1963.

Frank, H. E. *Organizational Structuring.* New York: McGraw-Hill, 1971.

Hall, C. L. *The Management Guide.* Standard Oil Company of California, Department of Organization, 1948.

Hodgetts, R. M., and Wortman, M. S., Jr. *Administrative Policy.* 2d ed. New York: John Wiley and Sons, 1980.

Holden, P. E., Fish, L. S., and Smith, H. L. *Top-Management Organization and Control.* New York: McGraw-Hill, 1941.

Hopwood, A. G. *Accounting and Human Behavior.* Englewood Cliffs, N.J.: Prentice-Hall, 1976.

Ishikawa, A. *Corporate Planning and Control Model Systems.* New York: New York University Press, 1975.

Jaques, E. *A General Theory of Bureaucracy.* New York: Halsted Press, 1976.

Kastens, M. L. *Long-Range Planning for Your Business.* New York: AMACOM, 1976.

Kolasa, B. J. *Responsibility in Business.* Englewood Cliffs, N.J.: Prentice-Hall, 1972.

Latham, G. P., and Wexley, K. N. *Increasing Productivity through Performance Appraisal.* Reading, Mass.: Addison-Wesley, 1980.

Lawler, E. E., and Rhode, J. G. *Information and Control in Organizations.* Pacific Palisades, Calif.: Goodyear Publishing Co., 1976.

LeBreton, P. P., and Henning, D. A. *Planning Theory.* Englewood Cliffs, N.J.: Prentice-Hall, 1961.

Leontiades, M. *Strategies for Diversification*

and Change. Boston: Little, Brown, 1980.

Lorange, P., and Vancil, R. F. *Strategic Planning Systems*. Englewood Cliffs, N.J.: Prentice-Hall, 1977.

MacMillan, I. C. *Strategy Formulation: Political Concepts*. St. Paul, Minn.: West, 1978.

McCarthy, D. J., Minichiello, R. J., and Curran, J. R. *Business Policy and Strategy*, rev. ed. Homewood, Ill.: Richard D. Irwin, 1979.

Mahler, W. *Structure, Power and Results*. Homewood, Ill.: Dow-Jones, 1975.

Migliore, R. H. *MBO: Blue-Collar to Top Executive*. Rockville, Md.: Bureau of National Affairs, 1977.

Miles, R. E., and Snow, C. C. *Organizational Strategy and Process*. New York: McGraw Hill, 1978.

Mitchell, F. H., and Mitchell, C. C. "Development, Application, and Evaluation of an Action-Reaction Planning Method." *Academy of Management Review* (January 1980), pp. 83–88.

Mockler, R. J. *The Management Control Process*. New York: Appleton-Century-Crofts, 1971.

Newman, W. H. *Constructive Control*. Englewood Cliffs, N.J.: Prentice-Hall, 1975.

Paine, F. T., and Naumes, W. *Strategy and Policy Formation*. Philadelphia: W. B. Saunders, 1978.

Paine, F. T., and Naumes, W. *Organizational Strategy and Policy*, 2d ed. Philadelphia: W. B. Saunders, 1978.

Pyhrr, P. A. *Zero-Base Budgeting, A Practical Management Tool for Evaluating Expenses*. New York: John Wiley and Sons, 1973.

Richards, M. D. *Organizational Goal Structures*. St. Paul, Minn.: West, 1978.

Robinson, S. J. Q.; Hickens, R. E.; and Wade, D. P. "The Directional Policy Matrix—Tool for Strategic Planning," *Long Range Planning* (June 1978), pp. 8–15.

Rose, T. G. *Top Management Accounting*. London: Sir Isaac Pitman and Sons, 1958.

Rose, T. G., and Farr, D. E. *Higher Management Control*. New York: McGraw-Hill, 1957.

Rumelt, R. P. *Strategy, Structure and Economic Performance*. Cambridge, Mass.: Harvard University Press, 1979.

Shirley, R. C., Peters, H. H., and El-Ansary, A. I. *Strategy and Policy Formulation: A Multifunctional Orientation*. New York: John Wiley and Sons, 1976.

Steiner, G. A. *Top Management Planning*. New York: Macmillan, 1969.

Steinmetz, L. L., and Todd, H. R., Jr. *First-Line Management: Approaching Supervision Effectively*. Dallas: Business Publications, 1979.

Strauss, G., and Sayles, L. R. *Personnel: The Human Problems of Management*. Englewood Cliffs, N.J.: Prentice-Hall, 1980.

Swieringa, R. J., and Moncur, R. H. *Some Effects of Participative Budgeting on Managerial Behavior*. New York: National Association of Accountants, 1975.

Thompson, A., and Strickland, A. *Strategy Formulation and Implementation*. Dallas: Business Publications, 1980.

U.S. Army Institute of Administration, *Fundamentals of Management*. Ft. Benjamin Harrison, Ind.: April 1978.

Vancil, R. F. "What Kind of Management Control Do We Need." *Harvard Business Review* (March–April 1973), pp. 75–86.

Verga, J. F., and Yanouzas, J. N. *The Dynamics of Organization Theory*. St. Paul, Minn.: West, 1979.

Wanous, J. P. *Organizational Entry*. Reading, Mass.: Addison-Wesley, 1980.

Weber, J. A. *Growth Opportunity Analysis*. Reston, Va.: Reston Publishing, 1976.

Weston, J. F., and Brigham, E. F. *Essentials of Management Finance*. Hinsdale, Ill.: Dryden Press, 1979.

Part II
Quantitative Methods

Chapter 2

Statistics for Industrial Engineers

Statistics may be defined as a branch of mathematics dealing with the collection, analysis, interpretation, and presentation of numerical data. In this text the term is extended to include the entire body of methods for studying masses of data and the tools for their consolidation into a few essential facts.

When the decisionmaker uses statistics as a fact-finding tool, he does not personally assemble a mass of data, reduce it to formulas, or run it through various statistical tests. Statistical specialists perform those tasks. But the decisionmaker should know what can be used, what can be done, what results can be reasonably expected, and—most important—how to interpret the results.

Evidence of the practical uses of numerical data can be seen throughout recorded history, but it was not until the twentieth century that statistical theory was widely applied to the problems of decisionmaking. One of the primary forces to influence the expanded use of statistics was the federal government during World War II. The need for vast amounts of high-quality materials within critical time limitations led the government to use the quality control methods then practiced by industry.

The following abridgment of the broad subject of statistics merely indicates the great potential of one of the decisionmaking tools now available to management.

FUNCTIONS OF STATISTICS

Statistics are used mainly in the areas of description, analysis and explanation, and inference or estimation. Description is the simplest application of the concepts of statistics. Any sample or quantity of data may be arranged in a frequency distribution, which may be defined as the quantitative classification of a group of items. The number of items in each class interval is the frequency of that class. Averages and measures of dispersion are computed and shown in charts. A mass of data is thus reduced to as small a set of numbers as possible, and such reduction provides an objective, concise mathematical and pictorial description of the distribution; it also allows for the comparison of distributions.

Statistical description may be entirely deductive, offering relevant information for a whole population. More often it is inductive, providing information on only a sample of the population and permitting generalization through inference. Description is, of course, only a means to the goal of analysis and explanation. In presenting the facts, and in establishing expected and occasionally unexpected relationships, description offers the relevant information for analysis and explanation.

Through analysis it is possible to gain an insight into relationships and perhaps detect hidden factors that affected the data; to determine whether a given sample could have arisen from a particular distribution; and to learn whether two given samples belong to the same population. However, analysis is not an end in itself. Analyses are performed for comprehension and for the purpose of making forecasts and inferences. Inference or estimation is the major effort of statistical inquiry. On

Parts of this chapter are based on Alfred N. Block, *On the Collection and Handling of Data*, Engineering Agency Manual no. 1 (Md.: Chemical Corps Engineering Agency, Army Chemical Center, 1 May 1952).

the basis of selected samples, it is possible to estimate the characteristics of a population. By definition, a sample is a selected part of a statistical population that is analyzed in order to make inferences about the whole population.

The statement of logical and accurate inferences requires the ability not only to analyze statistical data logically but also to refrain from inferring more than is warranted by the analysis. For example, the man who thought he had discovered that eminent musicians were also long-lived was correct in his data but careless in its application. He should have compared the average life span of these artists, not with that of all human beings, including those who die young, but with that of men who attained intellectual maturity. It would likewise be unfair to judge the skill of a surgeon by the number of his patients who have died unless the judgment also considers the total number of his patients. Such abuses of statistics could account for the generalization that anything can be proved by figures.

Statisticians do not perform experiments, nor do they claim expert knowledge of all important aspects of experimentation. Nevertheless, statisticians can and do provide valuable assistance in the evaluation of results.

In the planning phase of a test program, a draft of the proposed experiments is usually written in three parts: a statement of the objectives; a description of the experiments, covering such matters as the types of tests, the size of the tests, and the test apparatus; and an outline on the proposed statistical analysis of the results.

The objectives outline the problem to be solved and the questions to be answered. A statement of objectives might include the following: an examination of a hypothesis either directly or by the verification of predictions derived from it; a determination of the characteristics of a population from a sample survey; a comparative study of the effects of two or more testing processes or procedures on a chosen characteristic of a population; an investigation of samples in order to establish whether they are part of a given population; and an inspection of two or more processes or procedures to prove or disprove their similarity or the superiority of one over the other.

The statement of objectives should also include a detailed account of the one or more populations about which information is desired. The experimenter usually has some definite population in mind to which he plans to apply the results. Since it is seldom possible to draw worthwhile inferences on an extensive population from a single experiment, the scope of the test program should be determined to prevent the establishment of overambitious test plans.

The purpose of experimentation is the collection of adequate data. The test plan provides the collection pattern, defines and describes each process and procedure, and explains the expected role of each process and procedure in achieving the objectives. There is an art to setting up an efficient test program that is closely adapted to the objectives and that can be trusted to answer all questions. For example, it should be clearly established whether the object of a test is to determine the best among different procedures or whether it will also attempt to explain the reasons for the effects produced by the testing procedures.

The test plan often calls for a control—a factor of no particular interest or consequence except as a basis of comparison for the effectiveness of procedures under consideration. Suppose there is a need to compare the effectiveness of three procedures that are qualitatively similar, for example, the effectiveness of three decontaminants in aqueous solutions of prescribed concentration. The basis of comparison—the control—would be the cleaning of the contaminated test area with pure water.

Also included in the test plan should be the number of experimental runs, the types of experimental materials to be used, and the observations and measurements that are to be made. The accuracy of the tests depends largely on this information.

An integral part of a test program is the outline of the proposed statistical evaluation of the test results. This outline justifies the various phases of the test plan and indicates the methods and the reasoning to be used in drawing conclusions from the test results. The outline includes the arrangement of tables to show the results, and a statement of the planned statistical evaluation procedures. It also prescribes any significant tests, statistical examinations, and computations required to meet the objectives of the test program and to decide the issues involved.

Thus statisticians have developed the clear-cut requirements that data must meet to ensure correct interpretation. Statistical methods are merely tools that must be applied by qualified hands in order to turn out useful results.

A statistical procedure that is finding wide acceptance throughout the field of production management is that of quality control. Although the theories used in quality control are largely mathematical and technical in character, the basic concepts are relatively simple. This method is based upon the relationship between reliability and experience regarding a given set of facts. For example, an aircraft mechanic with a certain amount of experience in maintenance of specific aircraft types can predict reliability of engine performance. If the engine performs erratically, the estimate of reliability is said to be out of "control," and efforts are made to determine the factor responsible.

Thus, the relationship of an established reliability factor (performance, quality, strength, and so on) within a given set of facts is the basis for quality control. This technique is especially valuable in programs such as procurement, research and development, and personnel training—programs in which the maximum benefit to the organization is possible only if a certain reliability is maintained in all units. It can be expected that many of the procedures of quality control will change as the processes of automation are extended.

Another statistical concept used by the decisionmaker is that of sampling and inference. Since statistical decisions are based on observations and since obtaining a complete set of observations on a problem would seldom be practical from the standpoint of expense or time, the statistician develops a sampling process. From selected observations, he infers the condition of the whole problem area in question. And on the basis of these findings, the decisionmaker is better prepared to select a course of action.

In the sampling procedure, the statistician applies the theories of mathematical probability to the problem to determine the size of sample required. It is the responsibility of the manager to specify the tolerable degree of error and the risk he is willing to accept. The sampling procedure can be effectively adapted to decisionmaking, especially in those requirements related to the fields of production, procurement, supply, and distribution.

A simplified example of the use of sampling in decisionmaking can be drawn from a maintenance shop that receives a shipment of lumber. For the purposes of this illustration, the shop foreman must decide between two alternative courses of action: to accept or to reject the shipment.

The decision between these alternatives is based on the moisture content and amount of certain grain irregularities in the lumber. The shop foreman specifies the acceptable amount of moisture and irregularities and initiates a test of sampling. On the basis of information thus obtained, the foreman makes his decision in accordance with the previously established criterion.

Although statistics is a useful tool for the decisionmaker, the collection of masses of data is not an end in itself; in fact, the primary managerial function of statistics is to enable the decisionmaker to choose the best course of action in the face of uncertainty.

Much present-day investigation is based on systematic experimentation. Observational data are accumulated, for example, to establish a law, to determine the functioning of an apparatus, to test the quality of some material, or to verify the merits of techniques and processes. However, experiments that require repetitive operations usually yield widely varying results, and this variation introduces an element of uncertainty or even doubt into the conclusions drawn from the data. Further, numerical data may be difficult to understand because of the irrelevant material they contain. When that is the case, it is necessary to isolate the relevant information. To some extent, statistics can do this job by providing the methods for the study of masses of data and the means of consolidating such data into a few essential facts.

Consider, for example, tables containing information on the life expectancy of a specific type of radar tube used by the armed forces. The very mass of the numerical data would create confusion and make the information difficult to use. But if these figures could be reduced to a manageable number, they might present the necessary facts more clearly. In establishing that the average life of the tube, as manufactured, is 28.9 days, the statistician provides concrete information concerning the meaning of the original data. Of course, much more information is hidden in the tables, but some aspects of the data must be temporarily discarded to arrive at a convenient and easily understand general statement.

Almost without exception, a statistical analysis attempts to form an opinion on a very large universe by means of a study of a small part of it. In the example of the radar tubes, it would be impractical as well as impossible to test all tubes at the time of issue, since such a test would destroy their usefulness. The summarized numerical description of a representative sample, however, provides reliable information on the quality of the total number produced.

Most people have confidence in a conclusion stated in numerical language and supported by numerical facts. Statistical analysis represents just such information, and statistics provides the methods and processes used in attaining it, the methods and means for estimating its reliability, and the criteria for determining its significance.

Although quantitative data are unavoidably subject to inaccuracies, this does not affect their usefulness to the decisionmaker. Complete and precise data are not usually required for management decisions.

ORGANIZATION OF STATISTICAL DATA

The statistician seldom retains the incoming data in their original form, since they are too numerous to be handled easily. Such material is rearranged in some compact and orderly form to convey an idea on the general nature of the "distribution" at a glance. Thus the data are grouped, and this procedure is known as "tabulation."

Suppose that a table lists radar tube lives, which vary between 20 and 35 days—a range of 15 days. This range is then subdivided into a number of conveniently sized "class intervals," and the number of data falling under them is subdivided into "class frequencies." The sum of the class frequencies—the "frequency" (n) of the distribution—is, of course, identical with the total number of data being investigated. The "class marks" are the midpoints of the class intervals, and it is assumed that the class frequencies are concentrated at the class marks. Although small errors thus enter the evaluation process, they are fully justified by the saving in computation labor. When the data have been organized into a suitable table, they are ready for the first step in the analysis: the graphic representation of the frequency distribution.

A graphic display presents significant facts of a distribution and emphasizes relationships that otherwise would be difficult to comprehend or that might be overlooked entirely. A column of figures is overwhelming; the same data in graphic form tells an easily understood story. Relative quantities can be grasped visually with a comprehensiveness that is not possible by pure analysis.

The frequency chart or graph shows, for example, the approximate range of values within which the data are found. It indicates any tendency of the data to group about particular values, and it readily discloses the most probable or least probable data locations.

STATISTICAL MEASURES

Statistical methods make it possible to analyze the relationships existing within and among groups of related numbers; and through analysis, it is possible to understand the meaning of numbers. Some statistical measures—averages, means, medians, modes, dispersions, standard deviations, regression, and standard error of estimate—must be expressed in terms of the original data. That is, if the original data are expressed in tons, gallons, or miles, the statistical measurements will be computed in tons, gallons, or miles. Another statistical method, the coefficient of correlation, is used as the comparative measure of association and is expressed as a ratio or abstract number.

Measures of Central Tendency

After the statistician has grouped masses of data into frequency tables or charts to make their meaning clear, the next step is to compute averages that will in some way represent all the numbers of the group. Averages are probably the most widely used of all statistical tools. As a measure of clustering (central tendency) in the distribution, they can present much information. They are used to obtain information on a parent population from the measurement of a sample.

The three most commonly used averages are the arithmetic mean, the median, and the mode (Figure 2–1). The arithmetic mean of a series of data is their sum divided by their number. The formula for the arithmetic mean ($\overline{X}$) of a series of ungrouped measures is written

$$\overline{X} = \frac{\Sigma X}{n}$$

in which n is the number of items; X the values of the individual items; and the symbol Σ is the "sum of."

In an example from aircraft maintenance, the removal and replacement of a defective aircraft shuttle valve has required 20, 23, 22, and 19 minutes in four successive work cycles. The mean time can be determined as follows:

$$\frac{20 + 23 + 22 + 19}{4} = 21 \text{ minutes}$$

The median is the middle item in a series of data arranged according to magnitude. In the case of an even number of data, the midpoint is taken as the arithmetic mean of the two central items. In simple terms, the median is an average of position; the arithmetic mean, a calculated average.

In a frequency distribution the median is that value which divides the data into two equal groups. It is that point on the base scale of a frequency curve or polygon from which the perpendicular will divide the area under the curve exactly in half. The class intervals are set on the horizontal, or X-axis, and the frequencies, on the vertical, or Y-axis. The point of intersection of the basic lines is called 0, or the origin. The distance of a point from 0 on the X-axis is known as the abscissa; the distance of the point from 0 on the Y-axis is known as the ordinate.

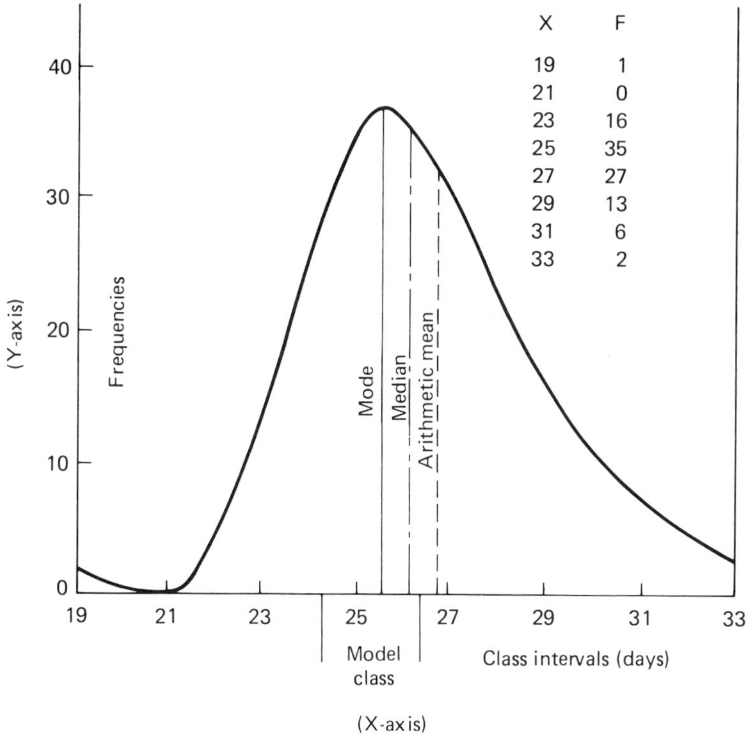

FIGURE 2–1. Representation of Data on the Lives of Radar Tubes.

The mode is an average in which an item appears the most number of times. The class interval that has the highest frequency is called the modal class, and its class mark is called the crude mode. Often an unstable measure of central tendency, the mode is useful when considered as a rough average to indicate the center of concentration in the distribution. For this purpose, it does not have to be calculated as carefully as the median or mean. Although any average is a single value that is supposed to represent a whole group of data, no average can be a valid measure of central tendency if there is a marked variation in the distribution.

For moderately asymmetrical (or skewed) distributions, an estimate of the value of the mode may be obtained from the relationship that exists between the locations of the three measures of central tendency. It has been found that for such a distribution, the distance between the mean and the median is one-third of the distance between the mean and the mode. Since the values of the mean and the median can be determined exactly, the value of the mode may be approximately established through this relationship:

$$\text{Mode} = \text{Mean} - 3\,(\text{Mean} - \text{Median})$$

Applied to the frequency curve of Figure 2–1, the following values are obtained:

Mean = 26.2
Median = 25.9
Mode = 26.2 − 3 (26.2 − 25.9) = 25.3

It should be pointed out that there is no one best average. The essential average is that needed by the decisionmaker, who may or may not be interested in the value that occurs most often or in the observations that fall between or outside certain limits. What is important, of course, is the answer to the question: What must be known about the population in order to make the best decision? In accordance with the established criteria, the decisionmaker must use relevant information, obtained by statistical or other methods, to select the best course of action from the alternatives.

Measures of Dispersion

While averages are used to show a value that is centrally representative of a number of items, measures of dispersion show how much items deviate from a point of central tendency. It may happen that two or more frequency distributions have identical averages even though the distributions are decidedly unlike. For example:

Distribution 1:	120	120	120	120	120
Distribution 2:	116	118	120	122	124
Distribution 3:	36	67	120	140	237

The arithmetic mean and the median of each distribution is 120. Yet there is a considerable difference between the degree of concentration of the data.

The simplest measure of the variation of a group of data is the range—the difference between the highest and the lowest recorded item of the series. The larger the range, the greater is the scatter of values in the series. Although much detailed information is hidden within the range of ages, wages, performance, rainfall, and so on, the quartile and decile deviations show where a certain quarter or a certain tenth of the items are located.

As the most common and useful measure of dispersion, the standard deviation is a valuable tool in statistical analysis. Use of the standard deviation allows the decisionmaker to weigh the element of variation in selecting a course of action from available information. Whereas the arithmetic mean measures the central tendency of a group of items, the standard deviation is used to measure the extent of variation in a frequency distribution, that is, the distance of the items from the mean. The basic formula for the standard deviation of ungrouped data is

$$\sigma = \sqrt{\frac{\Sigma x^2}{N}},$$

and for grouped data it is

$$\sigma = \sqrt{\frac{\Sigma f x^2}{N}}$$

A large standard deviation indicates that the items are widely scattered. Like averages, the standard deviation is expressed in the unit of the original data—tons, gallons, miles, and so on. An example of the calculation of standard deviation is given in Table 2–1, from data listing periodic maintenance inspections of a company fleet of small jet aircraft over a four-month period.

An unsymmetrical frequency distribution is said to be skewed. If there are scattered frequencies with small values, the distribution is skewed to the left, or negatively; if there are scattered frequencies of large values, the distribution is skewed to the right, or positively. When the distribution is perfectly symmetrical, the values of the mean, median, and mode coincide, and the skewness is zero.

When a measure of the degree of skewness is needed, Pearson's coefficient of skewness, as shown below, is generally used:

$$\text{Skewness} = \frac{3\,(\bar{X} - \text{median})}{\sigma_x},$$

TABLE 2-1
Calculation of Standard Deviation

	Aircraft Periodic Maintenance Inspections Completed per Month	Deviations from Arithmetic Mean	Deviation Squared
Mo.	X	$(X - \overline{X})$	$(X - \overline{X})^2 = x^2$
Jan.	29	29 − 30 = 1	1
Feb.	34	34 − 30 = 4	16
Mar.	27	27 − 30 = 3	9
Apr.	30	30 − 30 = 0	0
Total		0	26

Arithmetic mean $(\overline{X}) = 30$
Standard deviation squared = 8.67
Standard deviation $(\sigma_X) = \sqrt{8.67} = 2.94$ inspections.

Normal Distribution

Of the equations that have been formulated to apply to a variety of problems, the normal or Gaussian distribution is sufficiently general to be most useful. This distribution falls in a bell shape so that the two variations or slopes from the middle are uniform and in the shape of a normal probability curve. It is widely applied in statistical work, but not, as is sometimes supposed, because data naturally occur in this form. Most of the distributions found in experimental and observational work are, however, of nearly "normal" type—in which the frequency curves have a maximum near the center and a roughly symmetrical falling-off on either side (Figure 2–2). Experimental evidence has shown that the conclusions reached in theoretical statistics, nearly all of which are based on the assumption of normally distributed data, are not seriously invalidated by a slight departure from normality. This consideration, combined with the fact that the analytical expression of the normal frequency distribution lends itself to mathematical treatment, gives the normal distribution its important place in statistics.

The mean, median, and mode of the normal curve (Figure 2–2) coincide in $\overline{X}$. The curve has its maximum exactly at the center and is symmetrical with respect to the ordinate through $\overline{X}$. The concentration of usable data will be contained within points I_1 and I_2, which are located at a distance of σ (the standard deviation of the

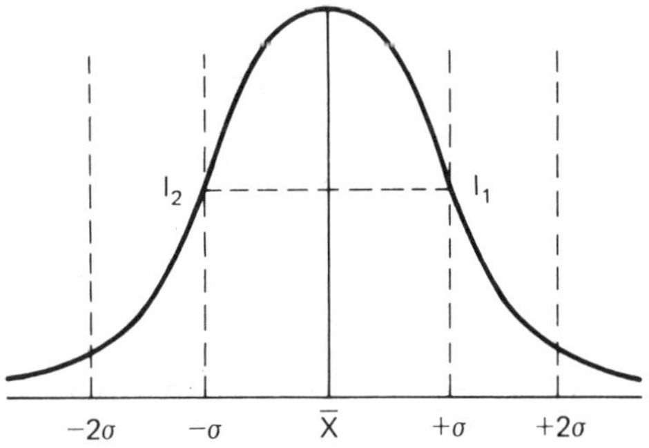

FIGURE 2–2. In the Symmetrical Distribution, or Normal Curve, the Mean, Median, and Mode Coincide.

normal distribution) from the ordinate through $\bar{X}$.

The mathematical equation of the normal probability distribution shows that the interval from

$(\bar{X} - \sigma)$ to $(\bar{X} + \sigma)$ includes 68.27% of all items

$(\bar{X} - 2\sigma)$ to $(\bar{X} + 2\sigma)$ includes 95.45% of all items

$(\bar{X} - 3\sigma)$ to $(\bar{X} + 3\sigma)$ includes 99.73% of all items.

Thus, the standard deviation σ is approximately one-sixth of the range.

If N is set at 1, σ at 1, and $\bar{X}$ at 0, the mathematical equation of the normal curve shows that the curve has its maximum $Y\sigma$ equals 0.3989 for x equals 0. The distribution is asymmetrical with respect to the Y-axis, and very little of the distribution is beyond x equals -3 in one direction and x equals $+3$ in the other direction. This form of the normal probability curve is called the unit normal curve (Figure 2–3). The values of the ordinates of this curve for various fractions and multiples of the standard deviations are assembled in tables, and they can be easily converted to fit any particular related problem.

Occasionally it is necessary to know how close an actual distribution approximates a theoretical distribution, such as the normal curve. The problem becomes one of determining the fit of the theoretical curve to actual data. For this purpose, a normal curve with the same frequency, mean, and variance as the actual data is fitted to the frequency distribution under study.

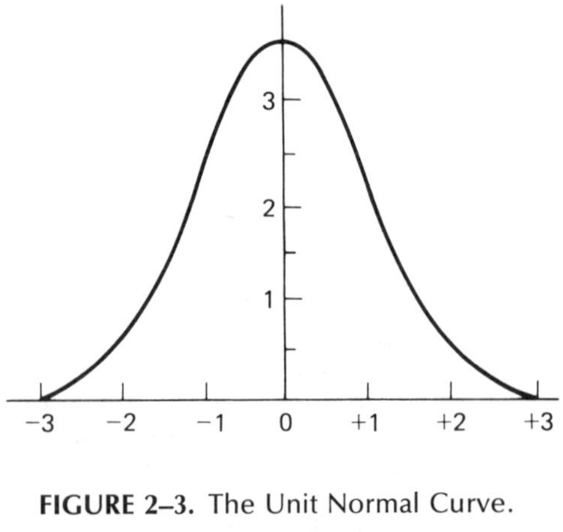

FIGURE 2–3. The Unit Normal Curve.

The first step is to plot the data in a frequency curve, letting the ordinates represent frequencies, and the abscissas, the values of X. The previously cited example of data on the life span of radar tubes shows these essential statistics:

$$N = \Sigma f = 100;\ \text{class width } w = 2;$$
$$\bar{X} = 26.2;\ \sigma_x = 2.48.$$

It has been established that the normal curve is symmetrical, and that the arithmetic mean, the median, and the mode coincide. In the case of the radar tubes, the maximum ordinate of the normal curve (the mode) has the abscissa $\bar{X} = 26.2$. Its value and the ordinates of other points on the curve can be computed with the equation of the normal curve, but it is advisable to use available tables that show ordinates of the unit normal curve at various distances from the mean.

The computations are first performed for the unit normal curve, and the results are then converted to the problem at hand. The table of ordinates shows that the unit normal curve has a height of 0.062 at a distance of 1.93 σ from the mean. The height of original units will be found by multiplying the tabular value by $N \cdot w/\sigma$. Thus:

$$\frac{N \cdot w}{\sigma_x} = \frac{100 \times 2}{2.48} = 80.645.$$

The desired ordinate at 1.93 from the mean will be $0.062 \times 80.645 = 5.0$.

The frequencies of the normal curve that fit the data of the life span of radar tubes can now be systematically computed by fitting the normal curve by ordinates: frequency $N = 100$; class width $w = 2$;

arithmetic mean $\overline{X} = 26.2$; standard deviation $\sigma = 2.48$. The computed maximum value of the normal curve at $\overline{X} = 26.2$; $Y_{max} = 32.2$. Computation factor $N \cdot w/\sigma_x = 80.645$. (See Table 2–2 and Figure 2–4.)

Standard Error

Mean, standard deviation, and variance give a fairly complete numerical description of a sample. They are also estimates

TABLE 2-2
Fitting the Normal Curve by Ordinates

Class Mark X	*Observed Frequency* f_0	*Deviation from Mean* x	*Deviation in* σ *Units* x/σ	*Tabular Value* ϕ	*Computed Frequency* $f_0 = 80.645.\psi$
19	1	−7.2	−2.90	.006	0.5
21	0	−5.2	−2.09	.045	3.6
23	16	−3.2	−1.29	.174	14.0
25	35	−1.2	−0.48	.356	28.7
27	27	0.8	0.32	.379	30.6
29	13	2.8	1.13	.211	17.0
31	6	4.8	1.93	.062	5.0
33	2	6.8	2.74	.009	0.7
35	0	8.8	3.55	.001	0.1

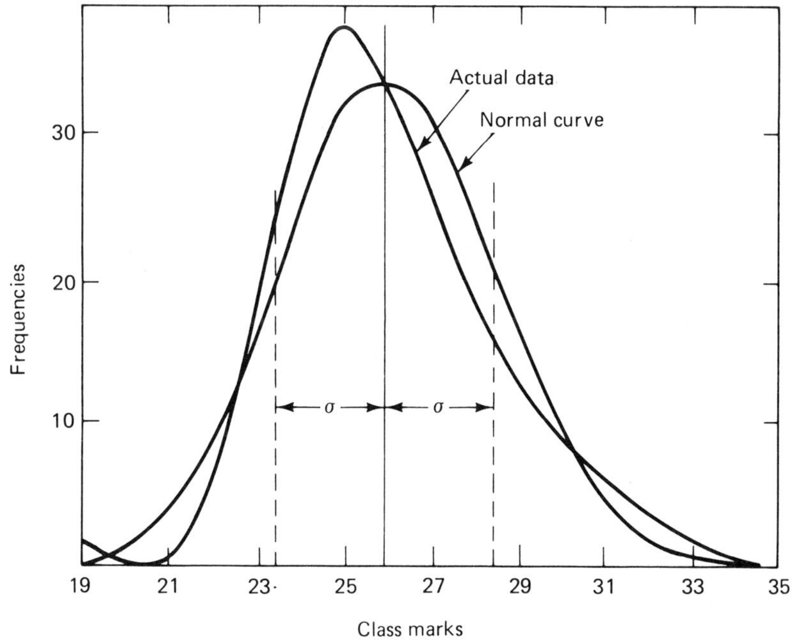

FIGURE 2–4. A Normal Curve Is Fitted to the Data on the Lives of Radar Tubes.

of the mean, standard deviation, and variance, respectively, of the parent population. Being estimates, they are subject to error, and the question arises as to how far a sample value can be expected to differ from the true value. That is, how reliable is an estimate that is based on a sample of a given size?

In answer to this question, a large number of samples are drawn from one population, with each sample having its own mean and standard deviation. These values will, therefore, differ from sample to sample; that is, the mean and standard deviation of the samples will have a distribution of their own. Thus the standard deviation of this random sampling distribution is a measure of the accuracy of the mean of a sample of the given size.

The standard deviation of the random sampling distribution of a statistic is called the standard error of the statistic. Obviously, an estimate based on a large sample will be more accurate than one based on a small sample. It is even possible to establish the degree of accuracy.

The standard error of the mean, for example, indicates the reliability of a particular arithmetic mean, and this reliability depends on the sample size. The standard error decreases as the square root of the sample size increases. If the sample size is increased by four, the standard error is halved. Also, the distribution of sample means tends rapidly to the normal form as the sample size increases.

TESTS OF SIGNIFICANCE

From a discussion of the organization of data and a summary of their parameters (characteristics or constants), it is logical to proceed to their interpretations. The data can be considered in several groups, which might be obtained at different times or under different conditions. The question arises as to whether the groups differ among themselves by more than could be reasonably expected because of experimental error or random sampling variations. For example, at the request of a large petrochemical firm, a series of chemical tests and analyses were made to obtain necessary data on material from a supplier. The results for the percentage of an impurity (shown in Table 2–3) were tabulated after triplicate analyses.

TABLE 2-3

Run	*Percentage of Impurity*			*Average*
1	1.1	1.4	1.2	1.23
2	1.7	1.3	1.5	1.50
3	1.0	1.0	1.4	1.13
4	1.2	1.6	1.5	1.43
5	1.6	1.8	1.4	1.60

These analyses indicate a considerable experimental error, but they do not establish whether the error accounts for the differences between the averages.

With each change in running conditions, a new set of data is obtained, and it is found that the new mean and the new standard deviation vary from the previous ones. Now the question is whether the differences can be attributed to random sampling fluctuations or process variations, or whether the change has affected the product. A hypothetical example follows. The process average and the standard deviation, estimated from tests over a long period, are 21.0 and 1.2, respectively. After a change in conditions, a series of ten tests gives an average of 22.5 and a standard deviation of 0.9. Has the average in fact increased, and has the process in fact become more uniform, or are the apparent improvements so small that they could be due simply to normal process variations?

Sometimes the answer will be obvious, as would be the case if the means differ widely and the standard deviations are small. Statistical tests would not then be necessary, although they might add to the precision of the answer and make it possible to set up quantitative limits. But frequently the answer is not obvious, and a statistical analysis is required to determine the issue.

The term *tests of significance* refers to the techniques used to establish whether statistics estimated from two or more samples differ among themselves or from standard values by more than would be expected in random sampling. Tests of significance distinguish the significant differences from those that are not significant—that is, those small enough to arise frequently because of random sampling variations alone. Where chance variations exist, the statistical method is the only logical one, since there is no other means of distinguishing between chance effects and the real effects of any particular factor, unless the latter are very large compared with the chance variations. Where chance variation exists, it is never possible to say definitely that any particular variation is not due to chance alone. However, statistical analysis states the odds against this, and if the odds are high enough, chance variations may be ruled out as the sole cause of the variation.

Null Hypothesis

A test of significance proceeds as follows: It is first assumed that the samples in question do not exhibit any real differences; that is, they are all random samples drawn from the same population. This hypothesis is known as the null hypothesis.

In the impurity percentage problem presented above, the null hypothesis would state that all runs have the same quality; and in the problem in which running conditions are changed, the null hypothesis would state that the change in running conditions has not affected the product.

On the assumption that the null hypothesis is valid, it is possible to determine the probability (P) that certain parameters of the samples, such as their means or their standard deviations, will have values lying outside given limits. Readily obtainable tables give these probabilities for the statistics required in tests of significance. If the probability is moderately high, the truth of the null hypothesis is not considered questionable on the basis of the available evidence. This does not mean, however, that the null hypothesis is proved true; in fact, a null hypothesis may be disproved, but never proved. If the probability is low, it is concluded that the null hypothesis is false.

As a result of experience in many fields, certain levels of probability, called significance levels, represent the dividing lines between low and high probabilities, and help insure against wrong conclusions.

The generally accepted significance levels are identified below:

1. $P > 10\%$—Not significant. No evidence to suggest that the null hypothesis is false.
2. $10\% > P > 5\%$—Possibly significant. Some doubt is cast on the null hypothesis, but further evidence is required before it can be rejected.
3. $5\% > P > 1\%$—Significant. The null hypothesis may be presumed false, but if the answer is very important, further evidence should be sought.
4. $P < 1\%$—Highly significant. The null hypothesis may be confidently rejected.

Degrees of Freedom

The degrees-of-freedom concept, which is based on the fact that the sum of the deviations from a mean must equal zero, is used in tests of significance and is of great importance in statistical theory and practice. The degrees of freedom (*df*) of a statistic may be defined as the effective number of data or observations on which the value of the statistic is based.

The arithmetic mean of a distribution, for example, is determined by its n (total number) data, and there are n degrees of freedom in the choice of these data. But if a group of data is expected to have a given arithmetic mean, the values of all items, except one, are free to vary. In that case, the number of degrees of freedom is one less than the number of items in the sample.

If it is stipulated that a group of data has given total frequency n, a given mean, and a given standard deviation, $(n-3)$ degrees of freedom remain available.

Statistical Tests

Three tests that are valuable in statistical work are the t-test, which provides a tool for interpretation of small sample statistics; the F-test, which is used in determining the significance of differences between two variances; and the chi-square (χ^2) test, which is useful for comparing actual data with hypothetical data.

The t-test. The t-test was devised for the evaluation of differences between two means. In research and engineering work, the mean and the standard deviation are estimated from relatively small samples and are therefore subject to some uncertainty. The t-test accounts for this element of uncertainty and thus provides a convenient tool for the interpretation of small sample statistics. A commonly used form of the t-test answers the question: Given a group of n data with sample mean ($\bar{X}$) and standard deviation (σ_x), can that distribution be assumed to be a random sample from a parent population of theoretical mean (μ)? Or does the sample mean $\bar{X}$ differ significantly from a theoretical mean?

The test is based on the investigation and interpretation of a statistic, called t, which is the difference of two given means, expressed in terms of the standard error of the mean:

$$t = \frac{\bar{X} - \mu}{\sigma_x/\sqrt{n}}.$$

Since the mean was established first, the standard deviation has $(n - 1)$ degrees of freedom, and the same applies for the t.

The possible values of t, computed for various probabilities and various actual degrees of freedom, are assembled in statistical tables that are readily available. The following example illustrates the application of this type of t-test and the use of the tables. A batch process was used in the manufacture of a certain product, and the theoretical yield was 680 pounds per batch. The process was experimentally based on 10 batches with the following results:

Batch No.	1	2	3	4	5	6	7	8	9	10
Yield:	600	570	580	650	700	630	560	620	710	580

The question arises as to whether the process gives a significantly lower yield than the theoretical expectation. With the theoretical mean given as 680, Table 2–4 is prepared for the computation of the mean and the standard deviation of the experimental results.

The following computations are made of the sample:

Arithmetic mean:

$$\bar{X} = \frac{\Sigma X}{n} = \frac{6{,}200}{10} = 620$$

Standard deviation:

$$\sigma_x = \sqrt{\frac{\Sigma X^2}{n}} = \sqrt{\frac{25{,}200}{10}} = \sqrt{2{,}520} = 50.2$$

Computation of t:

$$t = \frac{\bar{X} - \mu}{\sigma_x/\sqrt{n}} = \frac{620 - 680}{50.2/\sqrt{10}} = \frac{-60}{50.2/3.16} = \frac{-60 \times 316}{5020} = -3.77$$

Evaluation of t: The tables on percentage points of the t-distribution show that for 9 degrees of freedom,

TABLE 2-4
Tabulation of Data To Be Used in the *t*-test

Batch No.	*fX*	$x = X - \bar{X}$	x^2
1	600	20	400
2	570	50	2,500
3	580	40	1,600
4	650	30	900
5	700	80	6,400
6	630	10	100
7	560	60	3,600
8	620	0	0
9	710	90	8,100
10	580	40	1,600
$n = 10$	$\Sigma X = 6{,}200$	$\Sigma \chi = 0$	$\Sigma \chi^2 = 25{,}200$

P = .05 level, one tail-test; t = 1.83
P = .05 level, two tail-test; t = 2.26.

The computed *t* is thus found to be "highly significant," and the null hypothesis—that the sample mean does not differ significantly from the theoretical mean—must be rejected.

The F-Test. Just as the *t*-test was devised for the evaluation of differences between two means, the *F*-test (or variance ratio test) is used to determine the significance of differences between two variances. It tests whether or not two sets of data show basically different degrees of spread.

As a rule, the estimates of variance will vary, even with two samples taken from the same universe. A method is therefore necessary for establishing whether or not these estimates differ significantly. If they do, it can be justifiably concluded that the samples were drawn from universes having different variances.

The test is based on the investigation and interpretation of a statistic, called *F*, which is the ratio of the greater to the smaller variance:

$$F = \frac{V_1}{V_2}$$

where $V_1 > V_2$ and V_1 has $(n_1 - 1)$ degrees of freedom and V_2 has $(n_2 - 1)$ degrees of freedom. If both estimates are based on very large samples (so that they can be considered accurate) and if the samples come from the same universe, V_1 equals V_2 and *F* equals unity.

The fewer the degrees of freedom (that is, the fewer the number of specimens in a sample), the less precise are the estimates V_1 and V_2, and the more they may differ owing to sampling variations.

The values of *F*—which reflect sampling variations at given levels of probability and for various degrees of freedom—are assembled in readily available tables.

The chi-square test. The third statistical test to be considered—the chi-square (χ^2) test—is one of the most useful methods devised to compare actual data (results of experimentation) with hypothetical data. This test is based on the computation and interpretation of the statistic chi-square, which establishes the closeness of fit of the theoretical and observed distributions by means of the following formula:

$$\chi^2 = \Sigma \left[\frac{(f_0 - f_t)^2}{f_t} \right]$$

where f_o = the observing frequency in a class, and f_t = the corresponding theoretical frequency.

The degrees of freedom are determined by the number of classes whose frequencies can be chosen without violating any of the present totals. As a rule, equal totals of the observed and theoretical frequencies are required. Frequencies are divided among n classes and are assigned arbitrarily to $(n - 1)$ of them, which means that the statistician does not have the freedom to select the frequency of the nth class. Thus, $(n - 1)$ degrees of freedom are available. If it is further required that the two distributions have identical means and standard deviations, two more degrees of freedom are lost.

The possible values of χ^2, which have been computed for various probabilities and various actual degrees of freedom, are assembled in readily available tables. Although the χ^2-test does not reveal a great deal of information about the data, it does indicate conclusively a disparity between the observed and the theoretical frequencies that is too large to attribute to chance.

When table entries are large, the χ^2-test gives an estimate of divergence from hypothesis which is reasonably close to that obtained by other measures of probability. However, if computed from a table in which any theoretical frequency is less than 5, the χ^2-test is subject to considerable error.

STATISTICAL ANALYSIS

In statistical analysis, regression is the basis for comparing a series of data, variables, or significant relationships. When one member of two or more series of related data is selected, and that member has a given value, the second has on the average a lesser value and regresses toward the value for the mean of all members of the class. Thus, regression, which is generally thought of as the basic tool in a scientific and statistical analysis, involves the measurement of the relations between two or more series of related data. In the comparison of two variables, one is considered to be independent; the other, dependent. The independent variable—for example, supply, speed, heat—varies independently; the dependent variable; for example, price, distance, expansion—changes in relation to a unit of change in the independent variable. However, this does not mean that a cause-and-effect relationship necessarily exists between the independent and dependent variables. The independent series is measured on the X-axis; the dependent series, on the Y-axis.

An example is given to illustrate the procedures used in determining the effects of additions to the properties of synthetic rubber. Varying amounts and types of ingredients were used in the preparation of thirty specimens. The data on the hardness and abrasion loss of each specimen are assembled in Table 2–5. These figures show that high values of abrasion loss tend to coincide with low values of hardness; that is, some degree of relationship exists. The relationship can be more clearly represented by a graph in which one party is plotted against the other (Figure 2–5).

Such plotting of two associated sets of data is known as a scatter diagram—which is a graph of coordinate scales on which the paired values of the data of X and Y are located by dots or marks opposite the appropriate points on the two axes. If there is a relationship between the associated variables, the points will form a path across the coordinate system. In the case of a perfect relationship, all the points would coincide with a curve or line. But if the data are imperfectly related, the points will scatter about the line or curve.

In Figure 2–5, the abrasion loss of synthetic rubber shows a tendency to decrease with increasing values of hardness, and the relationship appears linear since the points tend to cluster about a diagonal line.

TABLE 2-5
Abrasion Loss and Hardness of Synthetic Rubber Specimens

Specimen No.	:	1	2	3	4	5	6	7	8	9	10
Hardness	X:	45	55	61	66	71	71	81	86	53	60
Abrasion loss	Y:	372	206	175	154	136	112	55	45	221	166
	No.:	11	12	13	14	15	16	17	18	19	20
	X:	64	68	79	81	56	68	75	83	88	59
	Y:	164	113	82	32	228	196	128	97	64	249
	No.:	21	22	23	24	25	26	27	28	29	30
	X:	71	80	82	89	51	59	65	74	81	86
	Y:	219	186	155	114	341	340	283	267	215	148

For a high degree of association, the scatter will be confined to a narrow path. The less perfect the relationship between the two sets of data, the greater will be the departure from the indicated line or course.

The spread of the points in the scatter diagram is due to real differences between the specimens; thus there is no definite mathematical relationship between the two properties of synthetic rubber. Whatever association exists is limited to that of a statistical nature. In fact, the results obtained may very well depend on the choice of specimens. For example, if the selection was limited to specimens 25 to 29, represented by the six outer and topmost points running diagonally from the top left-hand corner of the diagram, the apparent re-

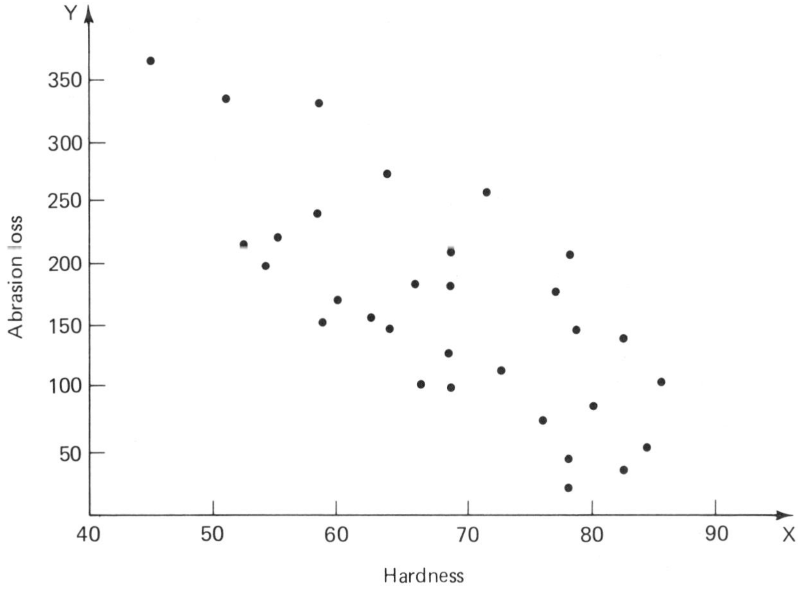

FIGURE 2–5. Data on Synthetic Rubber Specimens Are Plotted to Show the Correlation Between Two Variables—Abrasion, Loss and Hardness.

lationship between the two variables would be difficult. Actually, it is possible to select specimens so as to obtain any relationship desired between very wide limits. A natural and logical conclusion is that general inferences from the analysis of data of this kind are valid only with random selection of the specimens for test.

When a scatter diagram indicates a definite association between the variables, the statistician attempts to fit a line to it and thus establish a relationship. This line, called the regression line, describes the relationship between two variables on the basis of the average relationship between them.

When the deviations from the regression line are measured along the ordinates, it is assumed that *X* is the independent and *Y* the dependent variable, and the regression of *Y* upon *X* is the best line for estimating the *Y* for a given *X*.

Likewise, *Y* could be considered the independent and *X* the dependent variable. The regression of *X* upon *Y* is then the best line for estimating the *Y* for a given *X*.

Figure 2–6 shows that the best line for predicting abrasion loss from hardness is not the same as the best line for predicting hardness from abrasion loss (see also Figure 2–5). Therefore, it is seen that the regression of *Y* upon *X* is not equivalent to the regression of *X* upon *Y*.

The fact that two regression lines exist should not be confusing since the two lines represent two different problems. The process of obtaining the best estimate of *Y* from a knowledge of *X* is not the same as that of obtaining the best estimate of *X* from a knowledge of *Y*. It should be noted

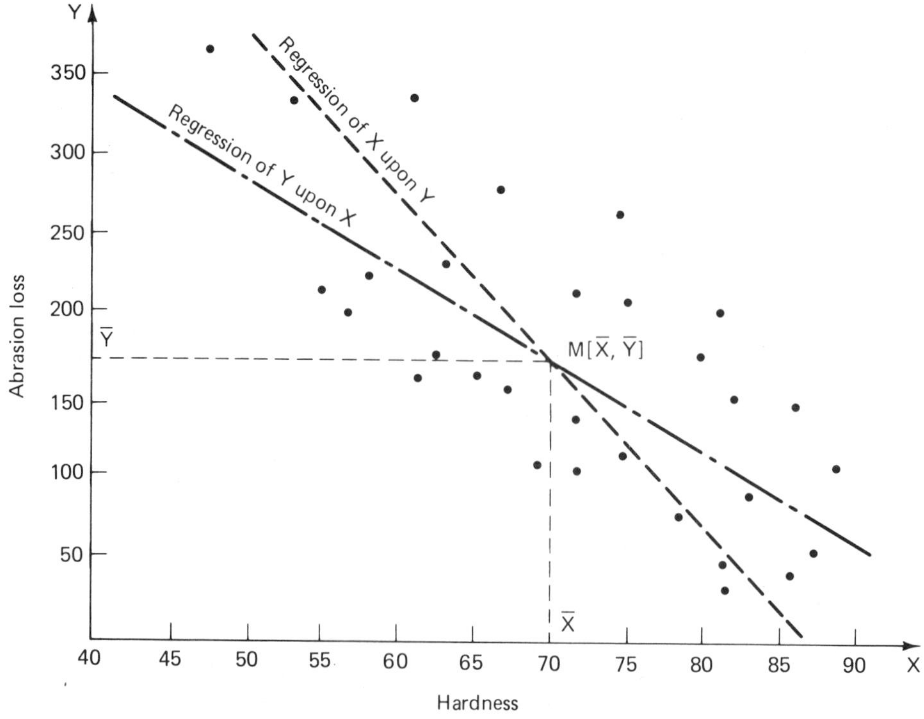

FIGURE 2–6. Graphic Presentation of Regression Lines.

that the two regression lines intersect in point M, whose coordinates are the means of the X and Y observations. M thus equals the point of averages.

If the relationship between the two basic sets of data is not perfect, the actual values of Y will not coincide with the computed values, as the scatter about the regression line would indicate. This scatter or variation may be compared to the dispersion of a frequency distribution about its mean, and this variability suggests a need to define a measure for the scatter about the regression line.

The measure used for this purpose, the standard error of estimate, is therefore similar to the standard deviation. Standard deviation is defined as the square root of the mean of the squared deviations of the items of a sample from its arithmetic mean. In the normal distribution, one standard deviation plus and minus from the arithmetic mean includes 68.27 percent of the items in the sample if the sample is large. Standard error of estimate is defined as the square root of the mean of the squared deviations between the actual values of the dependent variable from the line of regression (measured along the ordinates if X is the independent variable, and along the abscissas if Y is the independent variable).

The standard error of estimate for the regression of Y upon X is expressed by the following formula:

$$S_y = \sqrt{\frac{\Sigma(X - \eta)^2}{n}}$$

where Y = actual value, and η = computed value for a given X.

The standard error of estimate may be used in the same manner as the standard deviation. When measured off plus and minus about the line of regression, one standard error of estimate will include 68.27 percent of the cases; two standard errors of estimate will include 95.45 percent of the cases; and three standard errors of estimate will include 99.73 percent of the cases.

The size of the standard error of estimate is a measure for the degree of association between two sets of data or two variations. A zero standard error of estimate indicates that all values are located on the regression line, and the relationship is therefore perfect. The larger the standard error of estimate, the greater is the scatter about the regression line and the poorer is the relationship. However, standard errors cannot always be directly compared because such error is expressed in terms of the original unit of the variable it qualifies and frequently the units are different, for example, in the association of abrasion loss versus hardness of synthetic rubber. But if the standard error of estimate (for example, of Y upon X) is divided by the related standard deviation (in this case, of the Y-distribution), the resulting value will be a pure number and can be expressed in percentages.

FORECASTING FOR PRODUCTION PLANNING

The demand for production is felt everywhere within an enterprise, from the sales engineer's field office to the treasurer's sanctum, and from the table at which directors make decisions to the production line. Results, of course, are manifold, but this chapter is concerned with only three: (1) *sales forecasting*, (2) *production planning*, and (3) *control*. Before entering into a detailed discussion of these closely related results, it is well to define our terms.

Sales forecasting has various meanings, but in this text it will refer to the attempt to predict, on a sound basis, the volume of sales that can reasonably be expected by some future date. The sales forecast should be quantitative, for example, "sales of 2000 units." The estimate of future sales must be consistent with market forces and must be a result of planned company business activities. The estimate must rest on planned and expected results, not hoped or conservative minimums.

Production planning is the determinative phase of production management; during this phase, management determines what is to be done. It translates sales forecasts into production master schedules; picks material, equipment requirements, and personnel needs; and prepares detailed department schedules. It also establishes raw materials and finished goods maintained at properly selected levels. Finally, it prepares alternative plans of action as a way of meeting emergencies.

Control is considered to be the regulative phase in that it involves balancing production and inventories with the future sales estimate. Broadly, control can be defined as the process of determining what's being accomplished, evaluating it, and, if necessary, applying corrective measures so that performance takes place according to plans.

Need for a Technique

Sales forecasts for company's producers are, for the most part, based on past sales. Past sales history is adjusted in the light of expected market conditions and other known factors that affect future sales. Some of these factors are product obsolescence, the introduction of new products, sales promotion programs, component changes, and change in competitive position.

After the forecasts are firmed up on this basis, a technique is needed to indicate the change of important departures from the estimated sales trend. The further in advance of actual production that this technique can perform its alerting function, the more valuable it becomes as a tool, since components are not usually made to order but are stocked at an economic level to fill customer's orders.

Without a reliable tool to indicate the point at which corrective action should be taken to revise the sales forecast, there is a natural tendency to review and perhaps revise it on the basis of the sales picture and outlook at the time of consideration. When sales forecasts are reviewed on a monthly basis and it is found that there was a high order rate for the previous month, the result is usually an increased forecast and hence an accelerated production plan. Conversely, the forecast is reduced and the production schedule is cut back if the preceding month's orders were below expectations.

This unscientific approach leads to continuous changes rather than to some predictions on which management can rely as a control device for the production departments. The production departments may be forced to requisition materials, labor, and expand manufacturing facilities one month and then may find that their work and troubles were unnecessary in the light of the lower order rate of succeeding months. Conversely, skilled workers may be transferred to other jobs or laid off one month and urgently needed the next month. The production schedule becomes a constantly changing plan that the manufacturing organization cannot hope to achieve.

A statistical control technique can be used to overcome these problems. This technique automatically indicates when a revised forecast is warranted. These indications are reliable about 95 percent of the time. The technique is simple enough to be performed by clerical personnel until the sales order rate goes "out of control." (This is a good illustration of "management by exception.") When "out of control" is indicated, the forecast and the production schedule should be reviewed and a decision made as to revision.

Determining Control Limits

Business managers who have observed the monthly sales of a product have noted that variation from the average is the rule

TABLE 2-6
Computation of Control Limits

1 Month	2 1981 Monthly Sales in Units	3 Cumulative Monthly Sales Actual (Y)	4 Cumulative Monthly Sales Average (Y_1)	5 Difference ($Y-Y_1$)	6 Difference Squared $(Y-Y_1)^2$
January	79	79	70	9	81
February	87	166	140	26	676
March	79	245	210	35	1225
April	85	330	280	50	2500
May	45	375	350	25	625
June	52	427	420	7	49
July	57	484	490	− 6	36
August	54	538	560	−22	484
September	64	602	630	−28	784
October	58	660	700	−40	1600
November	91	751	770	−19	361
December	89	840	840	0	0

Sum (Σ) = 840

Average $\overline{X} = 70$

$$Sy = \sqrt{\frac{\Sigma(Y-Y_1)^2}{N-1}} = \sqrt{\frac{8421}{11}} = \sqrt{766} = 27.7 \text{ is the standard error of estimate}$$

N is the number of months

2 standard errors = 27.7 × 2 = 55.4

$$\text{Coefficient of variation } V = \frac{Sy}{\overline{X}} = \frac{\text{standard error of estimate}}{\text{average monthly sales}}$$

$$V = \frac{27.7}{70} \approx .04$$

rather than the exception. Consequently, no matter how accurate the forecasts for the year, random fluctuations that are independent of the estimated average can be expected to occur. Thus, one month's sales will be high and the next month's sales low. Over several months, they will strike an average. This change in monthly sales is shown in Table 2–6, with an average monthly sales of 70 (see columns 1 and 2).

Business statisticians have observed that the variations in the demand for a product over a period of time will approximate a normal distribution. That is to say, there is sales variation each month, but the variation is regularized. Monthly sales differ, but within limits. Moreover, the pattern of variation is fairly uniform; that is, there is as much variation below an average line as above an average line.

The statistical tool called *standard error of estimate* (symbolized: S_y) that we examined earlier is useful for estimating the natural dispersion or variation that will occur even when the sales forecast is good. The *standard error of estimate* (S_y) is computed as a square root of the mean of the squared deviations. The deviations are the monthly differences from the average monthly sales for the year, as shown in Table 2–6. The deviations of each month's sales from the year's monthly average is symbolized by $Y - Y_1$, which will be used in factored form: $(Y - Y_1)$.

It is advisable to include at least ten months' figures in the computation of S_y. The more historical sales data that can be included, the greater will be the degree of accuracy.

Statisticians state that if you solve the formula for the standard error of the estimate—the figure obtained (in the problem the figure is 27.7)—will represent the natural dispersions of a good forecast 68 percent of the time. The S_y of 27.7 indicates that it is normal for sales of this product (with an average of 70 per month) to vary as much as 27.7 plus or minus of the average; and that variation of sales—that is, plus or minus from the average—can be expected to occur 68.27 percent of the time. It can also be said that it will exceed 27.7 variation the remainder of the time (32 percent).

As a rule, statisticians suggest using 2 S_y. In our example 2 S_y is 55.4. With 2 S_y, 95.45 percent of the normal variation in sales will be included. Figure 2–7 shows the sales data from Table 2–6 plotted. The solid line, the line G, *average relationship*, is the cumulative monthly average of 70. The broken lines are set at 2 S_y, (55.4 units above and below the average) and are called *control limits*. Thus, slightly more than 95 percent of the sales, by months, will fall within a band of ± 2 S_y from the average line.

At the bottom of Table 2–6 you will notice that the coefficient of variation (V), was computed. This coefficient of variation (V) will be used to determine controls on the next year's forecast of this product.

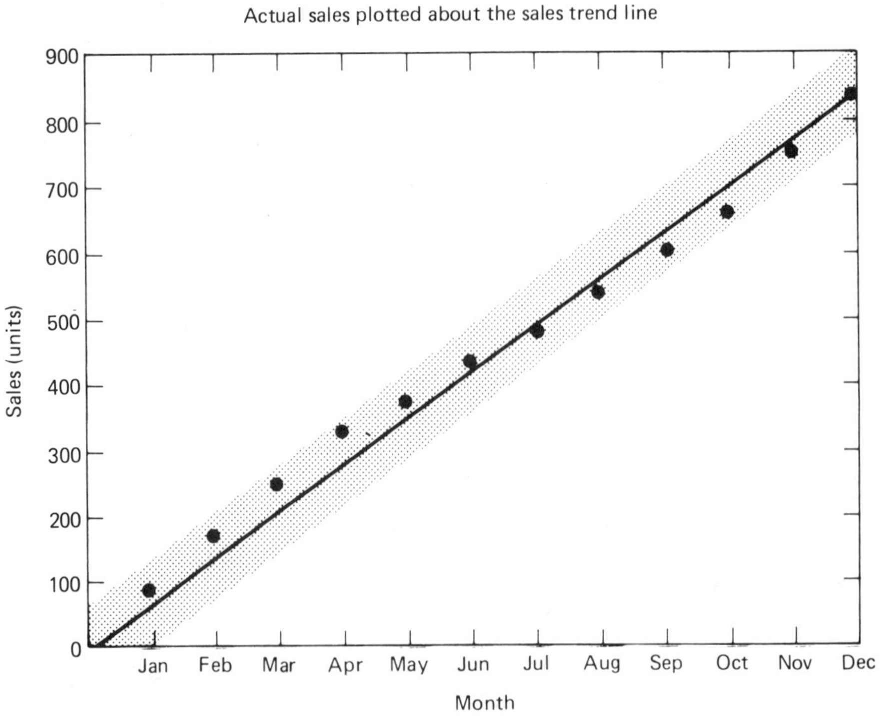

FIGURE 2–7. Actual Sales Plotted About the Sales Trend Line.

Assume that next year's (1982) forecast calls for an average monthly sale of 75 units; we can establish the new S_y and control limits for the sale forecast by multiplying the average (75) by the coefficient of variation:

$$S_y = V \times \text{New Mo. Avg.} = .4 \times 75 = 30. \quad 2\,S_y = 60.$$

Figure 2–8 shows the new (1982) forecast and new control limits set as before at 2 S_y, and the first four months sales are plotted on the graph. Note that the April sales plot has gone "out of control." The March sales plot indicated a probable out-of-control condition. The April sales figure indicates a change in sales demand and the need for a downward revision of the yearly sales estimate.

When the monthly sales plots fall outside the control area, this situation is an early warning that a decision must be made about revising the sales forecast. Usually when the plotted sales remain within the control limits, the forecast is presumed good.

Normal practice is to treat an unbroken sequence of five months' sales plottings (all above or below the cumulative forecast line) in the same manner as a plot outside the control limits. In either case an analysis is in order to determine the cause, if possible. A revised forecast may be indicated. In the event that two plots fall outside the control limit (on the same side), the need for a new forecast is strongly indicated.

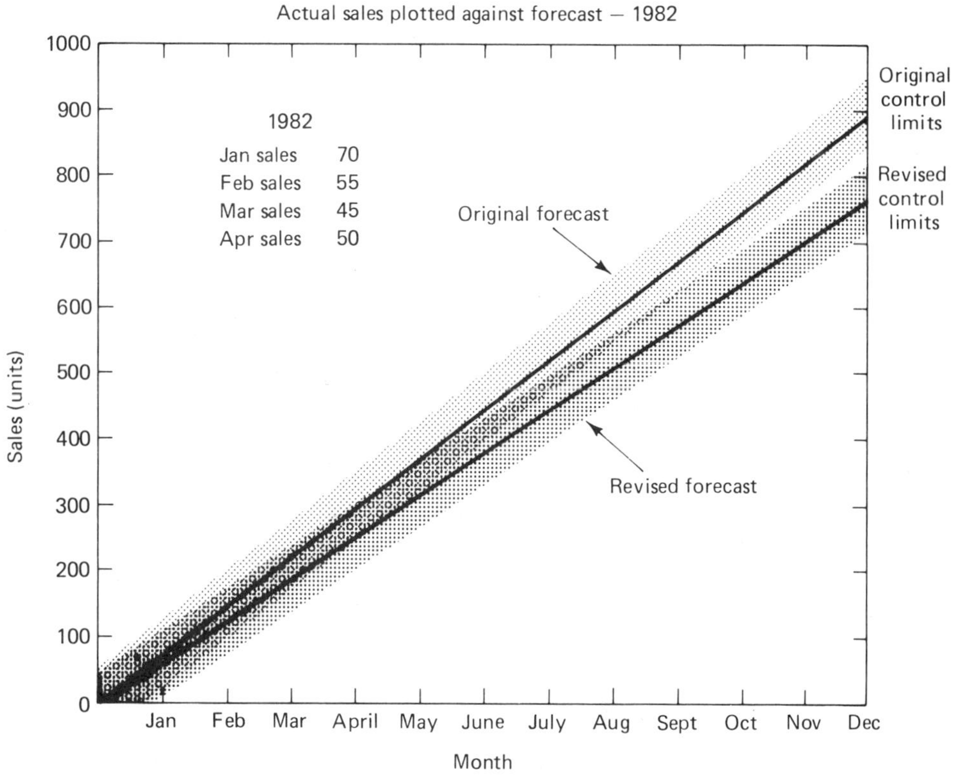

FIGURE 2–8. Actual Sales Plotted Against Forecast—1982.

The Revised Forecast

Figure 2–8 shows the revised forecast that was reduced to yearly sales of 770. The new trend line was drawn by inspection (the forecaster drew a line through the four plots and extended it), and the new control limits were applied to the indicated revised forecast. The new control limits were applied so that the out-of-control points were within them and on the low side.

When such a statistical technique is applied to the control of sales forecasts and sales performance is reviewed against forecast, the production schedule should improve and an economic inventory should be maintained.

Application to Inventory Control

Effective inventory control insures that adequate but not excessive units are on hand at all times to meet customers' orders. The economic inventory level for a product can also be determined by the use of the statistical control chart. Its application for inventory control involves the equation:

$$Q = Se\,(1 - V) - In$$

where Q = quantity to be manufactured during a given period, Se = estimated sales during this period, V = coefficient of variation, and In = present inventory.

Important Limitations

The standard error of the estimate does not, in any way, aid in determining the initial sales forecast. As we noted earlier, sales forecasts are generally based on a composite of past sales adjusted in the light of predicted business conditions and trends and other factors, such as product obsolescence, the introduction of new products, and the overall marketing program.

An occasional large order can cause a major distortion from the normal trend. These unusual orders should probably be omitted from the calculations of the control limits.

This technique is not applicable to products made to order for one customer. In such cases, requirements are usually known and statistical methods are not used.

Users of the Technique

This technique has been used with great success in establishing control over the sales forecast on aeronautical electronic products and automotive parts. The value of the technique has also been proved for many types of products in other industrial concerns.

Summary and Conclusions

It has often been stated that the only thing certain about the future is that it is uncertain. This limitation holds for statistical forecasting. As one friend of mine, a professor of business statistics, has put it: "The only thing you can be sure about in any forecast is that it will contain some error."

This topic section discussed the control and revision of forecasts and not how to forecast. The statistical technique just explained provides answers to the range of error to be expected and indicates at an early stage any occurrence of deviation from a sales estimate. On the basis of the plotted sales data and the concept of the control chart the sales forecaster can make a decision as to whether or not a revision of the forecast should be made.

Some of the savings that can accrue to the firms that apply the technique are as follows:

1. Well-balanced production of the product.

2. Reduction of overall labor costs and savings in manpower.
3. Elimination of wasted time and money spent to expedite production that fails to materialize.
4. Provision of sufficient time to meet normal customer commitments.
5. Maintenance of an economic inventory level of material and finished goods.

TIME SERIES ANALYSIS

A business enterprise, like the national economy, is characterized by fluctuations in business activity that affect the operations of business, the welfare of labor, and the policies of management. Every executive should understand the nature of these fluctuations and the factors that produce them. The technique of time series analysis has been developed for the most part by econometricians, but the study of time series is of interest to many people, including businessmen, industrial engineers, sociologists, and operations researchers.

Any economic series such as sales volume, production data, employment figures, chronologically classified, is in its raw form called original data. In the analysis of any series of economic data over a period of time, it is beneficial to separate the factors that are considered to be the result of the forces influencing the data. There are four major types of factors: (1) trend; (2) seasonal variation; (3) cyclical fluctuations; (4) irregular movements. The original data are equivalent to the four factors expressed in the following equation:

$$O = T \times S \times C \times I.$$

Economic statisticians are not in complete agreement concerning the meaning or the proper method of analyzing the various movements constituting time series. There is no widely applicable, tried-and-proved body of techniques for analyzing the factors making up the time series. In the analysis of time series, much attention has been given by statisticians to this problem. The techniques now used require formidable computations. With the widespread accessibility of electronic computers, this obstacle is gradually being overcome, but many conceptual as well as computational difficulties remain.

One of the major managerial interests is how to achieve and maintain stability and regularity of employment. Management is cognizant that irregularity of employment is expensive, that it increases production costs in virtually all cases, and that there are social reasons for undertaking a program of employment stabilization. Labor expects employers to offer steady work, and management has become aware of the losses arising from idle plant space, machines and equipment, the costs of unemployment insurance taxes, and the losses of trained and experienced workers.

For intelligent business planning, management must recognize and understand the various factors in the variation of employment. Appropriate methods of control vary with these factors, which can be isolated by statistical techniques.

Many statistical techniques are available to assist the analyst in isolating each element that affects a particular series and to help in appraising the various types of irregularity in employment that may be reflected in the experience of the firm. The objective of this analysis is the measurement of secular trend and fluctuations to serve as a basis for reliable conclusions as to the types and extent of the factors involved.

A carefully drawn chart of the monthly averages of employment extending over a number of years often suggests what type of instability has contributed to the whole panorama of change (see Figure 2–9).

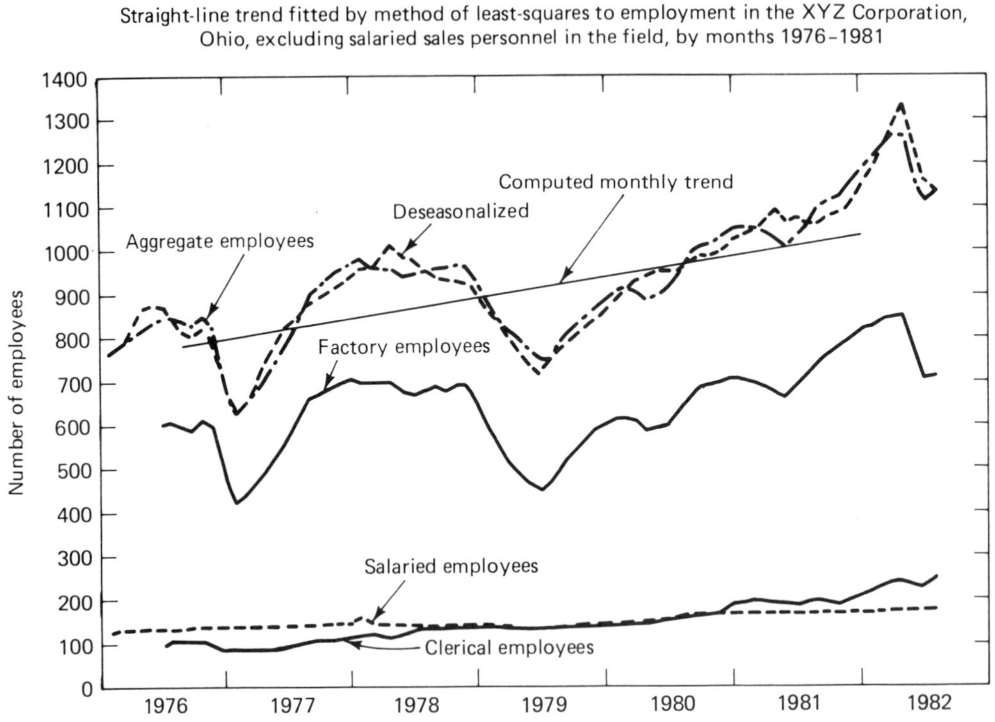

FIGURE 2–9. Dichotomies.

The Firm Under Study

The XYZ Corporation was incorporated in January 1930, under Ohio laws. The firm is engaged in the manufacture and sale of lubricating equipment, portable and automatic-type air tools, aviation oxygen equipment and environmental control systems, and specialized products.

The corporation owns two plants, which have a floor area of 300,000 sq. ft. and 40,000 sq. ft. and are located in an Ohio city.

Measurement of Secular Trend

This trend is the persistent underlying movement that has taken place in a series of data. It is the basic growth or decline that would exist if there were no cycles. The straight line that most closely approximates the growth in XYZ's labor force is figured by the method of least-squares. It is a line from which the sum of squared vertical deviations is a minimum. Such a trend for the employment data of Table 2–7 is illustrated in Figure 2–9, and the method of calculation is shown in Table 2–8 and summarized below.

Employment data for the six years 1976 through 1981 are probably considered too short a period for calculating a trend, but detailed records of employment data prior to this period are not available and it is necessary to figure trend to eliminate it from the series of data so that the other factors in the data can be isolated. The formula for the straight line is $Y_c = a + bX$ in which Y_c is the trend factor for each year expressed in terms of the original data. The annual trend equation has been converted

TABLE 2-7
Employment in The XYZ Corporation, Ohio, Excluding Salaried Sales Personnel in the Field, by months 1976-1981

Month \ Year	1976	1977	1978	1979	1980	1981	Total	Monthly Average $\overline{X}$
January	765	634	980	874	906	1045	5204	867
February	779	648	964	847	908	1044	5190	865
March	793	672	961	793	907	1041	5167	861
April	806	706	959	753	877	1025	5126	854
May	829	745	938	730	898	1010	5150	858
June	840	794	942	718	909	1030	5233	872
July	846	841	950	742	946	1055	5380	897
August	833	898	960	793	992	1093	5569	928
September	827	913	958	814	1016	1112	5640	940
October	850	933	968	849	1018	1118	5736	956
November	821	952	964	870	1031	1157	5795	966
December	707	965	935	879	1052	1186	5724	954
Yearly Total	9,696	9,701	11,479	9,662	11,460	12,916	64,914	
Monthly Average per year	808	808	957	805	955	1076		

to a monthly trend equation. The value of b is 3.881, which is the average monthly increase in employment for the period.

Employment Growth Rate

The rate of growth is figured by means of the formula for a geometric progression (GP), which is $l = ar^{n-1}$. Let us denote the first term of this GP by a, the common ratio by r, the number of terms by n, and the nth term by 1.

$l = 1076$	$1076 = 808r^5$	log of 1076 = 3.031812
$a = 808$		log of 808 = 2.907411 (subtract)
$r = ?$	$r^5 = \frac{1076}{808}$	5 $\overline{)50.124401-50}$
$n-1 = 5$	$r = \sqrt[5]{\frac{1076}{808}}$	antilog = 10.024880 − 10
	$r = 1.05896 \simeq 1.059$	

There has been a 5.9 percent average rate of growth over the five year period, 1976–1981.

Measurement of Seasonal Variations

A measure of the seasonal variation may be obtained by the ratio-to-moving-average method. The reason for measuring these kinds of variations is to study them and to isolate them. A 12-month moving average is calculated from the monthly data of

TABLE 2-8
Computation by Least-Squares Short Method of Straight Line Trend for Employment in the XYZ Corporation, Ohio 1976–1981

Year	Employment Y	X	XY	X^2
1976	9,696	0	0	0
1977	9,701	1	9,701	1
1978	11,479	2	22,958	4
1979	9,662	3	28,986	9
1980	11,460	4	45,840	16
1981	12,916	5	64,580	25

$\Sigma Y = 64{,}914 \quad \Sigma X = 15 \quad \Sigma XY = 172{,}065 \quad \Sigma X^2 = 55$

$$\frac{(\Sigma X)^2}{N} = \frac{225}{6} = 37.5 \qquad \frac{\Sigma X \cdot \Sigma Y}{N} = \frac{973{,}710}{6} = 162{,}285$$

$$\Sigma x^2 = \Sigma X^2 - \frac{(\Sigma X)^2}{N} = 55\text{-}37.5 = 17.5 \qquad \Sigma xy = \Sigma XY - \frac{\Sigma X \cdot \Sigma Y}{N} = 172{,}065\text{-}162{,}285 = 9780$$

$$\text{Annual } b = \frac{\Sigma xy}{\Sigma x^2} = \frac{9780}{17.5} = 558.86$$

$$\text{Monthly } b = \frac{558.86}{12 \times 12} = \frac{558.86}{144} = 3.881$$

$$a = \frac{\Sigma Y}{N} = \bar{Y} = \frac{64{,}914}{6} = 10{,}819 \quad \text{Height of line at middle of time period June 30, 1978}$$

$$a = \frac{\Sigma Y}{N} - \frac{b_m(N-1)}{2} = 10{,}819 - \frac{19.405}{2} = 10{,}819 - 9.70 = 10{,}809.30$$

Height of line at June 15, 1978

$$a = \frac{\Sigma Y}{12N} - \frac{b_m(12N-1)}{2} = \frac{64{,}914}{72} - \frac{3.881\,(12 \cdot 6 - 1)}{2} = 901.58 - 137.78 = 763.80$$

employment for the period, since it averages out the seasonal variations and irregular movements in the data. This means that the moving average contains the trend, and the cycle. The original data divided by the 12-month moving average gives a measure of the seasonal variation.

The basis for this procedure may be seen from the following equation:

$$\frac{T \times C \times S \times I}{T \times C} = S \times I.$$

The first step is to calculate a 12-month moving average of the employment data. This work is performed by dividing the 12-month moving total by 12 to get the moving average. A short-cut method of calculating a centered 12-month moving average, which is the method used, may be seen from the work sheets.

The next step is to divide the original data by the 12-month moving average; the result is called the *seasonal relative* and is expressed as a percent. For example, the employment figure of 846 for July 1976 is divided by the 12-month moving average for that month of 802.5 to yield a seasonal index of 105.42.

The purpose of the third step is to average, and, in the process of averaging, to eliminate the irregular factor. It is assumed that the high and low values of seasonal relatives for any month are caused by irregular factors. A modified arithmetic mean eliminates unusually high and low items for the months and then an average of the remaining items gives a typical seasonal relative, one for each month. This is called the crude seasonal index and it represents the seasonal element S in the purest form that can be achieved.

The fourth step is an adjustment to eliminate certain small discrepancies. The total of the 12 modified means from Table 2–9 is 1206.80, but that total should be 1200 or average 100; in consequence of rounding and other operations, the total is slightly higher. To reduce the total of the 12 modified means to 1200, a correction factor is applied (.9944), to each month's raw seasonal index, and thus a total of 1200 is attained—the goal of the analysis. This seasonal pattern has already been shown in Table 2–9.

The seasonal pattern in employment clearly shows a seasonal high in November and a seasonal low in April. Moreover, the entire period from September through November is the high, whereas the period from April through June is the low.

From a quantitative standpoint, seasonal variations are probably the most important cause of unemployment. Few industries completely escape seasonality, either in the demand for their products or in the raw materials they use. As a rule, industries producing nondurable consumer goods experience more seasonality than do production goods industries, but the effect of seasonality is so general that, for all industry in the nation, January is the lowest employment month, while October is the month of highest levels.

Adjustment for Seasonality. To adjust the data for seasonality, which means to deseasonalize the data, divide the original data for each month by the corresponding seasonal index for the month; or in algebraic form,

$$\frac{T \times C \times S \times I}{S} = T \times C \times I.$$

The seasonal index for January is the same for every January in the entire series, and so on for the twelve months. The deseasonalized value for January 1976 is 765 ÷ 101.85 = 751.1. Deseasonalized data by months for the years 1976 through 1981 are presented in Table 2–10 and graphically in Figure 2–9.

Measurement of Cyclical Fluctuations

Monthly data contain all four elements of the composite force, that is $T \times S \times C \times I$. Methods of measuring cyclical fluctuations of time series movement are probably of most interest to economic analysts. The most widely used method for measuring cyclical fluctuations is the residual method in which the cycle is found by eliminating the other factors in the data. The National Bureau of Economic Research has developed a statistical method of determining the cycle directly.

The residual method of calculating the cycle is based on the elimination of the trend and seasonal elements. Remembering that the original data = $T \times C \times S \times I$ and that deseasonalized data = $T \times C \times I$; divide the monthly deseasonalized data by the trend value for each month; that is, compute

$$\frac{\mathrm{T} \times C \times I}{T} = C \times I.$$

For example, the deseasonalized value for January 1976 was 751.10, and the trend value for this month was 763.8, making the

TABLE 2-9

Calculation of the Corrected Seasonal Index From the Raw Seasonal Index of The XYZ Corporation, Ohio, by Months 1976–1981

Month	*1976*	*1977*	*1978*	*1979*	*1980*	*1981*	*Raw Seasonal Index*	*Corrected Seasonal Index*[a]	*Monthly Employment as a Percentage of Total*
January		83.78	104.07	101.37	104.00	101.91	102.43	101.85	8.49
February		85.35	101.60	100.05	102.26	100.55	100.73	100.16	8.35
March		87.79	100.81	95.13	100.26	99.08	98.16	97.61	8.13
April		91.39	100.25	91.54	95.31	96.80	94.55	94.02	7.84
May		95.33	97.85	89.71	96.16	94.55	95.35	94.81	7.90
June		99.54	98.35	88.92	95.91	95.45	96.57	96.03	8.00
July	105.42	102.21	99.77	92.00	98.46		100.15	99.58	8.30
August	105.23	105.60	101.82	97.86	102.03		103.03	102.45	8.54
September	105.87	104.27	102.90	99.55	103.30		103.49	102.91	8.58
October	110.12	103.87	105.74	102.59	102.29		104.07	103.48	8.62
November	107.43	103.84	107.33	103.60	102.48		104.92	104.33	8.69
December	93.17	103.65	106.23	102.84	103.56		103.35	102.77	8.56
						Totals	1206.80	1200.00	100.00

[a]Correction Factor:
1200 ÷ 1206.8 = .9944

This is shifting the origin from an annual trend (June 30) to a monthly trend (January 15), which makes its origin at the center of a month. Fitting a trend value by least squares ($Y_c = a + bX$) to monthly data may be excessively time-consuming. Thus it is often more convenient to compute the trend equation from annual data and then convert this annual trend equation to a monthly trend equation.

TABLE 2-10
Deseasonalized Data of Employment in The XYZ Corporation, Ohio, by Months, 1976-1981

Month	1976	1977	1978	1979	1980	1981	1982
January	751.10	622.48	962.20	858.12	889.54	1026.02	1180.17
February	777.76	646.96	962.46	845.65	906.55	1042.33	1239.02
March	812.42	688.45	984.53	812.42	929.21	1066.49	1291.88
April	857.26	750.90	1020.00	800.89	932.78	1090.19	1343.33
May	814.38	785.78	989.35	769.96	947.16	1065.29	1237.21
June	874.73	826.82	980.94	747.68	946.58	1072.58	1160.05
July	849.57	844.55	954.01	745.13	949.99	1059.45	1138.78
August	813.08	876.53	937.04	774.04	968.28	1066.86	
September	803.61	887.18	930.91	790.98	987.27	1080.56	
October	821.41	901.62	935.45	820.45	983.76	1080.40	
November	786.93	912.49	923.99	833.89	988.21	1108.98	
December	687.94	938.99	909.80	855.31	1023.65	1154.03	

division equal 98.34, the cyclical-irregular relative. The cyclical-irregular movements as percentage of employment for each month of the study period are given in Table 2–11 and shown on Figure 2–10.

Periodograph Analysis

After the cyclical-irregular movements are obtained, a curve is fitted to the data. The simple procedure by the freehand method

TABLE 2-11
Cyclical-Irregular Movements From Deseasonalized Data of Employment in the XYZ Corporation, Ohio, by Months, 1976-1981

Month	1976	1977	1978	1979	1980	1981	1982
January	98.34	76.82	112.29	94.98	93.63	102.95	113.13
February	101.31	79.46	111.81	93.20	95.03	104.18	118.34
March	105.30	84.15	113.86	89.16	97.02	106.19	112.93
April	110.55	91.35	117.44	87.52	96.99	108.13	127.35
May	112.20	95.14	113.40	83.78	98.09	105.25	116.86
June	111.69	99.65	111.94	81.02	97.64	105.57	109.18
July	107.94	101.31	108.39	80.40	97.60	103.88	106.78
August	102.80	104.66	105.99	83.17	99.09	104.21	
September	101.10	105.44	104.84	84.64	100.63	105.15	
October	102.84	106.67	104.89	87.43	99.88	104.74	
November	98.05	107.46	103.16	88.50	99.94	107.11	
December	85.30	110.08	101.13	90.40	103.12	111.04	

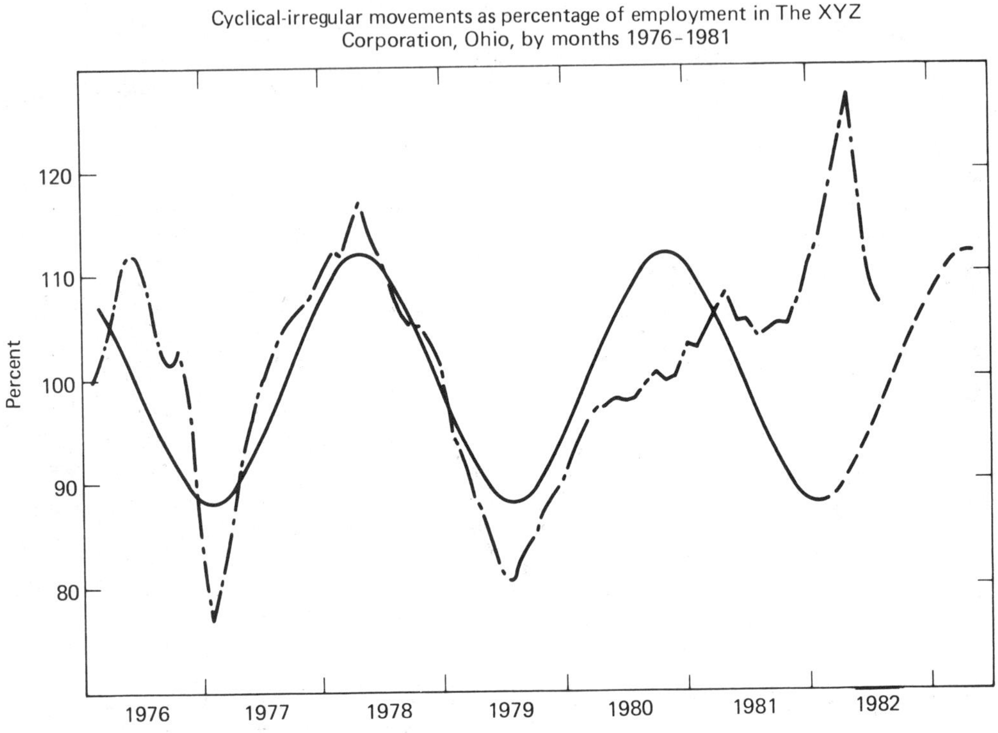

FIGURE 2–10. Binominal and Cumulative Binomial Distributions.

will seldom be found appropriate, since cycles seldom exhibit a simple periodicity, but the method is to be considered an introduction to more complex methods.

Having made a rough graph of the aggregate employment data since 1971, and having somewhat of an understanding of the background of this particular series, we can draw a curve through the data that describes the cycle. This method obviously is highly subjective, since the curve depicts what the individual statistician sees.

The periodicity is 30 months, that is, the period of time for the recurrence at regular interval from a peak to a peak or a trough to a trough. The trough is 88, whereas the peak is 112. The range from the high to low is 24. This curve is shown in Figure 2–10. Notice that the employment series has been out of phase with the cycle since the spring of 1980, when this series was first subjected to severe irregular influences. Prior to this time, production was of the fire-engine type, putting out fires created by unusual demands. Top management ordered that inventory be built up so that delivery of commercial products could be made promptly from finished inventory. During the early months of 1981, orders for aircraft products increased considerably and a corresponding backlog of unfilled orders developed. These two conditions existing almost simultaneously credited the need for a larger labor force.

From the summer of 1980 to the winter of 1981, there was a reorganization of the company in sales and production, and three staff departments were added, namely, marketing research, procurement and production planning, and industrial engineering. During this period plans were also developed to better coordinate sales forecasting, procurement and production planning, to interlock the sales forecast with production scheduling, and to give more careful consideration to all the contributing activities of management.

The latter part of 1982 marked the beginning of the balancing of sales, backlog of orders, and production, which should aid in bringing about steady employment. Many peaks and valleys in production loads are being studied to lessen the amplitude and to fit the production schedule to a more complete and accurate sales forecast.

Summary

The employment for December 1981 will summarize and help to explain the preceding material. The monthly employment for December 1981, when 1186 persons were employed, is corrected for seasonality by dividing it by the seasonal index for December (modified average seasonal index is used), $S_i = 102.77$ or as a decimal, 1.0277; then the seasonally corrected item then appears as

$$\frac{T \times C \times S \times I}{S} = 1154.03.$$

It means that, since January employment is typically 102.77 percent of the average month, if this seasonal influence were removed, the employment figure would be decreased to approximately 1154.03. The trend value for this month is, however, 1039.28 (least-square linear trend), a figure which means that, in conformity with this trend, the month should have had an employment, corrected for seasonal influence, of approximately 1039.28.

The seasonality corrected figure may now be corrected for this trend so that it becomes 111.04, that is,

$$\frac{T \times C \times I}{T} = C \times I$$

or

$$\frac{1154.03}{1039.28}$$

The figure 111.04 indicates that the month actually shows 111 percent of the employment to be expected in terms of the measured trend and seasonal influences. It suggests that a cyclical or an irregular factor has exerted a positive effect upon the situation. According to the explanation given above, it has been accounted for by irregular influences.

Questions

1. Define statistics.
2. What are the measures of central tendency?
3. Find the arithmetic mean, the median, and the mode for the following sets of measurement: 10, 8, 6, 0, 8, 3, 2, 2, 8, 0. Show the sum, $\Sigma(X - \bar{X}) = 0$.
4. What are the measures of dispersion?
5. Calculate s^2 and s for the following array of scores: 3, 4, 5, 5, 6, 7,.
6. What are the properties of a normal distribution?
7. What are some of the statistics tests? When is the chi-square test used?

8. How is a regression line fitted to a scatter of data points?
9. What are the various movements constituting a time series?
10. Define the standard error of the estimate.
11. What are the key parameters of the general normal distribution?

Bibliography

Bajpai, A. C., et al. *Statistical Methods for Engineers and Scientists.* New York: John Wiley and Sons, 1978.

Bethea, R. M., et al. *Statistical Methods for Engineers and Scientists.* New York: Dekker, Marcel, 1975.

Bhattacharyya, G. K., and Johnson, R. A. *Statistical Concepts and Methods.* New York: John Wiley and Sons, 1977.

Blank, L. *Statistical Procedures for Engineering, Management, and Science.* New York: McGraw-Hill, 1980.

Box, G., et al. *Statistics for Experimenters: An Introduction to Design Data Analysis and Model Building.* New York: Wiley Interservice, 1978.

Chatfield, C. *Statistics for Technology* (2nd ed.). New York: John Wiley and Sons, 1979.

Clark, C. T. *Statistical Analysis for Administrative Decisions* (3rd. ed.). Cincinnati, Oh.: South-Western, 1979.

Clark, C. T. *Statistical Analysis for Technology* (2nd ed.). New York: John Wiley and Sons, 1979.

Cochran, W. G., and Snedecor, G. W. *Statistical Methods.* Ames: Iowa State University Press, 1980.

Haber, A., and Runyon, R. P. *General Statistics* (2nd ed.). Reading, Pa.: Addison-Wesley, 1977.

Holmes, J. P. *Experimental Methods* (3d ed.). Hightstown, N.J.: McGraw-Hill, 1973.

Kennedy, J. B., and Neville, A. M. *Basic Statistics for Engineers and Scientists* (2nd ed.). New York: Harper & Row, 1976.

Levin, R. I. *Statistics for Management* (2nd ed). Englewood Cliffs, N.J.: Prentice-Hall, 1981.

Lindgren, B. W., and McElrath, G. *Introduction to Probability and Statistics.* New York: Macmillan, 1978.

Lipson, C., and Sheth, N. *Statistical Design and Analysis of Engineering Experiments.* New York: McGraw-Hill, 1973.

Mendahl, W., and Reinmuth, J. B. *Statistics for Management and Economics* (4th ed.). N. Scituate, Mass.: Duxbury Press, 1982.

Miller, I., and Freund, J. E. *Probability and Statistics for Engineers.* Englewood Cliffs, N.J.: Prentice-Hall, 1965.

Mood, A. M., et al. *Introduction to the Theory of Statistics* (3d ed.). New York: McGraw-Hill, 1974.

Neter, J., et al. *Applied Statistics.* Boston, Mass.: Allyn and Bacon, 1978.

Olson, C. L., and Picconi, M. J. *Statistics and Statistical Reasoning for Management Decisions.* Glenview, Ill.: Scott-Foresman, 1982.

Peters, W., and Summers, G. *Statistical Analysis for Business Decisions.* Englewood Cliffs, N.J.: Prentice-Hall, 1968.

Plane, D. R., and Opperman, E. B. *Statistics for Management Decisions.* Dallas, Tex.: Business Pub., 1977.

Schlaifer, R. *Probability and Statistics for Business Decisions.* Huntington, N.Y.: Kreiger, 1980.

Spiegel, M. L. *Probability and Statistics.* Schaum's Outline Series. New York: McGraw-Hill, 1975.

Ullman, J. *Quantitative Methods in Management.* Schaum's Outline Series. New York: McGraw-Hill, 1976.

U.S. Army Management Engineering Training Agency. *Management Statistics.* Course Book. Rock Island, Ill.: Author, 1970.

U.S. Army Ordance Center and School. *Operations Research in Maintenance.* Pamphlet No. 901-5. Aberdeen Proving Ground, Md.: 1970.

Wonnacott, T. H., and Wonnacott, R. J. *Introductory Statistics.* New York: John Wiley and Sons, 1977.

Young, H. D. *Statistical Treatment of Experimental Data.* New York: McGraw-Hill, 1962.

Chapter 3

Operations Research for Industrial Engineers

Introduction to Operations Research

A useful and productive analyst has the ability to formulate the problem, choose appropriate objectives, define the important environments or situations in which to test the alternatives, and judge the reliability of his cost and other data; such as analyst also has the ingenuity to invent new systems or alternatives to evaluate.

It is important for every industrial engineer to understand what researchers and systems analysts are trying to do, how they go about their work, and the type of information they can be expected to present. Remember, analysts are not decisionmakers; managers are. An analysis can be extremely helpful to the decisionmaker. This, then, is the purpose of courses in operations research. You will not be trained as a skilled operations research analyst in a few lessons. Rather, you will be equipped to pose problems suitable for analysis. You will learn how an analysis is conducted, and you will be shown how to judge the validity of conclusions and to use them to advantage.

Parts of this chapter are excerpted and updated, by permission of U.S. Army Ordnance Center and School, from "Introduction to Operations Research," Supplement Pamphlet 901–1. Aberdeen Proving Ground, Md. March 1970.

DEFINITION

There is no standard definition of operations research; like most disciplines, it merges and overlaps other disciplines. However, there is general agreement about the purpose of operations research. Operations research is concerned with the analysis of the consequences of alternative decisions regarding an operation. There is also agreement that operations research is strictly a staff function, a study function, designed to assist the decisionmaker through a comparison of the consequences of alternative decisions.

Types of decisions that are analyzed will vary, as will the problems facing the decisionmaker:

1. Logistics
2. Procurement
3. Manpower composition
4. Research and development
5. Production management decisions

The types of analyses are more easily categorized than decisions. Types of analysis are: (1) existing systems analysis, which deals with a comparison of effectiveness of alternate modes of production; and (2) proposed systems analysis, which is a comparison of effectiveness of alternative systems obtainable at equal cost.

Because there is no standard definition, there is disagreement on what operations research should be called. Preferred terminology includes:

1. Operations research
2. Operations evaluation
3. Operations analysis/systems analysis
4. Cost effectiveness
5. Operations research/management science
6. Systems analysis (engineering)

The essential elements of systems analysis, or cost effectiveness, are considered to be:

1. Identification of objectives.
2. Identification of operational environments or situations.
3. Identification or invention of alternative systems for satisfying objectives.
4. Definition of measures of effectiveness.
5. Determination of effectiveness in the various environments.
6. Determination of costs.
7. Presentation of cost-effectiveness comparisons.

HISTORY

Operations research started in the U.S. Armed Services in 1942. The first U.S. Army Air Force (USAAF) Operations Research Section was attached to the 8th Air Force in Britain. The first problem posed by the commanding general was, "How can I put twice as many bombs on my targets?" As a result of operations research studies of this group, ten times as many bombs reached their targets. By the war's end, a total of twenty-six sections were established at the various USAAF headquarters. An operations and analysis division in Washington served as a training and recruiting headquarters. The U.S. Navy established two independent activities: one in the field of mining and one concerned with antisubmarine warfare.

In 1945, the atomic bomb seemed to eliminate the need for operational analysis. However, it wasn't long before Russia had "the bomb." Also, a rash of small brush-fire wars broke out. These were caused by a new spirit of nationalism and were fanned by the Soviets. The increased international tensions contributed to the creation of new "think" factories. Among the earliest of these were the U.S. Army Operations Research Office established in 1948 in conjunction with Johns Hopkins University and the U.S. Air Force's RAND Corporation. In addition, a new tool came onto the scene—the digital computer.

The ENIAC, generally considered the first modern digital machine, was developed for Aberdeen Proving Ground to expedite calculations of firing tables. The high-speed calculation capability of the computer made practical the undertaking of complex systems analysis. One of the first such analyses occurred in 1950 when the U.S. Army Operations Research Office conducted a large-scale simulation of the defense of the U.S. population and industry against air attack by the use of NIKE batteries.

Development of large-scale systems required another revolution. This was in management sciences. The first major breakthrough was made in the development of program evaluation and review technique (PERT). This made possible the coordination necessary to manage large-scale research and development projects.

OPERATIONS RESEARCH APPROACH

Operations research consists of several steps:

1. In order to be effective, operations research has an objective. This objective is to furnish managers with a scientific basis for solving problems. These problems are the result of, and involve, the

working together of components of an organization in the best interests of the organization as a whole.

2. Operations research attempts to discover the best (optimum) decision to as large a part of the whole organization as possible. If, for example, there is a storage problem, operations research would consider the effect of alternative storage solutions on the rest of the operation: production, handling, shipping, sales, and so on. Operations research could even go all the way: for example, how will our solution to this local problem affect industry as a whole?
3. Operations research usually begins with more or less familiar problems of limited scope. However, as the research progresses, the scope enlarges. It is characteristic of operations research that in solving each problem, new ones are revealed. Thus, the greatest benefit can be realized by following through.

The operations research approach always looks for the optimum decision, policy, or design. Operations research doesn't look for merely a better answer; it seeks the best answer.

OPERATIONS RESEARCH PERSONNEL

Operations research personnel selection is primarily concerned with professional characteristics of people, along with their ability to communicate with nonprofessionals. The operations research man must be able to make effective lay presentation of technical matters. He must learn company jargon and must recognize and appreciate the skills that managers and workmen possess. Personnel selected for operations research should be selected for breadth of knowledge of company operations since operations research is vitally concerned with interrelationships. The person should be inclined toward quantitative thinking, but he doesn't need to be highly trained in advanced mathematics. It isn't necessary that he be a scientist or engineer; effective teams have included accountants and personnel from marketing, purchasing, and administration. A scientist intent upon pursuing knowledge for its own sake is a poor risk for an operations team; so is the man who is married to the laboratory. The complicated data of the real world are in too great a contrast to the controlled conditions of the laboratory. The perfectionist more intent upon the completeness of the result than meeting a deadline is also a poor risk.

Team Approach

Members of an organization research team should be method oriented; they should be researchers who are more interested in the way research is conducted than in specific items studied. Team members should be people who are interested in formulating problems and measuring intangibles. Authorities claim that in a two-man team, one member should be data oriented and the other theory oriented. A mixed team of specialists is highly desirable since researchers with different training supplement each other.

In the operations research team approach, the philosophy is that no single mind can contain all the potentially useful scientific information, but a team mind may. As a matter of fact, since operations research emerged out of other sciences, it borrows from them. Operations research is done by teams whose members come from different scientific and engineering disciplines.

When a scientist, for example, has a new problem, he tries to extract the essence of the problem and decide whether or not he has been up against this problem before in a different context, especially in his specialty. Once he finds an analogous problem, he inquires as to whether or not the methods he would use on the analogous problem in his own field can be applied to his new problem. This is how he goes at the new problem with methods he might not otherwise have used in this connection. Thus, when scientists from different disciplines do this collectively, the pool of possible approaches to the problem grows immensely. For example, an electronics engineer looking at a problem of production and inventory control might see that fluctuations in inventory are a function of time lapse between market changes and production-level adjustment. In other words, he sees the problem as one of coming up with a servo-control system that feeds information quickly and accurately to the production control center. In effect, he has translated the problem into one of servo theory and he knows how to find answers to such problems. A chemical engineer might look at the same problem and formulate it in terms of flow theory for which he has methods of solution. The research team examines alternatives to select an approach to the problem or develops a new one that borrows from several methods of attack.

The team approach also takes advantage of the fact that most man-machine systems have physical, biological, psychological, economic, and engineering aspects. These aspects of the system can best be understood and analyzed by those trained in these fields. The manager of a system may be unaware of one or more of these aspects and therefore have an incomplete picture of his system. One must review a system as a whole. The mixed team approach increases the number of aspects of the operation that can be examined in detail. When all of this has been accomplished, the manager can make the best possible decision.

Systems Analysis and Cost Effectiveness

OPERATIONS RESEARCH

Operations research is usually applied to studies of existing systems to uncover optimal or more effective ways to perform specific missions. Operations research is concerned with an overall understanding of optimal solutions to executive-type problems in organizations. It is applied decision theory.

The main steps of an operations research project are:

1. Formulating the problem.
2. Constructing a mathematical model to represent the system under study.
3. Deriving a solution from the model.
4. Testing the model and the solution derived from it.
5. Establishing controls over the solution.
6. Putting the solution to work—that is, implementation.

SYSTEMS ANALYSIS

Systems analysis is concerned with the broader and more complex problem of choice among some alternative future systems, with little possibility of quantitative optimization, not necessarily quantitative as opposed to operations research. We shall consider systems, subsystems, and system optimization.

A system includes boundaries, inputs, outputs, and a process operating within some constrained limits. It is important to know the concepts associated with systems analysis, such as broad, long-range, high-level, choice of objectives, problems, choice of a strategy, judgment, qualitative, and assistance to logical thinking. In operations research we deal with concepts like lower-level, overall minimization, mensuration, quantitative, means-to-an-end, and the optimal solution.

A system implies an interconnected complex of functionally related components. A business organization is a social system, a manufacturing plant is a man-machine system, whereas a motorcar is a mechanical system. The components of business and industrial systems include:

1. Management, which directs
2. Men, who control and operate
3. Machines, which convert
4. Materials into products or services, which are purchased by
5. Consumers, whose purchases are also sought by
6. Competitors,
7. Government, and the public.

A subsystem is usually an interdependent system within the total system under study. A subsystem objective is an isolated objective. An automobile is a system; the fuel tank, line, pump, and so on make up a subsystem usually called the fuel system.

In operations research and systems analysis, when we speak of optimum and optimization, we are talking about an essential characteristic. We are not looking for merely a better solution to a problem; we seek the best solution. System optimization is attained by manipulating system parameters within the constrained limits to achieve the highest degree of objective attainment.

By parameter, we mean an element of a problem that may be either a constant or a variable. For example, the demand for parts is a parameter in some logistics problems; and an analysis is conducted with assumed instead of actual or expected values. In the absence of data from experiments or other sources, parametric analyses are used to examine a problem, to identify sensitive parameters, and to obtain reasonable approximations of final results (upper and lower bounds). In a parametric analysis, a range of values for each parameter is assumed that will bracket the expected values of that parameter, and a solution to the problem is obtained for each set of assumed parameter values. In summary, a parametric analysis answers the figurative question: "If the values of the parameters were such and such, then what would the results be?"

Constraints are limits, controls, or conditions imposed when the problem is defined. For example, operations research couldn't effectively or meaningfully be applied to the production of men's shoes if there were no constraints such as size, style, percentage of leather, rubber, and so on.

Suboptimization occurs when isolated (subsystem) objectives rather than overall objectives of interdependent systems are considered. If there is no conflict between objectives, you can go ahead and solve a decision problem separately. However, if objectives are dependent, the optimization of one can result in a lower degree of attainment for the others. For example, suppose you decide to take a new job solely on the basis of your professional objective. Assume that your new job entails long hours and much traveling, although it is optimal in terms of your professional goal. The fact that the time you can spend with your family is sharply reduced may have such bad effects that your optimization in terms of one objective has produced a result far below optimal in terms of all your objectives. The problem of analysis must be broken into parts; alternatives at all levels cannot be analyzed simultaneously.

In other words, decisionmakers always compare alternative courses of action that pertain to a part of a problem. Also, some decisions are high-level and some are low-level, since all decisions cannot be made by one official or group.

COST-EFFECTIVENESS ANALYSIS

Cost-effectiveness analysis is an analytical technique for comparing ratios involving cost on one hand and some quantitative depiction of performance on the other. It compares alternative courses of action in terms of their costs and their effectiveness in attaining some specific objective. It is an attempt to minimize dollar cost subject to some mission requirement (which may not be measurable in dollar terms) or, conversely, to maximize some physical measure of output subject to a budget constraint.

The essential elements of cost-effectiveness or analysis are:

1. Identification of objectives.
2. Identification of operational environments or situations.
3. Identification or invention of alternative systems for satisfying objectives.
4. Definition of measures of effectiveness.
5. Determination of effectiveness in the various environments.
6. Determination of costs.
7. Presentation of cost-effectiveness comparisons.

A cost-effectiveness study must consider certain basic elements. These elements are:

1. An objective or a number of objectives.
2. Alternative means or systems by which the objective may be accomplished.
3. The costs or resources required by each system.
4. A mathematical or logical model or models; that is, a set of relationships among the objectives, the alternative means of achieving them, the environment, and the resources.
5. A criterion for choosing the preferred alternative. The criterion usually relates the objectives and the costs in some manner, for example, by maximizing the achievement of objectives for some assumed or given budget.

Costs are computed to help put a decision into perspective. In a sense, costs are used in cost-effectiveness studies simply as tools, as ways of insuring that the necessarily limited manpower and equipment resources that the dollars represent are used in the best way possible. The costs of all factors needed to make a system workable are to be included. This often means that the manpower resources for a system are more important than material costs. At the same time, it's important for the costs to be consistent from one alternative to another if the costs are to be unbiased. Also, money spent in the past is not relevant to future budgets. Another way of saying this is: "Inherited assets are free" (although operating costs must be considered).

Before we consider the models and mathematics involved in cost-effectiveness, certain other costs must be mentioned.

Sunk Costs. If you (and not a lending institution) own the car you drive, you don't have to put money aside in the future to pay for the car you already bought. The same principle applies to industrial decisions. Machines already bought and paid for, if available for the purpose being considered, do not have to be purchased again; a hooker is the phrase "if available . . . ." Suppose the decision being considered has to do with whether to recommend use of an old machine or a new one.

Opportunity Loss. If a decision is made, say, to move ten automatic screw machines from Chicago to the west coast, the loss of these units for use in the Chicago plant is an opportunity loss or an opportunity cost. The usefulness of moving them is equal to the difference between their value on the coast and their value in the Chicago plant.

In this presentation of cost-effectiveness essentials, we now come to models. like the chap who was pleased to discover that he had been speaking prose all his life, some people are surprised to find that they have been making and using models without calling them by name. When you talk about miles per litre, you are using a simple mathematical model. If you study a logistic system and combine numerical factors like capacity, distance, and speed in a logical way to find the number of tons that could be moved in certain circumstances in a week, you are also using a model; in this case, you may at the same time be setting up a measure of effectiveness. Models show relations among quantities. The form the model takes depends upon the problem. Some can take several forms: words, algebra, or graphs. Table 3–1 shows three examples in which the relation between factors is shown in words, then in algebraic symbols.

The three categories of models are:

Iconic Models. These models visually or pictorially represent certain aspects of a system. It looks like what it is. A model airplane is an iconic model of a real airplane.

Analogue Models. These employ one set of properties to represent some other set of properties possessed by the system under study. A very simple analogue is the graph. In graphs we use distance to represent such properties as time, number, percent, weight, and so on.

Symbolic models. These employ symbols, usually mathematical in character, to designate properties of the system under study. Symbolic models are mathematical models; the pertinent factors of a problem are

TABLE 3-1.
Examples of Models Expressed in Words and Algebraic Form

Quantity To Be Found	*Verbal Model*	*Algebraic Model*
Distance from ground zero covered by blast from atomic weapons of different yield.	Radius for a given overpressure equals a constant times the cube root of the yield in kilotons.	R = constant X $\sqrt[3]{Y}$
Tons of cargo delivered per day by a cargo carrier.	1. Tons delivered per day equals capacity times the number of trips possible per day. 2. In turn, number of trips equals the hours of operation per day divided by round-trip time, which is time for loading and unloading each trip together with travel time which depends on the distance and speed.	$T\text{ day} = CX\,n.$ $n = \dfrac{\text{hr/day}}{t},$ $t = L + U + \dfrac{2d}{s}$ $T\text{ day} = \dfrac{\text{hr/day} \times C}{L + U + 2d/s}$
Approximate water speed of marine craft.	To fair approximation, speed is equal to a constant times the sixth root of the capacity in short tons.	$S = 5.1\sqrt[6]{C}$

related in abstraction. A simple example is the equation for the area of a circle is $A = \pi r^2$ or $\pi/4\ d^2$.

As long as the model represents the real world, it is possible to predict the consequences of decisions from the model without having to actually manipulate the real-world system. The object of manipulating the model is to determine an optimum solution to the problem. The general form of an operations research model is: $E = f(C, u)$, where E is effectiveness, C represents the variables that can be controlled (independent variables) and u represents the variables that cannot be controlled. In other words, effectiveness is a function of the controllable and uncontrollable variables. A solution must be obtained from the model since a solution is a set of values for the controllable variables that yields optimum effectiveness. The value of the variables must also satisfy the constraints. Solutions may be obtained by deterministic methods, probabilistic methods, or simulation. A deterministic solution is obtained under conditions of certainty. A probabilistic solution is obtained under conditions of risk. A solution by simulation is obtained by imitating the conditions of the problem; it may be applied under conditions of certainty, risk, or uncertainty.

The final point to consider before we take up the techniques of analysis is the choice of a criterion or criteria. A customary and proven procedure is to choose one of two ways of comparing alternatives: hold the cost constant and measure the effectiveness. That is, buy for some specific sum as large quantities as possible of the first alternative you are considering, then for the same sum buy quantities of the second, and so on. Finally, measure the capabilities or effectiveness of the resultant quantities. The second alternative is to hold the effectiveness constant and find the cost. That is, consider the alternative systems in quantities such that each is just capable of doing the same job. Then find the costs of the required quantities of each alternative. At this point, you may ask: "Why isn't it just as reasonable not to hold either cost or effectiveness constant but instead simply to compare ratios of cost to effectiveness without worrying about anything being held constant?" In other words, why not, for example, find the effectiveness of one alternative for some particular cost, find the effectiveness of the next alternative for its cost, and so on, and then compare the ratios of cost to effectiveness for the various alternatives?

Ratios are not always independent of quantities. Sometimes there is an increase or decrease in cost depending on how much you buy or how great a quantity you intend to use.

If you consider buying a new design of helicopter, the cost of design, development, and initial tooling might, together with the production costs of the actual helicopters, bring the total cost for an initial order of 10 helicopters to some particular amount—say x dollars. The cost of 40 additional helicopters might conceivably be only an additional x dollars because now the design and development have already been paid for. Then, as we will see when we get to curves, still another 40 helicopters would cost somewhat less, typically about 85 or 90 percent of x, because the manufacturer could be expected to learn how to make each one more quickly and cheaply. This is our word model of the relation between cost and quantity. We can also make a graphic model of the relation between cost and quantity. We can also make a graphic model as shown in Figure 3–1. Note that in the graph the slope of a line from the origin to the point on the curve that represents the quantity being considered is a measure of the quantity per dollar for that quantity.

Now assume that for the purposes of our study the effectiveness of helicopters is proportional to their quantity. Then the cost-effectiveness ratio would change depending on how many were being consi-

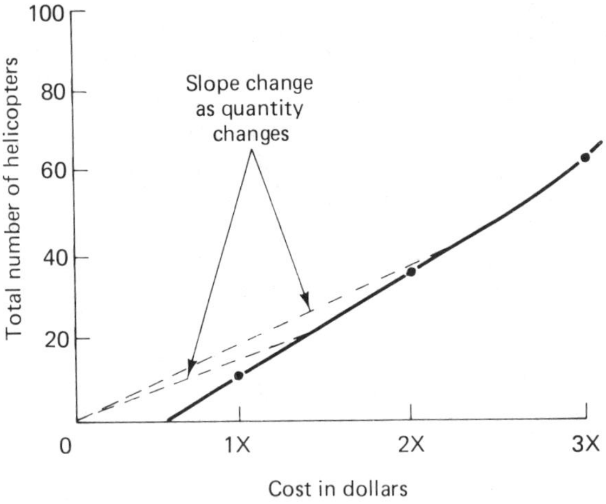

FIGURE 3–1. Graphic Model of the Relation Between Cost and Quantity.

dered, just as the quantity per dollar did. For this reason it might be misleading to use the ratio without in some way holding costs or quantities constant. The ratio might also change because of a difference in effectiveness. For some equipment there seems to be a law of diminishing returns—you wouldn't double the effectiveness of a factory if you doubled the number of punch press operators.

Finally, there's still another reason why cost-effectiveness ratios are to be avoided. It is possible to have a low cost-effectiveness ratio for a system that costs very little but that is also not very effective. It may just not achieve a suitable level of effectiveness.

LEARNING CURVES

The first time you make something or do something it takes longer than after you've had some practice. This also applies to manufacturing. In either case, the cost of doing a particular job is reduced as the time taken to do it gets shorter. The technique used in making cost estimates that reflects this decreased cost is called the learning curve.

The learning curve, in one sense, is a particular kind of cost-estimating relation. A learning curve is based on previous applicable experience. Usually it is expressed graphically as either *unit* cost versus quantity produced, or *average* cost versus quantity produced. Thus, if the first item cost \$100 and the second one \$80, the unit-cost graph would show that information directly. The average-cost graph would also show the \$100 point for the first item produced, but at the quantity "two," the graph would read \$90. This is the average of \$100 and \$80.

Learning curves are usually plotted on the basis of logarithmic scales (sometimes called ratio scales) on both the cost axis (usually vertical) and the quantity axis (usually horizontal). A straight line on such a paper is often a good fit to real data and it is thus found convenient. Another convenience of such a plot is that it represents a situation such that every time the quantity doubles, the unit cost goes down to some constant percentage of what it had been before doubling. Thus, if in going from a quantity of 5 to a quantity of 10, for example, the cost is reduced to 90 percent of the cost of 5, then going from 10 to 20 will reduce it to 90 percent of the cost of 10, and so on. The percentage to which the price is reduced for a doubled quantity is referred to as the slope of the learning curve.

Either the unit cost or the average cost can be the data basis for the straight line on the graph. To emphasize the fact that there is a difference between the two kinds of curves, Figure 3–2 shows how they are related.

If you pick the unit-cost curve as the basis, it is easy to compute the average cost from the line on the graph. For example, if your unit-cost data can be approximated by a straight line with a 90 percent slope, the straight line would look like the solid line in the drawing. (The data points are not shown.) The computed average cost is indicated by the circled points. Table 3–2

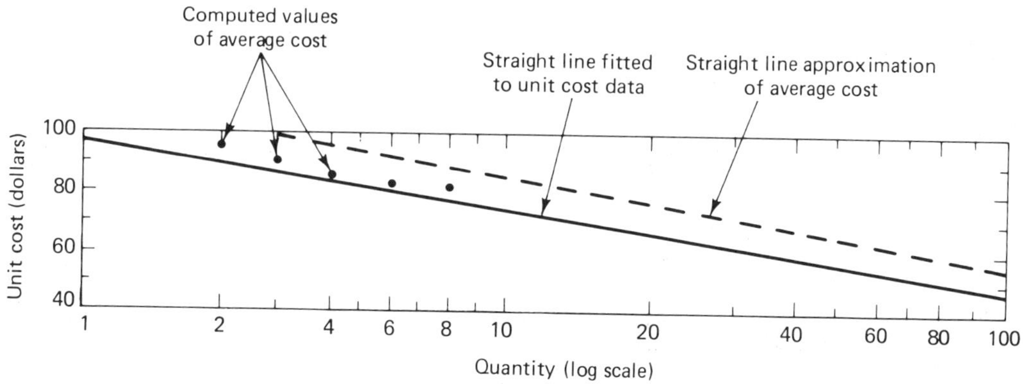

FIGURE 3–2. Relation Between Two Curves.

illustrates the data from Figure 3–2 in tabular form. It shows an example of the way some of the points were found. First, the unit costs were read off as shown in the first column; then the total-cost column was computed. Finally, the average of the total cost was found, as in the last column.

1. The average cost is always higher than the unit cost. Note that a straight line parallel to the unit cost approximates the average-cost points well for large quantities.
2. To give you an idea of the size of the cost reduction that results from learning, here are some typical slopes: for airframes for helicopters (curves are often based on man-hours per pound), 80 to 85 percent; for engines, piston or jet, 90 to 95 percent; for avionics, 90 to 95 percent; for total costs of helicopters, 85 to 90 percent.

(3) Learning curves apply to those costs that recur as the process of making or doing something is repeated. You should separate from recurring costs such one-time costs as long-lived tools, drawings, or research and development costs. Otherwise, you would have the learning effect and the one-time effects mixed together.

TABLE 3-2.

Quantity	*Unit Cost*	*Total Cost*	*Average Cost*
1	100	100	100
2	90	190	95
3	85	275	92
4	81	356	89

Summary

We have discussed some basic concepts and techniques of systems analysis and cost-effectiveness. With the current emphasis by industry and government on systems analysis, our primary objective was to become familiar with these methods of analysis, their uses, and their advantages. Gilbert Burch once said, "All the wrong decisions over the centuries from Darius' attack at Marathon to the birth of the Edsel have been the result of insufficient or inadequately processed knowledge." It is hoped that you, as a future decisionmaker in a position of responsibility, can use your basic understanding of these techniques to improve your estimates and decisions.

Glossary

Analogue Model: A model that uses one set of properties to represent some other set of properties possessed by the system being studied (the flow of water through pipes may be taken as an analogue of the flow of electricity in wires).

Cost: Any potential or real expenditure.

Cost Model: An ordered arrangement of data and equations that converts physical resources into costs.

Criterion: A rule or test by which one alternative can be chosen in preference to another.

Iconic Model: A model that pictorially or visually represents certain aspects of a system (as does a model airplane or a photograph).

Iteration: A procedure in which successive trials tend to approach an optimum solution or a process of successive approximation.

Learning Curve: The cost-quantity relationships for estimating costs of equipment.

Overall Optimum: Policy that takes account of the necessity of a split function in an organization.

Parameter: An element of a problem that may either be a constant or a variable.

Research and Development (R&D) Costs: The costs of developing a new capability to the point where it is ready for production.

State of Nature: The intransigence of society and nature; that is, natural, uncontrollable factors.

Strategy: Specific utilization of resources under the decisionmaker's control.

Symbolic Model: A model that uses symbols to designate properties of the system under study (by means of a mathematical equation or a set of such equations).

Simulation and Replacement

GENERAL COMMENTS

In the event that a particular operation is to be investigated and, at present, no historical data are available; or if the problem is too difficult to formulate mathematically, or if the problem has for an analytical solution a function or family of functions too difficult to manipulate; a technique referred to as simulation may be used. Simulation is a symbolic representation of a system or operation. In effect, it is an imitation of reality. The closer it can be connected to reality, the more meaningful the simulation model becomes. As a result, the probability distribution of a system is often used to establish a simulated model.

If you recall the discussion of models, you will remember that the iconic, analogue and symbolic models described are merely simulations. As a method for operations research problem solution, the symbolic model is the one that is manipulated.

In this section we will be concerned with the symbolic models.

The type of simulation that depends on random sampling from a probability density function is called the Monte Carlo procedure. In effect, the Monte Carlo method enables a researcher to predict the outcome of an event by using random numbers. This method cannot be used without a procedure for random sampling.

RANDOM NUMBERS

Random numbers provide a convenient method for selecting sample values from a probability density function. Tables are available from which random numbers may be obtained. These tables consist of rows and columns of digits (that is, 0, 1, 2, . . . , 9). These digits have been chosen in such a manner that each digit was given an equal chance of appearing at a given place in the table. The expected frequency of occurrence of each digit is 1/10. In order to obtain a series of random digits, select a random starting point in the table and use the required number of subsequent digits.

If two-digit random numbers are required, the same tables may be used. Select a random starting point and use the two successive digits appearing at that point in the table. The second random number would be the next two digits, and so on. The selection of random numbers may move vertically up or down a column(s) or it may move horizontally across a row(s) of the table. A table of random numbers is included at the end of this section (Table 3–10). Quite often such sampling procedures are performed by a computer. Random numbers may be fed into a computer from a table of random numbers. As an alternative, the computer may generate its own pseudorandom numbers by means of existing arithmetic procedures.

TABLE 3-3.

x	$p(x)$	*Random Numbers*
0	0.50	01-50
1	0.25	51-75
2	0.25	76-100 (00)

Since symbolic simulation requires that random samples be selected from probability density functions, there must be a method for converting random numbers to values of the distribution involved. This presents no problem in the case of discrete distributions because there is a given probability associated with each value of the distribution. For example, if the discrete random variable x has density function $p(x)$ and random numbers containing two digits are to be selected from the random number table (entering the table in some random fashion), then the conversion to x values is accomplished by Table 3–3, where the interval of random numbers is determined by $p(x)$. If a random of 51 were selected from the random number table, this would correspond to the occurrence of the value $x = 1$.

Another method must be found for converting random numbers to sampled values in the case of a continuous distribution. To illustrate this method, consider the probability density function, $f(x)$. The cumulative probability distribution is shown in Figure 3–3.

The steps for selecting a random value are as follows:

1. Pick a random number. Consider a two-digit random number for this example. Divide the cumulative probability scale into 100 equal parts from 01 to 100.
2. Find the random number on this scale.
3. Find the corresponding value of x on the abscissa, as shown in Figure 3–3.

The selected x values could be determined more precisely if more digits were included

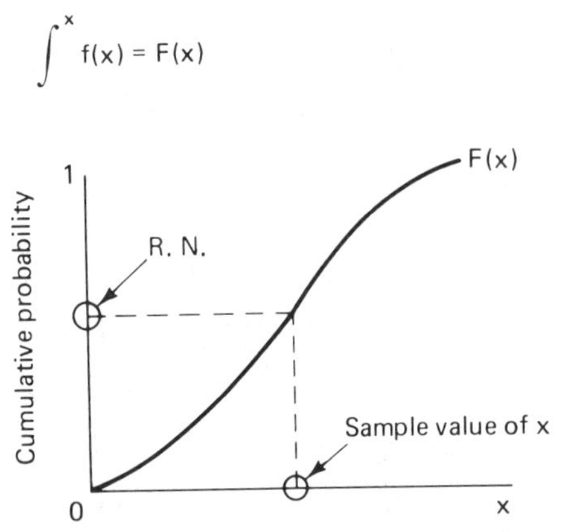

FIGURE 3–3. Cumulative Probability Distribution.

in the random number. This method can also be used for discrete distributions. For example, in the preceding discrete problem the selection of the random numbers would be associated with the values x for 0, 1, 2. In Figure 3–4, a random number of 62 would determine an x value of 1.

Other methods of obtaining random numbers are also available. In addition to computer routines, a roulette wheel, multi-sided dice, and an electronic generator

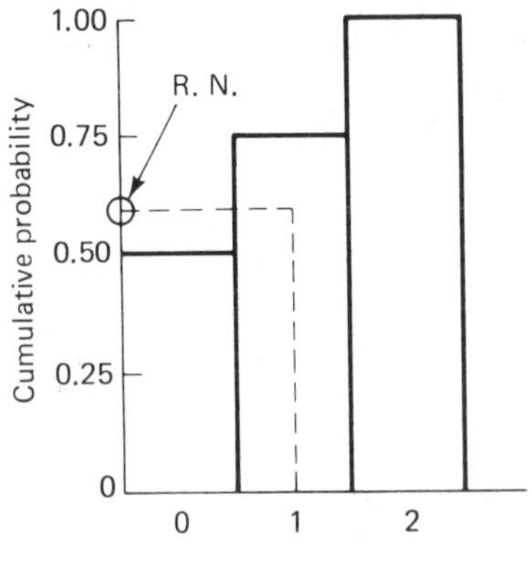

FIGURE 3–4. Discrete Distribution.

producing an infinite number of frequencies that are measured are but some of these. Using the table of random numbers (Table 3–10), we can now attempt to apply the methodology to simulation.

A MONTE CARLO APPROACH TO QUEUING

Consider an organization that has a large number of keypunch machines. At present, maintenance of these machines is performed under contract to an outside service organization. This arrangement has often presented problems in that repairmen aren't always immediately available when a machine breaks down. At the expiration of the contract, management has decided to hire permanent repairmen but is undecided as to whether one or two repairmen should be hired. The cost associated with a down machine has been set at \$16 per hour and a repairman's wages are \$8 per hour. No historical data concerning machine breakdown rate and time required to repair a machine are presently available. In order to decide upon the number of repairmen needed, it is necessary to collect the following data:

1. The breakdown data in Table 3–4 were obtained by observing the breakdown times during one day's operation. Table 3–5 shows the same data as a frequency table.
2. The machine repair times were recorded during a day's work by a repairman. During this particular day the repairman repaired 17 machines. The results are shown by Table 3–6. Table 3–7 is a frequency table for the same data.
3. It is noted that the collected data indicate variation in both the time between breakdowns and the time required to repair a machine. This information lends itself to a Monte Carlo simulation technique.

TABLE 3-4
Observed Breakdown Times

Machine Breakdown Time	*Minutes Between Breakdowns*
0803	–
0809	6
0816	7
0855	39
0907	12
0928	21
1056	88
1057	1
1206	69
1221	15
1230	9
1249	19
1250	1
1327	37
1505	98
1506	1
1517	11

Mean time between breakdowns = 27.1 minutes

TABLE 3-5
Observed Breakdown Times

Minutes Between Breakdowns	*Frequency*	*Cumulative Frequency*	*Cumulative Relative Frequency*
1	3	3	0.19
6	1	4	0.25
7	1	5	0.31
9	1	6	0.38
11	1	7	0.44
12	1	8	0.50
15	1	9	0.56
19	1	10	0.63
21	1	11	0.69
37	1	12	0.75
39	1	13	0.81
69	1	14	0.88
88	1	15	0.94
98	1	16	1.00

TABLE 3-6
Observed Machine Repair Times

Minutes to Repair Machine
5
28
11
3
27
37
61
29
32
7
25
53
14
58
4
81
3

Mean Repair Time = 28.1 Minutes

TABLE 3-7
Observed Machine Repair Times

Repair Time (Minutes)	*Frequency*	*Cumulative Frequency*	*Cumulative Relative Frequency*
3	2	2	0.12
4	1	3	0.18
5	1	4	0.24
7	1	5	0.29
11	1	6	0.35
14	1	7	0.41
25	1	8	0.47
27	1	9	0.53
28	1	10	0.59
29	1	11	0.65
32	1	12	0.71
37	1	13	0.76
53	1	14	0.82
58	1	15	0.88
61	1	16	0.94
81	1	17	1.00

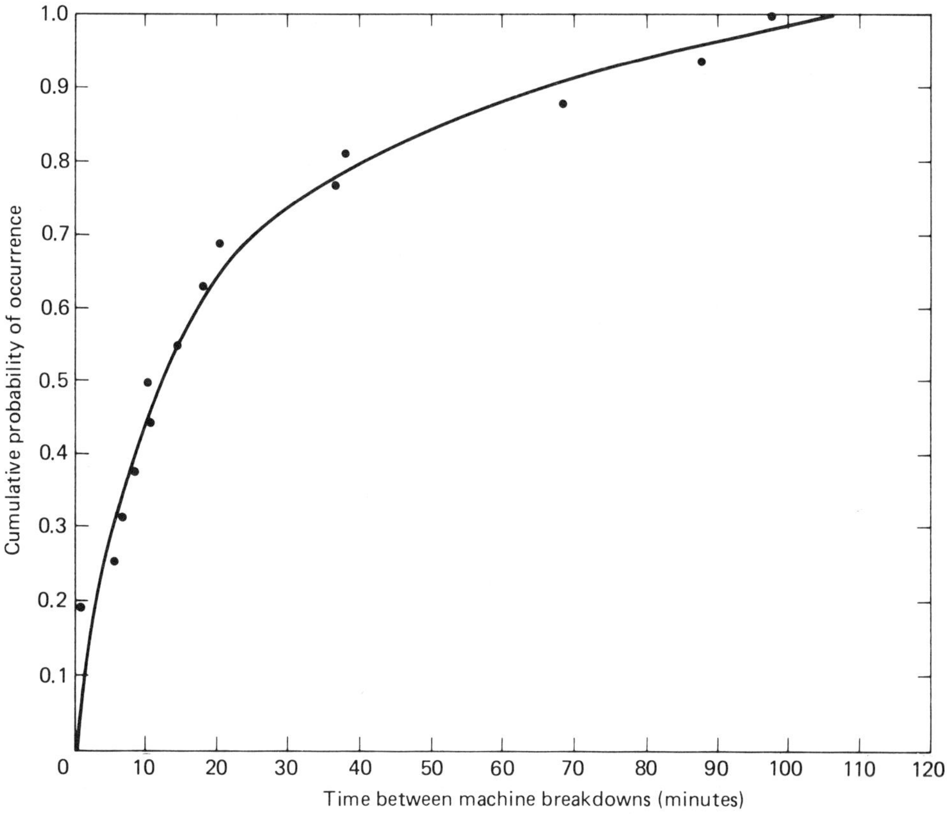

FIGURE 3–5. Cumulative Probability Distribution for Time Between Breakdowns.

4. The cumulative relative frequencies of times between breakdowns and repair times are plotted in Figures 3–5 and 3–6, respectively. A smooth curve has been drawn through these plotted points.
5. Table 3–8 is a simulation of one day's breakdowns and the associated repair times if one repairman is available full time:
   a. The first column is a random number from which times between breakdowns may be simulated.
   b. The second column is the time between breakdowns associated with the given random number. To determine this time from Figure 3–5, find the random number value of the probability (vertical) scale, proceed horizontally to the cumulative curve, proceed vertically to horizontal scale, and read the time between breakdowns.
   c. The third column is the time of breakdown as determined from the simulated breakdowns starting at 0800 a.m.
   d. The fourth and fifth columns simulate the time required to repair the machine. The random number is used to find the repair time from Figure 3–6.
   e. The sixth column shows when the repairman actually starts repairing the machine. This time is dependent up-

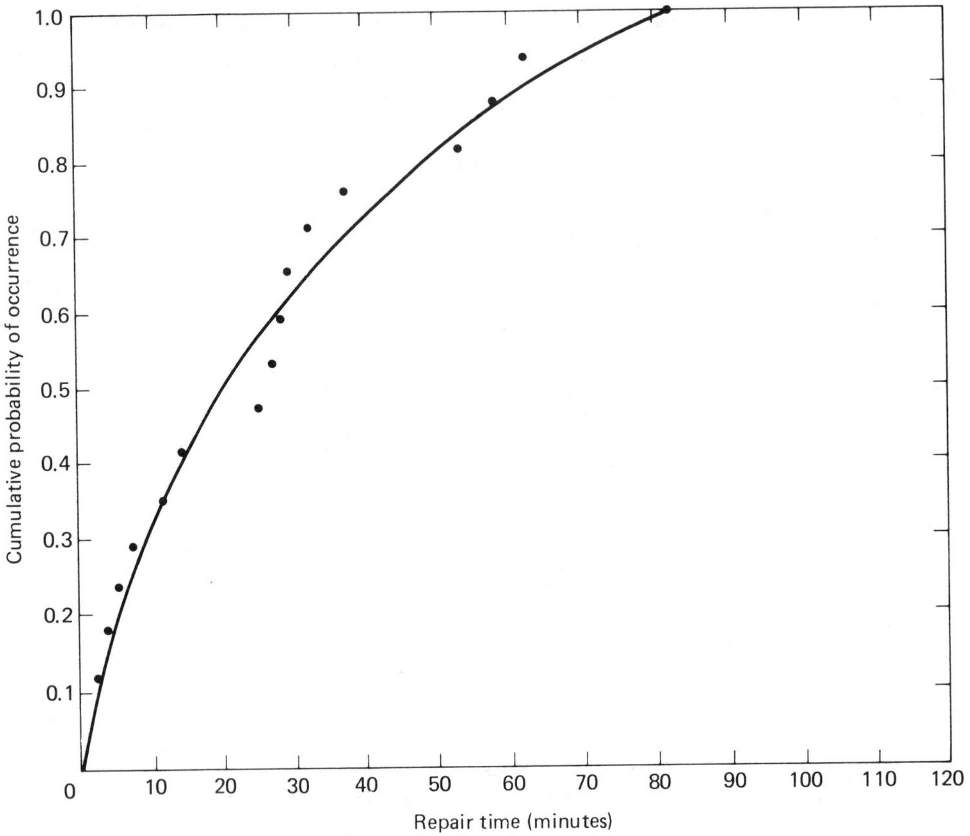

FIGURE 3–6. Cumulative Probability Distribution for Machine Repair Times.

on the availability of the repairman, but is as soon as possible after breakdown.

f. The seventh column shows when the repairman finishes repairing the machine and is found by adding the required repair time to the starting time.

g. The last column shows how long the machine is down, that is, the difference between the breakdown time and the completed repair time.

h. Table 3–9 is a simulation of one day's breakdowns if two repairmen are available full time. It differs from Table 3–8 only in that a column is added to identify which repairman works on the machine.

6. The costs associated with one day's breakdowns and one repairman are:

Total machine downtime = 2774 min	
= 46.2 hrs @ $16 =	$739.20
Total hours spent by repairman	
= 11.8 hrs @ $8 =	94.40
Total	= $833.60

7. Note: Table 3–8 indicates that the down time will continue to increase if only one repairman is available.

TABLE 3-8
Monte Carlo Simulation – One Repairman

R.N.	Minutes to next Breakdown	Breakdown Time	R.N.	Time Required for Repair (Min)	Time Repair Started	Time Repair Finished	Downtime (Min)
85	51	0851	22	6	0851	0857	6
39	8	0859	23	6	0859	0905	6
47	12	0911	40	14	0911	0925	14
09	2	0913	81	49	0925	1014	61
44	10	0923	39	13	1014	1027	64
33	6	0929	82	51	1027	1118	109
61	18	0947	93	66	1118	1224	157
10	2	0949	18	4	1224	1228	159
93	76	1105	92	61	1228	1329	144
68	23	1128	59	26	1329	1355	147
86	54	1222	63	30	1355	1425	123
53	14	1236	35	11	1425	1436	120
37	8	1244	91	63	1436	1539	175
90	64	1348	24	6	1539	1545	117
42	9	1357	77	44	1545	0829*	152
33	6	1403	82	51	0829	0920	197
92	70	1513	60	27	0920	0947	154
25	4	1517	68	34	0947	1021	184
05	1	1518	75	42	1021	1103	225
65	21	1539	28	8	1103	1111	212
23	4	1543	73	40	1111	1151	248

*Next day.

TABLE 3-9
Monte Carlo Simulation – Two Repairmen

R.N.	Minutes to next Breakdown	Breakdown Time	R.N.	Time Required for Repair (Min)	Repair Man	Time Repair Started	Time Repair Finished	Downtime (Min)
14	2	0802	54	23	A	0802	0825	23
68	23	0825	07	2	B	0825	0827	2
26	5	0830	91	63	A	0830	0933	63
85	52	0922	36	12	B	0922	0934	12
11	2	0924	97	74	A	0933	1047	83
16	3	0927	06	2	B	0934	0936	9
26	5	0932	30	9	B	0936	0945	13
95	84	1056	38	13	B	1056	1109	13
67	22	1118	94	68	A	1118	1226	68
97	92	1250	26	7	B	1250	1257	7
73	29	1319	32	10	A	1319	1329	10
75	32	1351	06	2	B	1351	1353	2
64	20	1411	76	43	A	1411	1454	43
26	5	1416	64	31	B	1416	1447	31
45	10	1426	19	4	B	1447	1451	25
01	1	1427	09	2	B	1451	1453	26
87	56	1523	80	48	B	1523	0811*	48
20	3	1526	34	11	A	1526	1537	11
01	1	1527	45	17	A	1537	1554	27
19	3	1531	02	1	A	1554	1555	25
36	7	1538	05	1	A	1555	1556	19
					Total downtime = 560			

*Next day.

TABLE 3-10

Table of Random Numbers

104	150	015	020	816	916	691	141	625	362	209	995	912	907	223
465	255	853	309	891	279	534	939	340	526	191	396	995	241	483
225	972	763	648	151	248	493	320	306	196	633	586	421	930	062
616	078	163	394	535	713	570	008	749	977	163	375	399	818	166
061	917	604	813	496	606	141	069	012	546	779	069	110	427	277
534	186	706	906	150	219	818	443	428	995	729	564	699	988	310
711	187	440	488	632	210	106	129	963	919	054	079	188	209	945
568	690	600	184	849	425	323	895	143	636	102	174	181	577	843
253	125	586	449	055	569	854	368	533	539	530	595	388	623	081
179	164	114	185	649	289	695	882	332	709	799	568	058	901	315
015	855	916	781	635	409	482	034	496	694	186	726	521	208	122
905	337	903	094	939	526	927	889	334	363	176	300	082	841	271
306	749	103	611	875	856	482	522	676	933	015	263	851	202	299
898	071	973	710	081	772	139	475	810	977	859	293	744	285	907
510	127	518	512	774	163	607	921	494	539	709	639	756	407	023
213	524	602	893	198	553	448	011	652	648	449	059	551	010	540
333	949	312	041	185	298	715	850	511	019	927	649	521	539	463
585	232	145	831	987	234	643	947	177	351	357	070	976	337	099
426	066	769	136	518	461	889	195	256	581	486	912	858	143	091
301	902	047	591	221	304	616	999	328	541	584	224	741	470	253
764	263	581	066	215	152	969	445	326	323	055	242	133	380	943
287	358	069	170	641	182	228	293	270	876	873	587	002	458	153
465	411	103	076	361	185	024	330	288	073	197	924	609	612	500
676	325	866	507	949	132	168	741	920	246	366	007	228	021	516
072	765	972	459	212	003	304	038	946	894	415	175	273	639	415
491	822	241	990	478	810	649	662	804	657	832	341	132	305	977
358	919	001	509	986	384	878	946	397	574	675	776	443	112	711
110	605	064	287	378	079	987	985	271	312	806	444	978	704	954
145	507	354	590	875	481	029	009	481	047	212	208	929	902	124
250	911	386	281	680	109	100	542	064	508	654	793	538	106	218
724	779	565	559	873	696	451	003	257	008	968	306	476	231	395
569	206	217	517	331	726	326	415	761	915	211	362	278	739	206
378	638	710	847	524	223	780	174	961	183	709	669	997	724	011
421	113	207	543	369	700	232	654	596	996	947	114	181	813	804
906	525	020	851	885	478	002	825	720	157	438	998	104	769	259
035	215	834	439	907	229	442	240	655	857	558	388	593	137	351
013	395	762	224	832	322	795	290	041	162	153	128	662	383	224
733	887	094	825	052	926	826	270	325	170	276	982	638	119	346
880	561	349	570	239	258	400	670	122	027	148	232	350	997	375
116	355	851	099	963	059	979	283	141	008	807	704	756	767	887
378	401	590	333	266	622	699	761	508	438	866	709	793	938	281
192	687	695	889	496	467	633	566	004	733	914	152	069	570	541
179	008	643	607	889	610	997	306	264	115	443	347	603	609	719
602	635	711	056	438	582	261	321	634	354	571	109	073	546	936
851	643	291	443	144	552	787	341	303	484	513	095	259	276	112
652	528	508	222	055	995	737	857	292	703	602	183	198	428	082
432	470	426	456	000	206	146	499	945	563	596	091	580	290	443
457	707	056	490	269	574	992	241	746	756	286	392	528	627	726
980	672	727	018	134	146	876	897	139	778	691	700	354	345	154
813	587	354	948	755	006	977	966	864	964	864	544	964	554	413

The costs associated with one day's breakdowns and two repairmen are:

Total machine downtime	
= 560 min = 9.3 hrs @ $16 =	$148.80
Total hours spent by repairmen	
= 16 hrs @ $8 =	128.00
Total	= $276.80

8. These simulated costs indicate that two repairmen should be hired. An actual simulation problem would be continued beyond a single day's breakdowns in order to get more reliable information.

Simulation Problems

Consider the following replacement problems using simulation to arrive at a solution.

1. A typical maintenance policy problem is as follows: The following failure rates have been observed for a certain type light bulb.

Light Bulb Age at Failure (Hours)	*Probability of Failure*	*Cumulative Probability Distribution*
1,000	0.10	0.10
2,000	0.10	0.20
3,000	0.15	0.35
4,000	0.14	0.49
5,000	0.12	0.61
6,000	0.10	0.71
7,000	0.08	0.79
8,000	0.06	0.85
9,000	0.05	0.90
10,000	0.04	0.94
11,000	0.03	0.97
12,000	0.02	0.99
13,000	0.01	1.00
	1.00	

Using the information in the table, simulate the replacement of light bulbs in one socket for 25,000 hours. Before starting the simulation, the student must properly interpret the information given. For example, notice that all bulbs fail by 13,000 hours and 90 percent fail by 9,000 hours. The 90 percent can be found by looking down the failure column until reaching 9,000 hours, then reading across the table until 90 percent is noticed under the cumulative probability distribution (CPD) column. The CPD is found by summing all the individual probabilities to that point. For instance, the 0.20 in the CPD column was found by summing the probabilities of failure of 1,000 hours (0.10) and 2,000 hours (0.10), thus equaling 0.20. In other words, after 2,000 hours, 20 percent of the bulbs fail. During the period zero hour to 1,000 hours, 10 percent, and from 1,000 hours to 2,000 hours, another 10 percent of the light bulbs fail. Notice the probabilities of failure add to 100 percent because all the light bulbs eventually fail. If you do not understand the explanation to this point, then reread the preceding paragraphs before going to the final solution.

2. A number of 16 mm projectors are used as visual aid equipment by a large Illinois educational institution. An inventory problem has developed concerning when to order replacement projection lamps. The policy of ordering twelve lamps every 5 days is being considered. Data collected for the last 100 days indicate the daily lamp usage to be as follows:

Usage per day	0	1	2	3	4	5	6
No. of days	3	4	12	16	30	19	16

The times between placement and receipt of orders for the last 100 orders are as follows:

Order lead time (days)	1	2	3	4
No. Orders	5	23	41	31

By simulation, find the average number of needed lamps that could not be provided from stock each day. In addition, determine the average number of lamps remaining in stock at the end of the day.

REPLACEMENT

The concept of replacement centers around failure. The idea is to determine when to replace an item, machine, or tool so that the overall cost of operation is minimized.

There are two types of failure: items may deteriorate over a period of time and use; or items may fail completely. The first type would cover televisions, automobiles, computers, airplanes, and the like, which, because of time or use, still operate and function, but at a less than desirable level. The second type would include items such as light bulbs, tires, and so on, which tend to operate efficiently throughout their life span but then reach a point at which they fail 100 percent.

Items deteriorating or operating at less than peak efficiency seem to be costly and complex in nature. Because of their cost and complexity, they must be maintained. Maintenance, of course, involves cost and, in general, is of two types—corrective maintenance and preventive maintenance. The longer an item operates, the more expensive, generally, is its preventive and corrective maintenance. If the item is not maintained, then it will eventually deteriorate and the cost incurred is that of the item operating at less than peak efficiency. If the item is replaced, the cost, in addition to the above, will include procurement and replacement costs. Therefore, the function of replacement theory is to determine the point in time at which the item should be replaced so that total cost may be minimized.

Another consideration in this area is that of obsolescence. Because of rapidly changing technology, new equipment is being developed that may increase capability and efficiency in such a manner that would cause operating costs to decrease. It must then be determined what policy should be effected to minimize overall cost. When considering problems in this area, one should have definite knowledge of the distribution of failure. The inability to establish maintenance and replacement policy is usually the result of not having this type of data.

When one is considering items that fail completely after time and use, the problem is to determine what kind of replacement policy will minimize the cost of replacing. Items of this type tend to be small, inexpensive, and less complex. The cost incurred is a result of how the failed item can affect operations and the cost of replacement. Items that are necessary for an operation must be replaced when they fail. Take, for example, a tractor-trailer truck that uses twenty-four tires. If a failed tire was not replaced, the added stress on the remaining tires would cause them to fail sooner. The possibility of a blowout is higher as the tires age. A blowout could cause the loss of the entire rig so it is important to establish a replacement policy that will consider the consequences of complete failure.

Many combinations exist, but consider two extremes—replace items only when they fail, and replace all items of a group when one fails. One policy minimizes the cost of procuring items and gives you the longest life span available for each item. However, the risk involved could be extremely high. A blowout of a weak tire could cause total loss of the equipment. The other policy is very expensive because it requires constant procurement and still there is a risk that damage or total loss of the equipment could occur from one failure. A common replacement policy might be to replace all items at designated intervals and replace those that fail in between immediately.

Another area of replacement study that is gaining prominence is labor and training losses. The concern here is attrition rates. If it can be determined which type of person is apt to leave, a replacement can be found and trained before he leaves so that the function or operation will continue smoothly. If, from investigation, a behavioral scheme can be determined, the operations researcher can model group characteristics. From this he is able to determine how many people should be recruited to efficiently staff a function for a given period of time. The model could also be applied to personnel policies to determine how they can be improved to reduce the attrition rate. Here, too, the operations research approach cannot limit itself to a simple "replace when worn out" concept or even end the investigation with a simple statement of replacement policy. Areas of recruitment, inventory, spare parts provisioning, obsolete equipment, retraining, and so on must all be a part of the end result of the study since all affect or are affected. Consider the following replacement problem using simulation to arrive at a solution.

Replacement Problems

1. The following failure rates have been observed for a certain type of light bulb.

t	*Pt*	*Cumulative Pt*
1	0.05	0.05
2	0.08	0.13
3	0.12	0.25
4	0.18	0.43
5	0.25	0.68
6	0.20	0.88
7	0.08	0.96
8	0.04	1.00

The cost of replacing an individual failed bulb is $3.75. The decision is made to replace all bulbs simultaneously at fixed intervals, and also to replace individual bulbs as they fail in service. If the cost of group replacement is 50 cents per bulb, what is the best interval between group replacements? At what group replacement price per bulb would a policy of strictly individual replacement become preferable to the adopted policy?

2. Machine A costs $13,000. Annual operating costs are $700 for the first year and they increase by $1600 every year. What is the best age to replace the machine? If the optimum replacement policy is followed, what will be the average yearly cost of owning and operating the machine? (Assume that the machine has no resale value when replaced, and that future costs are not discounted.)

3. Machine B costs $15,000. Annual operating costs are $900 for the first year and increase by $1,100 every year. You now

have a machine of type A that is one year old. Should you replace it with B, and if so, when?

4. A given computer has three integrated circuits (IC) of a given type. Each IC has a life that is normally distributed with a mean of 600 operating hours and a standard deviation of 100 hours. If all of these ICs are replaced at fixed intervals during the time the computer is not normally used, the total replacement cost is about $7.00 per IC. Since the computer is used 8 hours per day, the fixed replacement interval must be a multiple of 8 operating hours. However, if an IC fails during computer operation, immediate replacement of that IC costs about $10.00 for labor and parts plus the cost of computer down-time, which is about $100.00 for each such stoppage. At what interval should ICs be replaced—that is, what should be the replacement policy?

Simulation & Replacement Applications[1]

INTRODUCTION

It has been said that the concept of replacement centers around failure. With a little elaboration of this statement, you can become familiar with the theory of replacement. The idea is to determine when to replace an item, machine tool, or the like, so that the overall cost of operation is minimized.

The alternative to the increased cost of operating aging equipment is the cost of replacing old equipment with new. There is some age at which replacement of old equipment is more economical than continuation at the increased operating cost. At that age, the saving from use of new equipment more than compensates for its initial cost.

Replacement processes fall into two classes depending on the life pattern of the equipment involved: (1) the equipment deteriorates or becomes obsolete (less efficient) with use or new developments; or (2) the equipment does not deteriorate but is subject to failure or "death" (for example, light bulbs).

For deteriorating items the problem consists of timing the replacement so as to minimize the sum of the cost of new equipment, the cost of maintaining efficiency on the old, or the cost of loss of efficiency. For items that fail, the problem is one of determining which items to replace and the frequency to replace them in such a way as to minimize the sum of the cost of the equipment involved, the cost of replacing the units, and the cost associated with failure of the unit.

Maintenance problems can be considered a special class of replacement problems since maintenance usually involves the replacement of a component of a facility or a resource rather than the whole. Consequently, the same type of approach is applicable to both maintenance and replacement problems.

For those who remember their mathematics, this section should prove very stimulating. If you don't remember your math, including calculus, don't be unduly alarmed. The main thing is to learn the principles and methods that are used in replacement, reliability, and life cycle

[1]Parts excerpted and updated with permission from the U.S. Army Ordnance Center and School, from "Operations Research Application in Maintenance," Pamphlet 901–5. Aberdeen Proving Ground, Md., March 1970.

studies. The past twenty-five years have seen a very rapid development in the mathematics and statistics of renewal and replacement processes, and many mathematical models have been developed to help in selecting alternative systems. These are the "tools of the trade." You could doubtless list the main tools a carpenter uses to build a house without necessarily knowing how to use them. By the same token, you will learn that, for example, a convenient way to fit failure rate curves is an age-dependent exponential called the Weibull distribution.

REPLACEMENT AND MAINTENANCE PROBLEMS

Replacement and maintenance are essentially the same processes. The difference lies in what we consider an operating unit to be. For example, we can consider the replacement of a truck tire to be truck maintenance or replacement of a truck to be fleet maintenance. In other words, fleet maintenance is the process of replacing components. When we use the term "replacement," we also mean maintenance.

Replacement problems deal with the replacement of degenerating and nondegenerating units. In dealing with the replacement of degenerating units, we must balance the additional cost of new equipment against the increases in efficiency that result from new equipment. This balance changes, depending on the efficiency of the old equipment and, hence, on its age, and on the improvement provided by new equipment. Replacement problems involving nondegenerating units generally have certain characteristics: (1) equipment breaks down at various times; (2) each breakdown can be remedied, as it occurs, by replacement or repair and, of course, there is a certain cost associated with each replacement or repair; and (3) before a unit fails, each unit can be replaced or have preventive maintenance performed on it. Because of the quantity of work involved, the unit correction cost usually goes down in group replacement but the total number of unit corrections required goes up.

Between the two extremes (unit replacement after each failure versus group replacement before any failures) are many alternatives, each defined by the time at which group replacement is performed. Associated with each intermediate time is an expected number of individual replacements. The problem, then, is to select a time for group replacement that minimizes the sum of the expected costs due to each type of replacement.

RELIABILITY AND REPLACEMENT MODELS

In a previous section we discussed a symbolic model and learned that mathematical or logical operations can be used to formulate solutions to problems. In any discussion of reliability and replacement models, we become involved with random variables whose values depend on a parameter such as time. This is known as a stochastic process.

An integral part of the design and evaluation of any system is the determination of its reliability over time under the conditions in which it is expected to operate. The performance of equipment, supply systems, and even men deteriorates in time and may eventually fail, become overloaded, or incapacitated. To support its operating capability, rather complicated industrial systems have been developed such as repair shops, service centers, and supply centers.

In recent years a number of models have been developed to aid in the selection of alternative systems and their components and the specification of replacement or maintenance policies. In these models, system performance is most often expressed by an objective function that includes

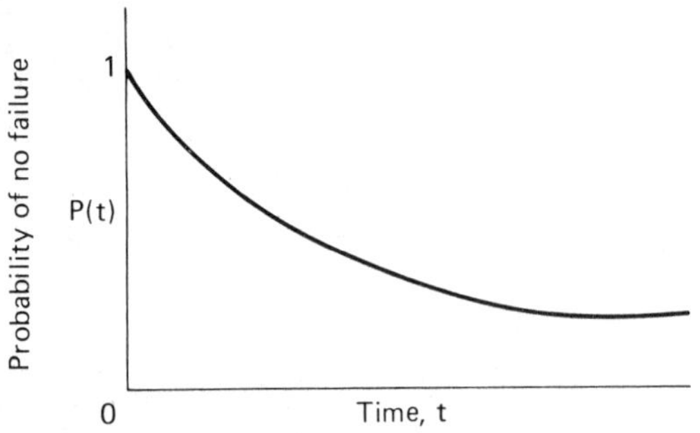

FIGURE 3–7. Typical Survival Curve.

$$P\,(\text{Failure between } t \text{ and } t + dt) = f(t)dt$$

$$P(t + dt) = P(t)\ 1 - f(t)dt \qquad (1)$$

$$P(t + dt) = P(t) + P'(t)dt \qquad (2)$$

$$f(t) = -P'(t)/P(t) \qquad (3)$$

$$f(t) = \frac{-\,d\,\ln P(t)}{dt_{t_1}} \qquad (4)$$

FIGURE 3–8. Relationship Between Survival Curve and Failure Rate.

values of effectiveness and reliability as well as the costs of development or acquisition, maintenance, and replacement. The key control variable in replacement studies is the life cycle or survival probabilities of the system and its components.

For the remainder of this section, let us consider equipment that is subject to failure and those operations made necessary by the fact that equipment failures do take place.

If we consider a new piece of equipment at the time it is first put into operation, there is a definite probability that after operating for a time it will still be in operating condition; that is, it will have not failed. A plot of the probability distribution against time (t) is typical of the form shown in Figure 3–7. At $t = 0$, $P(t) = 1$. As time goes on, $P(t)$ decreases continuously and finally approaches 0. This curve $P(t)$ against t is usually called the survival curve of the equipment.

Closely related to the survival curve is the failure rate of the equipment (see Figure 3–8). The failure rate, $f(t)$, is defined so that $f(t)dt$ is the probability that a piece of equipment that has not failed up to time t will fail between t and $t + dt$. To relate $P(t)$ and $f(t)$, we note that the probability, $P(t + dt)$, that a piece of equipment will survive for a time $t + dt$ is the product of the probabilitty, $P(t)$, that it will survive a time t, and the probability, $1 - f(t)\,dt$, that it will not fail between t and $t + dt$. Now the probability that the equipment will survive to time $t + dt$ can also be expressed in this form, where $P'(t)$ is the differential of $P(t)$ at time t. By equating the right sides of equations 1 and 2 and rearranging terms, we find that the failure rate, $f(t)$, is equal to the negative ratio $P'(t)/P(t)$.

For those of you who remember your calculus, this is equal to the differential of the natural log of the survival curve. If you haven't been able to follow this discussion in calculus, don't be concerned. The main thing is that the result, equation 4, provides a convenient way of finding the failure rate, which is difficult to measure directly from the survival curve, which can be obtained from extensive experimental data. If we plot the survival curve on a log plot, the negative of the slope of the resulting curve at any time t is $f(t)$, the failure rate at time t. A plot of the failure rate, $f(t)$, against t is called the life characteristic of the equipment.

TYPICAL LIFE CHARACTERISTIC

A typical form of the life characteristic is shown in Figure 3–9. It is sometimes referred to as the bathtub curve. There are generally three parts to the curve. During the first period of life, the failure rate is

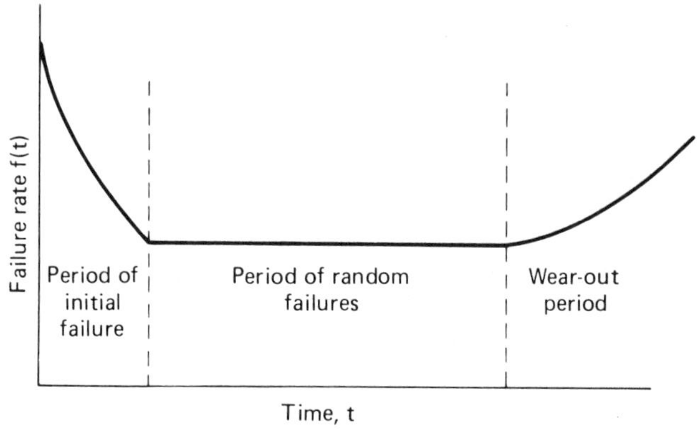

FIGURE 3–9. Typical Life Characteristics.

high. This is the so-called period of initial failures, the failures due to defective construction that appear very quickly. The second period is the so-called period of random failures, when failures seem to be due to purely chance causes. Finally, there is the wear-out period, when the main cause of failure is the accumulated wear and tear on the equipment. These periods are shown on the survival curve.

The period of initial failures (Figure 3–10) is usually short compared to the period of random failures or the wear-out period. Under these circumstances, it is possible to eliminate the initial failures by giving the equipment a break-in run of a duration equal to the length of the period

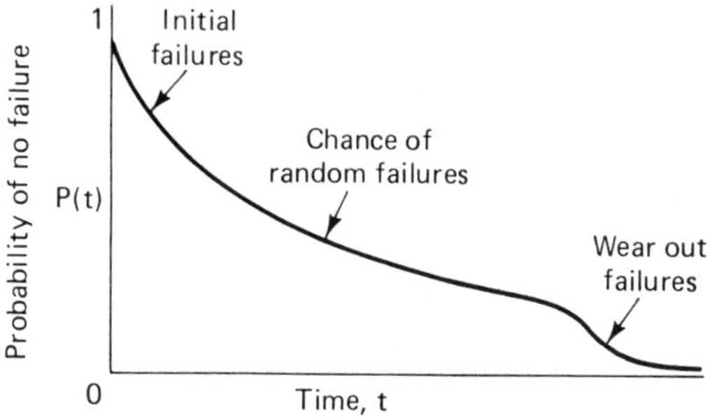

FIGURE 3–10. Typical Survival Curve.

of initial failures. Of course, a break-in does not actually prevent the initial failures. Instead, it causes them to occur under conditions that make the occurrence of a failure less costly. In the case of a jet engine for aircraft, for example, a static test run is made on the ground rather than in the air. If the break-in run is practiced, therefore, the survival curve is usually developed on the basis of the period following the break-in period.

Now, let us consider the simple cause in which the failure rate, $f(t)$, is a constant, say A:

$$f(t) = A$$

$$P(t) = e^{-\Lambda T}$$

$$L(t) = 1/A.$$

Then we find from the equation relating the survival curve to the failure rate that the probability of no failure by time t is the exponential distribution and the life expectancy, $L(t)$, is the reciprocal of the mean failure rate regardless of how long the equipment has operated.

If the equipment's life characteristic follows a random or chance curve, there is no value in scheduling replacement or preventive maintenance, because the probability that the new or maintained equipment will survive a specific time is no better than that for the original equipment. In fact, if a group replacement policy was used, replaced units might include some that are still subject to initial failure, in which case scheduled replacement will actually lead to more equipment failures.

On the other hand, the equipment may be following a wear-out curve in which the failure rate increases the longer the equipment is in operation or, in other words, the probability of surviving a given interval of time decreases with the age of the equipment. It is only when the equipment is experiencing a wear-out process that preventive maintenance or scheduled replacement may be justified depending upon the costs entailed in failure and support effort.

WEIBULL DISTRIBUTION

A special age-dependent exponential called the Weibull distribution is a convenient way to fit failure rate curves:

$$f(t) = Avt^{v-1} \qquad \text{increasing if } v > 1$$

$$P(t) = e^{-At^{v}} \qquad \text{decreasing if } v < 1.$$

In the Weibull distribution the failure rate function includes the parameter, v, so that the failure rate is proportional to the time the equipment has been in operation to the v minus 1 power. Obviously, if v is greater than 1, the failure rate is increasing, which is typical of the wear-out period. If v is less than 1, the failure rate is decreasing, which is typical of initial failure, and if $v = 1$, the failure rate equals the constant, A, which is simply the case of random failures. Thus, the probability of a failure by time t is given by this general exponential distribution. As a convenience to the analyst, Weibull probability paper is available for plotting data.

In practice, it is seldom possible to separate the causes of failure into the three distinct categories we have considered here: initial, random, and wear-out. The chance of random failures will occur throughout the life of the equipment. Inherent defects in the equipment may not become evident until after the break-in period, and the equipment may begin to wear out early. Nevertheless, usually one of these categories of failure predominates within particular segments of the equipment's life cycle, which can be determined by analysis of survival and life characteristic curves.

Once we have complete insight into the behavior of the equipment provided by the failure rate function, we are in a position to establish group replacement policies, develop preventive maintenance routines, or select the best piece of equipment from several alternatives. Deterministic models have been developed to solve most of these problems. Most of these models use calculus or iterative methods like dynamic programming.

SYSTEM REDUNDANCY

Let us consider a simple problem in which we wish to determine the optimum inspection interval for a system containing two parallel components, so arranged that if one fails the other will carry the load. The system then only fails if both of these components fail. In system design, frequent use is made of redundant parallel components to overcome the effects of random failures (Figure 3–11).

If we assume that both of these components have constant and equal failure rates A, then the average time before the first failure of a component is $1/2A$, and the average time from this failure to the failure of the next component is $1/A$. Hence, the mean life of the system is $1/2A + 1A$ or $3/2A$, which is a 50 percent increase over the life of a single component. But the true value of such an arrangement lies in the

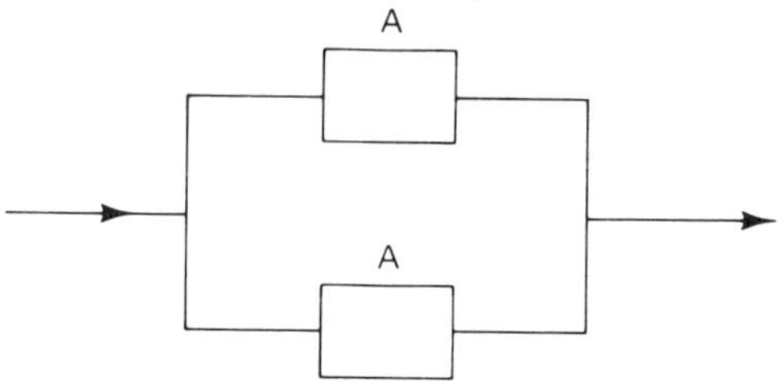

Component failure rate: $f(t) = A$ (1)

Mean life of system: $T = 1/2A + 1/A = 3/2A$ (2)

Probability of no system failure:

$$P(t) = e^{-At}e^{-At} + 2(1 - e^{-At})\,e^{-At}$$

$$P(t) = 2e^{-At} - e^{-2At} \quad (3)$$

If t — — 0

$$P(t) = 1 - (At)^2 \quad (4)$$

System failure rate:

$$f(t) = A^2\tau \quad (5)$$

Total variable cost:

$$c = I/\tau + A^2\tau B \quad (6)$$

Optimum inspection interval:

$$\tau * = \frac{I}{A}\sqrt{\frac{I}{B}} \quad (7)$$

FIGURE 3–11. System Redundancy.

fact that if the system is inspected frequently, the components that have failed can be detected and replaced before the system fails. We have already seen that preventive maintenance is of no value against random failures when redundancy is not used. Let us see what the situation is when the parallel arrangement is made.

The survival curve for the system with two components in parallel is the joint probability of neither component failing by time t plus the probability of one component failing times the probability of the other surviving, and since there are two ways this can happen the latter expression is multiplied by 2. By multiplying and collecting terms, we get this expression for the probability, that the system will survive until time t, equation 3. If At is small, it can be shown that this becomes approximately $1 - (At)^2$, so that if the system is inspected at small intervals, say τ, the probability of failure in one such interval is $(A\tau)^2$. Hence, the failure rate is $A^2\tau$, and it can be made as small as we please by making τ sufficiently small, equation 5.

In practice, of course, the frequency of inspection is limited by operating requirements and inspection costs. Let us assume that I is the cost of making an inspection and B is the cost of a system breakdown. The total variable cost is the inspection cost per inspection interval τ times the cost of breakdown, equation 6. Differentiating C with respect to τ and setting the result to zero gives us the minimum cost solution. If the inspection and breakdown costs, I and B, can be estimated, this determines the optimum inspection interval τ^*, equation 7.

If a system is made up of a series of independent components in which the failure of any component means the failure of the entire system, then the survival curve of the system is simply the product of the survival curves of its components, assuming all components are new at the beginning of the time period. But, in actual practice, this situation seldom arises. As components fail, they are replaced by new ones, so that after some period of operation the system becomes a mixture of components of all ages. If every component has a constant failure rate, this makes no essential difference. The failure rate of the system is simply the sum of the failure rates of its components.

SYSTEM WITH SERIAL COMPONENTS

If we designate the failure rate of the kth component (Figure 3–12) in a series such as A_k, then the total failure rate, A, is the sum of the component failure rates. The average life of the system, or the average

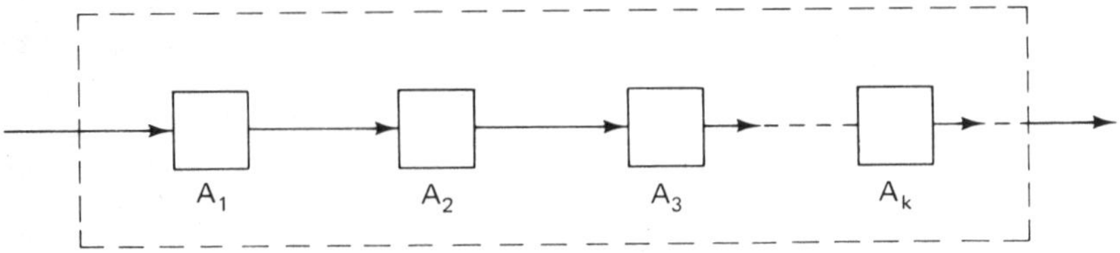

$$A = \sum_k A_k$$

$$L = 1/A = 1/(\sum_k \frac{1}{L_k})$$

FIGURE 3–12. A System with Serial Components.

time between system failures, L, is $1/A$ or 1 divided by the sum of the reciprocals of the average lives of the individual components, where L_k designates the average life of the kth component. As in the case of a simple unit, there is no advantage to a preventive maintenance policy for a system with components in series that fail by chance causes.

We have covered some of the more elementary aspects of reliability analysis. In more complex problems, the basic principles are the same. It is only the computations that become more complicated.

FIELD APPLICATIONS TO SIMULATION

Simulation is a form of experimentation that uses models for evaluation (Figure 3–13). Those models having a formal mathematical solution are classified as computational. Large and complex models may, however, require many millions of operations before a solution is obtained. Thus, probabilistic methods may be applied for evaluation. These, however, are still computational rather than simulated. In general, models developed by linear and dynamic programming techniques are closed in solution and are evaluated by means of computation. Other examples are grain mixes, resources allocation and scheduling, and transportation routes.

Evaluation through simulation is essentially a form of experimentation. Thus, the design of simulations is in many ways analogous to that of the design of experiments. The model, because it is abstracted from the real world, can be regarded, along with its expected behavior, as a hypothesis. Consequently, it is subject to test, verification, and modification as is any hypothesis. Simulation can be looked on as the method of testing and verification.

The observation, hypothesis, and simu-

Computation: Models having a closed solution or requiring counting and/or ordering (ARITHMETICAL AND COMBINATORIAL).

Example: (1) Critical path calculation (PERT/CPM).

(2) Optimum truck loading mix of assorted items.

Simulation: Models whose performance must be evaluated over a range of actual or probable outcomes (varying with respect to time or other independent variables). This class covers all of iconic and analogue models.

Example: Communications load study.

FIGURE 3–13. Methods of Model Evaluation.

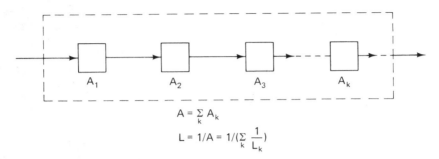

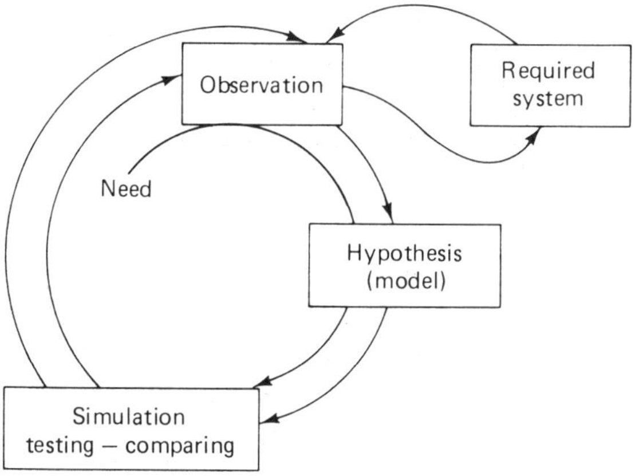

FIGURE 3–14. Simulation Cycle.

lation cycle (Figure 3–14) is like a spiral that originates from a recognized need. The end of the cycle is the development and implementation of the required system to meet the need. However, the need may vary with time, and the cycle may require many subsequent reentries to assure that the required system always meets the need.

Models that are evaluated through simulations are all iconic and analogous models and those symbolic models that represent physical properties rather than counting or ordering. Simulations can be subdivided into two major classes:

Deductive	*Inductive*
Physical Mathematical	Gaming

In formal logic there are two forms of reasoning: deductive and inductive, deductive being reasoning from the general to the specific or particular. For example, the ballistic equations of motion are general and are based on laws of physics. For most cases, these laws are those known as Newton's or Newtonian dynamics. If we desire to design a projectile with a specified level of performance, we first make assumptions (hypotheses) concerning the initial velocity and aerodynamic properties. We may also make specific assumptions about the environment (air, water, temperature, and so on). These assumptions then become the parameters that particularize the equations to the specific projectile and its environment being examined. The behavior of the system is then studied to see if the projectile performs to the desired level. If it does not, those parameters subject to control, such as thrust, weight, hardness, or aerodynamic properties, are varied until the desired characteristics are met. In this manner we have obtained a specific solution to the general laws and characteristics from which we commenced.

On the other hand, not all the relationships that exist may be well known. Therefore, it is necessary to draw (or infer) generalized conclusions from particular simulations (experiment). The classical example of this form of reasoning is that which caused Newton to develop his physical laws of motion. From studying astronomical observations, Newton made certain generalized conclusions concerning the nature of the universe and the laws governing the motions of bodies. These generalizations, of course, are the laws that were used to develop the equations of motion for the analysis of the projectile in the previous example. The generalizations made from particular observations may be completely or partially invalid. Consequently, it is important that enough particular applications of the law be observed to warrant their use. In simulation, gaming is a method whereby generalizations are made from the results of observations of particular applications

Deductive simulation exists in one or a combination of two forms: physical and mathematical. Physical simulation covers that area ranging from the evaluation of iconic models to simulations having one or more items of actual system hardware and men included as parts of the simulation.

Mathematical simulation covers the evaluation of models constructed symbolically, such as the ballistic equations of motion or the Markov chain. Simulation is accomplished by or on simulators. Simulators may range anywhere from large-scale computers to devices specifically constructed for the purpose, for example, field experimentation devices.

Inductive simulations are primarily the various forms of gaming, ranging from field tests to very elaborate forms of computer-assisted games. In most instances, these inductive simulations involve as part, or perhaps even all, of their structure a large number of deductive simulations. But the primary purpose of these simulations is to draw generalized laws rather than to evaluate specifics.

Perhaps one of the most important elements of simulation, and one that is often lightly passed over, is that of errors. This is not only true for deductive simulations, but it is equally true for gaming. Thus, during this discussion, the importance of error will be either explicit or implied at all times (Figure 3–15).

Three different elements in a complex system contribute to the overall error variance of the system. If the total variable error in a simulation is represented by σ_t, then the additive components contributed by the model, simulator, and the process are shown by equation one. Process, here, means the designed experiments required to be run in order to infer conclusions. Each of these contributions represents the total variable error developed by the source (that is, model, simulator, process). It should be noted that for simulations using stochastic models, the error contributed by the stimulator is small, originating mostly from number round-off. Equation 1 assumes that no coupling takes place between model, simulator, and process errors. Unfortunately, this is seldom, if ever, the case. When correlation exists between these three elements, which is generally the case, the relative importance of the root-mean-square error contributed by any one element increases quadratically with its relative size. Thus, if the simulator is accurate and the designed experiment is accurate, then improvement in these two will produce only a negligible reduction in overall error.

As mentioned previously, deductive simulation was defined as being composed

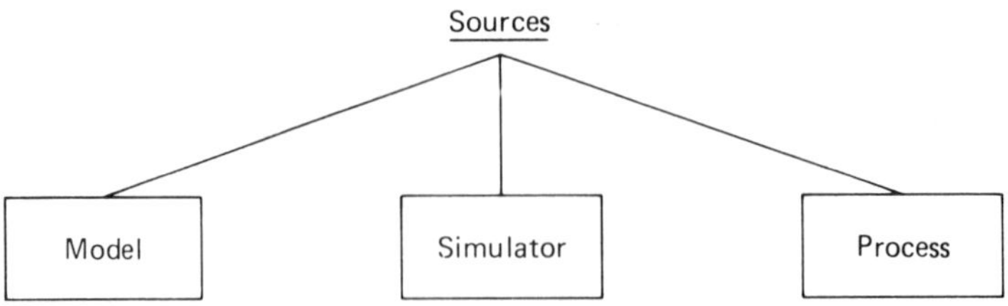

Uncorrelated contributions

(1) $\sigma T^2 = \sigma mt^2 + \sigma st^2 + \sigma pt^2$

(2) $\sigma T^2 = \sigma m^2 + \sigma s^2 + \sigma p^2 \pm 2r_{ms}\sigma_a\sigma_b \pm 2r_{mp}\sigma_a\sigma_b \pm 2r_{sp}\sigma_b\sigma_c \pm \cdots$

FIGURE 3–15. Errors in Simulation.

of two major types: physical and mathematical simulation. The role played by physical simulation in the development of systems is an important one. In general, physical simulation tries to create, under laboratory control, operating conditions that the actual system or components of the system might meet during the performance of its mission. The substitution of hardware or procedures, as the system is developed for its mathematical counterpart in simulation, makes possible the development of subsystems with a high degree of reliability. By thoroughly testing system components or procedures under simulated environmental and mission conditions, as they play their role in the operation of the system, we can study their reaction and interaction in the perspective of the system. In this manner, adverse effects can be rapidly ascertained and corrected long before the final design is completed. As components or procedures are developed, they are substituted in the simulation until the only remaining mathematical portions of the simulation are those events that cannot be built in the laboratory.

The general objectives of physical simulation are:

1. To provide an adequate and more realistic evaluation of system performance during each stage of development.
2. To evaluate subsystem, component, and procedure tolerances and uncertainties.
3. To obtain a performance comparison between hardware and personnel executing procedures with the analytic studies.
4. To provide a realistic basis for more effective test planning.

These objectives are, of course, not necessarily unique to just physical simulation. A number of difficulties can be encountered in physical simulation, and some of these problem areas are worth mentioning. First, special consideration must be given to the mathematical model to determine whether it is adequate to represent the required data. In particular, the simplifications and assumptions made should be studied to make certain that masking or filtering of system characteristics does not occur, and that artificial effects, such as damping, are not introduced into the system. In coupling hardware into the system, special transducers are often required, such as modulators and demodulators, pressure transducers, thermocouples, and so on. These transducers are often sources for the above experienced difficulties. Another source of error may occur from hydraulic and power sources utilized in the simulation. The characteristics of these devices must be determined, and in some cases altered, so that they may be consistent with the simulated system.

The difficulties are not insurmountable, but careful and exhaustive static and dynamic checks must be made of the system before results can be accepted as conclusive. However, it is precisely the checking procedures, which analyze the difference between actual and predicted behavior, that determine what modifications must be made in design to make it compatible with the system requirements. Checking procedures can be divided into three phases and are important enough to warrant some discussion.

1. *Checkout of mathematical model.* This is the portion that is simulated on the analog, combined analog-digital, or digital computer. Normal procedures for mechanization of models on computers are followed here.
2. *Subsystem, component part, and equipment checkout.* It is of primary importance that the system hardware and procedures be given a thorough open-loop functional checkout, especially from a frequency or time-response standpoint where this

is required. Deviations from predicted characteristics should be known and made available. Simultaneously with this, or subsequently, computer tie-in equipment should be checked. Once again, frequency-response characteristics are important. Perceptible lag between command and response in a pressure system, for example, may show up as an instability in the system. Sharp differences in the performance of hydraulic systems may show a system to be stable, whereas this may not be the case with the system's own hydraulics. Procedures and movements of personnel may require awkward and time-consuming functions. Other functional tests can be performed as dictated by the nature of the system.

3. *Checkout of entire physical simulation.* One of the first checks is to compare the results of runs made during the physical simulation with those made by a prior mathematical simulation or analysis to determine if the performance is within the predicted limits. Continuity checks can be made to establish the validity of tie-in gains and signs. Comparison runs can also be made substituting the mathematical model for the hardware or various parts of the hardware. This latter check can also serve as a design tool for modification, if required.

Physical simulation is not limited to evaluation of deterministic systems alone. It is equally applicable to probabilistic and correlative systems. For large-scale simulations of complex systems, all of the cause-effect relationships may form parts of the composite system simulation.

Mathematical simulation (Figure 3–16) uses only mathematical models that represent the characteristics of the system abstracted for analysis. Because model development is often predicted on the information required as part of the analytic process, the design of the simulation takes place early in the modeling process. This enables the model to be selected and designed to meet the simulation requirements: (1) generally, mathematical simulations are based on either one or a mixture of both of two causal relationships, deterministic (cause-effect) and probabilistic (risk); and (2) although in most analytical studies the use of mathematical simulation precedes physical simulation, the mathematical model represents a higher level of abstraction. Because of this higher level of abstraction, the system represented must be well known in order to define the meaningful system elements, parameters, and variables.

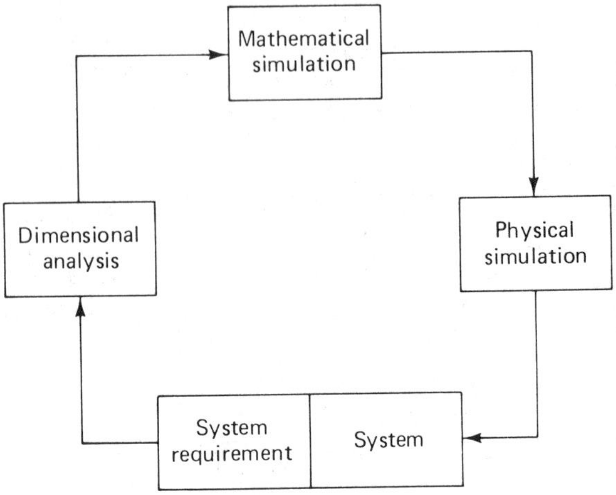

FIGURE 3–16. Mathematical Simulation.

Thus, planning mathematical simulation (or simulation using purely mathematical models) requires that a preliminary stage be performed. This stage, which we will call dimensional analysis, is a form of simulation that permits us to define the relative magnitudes of the various elements (variables) composing the mathematically simulated system. These magnitudes are analyzed within the parameters of interest or problem boundary conditions. Solutions outside of these boundary conditions should, until demonstrated otherwise, be regarded as invalid. The dimensional analysis also helps us to decide on the type of simulation required, that is, deterministic, probabilistic, or probabilistic-deterministic.

In this section, we have covered some of the aspects of simulation in general and of deductive simulation in particular. Only a quick overview of the subject is possible within the limited space. However, it is of paramount importance to remember that simulation is a form of experimentation, and, as such, simulation must be designed in accordance with acceptable experiment design practices.

Questions

1. What are the essential characteristics of operations research?
2. What contributions has operations research made to business and government in the United States?
3. List the main steps of an operations research project.
4. What are the essential elements of systems analysis or cost effectiveness?
5. How can models be classified?
6. What is the learning curve as applied to cost estimating? What type of industry is most likely to use this curve?
7. Describe a method for using a random number table to select sample values.
8. What is the Monte Carlo application to simulation?
9. What is a stochastic process?
10. Give and explain the typical life characteristic curve of a product.
11. What type of statistical distribution has been found to fit failure rate curves? Explain this distribution.
12. What are the various techniques associated with simulation?
13. List the general objectives of physical simulation.
14. How practical are mathematical models?

Bibliography

OPERATIONS RESEARCH

Au, Tung, and Stelson, Thomas E. *Introduction to Systems Engineering: Deterministic Models.* Reading, Mass.: Addison-Wesley, 1969.

Brennan, J., ed. *Operational Research in Industrial Systems.* New York: Elsevier-North Holland, 1972.

Budnick, Frank S., et al. *Principles of Operations Research for Management.* Homewood, Ill.: Richard D. Irwin, 1977.

Buffa, Elwood S., and Dyer, James S. *Essentials of Management Science—Opera-*

tions Research. New York: John Wiley and Sons, 1978.

———. *Management Science—Operations Research: Model Formulation and Solutions Methods*. New York: John Wiley and Sons, 1977.

Cabell, Randolph W., and Phillips, A. *Problems in Basic Operations Research Methods for Management*. New York: Robert E. Krieger, 1975.

Cabot, A. Victor, and Hartnett, Donald L. *Introduction to Management Science*. Reading, Mass.: Addison-Wesley, 1977.

Cook, Thomas M., and Russell, Robert A. *Introduction to Management Science*. Englewood Cliffs, N.J.: Prentice-Hall, 1977.

Cooper, Leon, et al. *Introduction to Operations Research Models*. Philadelphia, Pa.: W. B. Saunders, 1977.

Daellenbach, Hans G., and George, John A. *Introduction to Operations Research Techniques*. Rockleigh, N.J.: Allyn and Bacon, 1978.

Dean, Burton V., ed. *Operations Research in Research and Development*. New York: Robert E. Krieger, 1978.

Eck, Roger D. *Operations Research for Business*. Belmont, Calif.: Wadsworth, 1976.

Emshoff, James R., and Sisson, Roger L. *Design and Use of Computer Simulation Models*. New York: Macmillan, 1970.

Gal, Thomas. *Postoptimal Analysis, Parametric Programming and Related Topics*. New York: McGraw-Hill, 1979.

Gaver, Donald P., and Thompson, Gerald L. *Programming and Probability Models in Operations Research*. Monterey, Calif.: Brooks-Cole, 1973.

Ghosal & Ghosal, A. *Applied Cybernetics: Its Relevance to Operations Research*. New York: Gordon and Breach, 1975.

Gillett, Billy E. *Methods of Operations Research*. New York: McGraw-Hill, 1976.

Gupta, Shiv K., and Cozzolino, John M. *Fundamentals of Operations Research for Management*. San Francisco: Holden-Day, 1975.

Hammer L. Ivanescu, and Rudeanu, S. Boolean. *Methods in Operations Research and Related Areas*. New York: Springer-Verlag, 1968.

Hartley, Ronald V. *Operations Research: A Managerial Emphasis*. Santa Monica, Calif.: Goodyear, 1976.

Hillier, Frederick S., and Leberman, Gerald J. *Operations Research*, 2d ed. San Francisco: Holden-Day, 1974.

Johnson, Rodney D., and Siskin, Bernard R. *Quantitative Techniques for Business*. Englewood Cliffs, N.J.: Prentice-Hall, 1976.

Levin, Richard I., and Kirkpatrick, Charles A. *Quantitative Approaches to Management*, 4th ed. New York: McGraw-Hill, 1978.

McCloskey, Joseph F., et al. *Operations Research for Management*, Vols. I, II. Baltimore: Johns Hopkins Press, 1954.

Muth, Eginhard J. *Transform Methods with Applications to Engineering and Operations Research*. Englewood Cliffs, N.J.: Prentice-Hall, 1977.

Nagel, Stuart, and Neef, Marian. *Operations Research Methods*. Beverly Hills, Calif.: Sage, 1976.

Phillips, Don T., et al. *Operations Research: Principles and Practices*. New York: John Wiley and Sons, 1976.

Plane, Donald R., and Kockenberger, Gary A. *Operations Research for Managerial Decisions*. Homewood, Ill.: Richard D. Irwin, 1972.

Poege, Scott. *Quantitative Management Methods for Practicing Engineers*. Boston: CBI, 1970.

Ramalingani, P. *Operations Research and Management Science: An Applications Approach*. San Francisco: Holden-Day, 1979.

Richmond, Samuel B., *Operations Research*

for Management Decisions. New York: John Wiley and Sons, 1968.

Sasieni, Maurice W., et al. *Operations Research: Methods and Problems.* New York: John Wiley and Sons, 1959.

Shamblin, James E., and Stevens, G. T. *Operations Research.* New York: McGraw-Hill, 1974.

Sivazlian, B. D., and Stanfel, Larry E. *Optimization Techniques in Operation Research.* Englewood Cliffs, N.J.: Prentice-Hall, 1974.

Thesen, Arne. *Computer Methods in Operations Research.* New York: Academic Press, 1978.

Thierauf, Robert J. *An Introductory Approach to Operations Research.* New York: John Wiley and Sons, 1978.

Thornton, Billy M., and Preston, Paul. *An Introduction to Management Science: Quantitative Approach to Managerial Decisions.* Columbus, Oh.: Charles E. Merrill, 1977.

U.S. Army Ordnance Center and School. *Operations Research/Systems Analysis.* Course 901 and Supplement Pamphlets. Aberdeen Proving Ground, Md.: March 1970.

Wagner, Harvey M. *Principles of Operations Research: With Applications to Managerial Decisions.* 2nd ed. Englewood Cliffs, N.J.: Prentice-Hall, 1975.

SYSTEMS ANALYSIS

Bingham, John E., and Davies, Garth W. *A Handbook of Systems Analysis.* New York: Halsted, 1978.

Brauers, W. K. *System Analysis Planning and Decision Models.* New York: Elsevier-North Holland, 1976.

Churchman, C. West. *Design of Inquiring Systems, Basic Concepts in Systems Analysis.* New York: Basic Books, 1972.

Cleland, David I., and King, William R. *Systems Analysis and Project Management.* 2nd ed. New York: McGraw-Hill, 1975.

Cochin, Ira. *Analysis and Design of Dynamic Systems.* New York: Harper & Row, 1977.

Coldicott, P. R. *Principles of Systems Analysis.* Brooklyn Heights, N.Y.: Beekman, 1971.

Forrester, Jay W. *Collected Papers of Jay W. Forrester.* Cambridge, Mass.: MIT Press, 1975.

Frank, P. M. *Introduction to System Sensitivity Theory.* New York: Academic Press, 1978.

Gross, P., and Smith, R. D. *Systems Analysis and Design for Management.* New York: Harper and Row, 1976.

Hopeman, Richard. *Systems Analysis and Operations Management.* Columbus, Oh: Charles E. Merrill, 1969.

McMillan, Claude, and Gonzalez, Richard R. *Systems Analysis: A Computer Approach to Decision Models.* 3rd ed. Homewood, Ill.: Richard D. Irwin, 1973.

Mital, K. V. *Optimization Methods in Operations Research and Systems Analysis.* New York: Halsted, 1977.

Mossman, Frank H., et al. *Logistics Systems Analysis.* Washington, D.C.: University Press of America, 1977.

Pegels, C. C. *Systems Analysis for Production Operations.* New York: Gordon, 1976.

Silver, Gerald A., and Silver, Joan B. *Introduction to Systems Analysis.* Englewood Cliffs, N.J.: Prentice-Hall, 1976.

Smith, David B., and Rowland, George. *Systems Engineering and Management.* Reading, Mass.: Addison-Wesley, 1974.

Van Valkenburg, M. E. *Network Analysis.* 3rd ed. Englewood Cliffs, N.J.: Prentice-Hall, 1974.

Wets, Robert J., ed. *Stochastic Systems: Modeling Identification and Optimization I.* New York: Elsevier-North Holland, 1977.

Whitehouse, Gary E. *Systems Analysis and Design Using Network Techniques.* Englewood Cliffs, N.J.: Prentice-Hall, 1973.

SYSTEMS ENGINEERING

Au, Tung, and Stelson, Thomas E. *Introduction to Systems Engineering: Deterministic Models.* Reading, Mass.: Addison-Wesley, 1969.

Blanchard, Benjamin S. *Logistic Engineering and Management.* Englewood Cliffs, N.J.: Prentice-Hall, 1974.

Chase, Wilton P. *Management of Systems Engineering.* New York: Wiley-Interscience, 1974.

Chestnut, Harold. *Systems Engineering Methods.* New York: Wiley-Interscience, 1967.

Coutinho, John De S. *Advanced Systems Development Management.* New York: Wiley-Interscience, 1977.

DeNeufville, R., and Stafford, J. *Systems Analysis for Engineers and Managers.* New York: McGraw-Hill, 1971.

Machol, Robert E., et al. *System Engineering Handbook.* New York: McGraw-Hill, 1965.

Seely, Samuel. *Introduction to Engineering Systems.* Elmsford, N.Y.: Pergamon Press, 1972.

Shinners, Stanley M. *A Guide to Systems Engineering and Management.* Lexington, Mass.: Lexington Books, 1976.

Chapter 4

Engineering Economics

HISTORY OF ENGINEERING ECONOMICS

The early history of the teaching of university courses on engineering economics goes back to the formation of the Engineering Economy Committee of the Society for Promotion of Engineering Education (SPEE). The story of the early days of this committee is told by P.T. Norton, Jr. in the *Journal of Engineering Education,* September 1945.

The SPEE Committee on Engineering Economy was created in 1936 at the suggestion of William E. Wickenden, who as president of SPEE proposed that a joint conference on the teaching of engineering economy be held during the 1934 annual meeting. A conference on the teaching of engineering economy was held in Atlanta on June 25, 1935. The attendance was estimated to be eighty.

INTRODUCTION

Engineering is a science that has as its purpose satisfying the wants and needs of people. In accomplishing this objective, the aim of the engineer should be to attain maximum results in the most economical manner.

Unfortunately, the field of engineering economics has been neglected in the past. Instead, emphasis has been placed on the principles of theory, design, and development, with little consideration being given to the development of economic alternatives for accomplishing a given task.

This chapter is not intended as a complete course in engineering economics, which would require a lengthy text on the subject. A discussion of the principles and concepts underlying engineering economics has been omitted, and instead, emphasis has been placed on the various mechanical procedures used to arrive at solutions to practical engineering economic problems.

The chapter is divided into four parts:

Interest and Interest Formulas—time value of money.

Equivalence—practical application of interest formulas.

Depreciation.

Practical examples involving engineering economics.

Appendix—Interest Tables (A–T).

It is hoped that this chapter will provide some insight into the field of engineering economics, and that the student will not only develop the ability to solve practical problems, but will also strive to learn more about the principles and concepts of this field.

INTEREST AND INTEREST FORMULAS

In business, *interest* is usually defined as the charge for the use of money. If an individual borrows money, he pays interest to the lender; if an individual makes

---

Parts excerpted and adopted, by permission, from "Principles and Problems in Engineering Economics," Student Pamphlet. Ft. Belvoir, Va.: U.S. Army School, April 1971.

time deposits in a bank, he receives interest from the bank.

An individual can do several things with money. He can use it for personal satisfaction; he may hoard it, and hence not productively employ the money; or he may lend it interest-free. He might also invest it as capital, which may eventually produce a greater return than his investment; or he may lend it, charging interest.

As most businesses operate to obtain a profit, the last two alternatives are the most prevalent. Often, the choice to be made is between investing money in a bank or bonds with a lower but assured return, and investing money in capital to make a higher return while taking a greater risk. It is on the latter premise that most businesses operate.

At this point, it may be advisable to define the two terms, *interest rate* and *interest*. *Interest rate* is the ratio of the interest payments to the principal for a given period of time and is usually expressed as a percentage of the principal. *Interest* is the actual amount gained from an investment or paid for money borrowed.

Terminology

In economics, certain letters are used for common terms. These appear in interest formulas and in equivalence and depreciation calculations. Some of the more common symbols are:

i: Interest rate for a given interest period.

n: Number of interest periods involved, generally years.

c: Number of interest periods per year.

P: Principal sum at present time.

S: Future worth of a present sum after n interest periods at interest rate i, or the future worth or compounded amount of a series of equal payments at interest rate i.

R: A single payment in a series of n equal payments made at the *end* of each interest period.

B: A single payment in a series of n equal payments made at the *beginning* of each interest period.

L: Estimated salvage value of an asset at the end of its life.

g: Gradient quantity, which is subject to increasing standard increments of multipliers to produce the gradient series.

Interest Formulas

Money has a time value; that is, its value varies with respect to time. It varies at a rate called the interest rate. If the interest rate were zero, there would be no variance.

With no interest rate, $1 put aside now would still be $1 in ten years; $1 put aside each year would be $10 at the end of ten years. There would be no variance. But, with interest rates comes variance. For example, $1 deposited at 8 percent interest compounded annually will be $2.16 in ten years, and $1 deposited each year at 8 percent amounts to $14.49 at the end of ten years.

Interest formulas, then, are merely a means of relating money to time. There are seven major interest formulas:

Simple Interest. Simple interest means that the interest earned in a previous period is not considered along with the principal to accrue interest in the subsequent period. In other words, the interest earned each period is that on the principal sum only.

In normal borrower-lender contractual relations, unless "simple interest" is specified, business usage and custom will be implied by the courts to stipulate an annual compounding of the stipulated interest rate.

Practical applications involving simple interest are short-term loans, usually never running for more than one year.

The simple interest formula is derived as follows:

$$\begin{aligned} \text{At end of 1 year, } S_1 &= P + Pi = P(1 + i) \\ \text{At end of 2 years, } S_2 &= P + P(2i) = P(1 + 2i) \\ \text{At end of } n \text{ years, } S_n &= P + P(ni) = P(1 + ni) \\ \text{By factoring, } S &= P(1 + ni) \end{aligned}$$

Lending institutions usually consider the year to be made up of twelve months of thirty-day months. Thus, if \$10,000 was borrowed for sixty days at 6 percent, the interest charged would be (60/360 × 6%) \$10,000 or 1/6 × .06) × \$10,000 or \$100, which would amount to \$100/60 or \$1.67 per day. On this basis, some banks would charge interest on a \$10,000 loan for a full calendar year (365 days) as follows: 6 percent of \$10,000 = \$600 plus 5 (\$1.67) = \$608.35.

Single-payment Compound-amount Factor. In compound interest, the interest earned in the preceding interest period is allowed to remain with the principal sum and to accumulate interest in the subsequent period. Thus, the amount of interest earned each period increases. The single-payment compound-amount factor is derived as shown in Table 4–1.

This factor, $(1 + i)^n$, is called the single-payment compound-amount factor. In practical work in engineering economics, these factors are usually determined by the use of interest tables rather than by long, laborious calculations. Thus, to determine the single-payment compound-amount factor when $i = 8$ percent and $n = 10$ years, one would look in the interest tables under 8 percent; and, opposite n of 10, would find 2.159 is the factor. Computing

$$(1 + i)^n = (1 + 0.08)^{10} = 2.159$$

would also provide the same results. Tables used by lending institutions would be more precise than this; tables found in textbooks will not be as precise.

The single-payment compound-amount factor will be designated by mnemonic symbol as: $(caf' - i\% - n)$. Thus, at a given interest rate i, for a given number of interest periods n, knowing P, S can be determined.

For example, find the value in ten years of \$500 deposited now in a bank with interest at 8 percent compounded annually:

$P = \$500;\ i = 8\%;\ n = 10$

From Table O: $(caf' - 8\% - 10) = 2.159$

$S = P(caf' - 8\% - 10) = \$500\,(2.159) = \$1079.50.$

Single-payment Present-worth Factor. If the present worth of a future sum is desired, this factor is used. For instance, how much must be deposited now at a certain interest rate to be worth a certain amount at the end of n interest periods?

If $S = P(1 + i)^n$, as derived in the preceding section, then algebraically:

TABLE 4-1

	Total at Beginning of Yr.	*Interest*	*Accumulated*
At end of 1 period,	$S_1 = P$	$+ Pi$	$= P(1 + i)$
At end of 2 periods,	$S_2 = P(1 + i)$	$+ P(1 + i)i$	$= P(1 + i)^2$
At end of 3 periods,	$S_3 = P(1 + i)^2$	$+ P(1 + i)^2 i$	$= P(1 + i)^3$
At end of n periods,	$S_n = P(1 + i)^{n-1}$	$+ P(1 + i)^{n-1} i$	$= P(1 + i)^n$
Therefore,	$S = P(1 + i)^n$		

$$P = \frac{S}{(1+i)^n} = S\,\frac{1}{(1+i)^n}.$$

The factor

$$\frac{1}{(1+i)^n}$$

is the single-payment present-worth factor and will be designated as: $(pwf' - i\% - n)$. Thus, at a given interest rate i, for a given number of interest periods n, knowing S, P can be determined.

For example, find the amount that must be deposited at 7 percent compounded annually to be worth $1,000 in fifteen years:

$S = \$1{,}000;\ i = 7\%;\ n = 15$

From Table N: $(pwf' - 7\% - 15) = 0.3624$

$P = S(pwf' - 7\% - 15) = \$1{,}000\,(.3624) = \$362.40.$

Again, it should be noted that:

$$(pwf' - 7\% - 15) = \frac{1}{(1+i)^n}$$

$$= \frac{1}{(1+.07)^{15}} = \frac{1}{(1.07)^{15}} = 0.3624.$$

Equal-payment Series Compound-amount Factor. Thus far we have discussed the interest-time relationship between two amounts. The next four factors will relate one amount with a series of equal amounts or payments occurring at the end of each interest period. The first of these, the compound-amount factor, relates the series of payments with the future worth, S.

If $100 were deposited in a bank at 8 percent interest at the end of a year, it would earn $8.00 during the second year. If, at the end of the second year, another $100 were added to the fund, the ($100 + $8.00 + $100), or $208, would earn $16.64 in interest during the third year. If, at the end of the third year, another $100 were added, the new total of $100 + $8.00 + $100 + $16.64 + $100, or $324.64, would earn $25.97 in interest during the fourth year. And if $100 were added at the end of the fourth year, the total amount in the fund would equal $324.64 + $25.97 + $100, or $450.61.

This illustration shows that the first $100 deposit earned interest for three years, the second for two years, the third for one year, and the fourth, none. The equal payment was the $100, and the sum was $450.61. The equal-payment series compound-amount factor relates the series of equal payments with the sum and is derived as shown in Table 4–2.

TABLE 4-2

Year	Amount of Year-end Payment	X	Compound-amount Factor
1	R	X	$(1+i)^{n-1}$
2	R	X	$(1+i)^2$
3	R	X	$(1+i)^1$
$4 = n$	R	X	1
			S = compound amount of series

$$S = R + R(1+i) + R(1+i)^2 + \ldots R(1+i)^{n-1}$$

Factor at R from the right side of the equation so that

$$\text{(A) } S = R\,[1 + (1+i) + (1+i)^2 + \ldots (1+i)^{n-1}].$$

Multiply (A) by $(1 + i)$:

$$\text{(B) } S(1+i) = R(1+i) + R(1+i)^2 + R(1+i)^{n-1} + R(1+i)^n.$$

Subtract (A) from (B):

$$S(1+i) - S = R(1+i)^n - R$$

$$S + Si - S = R[(1+i)^n - 1]$$

$$Si = R[(1+i)^n - 1]$$

Thus, $$S = R\left[\frac{(1+i)^n - 1}{i}\right].$$

The factor,

$$\frac{(1+i)^n - 1}{i},$$

is the equal-payment series compound-amount factor. It may be computed, or obtained from interest tables by entering with the known values of n and i. It will be designated as: $(caf - i\% - n)$.[1] Given an interest rate i, and a series of equal payments, R, for n interest periods, the compound amount S, can be determined. For example, if \$100 is deposited at the end of each year for four years and the interest rate is 7 percent, find the compound amount, S, at the end of four years.

$R = \$100;\ i = 7\%;\ n = 4$

From Table N: $(caf - 7\% - 4) = 4.400$

$S = R(caf - 7\% - 4) = \$100\ (4.440) = \$444.00.$

You will also find that

$$\frac{(1+i)^n - 1}{i} = \frac{(1.07)^4 - 1}{.07},$$

which is equal to 4.440.

Equal-payment Series Sinking-fund Factor. In the preceding section, we discussed the compound-amount factor and its use in finding the sum, S, of a series of equal payments, R. In this section, we are concerned with finding the amount of the payment, R, which will provide a certain final amount, S. To do this we use the equal-payment series sinking-fund factor.

The derivation of this factor shows that it is merely the reciprocal of the compound-amount factor:

If $$S = R\left[\frac{(1+i)^n - 1}{i}\right]$$

then, $$R = S\left[\frac{i}{(1+i)^n - 1}\right].$$

The factor,

$$\frac{i}{(1+i)^n - 1},$$

is the sinking-fund factor and can also be obtained from interest tables. It will be designated as: $(sff - i\% - n)$. Given an interest rate i, the amount R, that must be paid each year to equal an amount S, at the end of n years can be determined. Using the tables, find the amount that must be deposited each year to have \$1,000 at the end of ten years if interest is 6 percent.

$S = \$1,000;\ i = 6\%;\ n = 10$

From Table M: $(sff - 6\% - 10) = .07587$

$R = S(sff - 6\% - 10)\ \$1,000(.07587) = \$75.87$

Equal-payment Series Capital-recovery Factor. Whereas the compound-amount factor and the sinking-fund factor related R and S, the next two interest factors relate P and R.

It may be desirable to know what payments can be made from a fund currently existing. Or, it may be necessary to pay back a loan or recoup an investment in yearly payments. For problems of this type, the capital-recovery factor is used.

The derivation of this factor is contingent upon the sinking-fund factor and is quite simple:

[1]There is no (') prime mark following the "compound amount factor" designation because the factor involves a series of end of the interest period payments.

If $R = S\left[\frac{i}{(1+i)^n - 1}\right]$ but $S = P(1+i)^n$

Then, $R = P\left[\frac{i(1+i)^n}{(1+i)^n - 1}\right]$

The factor,

$$\frac{1(1+i)^n}{(1+i)^n - 1},$$

is the equal-payment series capital-recovery factor, and will be designated as: $(crf - i\% - n)$. For a given interest rate i, the amount R, that must be paid for n years to be equivalent to a present sum P, can be determined.

With interest at 6 percent, find the amount R, that must be paid each year for fifteen years to pay off a mortgage of \$12,000.

$P = \$12,000;\ i = 6\%;\ n = 15$

From Table M: $(crf - 6\% - 15) = .10296$

$R = P(crf - 6\% - 15) = \$12,000(.10296) = \$1235.52.$

An important relation exists between the sinking-fund factor and the capital-recovery factor in that the sinking-fund factor plus the interest rate equals the capital-recovery factor or

$$\frac{i}{(1+i)^n - 1} + i = \frac{i}{(1+i)^n - 1}$$

$$+\,i\left[\frac{(1+i)^n - 1}{(1+i)^n - 1}\right] = \frac{i(1+i)^n - 1}{(1+i)^n - 1}.$$

This important relation proclaims that if we commence with the full sum or cost, it must be recouped, *plus* interest, over the life of an investment.

Equal-payment Series Present-worth Factor. If we desire the present-worth of a series of equal payments, we use the equal-payment series present-worth factor.

This factor is merely the reciprocal of the capital-recovery factor.

Thus: $P = R\left[\frac{(1+i)^n - 1}{(1+i)^n}\right].$

The factor,

$$\frac{(1+i)^n - 1}{i(1+i)^n},$$

is the equal-payment series present-worth factor, and will be designated as: $(pwf - i\% - n)$. Thus, for a given interest rate, the present worth P, of a series of n equal payments R, can be determined. With interest at 5½ percent, how much money must be in the bank to make eight annual payments of \$100?

$R = \$100;\ i = 5½\%;\ n = 8$

From Table L: $(pwf - 5½\% - 8) = 6.335$

$P = R(pwf - 5½\% - 8) = \$100(6.335) = \$633.50.$

It can be shown that:

$$(pwf - 5½\% - 8) = \frac{(1.055)^8 - 1}{(0.055)(1.055)^8} = 6.335$$

Interest Periods Other Than a Year. In engineering economics, an interest period is generally a year. Sometimes, however, interest may be compounded semiannually, quarterly, or monthly. In these cases, the effective annual interest rates will be higher than the nominal rate, because some interest earned in the first part of the year is also earning interest in the latter part of the year. The effective annual interest rate (EAIR) may be found by:

$$\text{EAIR} = \left(1 + \frac{i}{c}\right)^c - 1,$$

where i is the nominal interest rate, and c is the number of interest periods per year. Thus, the effective annual interest rate on money earning 6 percent compounded semiannually is:

$$\text{EAIR} = \left(1 + \frac{.06}{2}\right)^2 - 1 = 1.03^2 - 1$$
$$= 1.0609 - 1 = 0.609 = 6.09\%.$$

Compounding at a bimonthly rate would increase the effective annual interest rate to:

$$\text{EAIR} = \left(1 + \frac{0.06}{6}\right)^6 - 1 = 1.01^6 - 1$$
$$= 1.06152 - 1 = 6.152\%.$$

The consequence of infinite compounding would be developed by the following derivation:

Recall that

$$e = \lim_{x \to 0} (1 + x)^{\frac{1}{x}}.$$

$$\text{EAIR} = \left(1 + \frac{i}{c}\right)^c - 1,$$

where c approaches an infinitely small interval or the number of compounding periods per year approaches infinity. Let

$$\frac{i}{c} = x$$

or

$$c = \frac{i}{x}$$

therefore

$$\text{EAIR} = (1 + x)^{\frac{i}{x}} - 1$$
$$= [(1 + x)^{\frac{i}{x}}]^i - 1 = e^i - 1.$$

Infinite compounding at 6 percent for one year would give:

$$\text{EAIR} = e^{(0.06)} - 1 = 1.0619 - 1 = 6.19\%.$$

Note there is a fairly small increase produced in the effective interest rate as the nominal rate compounding interval becomes shorter.

Gradient Series Conversion. A gradient series is one that changes at the end of each accounting interval by successively increasing multiples of a fixed sum. It is to be noted that the gradient series does not commence until the end of the *second* accounting period. Therefore, the gradient series would manifest itself in the following graphic form.

0	1	2	3	4	5	6	$n-1$	n
		g	$2g$	$3g$	$4g$	$5g$	$(n-2)g$	$(n-1)g$

The g is known as the *gradient amount.*

Sum this gradient series in the following step manner considering the effect of interest.

0	1	2	3	4	5	$n-1$	n
		g	g	g	g	g	g

A. $S = g + g(1 + i) + g(1 + i)^2 + g(1 + i)^3 + \text{---}\ g(1 + i)^{n-3} + g(1 + i)^{n-2}$

Multiply A by $(1 + i)$

B. $S + Si = g(1 + i) + g(1 + i)^2 + g(1 + i)^3 + g(1 + i)^4 + \text{---}\ g(1 + i)^{n-2} + g(1 + i)^{n-1}$

Subtract A from B leaving:

$$Si = g(1 + i)^{n-1} - g$$

or $$S = g\left[\frac{(1 + i)^{n-1} - 1}{i}\right].$$

The next step would be to consider the series containing the second g multiple:

0	1	2	3	4	5	$n-1$	n
			g	g	g	g	g

C. $S = g + g(1 + i) + g(1 + i)^2 + g(1 + i)^3 + \text{---}\ g(1 + i)^{n-4} + (1 + i)^{n-3}$

Multiply C by $(1 + i)$

D. $S + Si = g(1 + i) + g(1 + i)^2 + g(1 + i)^3 + g(1 + i)^4 + \text{---}\ g(1 + i)^{n-3} + g(1 + i)^{n-2}$

Subtract (C) from (D) leaving:

$$Si = g(1 + i)^{n-2} - g$$

$$\text{or} \quad S = g\left[\frac{(1 + i)^{n-2} - 1}{i}\right].$$

It is readily observed that the modus operandi is similar to the equal-payment series compound-amount factor and that the summation of the sequence of remaining g elements in this series along with the first two developed above produces:

$$S = g\left[\frac{(1 + i)^{n-1} - 1}{i} + \frac{(1 + i)^{n-2} - 1}{i} \text{---} + \frac{(1 + i)^2 - 1}{i} + \frac{(1 + i) - 1}{i}\right]$$

$$S = \frac{g}{i}\left[(1 + i)^{n-1} + (1 + i)^{n-2} \text{---} + (1 + i)^2 + (1 + i) - (n - 1)\right]$$

$$S = \frac{g}{i}\left[(1 + i)^{n-1} + (1 + i)^{n-2} \text{---} + (1 + i)^2 + (1 + i) + 1\right] - \frac{ng}{i}.$$

NOTE: The term in the brackets is the same in essence as the "A" equation in the development of the equal-payment series compound-amount factor, thus from this prior development we may state

$$S = \frac{g}{i}\left[\frac{(1 + i)^n - 1}{i}\right] - \frac{ng}{i}.$$

Now multiply this equation by

$$\frac{i}{(1 + i)^n - 1}:$$

$$S\left[\frac{i}{(1 + i)^n - 1}\right] = \frac{g}{i} - \frac{ng}{i}\left[\frac{i}{(1 + i)^n - 1}\right].$$

Recall that

$$R = S\left[\frac{i}{(1 + i)^n - 1}\right].$$

The factor,

$$\frac{g}{i} - \frac{ng}{i}\left[\frac{i}{(1 + i)^n - 1}\right],$$

is the gradient series factor and converts the gradient series to an equivalent annual series of R magnitude. It will be designated as: $(gf - i\% - n)$.

Another correlation that is useful is to convert this gradient series into a present worth value. This is accomplished by: $(gf - i\% - n)$ $(pwf - i\% - n)$ and it will be designated as: $(gpwf - i\% - n)$. Thus, at a stipulated interest rate i, the amount R that must be paid each year to be economically equivalent to a gradient series of magnitude g, can be determined.

For example, maintenance and repair expenses on production tool machines may increase by a relative amount each period. Suppose a machine with an expected life of ten years has an initial annual power and maintenance cost of $3,000 and that this cost will increase $200 each year for the remainder of its life (maintenance goes up with use, as does power to operate, because wear makes the machine less efficient). Economists often assume that power and maintenance costs are lump sum payments at the end of the designated accounting interval (one year in this case). This is a convenience in calculation, and contributes insignificant error by its use. The maintenance and power cost can be more analytically employed by converting the cost from a gradient series to an equivalent annual series at whatever value money has to the machine owner, say 8 percent. This is accomplished as follows: $g = \$200$; $i = 8\%$; $n = 10$; $P = \$3,000$.

By calculation, or reference to Interest Table S (see appendix tables): $(gf - 8\% -$

10) = 3.87. Average annual power and maintenance cost = $R = P + g(gf - i\% - m)$ = \$3,000 + \$200 $(gf - 8\% - 10)$ = \$3,000 + \$200(3.87) = \$3,774.

Recall the development of the gradient factor formula and note the use of 10 as the time interval although there are only 9 actual financial payments in this particular gradient factor exercise. If, instead, the present worth of the ten-year power and maintenance expense was needed the calculation would be handled in the following manner:

P = \$3,000; g = \$200; $i = 8\%$; $n = 10$

From Table O: $(pwf - 8\% - 10) = 6.710$

From Table T: $(gpwf - 8\% - 10) = 25.98$

$$\begin{aligned} \text{P.W.} &= P(pwf - i\% - n) + g(gpwf - i\% - n) \\ &= \$3{,}000\ (6.710) + \$200(25.98) \\ &= \$20{,}130 + \$5{,}196 = \$25{,}326. \end{aligned}$$

See Problem 5 in the section "Practical Examples," for further use of gradient factors.

Summary

In this section we have briefly discussed interest formulas. We have seen that interest formulas serve the purpose of relating money to time. If there was no interest, money wouldn't change in value with respect to time, and there would be no need for interest formulas.

We have seen that, in addition to the simple-interest formula, there are four pairs of compound-interest formulas—one that relates P and S, one that relates R and S, one that relates P and R, and one that converts a gradient series to either R or P.

By use of these formulas, we can find the value of money at any time. These relationships will be extremely important as we go into equivalence and depreciation calculations.

EQUIVALENCE

In order to determine the most economical way in which to do a job, or the most economical plan to follow, it is necessary for the engineer to make comparisons between alternatives. These economic comparisons are equivalence calculations.

In order that a comparison may be made, each alternative must have the same basis. For instance, liters of water cannot be compared with kilograms of mercury until there is a conversion to an equivalent basis.

For things to be equivalent, they must have the same effect or the same value in exchange. For instance, the cost of doing a job one way must be compared with the cost of doing it another way. In other words, the effect is the same regardless of method, but the cost may differ. Or if the cost is the same regardless of method, the incomes from the finished products, or the results may be compared.

Three factors are involved in the equivalence of money: (1) total sum of money, (2) prevailing interest rate, and (3) time of occurrence.

Costs and incomes resulting from economic ventures must be compared on an equivalent basis. The interest formulas discussed in the first section enable the analyst to place these figures on an equivalent basis—that is, yearly, present, or some time in the future.

For instance, if plan A guarantees an income of \$2,000 per year for ten years, but plan B provides a lump sum of \$18,000 now, which plan is worth more if interest is 6 percent? Here interest formulas can be most logically employed to place each alternative on either the yearly basis or the present-worth basis. Using the capital-recovery factor, it will be found that plan B is equivalent to \$2,445.66 yearly, that is $(18{,}000 \times 0.13587)$, and is thus worth more than Plan A. Thus, we will see that equivalence calculations are in effect the practical application of interest formulas.

Basic Methods by Which Economic Ventures Can Be Compared

There are seven basic methods by which economic ventures can be compared:

1. Annual cost or annual income.
2. Present worth of costs or incomes.
3. Capitalized amount (benefit = interest on investment).
4. Rate of return.
5. Minimum cost points.
6. Break-even point analysis.
7. Payback analysis.

Annual Cost or Annual Income. In the previous section, we covered a very simple example using this basis of comparison. In essence, this method is simply the application of the sinking-fund and the capital-recovery factors. We will use another simple example and carry it through using both the present-worth and the capitalized-cost methods.

Suppose a company can buy a machine for $5,000 and use it for ten years, after which they will sell it for $100. Maintenance costs will average $45 per year. Or, the company can rent the machine for $710 per year, maintenance included. With interest at 6 percent, which is more profitable? In this comparison, you will note that the effect is the same; either way, the company has the use of the machine. Thus, we will compare the alternatives on the basis of annual cost.

First, convert the present purchase price to an equivalent annual cost by using the capital-recovery factor:

$$R = P(crf - i\% - n) = \$5{,}000\,(crf - 6\% - 10)$$
$$= \$5{,}000(0.13587) = \$679.35.$$

Next, find the annual equivalent of the salvage value by using the sinking-fund factor:

$$R = S(sff - i\% - n) = \$100\,(sff - 6\% - 10)$$
$$= \$100(0.07587) = \$7.59.$$

Annual cost of purchase less annual salvage recovery = $679.35 − $7.59 = $671.76. The above may also be determined as follows:

$$(\$5{,}000 - \$100)\,(crf - 6\% - 10) + (\$100 \times 6\%) = \$4{,}900\,(0.13587) + \$6.00 = \$671.76.$$

Then, the annual cost for purchase and upkeep is

$$\$679.35 - \$7.59 + \$45.00 = \$716.75.$$

Annual cost to rent is $710.00. Thus, renting is more economical by $6.76 per year.

Present Worth of Costs or Incomes. In the preceding section, we compared the rental costs of a machine with the costs of purchasing and maintaining the machine on an annual cost basis. If we wished to compare these alternatives on the basis of their present worths, we would merely bring all the costs and incomes, including salvage, to the present.

The present worth of owning the machine may be found in either of two ways. In the first, find the present worth of the annual cost (found previously by using the *crf* and *sff* factors):

$$P = R(pwf - i\% - n) = R(pwf - 6\% = 10)$$
$$= \$716.76(7.36) = \$5.275.36.$$

In the second, find the present worth of the annual maintenance cost and the final salvage cost:

Maintenance: $P = R(pwf - i\% - n) = \$45.00$ $(pwf - 6\% - 10)\ \$45.00(7.36)$ $= \$331.20$

Salvage: $P = S(pwf' - i - n)$ $= \$100.00(pwf' - 6\% - 10)$ $= \$100.00(0.5584) = \$55.84.$

Thus, the present-worth cost is:

$$P_{net} = \$5{,}000 + \$331.20 - \$55.84 = \$5{,}275.36.$$

By either method, the present-worth cost of purchasing and owning the machine is found to be $5,275.36.

Next, the present-worth cost of rental is found by the equal-payment present-worth factor:

$$P = R(pwf - i\% - n) = \$710.00$$
$$(pwf - 6\% - 10) = \$710.00\,(7.36) = \$5{,}225.60.$$

Thus, on the present-worth basis, the cost of purchasing and owning is $49.76 more than the cost of renting. This $49.76 may be verified by obtaining the present worth of the 10 annual savings computed in the first problem: $6.76 ($pwf - 6\% - 10$) = $6.76(7.36) = $49.76. Comparison on this basis means simply that an investment now of $5,225.60 would be required to rent the machine, whereas a present investment of $5,275.36 would pay for the purchase and upkeep of the machine.

Capitalized Amount. The capitalized basis of evaluation is used on long-term assets or programs, such as highways, dams, and power-generating plants. Under this system, annual incomes or annual costs are calculated on the assumption that they will continue forever. This assumption is quite realistic. In justification, note how the capital recovery factor approaches the interest rate in the 75-to-100-year intervals, particularly in the higher interest rates. Thus, it is necessary to find a single amount in the present having a return, at the prevailing rate, equal to the annual income, costs, or net incomes and costs.

Our example in itself is not a good example of a long-term asset. If, however, we consider that this machine is replaced every ten years under the given conditions, this may be considered a long-term asset.

The capitalized cost of purchase is:

$$\frac{\text{Annual cost}}{i} = \frac{\$716.76}{0.06} = \$11{,}946.00.$$

The capitalized cost of rental is:

$$\frac{\text{Annual cost}}{i} = \frac{\$710.00}{0.06} = \$11{,}833.33.$$

The capitalized cost of rental is less by $112.67. Thus, an investment of $11,946 yielding a 6 percent return is necessary to cover the cost of purchasing and maintaining the machine, while an investment of $11,833.33 at 6 percent is required for rental. These investments would then cover the annual costs forever.

It should be noted here that these three methods (annual cost, present worth, and capitalized) all yield the same results.

$$\frac{\text{Purchase}}{\text{Rental}} = \overset{\text{(A.C.)}}{\frac{\$716.76}{\$710.00}} = \overset{\text{(PW)}}{\frac{\$5{,}275.36}{\$5{,}225.60}} = \overset{\text{(Cap)}}{\frac{\$11{,}946.00}{\$11{,}833.33}} = 1.01$$

It should also be noted that, although our example was one of costs, comparisons are made on the basis of incomes, costs, net incomes, and net costs. The principles remain the same; the calculations merely become more difficult.

Rate of Return. Many times, opportunities are compared on the basis of rates of return. For instance, Proposal A requires an investment of $2,000, but returns $2,200 at the end of the year. The rate of return is

$$\frac{\$2{,}200 - \$2{,}000}{\$2{,}000}$$

or 10 percent. Proposal B requires an investment of $3,000, but returns $3,600 at the end of the year. Its rate of return is then

$$\frac{\$3{,}600 - \$3{,}000}{\$3{,}000}$$

or 20 percent.

On the basis of rate of return, Proposal B is then the better one.

Basically, rate-of-return calculations are similar to this simplified example. They consist of finding the interest rate for which the present worth of incomes and disbursements are equal. These are usually trial-and-error calculations using the interest tables in which the exact interest rate is bracketed and then found by interpolation.

As for the basic problem of whether to buy or rent in an earlier part of this section, it may be of value to determine at what interest rate the two alternatives are equal.

Try 5½%: $R = S(crf - 5½\% - 10)$ $R =$ \$4,900(0.13267) = \$650.08. Annual Cost of Purchase is: \$650.08 + (5½% of \$100.00) + \$45.00 = \$700.58. Note that at 5½ percent this annual purchase cost is less than rental by \$9.42, that is, (\$710.00 − \$700.58).

Try 6 percent: R = \$4,900(0.13587) = \$655.76. Annual Cost of Purchase is: \$655.76 + (6% of \$100.00) + \$45.00 = \$716.76. Note that at 6 percent this annual purchase cost is more than rental by \$6.76, that is, (\$716.76 − \$710.00). Also observe that by increasing the interest rate the annual cost of ownership increases because interest is higher on unrecovered elements of capital outlay. The equivalent interest rate is then

$$5\tfrac{1}{2}\% + \tfrac{1}{2}\%\left[\frac{\$9.42}{\$9.42 + \$6.76}\right] = 5.79\%.$$

This straight-line interpolation of the ½ percent interval of interest is reasonably correct since the accurate geometry of the exponential interest curves is not especially sharp.

Minimum-cost Points. In many engineering problems and financial situations, the total cost (y) is a function of several monetary items, some of which vary directly with a specified variable (v), such as (ax, $a'x$, $a''x$), and others that vary inversely with the same specified variable (x), such as:

$$\frac{b}{x}, \ \frac{b'}{x}, \ \frac{b''}{x}.$$

In its simplest form, this relationship may be expressed as:

$$y = ax + \frac{b}{x}$$

The minimum total cost will be indicated by employing the basic rule of calculus whereby the first derivative of the above equation is determined and set equal to zero. That is:

$$\frac{dy}{dx} = 0 = a - \frac{b}{x^2} \quad \text{or } x' = \sqrt{\frac{b}{a}}.$$

This equation indicates that the square root of the inversely varying costs divided by the directly varying costs of the variable influencing total costs will produce the minimum cost. It is easily observed that if

$$y = ax + a'x + a''x + \frac{b}{x} + \frac{b'}{x},$$

then at the minimum cost point

$$x = \sqrt{\frac{b + b'}{a + a' + a''}},$$

thus allowing a large number of items to play on the variable in both direct and inverse fashion.

In the daily operations of business and industrial organizations, many economic studies are made for the purpose of minimizing costs. When the total cost of an item or operation is the sum of a fixed cost, and a variable cost that increases directly with respect to some design variable, such as the number of units produced, and a second variable cost that is inversely proportional to the same design variable, then the total cost C is

$$C = ax + \frac{b}{x} + k,$$

where a, b and k are constants and x is the design variable that can be controlled.

A typical situation involving the minimum-cost concept is the procurement of goods for use or sale. Usually the goods or supplies are purchased periodically throughout the year in lots, and each lot is received at one time and put into storage. Thereafter, the supply is used as needed, sometimes at a fairly constant rate, until the supply is exhausted or diminished to a predetermined minimum inventory quantity, at which time a new order is placed. This situation is depicted in Figure 4–1.

In such a situation, the cost of processing an order is essentially constant regardless of the quantity ordered. Consequently, the order cost per unit varies inversely with the size of the order. On the other hand, a number of costs increase as the size of the order increases: for example, the amount of storage space and its costs, the interest on the average inventory in stock, insurance, and taxes all increase directly with the order quantity. These directly varying costs are known as carrying or holding costs. The cost per piece of material purchased is, in most cases and for a great range of quantities, independent of order size. Clearly, under these conditions there will be some order size that will be most economical, and this economic order quantity (EOQ) can be determined by the application of the equation

$$x' = \sqrt{\frac{b}{a}}.$$

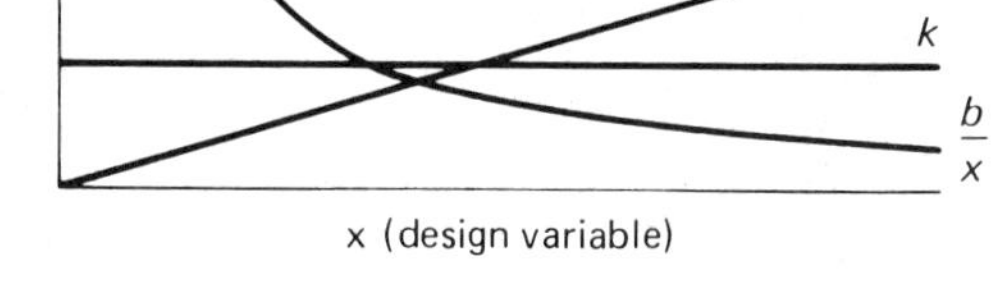

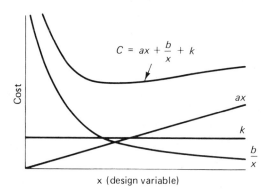

FIGURE 4–1. General Relationship of the Fixed Cost (k), Direct Variable Cost (ax), Inversely Variable Cost (b/x), and Total Cost (C).

The determination of a minimum cost point can be illustrated by an economic order quantity. Example: Find the EOQ and minimum cost if usage is 100 items per month, cost of placing an order is \$6.00 each, and carrying charge is 46¢ per month per item. Thus if,

A = Cost of placing an order, setup cost, etc.

u = Number of units consumed per unit of time (at a constant rate).

c = Carrying or holding cost per unit of product per unit of time, or cost to set up the machine to produce.

q = Production or order quantity, units.

t = Length of one inventory cycle, units of time (i.e., $t = q/u$).

C = Total cost per unit of time.

Here, $u = 100$, $A = 6$, $c = 0.46$. Setup cost: there are u/q setups per unit of time and their cost is Au/q. Carrying cost: the inventory on hand varies linearly from q at the beginning to 0 at the end. The average on hand is therefore $q/2$, and the cost of carrying it is $cq/2$. The total cost that is influenced by the choice of q is just the sum of the carrying cost and setup cost. Thus

$$C = \frac{Au}{q} + \frac{cq}{2}$$

To get a minimum, we differentiate with respect to q and set the results = 0.

$$\frac{dC}{dq} = -\frac{Au}{q^2} + \frac{c}{2} = 0$$

$$q^{*2} = \frac{2Au}{c} \text{ or } q^* = \sqrt{\frac{2Au}{c}} \quad (q^* \text{ is the EOQ})$$

$$C = Au\sqrt{\frac{c}{2Au}} + \frac{c}{2}\sqrt{\frac{2Au}{c}} = \sqrt{2Auc}.$$

Therefore, from our example:

$$q^* = \sqrt{\frac{2(6)100}{0.46}} = 51 \text{ items. Answer.}$$

$$C = \sqrt{2(6)(100)(0.46)} = \$24 \text{ per month}$$

Answer.

See Figure 4–2 for a graphic presentation of this example. Note that the C curve is quite flat at the optimal level.

Break-even Point Analysis. Most production organizations have as their primary goal the maximization of profits. As a result, one of the oldest and most widely used tools to analyze the cost-volume relationship is the break-even point analysis. Break-even point analysis provides a comparison of a firm's revenue with its cost structure at various potential levels of operation. It is particularly useful in profit projections, expense control, price determination, and decisionmaking when changes in the cost structure are involved. Comprehension of operating and marketing conditions is greatly facilitated by the "conspectus" of the interrelation between operating levels, sales revenue, costs and profits, as provided by the break-even chart. The break-even point is the level of operation at which total revenue equals total costs.

The break-even model is a deterministic model used to illustrate the relationship between revenues, costs, and profits. The model can answer such questions as: (1) What will be the break-even point in dollars, units, or capacity? (2) What will be the profit or loss in producing and selling various quantities of a product? (3) What level of production output and sales is needed to achieve a desired level of profit?

The following symbols are usually used:

BeP: Break-even point.

P: Selling price per unit.

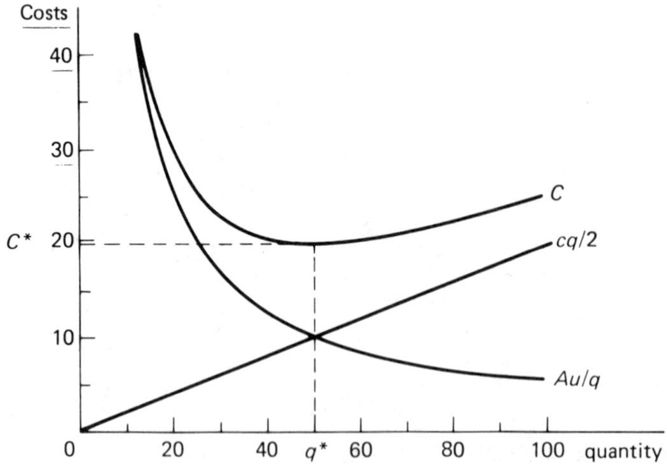

FIGURE 4–2. Graphic Model of a Simple Inventory Problem.

VC: Variable cost per unit.

FC: Fixed costs.

TC: Total costs.

Q: Number of units.

TR: Total revenue.

Using the symbols cited above, we can derive the break-even formula. First we define the equation for total costs: $TC = FC + (VC \times Q)$. Then we define total revenue: $TR = P \times Q$. At the break-even point, total costs equal total revenue. Therefore, equating these two:

$$P \times Q = (VC \times Q) + FC$$

Solving Q:

$$(P \times Q) - (VC \times Q) = FC$$

$$Q(P - VC) = FC$$

$$Q \text{ or } BeP = \frac{FC}{P - VC}$$

We also know that profit = total revenue − total costs.

It is understood that fixed costs remain fixed regardless of the level of production or activity. The insurance, taxes, and depreciation on a production facility must be paid regardless of whether or not it is being fully utilized. Costs that vary in close proportion to changes in output are known as variable costs. In a manufacturing plant the cost of materials used will depend on the number of units produced. Thus, the cost of materials would be a variable cost. Variable costs, then, are related to the activity itself, for example, producing a product, rather than providing the plant to produce the product.

Suppose the plant manager of an electronics firm is interested in how much the sales of one of the firm's products could decline before the product would lose money. This figure is necessary because a competitor is about to introduce a similar device. The following information has been made available by the plant comptroller.

P = \$26 per unit VC = \$15 per unit

Present Q sold = 80,000 units FC = \$95,000

$$\text{Thus } BeP = \frac{\$95{,}000}{\$26 - \$15} = 8{,}636 \text{ units.}$$

Since 80,000 units are being sold annually, and sales of 8,637 units enable the firm to break even, the plant manager knows that he can sell 71,364 fewer units without incurring a loss on the product.

Oftentimes managers must choose between alternative courses of action. In many cases the break-even model can be a useful aid. Let us assume that we have two design proposals for the same end product and we want to know the production quantity. Our objective is to determine which proposal (design 1 or design 2) will be most economical.

Fixed nonrecurring costs include engineering to design and develop the product; tooling costs of jigs, fixtures, and the like, necessary for the production of the product; testing the design to insure feasibility and user acceptance; and the planning of manufacturing processes, tools, and routing. Variable costs (recurring) include material per unit, labor to produce and assemble each unit, inspection, packing, tooling maintenance, and the engineering that accompanies production. In addition, many organizations allocate overhead on a direct labor-hour or direct labor-dollar basis and therefore include overhead as a variable cost.

The following symbols are used to derive the break-even point equation:

FC_1: Fixed cost of design 1.

FC_2: Fixed cost of design 2.

VC_1: Variable cost of design 1.

VC_2: Variable cost of design 2.

X: Break-even (crossover) point in terms of quantity.

At the break-even point,

$$FC_1 + V_1(X) = FC_2 + V_2(X)$$

$$(VC_1 - VC_2)X = FC_2 - FC_1$$

$$\text{Solve for } X = \frac{FC_2 - FC_1}{VC_1 - VC_2}.$$

For the example problem, the calculation is based on the following given information:

$$FC_1 = \$307{,}000 \qquad FC_2 = \$446{,}000$$

$$VC_1 = \$38.80 \qquad VC_2 = \$22.00$$

$$X = \frac{FC_2 - FC_1}{VC_1 - VC_2} = \frac{\$446{,}000 - \$307{,}000}{\$38.80 - \$22.00}$$

$$= \frac{\$139{,}000}{\$16.80} = \$8{,}274 \text{ units.}$$

If the expected order quantity $Q < 8{,}274$ use design 1; if $Q > 8{,}274$ use design 2. The production cost at break-even is determined by the equation:

$$TC_1 = FC_1 + (VC_1 X Q)$$

$$TC_1 = \$307{,}000 + (\$38.80 \times 8{,}274) = \$628{,}030$$

or $$TC_2 = \$446{,}000 + (\$22.00 \times 8{,}274) \cong \$628{,}030.$$

Figure 4–3 depicts the break-even point and the production cost at break-even for the above figure.

One of the shortcomings of break-even analysis is that no project really exists in isolation; one must consider not only the value of an individual project, but how it compares to other uses of funds and facilities. Nor does break-even analysis permit proper examination of cash flow.

Payback Analysis.[2] Payback analysis of capital investment proposals is one of the most widely used and misapplied concepts in industry today. The difficulties in providing accurate application are even further increased when attempts are made to account for the economic inflation factors associated with energy. Thus, because analysts attempt to provide economic justification to energy proposals subject to inflation, it is important that we examine a method to remedy this problem.

By defining simple payback as the length of time required for the cash inflows (savings) from a project to equal the cash outflows (cost) of the project, one can calculate the simple payback as follows:

Payback (yrs) = First Cost (\$) Annual Savings (\$/yr)[3]

Example 1: Your firm buys a new machine tool for \$10,000 with the expectation it will save \$1,000 a year over the old equipment it replaced. The new equipment will last 15 years (Figure 4–4).

Careful observation indicates a couple of obvious weaknesses in this method of analysis. First, payback analysis ignores all cash flows after payback, a fault that can hurt longer lived projects that generate smaller annual savings (as many energy proposals do). Second, payback does not consider the time value of money, which is a serious omission when a project involves the input of depreciable capital goods. A similar shortcoming of this analysis, closely related to the time-value-of-money concept, is the omission of inflation factors. One would have to be living in a vacuum not to recognize the existence of inflation, and in particular the inflation of energy costs above the inflation rate of the general economy. In other words, almost as an insight to the obvious, energy costs are rising faster than those costs associated with other sectors of the econ-

[2]Reprinted with permission from *Energy Channel*, December 1979, Oklahoma Dept. of Energy and Oklahoma State University, School of Industrial Engineering and Management, Stillwater, OK.

[3]Under the assumption that savings are constant throughout the life of the project.

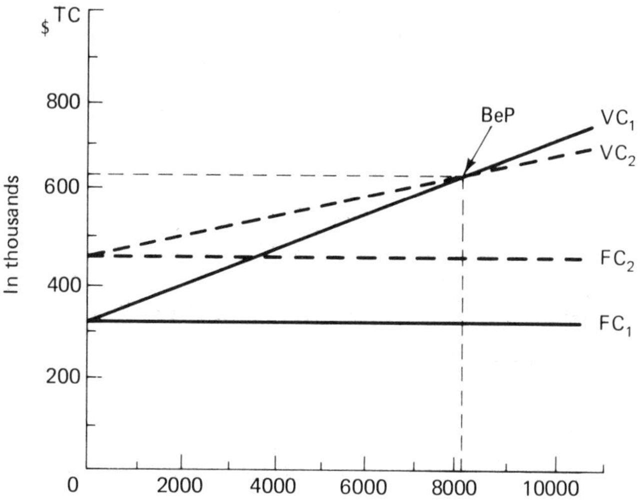

FIGURE 4–3. Break-Even Point Analysis.

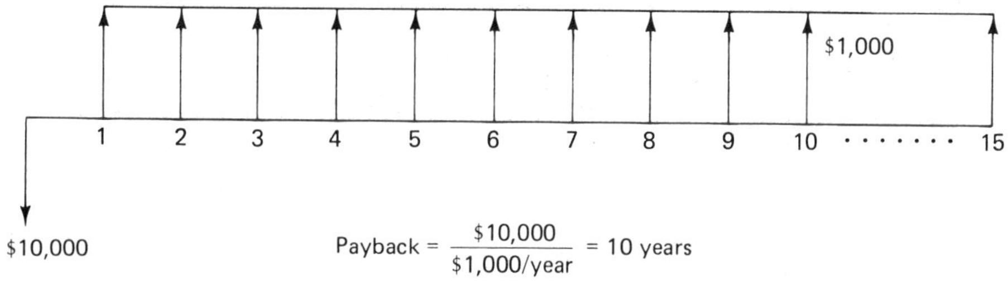

FIGURE 4–4. Payback Analysis of a Capital Investment Proposal.

omy, and the energy manager should include this in the economic analysis of all energy savings proposals.

To compensate for the time value of money, the method of discounted (or in the case of energy inflation, an inflated) payback calculation has been developed. Simply, this "inflated" payback recognizes that energy dollars saved today can be inflated to some dollar savings in the future owing to the expected higher costs of energy. Example 2 illustrates the effect of inflation on a project's savings.

Example 2: A thousand dollars a year in fuel oil can be saved by installing a more efficient boiler in the plate. Fuel oil saved is inflating at 20 percent a year. What is the effect of this inflation on future savings generated? Savings = $\$1{,}000\ (1 + .20)^n$, where n is the year in question. See Figure 4–5.

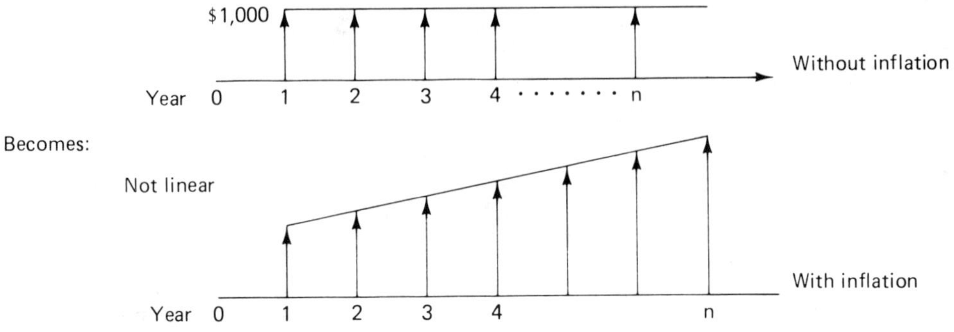

Year	1	2	3	4	········	n
Inflated savings	$1,200	$1,440	$1,728	$2,073.60	········	$1,000 (1.20)^n

FIGURE 4–5. A Cash Flow Diagram.

This principle is applied to payback analysis by inflating the cash (energy) savings at an appropriate rate. The succeeding examples show two incorrect applications of inflated payback and finally a correct method of calculation.

Example 3: Incorrect Inflated Payback Analysis (Table 4–3). A thousand dollars a year (at today's cost) in fuel oil can be saved by installing a more efficient boiler in the plant. Fuel oil is inflating at the general economy's inflation rate of j = 12 percent a year. The new boiler costs $10,000 and has an expected life of twenty years. Calculate the payback of this proposal (payback occurs when the unrecovered portion of the initial investment becomes non-negative).

This method of inflated payback is not correct and should not be used in the economic analysis of energy savings prop-

TABLE 4-3

End of Year	*Investment*	*Estimated Savings (Today's Dollars)*	*Then Current Dollars (j = 12%)*	*Unrecovered Balance*
0	$10,000			−10,000
1		$1,000	$1,120	−8,880
2		1,000	1,254.40	−7,625.60
3		1,000	1,404.93	−6,620.67
4		1,000	1,573.52	−4,647.15
5		1,000	1,763.34	−2,883.81
6		1,000	1,973.82	−909.99
7		1,000	2,210.68	+1,300.69

Payback = 6.41 years (occurs during the seventh year)

TABLE 4-4

End of Year	Investment	Estimated Savings (Today's Dollars)	Then Current Dollars (k = 20%)	Unrecovered Balance
0	−$10,000			−10,000
1		$1,000	$1,200	−8,800
2		1,000	1,440	−7,360
3		1,000	1,728	−5,632
4		1,000	2,073.60	−3,585.40
5		1,000	2,488.32	−1,070.08
6		1,000	2,985.98	+1,915.90

Payback = 5.35 years (occurs during the sixth year)

osals. Its fault lies in the assumption that energy is inflating *only* at the inflation rate of the general economy. It is assumed that for all projects savings are inflating at the rate of the general economy; therefore (energy related or not), we have failed to include the higher inflation of energy in this analysis. In other words, one could inflate the savings from Example 1, which are not energy related at 12 percent a year, and arrive at exactly the same payback period. Clearly, this is not a true representation of the respective energy and nonenergy-related proposals and should not be used.

Example 4: Incorrect Inflated Payback Analysis (Table 4–4). This example involves the same equipment as the previous example; however, in this instance the savings will be allowed to inflate at the energy inflation rate k = 20 percent.

The important fault to note with this method of calculation is that it does not recognize the contribution of general inflation to the energy inflation rate. Thus, we are overcrediting our savings and artificially forcing payback to an exaggerated value. This method of analysis, therefore, is not theoretically correct and cannot be used.

Obviously, a dilemma has presented itself to the analyst. The fact that energy is inflating at a rate above that of the general economy has been recognized; however, the contribution of that general inflation to energy inflation is not yet clear. To resolve this problem, Turner and Case[4] have developed a modified energy inflation rate that recognizes incremental inflation of energy above the general inflation. Applying this modified inflation factor to payback analysis, we can develop the following equation. Example 5 illustrates the calculations involved in economic analysis using this modified energy inflation rate.

$$\text{Payback} = \frac{P}{A\left(\sum_{L=1}^{n'} (1+K')^{L}\right)}$$

Where:

P = Installed (first) cost of the project.

A = Estimated uniform annual energy savings in today's dollars.

K' = Modified inflation rate of energy above the general economy's inflation rate.

$$\left(K' = \frac{(1 + \text{Energy Inflation Rate})}{(1 + \text{General Inflation Rate})} - 1\right)$$

[4]Turner, Wayne C. and Kenneth E. Case, *Economic Analysis of Energy Proposals*. Stillwater, Okla.: Oklahoma State University, 1979.

n^1 = The year in which the sum of accrued energy savings exceeds the installed cost of the project (i.e., when the unrecovered balance becomes non-negative).

Example 5: Correct Inflated Payback Analysis (Table 4–5). Using the same data as previous examples, we can calculate a modified energy inflation rate as follows:

Energy inflation rate: $K = 20\%$

General economy's inflation rate: $j = 12\%$

Modified energy inflation rate: K'

$$K' = \frac{(1 + .20)}{(1 + .12)} - 1 = .0714.$$

Note: $K' \neq k - j$.

In conclusion, four different methods of payback analysis have been illustrated. While none of these methods eliminates all of the problems associated with payback analysis, the modified energy inflated payback (using K') does correctly account for the higher rate of energy inflation. If a more theoretically sound method of investment analysis (such as net present value or internal rate of return) cannot be used and payback analysis is required, this modified payback should be applied.

The following references are cited pertaining to payback analysis of energy proposals:

1. Shelton, Ronald L. *Calculating the Discounted Payback Period for Energy Conservation Projects*. Oak Ridge, Tenn.: Union Carbide-Nuclear Division, 1979.
2. Snyder, W. T., and F. W. Symonds. "The Influence of Energy Escalation on Payback Analysis of Energy Cost Savings Opportunities," *Building Systems Design*. October/November, 1978.
3. Turner, Wayne C., and Kenneth E. Case. *Economic Analysis of Energy Proposals*. Stillwater, Okla.: Oklahoma State University, 1979.
4. White, John A., M. H. Agee, and Kenneth E. Case. *Principles of Engineering Economic Analysis*. New York: John Wiley and Sons, 1979.

Summary

In this section we have discussed equivalence calculations—in other words, the practical use of interest factors. In order for

TABLE 4-5.

End of Year	*Investment*	*Estimated Savings (Today's Dollars)*	*Then Current Saving ($K' = 0.0714$)*	*Unrecovered Balance*
0	$10,000			−$10,000.00
1		$1,000	$1,071.40	−8,928.60
2		1,000	1,147.90	−7,780.70
3		1,000	1,229.86	−6,055.84
4		1,000	1,317.67	−5,233.17
5		1,000	1,411.75	−3,821.42
6		1,000	1,512.55	−2,308.87
7	Pay back = 7.4 years	1,000	1,620.55	−688.32
8	(occurs during the eighth year)	1,000	1,736.25	+1,047.93

a person to make the most economical choice, he must choose from among alternatives. The most economical alternative cannot be chosen unless each alternative is on an equivalent basis. We discussed four of the more common bases of comparison—annual cost, present worth, capitalized cost, and rate of return. In addition, we discussed the development of minimum-cost points, break-even point analysis, and payback analysis. Some of the usual items of cost involved in equivalence computations are investment and depreciation, interest, labor, and operating costs. When all the factors involved in a comparison of alternatives are converted to equivalent bases of comparison, then the decision of which alternative to select is simplified considerably.

The reader should note that the shortcoming of the article by Larry D. Blevins, "Payback Analysis of Energy Proposals," in *Energy Channel* (Oklahoma Department of Energy), is that it does not include the time value of money in the analysis.

DEPRECIATION

Depreciation may be defined as the decrease in value of physical assets with the passage of time. Depreciation can be considered from various aspects, some of which may be defined as follows:

Physical depreciation: This is the decrease in value of an asset because of physical impairment or wear and tear. An example of this would be the depreciation of forklift trucks or a piece of machinery.

Functional depreciation: This is depreciation due to obsolescence or inadequacy. For instance, a new invention or innovation may make a product, process, or machine economically unjustified. A change in demand also comes into play here, an example of which might be the Bessemer converter for steelmaking.

Depletion: The piecemeal removal of assets, such as in a mine, forest, or oil well, constitutes depletion.

Fluctuation in price levels: The fluctuation of price levels may cause depreciation or appreciation. In real estate, appreciation, or the raising of price levels, is quite common. Seldom does the Internal Revenue Service allow land to be systematically depreciated.

Accidents: Accidents are a cause of sudden loss of value, or depreciation.

Capital Recovery with a Return

Capital recovery is defined as that income equal to the money invested in the machine or equipment. It is the cost of depreciation. If a machine depreciates $1,000 per year, $1,000 per year must be earned to recover this capital before any profit or return is possible.

Return is the income over and above that necessary to equal the cost of the investment, and is usually expressed as a percentage of the diminishing unrecovered balance of the capital invested. For instance, if the machine mentioned in the paragraph above was worth $10,000 at the beginning of the year, and $1,500 income was earned for the year, $1,000 would recover the year's depreciation while the additional $500 would represent return. This $500 represents a 5 percent ($500/$10,000) return for the first year. In the event this machine continued to perform with the same capability during the second year of ownership, and the $1,500 income continued, the $500 profit would then represent a 5.56 percent ($500/$9,000) return.

This varying percent return does not lend itself conveniently to accounting procedures or economic analysis of the machine. To overcome this, the capital recovery factor provides a convenient means of computing a percent return when two factors apply jointly to the same economic problem, namely: (1) net income before depreciation remains constant throughout the life of an asset; and (2) the sinking-fund method of depreciation is employed.

Methods of Depreciation

Four methods of depreciation are discussed in this section. The first two, the straight-line method and the sinking-fund method, are widely employed because of their historical vestiges. Convenience facilitated the use of these two depreciation systems when the inpact of income tax was either nonexistent or inconsequential. Fast supplanting the first two are the sum-of-the-digits and the declining-balance method. These last two methods provide a faster depreciation in the earlier life of property. This results in lower taxes in the first years of ownership (depreciation is an acceptable charge against income, which reduces the income to which the tax rate applies); hence, more after-tax income is in the hands of business and available for reinvestment.

Note carefully in this discussion of depreciation, that rate of return is purposely intertwined with depreciation. The depreciation methods developed are unique, and the system by which a particular depreciation method accounts for the future diminishment in property value greatly affects the rate of return. Judiciously observe the following depreciation systems and note the rate-of-return consequences. Tax impact will not be included in this discussion but will be considered in the section "Practical Examples," which follows. In the discussion of each of these four methods, the following example is applicable: A machine with a present cost of \$6,000 is expected to depreciate to \$1,500 in five years. The desired rate of return (interest) is 6 percent. Determine the depreciation (capital recovered) plus the return, using each of the four methods of depreciation.

Straight-line Method of Depreciation. In this method of depreciation, the amount of depreciation (capital recovered) is assumed to be equal for each year of the asset's life. Table 4-6 shows the above-mentioned example. Since the depreciation per year is assumed to be equal, the annual depreciation is found by:

$$\frac{(P - L)}{n} = \frac{(\$6{,}000 - \$1{,}500)}{5} = \$900.$$

This is shown in column 3 of Table 4-6. Column 4 shows the return on the unrecovered capital; this is 6 percent of the undiminished balance at the beginning of the year (column 2). The fifth column is the

TABLE 4-6
Straight-Line Depreciation

Year	*Balance at Beg. of Yr.*	*Capital Recovered during Year*	*Return on Unrecovered Capital*	*Sum of Cap. Rec. + Ret.*
(1)	(2)	(3)	(4)	(5)
1	\$6,000	\$900	0.06 × 6,000 = \$360	\$1,260
2	5,100	900	0.06 × 5,100 = 306	1,206
3	4,200	900	0.06 × 4,200 = 252	1,152
4	3,300	900	0.06 × 3,300 = 198	1,098
5	2,400	900	0.06 × 2,400 = 144	1,044

sum of the capital recovered (depreciation cost) and the return. Thus, it is seen that if a 6 percent return is to be realized from this investment, \$1,260 must be earned in the first year, \$1,206 in the second, and so on.

A formula for straight-line depreciation plus average interest can be developed as follows:

(a) Depreciation in n years $= (P - L)$.

(b) Depreciation per year $= \frac{(P - L)}{n}$.

(c) Interest on unrecovered balance, 1st year, $= (P - L)i + Li$.

(d) Interest on unrecovered balance, nth year $= \frac{(P - L)}{n} i + Li$.

(e) Therefore, average interest

$$= \left[(P - L) + \left(\frac{P - L}{n}\right)\right]\frac{i}{2} + Li$$

$$= \left[(P - L)\left(\frac{n+1}{n}\right)\right]\frac{i}{2} + Li.$$

From (b) and (e), we have the formula for straight-line depreciation plus average interest:

$$\text{“}D + AI\text{”} = \frac{P - L}{n} + \left[(P - L)\left(\frac{n+1}{n}\right)\right]\frac{i}{2} + Li.$$

However, it is imperative to note that this formula provides only approximate or average results. Use of this formula with the example dictates an answer of \$1,152, which is the average of the five figures in column 5. But, because of the time-interest scale, this is not a true average. Hence, for exact computations, it is necessary to set the given information in a tabular manner similar to that in Table 4–6.

Sinking-fund Method of Depreciation. In this method of depreciation, one of a series of equal amounts is assumed to be deposited into a sinking fund at the end of each year of the asset's life. This deposit may be a matter of bookkeeping. However, if the company is planning to purchase a replacement, an actual deposit may be made. At the end of the estimated life of the asset, the amount in the sinking fund will equal the amount of estimated depreciation. The total depreciation for each year is then that "deposit" plus interest on the sum already deposited: Table 4–7 shows our example

TABLE 4-7
Sinking Fund Depreciation

Year	*Depreciation (Capital Recovered) during Year*			*Total Depreciation to End of Yr.*	*Undepreciated Balance at End of Year*	*Return on Unrecovered Capital*	*Sum of Cap. Rec. + Return*
	Deposit	*Interest Earned Each Year*	*Total*				
(1)	(2)	(3)	(4)	(5)	(6)	(7)	(8)
0	\$000.00 +	\$000.00 =	\$000.00	\$000.00	\$6,000.00	—	—
1	798.30 +	000.00 =	798.30	798.30	5,201.70	\$360.00	\$1,158.30
2	798.30 +	0.06(798.30) =	846.20	1,644.50	4,355.50	312.10	1,158.30
3	798.30 +	0.06(1,644.50) =	896.97	2,541.47	3,458.53	261.33	1,158.30
4	798.30 +	0.06(2,541.47) =	950.79	3,492.26	2,507.74	207.51	1,158.30
5	798.30 +	0.06(3,492.26) =	1,007.84	4,500.10	1,499.90	150.46	1,158.30

set up in tabular form using the sinking-fund method of depreciation. The yearly "deposit" R, is determined by using the sinking-fund factor:

$$R = (P - L)(sff - i\% - n)$$
$$= \$4{,}500\ (sff - 6\% - 5)$$
$$= \$4{,}500(0.17740) = \$798.30.$$

The second column shows this "deposit." The total depreciation for the year (column 4) is the sum of the deposit (column 2) and the interest earned during the year (column 3) on the amount already in the sinking fund. Column 5 is the total depreciation to date. The return on the unrecovered capital (column 7) is specified at 6 percent of the undepreciated value at the beginning of the year. Thus, \$360 is 6 percent of \$6,000, \$312.10 is 6 percent of \$5,201.70, and so on. The sum of the capital recovered plus return (column 8) is the sum of the total depreciation for the year (column 4) and the return (column 7). It should be noted here that the sum of capital recovered plus return is equal for each year of the asset's life when the sinking-fund method of depreciation is used. The amount of depreciation increases and the return necessary decreases. Thus, in this example, in order to attain a 6 percent return on the investment, it will be necessary to earn \$1,158.30 each year when the sinking-fund method is used.

A more concise way of summarizing Table 4–7 is as follows:

Recovery of capital with interest = $(P-L)$ $(sff - i\% - n) + Pi$ OR $(P - L)(crf - i\% - n) + Li$

$$\$4{,}500(0.23740) + (\$1{,}500 \times 0.06) = \$1{,}158.30$$

$$\$1{,}608.30 + \$90.00 = \$1{,}158.30.$$

Declining-balance Method of Depreciation. This method produces the highest depreciation (which is a business charge against taxable income providing smaller tax consequences) in the first year of life, and the depreciation becomes progressively less as time approaches the last year of scheduled productive life. The amount of depreciation each year is equal to the unappreciated amount at the beginning of the year times D, a fixed percentage rate.

The Internal Revenue Service Law allows a declining balance of up to 200 percent of the straight-line (200%/5 = 40% in our example) for certain new equipment with a life of three or more years. The law allows a declining balance of up to 150 percent of the straight-line rate for certain used equipment.

The depreciation of the machine at 40 percent is shown in tabular form in Table 4–8. In this table, column 2 represents the depreciation for the year, which is the undepreciated balance at the end of the previous year (column 3) multiplied by 40 percent. When the allowable declining-balance rate is computed, any terminal salvage value (in this case \$1,500) is ignored. The return on the unrecovered balance (column 4) is again 6 percent of the undepreciated balance at the beginning of the year (balance at end of previous year, column 3). Column 5 shows the sum of capital recovered plus return, that is, column 2 plus column 4.

It should be noted here that, since the depreciation per year is always a fixed percentage of the remaining balance, an asset can never be depreciated to zero. It should also be noted that the law will not always allow a declining-balance rate equal to double the straight-line rate.

Sum-of-the-years-digits Method of Depreciation. This method of depreciation results in a decrease in value very similar in nature to that discussed in the preceding section. The main advantage of this system is that an asset can be reduced to zero.

If we let n equal the number of years of estimated life of the asset, the summation of these years becomes n.

$$n = 1 + 2 \text{---} + (n - 1) + n = \frac{n(n+1)}{2}$$

TABLE 4-8
Declining-Balance Depreciation

Yr.	Depreciation (Cap. Recovered)	Undepreciated Balance at End of Year	Return on Unrecovered Balance	Sum of Capital Recovered + Return
(1)	(2)	(3)	(4)	(5)
0	$ 000.00	$6,000.00	—	—
1	2,400.00	3,600.00	$360.00	$2,760.00
2	1,440.00	2,160.00	216.00	1,656.00
3	864.00	1,296.00	129.60	993.60
4	518.40	777.60	77.76	596.16
5	311.04	466.56	46.66	357.70

$$\text{depreciation in 1st year} = \frac{n}{\frac{n(n+1)}{2}}(P-L)$$

$$\text{depreciation in 2nd year} = \frac{n-1}{\frac{n(n+1)}{2}}(P-L)$$

and

$$\text{depreciation in last year} = \frac{n-(n-1)=1}{\frac{n(n+1)}{2}}(P-L)$$

The depreciation, by this method, of the machine in our example is shown in Table 4–9. In this example $(P - L) = \$4{,}500$. The depreciation factor is shown in column 2. The denominator is the sum-of-the-years-digits obtained by

$$\frac{n(n+1)}{2} = \frac{5(5+1)}{2} = 15,$$

and is constant. The numerator is arrived at by using n years (in this case $n = 5$) for the first year and subtracting 1 year for each successive year of depreciation. The return on the unrecovered capital (column 5) is calculated as before. Column 6 is the sum of columns 3 and 5.

TABLE 4-9
Sum-of-the-Years-Digits Method

Year	Depreciation Factor	Depreciation during Year	Undepreciated Balance at End of Year	Return on Unrecovered Capital	Sum of Cap. Recovered + Return
(1)	(2)	(3)	(4)	(5)[a]	(6)
0	0	$ 000	$6,000	—	—
1	5/15	1,500	4,500	$360	$1,860
2	4/15	1,200	3,300	270	1,470
3	3/15	900	2,400	198	1,098
4	2/15	600	1,800	144	744
5	1/15	300	1,500	108	408

[a]Note a decreasing factor of $18 in the column (i.e., $90, 72, 54, 36).

Summary

We have shown an asset depreciated by four different methods. A comparison of these four methods is shown in Figure 4–6.

It should be stressed here that depreciation calculations are all based on a standard or system that projects the diminishing value of disposition property from the time of acquisition to time of planned disposition. When the depreciation system is adopted, the accountant is generally committed to it, even though the value produced by the system of depreciation accounting does not truly reflect the market price for the used equipment as its useful life mature. The values that the depreciation method employed may develop at the end of each year for the property involved are known as book values.

If, for example, the owner has made a faulty estimate, and his machine wears out in three years and he sells it for salvage as $500, he suffers a loss called a sunk cost loss. This loss is the difference between the book value and the salvage value. It should be understood that the magnitude of this sunk cost loss in no way affects future economic comparison of alternatives, such as, considering whether to replace a machine before the end of its productive life when the machine book value is higher

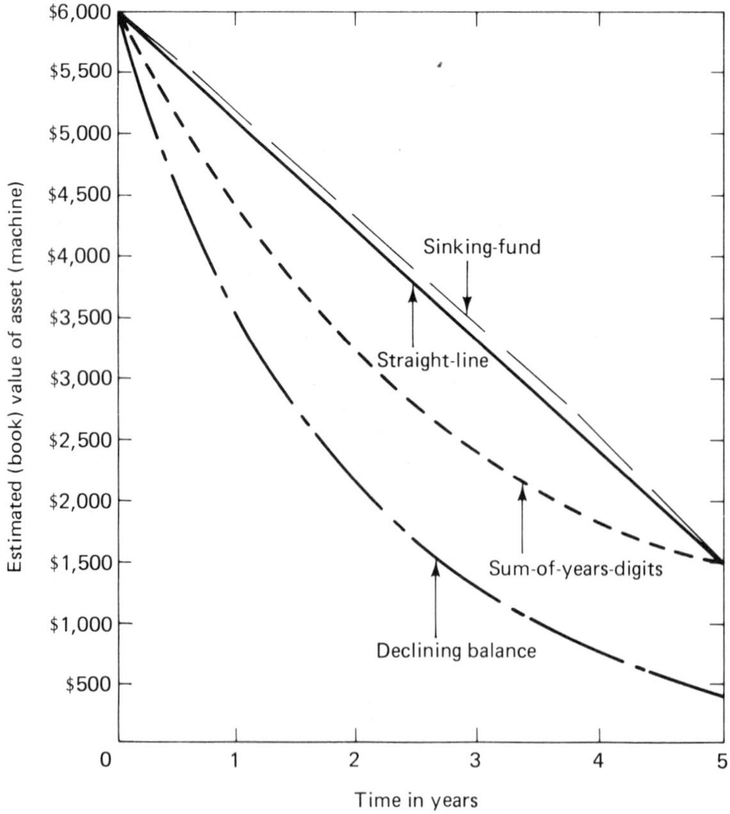

FIGURE 4–6. Comparison of Four Methods of Depreciation.

than its sales or trade-in value. If he uses straight-line depreciation, his loss is $3,300 − $500, or $2,800; for sinking-fund depreciation it is $3,458.53 − $500, or $2,958.53. For declining-balance depreciation, it is $1,296 − $500, or $796; and, for the digits method, $2,400 − $500, or $1,900. Sunk cost loss problems are generally more involved than this, but the basic principle stated herein remains true.

A person may use any method of depreciation, depending upon the particular situation and the applicable laws and regulations. However, once he has begun using one method, he can rarely switch to another under Internal Revenue Service Code.

Capital Recovery with a Return Equal for All Methods of Depreciation

It should be noted here that, although there is wide variation in the yearly values of capital recovered plus return, the final value of capital recovered plus return is exactly the same for any method used. We will show that here by finding the total, at the end of five years, of the yearly capital recovered plus return for our example using each of the four methods of depreciation. Note that use is made of more accurate interest factors than found in Tables 4–10 to 4–12.

Sinking-fund method. Annual sum of capital recovered + return = R = $1,158.30. Using compound-amount factor:

$$S = (caf - 6\% - 5) = \$1{,}158.30(5.6371) = \$6{,}529.45$$

Value of capital recovered + return after 5th year:	$6,529.45
+ income from salvage of item:	1,500.00
Total capital at the end of 5th year:	$8,029.45.

Note that regardless of which system is used, the end result differs by only a few pennies because of insufficient significant digits in the interest factors used. It should also be noted that, if the initial capital, $6,000, were deposited in a bank at 6 percent compounded annually, the total capital at the end of five years would be the same as above:

$$S = P(caf' - 6\% - 5) = \$6{,}000(1.3382) = \$8{,}029.20.$$

TABLE 4-10
Straight-line Method

Year	*Sum of Cap. Rec. + Ret.*		*Interest Factor*		*Value at End of 5th Yr.*
1	$1,260	×	(caf′ − 6% − 4) (1.2625)	=	$1,590.75
2	1,206	×	(caf′ − 6% − 3) (1.1910)	=	1,436.35
3	1,152	×	(caf′ − 6% − 2) (1.1236)	=	1,294.39
4	1,098	×	(caf′ − 6% − 1) (1.0600)	=	1,163.88
5	1,044	×	1	=	1,044.00
Total value at end of 5th yr. of cap. rec. + ret.				=	$5,495.81
Plus income from salvage of item:				=	$1,500.00
Total capital at end of 5th yr:					$6,995.81

TABLE 4-11
Declining-balance Method

Year	Sum of Cap. Rec. + Ret.		Interest Factor		Value at End of 5th Yr.
1	\$2,760.00	×	(caf' – 6% – 4) (1.2625)	=	\$3,484.50
2	1,656.00	×	(caf' – 6% – 3) (1.1910)	=	1,972.30
3	993.60	×	(caf' – 6% – 2) (1.1236)	=	1,116.41
4	596.16	×	(caf' – 6% – 1) (1.0600)	=	631.93
5	357.70	×	1	=	357.70
Total value at end of 5th yr. of cap. rec. + ret.				=	\$7,562.84
Plus income from salvage of item[a]:				=	466.56
Total capital end of 5th yr.:					\$8,029.40

[a] Note that in using this method the undepreciated balance at the end of the 5th year is \$466.56 and not \$1,500 as in the other methods.

TABLE 4-12
Sum-of-the-years-digits Method

Year	Sum of Cap. Rec. + Ret.		Interest Factor		Value at End of 5th Yr.
1	\$1,860	×	(caf'– 6% – 4) (1.2625)	=	\$2,348.25
2	1,470	×	(caf' – 6% – 3) (1.1910)	=	1,750.77
3	1,098	×	(caf' – 6% – 2) (1.1236)	=	1,233.71
4	744	×	(caf' – 6% – 1) (1.0600)	=	788.64
5	408	×	1	=	408.00
Total value at end of 5th yr. of cap. rec. + ret.				=	\$6,529.37
Plus income from salvage of item:				=	1,500.00
Total capital at end of 5th yr.:					\$8,029.37

This should verify the statement that a 6 percent return is a true return of 6 percent, regardless of the manner in which it is invested.

Summary

In this section, we have considered depreciation in the light of physical deterioration, functional obsolescence, depletion, price fluctuation, and disasters. We have covered the four main methods of depreciation and found that capital recovery with a return is the same for any method. Recall that only in the case of the sinking-fund depreciation method do interest table factors allow the rate-of-return approach to be summarized. All other methods require computations for each year of life to provide acceptable rate-of-return data.

The treatment of depreciation and its ramifications here is brief; therefore the serious student is encouraged to investigate more detailed textbooks on this particular subject.

PRACTICAL EXAMPLES

In this section some practical examples[5] are shown that illustrate and utilize the principles discussed in the preceding three sections.

Interest computations can be correct to the nearest penny if detailed interest tables are used. In the preceding section, more precise tables were used in order to illustrate refinement. However, in the interest of brevity and simplicity, less precise tables are commonly used in the solution of problems in engineering economics.

1. Use of interest factors.
   a. Mr. A deposits \$1,000 in the bank at 5 percent compounded annually. How much will he have in 15 years?

$$\begin{aligned} S &= P(caf' - i\% - n) \\ &= \$1{,}000\ (caf' - 5\% - 15) \\ &= \$1{,}000(2.079) = \$2{,}079. \end{aligned}$$

   b. If Mr. A deposited his \$1,000 at 5 percent with the intention of making a withdrawal each year, how much could he withdraw each year so that he had nothing at the end of 15 years?

$$\begin{aligned} R &= P(crf - i\% - n) \\ &= \$1{,}000\ (crf - 5\% - 15) \\ &= \$1{,}000(0.09634) = \$96.34. \end{aligned}$$

   c. If Mr. A took his withdrawals (from part b) and invested them in stocks which eventually earned him 8 percent, what would he have at the end of 15 years?

R_1 occurs at end of 1st year:
R_{15} at end of 15 years.

$$\begin{aligned} S &= R(caf - i\% - n) \\ &= \$96.34\ (caf - 8\% - 15) \\ &= \$96.34(27.152) = \$2{,}615.82. \end{aligned}$$

2. Use of interest factors.
   a. Mr. B., now 20 years old, would like to retire at 65 with an annual income of \$2,000 more than he will receive from retirement benefits, social security, and so on. If the interest rate is 4 percent, how much must he deposit yearly in order to draw off this additional amount for the rest of his life.

   Since Mr. B has no idea how long he will live, he must use only the interest on his deposit, leaving the principal intact. Thus, when he dies, the principal will still exist, which may be willed to his beneficiaries. The amount required at the end of this 65th year is then:

$$S = \frac{\$2{,}000}{i} = \frac{\$2{,}000}{0.04} = \$50{,}000.$$

   This can be considered a special application of the simple-interest factor or the compound-interest fac-

[5]Taken from Student Pamphlet on "Principles and Problems in Engineering Economics," Ft. Belvoir, Va.: U.S. Army Engineers School, April 1971.

tor in which the interest does not compound after the 65th year.

The yearly deposit required is then found by the sinking-fund factor:

$$R = S(sff - i\% - n)$$
$$= \$50{,}000\ (sff - 4\% - 45)$$
$$= \$50{,}000(0.00826) = \$413.00.$$

b. Suppose Mr. B estimates that he will live until he is 90, and desires to leave nothing at his death. What then will be his yearly deposit? The amount needed at the end of his 65th year is found by the equal-payment present-worth factor:

$$P = R(pwf - i\% - n)$$
$$= \$2{,}000(pwf - 4\% - 25)$$
$$= \$2{,}000(15.622) = \$31{,}244.$$

(Since P of the \$2,000 series must equal S of the deposit series at year 65) the yearly deposit required is:

$$R = S(sff - i\% - n)$$
$$= \$31{,}244(sff - 4\% - 45)$$
$$= \$31{,}244(0.00826) = \$258.08.$$

3. Equivalence.

Mr. C acquires a building for \$30,000 which he estimates he can sell in 30 years for \$20,000. He estimates that, over this 30-year span, his annual net income from rent will be \$2,000. What rate of return will he receive on his investment? The rate of return is the rate that causes the PW of expenditures and income to be equal.

$$\$30{,}000 = R(pwf - i\% - n) + L(pwf' - i\% - n)$$

Try $i = 6\%$:

$$P = \$2{,}000(pwf - 6\% - 30) + \$20{,}000(pwf' - 6\% - 30)$$

$$P = \$2{,}000(13.765) + \$20{,}000(0.1741)$$

$$P = \$27{,}530 + 3{,}482 = \$31{,}012.$$

Since this interest rate dictates more than \$30,000

Try $i = 7\%$:

$$P = \$2{,}000(pwf - 7\% - 30) + \$20{,}000(pwf' - 7\% - 30)$$

$$P = \$2{,}000(12.409) + \$20{,}000(0.1314)$$

$$P = \$24{,}818 + \$2{,}628 = \$27{,}446.$$

Since this is less than \$30,000, interpolate for i. By interpolation:

$$i = 0.06 + 0.01 \left[\frac{31{,}012 - 30{,}000}{31{,}012 - 27{,}446}\right] \text{ or}$$

$$0.07 - 0.01 \left[\frac{30{,}000 - 27{,}446}{21{,}012 - 27{,}446}\right]$$

$$= 0.06 + 0.01 \ \frac{1{,}012}{3{,}566} = 0.06 + 0.0028.$$

$i = 6.28\%$ = rate of return.

4. Equivalence—annual costs.

If Mr. D invests \$100,000 in a machine that will be worth \$10,000 in 20 years, what must the annual net income be for him to make an 8 percent return on his investment? First, reduce all net costs to the present.

Initial expenditure	=	\$100,000
less PW of salvage value		
$(pwf' - 8\% - 20)$		
\$10,000(0.2145):	=	−2,145
PW of net costs		\$ 97,855.

Find equivalent annual cost:

$$R = P(crf - i\% - n)$$
$$= \$97{,}855\ (crf - 8\% - 20)$$
$$= \$97{,}855(0.10185) = \$9{,}966.53.$$

Therefore, Mr. D's net annual income must be \$9,966.53 for him to earn an 8% return on his investment. This problem may also be solved by conceiving the economic situation as requiring the diminished value to be recouped over the economic life of the machine, plus the interest rate of return being applied to money tied up in the salvage value, as follows:

R = \$90,000(crf − 8% − 20) + \$10,000
@ 8% = \$90,000(0.10185) + \$800
= \$9,166.50 + \$800 = \$9,966.50.

5. Depreciation.

An asset valued at \$100,000 has an estimated salvage value of \$22,000 in 12 years. Economic projections for this asset indicate that in each of the 12 years of ownership the income derived from this asset will exceed the cost of operating it (excluding depreciation and taxes) by \$20,000 per year. Tax accountants anticipate the average state and federal income taxes for the period the corporate owner operates this asset to be 56 percent. What will be the after-taxes prospective rate of return from this asset if the sum-of-the-years-digits method of depreciation is employed? Also, assume the investment tax credit of 7 percent applies. This tax credit is a subsidy allowing a percentage of commercial asset value to be deducted from tax liability in the first year of ownership if certain fairly common conditions are met.

The sum of digits

$$= \frac{n(n+1)}{2} = \frac{(12)(13)}{2} = 78$$

First year depreciation

$$= \frac{12}{78}(\$100{,}000 - \$22{,}000)$$

= \$12,000, etc.

Compare on a present-worth basis by assuming a rate of return—say 10 percent:

− \$93,000 + \$15,520(pwf − 10% − 12) − \$560($gpwf$ − 10% − 12) + \$22,000 (pwf' − 10% − 12).

− \$93,000 + \$15,520(6.814) − \$560(29.90) + \$22,000 (0.3186).

− \$93,000 + \$105,753 − \$16,744 + \$7,009 = \$3,018.

Say 12 percent:

− \$93,000 + \$15,520(pwf − 12% − 12) − \$560($gpwf$ − 12% − 12) + \$22,000(pwf' − 12% − 12).

− \$93,000 + \$15,520(6.194) − \$560(25.95) + \$22,000(0.2567).

− \$93,000 + \$96,131 − \$14,532 + \$5,647 = −\$5,754.

Rate of Return by interpolation:

$$i = 10\% + 2\%\,[3018 \div 5754] = 10.69\%.$$

6. A new highway is to be constructed. Design A calls for a concrete pavement costing \$30 per foot with a 20-year life, paved ditches costing \$1 per foot each, and 3 box culverts per mile costing \$3,000 each with 20-year lives. Annual maintenance will cost \$600 per mile; the culverts must be cleaned every 5 years at a cost of \$150 each.

Design B calls for a bituminous pavement costing \$15 per foot with a 10-year life, sodded ditches costing \$.50 per foot each, and 3 pipe culverts per mile costing \$750 each with 10-year lives. The replacement culverts will cost \$800 each. Annual maintenance will cost \$900 per mile; the culverts must be cleaned yearly at \$75 each; and the annual ditch maintenance will cost \$.50 per foot per ditch.

Find the most economical design on the basis of annual cost, present worth, and capitalized cost if the current interest rate is 6 percent.

Compare the two designs on the basis of a mile for a 20-year period.

Design A

Initial pavement cost:
$30/ft × 5,280 ft/mile = $158,400/mile

Initial ditch cost:
$1/ft × 5,280 ft/mile × 2 = $10,560/mile

Find annual cost:

Pavement: $(P - L)(crf - 6\% - 20)$
= $158,400(0.08718) = $13,809.31

Box culverts: 3× $3,000($crf - 6\% - 20$)
= $9,000(0.08718) = 784.62

Ditches: $10,560($crf - 6\% - 20$)
= $10,560(0.08718) = 920.62

Maintenance: 600.00

Amount set aside for culvert cleaning:
3 × $150($sff - 6\% - 5$)
= $450(0.17740) = 79.83

Annual cost of design A $16,194.38

Present-worth cost of design A
= $16,194.38($pwf - 6\% - 20$)
= $16,194.38(11.470) = $185,749.54

Capitalized cost of design A

$$= \frac{R}{i} = \frac{\$16{,}194.38}{0.06} = \$269{,}906.33$$

Design B

Initial pavement cost:
$15/ft × 5,280 ft/mile = $79,200/mile

Sodded ditch cost:
$0.50/ft. × 5,280 ft/mile × 2
= $5,280/mile

Ditch maintenance cost: $0.50/ft/yr
× 5,280 ft/mile × 2 = $5,280/mile/yr

Present-worth cost:

Original pavement:
$79,200 × 1 = $ 79,200.00

Replacement pavement:
$79,200($pwf' - 6\% - 10$)
= $79,200(0.5584) = 44,225.28

Original culverts: 3 × $750 = 2,240.00

Replacement culverts:
3 × $800($pwf' - 6\% - 10$)
= $2400(0.5584) = 1,340.16

Ditches: $5,280 × 1 = 5,280.00

Annual ditch maintenance:
$5,280 ($pwf - 6\% - 20$)
= $5,280 (11.470) = 60,561.60

Annual road maintenance:
$900($pwf - 6\% - 20$)
= $900(11.470) = 10,323.00

Yearly culvert cleaning:
3 × $75($pwf - 6\% - 20$)
= $225(11.470) = 2,580.75

Present-worth cost of Design B $205,760.79

Annual cost of design B
= $P(crf - 6\% - 20)$
= $205,760.79(0.08718) = $ 17,938.22

Capitalized cost of design B $= \frac{R}{i}$

$$= \frac{\$17{,}938.22}{0.06} = \$298{,}970.33$$

Comparison of Costs Per Mile

	AC	*PW*	*Cap Cost*
Design A	$16,194.38	$185,749.54	$269,906.33
Design B	$17,938.22	$205,760.79	$298,970.33

Thus, Design A is the more economical engineering design.

BeP Problems

Show calculations for each solution to problem.

Questions 1 through 9 are based upon the following special situation:

The ABC Company has just completed producing 900 units on an order calling for delivery of 8,000 units. To set up for this order, the company incurred costs of \$3,500 for reproduction tooling, \$3,000 for production engineering, and \$2,000 for planning. The material for each unit costs \$10. Each unit requires 2.5 man-hours of direct labor.

The value engineering group has just completed a VE study with apparent merit. The proposal will reduce material costs to \$5 per unit. Because of time considerations, the change cannot be implemented until another 600 units have been produced. The proposal will reduce direct labor requirements to 2.0 man-hours. Other costs associated with this proposal are as follows: new drawings \$1,500, revision of technial manuals \$800, new tooling \$3,200, added testing \$4,500. The regular charge for labor is \$4 per hour and overhead is 200 percent of the direct labor charge.

Where

Fa = fixed cost of method A

Fb = fixed cost of method B

Va = variable cost of method A

Vb = variable cost of method B

X = number of units at break-even point

1. The basic formula for the break-even technique is:

   a. $Fa - Fb = (Va - Vb)\,X$
   b. $Fa - Fb = (Vb - Va)\,X$
   c. $Fa + Vb\,(x) = Fb + Va\,(X)$
   d. $Fa + Va = Fb + Vb$

2. The total fixed charge for the present procedure described in the situation above was:

   a. \$8,500 c. \$5,000
   b. \$6,500 d. \$3,500

3. The total variable cost per unit for the present method is:

   a. \$45 c. \$30
   b. \$40 d. \$10

4. The total fixed charge for the proposed method is:

   a. \$15,500 c. \$8,500
   b. \$18,500 d. \$10,000

5. The total variable cost per unit for the proposed method is:

   a. \$13 c. \$29
   b. \$24 d. \$40

6. If the two methods had been considered before production had begun, the break-even quantity would have been:

   a. 95 units c. 200 units
   b. 56 units d. 137 units

7. The production quantity at which the break-even point can be reached is:

   a. 3,000 units c. 1,700 units
   b. 2,410 units d. 1,500 units

8. Because the proposed method was not developed until after production had started, the break-even quantity now is:

   a. 910 units c. 371 units
   b. 625 units d. 200 units

9. The net savings that this proposal will produce is:

   a. \$61,500 c. \$94,000
   b. \$71,500 d. \$104,000

Questions

1. Define and discuss engineering economics.
2. Define and give examples of interest, interest rate, simple interest, single-payment component-amount factor, single payment present-worth factor, and equal-payment series compound-amount factor.
3. What is the equal payment series sinking-fund factor, equal-payment series capital-recovery factor, and equal-payment series present-worth factor?
4. What three factors are involved in the equivalence of money?
5. List and briefly explain each of the basic methods on which economic ventures may be compared.
6. How is the minimum cost point determined in an economic order quantity or economic production lot size?
7. Plot a break-even chart and identify the break-even point. What are some of the shortcomings of break-even analysis?
8. What are the difficulties encountered in using payback analysis of capital investment proposals?
9. Define depreciation. Compare the advantages and disadvantages of each depreciation method allowed by the U.S. Internal Revenue Service.
10. Select three odd or even problems from each of the three examinations on engineering economics. Show all calculations for each problem.

Table of Mnemonic Correlation

Long hand means of describing an interest (i) condition for n periods	*Symbols used in solutions manual*	*Mnemonic symbols used in text*
Future amount of a present sum of money	(F/P-i-n)	(caf′-i-n)
Present amount of a future sum of money	(P/F-i-n-)	(pwf′-i-n)
Equal series recovery of an invested sum	(A/P-i-n)	(crf-i-n)
Equal series payments to produce a future sum	(A/F-i-n)	(sff-i-n)
Present amount of an equal payment series	(P/A-i-n)	(pwf-i-n)
Future amount of an equal payment series	(F/A-i-n)	(caf-i-n)
Equal series amount of a series increasing uniformly	(A/G-i-n)	(gf-i-n)
Present worth of a uniformly increasing series of money	(P/G-i-n)	(gpwf-i-n)

Student Exercises[6]

EXAMINATION 1: INTEREST AND RATE OF RETURN

Answer the following multiple-choice exercises. Each exercise has four possible choices with only one best answer.

1. If money is worth 8 percent per annum, compounded semiannually, how much can an individual afford to spend now to avoid an expenditure of $1000 eight years from now?

   a. 560 c. 610
   b. 534 d. 490

2. Smith has $10,000 he desires to invest for 10 years. A thrift institution in his own state will pay him 6 percent interest compounded annually. A similar thrift operation out of state will pay 6 percent compounded bimonthly. How many dollars will he lose by dealing in-state (more convenient, knows the people, will aid state economic development, etc.) assuming that all interest payments and principal repayment will occur only at the 10-year loan maturity?

   a. 550 c. 720
   b. 260 d. 420

3. Jones has an annuity from an uncle's estate that is scheduled to pay $3,000 per year commencing 8 years from now, this annuity continuing for a total of 20 payments. A bank will buy this annuity from Jones today by discounting it 6 percent. How many dollars does the bank pay Jones?

   a. 24,401 c. 22,032
   b. 22,886 d. 23,927

4. A small manufacturer required some additional working capital and borrowed $200,000 from the bank at 6 percent interest for one year. He agreed to maintain $100,000 at the bank in a checking account (which draws no interest) as a "compensating balance," or the loan would be called. Furthermore the bank discounted this loan. What actual interest rate did the manufacturer pay?

   a. 11.56 c. 13.24
   b. 14.42 d. 13.64

5. What is the effective interest rate percent stemming from compounding a principal amount continuously at a nominal interest rate of 10 percent?

   a. 12.22 c. 11.65
   b. 10.52 d. 11.00

6. A car was sold under an agreement whereby the purchaser made a 30 percent down payment and 30 ensuing monthly payments oriented to a 15 percent annual interest rate. The purchaser has now made 10 payments and the car dealer is agreeable to a lump sum payment of $2,474.95 to complete the purchase price obligation. If the car dealer is allowing the purchaser the same rate of interest the dealer is charging, what is the sales price (in dollars) of the car?

   a. 5,400 c. 5,000
   b. 4,800 d. 5,200

7. An investor desires a return of 6 percent compounded semiannually on his money; $1,000 face value 4 percent Podunk Municipal Waterworks bonds issued 5 years ago are available. The bonds are to mature 20 years after issue and pay interest semiannually. What price (in dollars) should this

[6] Used, by permission, from *Engineering Economics and Practice,* Pamphlet No. 446. Ft. Belvoir, Va.: U.S. Army School, June 1977.

investor pay for these bonds to realize his rate-of-return criteria?

a. 804 c. 784
b. 794 d. 774

8. After down payments, Mr. Doe is apparently $17,000 shy of the purchase price for a new house so he applied for a 6 percent FHA financing loan. Mr. Doe finds his closing costs (usually only $50 for recording the deed of bargain and sale) will be increased by the tabulated items below if he obtains the FHA loan:

Closing Costs	
Credit report	$10
Recording deed of trust	44
Appraisal fee	30
Inspection fees	30
Survey of lot	50
Title examination and attorney fee	200
Title insurance	50
Origination charge (1 percent of loan)	176
Drawing deed of trust and note	10
Total increasing closing costs	$600

It is thus apparent that in order to obtain the loan Mr. Doe will have to pay $600 more at the time the loan is made. Mr. Doe also finds there is a $7.25 FHA premium added to his monthly repayments to cover FHA deficiency guarantees on foreclosure of FHA loans. What percentage nominal annual interest will Mr. Doe pay on this loan if he makes monthly repayments amortizing the loan in 30 years? (Assume all payments are made at the end of the month.)

a. 6.54 c. 7.23
b. 6.24 d. 6.96

9. A town council proposes a bond issue, proceeds of which are to be used to purchase the privately owned water system now serving the town. The bonds are to bear 4 percent interest and are to be retired in 20 years. Assume the town can invest a 4 percent sinking fund that provides for semiannual compounding. A syndicate will buy up the issue, but conditions the purchase on the premise that the annual net income from the operation of the water system must exceed the annual cost of amortizing the debt by 30 percent. Semiannual net earnings are estimated at $325,000. What is the highest dollar value that may be offered for the water system assuming a semiannual payment of interest and principal compounding?

a. 6,751,000 c. 8,012,000
b. 6,838,000 d. 7,021,000

10. Nelso needs $20,000 to purchase a new house. The best arrangement that can be made is to borrow the money at 6 percent from the bank. The bank rationalizes that a 6 percent interest rate is inadequate return (6 percent is the maximum usury laws allow) for the existing money market. To provide a respectable return for the bank, the bank demands 8 points to make this loan of $20,000 for 10 years, the loan to be repaid in end-of-the-year installments of constant or unvarying payment magnitude. The charging of 8 points results in the borrowed having to pay the bank 8 percent of $20,000, or $1,600, at the time the loan is made. This payment is nonrefundable and it does not reduce the $20,000 principal to be repaid at 6 percent. What is the true rate of interest to obtain this loan under these terms?

a. 7.20 c. 6.54
b. 8.09 d. 7.81

EXAMINATION 2: COST COMPARISON AND CONTROL

The following are multiple-choice exercises and the instructions for solving them and indicating your answers are the same as for examination 1.

1. A metal fence post costs $1.40 and has an expected life of 8 years. A protective coating for this metal will increase the cost to $2.00 per unit. If money is worth 7 percent, determine the life span of the protected metal to justify investing in it.

   a. 14.34
   b. 13.87
   c. 13.46
   d. 13.22

2. An investor desires to build an apartment house and is considering two proposals. One building (plan A) will cost $200,000 and will produce $24,000 gross annual income with operating expenses of $10,000. By altering the basic plan and investing $240,000 in the building (plan B), annual gross revenue can be increased to $31,000 and the operating costs will increase to $13,000. The investor figures his annual depreciation as 2½ percent of total investment based on the straight-line method (assume zero salvage value) for both plan A and plan B.

   What percentage rate of return will this investor receive on the extra money invested in plan B?

   a. 8.94
   b. 9.75
   c. 9.40
   d. 10.01

3. A water resources district is considering alternate plans for an impounding dam. The following are engineering cost estimates:

   Concrete Dam:

   First cost $450,000; annual maintenance $5,000; desilting every 25 years at $50,000; and a 75-year life.

   Earth Dam:

   First cost $300,000; annual maintenance $10,000; desilting every 10 years at $30,000; replacing rodent barrier every 20 years at $20,000; and replace rip-rap every 36 years at $40,000. The life of the earth fill is permanent.

   Which facility has an economic advantage on an annual dollar cost comparison? Use a 6 percent interest rate.

   a. earth by 2,100
   b. concrete by 1,740
   c. earth fill by 640
   d. earth fill by 780

4. The State Highway Commission is evaluating two bridge designs for which data are as follows:

	Bridge A	*Bridge B*
Initial cost	$45,000	$80,000
Estimated life, years	20	50
Replacement cost	$30,000	$60,000
Annual maintenance	$ 1,000	$ 200
Repairs (every 5 years)	$ 2,500	$ 1,500
Salvage value	$ 5,000	$10,000

   Highway funds are available for initial cost; other expenditures are secured by a 4 percent sinking fund. Which is the more economical dollar investment via the annual cost method?

   a. bridge A is favored by 68
   b. bridge A is favored by 31
   c. bridge B is favored by 287
   d. bridge B is favored by 114

5. Using the same data as in exercise 4, except with an interest rate of 6 percent, which bridge is more economical on the basis of capitalized cost?

   a. bridge A by 840
   b. bridge B by 10,360
   c. bridge B by 8,420
   d. bridge B by 3,080

6. Compare the two plans below, using the present-worth method with interest at 8 percent.

	Plan A	Plan B
First cost	$20,000	$30,000
Life	12 yrs.	8 yrs.
Salvage at end of life	$ 2,000	$ 4,000
Overhaul at end of 8th year of life	$ 5,000	n/a
Annual operations and maintenance cost	$ 8,000	$ 4,000
Annual taxes expressed as a percentage of first cost	10%	10%

Note: The plan selected must not be greater than the imposed ceiling of $12,000.

a. select plan B
b. select plan A
c. plans A and B are equivalent
d. plans A and B exceed the imposed ceiling

7. A company is investigating the question of insulating a bare steam pipe. A study indicates a heat loss of 2,000 BTU's per hour per linear foot, 3,000 hours of operation per year, and a fuel cost of $0.60 per million BTU's for heat losses.

Data on the insulation being considered are:

	1 inch	2 inch	3 inch
Efficiency, percent	80	90	95
Cost per linear foot	$2.50	$4.50	$7.00

The life of the insulation is estimated at 12 years and it will have no salvage value. The company uses the sinking-fund method of depreciation with an interest rate of 10 percent. What is the most economical alternative on the basis of annual cost?

a. bare pipe
b. 1-inch insulation
c. 2-inch insulation
d. 3-inch insulation

8. Two heating systems are being considered for a proposed structure. One is of traditional design; the other employs some newly developed concepts. With data as follows, compute the break-even point in minimum expected life of the new equipment.

	Conventional System	New Type System
First Cost	$10,000	$5,000
Life	20 yrs.	Unknown
Salvage value	0	0
Annual maintenance	$ 50	$ 300
Annual energy cost	$ 150	$ 50
Interest rate	10%	

a. 5 years
b. 9 years
c. 7 years
d. 8 years

9. A chemical process plant is planning to install a new 3,000 gallon steam-jacketed kettle. Operating conditions and chemical reactions are so severe that only stainless steel or high-grade cast iron may be used. The cast iron kettle costs $6,750 delivered, has a service life of 5 years, and has a salvage value estimated at $250. The stainless steel kettle costs $10,000 delivered, has a service life of 9 years, and a residual value of 10 percent. Installation and operating costs are equal. At what interest percentage rate would the cost of these competing units be equal?

a. 11.43
b. 14.09
c. 10.76
d. 12.86

10. Two water distribution systems are to be economically evaluated to provide service in a new area being developed. Select the most desirable system on the basis of a dollar annual cost comparison and money being worth 8 percent. It is estimated that the water system

will be obsolete 50 years from original construction owing to the fact that water needs will be supplied by individual purifying and recycling units.

Plan A: Construct 10,000 feet of 12-inch line now at a cost of $12 per foot and build a $40,000 pumping station. Fifteen years from now build another parallel 10,000 feet of 12-inch line at a cost of $14 per foot and add the recondition pumps at a cost of $5,000. Replace pumps 30 years from now at a cost of $8,000. Pumping and maintenance costs will commence at $2,000 per year and increase at the rate of $400 per year for each year thereafter until the addition is made. When the new additional system is installed in 15 years, the pumping cost will be $6,000 for the first year after the new system is installed and will increase at the rate of $300 for each year thereafter.

Plan B: Construct 10,000 feet of 18-inch line now at a cost of $19 per foot and build a $43,000 pumping station. Twenty-five years from now replace the pumps and touch up the pumping station at a cost of $7,000.

Pumping and maintenance costs will commence at $1,500 per year and increase at the rate of $200 per year throughout the life of this plan.

a. A by 370 c. B by 3,170
b. A by 1,790 d. B by 640

EXAMINATION 3: PROBLEMS OF SELECTION AND OWNERSHIP

The following are multiple-choice exercises and the instructions for solving them and indicating your answers are the same as for the previous examinations.

1. A mechanism costs $11,000 and installation and shipping costs are $1,000. The salvage value at the end of 5 years of design-useful life is $2,000. If the tax depreciation write-off in the fourth year of ownership is computed on the straight-line method, the sum-of-the-digits approach and the 10 percent sinking-fund method, what will be the amount (in dollars) that separates the maximum and minimum of these three depreciation charges in the fourth year of ownership?
   a. 847 c. 667
   b. 683 d. 304

2. A community proposes to issue a $2.5 million face value bond issue at 4 percent interest. The improvements that will be financed by this revenue bond issue will generate bond servicing income the first year of $104,000 and this income will increase $3,000 per year for each year thereafter. These bonds (in $1000 denominations) will be periodically retired promptly according to serial number with any yearly income funds remaining after the bond issue interest has been paid yearly. Assume that the interest saved each year from not having to pay interest on the bonds previously retired will have to be spent on the increasing cost of maintenance on the improvements. What is the minimum period of time in years in which this bond issue may be completely retired?
   a. 40 c. 50
   b. 35 d. 45

3. A certain well-established manufacturing plant with a payroll of $100,000 per month pays 5 percent of payroll as premium on workmen's compensation insurance. A study shows that by undertaking an extensive industrial safety program, including considerable point-of-operation machine guarding and safety equipment, compensation-insurance premiums will be reduced to

2 percent. Administrative costs of the program will be $18,000 per year. With money worth 8 percent, how much is the company justified in investing in the machine guards and safety equipment, assuming this investment is capitalized disregarding any irreducibles such as humanitarianism and production benefits?

a. 225,000 c. 300,000
b. 24,000 d. 225,000

4. A company producing crenelated widgets has costs as follows:

Fixed costs per lot: $200

Variable outlay per widget: $0.60

Apportioned charge per widget: $0.75

Storage costs per year (widgets are unique and may not be housed in storage suitable for other products): $0.05

Property tax and insurance (based on book value): 2 percent

Maximum production rate per year: 150,000

Demand rate per year: 25,000

Interest on inventory (high due to obsolescence factor): 30 percent

What is the optimum lot size in running off a batch of widgets? (This computed optimum should be adjusted to provide a whole number yearly.)

a. 8,050 c. 6,380
b. 5,820 d. 7,140

5. Two competing improvements for the widget production line (exercise 4) are available which cost the same. Widgets Galore will increase the fixed costs per lot by $50, decrease the variable cost per widget by three cents, and the apportioned charge per widget by five cents, but the annual maximum production rate would increase to 200,000. Scotch widgets perfects its use in decreasing the fixed cost per lot by $60. Which investment should be made on the basis of an annual method of accounting in dollars?

a. Galore is better by 57
b. Galore is better by 228
c. Scotch is better by 642
d. Scotch is better by 284

6. It is proposed to run a new car that cost $4,200 the same distance each year. The trade-in value is $3,000 at the end of the first year, and this $1,200 first-year depreciation will decrease $200 per year for each remaining year of life. Annual expenses and maintenance cost $500 the first year and increase each year thereafter at the rate of $300 per year; cost consideration is assumed for the purpose of the exercise.

How many years after purchase should this car be traded in for a new model if money is worth 10 percent?

a. 2 c. 4
b. 3 d. 5

7. The PDQ Corporation has an unlimited line of credit with an insurance company as long as the corporation can demonstrate a 15 percent return on its investments. PDQ is contemplating the replacement of a supplier through the purchase of a specialty machine to produce certain parts. The least-cost machine is designated as plan A, and plans B through E represent various

Plan	*A*	*B*	*C*	*D*	*E*
Equipment cost	100,000	140,000	190,000	230,000	300,000
Savings generated	16,000	32,000	40,000	49,000	60,000
Return on total invested	11.80%	20.38%	18.19%	18.50%	16.90%

refinements and accessories available for this basic machine (such as cheaper fuels, sealed housings, fail-safe features, remote controls, automatic programming, etc.).

The machine and accessories have a 12-year life and the potential of a salvage value is not to be considered because of the dynamic technology being pursued in the general area of the product to be manufactured.

Select the wisest machine investment plan.

a. B
b. C
c. D
d. E

8. A corporation purchases a machine for \$240,000 that will have a salvage value in 20 years of \$30,000. The machine will provide income to the corporation's operations of \$40,000 the first year the machine is in service and this income will diminish at the rate of \$1,500 per year each of the remaining years of life. The reason for this steady reduction in income is that repairs and down time will increase, product quality may suffer, etc. What is the before-tax rate of return (in percent) from this investment?

a. 11.97
b. 11.59
c. 11.00
d. 10.41

9. Timbering rights for 10 years on a large parcel of land can be secured by the payment of \$200,000 at the beginning of the 10-year period. Annual gross sales are estimated at 85,000 dollars, with annual expenses, taxes, insurance and all other annual costs at \$48,000. Compute the prospective rate of return.

a. 12.5
b. 14.2
c. 14.1
d. 13.2

10. A privately owned steam power plant of 12,000-kilowatt capacity was built 15 years ago at a cost of \$210 per kilowatt. Its life was estimated at 25 years with 6 percent residual (salvage) value, and this estimate is still considered valid. Annual demand has averaged 55,000,000 kilowatt hours, for which operating costs have averaged \$300,000. These figures are expected to continue essentially unchanged.

A new diesel plant costing \$240 per kilowatt is being considered for replacement of the old steam plant. The diesel plant has an estimated life of 25 years with 10 percent residual value, and estimated annual operating costs of \$165,000. For both plants, taxes and insurance amount to 2½ percent of first cost.

If the company can sell the old steam plant for \$750,000 and figures its money is worth 6 percent, which plant has the better dollar justification at this time on the basis of an annual cost comparison?

a. steam by 3,600
b. steam by 12,400
c. diesel by 1,400
d. diesel by 7,800

Bibliography

American Telephone and Telegraph Co. *Engineering Economy*. 3rd ed. New York: McGraw-Hill, 1977.

Barish, N. N. *Economic Analysis for Engineering and Managerial Decision-Making*. New York: McGraw-Hill, 1962.

Bussey, Lynne. *The Economic Analysis of Industrial Projects*. Englewood Cliffs, N.J.: Prentice-Hall, 1972.

Canada, J. R. *Intermediate Economic Analysis for Management and Engineering*. Englewood Cliffs, N.J.: Prentice-Hall, 1971.

De Garmo, E. P. *Engineering Economy*. 6th ed. New York: Macmillan, 1979.

De Garmo, E. P., and Canada, J. R. *Engineering Economy*. 5th ed. New York: Macmillan, 1973.

"Engineering Economics and Practices." Pamphlet No. 446. Fort Belvoir, Va.: U.S. Army Engineering Corps, June 1977.

Grant, E. L., Ireson, W. G., and Leavenworth, R. S., *Principles of Engineering Economy*. 6th ed. New York: Ronald Press, 1976.

Happel, J. *Chemical Process Economics*. New York: John Wiley and Sons, 1968.

Jelen, F. C. *Cost and Optimization Engineering*. New York: McGraw-Hill, 1970.

Morris, W. T. *Engineering Economy: The Analysis of Management Decisions*. Homewood, Ill.: Richard D. Irwin, 1964.

Newnan, D. G. *Engineering Economic Analysis* 2nd ed. San Jose, Calif.: Engineering Press, 1983.

"Principles and Problems Engineering Economics." Student Pamphlet. Fort Belvoir, Va.: U.S. Army Engineer School, April 1971.

Reisman, A. *Managerial and Engineering Economics*. Boston: Allyn and Bacon, 1971.

Riggs, J. L. *Engineering Economics*. New York: McGraw-Hill, 1977.

Smith, G. A. *Engineering Economy*. 3rd ed. Ames: Iowa State University Press, 1979.

Tarquin, A. J., and Blank, L. T., *Engineering Economy: A Behavioral Approach*. New York: McGraw-Hill, 1976.

Taylor, G. A. *Managerial and Engineering Economy: Economy Decision Making*. New York: Van Nostrand Reinhold, 1980.

Thuesen, H. G., Fabrycky, W. J., and Thuesen, G. J. *Engineering Economy*. 5th ed. Englewood Cliffs, N.J.: Prentice-Hall, 1977.

White, J. A., Agee, M. H., and Case, K. E. *Principles of Engineering Economic Analysis*. New York: John Wiley and Sons, 1977.

Woods, D. R. *Financial Decision Making in the Process Industry*. Englewood Cliffs, N.J.: Prentice-Hall, 1975.

TABLE A
1% Compound Interest Factors

n	SINGLE PAYMENT		UNIFORM ANNUAL SERIES			
	Compound Amount Factor caf'	*Present Worth Factor pwf'*	*Sinking Fund Factor sff*	*Capital Recovery Factor crf*	*Compound Amount Factor caf*	*Present Worth Factor pwf*
	Given P to find S $(1+i)^n$	*Given S to find P* $\frac{1}{(1+i)^n}$	*Given S to find R* $\frac{i}{(1+i)^n-1}$	*Given P to find R* $\frac{i(1+i)^n}{(1+i)^n-1}$	*Given R to find S* $\frac{(1+i)^n-1}{i}$	*Given R to find P* $\frac{(1+i)^n-1}{i(1+i)^n}$
1	1.010	0.9901	1.00000	1.0100	1.000	0.990
2	1.020	0.9803	0.49751	0.50751	2.010	1.970
3	1.030	0.9706	0.33002	0.34002	3.030	2.941
4	1.041	0.9610	0.24628	2.25628	4.060	3.902
5	1.051	0.9515	0.19604	0.20604	5.101	4.853
6	1.062	0.9420	0.16255	0.17255	6.152	5.795
7	1.072	0.9327	0.13863	0.14863	7.214	6.728
8	1.083	0.9235	0.12069	0.13069	8.286	7.652
9	1.094	0.9143	0.10674	0.11674	9.369	8.566
10	1.105	0.9053	0.09588	0.10558	10.462	9.471
11	1.116	0.8963	0.08645	0.09645	11.567	10.368
12	1.127	0.8874	0.07885	0.08885	12.683	11.255
13	1.138	0.8787	0.07241	0.08241	13.809	12.134
14	1.149	0.8700	0.06690	0.07690	14.947	13.004
15	1.161	0.8613	0.06212	0.07212	16.097	13.865
16	1.173	0.8528	0.05794	0.06794	17.258	14.718
17	1.184	0.8444	0.05426	0.06426	18.430	15.562
18	1.196	0.8360	0.05098	0.06098	19.615	16.398
19	1.208	0.8277	0.04805	0.05805	20.811	17.226
20	1.220	0.8195	0.04542	0.05542	22.019	18.046
21	1.232	0.8114	0.04303	0.05303	23.239	18.857
22	1.245	0.8034	0.04086	0.05086	24.472	19.660
23	1.257	0.7954	0.03889	0.04889	25.716	20.456
24	1.270	0.7876	0.03707	0.04707	26.973	21.243
25	1.282	0.7798	0.03541	0.04541	28.243	22.023
26	1.295	0.7720	0.03387	0.04387	29.526	22.795
27	1.308	0.7644	0.03245	0.04245	30.821	23.560
28	1.321	0.7568	0.03112	0.04112	32.129	24.316
29	1.335	0.7493	0.02990	0.03990	33.450	25.066
30	1.348	0.7419	0.02875	0.03875	34.785	25.808
31	1.361	0.7346	0.02768	0.03768	36.133	26.542
32	1.375	0.7273	0.02667	0.03667	37.494	27.270
33	1.389	0.7201	0.02573	0.03573	38.869	27.990
34	1.403	0.7130	0.02484	0.03484	40.258	28.703
35	1.417	0.7059	0.02400	0.03400	41.660	29.409
40	1.489	0.6717	0.02046	0.03046	48.886	32.835
45	1.565	0.6391	0.01771	0.02771	56.481	36.095
50	1.645	0.6080	0.01551	0.02551	64.463	39.196
55	1.729	0.5785	0.01373	0.02373	72.852	42.147
60	1.817	0.5504	0.01224	0.02224	81.670	44.955
65	1.909	0.5237	0.01100	0.02100	90.937	47.627
70	2.007	0.4983	0.00993	0.01993	100.676	50.169
75	2.109	0.4741	0.00902	0.01902	110.913	52.587
80	2.217	0.4511	0.00822	0.01822	121.672	54.888
85	2.330	0.4292	0.00752	0.01752	132.979	57.078
90	2.449	0.4084	0.00690	0.01690	144.863	59.161
95	2.574	0.3886	0.00636	0.01636	157.354	61.143
100	2.705	0.3697	0.00587	0.01587	170.481	63.029

TABLE B
1¼% Compound Interest Factors

n	SINGLE PAYMENT		UNIFORM ANNUAL SERIES			
	Compound Amount Factor caf′	Present Worth Factor pwf′	Sinking Fund Factor sff	Capital Recovery Factor crf	Compound Amount Factor caf	Present Worth Factor pwf
	Given P to find S $(1+i)^n$	Given S to find P $\frac{1}{(1+i)^n}$	Given S to find R $\frac{i}{(1+i)^n-1}$	Given P to find R $\frac{i(1+i)^n}{(1+i)^n-1}$	Given R to find S $\frac{(1+i)^n-1}{i}$	Given R to find P $\frac{(1+i)^n-1}{i(1+i)^n}$
1	1.012	0.9877	1.00000	1.01250	1.000	0.988
2	1.025	0.9755	0.49689	0.50939	2.012	1.963
3	1.038	0.9634	0.32920	0.34170	3.038	2.927
4	1.051	0.9515	0.24536	0.25786	4.076	3.878
5	1.064	0.9398	0.19506	0.20756	5.127	4.818
6	1.077	0.9282	0.16153	0.17403	6.191	5.746
7	1.091	0.9167	0.13759	0.15009	7.268	6.663
8	1.104	0.9054	0.11963	0.13213	8.359	7.568
9	1.118	0.8942	0.10567	0.11817	9.463	8.462
10	1.132	0.8832	0.09450	0.10700	10.582	9.346
11	1.146	0.8723	0.08537	0.09787	11.714	10.218
12	1.161	0.8615	0.07776	0.09026	12.860	11.079
13	1.175	0.8509	0.07132	0.08382	14.021	11.930
14	1.190	0.8404	0.06581	0.07831	15.196	12.771
15	1.205	0.8300	0.06103	0.07353	16.386	13.601
16	1.220	0.8197	0.05685	0.06935	17.591	14.420
17	1.235	0.8096	0.05316	0.06566	18.811	15.230
18	1.251	0.7996	0.04988	0.06238	20.046	16.030
19	1.266	0.7898	0.04696	0.05946	21.297	16.819
20	1.282	0.7800	0.04432	0.05682	22.563	17.599
21	1.298	0.7704	0.04194	0.05444	23.845	18.370
22	1.314	0.7609	0.03977	0.05227	25.143	19.131
23	1.331	0.7515	0.03780	0.05030	26.457	19.882
24	1.347	0.7422	0.03599	0.04849	27.788	20.624
25	1.364	0.7330	0.03432	0.04682	29.135	21.357
26	1.381	0.7240	0.03279	0.04529	30.500	22.081
27	1.399	0.7150	0.03137	0.04387	31.881	22.796
28	1.416	0.7062	0.03005	0.04255	33.279	23.503
29	1.434	0.6975	0.02882	0.04132	34.695	24.200
30	1.452	0.6889	0.02768	0.04018	36.129	24.889
31	1.470	0.6804	0.02661	0.03911	37.581	25.569
32	1.488	0.6720	0.02561	0.03811	39.050	26.241
33	1.507	0.6637	0.02467	0.03717	40.539	26.905
34	1.526	0.6555	0.02378	0.03628	42.045	27.560
35	1.545	0.6474	0.02295	0.03545	43.571	28.208
40	1.644	0.6084	0.01942	0.03192	51.490	31.327
45	1.749	0.5718	0.01669	0.02919	59.916	34.258
50	1.861	0.5373	0.01452	0.02702	68.882	37.013
55	1.980	0.5050	0.01275	0.02525	78.422	39.602
60	2.107	0.4746	0.01129	0.02379	88.575	42.035
65	2.242	0.4460	0.01006	0.02256	99.377	44.321
70	2.386	0.4191	0.00902	0.02152	110.872	46.470
75	2.539	0.3939	0.00812	0.02062	123.103	48.489
80	2.701	0.3702	0.00735	0.01985	136.119	50.387
85	2.875	0.3479	0.00667	0.01917	149.968	52.170
90	3.059	0.3269	0.00607	0.01857	164.705	53.846
95	3.255	0.3072	0.00554	0.01804	180.386	55.421
100	3.463	0.2887	0.00507	0.01757	197.072	56.901

TABLE C
1½% Compound Interest Factors

n	SINGLE PAYMENT		UNIFORM ANNUAL SERIES			
	Compound Amount Factor caf'	Present Worth Factor pwf'	Sinking Fund Factor sff	Capital Recovery Factor crf	Compound Amount Factor caf	Present Worth Factor pwf
	Given P to find S $(1+i)^n$	Given S to find P $\frac{i}{(1+i)^n}$	Given S to find R $\frac{i}{(1+i)^n-1}$	Given P to find R $\frac{i(1+i)^n}{(1+i)^n-1}$	Given R to find S $\frac{(1+i)^n-1}{i}$	Given R to find P $\frac{(1+i)^n-1}{i(1+i)^n}$
1	1.015	0.9852	1.00000	1.01500	1.000	0.985
2	1.030	0.9707	0.49628	0.51128	2.015	1.956
3	1.046	0.9563	0.32838	0.34338	3.045	2.912
4	1.061	0.9422	0.24444	0.25944	4.091	3.854
5	1.077	0.9283	0.19409	0.20909	5.152	4.783
6	1.093	0.9145	0.16053	0.17553	6.230	5.697
7	1.110	0.9010	0.13656	0.15156	7.323	6.598
8	1.126	0.8877	0.11858	0.13358	8.433	7.486
9	1.143	0.8746	0.10461	0.11961	9.559	8.361
10	1.161	0.8617	0.09343	0.10843	10.703	9.222
11	1.178	0.8489	0.08429	0.09929	11.863	10.071
12	1.196	0.8364	0.07668	0.09168	13.041	10.908
13	1.214	0.8240	0.07024	0.08524	14.237	11.732
14	1.232	0.8118	0.06472	0.07972	15.450	12.543
15	1.250	0.7999	0.05994	0.07494	16.682	13.343
16	1.269	0.7880	0.05577	0.07077	17.932	14.131
17	1.288	0.7764	0.05208	0.06708	19.201	14.908
18	1.307	0.7649	0.04881	0.06381	20.489	15.673
19	1.327	0.7536	0.04588	0.06088	21.797	16.426
20	1.347	0.7425	0.04325	0.05825	23.124	17.169
21	1.367	0.7315	0.04087	0.05587	24.471	17.900
22	1.388	0.7207	0.03870	0.05370	25.838	18.621
23	1.408	0.7100	0.03673	0.05173	27.225	19.331
24	1.430	0.6995	0.03492	0.04992	28.634	20.030
25	1.451	0.6892	0.03326	0.04826	30.063	20.720
26	1.473	0.6790	0.03173	0.04673	31.514	21.399
27	1.495	0.6690	0.03032	0.04532	32.987	22.068
28	1.517	0.6591	0.02900	0.04400	34.481	22.727
29	1.540	0.6494	0.02778	0.04278	35.999	23.376
30	1.563	0.6398	0.02664	0.04164	37.539	24.016
31	1.587	0.6303	0.02557	0.04057	39.102	24.646
32	1.610	0.6210	0.02458	0.03958	40.688	25.267
33	1.634	0.6118	0.02364	0.03864	42.299	25.879
34	1.659	0.6028	0.02276	0.03776	43.933	26.482
35	1.684	0.5939	0.02193	0.03693	45.592	27.076
40	1.814	0.5513	0.01843	0.03343	54.268	29.916
45	1.954	0.5117	0.01572	0.03072	63.614	32.552
50	2.105	0.4750	0.01357	0.02857	73.683	35.000
55	2.268	0.4409	0.01183	0.02683	84.530	37.271
60	2.443	0.4093	0.01039	0.02539	96.215	39.380
65	2.632	0.3799	0.00919	0.02419	108.803	41.338
70	2.835	0.3527	0.00817	0.02317	122.364	43.155
75	3.055	0.3274	0.00730	0.02230	136.973	44.842
80	3.291	0.3039	0.00655	0.02155	152.711	46.407
85	3.545	0.2821	0.00589	0.02089	169.665	47.861
90	3.819	0.2619	0.00532	0.02032	187.930	49.210
95	4.114	0.2431	0.00482	0.01982	207.606	50.462
100	4.432	0.2256	0.00437	0.01937	228.803	51.625

TABLE D
$1\frac{3}{4}$% Compound Interest Factors

	SINGLE PAYMENT		UNIFORM ANNUAL SERIES			
n	*Compound Amount Factor caf'*	*Present Worth Factor pwf'*	*Sinking Fund Factor sff*	*Capital Recovery Factor crf*	*Compound Amount Factor caf*	*Present Worth Factor pwf*
	Given P to find S $(1+i)^n$	*Given S to find P* $\frac{1}{(1+i)^n}$	*Given S to find R* $\frac{i}{(1+i)^n-1}$	*Given P to find R* $\frac{i(1+i)^n}{(1+i)^n-1}$	*Given R to find S* $\frac{(1+i)^n-1}{i}$	*Given R to find P* $\frac{(1+i)^n-1}{i(1+i)^n}$
1	1.018	0.9828	1.00000	1.01750	1.000	0.983
2	1.035	0.9659	0.49556	0.51316	2.018	1.949
3	1.053	0.9493	0.32757	0.34507	3.053	2.898
4	1.072	0.9330	0.24353	0.26103	4.106	3.831
5	1.091	0.9169	0.91312	0.21062	5.178	4.748
6	1.110	0.9011	0.15952	0.17702	6.269	5.649
7	1.129	0.8856	0.13553	0.15303	7.378	6.535
8	1.149	0.8704	0.11754	0.13504	8.508	7.405
9	1.169	0.8554	0.10356	0.12106	9.656	8.260
10	1.189	0.8407	0.09238	0.10988	10.825	9.101
11	1.210	0.8263	0.08323	0.10073	12.015	9.927
12	1.231	0.8121	0.07561	0.09311	13.255	10.740
13	1.253	0.7981	0.06917	0.08667	14.457	11.538
14	1.275	0.7844	0.06366	0.08116	15.710	12.322
15	1.297	0.7709	0.05888	0.07638	16.984	13.093
16	1.320	0.7576	0.05470	0.07220	18.282	13.850
17	1.343	0.7446	0.05102	0.06852	19.602	14.595
18	1.367	0.7318	0.04774	0.06524	20.945	15.327
19	1.390	0.7192	0.04482	0.06232	22.311	16.046
20	1.415	0.7068	0.04219	0.05969	23.702	16.753
21	1.440	0.6947	0.03981	0.05731	25.116	17.448
22	1.465	0.6827	0.03766	0.05516	26.556	18.130
23	1.490	0.6710	0.03569	0.05319	28.021	18.801
24	1.516	0.6594	0.03389	0.05139	29.511	19.461
25	1.543	0.6481	0.03223	0.04973	31.027	20.109
26	1.570	0.6369	0.03070	0.04820	32.570	20.746
27	1.597	0.6260	0.02929	0.04679	34.140	21.372
28	1.625	0.6152	0.02798	0.04548	35.738	21.987
29	1.654	0.6046	0.02676	0.04426	37.363	22.592
30	1.683	0.5942	0.02563	0.04313	39.017	23.186
31	1.712	0.5840	0.02457	0.04207	40.700	23.770
32	1.742	0.5740	0.02358	0.04108	42.412	24.344
33	1.773	0.5641	0.02265	0.04015	44.154	24.908
34	1.804	0.5544	0.02177	0.03927	45.927	25.462
35	1.835	0.5449	0.02095	0.03845	47.731	26.007
40	2.002	0.4996	0.01747	0.03497	57.234	28.594
45	2.183	0.4581	0.01479	0.03229	67.599	30.966
50	2.381	0.4200	0.01267	0.03017	78.902	33.141
55	2.597	0.3851	0.01096	0.02846	91.230	35.135
60	2.832	0.3531	0.00955	0.02705	104.675	36.964
65	3.088	0.3238	0.00838	0.02588	119.339	38.641
70	3.368	0.2969	0.00739	0.02489	135.331	40.178
75	3.674	0.2722	0.00655	0.02405	152.772	41.587
80	4.006	0.2496	0.00582	0.02332	171.794	42.880
85	4.369	0.2289	0.00519	0.02269	192.539	44.065
90	4.765	0.2098	0.00465	0.02215	215.165	45.152
95	5.197	0.1924	0.00417	0.02167	239.840	46.148
100	5.668	0.1764	0.00375	0.02125	266.752	47.061

TABLE E
2% Compound Interest Factors

n	*SINGLE PAYMENT*		*UNIFORM ANNUAL SERIES*			
	Compound Amount Factor caf'	*Present Worth Factor pwf'*	*Sinking Fund Factor sff*	*Capital Recovery Factor crf*	*Compound Amount Factor caf*	*Present Worth Factor pwf*
	Given P to find S $(1+i)^n$	*Given S to find P* $\frac{1}{(1+i)^n}$	*Given S to find R* $\frac{i}{(1+i)^n-1}$	*Given P to find R* $\frac{i(1+i)^n}{(1+i)^n-1}$	*Given R to find S* $\frac{(1+i)^n-1}{i}$	*Given R to find P* $\frac{(1+i)^n-1}{i(1+i)^n}$
1	1.020	0.9804	1.00000	1.02000	1.000	0.980
2	1.040	0.9612	0.49505	0.51505	2.020	1.942
3	1.061	0.9423	0.32675	0.34675	3.060	2.884
4	1.082	0.9238	0.24262	0.26262	4.122	3.808
5	1.104	0.9057	0.19216	0.21216	5.204	4.713
6	1.126	0.8880	0.15853	0.17853	6.308	5.601
7	1.149	0.8706	0.13451	0.15451	7.434	6.472
8	1.172	0.8535	0.11651	0.13651	8.583	7.325
9	1.195	0.8368	0.10252	0.12252	9.755	8.162
10	1.219	0.8203	0.09133	0.11133	10.950	8.983
11	1.243	0.8043	0.08218	0.10218	12.169	9.787
12	1.268	0.7885	0.07456	0.09456	13.412	10.575
13	1.294	0.7730	0.06812	0.08812	14.680	11.348
14	1.319	0.7579	0.06260	0.08260	15.974	12.106
15	1.346	0.7430	0.05783	0.07783	17.293	12.849
16	1.373	0.7284	0.05365	0.07365	18.639	13.578
17	1.400	0.7142	0.04997	0.06997	20.012	14.292
18	1.428	0.7002	0.04670	0.06670	21.412	14.992
19	1.457	0.6864	0.04378	0.06378	22.841	15.678
20	1.486	0.6730	0.04116	0.06116	24.297	16.351
21	1.516	0.6598	0.03878	0.05878	25.783	17.011
22	1.546	0.6468	0.03663	0.05663	27.299	17.658
23	1.577	0.6342	0.03467	0.05467	28.845	18.292
24	1.608	0.6217	0.03287	0.05287	30.422	18.914
25	1.641	0.6095	0.03122	0.05122	32.030	19.523
26	1.673	0.5976	0.02970	0.04970	33.671	20.121
27	1.707	0.5859	0.02829	0.04829	35.344	20.707
28	1.741	0.5744	0.02699	0.04699	37.051	21.281
29	1.776	0.5631	0.02578	0.04578	38.792	21.844
30	1.811	0.5521	0.02465	0.04465	40.568	22.396
31	1.848	0.5412	0.02360	0.04360	42.379	22.938
32	1.885	0.5306	0.02261	0.04261	44.227	23.468
33	1.922	0.5202	0.02169	0.04169	46.122	23.989
34	1.961	0.5100	0.02082	0.04082	48.034	24.499
35	2.000	0.5000	0.02000	0.04000	49.994	24.999
40	2.208	0.4529	0.01656	0.03656	60.402	27.355
45	2.438	0.4102	0.01391	0.03391	71.893	29.490
50	2.692	0.3715	0.01182	0.03182	84.579	31.424
55	2.972	0.3365	0.01014	0.03014	98.587	33.175
60	3.281	0.3048	0.00877	0.02877	114.052	34.761
65	3.623	0.2761	0.00763	0.02763	131.126	36.197
70	4.000	0.2500	0.00667	0.02667	149.978	37.499
75	4.416	0.2265	0.00586	0.02586	170.792	38.677
80	4.875	0.2051	0.00516	0.02516	193.772	39.745
85	5.383	0.1858	0.00456	0.02456	219.144	40.711
90	5.943	0.1683	0.00405	0.02405	247.157	41.587
95	6.562	0.1524	0.00360	0.02360	278.085	42.380
100	7.245	0.1380	0.00320	0.02320	312.232	43.098

TABLE F
$2\frac{1}{2}$% Compound Interest Factors

n	SINGLE PAYMENT		UNIFORM ANNUAL SERIES			
	Compound Amount Factor caf'	Present Worth Factor pwf'	Sinking Fund Factor sff	Capital Recovery Factor crf	Compound Amount Factor caf	Present Worth Factor pwf
	Given P to find S $(1+i)^n$	Given S to find P $\frac{1}{(1+i)^n}$	Given S to find R $\frac{i(1+i)^n}{(1+i)^n-1}$	Given P to find R $\frac{i(1+i)^n}{(1+i)^n-1}$	Given R to find S $\frac{(1+i)^n-1}{i}$	Given R to find P $\frac{(1+i)^n-1}{i(1+i)^n}$
1	1.025	0.9756	1.00000	1.02500	1.000	0.976
2	1.051	0.9518	0.49383	0.51883	2.025	1.927
3	1.077	0.9286	0.32514	0.35014	3.076	2.856
4	1.104	0.9060	0.24082	0.26582	4.153	3.762
5	1.131	0.8839	0.19025	0.21525	5.256	4.646
6	1.160	0.8623	0.15655	0.18155	6.388	5.508
7	1.189	0.8413	0.13250	0.15750	7.547	6.349
8	1.218	0.8207	0.11447	0.13947	8.736	7.170
9	1.249	0.8007	0.10046	0.12546	9.955	7.971
10	1.280	0.7812	0.08926	0.11426	11.203	8.752
11	1.312	0.7621	0.08011	0.10511	12.483	9.514
12	1.345	0.7436	0.07249	0.09749	13.796	10.258
13	1.379	0.7254	0.06605	0.09105	15.140	10.983
14	1.413	0.7077	0.06054	0.08554	16.519	11.691
15	1.448	0.6905	0.05577	0.08077	17.932	12.381
16	1.485	0.6736	0.05160	0.07660	19.380	13.055
17	1.522	0.6572	0.04793	0.07293	20.865	13.712
18	1.560	0.6412	0.04467	0.06967	22.386	14.353
19	1.599	0.6255	0.04176	0.06676	23.946	14.979
20	1.639	0.6103	0.03915	0.06415	25.545	15.589
21	1.680	0.5954	0.03679	0.06179	27.183	16.185
22	1.722	0.5809	0.03465	0.05965	28.863	16.765
23	1.765	0.5667	0.03270	0.05770	30.584	17.332
24	1.809	0.5529	0.03091	0.05591	32.349	17.885
25	1.854	0.5394	0.02928	0.05428	34.158	18.424
26	1.900	0.5262	0.02777	0.05277	36.012	18.951
27	1.948	0.5134	0.02638	0.05138	37.912	19.464
28	1.996	0.5009	0.02509	0.05009	39.860	19.965
29	2.046	0.4887	0.02389	0.04889	41.856	20.454
30	2.098	0.4767	0.02278	0.04778	43.903	20.903
31	2.150	0.4651	0.02174	0.04674	46.000	21.395
32	2.204	0.4538	0.02077	0.04577	48.150	21.849
33	2.259	0.4427	0.01986	0.04486	50.354	22.292
34	2.315	0.4319	0.01901	0.04401	52.613	22.724
35	2.373	0.4214	0.01821	0.04321	54.928	23.145
40	2.685	0.3724	0.01484	0.03984	67.403	25.103
45	3.038	0.3292	0.01227	0.03727	81.516	26.833
50	3.437	0.2909	0.01026	0.03526	97.484	28.362
55	3.889	0.2572	0.00865	0.03365	115.551	29.714
60	4.400	0.2273	0.00735	0.03235	135.992	30.909
65	4.978	0.2009	0.00628	0.03128	159.118	31.965
70	5.632	0.1776	0.00540	0.03040	185.284	32.898
75	6.372	0.1569	0.00465	0.02965	214.888	33.723
80	7.210	0.1387	0.00403	0.02903	248.383	34.452
85	8.157	0.1226	0.00349	0.02849	286.279	35.096
90	9.229	0.1084	0.00304	0.02804	329.154	35.666
95	10.442	0.0958	0.00265	0.02765	377.664	36.169
100	11.814	0.0846	0.00231	0.02731	432.549	36.614

TABLE G
3% Compound Interest Factors

n	SINGLE PAYMENT		UNIFORM ANNUAL SERIES			
	Compound Amount Factor caf'	*Present Worth Factor pwf'*	*Sinking Fund Factor sff*	*Capital Recovery Factor crf*	*Compound Amount Factor caf*	*Present Worth Factor pwf*
	Given P to find S $(1+i)^n$	*Given S to find P* $\frac{1}{(1+i)^n}$	*Given S to find R* $\frac{i}{(1+i)^n-1}$	*Given P to find R* $\frac{i(1+i)^n}{(1+i)^n-1}$	*Given R to find S* $\frac{(1+i)^n-1}{i}$	*Given R to find P* $\frac{(1+i)^n-1}{i(1+i)^n}$
1	1.030	0.9709	1.00000	1.03000	1.000	0.971
2	1.061	0.9426	0.49261	0.52261	2.030	1.913
3	1.093	0.9151	0.32353	0.35353	3.091	2.829
4	1.126	0.8885	0.23903	0.26903	4.184	3.717
5	1.159	0.8626	0.18835	0.21835	5.309	4.580
6	1.194	0.8375	0.15460	0.18460	6.468	5.417
7	1.230	0.8131	0.13051	0.16051	7.662	6.230
8	1.267	0.7894	0.11246	0.14246	8.892	7.020
9	1.305	0.7664	0.09843	0.12843	10.159	7.786
10	1.344	0.7441	0.08723	0.11723	11.464	8.530
11	1.384	0.7224	0.07808	0.10808	12.808	9.253
12	1.426	0.7014	0.07046	0.10046	14.192	9.954
13	1.469	0.6810	0.06403	0.09403	15.618	10.635
14	1.513	0.6611	0.05853	0.08853	17.086	11.296
15	1.558	0.6419	0.05377	0.08377	18.599	11.938
16	1.605	0.6232	0.04961	0.07961	20.157	12.561
17	1.653	0.6050	0.04595	0.07595	21.762	13.166
18	1.702	0.5874	0.04271	0.07271	23.414	13.754
19	1.754	0.5703	0.03981	0.06981	25.117	14.324
20	1.806	0.5537	0.03722	0.06722	26.870	14.877
21	1.860	0.5375	0.03487	0.06487	28.676	15.415
22	1.916	0.5219	0.03275	0.06275	30.537	15.937
23	1.974	0.5067	0.03081	0.06081	32.453	16.444
24	2.033	0.4919	0.02905	0.05905	34.426	16.936
25	2.094	0.4776	0.02743	0.05743	36.459	17.413
26	2.157	0.4637	0.02594	0.05594	38.553	17.877
27	2.221	0.4502	0.02456	0.05456	40.710	18.327
28	2.288	0.4371	0.02329	0.05329	42.931	18.764
29	2.357	0.4243	0.02211	0.05211	45.219	19.188
30	2.427	0.4120	0.02102	0.05102	47.575	19.600
31	2.500	0.4000	0.02000	0.05000	50.003	20.000
32	2.575	0.3883	0.01905	0.04905	52.503	20.389
33	2.652	0.3770	0.01816	0.04816	55.078	20.766
34	2.732	0.3660	0.01732	0.04732	57.730	21.132
35	2.814	0.3554	0.01654	0.04654	60.462	21.487
40	3.262	0.3066	0.01326	0.04326	75.401	23.115
45	3.782	0.2644	0.01079	0.04079	92.720	24.519
50	4.384	0.2281	0.00887	0.03887	112.797	25.730
55	5.082	0.1968	0.00735	0.03735	136.072	26.774
60	5.892	0.1697	0.00613	0.03613	163.053	27.676
65	6.830	0.1464	0.00515	0.03515	194.333	28.453
70	7.918	0.1263	0.00434	0.03434	230.594	29.123
75	9.179	0.1089	0.00367	0.03367	272.631	29.702
80	10.641	0.0940	0.00311	0.03311	321.363	30.201
85	12.336	0.0811	0.00265	0.03265	377.857	30.631
90	14.300	0.0699	0.00226	0.03226	443.349	31.002
95	16.578	0.0603	0.00193	0.03193	519.272	31.323
100	19.219	0.0520	0.00165	0.03165	607.288	31.599

TABLE H
3½% Compound Interest Factors

n	SINGLE PAYMENT		UNIFORM ANNUAL SERIES			
	Compound Amount Factor caf'	*Present Worth Factor pwf'*	*Sinking Fund Factor sff*	*Capital Recovery Factor crf*	*Compound Amount Factor caf*	*Present Worth Factor pwf*
	Given P to find S $(1+i)^n$	*Given S to find P* $\frac{1}{(1+i)^n}$	*Given S to find R* $\frac{i}{(1+i)^n-1}$	*Given P to find R* $\frac{i(1+i)^n}{(1+i)^n-1}$	*Given R to find S* $\frac{(1+i)^n-1}{i}$	*Given R to find P* $\frac{(1+i)^n-1}{i(1+i)^n}$
1	1.035	0.9662	1.00000	1.03500	1.000	0.966
2	1.071	0.9335	0.49140	0.52640	2.035	1.900
3	1.109	0.9019	0.32193	0.35693	3.106	2.802
4	1.148	0.8714	0.23725	0.27225	4.215	3.673
5	1.188	0.8420	0.18648	0.22148	5.362	4.515
6	1.229	0.8135	0.15267	0.18767	6.550	5.329
7	1.272	0.7860	0.12854	0.16354	7.779	6.115
8	1.317	0.7594	0.11048	0.14548	9.052	6.874
9	1.363	0.7337	0.09645	0.13145	10.368	7.608
10	1.411	0.7089	0.08524	0.12024	11.731	8.317
11	1.460	0.6849	0.07609	0.11109	13.142	9.002
12	1.511	0.6618	0.06848	0.10348	14.602	9.663
13	1.564	0.6394	0.06206	0.09706	16.113	10.303
14	1.619	0.6178	0.05657	0.09157	17.677	10.921
15	1.675	0.5969	0.05183	0.08683	19.296	11.517
16	1.734	0.5767	0.04768	0.08268	20.971	12.094
17	1.795	0.5572	0.04404	0.07904	22.705	12.651
18	1.857	0.5384	0.04082	0.07582	24.500	13.190
19	1.923	0.5202	0.03794	0.07294	26.357	13.710
20	1.990	0.5026	0.03536	0.07036	28.280	14.212
21	2.059	0.4856	0.03304	0.06804	30.269	14.698
22	2.132	0.4692	0.03093	0.06593	32.329	15.167
23	2.206	0.4533	0.02902	0.06402	34.460	15.620
24	2.283	0.4380	0.02727	0.06227	36.667	16.058
25	2.363	0.4231	0.02567	0.06067	38.950	16.482
26	2.446	0.4088	0.02421	0.05921	41.313	16.890
27	2.532	0.3950	0.02285	0.05785	43.759	17.285
28	2.620	0.3817	0.02160	0.05660	46.291	17.667
29	2.712	0.3687	0.02045	0.05545	48.911	18.036
30	2.807	0.3563	0.01937	0.05437	51.623	18.392
31	2.905	0.3442	0.01837	0.05337	54.429	18.736
32	3.007	0.3326	0.01744	0.05244	57.335	19.069
33	3.112	0.3213	0.01657	0.05157	60.341	19.390
34	3.221	0.3105	0.01576	0.05076	63.453	19.701
35	3.334	0.3000	0.01500	0.05000	66.674	20.001
40	3.959	0.2526	0.01183	0.04683	84.550	21.355
45	4.702	0.2127	0.00945	0.04445	105.782	22.495
50	5.585	0.1791	0.00763	0.04263	130.998	23.456
55	6.633	0.1508	0.00621	0.04121	160.947	24.264
60	7.878	0.1269	0.00509	0.04009	196.517	24.945
65	9.357	0.1069	0.00419	0.03919	238.763	25.518
70	11.113	0.0900	0.00346	0.03846	288.938	26.000
75	13.199	0.0758	0.00287	0.03787	348.530	26.407
80	15.676	0.0638	0.00238	0.03738	419.307	26.749
85	18.618	0.0537	0.00199	0.03699	503.367	27.037
90	22.122	0.0452	0.00166	0.03666	603.205	27.279
95	26.262	0.0381	0.00139	0.03639	721.781	27.484
100	31.191	0.0321	0.00116	0.03616	862.612	27.655

TABLE I
4% Compound Interest Factors

n	SINGLE PAYMENT		UNIFORM ANNUAL SERIES			
	Compound Amount Factor caf'	*Present Worth Factor pwf'*	*Sinking Fund Factor sff*	*Capital Recovery Factor crf*	*Compound Amount Factor caf*	*Present Worth Factor pwf*
	Given P to find S $(1+i)^n$	*Given S to find P* $\frac{i}{(1+i)^n}$	*Given S to find R* $\frac{i}{(1+i)^n-1}$	*Given P to find R* $\frac{i(1+i)^n}{(1+i)^n-1}$	*Given R to find S* $\frac{(1+i)^n-1}{i}$	*Given R to find P* $\frac{(1+i)^n-1}{i(1+i)^n}$
1	1.040	0.9615	1.00000	1.04000	1.000	0.962
2	1.082	0.9246	0.49020	0.53020	2.040	1.886
3	1.125	0.8890	0.32035	0.36035	3.122	2.775
4	1.170	0.8548	0.23549	0.27549	4.246	3.630
5	1.217	0.8219	0.18463	0.22463	5.416	4.452
6	1.265	0.7903	0.15076	0.19076	6.633	5.242
7	1.316	0.7599	0.12661	0.16661	7.898	6.002
8	1.369	0.7307	0.10853	0.14853	9.214	6.733
9	1.423	0.7026	0.09449	0.13449	10.583	7.435
10	1.480	0.6756	0.08329	0.12329	12.006	8.111
11	1.539	0.6496	0.07415	0.11415	13.486	8.760
12	1.601	0.6246	0.06655	0.10655	15.026	9.385
13	1.665	0.6006	0.06014	0.10014	16.627	9.986
14	1.732	0.5775	0.05467	0.09467	18.292	10.563
15	1.801	0.5553	0.04994	0.08994	20.024	11.118
16	1.873	0.5339	0.04582	0.08582	21.825	11.652
17	1.948	0.5134	0.04220	0.08220	23.698	12.166
18	2.026	0.4936	0.03899	0.07899	25.645	12.659
19	2.107	0.4746	0.03614	0.07614	27.671	13.134
20	2.191	0.4564	0.03358	0.07358	29.778	13.590
21	2.279	0.4388	0.03128	0.07128	31.969	14.029
22	2.370	0.4220	0.02920	0.06920	34.248	14.451
23	2.465	0.4057	0.02731	0.06731	36.618	14.857
24	2.563	0.3901	0.02559	0.06559	39.083	15.247
25	2.666	0.3751	0.02401	0.06401	41.646	15.622
26	2.772	0.3607	0.02257	0.06257	44.312	15.983
27	2.883	0.3468	0.02124	0.06124	47.084	16.330
28	2.999	0.3335	0.02001	0.06001	49.968	16.663
29	3.119	0.3207	0.01888	0.05888	52.966	16.984
30	3.243	0.3083	0.01783	0.05783	56.085	17.292
31	3.373	0.2965	0.01686	0.05686	59.328	17.588
32	3.508	0.2851	0.01595	0.05595	62.701	17.874
33	3.648	0.2741	0.01510	0.05510	66.210	18.148
34	3.794	0.2636	0.01431	0.05431	69.858	18.411
35	3.946	0.2534	0.01358	0.05358	73.652	18.665
40	4.801	0.2083	0.01052	0.05052	95.026	19.793
45	5.841	0.1712	0.00826	0.04826	121.029	20.720
50	7.107	0.1407	0.00655	0.04655	152.667	21.482
55	8.646	0.1157	0.00523	0.04523	191.159	22.109
60	10.520	0.0951	0.00420	0.04420	237.991	22.623
65	12.799	0.0781	0.00339	0.04339	294.968	23.047
70	15.572	0.0642	0.00275	0.04275	364.290	23.395
75	18.945	0.0528	0.00223	0.04223	448.631	23.680
80	23.050	0.0434	0.00181	0.04181	551.245	23.915
85	28.044	0.0357	0.00148	0.04148	676.090	24.109
90	34.119	0.0293	0.00121	0.04121	827.983	24.267
95	41.511	0.0241	0.00099	0.04099	1012.785	24.398
100	50.505	0.0198	0.00081	0.04081	1237.624	24.505

TABLE J
$4\frac{1}{2}\%$ Compound Interest Factors

	SINGLE PAYMENT		UNIFORM ANNUAL SERIES			
n	Compound Amount Factor caf'	Present Worth Factor pwf'	Sinking Fund Factor sff	Capital Recovery Factor crf	Compound Amount Factor caf	Present Worth Factor pwf
	Given P to find S $(1+i)^n$	Given S to find P $\frac{1}{(1+i)^n}$	Given S to find R $\frac{i}{(1+i)^n-1}$	Given P to find R $\frac{i(1+i)^n}{(1+i)^n-1}$	Given R to find S $\frac{(1+i)^n-1}{i}$	Given R to find P $\frac{(1+i)^n-1}{i(1+i)^n}$
1	1.045	0.9569	1.00000	1.04500	1.000	0.957
2	1.092	0.9157	0.48900	0.53400	2.045	1.873
3	1.141	0.8763	0.31877	0.36377	3.137	2.749
4	1.193	0.8386	0.23374	0.27874	4.278	3.588
5	1.246	0.8025	0.18279	0.22779	5.471	4.390
6	1.302	0.7679	0.14888	0.19388	6.717	5.158
7	1.361	0.7348	0.12470	0.16970	8.019	5.893
8	1.422	0.7032	0.10661	0.15161	9.380	6.596
9	1.486	0.6729	0.09257	0.13757	10.802	7.269
10	1.553	0.6439	0.08138	0.12638	12.288	7.913
11	1.623	0.6162	0.07225	0.11725	13.841	8.529
12	1.696	0.5897	0.06467	0.10967	15.464	9.119
13	1.772	0.5643	0.05828	0.10328	17.160	9.683
14	1.852	0.5400	0.05282	0.09782	18.932	10.223
15	1.935	0.5167	0.04811	0.09311	20.784	10.740
16	2.022	0.4945	0.04402	0.08902	22.719	11.234
17	2.113	0.4732	0.04042	0.08542	24.742	11.707
18	2.208	0.4528	0.03724	0.08224	26.855	12.160
19	2.308	0.4333	0.03441	0.07941	29.064	12.593
20	2.412	0.4146	0.03188	0.07688	31.371	13.008
21	2.520	0.3968	0.02960	0.07460	33.783	13.405
22	2.634	0.3797	0.02755	0.07255	36.303	13.784
23	2.752	0.3634	0.02568	0.07068	38.937	14.148
24	2.876	0.3477	0.02399	0.06899	41.689	14.495
25	3.005	0.3327	0.02244	0.06744	44.565	14.828
26	3.141	0.3184	0.02102	0.06602	47.571	15.147
27	3.282	0.3047	0.01972	0.06472	50.711	15.451
28	3.430	0.2916	0.01852	0.06352	53.993	15.743
29	3.584	0.2790	0.01741	0.06241	57.423	16.022
30	3.745	0.2670	0.01639	0.06139	61.007	16.289
31	3.914	0.2555	0.01544	0.06044	64.752	16.544
32	4.090	0.2445	0.01456	0.05956	68.666	16.789
33	4.274	0.2340	0.01374	0.05874	72.756	17.023
34	4.466	0.2239	0.01298	0.05798	77.030	17.247
35	4.667	0.2143	0.01227	0.05727	81.497	17.461
40	5.816	0.1719	0.00934	0.05434	107.030	18.402
45	7.248	0.1380	0.00720	0.05220	138.850	19.156
50	9.033	0.1107	0.00560	0.05060	178.503	19.762
55	11.256	0.0888	0.00439	0.04939	227.918	20.248
60	14.027	0.0713	0.00345	0.04845	289.498	20.638
65	17.481	0.0572	0.00273	0.04773	366.238	20.951
70	21.784	0.0459	0.00217	0.04717	461.870	21.202
75	27.147	0.0368	0.00172	0.04672	581.044	21.404
80	33.830	0.0296	0.00137	0.04637	729.558	21.565
85	42.158	0.0237	0.00109	0.04609	914.632	21.695
90	52.537	0.0190	0.00087	0.04587	1145.269	21.799
95	65.471	0.0153	0.00070	0.04570	1432.684	21.883
100	81.589	0.0123	0.00056	0.04556	1790.856	21.950

TABLE K
5% Compound Interest Factors

n	SINGLE PAYMENT		UNIFORM ANNUAL SERIES			
	Compound Amount Factor caf'	Present Worth Factor pwf'	Sinking Fund Factor sff	Capital Recovery Factor crf	Compound Amount Factor caf	Present Worth Factor pwf
	Given P to find S $(1+i)^n$	Given S to find P $\frac{1}{(1+i)^n}$	Given S to find R $\frac{i}{(1+i)^n-1}$	Given P to find R $\frac{i(1+i)^n}{(1+i)^n-1}$	Given R to find S $\frac{(1+i)^n-1}{i}$	Given R to find P $\frac{(1+i)^n-1}{i(1+i)^n}$
1	1.050	0.9524	1.00000	1.05000	1.000	0.952
2	1.103	0.9070	0.48780	0.53780	2.050	1.859
3	1.158	0.8638	0.31721	0.36721	3.153	2.723
4	1.216	0.8227	0.23201	0.28201	4.310	3.546
5	1.276	0.7835	0.18097	0.23097	5.526	4.329
6	1.340	0.7462	0.14702	0.19702	6.802	5.076
7	1.407	0.7107	0.12282	0.17282	8.142	5.786
8	1.477	0.6768	0.10472	0.15472	9.549	6.463
9	1.551	0.6446	0.09069	0.14069	11.027	7.108
10	1.629	0.6139	0.07950	0.12950	12.578	7.722
11	1.710	0.5847	0.07039	0.12039	14.207	8.306
12	1.796	0.5568	0.06283	0.11283	15.917	8.863
13	1.886	0.5303	0.05646	0.10646	17.713	9.394
14	1.980	0.5051	0.05102	0.10102	19.599	9.899
15	2.079	0.4810	0.04634	0.09634	21.579	10.380
16	2.183	0.4581	0.04227	0.09227	23.657	10.838
17	2.292	0.4363	0.03870	0.08870	25.840	11.274
18	2.407	0.4155	0.03555	0.08555	28.132	11.690
19	2.527	0.3957	0.03275	0.08275	30.539	12.085
20	2.653	0.3769	0.03024	0.08024	33.066	12.462
21	2.786	0.3589	0.02800	0.07800	35.719	12.821
22	2.925	0.3418	0.02597	0.07597	38.505	13.163
23	3.072	0.3256	0.02414	0.07414	41.430	13.489
24	3.225	0.3101	0.02247	0.07247	44.502	13.799
25	3.386	0.2953	0.02095	0.07095	47.727	14.094
26	3.556	0.2812	0.01956	0.06956	51.113	14.375
27	3.733	0.2678	0.01829	0.06829	54.669	14.643
28	3.920	0.2551	0.01712	0.06712	58.403	14.898
29	4.116	0.2429	0.01605	0.06605	62.323	15.141
30	4.322	0.2314	0.01505	0.06505	66.439	15.372
31	4.538	0.2204	0.01413	0.06413	70.761	15.593
32	4.756	0.2099	0.01328	0.06328	75.299	15.803
33	5.003	0.1999	0.01249	0.06249	80.064	16.003
34	5.253	0.1904	0.01176	0.06176	85.067	16.193
35	5.516	0.1813	0.01107	0.06107	90.320	16.374
40	7.040	0.1420	0.00828	0.05828	120.800	17.159
45	8.985	0.1113	0.00626	0.05626	159.700	17.774
50	11.467	0.0872	0.00478	0.05478	209.348	18.256
55	14.636	0.0683	0.00367	0.05367	272.713	18.633
60	18.679	0.0535	0.00283	0.05283	353.584	18.929
65	23.840	0.0419	0.00219	0.05219	456.798	19.161
70	30.426	0.0329	0.00170	0.05170	588.529	19.343
75	38.833	0.0258	0.00132	0.05132	756.654	19.485
80	49.561	0.0202	0.00103	0.05103	971.229	19.596
85	63.254	0.0158	0.00080	0.05080	1245.087	19.684
90	80.730	0.0124	0.00063	0.05063	1594.607	19.752
95	103.035	0.0097	0.00049	0.05049	2040.694	19.806
100	131.501	0.0076	0.00038	0.05038	2610.025	19.848

TABLE L

$5\frac{1}{2}$% Compound Interest Factors

n	SINGLE PAYMENT		UNIFORM ANNUAL SERIES			
	Compound Amount Factor caf'	Present Worth Factor pwf'	Sinking Fund Factor sff	Capital Recovery Factor crf	Compound Amount Factor caf	Present Worth Factor pwf
	Given P to find S $(1+i)^n$	Given S to find P $\frac{1}{(1+i)^n}$	Given S to find R $\frac{i}{(1+i)^n-1}$	Given P to find R $\frac{i(1+i)^n}{(1+i)^n-1}$	Given R to find S $\frac{(1+i)^n-1}{i}$	Given R to find P $\frac{(1+i)^n-1}{i(1+i)^n}$
1	1.055	0.9479	1.00000	1.05500	1.000	0.948
2	1.113	0.8985	0.48662	0.54162	2.055	1.846
3	1.174	0.8516	0.31565	0.37065	3.168	2.698
4	1.239	0.8072	0.23029	0.28529	4.342	3.505
5	1.307	0.7651	0.17918	0.23418	5.581	4.270
6	1.379	0.7252	0.14518	0.20018	6.888	4.996
7	1.455	0.6874	0.12096	0.17596	8.267	5.683
8	1.535	0.6516	0.10286	0.15786	9.722	6.335
9	1.619	0.6176	0.08884	0.14384	11.256	6.952
10	1.708	0.5854	0.07767	0.13267	12.875	7.538
11	1.802	0.5549	0.06857	0.12357	14.583	8.093
12	1.901	0.5260	0.06103	0.11603	16.386	8.619
13	2.006	0.4986	0.05468	0.10968	18.287	9.117
14	2.116	0.4726	0.04928	0.10428	20.293	9.590
15	2.232	0.4479	0.04463	0.09963	22.409	10.038
16	2.355	0.4246	0.04058	0.09558	24.641	10.462
17	2.485	0.4024	0.03704	0.09204	26.996	10.865
18	2.621	0.3815	0.03392	0.08892	29.481	11.246
19	2.766	0.3616	0.03115	0.08615	32.103	11.608
20	2.918	0.3427	0.02868	0.08368	34.868	11.950
21	3.078	0.3249	0.02646	0.08146	37.786	12.275
22	3.248	0.3079	0.02447	0.07947	40.864	12.583
23	3.426	0.2919	0.02267	0.07767	44.112	12.875
24	3.615	0.2767	0.02104	0.07604	47.538	13.152
25	3.813	0.2622	0.01955	0.07455	51.153	13.414
26	4.023	0.2486	0.01819	0.07319	54.966	13.662
27	4.244	0.2356	0.01695	0.07195	58.989	13.898
28	4.478	0.2233	0.01581	0.07081	63.234	14.121
29	4.724	0.2117	0.01477	0.06977	67.711	14.333
30	4.984	0.2006	0.01381	0.06881	72.435	14.534
31	5.258	0.1902	0.01292	0.06792	77.419	14.724
32	5.547	0.1803	0.01210	0.06710	82.677	14.904
33	5.852	0.1709	0.01133	0.06633	88.225	15.075
34	6.174	0.1620	0.01063	0.06563	94.077	15.237
35	6.514	0.1535	0.00997	0.06497	100.251	15.391
40	8.513	0.1175	0.00732	0.06232	136.606	16.046
45	11.127	0.0899	0.00543	0.06043	184.119	16.548
50	14.542	0.0688	0.00406	0.05906	246.217	16.932
55	19.006	0.0526	0.00305	0.05805	327.377	17.225
60	24.840	0.0403	0.00231	0.05731	433.450	17.450
65	32.465	0.0308	0.00175	0.05675	572.083	17.622
70	42.430	0.0236	0.00133	0.05633	753.271	17.753
75	55.454	0.0180	0.00101	0.05601	990.076	17.854
80	72.476	0.0138	0.00077	0.05577	1299.571	17.931
85	94.724	0.0106	0.00059	0.05559	1704.069	17.990
90	123.800	0.0081	0.00045	0.05545	2232.731	18.035
95	161.802	0.0062	0.00034	0.05534	2923.671	18.069
100	211.469	0.0047	0.00026	0.05526	3826.702	18.096

TABLE M
6% Compound Interest Factors

n	SINGLE PAYMENT		UNIFORM ANNUAL SERIES			
	Compound Amount Factor caf′	*Present Worth Factor pwf′*	*Sinking Fund Factor sff*	*Capital Recovery Factor crf*	*Compound Amount Factor caf*	*Present Worth Factor pwf*
	Given P to find S $(1+i)^n$	*Given S to find P* $\frac{1}{(1+i)^n}$	*Given S to find R* $\frac{i}{(1+i)^n-1}$	*Given P to find R* $\frac{i(1+i)^n}{(1+i)^n-1}$	*Given R to find S* $\frac{(1+i)^n-1}{i}$	*Given R to find P* $\frac{(1+i)^n-1}{i(1+i)^n}$
1	1.060	0.9434	1.00000	1.06000	1.000	0.943
2	1.124	0.8900	0.48544	0.54544	2.060	1.833
3	1.191	0.8396	0.31411	0.37411	3.184	2.673
4	1.262	0.7921	0.22859	0.28859	4.375	3.465
5	1.338	0.7473	0.17740	0.23740	5.637	4.212
6	1.419	0.0750	0.14336	0.20336	6.975	4.917
7	1.504	0.6651	0.11914	0.17914	8.394	5.582
8	1.594	0.6274	0.10104	0.16104	9.897	6.210
9	1.689	0.5919	0.08702	0.14702	11.491	6.802
10	1.791	0.5584	0.07587	0.13587	13.181	7.360
11	1.898	0.5268	0.06679	0.12679	14.972	7.887
12	2.012	0.4970	0.05928	0.11928	16.870	8.384
13	2.133	0.4688	0.05296	0.11296	18.882	8.853
14	2.261	0.4423	0.04758	0.10758	21.015	9.295
15	2.397	0.4173	0.04296	0.10296	23.276	9.712
16	2.540	0.3936	0.03895	0.09895	25.673	10.106
17	2.693	0.3714	0.03544	0.09544	28.213	10.477
18	2.854	0.3503	0.03236	0.09236	30.906	10.828
19	3.026	0.3305	0.02962	0.08962	33.760	11.158
20	3.207	0.3118	0.02718	0.08718	36.786	11.470
21	3.400	0.2942	0.02500	0.08500	39.993	11.764
22	3.604	0.2775	0.02305	0.08305	43.392	12.042
23	3.820	0.2618	0.02128	0.08128	46.996	12.303
24	4.049	0.2470	0.01968	0.07968	50.816	12.550
25	4.292	0.2330	0.01823	0.07823	54.865	12.783
26	4.549	0.2198	0.01690	0.07690	59.156	13.003
27	4.822	0.2074	0.01570	0.07570	63.706	13.211
28	5.112	0.1956	0.01459	0.07459	68.528	13.406
29	5.418	0.1846	0.01358	0.07358	73.640	13.591
30	5.743	0.1741	0.01265	0.07265	79.058	13.765
31	6.088	0.1643	0.01179	0.07179	84.802	13.929
32	6.453	0.1550	0.01100	0.07100	90.890	14.084
33	6.841	0.1462	0.01027	0.07027	97.343	14.230
34	7.251	0.1379	0.00960	0.06960	104.184	14.368
35	7.686	0.1301	0.00897	0.06897	111.435	14.498
40	10.286	0.0972	0.00646	0.06646	154.762	15.046
45	13.765	0.0727	0.00470	0.06470	212.744	15.456
50	18.420	0.0543	0.00344	0.06344	290.336	15.762
55	24.650	0.0406	0.00254	0.06254	394.172	15.991
60	32.988	0.0303	0.00188	0.06188	533.128	16.161
65	44.145	0.0227	0.00139	0.06139	719.083	16.289
70	59.076	0.0169	0.00103	0.06103	967.932	16.385
75	79.057	0.0126	0.00077	0.06077	1300.949	16.456
80	105.796	0.0095	0.00057	0.06057	1746.600	16.509
85	141.579	0.0071	0.00043	0.06043	2342.982	16.549
90	189.465	0.0053	0.00032	0.06032	3141.075	16.579
95	253.546	0.0039	0.00024	0.06024	4209.104	16.601
100	339.302	0.0029	0.00018	0.06018	5638.368	16.618

TABLE N
7% Compound Interest Factors

	SINGLE PAYMENT		UNIFORM ANNUAL SERIES			
n	*Compound Amount Factor caf'*	*Present Worth Factor pwf'*	*Sinking Fund Factor sff*	*Capital Recovery Factor crf*	*Compound Amount Factor caf*	*Present Worth Factor pwf*
	Given P to find S $(1+i)^n$	*Given S to find P* $\frac{1}{(1+i)^n}$	*Given S to find R* $\frac{i}{(1+i)^n-1}$	*Given P to find R* $\frac{i(1+i)^n}{(1+i)^n-1}$	*Given R to find S* $\frac{(1+i)^n-1}{i}$	*Given R to find P* $\frac{(1+i)^n-1}{i(1+i)^n}$
1	1.070	0.9346	1.00000	1.07000	1.000	0.935
2	1.145	0.8734	0.48309	0.55309	2.070	1.808
3	1.225	0.8163	0.31105	0.38105	3.215	2.624
4	1.311	0.7629	0.22523	0.29523	4.440	3.387
5	1.403	0.7130	0.17389	0.24389	5.751	4.100
6	1.501	0.6663	0.13980	0.20980	7.153	4.767
7	1.606	0.6227	0.11555	0.18555	8.654	5.389
8	1.718	0.5820	0.09747	0.16747	10.260	5.971
9	1.838	0.5439	0.08349	0.15349	11.978	6.515
10	1.967	0.5083	0.07238	0.14238	13.816	7.024
11	2.105	0.4751	0.06336	0.13336	15.784	7.499
12	2.252	0.4440	0.05590	0.12590	17.888	7.943
13	2.410	0.4150	0.04965	0.11965	20.141	8.358
14	2.579	0.3878	0.04434	0.11434	22.550	8.745
15	2.759	0.3624	0.03979	0.10979	25.129	9.108
16	2.952	0.3387	0.03586	0.10586	27.888	9.447
17	3.159	0.3166	0.03243	0.10243	30.840	9.763
18	3.380	0.2959	0.02941	0.09941	33.999	10.059
19	3.617	0.2765	0.02675	0.09675	37.379	10.336
20	3.870	0.2584	0.02439	0.09439	40.995	10.594
21	4.141	0.2415	0.02229	0.09229	44.865	10.836
22	4.430	0.2257	0.02041	0.09041	49.006	11.061
23	4.741	0.2109	0.01871	0.08871	53.436	11.272
24	5.072	0.1971	0.01719	0.08719	58.177	11.469
25	5.427	0.1842	0.01581	0.08581	63.249	11.654
26	5.807	0.1722	0.01456	0.08456	68.676	11.826
27	6.214	0.1609	0.01343	0.08343	74.484	11.987
28	6.649	0.1504	0.01239	0.08239	80.698	12.137
29	7.114	0.1406	0.01145	0.08145	87.347	12.278
30	7.612	0.1314	0.01059	0.08059	94.461	12.409
31	8.145	0.1228	0.00980	0.07980	102.073	12.532
32	8.715	0.1147	0.00907	0.07907	110.128	12.647
33	9.325	0.1072	0.00841	0.07841	118.933	12.754
34	9.978	0.1002	0.00780	0.07780	128.259	12.854
35	10.677	0.0937	0.00723	0.07723	138.237	12.948
40	14.974	0.0668	0.00501	0.07501	199.635	13.332
45	21.002	0.0476	0.00350	0.07350	285.749	13.606
50	29.457	0.0339	0.00246	0.07246	406.529	13.801
55	41.315	0.0242	0.00174	0.07174	575.929	13.940
60	57.946	0.0173	0.00123	0.07123	813.520	14.039
65	81.273	0.0123	0.00087	0.07087	1146.755	14.110
70	113.989	0.0088	0.00062	0.07062	1614.134	14.160
75	159.876	0.0063	0.00044	0.07044	2269.657	14.196
80	224.234	0.0045	0.00031	0.07031	3189.063	14.222
85	314.500	0.0032	0.00022	0.07022	4478.576	14.240
90	441.103	0.0023	0.00016	0.07016	6287.185	14.253
95	618.670	0.0016	0.00011	0.07011	8823.854	14.263
100	867.716	0.0012	0.00008	0.07008	12381.662	14.269

TABLE O

8% Compound Interest Factors

n	*SINGLE PAYMENT*		*UNIFORM ANNUAL SERIES*			
	Compound Amount Factor caf'	*Present Worth Factor pwf'*	*Sinking Fund Factor sff*	*Capital Recovery Factor crf*	*Compound Amount Factor caf*	*Present Worth Factor pwf*
	Given P to find S $(1+i)^n$	*Given S to find P* $\frac{1}{(1+i)^n}$	*Given S to find R* $\frac{i}{(1+i)^n-1}$	*Given P to find R* $\frac{i(1+i)^n}{(1+i)^n-1}$	*Given R to find S* $\frac{(1+i)^n-1}{i}$	*Given R to find P* $\frac{(1+i)^n-1}{i(1+i)^n}$
1	1.080	0.9259	1.00000	1.08000	1.000	0.926
2	1.166	0.8573	0.48077	0.56077	2.080	1.783
3	1.260	0.7938	0.30803	0.38803	3.246	2.577
4	1.360	0.7350	0.22192	0.30192	4.506	3.312
5	1.469	0.6806	0.17046	0.25046	5.867	3.993
6	1.587	0.6302	0.13632	0.21632	7.336	4.623
7	1.714	0.5835	0.11207	0.19207	8.923	5.206
8	1.851	0.5403	0.09401	0.17401	10.637	5.747
9	1.999	0.5002	0.08008	0.16008	12.488	6.247
10	2.159	0.4632	0.06903	0.14903	14.487	6.710
11	2.332	0.4289	0.06008	0.14008	16.645	7.139
12	2.518	0.3971	0.05270	0.13270	18.977	7.536
13	2.720	0.3677	0.04652	0.12652	21.495	7.904
14	2.937	0.3405	0.04130	0.12130	24.215	8.244
15	3.172	0.3152	0.03683	0.11683	27.152	8.559
16	3.426	0.2919	0.03298	0.11298	30.324	8.851
17	3.700	0.2703	0.02963	0.10963	33.750	9.122
18	3.996	0.2502	0.02670	0.10670	37.450	9.372
19	4.316	0.2317	0.02413	0.10413	41.446	9.604
20	4.661	0.2145	0.02185	0.10185	45.762	9.818
21	5.034	0.1987	0.01983	0.09983	50.423	10.017
22	5.437	0.1839	0.01803	0.09803	55.457	10.201
23	5.871	0.1703	0.01642	0.09642	60.893	10.371
24	6.341	0.1577	0.01498	0.09498	66.675	10.529
25	6.848	0.1460	0.01368	0.09368	73.106	10.675
26	7.396	0.1352	0.01251	0.09251	79.954	10.810
27	7.988	0.1252	0.01145	0.09145	87.351	10.935
28	8.627	0.1159	0.01049	0.09049	95.339	11.051
29	9.317	0.1073	0.00962	0.08962	103.966	11.158
30	10.063	0.0994	0.00883	0.08883	113.283	11.258
31	10.868	0.0920	0.00811	0.08811	123.346	11.350
32	11.737	0.0852	0.00745	0.08745	134.214	11.435
33	12.676	0.0789	0.00685	0.08685	145.951	11.514
34	13.690	0.0730	0.00630	0.08630	158.627	11.587
35	14.785	0.0676	0.00580	0.08580	172.317	11.655
40	21.725	0.0460	0.00386	0.08386	259.057	11.925
45	31.920	0.0313	0.00259	0.08259	386.506	12.108
50	46.902	0.0213	0.00174	0.08174	573.770	12.233
55	68.914	0.0145	0.00118	0.08118	848.923	12.319
60	101.257	0.0099	0.00080	0.08080	1253.213	12.377
65	148.780	0.0067	0.00054	0.08054	1847.248	12.416
70	218.606	0.0046	0.00037	0.08037	2720.080	12.443
75	321.205	0.0031	0.00025	0.08025	4002.557	12.461
80	471.955	0.0021	0.00017	0.08017	5886.935	12.474
85	693.456	0.0014	0.00012	0.08012	8655.706	12.482
90	1018.915	0.0010	0.00008	0.08008	12723.939	12.488
95	1497.121	0.0007	0.00005	0.08005	18701.507	12.492
100	2199.761	0.0005	0.00004	0.08004	27484.516	12.494

TABLE P
10% Compound Interest Factors

n	*SINGLE PAYMENT*		*UNIFORM ANNUAL SERIES*			
	Compound Amount Factor caf'	*Present Worth Factor pwf'*	*Sinking Fund Factor sff*	*Capital Recovery Factor crf*	*Compound Amount Factor caf*	*Present Worth Factor pwf*
	Given P to find S $(1+i)^n$	*Given S to find P* $\frac{1}{(1+i)^n}$	*Given S to find R* $\frac{i}{(1+i)^n-1}$	*Given P to find R* $\frac{i(1+i)^n}{(1+i)^n-1}$	*Given R to find S* $\frac{(1+i)^n-1}{i}$	*Given R to find P* $\frac{(1+i)^n-1}{i(1+i)^n}$
1	1.100	0.9091	1.00000	1.10000	1.000	0.909
2	1.210	0.8264	0.47619	0.57619	2.100	1.736
3	1.331	0.7513	0.30211	0.40211	3.310	2.487
4	1.464	0.6830	0.21547	0.31547	4.641	3.170
5	1.611	0.6209	0.16380	0.26380	6.105	3.791
6	1.772	0.5645	0.12961	0.22961	7.716	4.355
7	1.949	0.5132	0.10541	0.20541	9.487	4.868
8	2.144	0.4665	0.08744	0.18744	11.436	5.335
9	2.358	0.4241	0.07364	0.17364	13.579	5.759
10	2.594	0.3855	0.06275	0.16275	15.937	6.144
11	2.853	0.3505	0.05396	0.15396	18.531	6.495
12	3.138	0.3186	0.04678	0.14676	21.384	6.814
13	3.452	0.2897	0.04078	0.14078	24.523	7.103
14	3.797	0.2633	0.03575	0.13575	27.975	7.367
15	4.177	0.2394	0.03147	0.13147	31.772	7.606
16	4.595	0.2176	0.02782	0.12782	35.950	7.824
17	5.054	0.1978	0.02466	0.12466	40.545	8.022
18	5.560	0.1799	0.02193	0.12193	45.599	8.201
19	6.116	0.1635	0.01955	0.11955	51.159	8.365
20	6.727	0.1486	0.01746	0.11746	57.275	8.514
21	7.400	0.1351	0.01562	0.11562	64.002	8.649
22	8.140	0.1228	0.01401	0.11401	71.403	8.772
23	8.954	0.1117	0.01257	0.11257	79.543	8.883
24	9.850	0.1015	0.01130	0.11130	88.497	8.985
25	10.835	0.0923	0.01017	0.11017	98.347	9.077
26	11.918	0.0839	0.00916	0.10916	109.182	9.161
27	13.110	0.0763	0.00826	0.10826	121.100	9.237
28	14.421	0.0693	0.00745	0.10745	134.210	9.307
29	15.863	0.0630	0.00673	0.10673	148.631	9.370
30	17.449	0.0573	0.00608	0.10608	164.494	9.427
31	19.194	0.0521	0.00550	0.10550	181.943	9.479
32	21.114	0.0474	0.00497	0.10497	201.138	9.526
33	23.225	0.0431	0.00450	0.10450	222.252	9.569
34	25.548	0.0391	0.00407	0.10407	245.477	9.609
35	28.102	0.0356	0.00369	0.10369	271.024	9.644
40	45.259	0.0221	0.00226	0.10226	442.593	9.779
45	72.890	0.0137	0.00139	0.10139	718.905	9.863
50	117.391	0.0085	0.00086	0.10086	1163.909	9.915
55	189.059	0.0053	0.00053	0.10053	1880.591	9.947
60	304.482	0.0033	0.00033	0.10033	3034.816	9.967
65	490.371	0.0020	0.00020	0.10020	4893.707	9.980
70	789.747	0.0013	0.00013	0.10013	7887.470	9.987
75	1271.895	0.0008	0.00008	0.10008	12708.954	9.992
80	2048.400	0.0005	0.00005	0.10005	20474.002	9.995
85	3298.969	0.0003	0.00003	0.10003	32979.690	9.997
90	5313.023	0.0002	0.00002	0.10002	53120.226	9.998
95	8556.676	0.0001	0.00001	0.10001	85556.760	9.999
100	13780.612	0.0001	0.00001	0.10001	137796.123	9.999

TABLE Q
Capital Recovery Factors for Interest Rates from 0% to 25%

n. \ i	0%	2%	4%	6%	8%	10%	12%	15%	20%	25%
1	1.00000	1.02000	1.04000	1.06000	1.08000	1.10000	1.12000	1.15000	1.20000	1.25000
2	0.50000	0.51505	0.53020	0.54544	0.56077	0.57619	0.59170	0.61512	0.65455	0.69444
3	0.33333	0.34675	0.36035	0.37411	0.38803	0.40211	0.41635	0.43798	0.47473	0.51230
4	0.25000	0.26262	0.27549	0.28859	0.30192	0.31547	0.32923	0.35027	0.38629	0.42344
5	0.20000	0.21216	0.22463	0.23740	0.25046	0.26380	0.27741	0.29832	0.33438	0.37184
6	0.16667	0.17853	0.19076	0.20336	0.21632	0.22961	0.24323	0.26424	0.30071	0.33882
7	0.14286	0.15451	0.16661	0.17914	0.19207	0.20541	0.21912	0.24036	0.27742	0.31634
8	0.12500	0.13651	0.14853	0.16104	0.17401	0.18744	0.20130	0.22285	0.26061	0.30040
9	0.11111	0.12252	0.13449	0.14702	0.16008	0.17364	0.18768	0.20957	0.24808	0.28876
10	0.10000	0.11133	0.12329	0.13587	0.14903	0.16275	0.17698	0.19925	0.23852	0.28007
11	0.09091	0.10218	0.11415	0.12679	0.14008	0.15396	0.16842	0.19107	0.23110	0.27349
12	0.08333	0.09456	0.10655	0.11928	0.13270	0.14676	0.16144	0.18448	0.22526	0.26845
13	0.07692	0.08812	0.10014	0.11296	0.12652	0.14078	0.15568	0.17911	0.22062	0.26454
14	0.07143	0.08260	0.09467	0.10758	0.12130	0.13575	0.15087	0.17469	0.21689	0.26150
15	0.06667	0.07783	0.08994	0.10296	0.11683	0.13147	0.14682	0.17102	0.21388	0.25912
16	0.06250	0.07365	0.08582	0.09895	0.11298	0.12782	0.14339	0.16795	0.21144	0.25724
17	0.05882	0.06997	0.08220	0.09544	0.10963	0.12466	0.14046	0.16537	0.20944	0.25576
18	0.05556	0.06670	0.07899	0.09236	0.10670	0.12193	0.13794	0.16319	0.20781	0.25459
19	0.05263	0.06378	0.07614	0.08962	0.10413	0.11955	0.13576	0.16134	0.20646	0.25366
20	0.05000	0.06116	0.07358	0.08718	0.10185	0.11746	0.13388	0.15976	0.20536	0.25292
25	0.04000	0.05122	0.06401	0.07823	0.09368	0.11017	0.12750	0.15470	0.20212	0.25095
30	0.03333	0.04465	0.05783	0.07265	0.08883	0.10608	0.12414	0.15230	0.20085	0.25031
40	0.02500	0.03656	0.05052	0.06646	0.08386	0.10226	0.12130	0.15056	0.20014	0.25003
50	0.02000	0.03182	0.04655	0.06344	0.08174	0.10086	0.12042	0.15014	0.20002	0.25000
100	0.01000	0.02320	0.04081	0.06018	0.08004	0.10001	0.12000	0.15000	0.20000	0.25000
∞		0.02000	0.04000	0.06000	0.08000	0.10000	0.12000	0.15000	0.20000	0.25000

TABLE R
Present Worth Factors for Interest Rates from 0% to 25%

n. \ i	0%	2%	4%	6%	8%	10%	12%	15%	20%	25%
1	1.0000	0.9804	0.9615	0.9434	0.9259	0.9091	0.8929	0.8696	0.8333	0.8000
2	1.0000	0.9612	0.9246	0.8900	0.8473	0.8264	0.7972	0.7561	0.6944	0.6400
3	1.0000	0.9423	0.8890	0.8396	0.7938	0.7513	0.7118	0.6575	0.5787	0.5120
4	1.0000	0.9238	0.8548	0.7921	0.7350	0.6830	0.6355	0.5718	0.4823	0.4096
5	1.0000	0.9057	0.8219	0.7473	0.6806	0.6209	0.5674	0.4972	0.4019	0.3277
6	1.0000	0.8880	0.7903	0.7050	0.6302	0.5645	0.5066	0.4323	0.3349	0.2621
7	1.0000	0.8706	0.7599	0.6651	0.5835	0.5132	0.4523	0.3759	0.2791	0.2097
8	1.0000	0.8535	0.7307	0.6274	0.5403	0.4665	0.4039	0.3269	0.2326	0.1678
9	1.0000	0.8368	0.7026	0.5919	0.5002	0.4241	0.3606	0.2843	0.1938	0.1342
10	1.0000	0.8203	0.6756	0.5584	0.4632	0.3855	0.3220	0.2472	0.1615	0.1074
11	1.0000	0.8043	0.6496	0.5268	0.4289	0.3505	0.2875	0.2149	0.1346	0.0859
12	1.0000	0.7885	0.6246	0.4970	0.3971	0.3186	0.2567	0.1869	0.1122	0.0687
13	1.0000	0.7730	0.6006	0.4688	0.3677	0.2897	0.2292	0.1625	0.0935	0.0550
14	1.0000	0.7579	0.5775	0.4423	0.3405	0.2633	0.2046	0.1413	0.0779	0.0440
15	1.0000	0.7430	0.5553	0.4173	0.3152	0.2394	0.1827	0.1229	0.0649	0.0352
16	1.0000	0.7284	0.5339	0.3936	0.2919	0.2176	0.1631	0.1069	0.0541	0.0281
17	1.0000	0.7142	0.5134	0.3714	0.2703	0.1978	0.1456	0.0929	0.0451	0.0225
18	1.0000	0.7002	0.4936	0.3503	0.2502	0.1799	0.1300	0.0808	0.0376	0.0180
19	1.0000	0.6864	0.4746	0.3305	0.2317	0.1635	0.1161	0.0703	0.0313	0.0144
20	1.0000	0.6730	0.4564	0.3118	0.2145	0.1486	0.1037	0.0611	0.0261	0.0115
25	1.0000	0.6095	0.3751	0.2330	0.1460	0.0923	0.0588	0.0304	0.0105	0.0038
30	1.0000	0.5521	0.3083	0.1741	0.0994	0.0573	0.0334	0.0151	0.0042	0.0012
40	1.0000	0.4529	0.2083	0.0972	0.0460	0.0221	0.0107	0.0037	0.0007	0.0001
50	1.0000	0.3715	0.1407	0.0543	0.0213	0.0085	0.0035	0.0009	0.0001	—
100	1.0000	0.1380	0.0198	0.0029	0.0005	0.0001	—	—	—	—

TABLE S
Factors to Convert a Gradient Series to an Equivalent Uniform Annual Series

This table contains multipliers for a gradient g to convert the n-year end-of-year series $0, g, 2g, \ldots (n - 1)g$ to an equivalent uniform annual series for n years.

n	1%	2%	3%	4%	5%	6%	7%	8%	10%	n
2	0.50	0.50	0.49	0.49	0.49	0.49	0.48	0.48	0.48	2
3	0.99	0.99	0.98	0.97	0.97	0.96	0.95	0.95	0.94	3
4	1.49	1.48	1.46	1.45	1.44	1.43	1.42	1.40	1.38	4
5	1.98	1.96	1.94	1.92	1.90	1.88	1.86	1.85	1.81	5
6	2.47	2.44	2.41	2.39	2.36	2.33	2.30	2.28	2.22	6
7	2.96	2.92	2.88	2.84	2.81	2.77	2.73	2.69	2.62	7
8	3.45	3.40	3.34	3.29	3.24	3.20	3.15	3.10	3.00	8
9	3.93	3.87	3.80	3.74	3.68	3.61	3.55	3.49	3.37	9
10	4.42	4.34	4.26	4.18	4.10	4.02	3.95	3.87	3.73	10
11	4.90	4.80	4.70	4.61	4.51	4.42	4.33	4.24	4.06	11
12	5.38	5.26	5.15	5.03	4.92	4.81	4.70	4.60	4.39	12
13	5.86	5.72	5.59	5.45	5.32	5.19	5.06	4.94	4.70	13
14	6.34	6.18	6.02	5.87	5.71	5.56	5.42	5.27	5.00	14
15	6.81	6.63	6.45	6.27	6.10	5.93	5.76	5.59	5.28	15
16	7.29	7.08	6.87	6.67	6.47	6.28	6.09	5.90	5.55	16
17	7.76	7.52	7.29	7.07	6.84	6.62	6.41	6.20	5.81	17
18	8.23	7.97	7.71	7.45	7.20	6.96	6.72	6.49	6.05	18
19	8.70	8.41	8.12	7.83	7.56	7.29	7.02	6.77	6.29	19
20	9.17	8.84	8.52	8.21	7.90	7.61	7.32	7.04	6.51	20
21	9.63	9.28	8.92	8.58	8.24	7.92	7.60	7.29	6.72	21
22	10.10	9.70	9.32	8.94	8.57	8.22	7.87	7.54	6.92	22
23	10.56	10.13	9.71	9.30	8.90	8.51	8.14	7.78	7.11	23
24	11.02	10.55	10.10	9.65	9.21	8.80	8.39	8.01	7.29	24
25	11.48	10.97	10.48	9.99	9.52	9.07	8.64	8.23	7.46	25
26	11.94	11.39	10.85	10.33	9.83	9.34	8.88	8.44	7.62	26
27	12.39	11.80	11.23	10.66	10.12	9.60	9.11	8.64	7.77	27
28	12.85	12.21	11.59	10.99	10.41	9.86	9.33	8.83	7.91	28
29	13.30	12.62	11.96	11.31	10.69	10.10	9.54	9.01	8.05	29
30	13.75	13.02	12.31	11.63	10.97	10.34	9.75	9.19	8.18	30
31	14.20	13.42	12.67	11.94	11.24	10.57	9.95	9.36	8.30	31
32	14.65	13.82	13.02	12.24	11.50	10.80	10.14	9.52	8.41	32
33	15.10	14.22	13.36	12.54	11.76	11.02	10.32	9.67	8.52	33
34	15.54	14.61	13.70	12.83	12.01	11.23	10.50	9.82	8.61	34
35	15.98	15.00	14.04	13.12	12.25	11.43	10.67	9.96	8.71	35
40	18.18	16.89	15.65	14.48	13.38	12.36	11.42	10.57	9.10	40
45	20.33	18.70	17.16	15.70	14.36	13.14	12.04	11.04	9.37	45
50	22.44	20.44	18.56	16.81	15.22	13.80	12.53	11.41	9.57	50
60	26.53	23.70	21.07	18.70	16.61	14.79	13.23	11.90	9.80	60
70	30.47	26.66	23.21	20.20	17.62	15.46	13.67	12.18	9.91	70
80	34.25	29.36	25.04	21.37	18.35	15.90	13.93	12.33	9.96	80
90	37.87	31.79	26.57	22.28	18.87	16.19	14.08	12.41	9.98	90
100	41.34	33.99	27.84	22.98	19.23	16.37	14.17	12.45	9.99	100

TABLE S
(continued)
Factors to Convert a Gradient Series to an Equivalent Uniform Annual Series

This table contains multipliers for a gradient g to convert the n-year end-of-year series $0, g, 2g, \ldots (n \quad 1)g$ to an equivalent uniform annual series for n years.

n	12%	15%	20%	25%	30%	35%	40%	45%	50%	n
2	0.47	0.47	0.45	0.44	0.43	0.43	0.42	0.41	0.40	2
3	0.92	0.91	0.88	0.85	0.83	0.80	0.78	0.76	0.74	3
4	1.36	1.33	1.27	1.22	1.18	1.13	1.09	1.05	1.02	4
5	1.77	1.72	1.64	1.56	1.49	1.42	1.36	1.30	1.24	5
6	2.17	2.10	1.98	1.87	1.77	1.67	1.58	1.50	1.42	6
7	2.55	2.45	2.29	2.14	2.01	1.88	1.77	1.66	1.56	7
8	2.91	2.78	2.58	2.39	2.22	2.06	1.92	1.79	1.68	8
9	3.26	3.09	2.84	2.60	2.40	2.21	2.04	1.89	1.76	9
10	3.58	3.38	3.07	2.80	2.55	2.33	2.14	1.97	1.82	10
11	3.90	3.65	3.29	2.97	2.68	2.44	2.22	2.03	1.87	11
12	4.19	3.91	3.48	3.11	2.80	2.52	2.28	2.08	1.91	12
13	4.47	4.14	3.66	3.24	2.89	2.59	2.33	2.12	1.93	13
14	4.73	4.36	3.82	3.36	2.97	2.64	2.37	2.14	1.95	14
15	4.98	4.56	3.96	3.45	3.03	2.69	2.40	2.17	1.97	15
16	5.21	4.75	4.09	3.54	3.09	2.72	2.43	2.18	1.98	16
17	5.44	4.93	4.20	3.61	3.13	2.75	2.44	2.19	1.98	17
18	5.64	5.08	4.30	3.67	3.17	2.78	2.46	2.20	1.99	18
19	5.84	5.23	4.39	3.72	3.20	2.79	2.47	2.21	1.99	19
20	6.02	5.37	4.46	3.77	3.23	2.81	2.48	2.21	1.99	20
21	6.19	5.49	4.53	3.80	3.25	2.82	2.48	2.21	2.00	21
22	6.35	5.60	4.59	3.84	3.26	2.83	2.49	2.22	2.00	22
23	6.50	5.70	4.65	3.86	3.28	2.83	2.49	2.22	2.00	23
24	6.64	5.80	4.69	3.89	3.29	2.84	2.49	2.22	2.00	24
25	6.77	5.88	4.74	3.91	3.30	2.84	2.49	2.22	2.00	25
26	6.89	5.96	4.77	3.92	3.30	2.85	2.50	2.22	2.00	26
27	7.00	6.03	4.80	3.94	3.31	2.85	2.50	2.22	2.00	27
28	7.11	6.10	4.83	3.95	3.32	2.85	2.50	2.22	2.00	28
29	7.21	6.15	4.85	3.96	3.32	2.85	2.50	2.22	2.00	29
30	7.30	6.21	4.87	3.96	3.32	2.85	2.50	2.22	2.00	30
31	7.38	6.25	4.89	3.97	3.32	2.85	2.50	2.22	2.00	31
32	7.46	6.30	4.91	3.97	3.33	2.85	2.50	2.22	2.00	32
33	7.53	6.34	4.92	3.98	3.33	2.86	2.50	2.22	2.00	33
34	7.60	6.37	4.93	3.98	3.33	2.86	2.50	2.22	2.00	34
35	7.66	6.40	4.94	3.99	3.33	2.86	2.50	2.22	2.00	35
40	7.90	6.52	4.97	4.00	3.33	2.86	2.50	2.22	2.00	40
45	8.06	6.58	4.99	4.00	3.33	2.86	2.50	2.22	2.00	45
50	8.16	6.62	4.99	4.00	3.33	2.86	2.50	2.22	2.00	50
60	8.27	6.65	5.00	4.00	3.33	2.86	2.50	2.22	2.00	60
70	8.31	6.66	5.00	4.00	3.33	2.86	2.50	2.22	2.00	70
80	8.32	6.67	5.00	4.00	3.33	2.86	2.50	2.22	2.00	80
90	8.33	6.67	5.00	4.00	3.33	2.86	2.50	2.22	2.00	90
100	8.33	6.67	5.00	4.00	3.33	2.86	2.50	2.22	2.00	100

TABLE T

Factors To Compute the Present Worth of a Gradient Series–Interest Rates from 3% to 20%

This table contains multipliers for a gradient g to find the present worth of the n-year end-of-year series 0, $g, 2g, \ldots (n-1)g$.

n	3%	4%	5%	6%	7%	8%	10%	12%	15%	20%	n
2	0.94	0.92	0.91	0.89	0.87	0.86	0.83	0.80	0.76	0.69	2
3	2.77	2.70	2.63	2.57	2.51	2.45	2.33	2.22	2.07	1.85	3
4	5.44	5.27	5.10	4.95	4.79	4.65	4.38	4.13	3.79	3.30	4
5	8.89	8.55	8.24	7.93	7.65	7.37	6.86	6.40	5.78	4.91	5
6	13.08	12.51	11.97	11.46	10.98	10.52	9.68	8.93	7.94	6.58	6
7	17.95	17.06	16.23	15.45	14.71	14.02	12.76	11.64	10.19	8.26	7
8	23.48	22.18	20.97	19.84	18.79	17.81	16.03	14.47	12.48	9.88	8
9	29.61	27.80	26.13	24.58	23.14	21.81	19.42	17.36	14.75	11.43	9
10	36.31	33.88	31.65	29.60	27.72	25.98	22.89	20.25	16.98	12.89	10
11	43.53	40.38	37.50	34.87	32.47	30.27	26.40	23.13	19.13	14.23	11
12	51.25	47.25	43.62	40.34	37.35	34.63	29.90	25.95	21.18	15.47	12
13	59.42	54.45	49.99	45.96	42.33	39.05	33.38	28.70	23.14	16.59	13
14	68.01	61.96	56.55	51.71	47.37	43.47	36.80	31.36	24.97	17.60	14
15	77.00	69.73	63.29	57.55	52.45	47.89	40.15	33.92	26.69	18.51	15
16	86.34	77.74	70.16	63.46	57.53	52.26	43.42	36.37	28.30	19.32	16
17	96.02	85.96	77.14	69.40	62.59	56.59	46.58	38.70	29.78	20.04	17
18	106.01	94.35	84.20	75.36	67.62	60.84	49.64	40.91	31.16	20.68	18
19	116.27	102.89	91.33	81.31	72.60	65.01	52.58	43.00	32.42	21.24	19
20	126.79	111.56	98.49	87.23	77.51	69.09	55.41	44.97	33.58	21.74	20
21	137.54	120.34	105.67	93.11	82.34	73.06	58.11	46.82	34.64	22.17	21
22	148.51	129.20	112.85	98.94	87.08	76.93	60.69	48.55	35.62	22.55	22
23	159.65	138.13	120.01	104.70	91.72	80.67	63.15	50.18	36.50	22.89	23
24	170.97	147.10	127.14	110.38	96.25	84.30	65.48	51.69	37.30	23.18	24
25	182.43	156.10	134.23	115.97	100.68	87.80	67.70	53.11	38.03	23.43	25
26	194.02	165.12	141.26	121.47	104.98	91.18	69.79	54.42	38.69	23.65	26
27	205.73	174.14	148.22	126.86	109.17	94.44	71.78	55.64	39.29	23.84	27
28	217.53	183.14	155.11	132.14	113.23	97.57	73.65	56.77	39.83	24.00	28
29	229.41	192.12	161.91	137.31	117.16	100.57	75.41	57.81	40.31	24.14	29
30	241.36	201.06	168.62	142.36	120.97	103.46	77.08	58.78	40.75	24.26	30
31	253.35	209.95	175.23	147.29	124.66	106.22	78.64	59.68	41.15	24.37	31
32	265.40	218.79	181.74	152.09	128.21	108.86	80.11	60.50	41.50	24.46	32
33	277.46	227.56	188.13	156.77	131.64	111.38	81.49	61.26	41.82	24.54	33
34	289.54	236.26	194.42	161.32	134.95	113.79	82.78	61.96	42.10	24.60	34
35	301 62	244.88	200.58	165.74	138.13	116.09	83.99	62.61	42.36	24.66	35

Part III

Production and Operations Activities

Chapter 5

The Industrial Engineer as a Manager

Concepts of Management

INTRODUCTION

Management is an elusive term, having almost as many definitions as there are writers in the field. Some refer to management as either an art or a science; others believe it is both. Art is defined as "a skill in performance, acquired by experience, study, and/or observation." Science is defined as "accumulated knowledge, systematized and formulated with reference to the discovery of general truths and the operation of general laws." Therefore, management is both an art and a science.

APPROACHES TO THE MANAGEMENT PROBLEM

Since management is an art as well as a science, individuals will use different approaches in solving management problems. The three basic approaches are: the idealistic approach, the realistic approach, and the pragmatic approach. Rarely will an individual use only one of these approaches. Normally, one will use two or possibly all three, with one of them dominating.

1. The idealist exhorts the philosophy of goodness in management by stressing the importance of personal relations and the recognition of individuals and the social sciences.
2. The realist sees management from a functional viewpoint and stresses the use of mathematics, statistics, and the physical sciences.
3. The pragmatist envisions management in the cold light of practicality and holds that management is simply a matter of using proven or workable techniques and procedures in a manner that recognizes their limitations.

AN INDIVIDUAL CONCEPT OF MANAGEMENT

The individual must relate his own role as a manager to the task performed. This development becomes the basis for an individual concept or philosophy of management. Philosophy, in this respect, is defined as management concepts that serve as the basis for action. Every individual, whether he recognizes it or not, has a philosophy upon which he relies in doing his job. He may find it difficult to express his philosophy in words, but he has it just the same.

The development of this personal philosophy is deeply rooted in the attitudes and experiences of the individual. Behavior is action based on attitudes that have developed into beliefs, habits, mannerisms, knowledge, and skills. The individual is aware of certain of his attitudes; there are others of which he is unaware. Continual self-analysis of attitudes and correction, where necessary, are essential to good management practices.

Continual self-analysis is also necessary to determine if one subscribes to the idealistic, the realistic, or the pragmatic approach to management, or a combination of all three of these approaches. This determination will assist in self-understanding and in the identification of those beliefs that tend to inhibit, control, or modify desires, impulses, or interests. The personal goal of the manager is an extremely important consideration. His determination and initiative may develop from pride, from profit, or from selfish motives.

Important beliefs are embodied in the moral and ethical considerations that constitute a value scale governing the individual's behavior. Loyalty and honesty with oneself and with one's associates rank high in this regard. Recognizing these traits in other people provides the manager insight as a basis for making decisions concerning these individuals.

Summary

There are different doctrines, definitions, philosophies, and approaches to management. No single concept will provide a workable answer in all situations. These variables make it necessary for one to adopt, and to adhere to, a personal concept of management that fills one's own needs, and within which one can work effectively.

The Functions of the Manager

INTRODUCTION

This section deals with the personal actions of the individual manager, to achieve effective management and to accomplish his task. In contrast to the functions of management as discussed from the viewpoint of the organization in the preceding section, this section describes the process by which a manager can insure that his individual responsibilities are being fulfilled.

THE SEVEN FUNCTIONS OF THE MANAGER

The functions of the manager are:

1. Establishing objectives.
2. Motivating.
3. Communicating.
4. Innovating.
5. Maintaining cooperation.
6. Developing subordinates.
7. Decisionmaking.

Table 5–1 tabulates the various tasks associated with these functions of the manager.

The manager executes each of these functions by example and direction in such a manner that he receives the confidence and respect of all his associates. This is leadership in that it involves personality, vision, knowledge, courage, judgment, mental flexibility, and integrity.

Establishing Objectives

Establishing objectives means setting specific goals that provide the targets for the overall plans and policies of the organization.

An objective is an end to be achieved or a purpose to be fulfilled. Establishing objectives sets specific goals that direct the overall plans and policies of the organization. Establishing objectives contributes directly and vitally to management of an organization. This contribution will be good, bad, or indifferent in direct proportion to the effectiveness with which the manager applies himself to this vital and continuing task.

Need for Establishing Objectives. The need is obvious—an organization exists to execute a mission. All organizations are composed of parts, or elements, each headed

TABLE 5-1.
Functions of the Manager

The total responsibility of the manager is to accomplish his mission by using his human, material and time resources most effectively. This responsibility is subdivided into the functions described below. They are supplementary, mutually supporting, and are performed individually, collectively, and concurrently.

Establishing Objectives	*Motivating*	*Communicating*	*Innovating*	*Maintaining Cooperation*	*Developing Subordinates*	*Decisionmaking*
1. Consider thoroughly what must be accomplished, distinguish between short- and long-term goals. 2. Examine requirements and balance them with current and attainable resources. 3. Consider time, priorities and the practicability of the ramifications of participatory goal setting. 4. On the basis of the above considerations prescribe achievable and measurable goals.	1. Appreciate the needs of the individual. Recognize and use individual abilities. Where practicable and feasible have people do the work that they do best, the work in which they are most interested, and that which challenges the the best within them. 2. Integrate interests of the individual with those of the organization. When practicable, gain individual acceptance of organizational objectives through participation. 3. Recognize both good and poor performance. Be prompt, decisive, and constructive in counseling, rewarding, and disciplining. 4. Set a personal example of optimum performance, attitude, and behavior; generate confidence in management.	1. Clarify your own ideas, desires, and purposes before communicating. 2. Consider timeliness and environment to facilitate communication. 3. Use words that your listeners and readers understand. 4. See that your actions and attitudes before, during, and after your communication support your oral and/or written message. Encourage interaction. 5. See that informal communications via the "grapevine" work for the organization. 6. Remember, the one communicating is responsible for proper understanding by the receiver.	1. Express a desire for change that will result in improvement. 2. Foster and maintain a climate wherein change for improvement is normal. 3. Provide a mechanism for orderly and rapid processing of ideas for improvement. 4. Provide for periodic review of policies and procedures to determine if improvement can be effected. 5. Have the courage to delegate and to assume the risk of failure inherent in change.	1. Maintain unity of purpose throughout the organization. 2. Encourage freedom of communication and teamwork. 3. Broaden individual understanding of the organization and its goals. 4. Where practicable, encourage maximum individual participation in establishing objectives and standards of performance. 5. Balance requirements of the organization with interests and capabilities of individuals. Maintain the dignity of the individual. 6. Be prompt, decisive, and fair in action. Demonstrate attitudes and behavior that make for a cohesive atmosphere.	1. Provide opportunities for self-development. 2. Clearly define subordinates' duties and standards of performance required. 3. To the extent possible, delegate to subordinates the responsibility to make decisions. Hold subordinates responsible for these decisions and be willing to assume the risk inherent in this practice. 4. Reward and publicize outstanding performance of subordinates promptly. 5. Counsel subordinates periodically in a fair and frank manner. Stress developing subordinates' strong points and talents rather than pointing out minor weaknesses.	1. Collect within time available all pertinent facts. All information is rarely available. A timely, practical decision is better than a brilliant decision made too late. 2. Develop as many courses of action for consideration as possible. 3. Weigh each course of action against available facts and existing conditions. Assess long-range effects of short-range decisions. 4. Select preferred course of action. Reword if necessary as a decision. 5. Communicate decision to those responsible for its implementation. 6. Avoid indecision. Never allow delegation to become abdication of authority.

Source: Reprinted by permission of the U.S. Army Logistics Management Center, *Army Management,* ALM61-3549-H, pp. 4-56. Ft. Lee, Va., July 1976.

by a manager, or a staff officer, or supervisor, from the first-line supervisor to the head of the entire organization; from the group leader or clerical supervisor, to the president. Each element is an organization in itself, containing at least one manager or leader and corresponding groups of people who assist the manager in accomplishing the mission of the organization. If these individuals are to make their best contribution to the accomplishment of the mission, they must know and understand the objectives of their organization. If they do not, or if this knowledge is vague, they will be working for the sake of working, and not for the sake of getting the job done. Establishing objectives must then receive continuing attention from the individual manager if his organization is to be successful.

Nature of Objectives. The nature of organizational objectives will vary somewhat with the type and task of the organization. However, there are some common characteristics:

1. Objectives must be attainable, and stated in measurable terms.
2. Objectives must recognize and contribute to those of the parent organization.
3. They should be so stated that individual responsibilities can be directly related to them.
4. Typically they are short-range and long-range.
5. Those of short span should be so prescribed that their attainment facilitates progress toward the ultimate goals.
6. They are of limited value unless they are accepted by those responsible for their accomplishment.

Acceptance of Objectives. Objectives should be established so that the result is attainable. There is overwhelming evidence that acceptance of the objectives by the individuals who must attain them is a vital prerequisite to their successful accomplishment. Time permitting, it behooves the individual manager to do all that he can to assure this acceptance. If the manager has difficulty believing that acceptance is a prerequisite for the success of his unit, he may wish to reflect on the following: some students of management and leadership believe that the day of blind obedience to orders by supervisory personnel is long past.

A person believing in the dignity of the individual feels a need to know why he is doing what he is doing, and why his organization is doing what it is doing. The degree to which a subordinate knows these things will directly affect his contribution as a member of the organization. Understanding the purpose or intent of the organization is a prerequisite to acceptance of the organization's objectives.

Many research reports substantiate that participatory leadership results in higher levels of motivation toward organizational goals, a higher sense of progress toward those goals, and more favorable attitudes toward the leader. The logic in this rests on both the sociology and psychology of participation. By the very act, subordinates have become morally committed to the successful attainment of the objectives. Where a subordinate shares in the decision process, he can become more committed to decisions, and can more fully appreciate the goals of the organization of which he is a part.

There are frequently many organizational objectives over which the individual industrial manager has little or no control. However, on these occasions he will do well to communicate the inflexibility of those objectives to his subordinates, and to tell them why. The industrial manager must separate the inflexible from the flexible, and then identify areas that will lend themselves to the participatory setting of objectives. This in itself will require subtle managerial skill, which should increase with experience. Participation is an aid to leadership, not a substitute for it.

Motivating

Motivation is the artery that runs through all managerial tasks. The most successful industrial manager is the one who gets people to work with him. To him, men are not just resources. They are vital, creative beings with hopes, aspirations, and needs. The success of the manager is measured to a considerable degree by the extent to which he can tap the unused potential of his people. There is no simple formula that will guarantee success in this area.

Motivating is developing within people as individuals and groups the willingness to accomplish required results. Motivation may be classed as primary or secondary. Primary motivation begins within the individual, secondary motivation comes from without. The manager must develop and learn to use both types.

Elements of Motivation. Among many others, motivation includes the following salient elements:

1. Appreciating and integrating organizational and personal needs.
2. Providing opportunity, where practicable, for individuals to participate in establishing goals and standards of performance. Such participation fosters ready acceptance of objectives and stimulates subordinates through identification of their personal interests with the aims of the organization.
3. Setting a personal example of optimum performance.
4. Recognizing both good and poor performance of subordinates.
5. Being decisive and fair in counseling, rewarding, and disciplining.

Group Motivation. American corporations believe in the development of their personnel. Equitable and realistic personnel policies and programs are motivating influences. These personnel programs and objectives of the firm provide the basic structure upon which the manager should build the organizational development program of subordinates. He can energize or defeat such a development program by his own actions, policies, and attitudes.

Industrial personnel programs are not a substitute for the manager's responsibility to motivate his subordinates. The company's promotion systems, its education programs, and its job rotation policy provide incentive for the people to be productive, and encourage self-motivation. Such incentives have been referred to as the "hygienic" factors. They motivate to a degree, but these personnel programs and systems in themselves are not enough. They do not provide the motivation that a manager needs to achieve an efficient organization. He must accomplish this himself, by constructive attitude and behavior, in order to achieve objectives through his people and through his organization. Results are obtained through people in the following ways, named in order of effectiveness and desirability: satisfaction, reward, persuasion, authority, fear, and force.

Individual Motivation. All people react differently to different stimuli. Individuals are like fractions, 1/8, 3/8, 5/8—basically the same, but all different in intelligence and personality.

When dealing with individuals, recognize that emotions are facts. Needs that affect people must be considered by the manager in his relations with his subordinates. The fulfillment of these needs motivates the individual. Compensation is only one motivating factor in the majority of cases. The manager, however, can usually bring only limited influence to bear on this factor. He must look for other motivating factors to inspire his people to top performance. There is a wide variety of such factors. Different ones appeal more to different individuals. A few that are generally accepted as having the strongest appeal are:

1. Being praised when praise is merited.
2. Having the opportunity to advance in pay and position.
3. Taking part in forming plans, policies, and procedures.
4. Having a general feeling of belonging to the group.
5. Knowing where one stands with the boss.
6. Being certain that awards and promotions go to the best-qualified individuals.

7. Performing useful and challenging work.
8. Having security against whimsical or capricious actions.

Individuals want fairness and judicious decisiveness, whether they be at the executive or administrative level. By satisfying these needs whenever practicable, the manager will generate efficient activity and organization esprit.

Hierarchy of Needs. The hierarchy of needs is arranged in a pyramid of five levels, from basic physiological drives at the bottom to the desire for self-realization. The hierarchy of needs[1] is arranged in a pyramid of five levels, from basic physiological drives at the bottom to the desire for self-realization, the highest expression of the human spirit, at the apex.

A brief word of explanation of each of the five levels of needs is as follows:

Physiological needs: Oxygen, food, water, shelter, rest, and so on. These needs dominate so long as they are not filled. Once satisfied, however, they cease to be important motivating factors.

Safety needs: Protection from physical and economic dangers, such as attack, war, fire, accidents, criminal assault, old age risks, and so on. Among the healthy adults of our society, these needs afford a minimal satisfaction, so consequently their motivating force is a diminished one.

Social needs: Love, affection, togetherness, belonging, and so on. Unlike physiological and safety needs, social needs are not readily satisfied in our society. Consequently, they have become a dominant motivating force.

Esteem needs: Personal worth, dignity, achievement, recognition, status, prestige, reputation, and so on. These needs are obviously important determinants of behavior. They can be satisfied in the American culture, but require a great effort if they are to be gratified. Accordingly, fulfilling the needs for esteem is today an important motivating force in our behavior.

Self-realization needs: This is the ultimate in the hierachy of needs. It entails the fulfillment of one's highest potential. It requires making maximum use of all one has, becoming everything that one is capable of becoming. As more people have more and more of their lower needs satisfied, a greater number will work toward fulfilling their self-realization need.

The Manager's Responsibility. Local leadership can translate the individual's needs into a tangible effort and create an organization *esprit de corps*. To do this, individuals must be given the opportunity to develop the maximum of their capabilities. They should be encouraged to seek better ways to perform their duties and to develop better ideas. The manager must foster initiative, imagination, and teamwork.

The manager must first clearly define the duties of each individual and the standards of performance he desires in the execution of these duties. This requires the manager to know what he wants done and who he wants to do it. To the extent possible, these duties, goals, and standards should be set cooperatively. Next, the individuals must be informed of the relationship between their duties and the duties of the section, department and organization. This will promote group effort, integrate the group and individual goals, and promote teamwork.

Assignment of responsibility and delegation of authority are interrelated. The manager must delegate authority commensurate with the responsibility assigned. For effective results, the person must know

[1]Abraham H. Maslow, *Motivation and Personality* (New York: Harper & Row, 1970). Used by permission.

that he has the authority to carry out his responsibilities and the support of the manager in doing so. The temptation is always present for the manager to make decisions for his next lower echelon. However, the individual cannot be held responsible if he lacks the authority and control to make his own decisions. If and when a mistake or poor decision is made, the junior must be supported and afforded both understanding and fair judgment by his senior. If his authority is taken away, or if he is reprimanded unjustly, the subordinate may fail to develop properly and his effectiveness and productivity may be decreased. Proper delegation of authority to juniors will free the manager from many routine operations and provide him with time to concentrate on the overall management of the organization.

Appraisal and recognition of job performance are essential in motivating personnel. It is the responsibility of the manager to make appraisals of performance, both formally and informally. Efficiency reports or rating sheets are not a sufficient evaluation in themselves. Direct, personal contact should be made with a person to discuss both his strong points and the areas in which he may be weak. The manager should counsel the individual and offer guidance for improvement when necessary. Criticism should be constructive and given in private. Public reprimands tend to lower morale, both of the individual and the work group as a whole.

Communicating

Communicating is any behavior that results in an exchange of understanding. It is transferring intent through creation of mutual understanding and is one of the most difficult and important areas of management responsibility. The effective manager recognizes and accepts the fact that adequate communication is a prerequisite for the successful operation of his department. Certainly communication cannot achieve its maximum effectiveness without understanding and cooperation on the part of both the communicator and the receiver. Usually employees want to do a good job. In order for them to do so, it is essential that they know and understand what their jobs are and what they are expected to do. The degree to which the industrial manager communicates his decisions understandably and creates ready acceptance of them determines his effectiveness as a manager.

Elements of Communication. The main elements of communication are:

1. Anticipating the reactions of recipients.
2. Using language that is understood. Conciseness and clarity of expression are essential.
3. Stimulating recipients to want to receive and understand the information transmitted, and encouraging interaction and personal contacts.
4. Being an attentive listener and evidencing a willingness to react to constructive suggestions and changing developments.
5. Realizing the impacts of attitude and behavior on effectively conveying intent and motivation.

Difficulty in communication has implications in every element of an organization. Without effective communication there can be no cooperative action. The limitations of communication are also limitations of decisionmaking itself. The decisionmaking process depends upon the reliability of information brought to bear on the issues to be resolved.

Communication may be either verbal or nonverbal, written or oral. The need for the written is obvious, but exclusive reliance on it can retard any operation. Oral messages are frequently more effective because of timeliness, and the opportunity for mutual understanding.

Nonverbal communication is more difficult to understand or to discuss, since it involves implications transmitted through attitude and behavior. The nonverbal communication should be used to support the verbal message. The signature of the manager on a paper, or his acceptance of a report, will be less effective if, by his behavior, he indicates disapproval, lukewarm approval, or doubt. On the other hand, enthusiasm visually displayed often expresses acceptance without further communication. The manager must constantly evaluate the manner in which his own actions affect the voluntary and cooperative flow of information.

An adequate formal communication system consists of three channels—down, up, and across. The down channel is obvious. It is the channel through which management policies and decisions are executed. The up channel is the channel through which reports are made and through which the operators make their ideas, wants, and needs known to higher management. The proper understanding and use of this channel enables management to feel the pulse of its own effectiveness. It is used improperly too frequently. The across channel enables peers to coordinate their performance of the functions of management laterally through the entire organization. This channel, when well used, reduces parochialism, fosters teamwork, and assures unified effort. These three channels, when kept open, are both complementary and supplementary circuits of communication.

In every organization there always exists an informal channel of communication called the grapevine. The grapevine transmits considerable speculative and hearsay information throughout the organization with no relation to specific line or channel. The wise manager, instead of trying to eliminate or ignore it, feeds it accurate and complete information, thereby putting it to work for the organization. If left alone and permitted to breed on false rumors and half-truths, the grapevine can become a demoralizing and disruptive influence within the organization.

Adequate Communication. It is the responsibility of the manager to keep his subordinates informed. It is not enough to issue an order with the expectation that it will be executed exactly as visualized in the mind of the originator. The manager should give his subordinates every opportunity to participate in the development of plans, policies, procedures, and objectives. Subordinates, through participation, will have better understanding of the problem and the reasons for the decision.

Having issued his decision, the manager must follow through with proper communication to assure understanding and implementation. This is necessary even though subordinates may have participated actively in previous discussions concerning the matter.

The passing down of information should not be limited to orders or directives. Background and related information should also be transmitted to subordinates. This additional information helps the recipients to understand what is wanted and enables them to do a better job. The manager's willingness to pass on all information gives the recipients a satisfying feeling of being well-informed members of the team. The result is job satisfaction and increased productivity. When an individual feels left out, and not a member of the team, his effectiveness and productivity are often impaired.

While it is normal procedure to issue orders or guidance in writing, it is often effective to provide related information orally to subordinates. When using both methods to transmit information, the manager must be consistent, clear, and concise and have a thorough understanding of the objectives to be attained. If he fails to do this, his written orders may be jeopardized by an erroneous interpretation of his orally transmitted information. Faulty communication can reduce effectiveness at lower and higher echelons. Cooperative action is jeopardized and the decision itself may be adversely affected.

To be effective, the manager must be appropriately responsive to reports he receives. He should clearly state the adequacy of reports and actions taken, and eliminate or combine reports when appropriate. The periodic review and analysis of the organization's operations will be worthwhile or worthless depending upon the interest displayed by the manager. If he participates actively in these reviews and analyses and requires that his subordinates be objective and constructive, the manager will not only obtain an overall evaluation of his operation, but the other subordinates will also become better informed. These periodic reviews and analyses further provide the manager an opportunity to make known the type and amount of information required.

Reports alone will not satisfy the manager's need for information. Reports must be supplemented with visits and inspections. Subordinates must be advised as to the manager's requirements for information so they can keep him informed. For the more experienced individuals, the usual expression, "keep me informed," may be sufficient. Others require detailed guidance. Regardless of how detailed this guidance may be, the flow of information is affected by the receptivity and attitude of the manager and to a considerable degree by his ability to be a listener. The manager must constantly evaluate the managerial climate within his organization and the manner in which his own attitudes and behavior affect the cooperative nature of that climate.

Staff and subordinates have a joint responsibility to keep the manager informed. The mere lack of definite guidance must not be used as an alibi or excuse for failure to keep the manager informed. Fear of being criticized or penalized, a lack of desire to complete corrective action, or failure to meet objectives are often the underlying reasons for failure of subordinates to report information promptly.

A major cause of breakdown in communication within an organization is the lack of a common language. Communication between and among elements of an organization must be prepared with the view of meeting the needs of the recipients. Adherence to terms defined in standard dictionaries is desirable. Local terms and expressions, words of limited use, and words peculiar to the operation of only one element of an organization should be avoided. A meeting of the minds between the individual sending the message and the recipient is essential in the various elements of an organization if they are to work together as a team in executing the decisions and policies of the manager.

Since Shakespeare's time, the number of words in the English language has quintupled, increasing from about 140,000 to between 700,000 and 800,000. About 500–800 of these words are basic to simple conversation, but since these basic words have over 14,000 meanings, our language itself complicates the communication problem.

A judicious balance between the various means of communication must be maintained. Remember, it's almost impossible not to communicate. The challenge is to communicate properly what is required.

Innovating

Innovating means doing things differently for the purpose of improvement. All variations of the word have a connotation of the new and different; all involve elements of change. The term embraces all acts, both of omission and commission, tending to cause a climate that encourages creative thinking and different ideas for improvement. If a creative climate prevails, individuals will feel motivated to think creatively, and they and their superiors will feel motivated to sponsor new ideas actively and vigorously.

It is unlikely that there will ever be enough dollars or personnel for industry to do all of its jobs in the manner it would like. With resources outstripped by tasks and crises, industrial managers at all levels must perform the continuing tasks of allocating shortages. This is far more difficult than the allocation of resources. Missions and tasks invariably increase out of proportion to resources. The industrial manager must manage better and accomplish more with less. He must seek and find new and more economical ways of accomplishing missions. One answer is innovation—creativity!

The industrial engineering manager can be innovative by:

Expressing a desire for change that will result in improvement. The manager must foster progress and should be imaginative himself. He must be receptive to the creative thinking of those about him.

Fostering and maintaining a climate in which change for improvement is normal. The successful manager proves the sincerity of his expressed desire for improvement changes by being enthusiastic and by setting the example! He openly encourages imaginative and different thinking by being willing to accept new solutions to old problems when they are proposed by subordinates.

Providing a mechanism for orderly and rapid processing of ideas for improvement. The wise manager creates a climate that encourages creative initiative and problem solving, and ensures that there is a system, prepared and in operation ahead of time, to process and evaluate creative suggestions appropriately and rapidly. The good ideas must be put into practice promptly and appropriate credit publicized rapidly throughout the organization.

Having the courage to delegate—and to assume the risk of mistakes and failures inherent in change. Good managers must emphasize the principle of delegation; enunciate clearly the areas in which subordinates can operate freely, and then permit them to operate. Wise managers must abide by these boundaries and be willing to accept occasional failure on the part of subordinates in the implementation of different solutions to problems.

Innovation and Change. The keynote in any definition of innovation is change. The very word *change* and all it connotes may be the greatest single obstacle the industrial manager faces. Human beings are creatures of habit and as such they are typically not receptive to change, which is often perceived as a threat to such important individual values as personal or economic security and existing desirable personal relationships.

Change instituted or directed by higher authority is different in some respects from that generated from within. Implementing a directed change demands a high level of managerial skill. The manager becomes the critical variable in his organization and his personal actions and attitudes will largely determine whether the change is truly instituted as intended, or whether it will be given lip service only and be regarded as a paper exercise. If he gives the implementation his wholehearted support, his subordinates will probably do the same. He has a responsibility, however, to ensure that the change and all pertinent facts, including the need for it locally and by corporate headquarters, are explained to and understood by all. He has a further responsibility in that after the change has been in effect for a period of time he should evaluate every aspect of it and report his findings to the next higher organizational element. In so doing he has discharged his responsibility to himself, to his organization, and to the larger organization of which his unit is a part. Change that is generated from within is commonly evolutionary and results from the imagination and initiative of the manager and his subordinates.

The Creative Climate. A starting point for fostering a creative climate in a large organization is the realization that it is possible to improve any rule. Rules are printed on paper, not hewn in stone! However, considerable time and effort are often devoted to improving a device when the use of the device itself should be questioned. If the manager can ensure continuing evaluation of current policies, methods, and procedures with a view toward improvement, there will be an orderly process of evolution going on at all times. Care should always be taken that any analysis of one particular area of operations be closely coordinated with similar areas in the larger organization of which it is a part. Otherwise, an improvement in one area may well produce undesirable effects in another. Evolution is not simple. It will occur either for good or for evil; but careful attention to it may well result in improved management.

One action on the part of the industrial manager that will help him establish this creative climate is his open, enthusiastic, complete, and sincere support of the suggestion program. Individuals must feel free and motivated to think up new ideas, to submit them, and to resubmit them, when justified.

There is nothing so lethal to a new idea as the first negative answer because people tend to support that which they create. Research on new ideas that have been adopted shows that the better ones had been previously rejected. The industrial manager will not achieve the desired climate of creativity until the people of his organization feel free to try and try again to sell new ideas. One way to encourage objective and impartial analyses and evaluation of new ideas is to establish standard operating procedure (SOP) within the organization requiring that all new ideas submitted to supervisors be sent up the chain of command to at least two higher supervisors before they can be disapproved. If such an SOP is used, care should be taken by the industrial manager to ensure that all supervisors understand the purpose of the SOP, and that it does not usurp the prerogatives of the supervisors. An effective way to stifle suggestions and creativity is for the senior to present his own ideas and opinions first, before his subordinates can participate in the exercise.

The answer to generating a creative climate and effecting innovation is neither easy nor readily apparent; there is no magic formula. Much will depend upon the situation and environment in which the manager finds himself and his organization. He must be prepared to stand apart, for innovation spells risk and loneliness, and his effectiveness in performing this function will materially bear on the effectiveness and success of his entire organization, and on any larger organization of which it may be a part.

To build a creative climate, the effective industrial manager must welcome opportunity to depart from the known and understood, and be willing to change the successful and the seemingly successful. Successful routine tends to destroy creativity. Successful businesses have emerged, risen to a zenith of status quo, then fallen.

Accelerating change and upheaval have become the pattern. While experience is extremely valuable, history serves mainly to clarify the present. Creative successes of the future will not result from targets of the past nor fashions of the moment. Any pattern soon becomes dated and antiquated. The real challenge to the manager lies in viewing today's problems in terms of the future.

Intellectual restlessness produces discontent. Constructive discontent with the moderately successful status quo is the first essential of progress. There will be no progress without change, no change without ideas, and no good ideas without creative thinking. Satisfaction with the past will not produce progress; contentment with the present will not improve the future. Innovation and creativity involve the unfamiliar; tomorrow-mindedness demands creative initiative, visionary boldness, and imaginative evaluation.

Maintaining Cooperation

It is normally the responsibility of the manager to determine the type of organization that is best suited to execute the tasks assigned. But organization charts are simply charts until the manager breathes life into them. He alone is responsible for the efficient functioning of the organization. Regardless of what the organization chart theoretically proclaims the organization structure to be, it is the manager who by his actions, manners, attitude, and personality determines to a great degree how successfully or poorly the organization will operate.

The manager may well have a one-man show if he decides to run the organization alone, and in small organizations with simple problems, this is possible. In today's industries, however, because of their size, complexity, worldwide scope of operations, and cost, plus the need to expand quickly in time of national emergency and to reduce scale of operation in times of economic recession, it is essential that managers use effectively the skills, training, and professional qualifications of their subordinates. In so doing, the industrial manager must obtain the wholehearted support of each individual in his organization if he is to accomplish his assigned missions with the minimum cost of men, material, money, and time. The atmosphere or climate in which they work will decide to a considerable degree the overall productivity of the manager's staff, his subordinates and his organization.

It is the responsibility of the manager to create an environment in which each member of his organization believes that his contributions or efforts are important and worthwhile. It should be an atmosphere in which each individual believes that he is a member of an aggressive and progressive organization and that his manager is receptive to new ideas and to creative thinking. He is convinced that the actions of his manager are the best for the accomplishment of the assigned missions. In brief, the manager's personal philosophy of management is the hidden force that will permeate an organization and mold its character.

A manager who effects and maintains cooperation throughout his organization enhances the chances for success. This function is intimately associated with motivating, communicating with, and developing subordinates. It creates and continually strengthens unity of purpose by keeping organizational needs and individual interests in balance. It includes: fostering unity of aims and freedom of communication, broadening subordinates' concepts of the organization, and integrating the requirements of the organization with the interests and capabilities of the group and the dignity of the individual.

In establishing and maintaining a cooperative system, the manager must establish realistic standards that are attainable by the organization. These standards should not be set by the manager arbitrarily, but, whenever appropriate, with his subordinates actively participating in their initial preparations. If the subordinates participate in establishing standards of performance, the manager will benefit not only from the standards being met or exceeded, but he will also benefit in that frequently the standards so determined will be higher than those he might develop alone. Standards must be revised when appropriate, with the subordinates participating in the revision. Revisions of standards must not penalize good performance but should provide for improved methods and procedures.

In his development of a management team, the manager must minimize and in time eliminate parochialism. The full effectiveness of an organization will not be realized until each element of the organization functions as an integral and inseparable part of that organization.

Developing Subordinates

Developing subordinates means providing an opportunity for the individual to improve his capabilities and realize his goals. This task is closely interwoven with all the other personal functions of the leader or manager, and it will normally result from their proper execution. It is closely allied with motivating, communicating, and maintaining cooperation and it will thrive in that environment where the manager performs them properly and exercises the principle of delegation appropriately.

Developing subordinates is basically a training process. Prior to beginning the training, it is necessary to know its objectives. Answers to the following four questions will assist in relating the training needs to the objectives:

1. What does the job require that the individual doesn't know or is not able to do?
2. How can the manager plan the instruction so that the individual will learn quickly and easily?
3. What must the manager take into consideration to assist a particular individual to learn rapidly?
4. How can the manager determine that the individual has learned what others have tried to teach him?

While these questions refer to teaching a specific skill, the same approach is useful in analyzing subordinates and forming a general plan for their development.

Developing subordinates involves:

Announcing and adhering to realistic policies and plans for development and promotion of individuals. Imaginative plans and policies must be practicable, down to earth, and flexible. Policies and plans must be reviewed and modernized frequently.

Providing an appropriate environment by practicing optimum delegation of authority, supporting subordinates in their actions, integrating organizational and individual needs, and providing incentives and rewards. This includes the manager's responsibility to create and maintain throughout the organization an atmosphere that encourages initiative, imagination, and teamwork.

Defining duties, constantly reviewing standards of performance desired, and informing individuals about organization relationships.

Permitting, where practicable, individuals to participate in establishing goals and standards of performance.

Appraising performance and counseling subordinates.

Providing the necessary time, facilities, and money for various training activities.

Techniques of Developing Subordinates. There are many effective techniques that assist in developing subordinates; many are used constantly, but largely unconsciously, in every contact between individuals. Some of them are as follows:

Coaching and counseling: Cooperative attack with subordinates of the problems of how best to do a job or how to improve an effort that is unsatisfactory. Discussing strengths and weaknesses as displayed in the day-to-day handling of job assignments.

Temporary replacement for a supervisor: Develops confidence and ability to make decisions. Discloses weaknesses.

Job rotation: Broadens experience and promotes cooperation.

Conference and committee assignments: Develop ability to get ideas across and to think on one's feet. Broaden knowledge and experience. If representing superior, foster feeling of responsibility.

Special task assignments: Increase knowledge in a specific field. Give unusual opportunity for coaching and counseling. Train in submission of findings, recommendations, and so on.

Developmental reading: A basic method of expanding theoretical knowledge in any desired field regardless of experience or lack of it.

Professional societies:

a. Increase interest and knowledge in primary field of endeavor. Provide social and professional contacts that will prove useful.

b. Keep individual abreast of the latest developments, techniques, and advances in selected fields of interest.

Community activities:

a. Broaden the outlook and provide contact with others in related fields of endeavor.

b. Tend to increase individual and company's prestige and standing in the community.

c. Create an awareness of the reaction an individual's company or organization, and its policies, have on the community.

Academic instruction: Provides formal training which, coupled with experience, makes for the most rapid development of the individual. Attendance of evening college classes at a local college or university, or full-time graduate study in business and engineering at a well-recognized university.

It is generally accepted that subordinates develop in stature more rapidly and more effectively under an individual who practices good leadership principles rather than under one who is a driver. There are times when it is absolutely necessary for any leader to be a driver but careful considerations should be given to the possible consequences. It is even more important for the leader to recognize and be familiar with the characteristics of a so-called driver.

Decisionmaking

All functions of the manager are performed cyclically and concurrently and there is no order of priority or sequence in which these functions can be listed. However, one of the more vital steps in executive action is making the decision. The decision is the moment of climax in the manager's activity. Making the decision may be lonely business, and the greater the responsibility, the more intense is the loneliness. Making a decision is painstaking work, directed toward the area in which change is to be executed. The responsibility for risk and all the implications of making the decision are upon the manager; the burden is the manager's own, and his alone. Decisionmaking is the most all-inclusive of the manager's responsibilities because he makes decisions in performing all his other functions. The art and science of managing is, within itself, decisionmaking, and all the preparation leading up to that climax.

Decisionmaking is selecting a course of action, from alternative courses of action, to achieve a prescribed objective. Decisions may be made by an individual, or by a group of individuals. A widely accepted method of decisionmaking is for a group of individuals—the staff or a committee—to study the impacts of the feasible alternatives; and to make recommendations, in order of desirability, to the manager, who will make the final decision between alternatives. Frequently, however, the manager will have to make a difficult decision on his own, one that his staff does not support. Having consulted with them and having kept them informed, the manager will have created an atmosphere in which the unpopular decisions will be more acceptable to all concerned. They will feel that their views have been thoroughly considered and evaluated.

The manager must ultimately be responsible for all decisions made at different echelons of his organization. The decisions made at the top echelon are normally policy decisions and action decisions having long-range effect, while at the lower echelons the decisions are invariably action decisions of a short-range effect—the routine day-to-day decisions affecting current operations.

Phases in Decisionmaking. The phases in decisionmaking will vary with the type of problem that confronts the manager. One category of problems is the type that can be answered with facts or data.

A second category of problems, which lends itself to a slightly different series of steps, is the type that calls for a judicial answer. Decisionmaking for this type of problem may vary from the intuitive yes, no, or maybe to the lengthy processes of engineering systems analysis and market research. The decision on such a matter as new product selection and introduction is a prime example of use of this process.

There is a third category of problems for which the methodology is not as clear-cut or logical. This may best be described as creative. Invention, innovation, and change call for ideas, imagination, and many alternatives. The past decade has seen notable progress in the formulation and development of processes to solve this type of problem. Basic to the phases of decisionmaking for this category is the theory—now well documented—that judgment should be separated, at least in time, from the creative steps. Since the phases of creative problem solving and decisionmaking encompass the phases and steps of the first two categories mentioned above, the description of the four-phase process is summarized as follows:

The Intelligence Phase. This starts with being sensitive to conditions requiring a decision. In both business and government, the mission or the need for decision may frequently be communicated from above or below. The energetic manager keeps himself constantly abreast of situations requiring decisions and is ever sensitive to conditions that may develop into problems. Whether the problem is imposed from outside, or arises from within, determination of its aspects and requirements is vital. Research for fact finding and analysis is essential. The manager should not constantly await developments; he must actively seek those areas requiring a decision. This phase also involves careful and imaginative definition of what needs to be solved. Redefining problems may be necessary, for each may well generate subproblems requiring definition and separate treatment or attack for solution. Sometimes proper definition makes the solution apparent. Too often, decisions are based upon a faulty analysis, or on some unanticipated or very restrictive aspect. Frequently the manager must stop to reassess, even to request clarification from above.

The Creative Attack Phase. This is accumulating ideas for alternate courses of action. In this phase, the manager thinks up tentative ideas and uses his imagination to accumulate as many leads as possible. He motivates his staff and subordinates to exercise their imaginations in accumulating as many ideas on solution of the problem as possible for later evaluation. He asks questions, suggests alternatives, and proposes goals that will stimulate progress. It is important in this phase that judgment and evaluation be deferred until the next phase. In creative attack we should not be dampened, or dampen our associates, by considering reasons why a possible solution will or will not work. We want to get the largest number of possible solutions before us that we can, without regard at this time for feasibility.

The Judgment Phase. This is defining and selecting the best of the alternatives. In the judgment phase, the manager is confronted with people and things, facts and implications. He views the entire problem with all of its elements and considers imaginatively the ideas and recommendations of his subordinates.

The Execution Phase. The best decision or course of action is useless until something is done with it. A fair decision put to use may do more good than the most brilliant idea that is never followed up. It is the manager's job to formulate plans for implementation of his decisions, sell them through generating understanding and acceptance, and follow up on the action directed.

The phases of decisionmaking are listed above in chronological order but their execution is cyclical and the cycle of activity is far more complex than the orderly sequence suggests. Each phase of solving a particular problem is in itself a complicated decisionmaking process. A subsequent phase may well demand return to the activity that preceded it. There is much concurrent mental activity similar to several concentric circles revolving in opposite directions—wheels within wheels turning counter to each other.

Other Elements of Decisionmaking. Timing is an important element in decisionmaking. The industrial manager in the office or in the plant is frequently required to make an early decision without complete information. Too many decisions are made in the absence of obtainable facts, but all desirable information will rarely if ever be available in time. The manager must realize that if he waits too long, events may overtake him, generating a greater and more complex problem and that his most difficult decision may be to decide when to decide. The urgent will always take priority over the important and frequently the manager must decide what is urgent, important, and routine. The horizontal priority list where everything is urgent is a breeding ground for confusion and inefficiency.

Once the decision is made, the manager must assure himself that it is stated in terms that will be clearly understood and not be subject to distortion and misinterpretation. Here, lessons in communicating come into play. Speak the language of the listeners, write the language of the reader, avoid the opium haze of ambiguity. Be clear!

Indecision is the cancer of effective management; indecisiveness is infectious and epidemic. Subordinates properly expect the manager to make positive decisions; they do not expect him to use his authority to let nature take its course.

One of the contributors to indecision and lack of desire to make decisions is the fear of conflict. If a problem involves conflict, the tendency is to leave the problem unresolved. To avoid being indecisive, the manager should develop as much comfort with conflict as he can endure.

Summary

The manager, one who has the delegated authority to direct an organization, utilizes and conserves resources to accomplish the objectives of that organization. He is the caretaker of the functions of the manager and ensures that they are carried out within his organization. With a full understanding of management, getting things done through people, the manager motivates and directs his people by always setting the example so as to obtain their confidence and respect. The manager's task is facilitated by a thorough understanding and practice of the functions of the manager, which influence people to cooperate toward attaining a common goal.

Management Theories and Thought

INTRODUCTION

A systematic search for a structure or theory underlying management has for the most part taken place during the twentieth century, and more especially after World War II. Early practitioners of industrial management theories and thought were Henri Fayol, James Mooney, Chester Barnard, and Lyndall Urwick. They began an orderly analysis of management during 1910–1920, and later some other practitioners followed up on this work. However, the behaviorists later began to consider the tenets of psychology and sociology as the basis of management theory.

THEORIES OF MANAGEMENT

Now that we have looked at definitions, principles, and functions of management, it is appropriate to look at the whole management process from the viewpoint of the basic theories that have evolved over the years. There are three basic philosophies of management that attempt to describe the process of management.

Scientific Management

The principal belief of this school of thought is that man seeks order and structure in his environment. Man seeks order and stability in all matters. Using this as a basic premise, we will see how scientific management started and trace it up to its present status.

During the latter part of the nineteenth century, Frederick W. Taylor, the father of scientific management, and others analyzed the basic tasks of the individual worker. The objective was to reduce the contributions of each workman to the smallest, most specialized unit of work possible and to eliminate any uncertainty about the expected outcome. Elementary to such analysis are work simplification studies, which break down manual labor tasks into definite repetitive movements, and motion studies which establish time standards for the accomplishment of each movement. The work simplification studies utilized a type of scientific method in their approach to analyzing the various tasks. The application of the scientific method tended to reduce the skills of the craftsman to routine procedures that were predictable sequences of movement.

From this rather simple start, scientific management has, over the years, continued to broaden its scope. It has advanced from studying single tasks to analyzing the entire manufacturing process. Analysts now study the system as a whole. Included might be such things as the flow of material from its source to the plant, the relationship of all the tasks to be performed in the plant, as well as the flow of manufactured products from the plant to the consumer.

Individuals are now analyzed on a scientific basis. Tests have been designed to measure the intellectual potential of individuals. The idea is to measure people on a predictive basis and fit the right man to the right task at the proper pay.

Scientific management is now being applied to a great variety of situations, some extremely complex in nature. Mathematical techniques are constantly being employed as a tool to assist in this endeavor. Today we constantly hear of such things as operations research, queuing theory, linear programming, models, and systems. Decisions at the top levels of management are based on factual data about variables that affect the entire system rather than on isolated segments. Computers are one of the chief tools used in the handling of the data. As the data-handling capability of computers continues to improve, there is every reason to believe that attempts will be made to bring order and predictiveness to increasingly complex aspects of society.

Some individuals fear that scientific management will reduce people to robots, and there is some basis for this fear. We certainly can see the results of programmed activity in our large manufacturing enterprises. Automobile assembly lines are good examples. However, it is not the goal of scientific management to reduce man to a mechanical being.

It takes creative people to reduce disorder and bring predictiveness to complex situations. There are so many constantly shifting factors in our environment that complete certainty in all matters is highly unlikely. A manager who advocates the scientific philosophy, however, is constantly seeking to identify areas or aspects of this environment that are unstructured. After these areas are determined, he attempts to structure the organization in such a way that this aspect of the environment now has a high degree of order, and feedback systems are developed to tell the manager if things are going as he desires. The manager must constantly be aware of his environment so that as conditions change, the predictiveness of the system will remain intact. Once operations become routine, the manager is then free to tackle other aspects of his environment that need to be structured.

The manager of the future will have to be creative and will require a broad spectrum of knowledge. He will have to learn how to use the new management tools that are being made available to him. His tasks will become more demanding and his training more rigorous. The benefits should be better decisions and more efficient employees.

Administrative Management

The theory of administrative management has as one of its main ingredients the idea that rules and principles can be used to ensure efficient operation of an organization. These principles of management should be formulated in such a manner that they will have universal application.

One of the early writers of this school of thought was a German, Max Weber. Weber's ideas on the best way to organize were based on studies of the civil service organization in Prussia, and were written about the same time as Frederick Taylor was doing his early work. Some of his principles were:

1. All tasks necessary for the accomplishment of the goals are broken down into the smallest possible unit; the division of labor is carried out to the extent that specialized experts are responsible for the successful performance of specialized duties.

2. Each task is performed according to a "consistent system of rules" to assure uniformity and coordination of different tasks.

3. Each member of an organization is accountable to a superior for his decisions, as well as those of his subordinates.

4. Each official in the organization conducts the business of his office in an impersonal, formalistic manner. The purpose of this approach is to assure that personalities do not interfere with the efficient accomplishment of the mission.

5. Employment in the organization is based on technical qualifications and is protected against arbitrary dismissal. Promotions are based on seniority and achievement. Because employment is secure, a high degree of loyalty for the organization is engendered in the members.

Another notable scholar who formulated principles during 1860–1890 was the French industrialist, Henri Fayol. Woodrow Wilson, an early spokesman for this school, advocated efficiency in government by utilization of organization theory, personnel practice, budget controls, and planning. Other theorists of this school include Professor Harold Koontz, the late Dr. Cyril O'Donnell, and Peter Drucker. However, Drucker is difficult to classify in view of the breadth of his contributions.

Some of the basic premises underlying these principles regard the manner in which people behave. The basic premise is that man's behavior can be controlled by rewards and punishment. The individual is viewed as an inert instrument performing the tasks assigned to him. Also, the individual is viewed as being basically lazy, and he has an inherent dislike of work and will avoid it if he can. Most people must be coerced, controlled, and directed to put out adequate effort to achieve objectives. One theory claims that, "Man is lazy, short-sighted, selfish, likely to make mistakes, has poor judgment, and may even be a little dishonest." Another theory claims there are three assumptions about man that are attributed to this school of thought:[2] (1) "man is a rational animal concerned with maximizing his economic gains"; (2) "each individual responds to economic incentives as an isolated individual"; and (3) "man, like machines, can be treated in a standardized fashion."

The administrative philosophy of management is today practiced by many organizations, the best example being the U.S. government. This bureaucratic form of organization is based on management principles and has many aspects that support the views about human behavior that were discussed earlier. A manager, using these basic assumptions as his guide, tends to manage "by the book" and controls people by assuring that they follow the rules.

Humanistic Management

It was only during the 1930s that the scientific and administrative philosophies were challenged. The emphasis of this challenge was that man is not a constant in an organization. Evidence was gathered to show that people in an organization change their work environment to meet their individual and group needs. The changing of the environment was related to the factors that motivate people.

The first evidence on this subject was gathered during tests at the Hawthorne Works, Cicero, Illinois, a division of the Western Electric Company. Engineers were attempting to determine the relationships between certain variables and the rate of production. They found that regardless of the type of working conditions, good or bad, the production of the test group increased. They found that production increased because of factors other than working conditions. What they deter-

---

[2]For an explanation of these theories, see Douglas McGregor, *The Human Side of Enterprise* (New York: McGraw Hill, 1960).

mined was that man, as a worker, does not exist in isolation, but as a member of a group, and that economic incentives are not necessarily the primary motivation of the worker. These insights into human behavior were used to explain the long-standing mystery of why workers would restrict output and produce far below standards established by exacting analyses.

Elto Mayo and Kurt Lewin made great contributions to the formation of the humanistic philosophy of management. Mayo initiated the human relations program at the Harvard Business School in 1926, and Lewin founded the Research Center for Group Dynamics at the Massachusetts Institute of Technology. Douglas McGregor in his book *The Human Side of Enterprise* lists the basic ingredients of this philosophy.[3]

Humanistic management stresses the ideas that individuals bring to their organization's attitudes, values, and goals. It is management's job to insure that these goals, attitudes, and values are meshed so that they are in harmony with the organization's goals and objectives. Management must create an environment so that the worker can satisfy his needs best by commitment to the goals of the organization. If management does not consider the needs of the employees, the results of industrialization will be social disorganization and unhappy individuals.

The practical application of human relations theory is influenced by the behavioral sciences, psychology, sociology, and cultural anthropology. Consideration is now given to the informal organization among employees, work teams, and symbols that evoke worker response. Labor unions are viewed as making a contribution to effective organization. Participative management, employee education, group decisions, and industrial counseling have become important means for improving the performance of workers in organizations. The premise that has become the focal point of humanistic management is that every human being earnestly seeks a secure, friendly, and supportative relationship, and one that gives him a sense of personal worth in the everyday groups most important to him. If management wants an effective organization, conditions must be created so that these human needs can be satisfied.

As you can see, application of the humanistic philosophy of management requires a great deal of knowledge about the needs of people and what motivates them. Mathematics and statistics have influenced greatly the development of this philosophy. Managers following the philosophy are generally creative and acutely aware of their environment.

SCHOOLS OF MANAGEMENT THOUGHT

It is possible to identify meaningful groupings of management theories, but because they may be classified in many different ways, there is no universally accepted listing. However, one logical way of classifying the various schools of management thought is to place them in six main groups.

Long experience with managing in a variety of situations can be grounds for distillation of basic truths or principles having a clarifying and predictive value in the understanding and improvement of management.

The Operational School

Managing is an operational process best dissected intellectually by analyzing managerial functions. Managing is an art that, like medicine and engineering, should rely on thorough grounding in principles. These principles can become focal points for useful

[3] *Ibid.*

research both to ascertain their validity and to improve their applicability. Such principles can furnish elements, at least until disproved and certainly until sharpened, of a useful theory of management.

Management principles, like those of logical and physical sciences, are nonetheless true even if a practitioner in a given situation chooses to ignore them and the costs involved in so doing, or attempts to seek some other benefits that offset the costs incurred.

While the total culture and the phsyical and biological universe variously affect the manager's environment, as they do every level of science and art, management theory need not encompass all knowledge in order for it to serve as scientific foundation of management principles.

The Empirical School

This school analyzes management by a study of experience, sometimes with the intention of drawing generalizations, but usually as a means of transferring experience to the student. Typical of this school are those who teach management of "policy" by the study and analysis of cases. Proponents of this school are likely to say that in analyzing cases or history they draw from them certain generalizations to be applied as useful guides for future thought or action.

The Human Behavior School

The thesis here is that, since managing involves getting things done with and through people, the study should be centered on interpersonal values. Variously called the human relations, leadership, or behavioral sciences approach, this school is concerned with existing and newly developed theories, methods, and techniques of phenomena, ranging fully from the personality dynamics of individuals at one extreme to the relations of cultures at the other. The focus is the individual and his motivations as a sociopsychological being.

The Social System School

This school is closely related to the human behavior school and often confused with it. It includes considerations that look upon management as a social system, that is, a system of cultural relationships. The system is said to be a cooperative one in which people are able to communicate with each other and are willing to contribute action toward a common purpose.

This school has made many noteworthy contributions to management. The recognition of organized enterprise as a social organism, subject to all the pressures and conflicts of the cultural environment, has been helpful to both theorist and practicing manager.

The Decision Theory School

This school concentrates on rational decision—the selection, from among possible alternatives, of a course of action. Decision theorists may deal with the decision itself, with the process of organized groups making the decision, or with an analysis of the decision process. Some limit themselves to the economics of the decision while others cover anything related to the decision or the process of decisionmaking.

There are those who believe that, since management is characterized by decisionmaking, the future development of management theory will use the decision as its central focus and that the rest of management theory will hang on this structural center.

The Mathematical School

Although mathematical methods can be used by any school of management theory, this school refers to theorists who see management as a system of mathematical models and processes. Perhaps the most widely known of these are the operations researchers or operations analysts, who sometimes call themselves management scientists. The belief of this group is that if management or organization planning or decisionmaking is a logical process, it can be expressed in mathematical symbols and relationships. There is much argument as to whether mathematics should be a separate school of management theory or a powerful tool for solving or simplifying complex phenomena.

Proponents of this school have shown management the means and desirability of seeing many problems more clearly; they have pressed on both students and managers the need for establishing goals and ways of measuring effectiveness; they have been helpful in promoting the concept of management as a logical system of relationships; and they have caused people in management to review and occasionally reorganize information sources and systems so that mathematics can be given sensible quantitative meaning.

Summary

Because these schools have been treated extensively in management literature, there is no point in undertaking an extensive analysis and evaluation here. Suffice it to say that these different approaches to the development of management theory have important insights to offer that can help give greater breadth and depth to the managing process and to the emerging discipline itself. Management theorists will have to sort and combine the contributions of these different schools of thought into a logical structure of management theory.

The various schools or patterns of management analysis all have essentially the same goals and deal with essentially the same subject. Two of the major differences are in concepts and semantics.

You are encouraged to become students of the management process. Be motivated to construct your own framework and always question everything that occurs in your organization as related to principles, theories, and functions of management. It is indeed a responsibility of management to know what is going on, but the real challenge for management is to understand what is behind what is going on.

Questions

1. Define management. Why is it defined as an art and a science?
2. What are the three basic approaches to solving management problems?
3. List and briefly define each of the seven functions of the manager as given by the author of this book.
4. Can engineering management be categorized as a profession?
5. Explain Maslow's hierachy of needs theory.
6. Why is communication an essential part of an organization? What are some of the elements of communication in an industrial enterprise?
7. How does innovation differ from creativity?

8. What can a manager do to obtain and maintain cooperation in an industrial organization other than explain and disseminate copies of the organization chart?
9. What are the necessary prerequisities in developing subordinates?
10. List some of the techniques used in the developing of subordinates?
11. What are some decisionmaking approaches?
12. What are the three basic philosophies of management that attempt to describe the process of management?
13. List and briefly describe the schools of management thought put forth by the author of this book.

Bibliography

Donnelly, James H., Jr., Gibson, James L., and Ivancevich, John M. *Fundamentals of Management.* Plano, Tex.: Bus. Pub., Inc., 1981.

Drucker, Peter. *Management: Tasks, Responsibilities, Practices.* New York: Harper and Row, 1974.

George, Claude S., Jr. *Management for Business and Industry.* Englewood Cliffs, N.J.: Prentice-Hall, 1970.

George, Claude S., Jr. *The History of Management Thought.* Englewood Cliffs, N.J.: Prentice-Hall, 1968.

Gilbert, Thos. F. *Human Competence: Engineering Worthy Performance.* New York: McGraw-Hill, 1978.

Koontz, Harold, O'Donnell, Cyril, and Weihrich, Heinz. *Essentials of Management.* New York: McGraw-Hill, 1982.

Koontz, Harold, ed. *Towards Unified Theory of Management.* New York: McGraw-Hill, 1964.

Krast, Fremont K., and Rosenzweig, J. *Organization and Management: A Systems and Contingency Approach.* 3rd ed. New York: McGraw-Hill, 1979.

Lee, J. A. *The Gold and the Garbage in Management Theories and Prescriptions.* Athens: Ohio University Press, 1980.

Likert, R. *New Patterns of Management.* New York: McGraw-Hill, 1961.

Litterer, J. A. *An Introduction to Management.* New York: John Wiley and Sons, 1979.

Maslow, A. H. *Motivation and Personality.* New York: Harper and Row, 1954.

McGregor, D. M. *The Professional Manager.* New York: McGraw-Hill, 1967.

McGregor, Douglas. *The Human Side of Enterprise.* New York: McGraw-Hill, 1960.

Miles, R. E. *Theories of Management.* New York: McGraw-Hill, 1975.

Petit, T. A. *Fundamentals of Management.* New York: John Wiley and Sons, 1975.

Scanlan, B., and Keys, J. B. *Management and Organizational Behavior.* New York: John Wiley and Sons, 1979.

Theirauf, R. J., et al. *Management Principles and Practices: A Contingency and Questionnaire Approach.* New York: John Wiley and Sons, 1977.

U.S. Army Institute of Administration. *Fundamentals of Management.* Fort Benjamin Harrison, Ind., April 1978.

U.S. Army Logistics Management Center. *Army Management.* ALM 61–3549–H. Ft. Lee, Va., July 1976.

Chapter 6

Industrial Engineering Support to Production Engineering

INTRODUCTION

Industrial engineering has become increasingly important, as industry, under the stimulus of keen competition, has intensified its efforts to improve methods and reduce the cost of its products. Many large companies have established industrial engineering departments staffed with personnel formally trained as industrial engineers, or with individuals capable of handling certain phases of cost-reduction techniques such as time and motion study. Some think industrial engineering is limited mainly to time and motion study and wage incentives. Others broaden the meaning to include every cost-reduction activity. Still others consider it to embrace nearly every staff function connected with manufacturing. There are so many techniques and functions related to industrial engineering that it is difficult to strictly define it. It is difficult to clearly define the mission of industrial engineering with respect to effort, time frame, expenditures, and results.

DEFINITIONS

Industrial engineering: Industrial engineering is the engineering activity concerned with the design, development, production, and inspection of material. It consists of the several activities that are accomplished before a decision is made to produce material for industrial and consumer use.

Product engineering: Product or component engineering is that phase of industrial engineering that involves the technical evaluation and resolution of new and novel ideas. This activity overcomes problems and product deficiencies by design or redesign to insure producibility, reliability, economy, durability, interchangeability, serviceability, and compatibility with associated items and intended usage.

Standardization engineering: Standardization engineering is that phase of industrial engineering that encompasses the process of establishing, by common agreement, engineering criteria, terms, principles, practices, materials, processes, and equipment, required to achieve the greatest practical uniformity of engineering practices and to effect optimum interchangeability of parts, assemblies, and components.

Value engineering: Value engineering is an organized effort directed at analyzing the function of systems, equipment, and supplies, for the purpose of achieving the required function at the lowest cost consistent with performance requirements.

Process engineering: Process engineering is that phase of industrial engineering that establishes the methods and sequence of operations pertinent to the fabrication of an item within economic and facility limitations.

Production engineering: Production engineering is that phase of industrial engineering that establishes machinery, tools, methods and procedures, production fixtures and jigs, and test and inspection equipment for items manufactured, to ensure conformity to engineering design requirements and specifications.

Inspecting engineering: Inspection engineering encompasses the development and provisioning of inspection acceptance and test equipment, methods, procedures, and quality control measures, to ensure conformity to engineering design requirements and specifications.

INDUSTRIAL ENGINEERING MISSION

Definition: The industrial engineering mission is defined as the planning, direction, appraisal of the development, provision, and maintenance of the technical resources essential to the accomplishment of production. This includes:

1. Prestandardization engineering liaison, studies, estimates, and evaluations essential to the transition of newly developed items into quantity production.
2. Engineering for efficient mass production, which encompasses: product engineering to improve quality, producibility, and maintainability, and to substitute materials; process engineering; engineering assistance to producers; and inspection engineering.
3. Control of all technical data necessary for the procurement, manufacture, inspection, and acceptance of items approved for quantity production.
4. Development and direction of the standardization program.
5. Provision and maintenance of technical instructions for maintenance.

INDUSTRIAL ENGINEERING SUPPORT MISSION

Definition: The industrial engineering support mission is defined as the development and provision of the technical resources necessary to support the engineering mission. This includes:

1. Engineering support in the transition from research and development to quantity production, such as:
   a. Keeping abreast of new items prior to release for production engineering.
   b. Initial production engineering of items to include: technical supervision of supply contracts; transferring and completing of research and development technical data to drawings; preparation of specifications; and development of inspection data suitable for acceptance inspection of production quantities.
   c. Furnishing information to responsible development departments on methods of manufacturing material adaptable to new designs.
2. Continued support in the area of major drawing revisions, drafting of specifications, and preparation of inspection procedures, after quantity production has started.
3. Continued engineering activity to improve the product and the process, in addition to eliminating bottlenecks in production.

Production Engineering

INTRODUCTION

There had been a tendency for many years to bypass certain essential steps in the transition of a product from a prototype to mass production. After the desired characteristics were obtained in the prototype, the product was rushed into mass production following the pattern of a crash program. In essence, the crash program neglects or minimizes the producibility aspects and forces an early prototype into production and use. While a crash program may be used under certain conditions, it would be unwise to "crash" all items. This is especially true with respect to the ability of this country's industrial might to provide material in the quantities needed as well as its ability to maintain products in serviceable condition in field use.

The major objection to developing and fulfilling the industrial and maintenance requirements jointly with the development effort has been the time and money involved. However, such needs can be readily fulfilled by the timely telescoping of the research and development (R&D) effort with the industrial and maintenance efforts without any significant loss in time and with the conservation of hundreds of millions of dollars, endless man-hours of critical skills, and tons of critical materials.

Engineering for production provides the means for this most effective production of material. The word *effective* is to be interpreted in its broadest sense, considering all factors involved, such as economy of resources and labor as well as the quantity and reliability of the product.

PURPOSE AND OBJECTIVES OF PRODUCTION ENGINEERING

Purpose

Considerable emphasis has been placed on this subject as a result of serious difficulties experienced during World War I and II, and to a lesser extent in the Korean and Vietnam wars. Crash programs to get items into production without an extensive production engineering effort resulted in intolerable delays and tremendous manufacturing costs. Today, new items are becoming more and more complex and require much more of our resources to produce them in quantity. Moreover, the availability of our natural resources is becoming limited.

Objectives

The objective of engineering for production is to provide mankind with the most advanced products possible. Some of the results of an effective engineering-for-production program are as follows:

1. Provides all of the technical information required to effect quantity production (including drawings, specifications, descriptions of manufacture, and gauge drawings).
2. Provides products in quantity with the degree of reliability established by the research and development engineers in conjunction with the reliability engineers.
3. Minimizes manufacturing costs, including in-process inspection costs.
4. Minimizes capital costs.
5. Minimizes customer acceptance inspection costs and destructive testing.
6. Minimizes requirements for special equipment and techniques.
7. Minimizes or eliminates use of critical materials.
8. Minimizes requirements for labor, particularly the skilled type.
9. Minimizes or eliminates waste products and air and stream pollution.
10. Minimizes lead time for mass production.
11. Promotes the use of standard parts and components.
12. Injects human engineering into product designs to assure that parts are put

together properly and that field handling is facilitated.

METHODS OF PRODUCTION ENGINEERING

General

Soon after mass production is initiated, numerous problems will arise. For example, the research and development personnel who are familiar with the product(s), and who have led it through successful development, are placed on new projects and are not available for consultation during production; or there is not enough of a particular material to produce the quantity of items desired; or it is discovered that parts do not function correctly because an on-the-spot change was made during production that was not reflected in the engineering drawings. This is when we recognize the need for production engineering. When and how should production engineering be accomplished? Numerous methods have been utilized, five of which are listed in Table 6–1, which indicates their good and bad features.

Method 1

The first method may be considered as no engineering for production prior to mass production. Any such studies would be accomplished after initiation of quantity production. Here, only a technical data package would be required to give to the manufacturing arm all information considered essential to effect production. The disadvantages of such a scheme are: (1) unbalanced productive capacity among the various segments of the production line—resulting in excessive capital investment; (2) overdesign of the product and process, which also leads to excessive capital investment; (3) excessive costs and delays in initiating and maintaining production due to inadequacies of the equipment and process; (4) possible compromise on quality in order to meet the schedules involved; and (5) hesitancy to change the process or product, once production has been established, in order not to interfere with production schedules. The only advantage of such a method is that it makes immediate production of a product possible in limited quantities. Such quantities could be obtained, for example, by screening out the good from the bad. However, long delays may be encountered in providing quality material in the quantities needed. This is essentially the crash program approach.

Method 2

Another method of engineering for production is to conduct a so-called desk or paper engineering study of the R&D prototype after final R&D engineering tests. Additional studies, if any, would be conducted after initiation of mass production. Some advantage is gained over the first method with respect to overdesign of the product; however, only limited and superficial changes will be made in the design or processes to avoid repeating any engineering tests. Moreover, there is the danger that some of these changes may yield an unsatisfactory product.

Method 3

A third method is to produce pilot lots after final R&D engineering tests. Advantages of this method are: (1) experience is obtained in the manufacture of the items by using production-type equipment; (2) many potential production problems are resolved by using essentially the R & D design of the item; and (3) chance of unbalanced capacity in the eventual mass production line is reduced. The disadvan-

TABLE 6-1.
Production Engineering Methods

Method	Description	Disadvantages	Advantages
1	No engineering for production.	Unbalanced production lines. Overdesign of product. Delays in initiating and maintaining production. Excessive cost in shakedown of plant. Compromise on quality. Hesitancy to change process or product.	Permits immediate production of limited quantities.
2	Engineering paper study.	Only superficial changes will be made. Danger that unsatisfactory product may result.	Some improvement over method 1 with respect to unbalanced production lines and overdesign of product.
3	Pilot lot manufacture.	Hesitancy to make major changes. Process and products will remain essentially the same as for R & D.	Production-type equipment experience gained. Many potential production problems resolved. Reduced chance of unbalanced production lines.
4	Comprehensive engineering for production.	Longest time to production.	Economical product and process.
5	Comprehensive engineering for production parallel with functional design.	More money and manpower required for production engineering effort.	Least time to production of a production engineering item. Economical product and process.

tages of only pilot lot manufacture are: (1) there is a hesitancy to make major changes because of a natural desire to produce satisfactory pilot lots expeditiously; and (2) the process and product will remain essentially the same as for the R&D prototype, except that larger capacity or production-type equipment is utilized.

Method 4

The fourth method calls for a comprehensive study to be initiated after successful preliminary R&D engineering tests. This comprehensive study includes a paper engineering study, the manufacture and test of sample items, and, finally, the production of limited production quantities to prove out the proposed product design and process. This procedure may require the longest time for accomplishment, but it provides proven product designs and processes suitable for economical quantity production. Considerable time can be saved with a system containing many components, if the individual components are production engineered one at a time as they are developed without waiting for the entire system to be developed.

Method 5

The fifth method, which is similar to method 4, calls for a comprehensive engineering-for-production study to be conducted along with functional design in order to minimize the time prior to mass production. The disadvantage of this procedure is that production engineering personnel would be continuously evaluating preliminary designs of an item, many of which would be discarded along the way because of design deficiencies. This means more money and manpower are required for the industrial engineering effort. The advantages of this method are similar to those for method 4, and it has the added advantage of minimum time to production.

COMPARISON OF METHODS

Comparison chart

Table 6–2 shows the relative order of the five methods of engineering for production in terms of economics (that is, manufacturing costs and capital investment), probability of successful quantity production, lead time to quantity production, quality of the end product, utilization of critical materials, and cost of the effort involved.

Results of Comparison

The comparison chart can be summarized in the following way. Where the item (and this can be product, process, or inspection technique) is essentially equivalent to one already in mass production, then the immediate building of production plants and subsequent mass production would appear to be most desirable. However, with many of the radically new items emerging from the research and development effort, the use of method 1 would be foolhardy. Method 2 is very similar to method 1 and only superficial changes would be made using this second method. Method 3 is valuable where extensive engineering studies cannot be justified on a cost or time basis. For new, unconventional products, method 4 would appear to be most suitable. Method 5 should be used for critical items where the time factor is extremely important. No one method would appear to be applicable across the board. For consumer and industrial products, method 4 is being used more than any other. There has not, however been a systematic or scientific method developed for selecting the most effective method for a specific item or situation. It has been a matter of exercising executive and engineering judgment in most cases. An attempt is being made through operations research techniques to arrive at a more scientific method for selecting the approach to be used.

CONSIDERATIONS

General

To answer the question of how much engineering for production should be performed, consider the following. When the research and development design is examined for production, usually various degrees of effort can be expended, depending on the uniqueness of the design, the processes required for its manufacture, and the numbers to be produced. Among the studies that can be made are studies to establish alternate manufacturing processes more applicable to quantity production,

TABLE 6-2.
Comparison of Methods of Engineering for Production

Method	*Description*	*Least Mfg. Cost*	*Least Capital Investment*	*Greatest Probability of Successful Production*	*Least Time to Initiate Production*	*Highest Quality or Efficiency*	*Least Utilization of Critical Material*	*Least Cost of Production Engineering*
1	No engineering for production	5	5	4	1 or 2[a]	4	5	1
2	Engineering paper study.	4	4	5	3[a]	5	3	2
3	Pilot lot manufacture.	3	3	3	4	3	4	3
4	Comprehensive engineering for production.	1 or 2	1 or 2	1 or 2	5	1 or 2	1 or 2	4
5	Comprehensive engineering for production parallel with functional design.	1 or 2	1 or 2	1 or 2	1 or 2	1 or 2	1 or 2	5

substitution of less critical or less costly materials, relaxation of noncritical tolerances or other related requirements, and redesign to permit the use of more economical mass production techniques. This also includes minimizing the number of parts required or utilizing standard parts, development of new or special processes and inspection techniques or equipment, and automation of operations. As a minimum, however, it will be necessary to provide the procuring activity with a complete technical data package (drawings, specifications, gauge lists, inspection equipment, and so on). Assuming that there are no limitations on funds, engineering manpower, or on time for accomplishment, all of the aspects discussed in method 1 should be fully and completely evaluated.

Limitations

There are, unfortunately, limitations on how much money can be spent, on the manpower and facilities that can be assigned for this engineering effort, and, most important, on the amount of time that can be allowed prior to quantity production. With respect to this time factor, we are always faced with considerations such as:

1. If we take too long, we may never utilize the product or process.

2. If we do nothing, our product costs may be so high as to make production of the item unjustified.
3. If we start before the initial product has passed final engineering tests, we stand the risk of losing the costs of the study in both money and scarce engineering time if the product does not pass final tests.

Inspection

The inspection problem may be examined with a view toward reducing costs and the expenditure of critical manpower. It had been the practice, more or less, to establish the inspection procedures and techniques after the design had been finalized. Currently, however, the R&D design is analyzed for ease of inspection and features are actually incorporated in the final design to facilitate inspection. A concerted effort is made to minimize component inspection and maximize end item go-no-go functional inspection on a 100 percent automatic basis, insofar as it is economically feasible. In other words, instead of inspection after the fact, inspection has become a part of the fact.

PHASING PRODUCTION ENGINEERING

General

Functional design and engineering for production should be considered as two interdependent functions that run parallel to one another for a major part of the entire development cycle. At the very beginning, emphasis must necessarily be on design that will meet the specific requirements. However, as the functional design features become more firm, the producibility aspects are given more and more consideration until development releases the item for quantity production. The degree of effort exerted on functional design and on manufacturability at various stages of development will, of course, depend on the product. The production engineering effort must be considered a part of the development of the product, and this effort can make a contribution on an informal or consultant basis, even at the very early stages of development. The production engineer may present an entirely new perspective to the problem, which can, in some cases, lead to final and successful acceptance of a new item. He certainly should not be thought of as passing judgment on the adequacy of the work of the functional designer. He is there to assure that the product will be acceptable from a production standpoint.

Phasing Diagram

How is this engineering-for-production effort phased into the overall development of a product? How is it telescoped in with the development work? Method 4 will serve as an example to illustrate the process in the life cycle of a product. A phasing diagram (Figure 6–1) depicts the various stages established between research and development and mass production for typical products.

1. When a project has been established for the development of a product, it is carried through a period that encompasses various phases; namely, research, feasibility study, engineering design, component development, system demonstration, and engineering tests.
2. When it is felt that the design, as established, is basically sound and can be developed into a satisfactory product by refinements in design (normally upon success in preliminary engineering tests), the status of the product is considered such that a production engineering study can be initiated. This stage

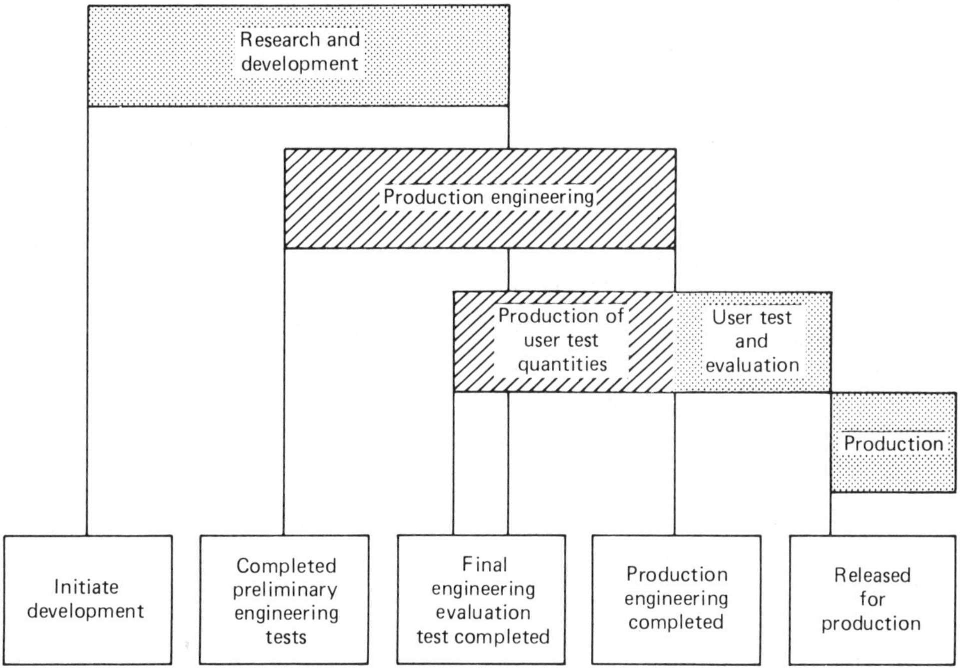

FIGURE 6–1. Phasing Diagram from Research and Development to Mass Production.

occurs when industrial engineering technically and formally evaluates the design in terms of mass producibility.

3. Note that development continues concurrently with production engineering to a point where the final engineering tests have proven to be successful. Any changes made by the R&D engineers are fully coordinated to assure that the production engineering design includes the latest features of the R&D item. Any changes developed by industrial engineering, during this period, are similarly coordinated with R&D.
4. Production engineering is continued, after the final engineering tests, to a point where sufficient hardware has been produced and engineering tests conducted to prove out the anticipated producibility of the production engineered version. The engineering tests also assure that the quality of the R&D design has not been compromised in terms of the established characteristics, safety, and field service interchangeability.
5. Transfer of responsibility for the product from R&D to industrial production, including the preparation of test quantities, occurs at the end of development. Upon completion of production engineering, the customer is furnished with the quantities of material required for user testing. The hardware for the tests will be that obtained from the production engineering effort. As stated before, furnishing a production-engineering item to the customer will give the customer much more assurance that he is testing a product that is exactly the

same as will be subsequently furnished in mass production quantities without further change. The customer will also feel more confident that, if the product is successful in these tests, the production quantities will be available at an early date.

6. When production engineering is completed and the test quantities have been delivered, the design may be released for production, depending upon the need to meet urgent deadlines. At this point a complete technical data package is finalized, pending acceptance of the item by the user, and is type classified as a standard product. The technical data package, consisting of all drawings, specifications, gauge drawings, descriptions of manufacture for parts, and so on, is then transferred to production status.
7. For some products, for which time schedules are very tight and the product is critical, this scheme may be modified. The product will remain under the control of the development activity through manufacture of the user test quantities, until the product is released for production. The industrial engineer still carries out his responsibilities concurrently with the development engineer.

Exceptions

Figure 6–1 covers primarily products that are required in considerable quantities, or high-density items; however, many of the same considerations apply to low-density items, although much more emphasis is placed on reliability, proprietary, and sole source aspects, as opposed to cost savings.

Funds

Finally, the telescoping of R&D and engineering for production requires timely funding. Without timely funding, many of the benefits of production engineering usually cannot be realized in initial production, as sufficient lead time to incorporate a production engineered item into the initial production may not be available. If funds are made available where needed, the loss in lead time may be insignificant (two to four months).

Specifications

NEED FOR SPECIFICATIONS

Before industry can ever hope to fulfill its mission, it must have the necessary types and quantities of materials, products, and services at the appointed places and at the appropriate times. These necessities can be of maximum use and benefit to the prospective user if complete descriptions convey to a prospective seller, accurately and precisely, what the buyer wishes to purchase. Almost all articles and services procured by industry can be described in terms of specifications. The use of specifications gives clarity to a requirement; the application of specifications to as large a number of items as possible necessarily results in a high degree of standardization. Through the use of specifications and standards, industry, trade associations, and government hope to obtain standardization of manufacture, packaging, inspection, and acceptance; uniformity and interchangeability of equipment; and uniform terminology for accurate description.

DEFINITION

A specification is a clear and accurate description of the technical requirements for a material, a product, or service, including the procedure by which it can be determined that the requirements have been met. The scope of this definition embraces documents used in invitations for bids, proposals, and contracts. These documents describe and establish the technical and physical characteristics or performance requirements of specific materials, products, or services, including the packaging and packing, marking, or other essential characteristics or requirements, together with the prescribed methods of inspection and testing for determining that these requirements are met by suppliers. When qualification approval is required, specifications include appropriate qualification tests. In other words, a specification is a procurement instrument that conveys to the seller what the buyer desires to purchase.

Questions

1. Distinguish between product engineering and production engineering.
2. What is the industrial engineering mission as it relates to the accomplishment of production?
3. What are the objectives of production engineering and the results of an effective production engineering program?
4. What production engineering methods are most prevalent in new product production? Give the advantages and disadvantages of each method.
5. Of the five production engineering methods, which method usually has the least manufacturing cost, and which method usually has the least time to initiate production?
6. Draw a phasing diagram of the various stages of the new product planning and development process.
7. Define a specification. How does it differ from a description of the technical and physical characteristics of a material or product?

Bibliography

DeGarmo, Paul E. *Materials and Processes in Manufacturing*. 5th ed. New York: Macmillan, 1979.

Matisoff, Bernard S. *Handbook of Electronic Manufacturing Engineering*. New York: Van Nostrand Reinhold, 1978.

Moshi, Bruno A. *Manufacturing Management and Engineering Handbook*. Englewood Cliffs, N.J.: Prentice-Hall, 1977.

Niebel, B. W., and Draper, A. B. *Product Design and Process Engineering*. New York: McGraw-Hill, 1974.

Niebel, Benjamin, and Gjesdahl, Maurice S. *Production Engineering*. New York: Unipub, 1975.

Pressman, R. S., and Williams, J. E. *Numerical Control and Computer-Aided Manufacturing*. New York: John Wiley and Sons, 1977.

Rudd, Dale F., and Watson, Charles C. *Strategy and Process Engineering*. New York: John Wiley and Sons, 1968.

Schey, John A. *Introduction to Manufacturing Processes*. New York: McGraw-Hill, 1977.

Society of Manufacturing Engineers. *Tool and Manufacturing Engineers Handbook*. 3rd ed. New York: McGraw-Hill, 1976.

U.S. Army Ordnance Center and School. *Engineering for Production*. Memorandum No. 516. Aberdeen Proving Ground, Md., July 1964.

Waither, Rudolph. *Technical Dictionary of Production Engineering*. Elmsford, N.Y.: Pergamon Press, 1973.

Wilhelm, Wilbert E. *Manufacturing Engineering Models for Design and Analysis of Production Systems*. Norcross, Ga.: AIIE, 1978.

Wright, J. R., and Jensen, T. R. *Manufacturing*. S. Holland, Ill.: Goodheart-Wilcox, 1976.

Chapter 7

Value Analysis and Engineering

In value analysis, an intensive study of the product or item is made in an attempt to reduce manufacturing costs. The usual methods used to accomplish this are:

1. Eliminate, reduce or combine parts.
2. Simplify the complete product or its component parts.
3. Alter it to increase automation or mechanization.
4. Alter it so that standard parts or materials can be used.
5. Redesign the product for automatic assembly.
6. Use lower cost, substitute materials.
7. Use lower cost processes or manufacturing methods.
8. Use a higher cost material, which affords simplified design or facilitates lower cost assemblies.
9. Change fabrication methods.
10. Increase reliability.
11. Ensure easy maintainability.
12. Reduce operating and maintenance costs.

BACKGROUND AND PURPOSE

Introduction

Value analysis is a new engineering specialty that pays large dividends. It originated in industry and was soon adopted by U.S. Naval shipyards where it achieved great success.

Definition

Value analysis is the objective appraisal of each area (or element) of design, development, manufacture, and procurement to achieve the necessary functioning and reliability at the minimum cost. It is a technique applied to purchased and manufactured material. Value analysis starts with the verification of the essential function of the item and sysematically develops a means of achieving this function in the most economical manner. It involves a team effort of individuals with diversified experience in design, manufacture, and procurement.

Lawrence D. Miles, the pioneer of value analysis, defines value analysis as follows: Value analysis is a philosophy implemented by the use of a specific set of techniques, a body of knowledge, and a group of learned skills. It is an organized creative approach which has, for its purpose, the efficient identification of unnecessary cost, i.e. cost which provides neither quality nor use nor life nor appearance nor customer features. Value analysis serves all branches of an enterprise: engineering, manufacturing, procurement, marketing, and management.[1]

Purpose

Through widespread acceptance and backing by industry and U.S. Department of Defense personnel (DOD), value analysis is rapidly expanding from an art to an exact

[1]Miles, Lawrence D. *Techniques of Value Analysis and Value Engineering*. (New York: McGraw-Hill, 1961, p. 1).

science. Its purpose is to make a high-quality product at a competitive and reasonable cost. Value analysis ensures that each part of a given design is functionally essential and absolutely necessary to achieve the product's function. It is necessary to analyze the function and efficiency of each part and, then, to produce the part as economically as possible through design and manufacturing simplicity and the proper choice of materials. This method of preliminary evaluation, combined with today's new materials and improved manufacturing techniques, makes it possible to produce a better product at a relatively lower cost. Remember, the cost reductions made possible by the use of value analysis are not intended to cheapen the product. Functional design simplicity and the more efficient use of materials actually improve both the product's quality and reliability.

Difference between Cost Reduction and Value Analysis

Some of the value analysis techniques were previously known to both industry and the DOD as successful cost-reduction methods. However, two distinct differences exist between the conventional cost-reduction procedures and the newer value analysis concepts:

1. Value analysis does not reduce the end-product cost by compromising quality or performance. It seeks to reduce end-product cost by minimizing the cost of accomplishing the required end-product functions.
2. Value analysis techniques are systematically applied during all stages of design, purchasing, and manufacture. The techniques are not applied as individual or specialized cost-reduction methods, sporadically applied without preplanning or coordination, either during manufacture or afterward.

Historical Background

Origin. The conventional cost-reduction committees have long been familiar to both industry and the U.S. government. However, in 1947 the General Electric Company went a step further and established what it called a value analysis program. In the beginning, the entire staff for this new program consisted of one man. He spent a great deal of time working on ways and means of reducing costs without compromising performance. The program improved and expanded with time, usage, and experience. It was soon recognized as a unique effort of considerable achievement and a program with a future. The company's original one-man value analysis team has expanded until there are now over 100 professional value specialists and over 3,000 other personnel who have been trained in the field.

First Military Use. In 1954, the spiraling costs of military equipment, combined with a relatively fixed budget, prompted the Navy Bureau of Ships to initiate its own program of value analysis patterned on the General Electric plan. In order to shift the emphasis from procurement to engineering, the program was called value engineering. This was the beginning of value analysis in defense. The new program permitted the Bureau of Ships to alter designs during development and before production was begun. In actual practice, the program operates at all levels of design, development, and production. Since 1954, value engineering has expanded greatly within the defense establishment. Early in 1959, the Office of the Chief of Ordnance issued an administrative order to the effect that ordnance installations with a design and procurement responsibility would establish a value analysis unit within their organizations.

PHILOSOPHY

Roadblocks

To be successful, value analysis must be recognized as a useful tool. Understanding the term *value analysis* is fundamental to the effective use of its techniques. Many value analysis techniques are known, but, until recently, they have not been coordinated and formulated into an effective program. It may be well to review the definition of value analysis presented before. Note that nothing is mentioned about cheapening or reducing product quality. The success and popularity of value analysis are attributed to the key phrases "team effort" or "organized approach." Outwardly, it may appear that value analysis is self-selling; that presentation of value analysis techniques would be sufficient to interest persons concerned with material. In truth, people must be convinced of the savings resulting from an effective value analysis program. There are those who limit their economy measures to such things as turning out lights and saving pencil stubs, followed by those who are satisfied with insignificant cost reductions of their product. Finally, there are those unimaginative persons who make such statements as:

1. It can't work.
2. We've tried that before.
3. We haven't had a failure in forty years, why change now?
4. We have always made it on a screw machine.
5. It's not company policy.

Creative Thinking

This brings us to key words in value analysis techniques—creative thinking. The statements of unimaginative people are good examples of noncreative or destructive thinking. If judicial thinking and fear of failure are enemies of value analysis, creative thinking is its best ally. Basically, the problem is to reduce the cost of a product without compromising on quality or reliability. The imagination must bring forth ideas. Radical as they may be, the most farfetched ideas many times provide the best solutions to the problem. Best results are usually obtained when there is an exchange of ideas as in a creative thinking session of persons with diverse training and experience.

Concentrate the Effort in the Engineering

Value analysis programs to reduce costs originated as an after-the-fact review of items. However, the object is to achieve maximum savings and, to do this, a before-the-fact program must be used. Such a program would concentrate the value analysis effort in the engineering department, so that value analysis work is conducted while the item is undergoing design and development. Engineering and specification changes on paper are easier and considerably less costly than changes in tooling.

Keep Value Analysis Close to Design

The design section plays the basic role in the economy of a product. If all desirable design changes could be made before the drawing of a product leaves the engineering department, a tremendous number of man-hours would be saved. This should be our goal. The design engineer carries a tremendous load. First, he must turn out a design that works, often within a very close time schedule. He also has to stay abreast of the latest developments in his own and other fields in order to incorporate the latest advances in his designs. He must keep accurate up-to-date cost information on materials, methods, and processes. To deliver the best designs, he must seek out specialists and obtain their advice on costs, methods, and so on. At the rate engineering technology is advancing today, this man is virtually swamped. The solution is to form a design team composed of the designer and specialists with diversified experience in purchasing, materials, manufacturing processes, and production. The more information that the specialists can provide to the designer, the more time he can spend on creative designs. The results will be fewer changes, more advanced designs, and more dollars saved.

RESOURCES

General

The value analyst or value engineer has tremendous resources available for his use. From these resources he may draw a wealth of information that can be brought to bear on a problem. Some of these resources include company employees, company and industrial specialists, and suppliers or vendors.

Industrial Employees

The value ability of industrial employees in this field of endeavor must not be overlooked. For best results, the employee must be informed of the present cost as well as the need for a cost reduction in the particular part under value analysis. Incentives, such as employee suggestion plans, provide further ideas for the value analyst. Approximately 5 percent of the cost of the product may be expected in savings in this area of know-how.

Technical Specialists

Trained industrial personnel such as production engineers, methods men, and standards specialists may be expected to reduce product costs about 10 to 15 percent. Their methods involve dividing the product into meaningful groups such as cost per year, cost per pound of material, cost of overhead and labor, and so on. This group has the same functions with respect to cost as the conventional cost-reduction committee.

Value-trained Personnel

Unfortunately, the number of people who fit into this category are limited. Trained staff personnel and company consultants cannot possibly cover all areas in which value analysis would contribute significantly. If organizational personnel can receive advance value training through value analysis seminars, classes, or other means, significant cost reductions can be expected. In an organization that has had extensive value analysis training, continuous and organized value analysis efforts may bring about cost reductions of 30 to 45 percent.

Vendor Know-how

A vendor is considered to be the basic material supplier, owner of a particular process, or the producer of a product. The relationship of the vendor and the value analyst should be one of mutual assistance. The value analyst must provide fair evaluation of the vendor's product in order that improvements or changes can be made. In turn, the vendor can make technical contributions and provide special products or processes and other information which can help the value analyst determine how and where cost reductions are possible. This interchange of information is profitable to the vendor as well as to the purchaser.

TECHNIQUES

You may find many different names given to the various value analysis techniques. However, they are all related to one general technique: namely, the functional approach. Problem solving by the functional approach may be accomplished in several ways. These methods will be discussed in the following paragraphs.

Evaluate the Function

The first method of analyzing an item of material involves answering a set of five questions:

1. What is the part?
2. What does it do?
3. What does it cost?
4. What else will do the job?
5. What would that cost?

Evaluate the Part versus the Function

1. First, take any item without revealing its function, then ask several people to evaluate the part. On the basis of the materials used and labor performed on the part, a reasonable estimate of the value of the item may be obtained. Second, describe the function and ask for the evaluation of the function in monetary terms. If the amount of the first answer consistently exceeds the amount of the second answer, it is obvious that this is an area where analysis is needed.
2. One small item evaluated was a drilled cylinder of metal with two drilled and tapped holes in the outside diameter. The cost of this part was placed between 95 cents and $2.90. The actual cost was slightly over $1.50. However, when the same people were informed of its function and asked to evaluate the function, their evaluation was 15 to 25 cents. As a result of considering the functional value against the part itself, the same part is now being made for 17 cents.
3. It is important, in the evaluation of a part, to consider only the value of the function itself. Should the part fail, the consequences of failure are not a fair criterion against which to measure value. A brake cylinder on your automobile has a functional value of only a couple of dollars, yet failure of this part could cause you to have an expensive accident, even to the extent of endangering human lives. Nevertheless, it is inconceivable that a brake cylinder is worth $10,000, $1,000, or even $100.
4. Remember, the definition of value analysis states that value is determined by the lowest cost for reliably providing a function.

Divide Cost into Functional Areas

1. A slightly different approach is to consider a product as a group of functions and to evaluate each functional area with respect to cost and functional value. For example: a commercial switch rated at 600 volts and 10 amperes originally cost $118. This switch protected $80,000 worth of equipment, but, once again, you don't pay for the consequences of failure, but for the essential quality and functioning. Breakdown of the cost into functional areas revealed the following:

a.	Electrical	$13
b.	Mechanical	10
c.	Case and cover	50
d.	Labor and overhead	45
e.	Total	$118

2. At first glance, it is obvious that the cost of the case and cover was disproportionately high and that it far exceeded its functional value. Two months of analysis reduced the cost to:

a.	Electrical	$ 6
b.	Mechanical	10
c,	Case and cover	14
d.	Labor and overhead	35
e.	Total	$65

3. As seen in the example, this method of dividing the costs into functional areas is valuable in analyzing existing designs in that it may indicate where value analysis should start.

Evaluate Functional Areas

This approach is almost the reverse of the previous method. In this method, as soon as the design is conceived, the various functional areas are listed. These functional areas are then evaluated and compared. The values of the functional areas are added to see if they fall within the total cost of the product. This method is helpful in determining if more money can be spent on important functional areas and less on items required as a consequence of the design.

Representatives of the General Electric program claim a tremendous potential for value analysis in the military; they say that by its application three times the quantity of weapons now being purchased could be purchased for the same cost. Even if this optimistic statement is only half right, the application of value analysis will save millions each year and allow pursuit of necessary programs that have had to be neglected owing to budget limitations.

Value Engineering

DEFINITION

Value engineering can be defined as an intensive appraisal of all the elements of the design, manufacture, inspection, procurement, installation, and maintenance of a product and its components, including the applicable specifications and operational requirements in order to achieve the necessary performance, reliability, and maintainability of a product at minimum cost. The purpose of value engineering is to make certain that every element of cost (design, labor, materials, supplies, and services) contributes proportionately to the function of the product.

The engineering design of a product can usually be improved the second time around, as dictated through value analysis work. But value engineering has the advantage of working before the fact, so that such redesign becomes less imperative, and, in many cases, uneconomical. Value engineering uses many of the same techniques as value analysis, but it starts at the drawing table for any product.

VALUE ENGINEERING METHODOLOGY

There are seven basic elements of value engineering methodology. These are not always distinct and separate; often they merge or overlap. The seven elements are:

Product selection: The selection of the hardware system subsystem, or component to which value engineering efforts are to be applied.

Determination of function: The analysis and definition of function(s) that must be performed by this hardware.

Information gathering: The pulling together of all pertinent facts concerning the product—present cost, quality and reliability requirements, development history, and so forth.

Development of alternatives: The creation of ideas for alternatives to the established design.

Cost analysis of alternatives: The development of estimates of the cost of alternatives, and the selection of one or more of the economical alternatives for further testing of technical feasibility.

Testing and verification: Proof that the alternative(s) will not jeopardize fulfillment of performance (functional) requirements.

Proposal submission and follow-up: Preparation and submission of a formal value engineering change proposal (VECP).

The foregoing elements are based on the supposition that the goals of hardware designers have been achieved, or at least achieved to the extent that the designers will recommend that a prototype of the hardware be produced for operational testing.

Another means of describing the substance of the seven elements is to say that doing them provides answers to the questions, What is the item? What does the item do? What does it cost? What must it do? What else will do the job? What will it cost? These types of questions are usually answered by using a job plan, which comprises six steps. These steps are presented in Figure 7–1.

WHEN, WHERE, AND TO WHAT EXTENT TO APPLY VALUE ENGINEERING

In the preceding sections we defined value engineering and indicated how value engineering concepts are applied. Now we turn to the criteria for deciding when, where, and to what extent value engineering concepts should be applied.

Value engineering may be applied to a product at any time after preliminary design. For a product already in production, it should be applied as early as possible. For a product in development, value engineering should be applied before production, but after preliminary design.

There are two views on the proper point of application. Some argue that in order to obtain maximum savings, value engineering should be applied as early as possible in the life cycle of a product. Too early an application, say immediately after the first design attempt, is not desired because of possible wasted effort if the first designs are subsequently modified or changed. From the standpoint of achieving maximum efficiency, then, it is said that value engineering should be applied sometime before mass production begins, but after the design has been firmed up.

Others say that the timing of value engineering should be related to the ease or difficulty of actually accomplishing value engineering. The process is easier to carry out if the product exists in physical form. It has been found that evaluation is easier if the product actually exists, because costs are easier to gather and estimate. These considerations are arguments for the introduction of value engineering downstream in the product's life cycle.

To resolve these conflicts, it seems best

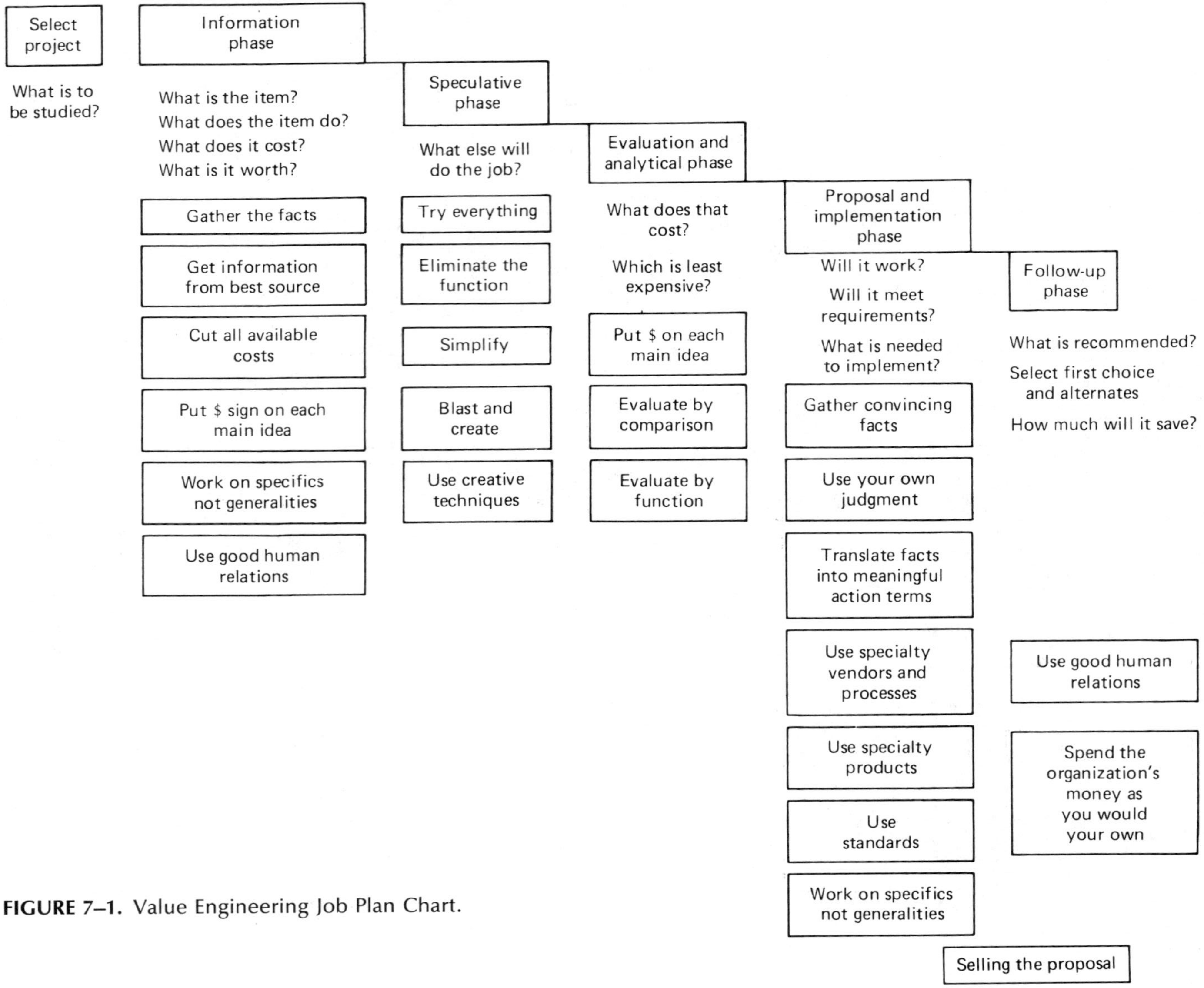
Select project
What is to be studied?
Information phase
What is the item?
What does the item do?
What does it cost?
What is it worth?
Gather the facts
Get information from best source
Cut all available costs
Put $ sign on each main idea
Work on specifics not generalities
Use good human relations
Speculative phase
What else will do the job?
Try everything
Eliminate the function
Simplify
Blast and create
Use creative techniques
Evaluation and analytical phase
What does that cost?
Which is least expensive?
Put $ on each main idea
Evaluate by comparison
Evaluate by function
Proposal and implementation phase
Will it work?
Will it meet requirements?
What is needed to implement?
Gather convincing facts
Use your own judgment
Translate facts into meaningful action terms
Use specialty vendors and processes
Use specialty products
Use standards
Work on specifics not generalities
Follow-up phase
What is recommended?
Select first choice and alternates
How much will it save?
Use good human relations
Spend the organization's money as you would your own
Selling the proposal

FIGURE 7–1. Value Engineering Job Plan Chart.

to apply value engineering at some point between design and production, the selection of the specific point being a function of the product, the organization's already established procedure, present control points, and the manufacturing process itself.

Even though this discussion has focused on the development of new products, products already in use may benefit considerably from initial or subsequent value engineering application.

For the same amount of time and effort, the benefits that can accrue from analyzing one item seldom are the same as can be achieved from analyzing another item. Usually, a preliminary analysis of all components and/or subsystems of a system enables the value engineer to select those items that will offer cost-reduction opportunities. A preliminary analysis of all components enables the value engineer to select and assign priorities to the components in accordance with their potential value improvement.

The cost of the present design of a subsystem or an item should be determined in as much detail as possible. When a value engineering study is being conducted on a product in an early stage of development, it is necessary to rely on estimates of what the cost will be. Later in the life cycle, it will be possible to use projected costs that are based on previous costs.

Evaluation of costs serves to identify the high-cost elements and thus aids in establishing the priority of individual studies to be undertaken. Usually, high-cost areas represent the greatest savings opportunities and should be investigated first. Studies have shown that generally costs are distributed in accordance with Pareto's law; that is, a few areas, generally 20 percent or less, represent 80 percent or more of the costs. This law is illustrated in Figure 7–2.

The manager of value engineering must not only decide when and where to focus

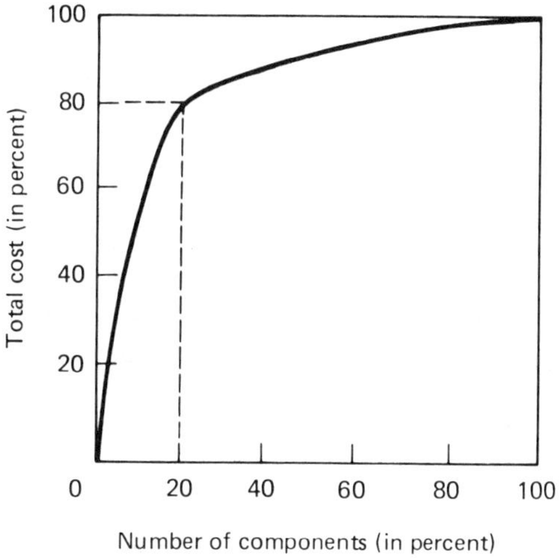

FIGURE 7–2. Pareto's Law of Distribution.

value engineering effort, but he must also decide how much time and money he can afford to spend on a particular job. Experience has proved that value engineering effort can be time-consuming and costly.

A rule of thumb that can be used by the manager of value engineering to determine the amount of effort to expend is that if $1 of additional effort applied to a component part is likely to yield $10 or more of savings in the current project, then the effort should be expended. Otherwise, shift the effort to another component of the overall value engineering job to be done. Thus, a reasonable rate of return is 10:1; that is, $10 of savings are generated for every $1 spent on value engineering.

FUNCTION, COST, AND RELIABILITY

Figure 7–3 shows function, cost, and reliability arranged in the form of a triangle. The proper combination of all three requirements would place a design somewhat in the center of the triangle, as in the case of good competitive market design. In

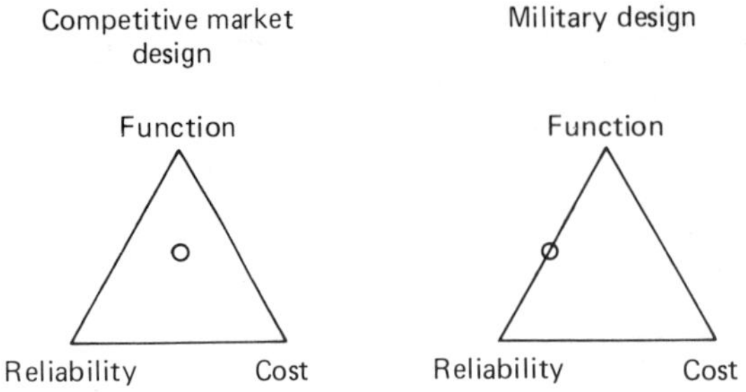

FIGURE 7–3. Function, Cost, and Reliability.

the automotive field the blending of function and cost is probably more nearly achieved than in any other field of engineering. An automobile battery guaranteed for twenty-four months usually lasts just that long. A few give out sooner and a few last longer, but the majority last only as guaranteed.

NEW PRODUCT PLANNING AND DEVELOPMENT

Product planning is a broad and creative activity (characterized by objectivity), whereas *product development* is an analytical and specific activity (characterized by subjectivity).

New product planning generally refers to the activities concerned with: choosing the product to make; deciding on the product specifications; determining the time when and place where it should be made; establishing price and price policy; and establishing procedures for the successful introduction of the product. It is a high-level staff function.

Product development is therefore considered to be somewhat more restricted. It is chiefly concerned with finding and developing ideas within the framework established by product planning. In most instances, it is an exceedingly complex activity and is thought to encompass initial development, subsequent change to incorporate new ideas, and the determination of new applications or uses.

It can be stated that whereas product planning is not directly concerned with problems relating to product idea and to product completion, new product development is directly concerned with such problems. New product development encompasses work directed toward the production of useful products to meet specific performance requirements. This includes advanced design engineering, product engineering, pilot plant operation, and preliminary marketing.

When a manufacturer plans to introduce a new technical product, he realizes that he should do some market research to determine what the prospective customers want and the price they will pay for it.

If the product is a radical innovation, customers seldom know what they want. The candid customers will tell you their wants are nebulous and that they have not yet figured them out. They generally say something like, "I'll take the product that does the most at the lowest price."

The problems of new product development and planning involve the state of the art, the entrepreneur's capabilities, and the customer's wants. They are all interdependent in a complex way. Electronic equipment producers need transistors, diodes, and intergrated circuits today, whereas in the past receiving tubes were adequate. Solid state devices would have been very useful but they were not available, so no one gave them a thought. Now the state of the art and the capability of electronic component producers is such that all kinds of original equipment producers need solid state devices.

When a customer becomes aware that he needs a product, he is not certain of the operating and physical characteristics it should have or the price he can afford to pay for it. Oftentimes he undertakes a great deal of study and trial before he knows these things well enough to intelligently purchase the product.

Now, assume that the manufacturer is aggressive and wants to be a jump ahead of his competitors. He wants to market a product before the need for it becomes general so that he can benefit from the initial high-profit period. To do this, he must have good timing to detect when the state of the art is ready for product development and acceptance by customers. An entrepreneur needs sufficient development time and he doesn't want to risk development expenditures on a product that is too far ahead of the state of the art. Unfortunately, an entrepreneur cannot rely upon customers to tell him these things.

VALUE ENGINEERING AND SYSTEMS APPROACH

So many factors interact in new product planning and development that the value engineering and the systems engineering approach—in which all the variables can be related and the product optimized over the entire set—is well worth exploring. Such an approach, when properly executed, can result in a much better impedance match between product function and price. The common goal of the entire system is subject to the design goals of each of its small components.

Figure 7–4 presents a sketch of the market for a complex technical product. The arrows between boxes indicate that each element helps to determine another. The focal point of the system is the block at the upper left marked "functions to be performed by product." This is the link that unites the manufacturer and the customer for the product.

Products perform functions, which include operational characteristics, physical characteristics, appearance, and relationships between the elements that have beneficial effects on the customers' operations. An oscilloscope, for example, may be valuable in a research laboratory but of no use in a hardware store. The beneficial effect of the research in which the oscilloscope plays a part may have a monetary worth to the customer. But the customer's idea of this monetary worth may not be accurate—usually it is underestimated. Promotional efforts, such as advertising and personal selling, can communicate facts to prospective customers that will enlarge their appreciation of such values. Nevertheless, the customer is bound to equate the monetary worth of the product's beneficial effects with the selling price of the nearest equivalent product or, perhaps, with the cost of making a change in present products used in plant operations.

Product functions dictate design. Design, in turn, affects manufacturing costs, which, in conjunction with unit overhead and distribution costs, plus profit, determine the selling price.

At the top of the figure, there is a box labeled "state of the art." It influences at least three other elements directly. They are product design, customer's operations, and the nearest equivalent product. The customer makes a comparison between his allowable buying price and the selling price of the product. If it appears favorable to him, he will make the purchase. The sum of many purchases made by many customers will cause a reduced per-unit overhead and distribution costs, thus providing a feedback that lowers selling price and generates additional sales. In turn, the increased sales make possible the adoption of production processes to high-volume production, providing a second feedback that further reduces selling price and generates still more sales.

The system is regenerative, if it goes at all, because the parts have to contribute to the favorable comparison at the bottom. Systems engineering goes about exploring this system in a methodical way, to deter-

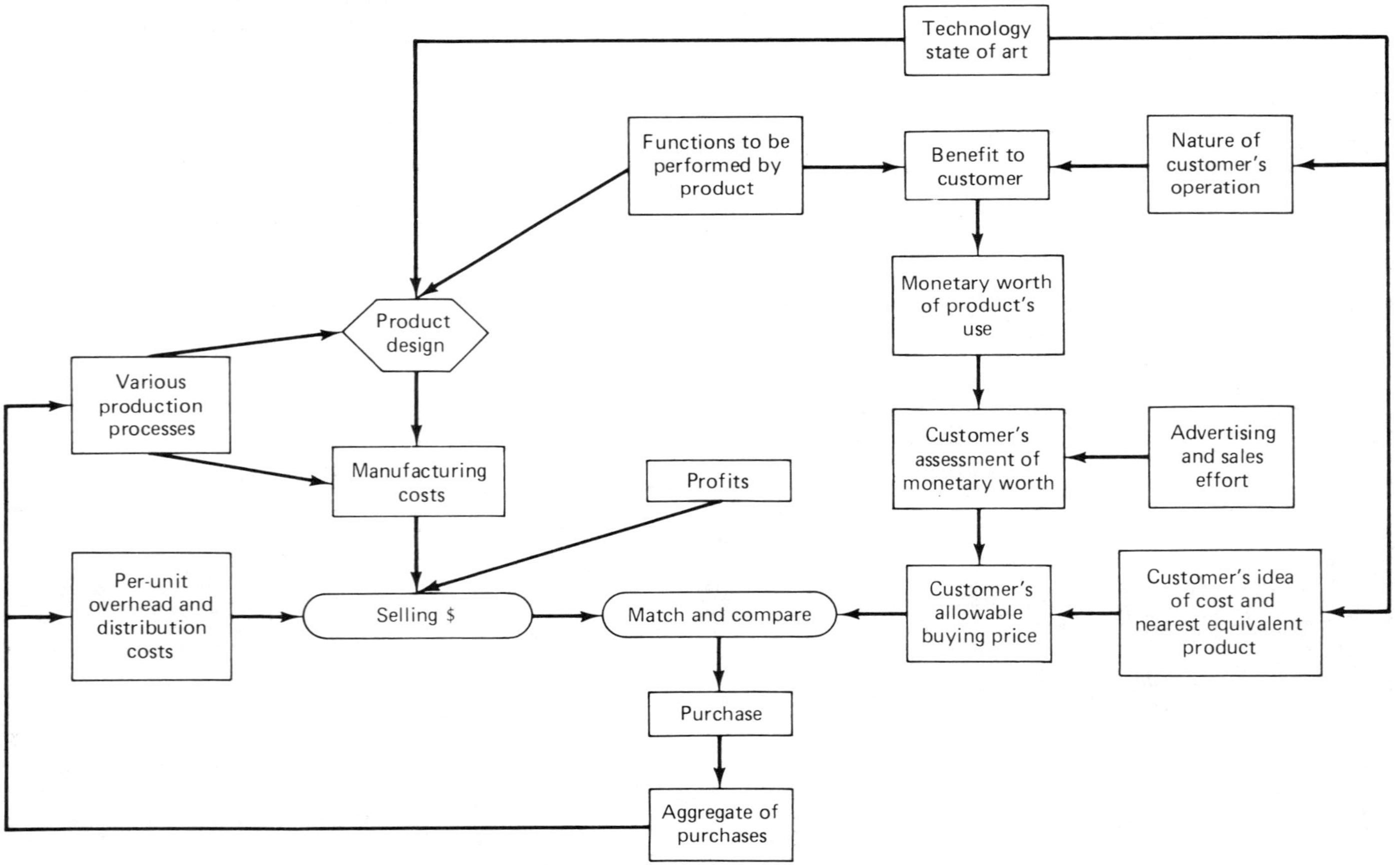

FIGURE 7–4. Flow Diagram of New Product Development, Production, and Marketing.

mine ahead of time whether all the parts will work and come together to bring about a profitable product. The first step is to study the whole diagram in relation to the proposed product. This includes a preliminary list of functions and specifications, state of the art in the design of this kind of product, nature of operation by customers, competing products, manufacturing processes available to make the product, and state-of-the-art advances in customer's operation. From these data a given set of specifications will probably be conceived from which a model of the product should be made.

Summary

Value engineering is concerned with the elimination or modification of anything that contributes to the cost of a product that is not necessary for needed performance, reliability, or quality. Specifically, value engineering constitutes a systematic and creative effort directed toward analyzing each component to ensure that its essential function is provided at the lowest overall cost.

Value engineering is not an isolated function. It serves all organizational divisions: design engineering, manufacturing, procurement, marketing, accounting, and top management. When value engineering methodology and techniques are applied to new product planning and development, the net results should be a marketable product at an increased profit, an improved competitive position, and a more active and alert organization.

Questions

1. Comment on the following statement. Value analysis is nothing more than cost reduction.
2. Describe the functional approach to value analysis.
3. How does Lawrence Miles define value analysis?
4. What are the usual methods used in a value analysis study?
5. What is value engineering? How does it differ from value analysis?
6. What are the seven basic elements of value engineering methodology?
7. List the six phases of a value engineering job plan and what is done under each phase.
8. Pareto's law was developed by Alfredo Pareto, an Italian, while studying the concentration of wealth and income in his native country. What interest does a value engineer have in applying this law?
9. What rule of thumb can be used by a manager of value engineering to determine the amount of effort to expend on a particular product or component?

10. Distinguish between new product planning and new product development.
11. Should a product design engineer design to cost or to function? Why?
12. Describe the flow diagram for new product development, production, and marketing.
13. Select an existing product or component that you strongly believe could benefit from value engineering. Consider function, design, material and production costs, quality, reliability, and maintainability. Present your suggestions to your classmates or supervisor.

Bibliography

American Society of Tool and Manufacturing Engineers. *Value Engineering in Manufacturing*. Englewood Cliffs, N.J.: Prentice-Hall, 1967.

Fallow, Carlos. *Value Analysis to Improve Productivity*. New York: Wiley Interscience, 1971.

Heller, Edward D. *Value Management: Value Engineering and Cost Reduction*. Menlo Park, Calif.: Addison-Wesley, 1971.

Herzog, Donald R. "Value Engineering in Defense Contracting." Paper presented at the American Society of Mechanical Engineers Winter Annual Meeting, November 16–20, 1969, Los Angeles. ASME Pub. No. 69–WA/Mgt-2.

———. "New Product Planning and Development for the Defense Market." Paper presented to the Lockheed-California Co. management and published by the Lockheed Training Department, 90–16, September 3, 1963, 22 pp.

———. "New Product Planning and Pricing." *Data on Defense and Civil Systems*. (July 1968), 56 pp.

Miles, Lawrence D. *Techniques of Value Analysis and Engineering*. 2nd ed. New York: McGraw-Hill, 1972.

Mudge, Arthur E. *Value Engineering: A Systematic Approach*. New York: McGraw-Hill, 1971.

Materials Handling Principles and Equipment

Chapter 8

Materials Handling and Plant Layout

GENERAL PRINCIPLES

Materials handling is the movement of materials and supplies from one place of operation to another without affecting its value or performing any productive operation. Materials handling practices vary; however, the basic principles remain constant. Because these principles are often overlooked, the broad principles of materials handling are presented below:

1. Least handling is the best handling. The greatest economy in moving materials is secured by not handling the material at all. Since this situation rarely exists, an attempt must be made to keep handling to a minimum.
2. Standardization of methods and equipment aids the materials handling activity. Standardization of equipment results in the reduction of costs of operation, in that maintenance and repair are simplified.
3. Materials handling equipment must be selected for a number of applications. Equipment should be chosen for its flexibility; that is, make sure it can be used for multiple operations. Therefore, emphasis must be given to the flexibility with which equipment can be converted to handle other jobs.
4. Specialized equipment should be kept to a minimum. Materials handling operations requiring special equipment are costly. Normally, first cost, cost of operation, and maintenance costs are greater for special equipment than for standard equipment.
5. Volume dictates the method of handling materials. The number of pieces to be moved determines the method of handling. Regardless of the size, shape, or value of an item to be moved, the first question to be answered before the selection of method for moving is, How many pieces are to be moved?
6. Advanced planning on materials handling methods and equipment should be carried on simultaneously with other planning activities and undertakings, with full recognition of present and future factors. The most essential phase of any program is planning. To be effective, planning activities in any organization must be coordinated. As an example, some of the factors requiring advanced planning are:
   a. Protection required against weather or breakage.
   b. Legal and physical restrictions in reference to transportation.
   c. The possibility of using utilized loads.
   d. The standardization of equipment and methods.
   e. Combining materials handling methods.
   f. Safety hazards involved.
7. Lengths and number of moves of materials should be kept to a minimum. Movement paths of material should be studied for the possibility of reducing back-hauling and distance of moves,

with a view to improving utilization of equipment and personnel.

8. The rated capacities of equipment should never be exceeded. Overloading causes excessive wear of equipment and creates additional accident potential.
9. All materials handling operations should be analyzed for improvement possibilities by elimination, combination, or simplification. Combination of operations may result in the simplification and reduction of the number of times that material has to be handled.
10. Selection of materials handling equipment is based on the economies of operation. These economies are measured in cost of moving the materials. Greater payloads for each handling operation will result in less handling cost per piece.
11. Physical state of materials is a factor in determining what materials handling equipment is needed. Those familiar with materials handling recognize this principle. Molten metal cannot be contained in a plastic container as it requires a container capable of withstanding intense heat. Likewise, acids cannot be contained in a cardboard container.
12. Straight-line flow. The shortest distance between two given points is a straight line. The time required to travel a given distance is reduced by following a straight line.
13. All materials handling operations should follow a defined method. What causes variation in the length of time required for handling a given product? The method used in picking up, carrying to, setting down, and returning from is always the source of variation. The standardization of the method will provide a basis for determining handling requirements. It should be recognized that normally the establishment of this method will not require refinement to be as detailed as it is in studies such as micromotion analysis.
14. Short, irregular moves lend themselves to manual materials handling. Some materials handling operations do not occur with any degree of repetitiveness. The use of equipment for such an operation may be much more costly than manpower. When moves are short and irregular, and load capacity of men is not exceeded, it may be more economical to use manpower.
15. Wherever practicable, materials should be pre-positioned for the handling operations. Consideration should be given to the following handling operations, that is, pre-positioning moves such as placing:
    a. Containers in a position to facilitate picking up.
    b. Containers on a conveyor in such a manner as to reduce accidents and lessen equipment damage.
    c. Materials so as not to obstruct other materials movements, will result in reduced materials and equipment damage and a reduction in number of accidents.
16. Wherever practicable, materials should be moved in horizontal plane or with the aid of gravity. When loading and unloading, personnel have to reach either down or up, and excessive effort is used which might have been greatly reduced if the workplace layout had been planned. The ideal lifting position is at the waist. The nearer to the waist that a container or part can be picked up and disposed, the greater will be the efficiency.

The main principles of materials handling are listed in Figure 8–1.

1. PRINCIPLE OF STRAIGHT-LINE FLOW. THE MOVEMENT OF MATERIAL BETWEEN ANY TWO POINTS SHOULD TRAVEL BY WAY OF THE SHORTEST DISTANCE. This is based on the old principle that "a straight line is the shortest distance between two points." In our consideration, it does not have to be a STRAIGHT line, but should always be the SHORTEST distance.
2. PRINCIPLE OF CONTINUOUS FLOW. MATERIAL SHOULD MOVE CONTINUOUSLY ALONG ANY PRODUCTION LINE. Material should always move as smoothly as possible. Spasmodic or interrupted flow causes confusion and delay.
3. PRINCIPLE OF CONCENTRATION OF OPERATION. IN MOVEMENT OF MATERIAL, THE OPERATION SHOULD BE LIMITED IN DISTANCE AND AREA COVERED. This principle stresses the idea that operations spread over too much area cause problems in handling and supervision, which do not occur in more compact operations. However, it is unwise to limit a "production line" or area to the point of congestion.
4. PRINCIPLE OF EFFICIENT HANDLING. IN THE MOVEMENT OF MATERIAL THERE SHOULD BE THE LEAST POSSIBLE AMOUNT OF HANDLING. The constant picking up and setting down of material is wasteful of time and energy, ties up the use of equipment, and causes damage. The principle can be applied to both manual and mechanical operations as follows:
   a. Principle of Efficient Handling as Applied to Manual Movement: IN MOVING MATERIAL THERE SHOULD BE AS LITTLE MANUAL HANDLING AS POSSIBLE. Although it is the basis for all materials handling, manual handling should be reduced whenever possible.
   b. Principle of Efficient Handling as Applied to Mechanical Movement: To reduce handling, MATERIAL SHOULD BE MOVED WITH MECHANICAL EQUIPMENT WHENEVER POSSIBLE AND EFFICIENT. PROPER USE OF MECHANICAL EQUIPMENT IS ONE OF THE BEST WAYS FOR LOWERING COST AND INCREASING SPEED.
5. PRINCIPLE OF WORK. THE GREATEST AMOUNT OF WORK SHOULD BE DONE IN THE LEAST AMOUNT OF TIME (MAN-HOURS). Mere speed of movement does not necessarily mean a good operation. The PRINCIPLE OF WORK suggests the most efficient handling for the amount of time spent. Often, apparently slow movements may be efficient if they are steady, continuous, direct, and synchronized—balanced operation of work is the most pressing problem in manufacturing today.

FIGURE 8–1. Main Principles of Materials Handling.

CONVEYORS

A conveyor, excluding mobile units, is defined as a device to move materials along a defined path. The storage and shipment of units in large quantities and materials handling depend upon each other. Since conveyors are one of the major devices for the handling of materials, the task of getting the highest efficiency and economy out of the use of conveyors involves selecting the right conveyor or system of conveyors for the job. Today, the conveyor is recognized as one of the more important tools in the materials handling field. It is a cost-saving, energy-saving, and profit-making modern mechanism. The principles of its use are:

1. Before a conveyor is selected as a purely transporting medium, the economics involved should be studied. The cost of placing the item on, or removing it from, the conveyor may exceed the value gained through the use of the conveyor.
2. Gravity conveyors should be used where practicable. When a movement analysis indicates that some type of conveyance is required to facilitate the manufacturing operation, roller-feed gravity conveyors are used to advantage in the loading or unloading of small containers as they reduce handling and the need for industrial trucks, and thus reduce detention time. Maintenance cost for gravity feed conveyors is considerably lower than for other means of conveyance.
3. Conveyor speed controls rate of materials delivery. The rate at which materials are delivered can be controlled by conveyors.
4. Whenever practicable, conveyors and conveyor fixtures should be standardized. The standardization of conveyor specifications for the purpose of being able to make repairs and replacements aids in the reduction of operating costs.
5. Where practicable, conveyor loading and unloading should be done by direct labor or mechanical handling devices. A basic principle in any operation improvement program is, "If you can't remove it, improve it." If the material must be moved, attempt to combine other operations with the move. Utilize direct labor where practicable by combining operations and moves. Inspection activities may lend themselves to this type of improvement. An example of this might be as follows: Two lines are running parallel. The material is to be transferred from one line to the other. An inspection operation could be given in the routing. The inspection should be carried on by the person moving the material from one line to another. The mechanical handling device would be a matter of removing the personnel and thus reducing manual handling.
6. Conveyor fixtures should be easy to load and unload. Efficiency decreases, if in the loading and unloading of con-

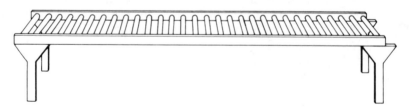

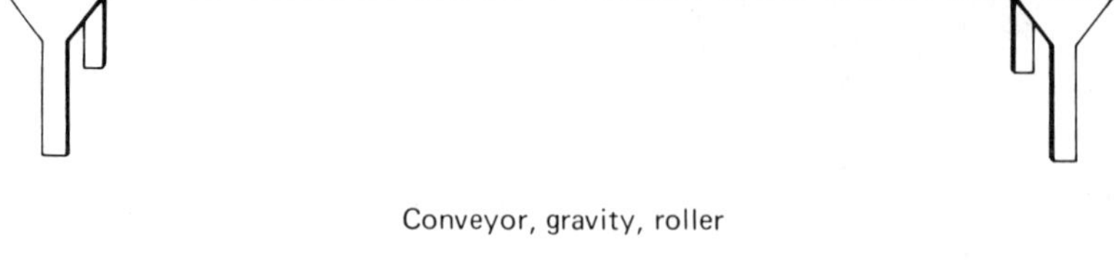

Conveyor, gravity, roller

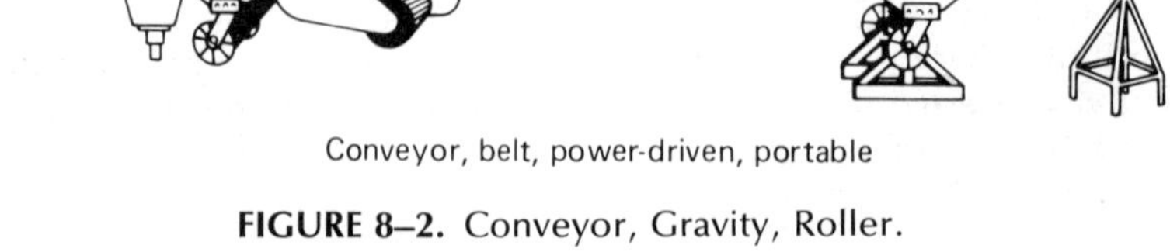

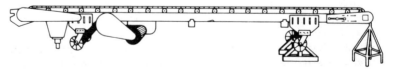

Conveyor, belt, power-driven, portable

FIGURE 8–2. Conveyor, Gravity, Roller.

veyor fixtures, there is difficulty in loading or removing parts from conveyor fixtures.

7. Synchronization of conveyors eliminates waits at transfer points and destination. Another advantage of the variable speed conveyor is that it can be set so as to tie in with other lines or operations.
8. Conveyor installations must provide adequate clearances for industrial trucks. This applies not only to the vertical plane, but also to the horizontal plane. In conveyor installations, ample clearance should be provided for industrial trucks and loads to be carried.

Figure 8–2 depicts the gravity-type roller conveyor, and the portable, power-driven belt conveyor powered by a gasoline engine or electric motor.

INDUSTRIAL TRUCKING

Industrial trucks are defined as mobile equipment and accessories designed for handling materials in intraplant or on-area facilities. This covers a wide variety of mechanical equipment, each designed to perform some materials handling job efficiently. No one unit will perform all operations. Rules for economic utilization of industrial trucks are as follows:

1. Maximum utilization of equipment requires accurate movement data. The answers to the questions, How long does it take a fork truck to go to storage area? or Where will truck No. 7 be at 10:30 A.M.? would aid in the utilization of industrial trucks. Complete movement data will aid planning activities of the organization.
2. An economic balance exists between the amount of equipment used and the volume of materials handled. Too often the amount of equipment available is not sufficient. This results in the use of more costly means of moving materials or failure to keep up with the schedule. Sometimes too many units are available; consequently, some units are idle. Through proper performance records and planning, the most economical number of operating units can be determined.
3. The distance to be traveled is the principal factor in determining the proper equipment. How far? will determine the equipment to be used. A truck train is more economical to use for long hauls than the fork truck. In some instances manual movement is more economical when the distance is just a few feet.
4. Industrial trucking operational costs should be analyzed. It is important that an operational cost record be kept of every unit of equipment to provide information which, among other things, may be used to improve preventive maintenance and the selection of new equipment.

Figure 8–3 shows a typical forklift truck used for in-plant hauling.

AUTOMATIC STORAGE AND RETRIEVAL SYSTEMS[1]

Automatic storage and retrieval systems (AS/RS) were first used in warehouses and distribution centers where inventory control and high-volume order filling were of foremost importance. However, there is now a growing tendency to apply AS/RS in manufacturing facilities, and to link the storage system with manufacturing floor operations.

AS/RS has the capacity to store a multitude of unit loads and retrieve any specific

[1]The following material is excerpted, by permission, from *Basics of Materials Handling* (Pittsburgh: Material Handling Institute, 1981).

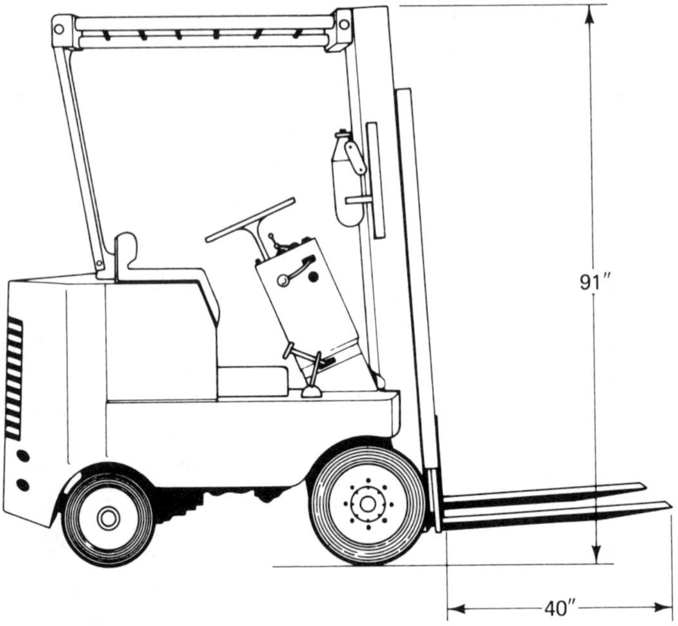

Truck, forklift, solid or semi-solid rubber tires, 4,000-pound, 144-inch lift

Type of power: Gasoline or electric

Load center: 24 inches

Standard operating aisle: 10 feet with 40″ load length

Application: This model is most widely used in the manufacturing industries. Because of its versatility, it can be used for most general medium-duty inside factories and warehouses. It is capable of entering rail cars for loading and unloading, as well as stacking supplies to a height of 20 feet.

FIGURE 8–3. Truck, Forklift, Solid or Semisolid Rubber Tires.

one within a couple of minutes. Computers are being used to direct the activities of AS/RS. They are also used with systems involving conveyors, stacker cranes, order-picking trucks, and others. The computers involved are medium-power units costing much less than the traditional business computers.

The system illustrated in Figure 8–4 is currently in operation at a manufacturing plant. A three-aisle unit-load storage system and a six-aisle miniload system operate together to supply materials to the manufacturing floor within precise schedules. The primary function of the unit-load system is to supply materials to the miniload

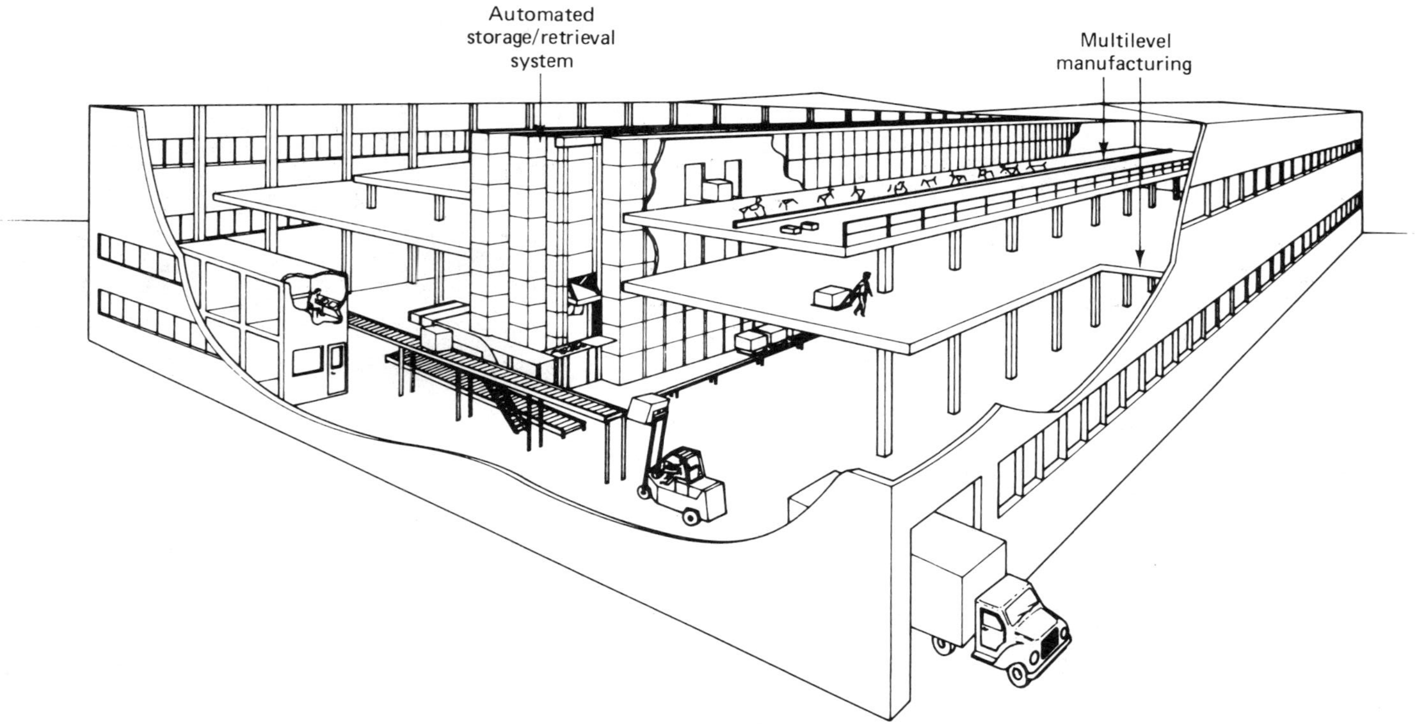

FIGURE 8–4. Automated S/R System.

parts storage area, where parts to be assembled are stored in kits. Operators place retrieved parts in containers that are conveyed to the manufacturing area and automatically diverted through drop zones to work stations.

In some cases, throughput levels may not justify the use of conveyors, but other equally efficient methods of transporting materials between storage and operations are desired. Depending on the levels of automation required, alternative approaches may include transfer cars traveling along rails to work stations, or electronically controlled robot vehicles following flexible guidewire paths in the floor. Having automated forward and reverse travel and self-loading and unloading capabilities, robot vehicles can operate without operator intervention. Whatever method is used, the linking of automated storage and retrieval with manufacturing represents a new dimension in industrial operations and a major step toward the ideal of the automated factory.

Economic justification for AS/RS is often complex. Labor savings alone are not enough. Some other factors that are often included in the justification are:

- Lower building cost
- 100 percent inventory control
- Lower land cost
- Improved deliveries
- Less damage to product
- Ability to put the system under computer control

The more sophisticated AS/RS are usually installed in new facilities. The trend is toward greater heights and speed, also toward more sophisticated controls. Installations keep getting bigger. You can buy preengineered modules for smaller plants and warehouses. You have a choice of control by push button, punch card, tape, or mini-computer.

At the lower level of the cost scale, you'll find the manual picking machine. Basically, it is a small, operator-controlled version of the floor-mounted automatic storage machine. It is available with or without shuttle table for fast picking of partial or full unit loads. A *unit load* is a number of items, or bulk material so arranged or restrained that the load can be picked up and moved as a single object too large or bulky for manual handling, and which upon being released will retain its initial arrangement for later movement. It is understood that large single objects too large for manual handling are also considered as unit loads. A unit will service racks up to 40 feet or more and works with payloads under 3,000 pounds (although heights and capacities will undoubtedly increase).

Figure 8–5 depicts a driverless R-Car (controlled electrically) that has been storing and retrieving pallet loads in conventional pallet racks at a raw material storage distribution facility of Texas Instruments.

FIGURE 8–5. Driverless R-Car Puts Load in a Rack.

FIGURE 8–6. The Man-A-Board Storage and Retrieval System.

The R-Cars are an integral part of a midrise storage and retrieval system. Rapistan, a division of Lear Siegler, Inc., Grand Rapids, Michigan, served as prime contractor for the system. Figure 8–6 illustrates another type of storage and retrieval system.

Facilities or Equipment Layout

This section is devoted to facilities layout and materials handling. These two activities are so closely related and normally have such an impact on each other that they have to be discussed together. The arrangement of the equipment in a plant greatly affects the distance a product must flow from start to finish. Similarly, the flow of the products should be the governing factor in the re-layout of all facilities and the planning for new facilities. That is, the equipment should be arranged to provide for the minimum total distance traveled for all products produced.

INTRODUCTION

Facilities layout is the functional arrangement of equipment in an existing or contemplated work system. It includes the planning necessary to determine and develop a physical relationship between the grounds, buildings, equipment, and operations in order to provide the maximum degree of economy and effectiveness in processing. The term *work system* refers to all systems that perform work regardless of the type. It includes not only industrial plants but also offices, electronic data processing centers, service facilities, and R&D laboratories.

The primary objective of facilities layout is to locate the equipment and facilities in such a manner as to permit the flow of materials at the lowest cost, with the least amount of handling, and in the shortest amount of time. A poor layout will cause increased costs owing to the necessity of handling materials over longer distances, and the need for additional handling of equipment, closer supervision, more in-process storage, and so on.

The layout of any production facility should be such that the material flows through it as quickly and as easily as possible. Under ideal conditions the materials will enter into receiving, flow through the processes in a straight line, and exit at the shipping department as a finished product. However, this is not often the case, since ideal conditions are seldom possible. The closest one can come to this situation is the continuous mass production of a single product.

LAYOUT ARRANGEMENTS

There are three main layout arrangements with which the industrial engineer should be familiar. It should be pointed out that many manufacturing organizations may have more than one of these layouts in existence.

1. Product layout
2. Process layout
3. Fixed material layout

Product Layout

Layout by product is also commonly called production-line or assembly-line layout. It is typical for automobiles and household appliance manufacturing associated with mass production. The equipment and work places are arranged in a line in the sequence that operations are performed on the product. With the current trend toward more automation, product layout will be more common in factories in the future.

In this type of layout, the production rate is based upon the speed of the slowest machine. Thus, it is evident that there can be much idle machine time. For this reason, layout by product is usually feasible only when:

1. There is relatively high volume over a long period of time.
2. There is one (or a few) standard product(s).
3. The demand is fairly constant.

The advantages of the layout by product include:

1. Less time in process.
2. Less in-process inventory.
3. Less flow space requirements.
4. Lower skill levels required, usually semiskilled operators.
5. Less need for detailed scheduling of production control.
6. Conveyorized movement of materials.

The disadvantages include:

1. Idle machine capacity—one machine depends on the output of the previous one.
2. Duplication of equipment—if the same type of equipment is used twice in the cycle, it is common practice to have two pieces of the same equipment.
3. A breakdown or delay at any point in the line can shut down the entire line.
4. Specialized machines have little flexibility.

Process Layout

In a layout by process all machines and work of the same nature are grouped together in the same area or department. Thus, the products or materials are moved between departments or cost centers, in accordance with the sequence of operations for that product. The same types of machines are grouped together, for example, drill presses, lathes, milling machines, and so on.

Layout by process is usually best when:

1. There is relatively low volume on individual items.
2. There is a wide variety of products.
3. Equipment is expensive and difficult to move.
4. There is an intermittent demand for the product.

These conditions adequately describe most of the work found in intermittent activities. Thus, this type of layout is used widely in various manufacturing and repair installations.

The advantages of a layout by process include:

1. Better machine utilization—machines are not dependent upon others.
2. Breakdowns do not delay other machines.
3. Lower investment in machines is possible.
4. Great flexibility is possible in output, design of products, and methods of fabrication.

The disadvantages include:

1. Higher in-process inventory—materials are stacked adjacent to machines to prevent delays.
2. Greater amount of floor space required.
3. Frequent movement of materials between operations and departments.
4. More highly skilled people required to handle the variety of work a machine can accomplish.
5. Many inspections required during a sequence of operations.
6. Problems arise in maintaining good labor and equipment balance.

Fixed Material Layout

In this layout the major components or material remains in a fixed position. It does not move. All tools, equipment, material, and men are brought to it. Rebuild, repair, and assembly work is performed with layout by fixed position in many instances.

This type of layout is used when

1. The cost of moving the major piece of material is high.
2. There is low volume.

This layout would be used in shipyards, or for large construction projects. However, it should be noted that the various shops that produce parts in support of the operations would be laid out by process.

Combinations

The three basic types of layout described above are seldom found in their pure form. Most manufacturing organizations use some combination or mixture of these types of layout.

GENERAL PROCEDURE

The best means of achieving an effective facilities layout is to follow a prescribed and systematic procedure. As no two layouts are ever alike, there are no detailed procedures available that take into consideration each and every phase of a layout problem.

State the Problem

Clearly define the scope and nature of the problem:

1. Location of the area to be laid out.
2. General overall layout.
3. Planning the detailed layout.
4. Installation of the layout.

Gather All the Basic Data

A solution to a problem usually becomes readily apparent if the "right" facts are gathered and analyzed in the proper perspective. For a facilities layout project, information is gathered on materials and products, machinery and equipment, men, and other factors that may be involved. Some of the most important details usually required are:

Process sheets and material flow
Product specifications
Production schedule (volume and rate)
Time standards
Operations to be performed pcApp

- Manufacturing services needed (for example, compressed gases or compressed air)
- Equipment lists and the specifications of the equipment
- Inventory policies
- Productive capacity of machines involved
- Availability of space and requirements
- Bills of materials
- Building plans and specifications
- Safety and fire restriction

Analyze the Data

These data will necessarily determine the development of the ideal layout and all facets must be thoroughly analyzed for the optimum interrelationships.

The layout is normally the first step in the planning phase of a new plant, and the building is then designed about the layout. This is most important in process industry, such as chemical and pharmaceutical plants. However, the layout is seldom complete at this stage since many changes are made in compromises with the architect to allow for economical building design and construction.

The re-layout of existing facilities and the layout of expansion to existing facilities require that consideration be given to all restrictions to the layout during the design stage. Perhaps one of the best ways to ensure that the effects of all restrictions are allowed for is to take a blueprint of the building into the area and check that each column, fire sprinkler, and so on, are shown on the blueprint.

Flow Pattern and Work Stations

An analysis and evaluation of the basic data will indicate the basic plan for the layout, that is, process or product. After the selection of the basic plan, a general pattern of the product flow should be determined. Oftentimes industrial plants are a mix of the two basic types of plant layout.

A useful tool that can be used to help determine the flow of materials between departments or work centers is the travel chart or the from–to chart. This chart is very useful in determining the distance, the volume, or distance-volume that materials must be moved among the various work centers.

The individual work stations or production center should be laid out for the most effective performance of the operation, taking into consideration space for storage of tools and equipment, and materials, ease of servicing the equipment, and worker safety and comfort.

Making the Layout. The preliminary layout may be accomplished during the analysis phase since the two steps are normally performed together. Every shift or change made to the layout may and usually does require further analysis to determine its effect upon the entire system.

Two types of layout models commonly made today are the two-dimensional and three-dimensional layout. *Two-dimensional* layout is the most common and least expensive to make. The primary disadvantage of this layout is its lack of the third dimension—height. Thus, additional care must be taken to allow height restrictions.

This layout shows the floor area required by the pieces of equipment, workplaces, departments, and so on. It can be made by drawing the outline of the equipment to scale directly on the layout paper. However, an easier way widely followed today is to use plastic templates with adhesive backs and plastic grid paper for the layout sheet. Both items can be obtained with a matte finish that allows writing on the layout. The great advantage of these materials is the ease of changing the layout. Another advantage of the plastic templates is that they can be obtained with dotted lines showing the outline of the path of all movable parts on pieces of equipment. Thus they assist the layout man by ensuring that adequate space is provided for the equipment.

Three-dimensional layout provides for an excellent presentation and assists the plant layout engineer because it includes the third dimension, height. These models are often made with all structural members and overhead equipment also included. The building is usually sealed in clear plastic, which is easily removable.

The expense of this type of layout can sometimes be justified if visualization of the layout is enhanced (models can be shifted quickly for study of optional arrangements) or if process equipment is so complex that a three-dimensional layout is necessary to ensure that all factors are considered.

The sequence of operations is the basis for the flow of materials in many layout plans. As a result, the process chart in its various forms is the most helpful of all devices. The from–to chart showing the flow of materials between each origin point and each destination is particularly useful in conjunction with other types of charts used in the analysis of flow.

The information used in the various types of forms is then transferred into a flow diagram, which graphically presents the relationships from the product flow. Several changes usually are made to get an optimum flow diagram. This then becomes the basis for a layout of the departmental flow space requirements. The required floor area for each department is then fitted into an initial area diagram, later to be revised until a final area diagram is approved.

Final Layout

Now that the area layout is complete, the work of actual placement of the equipment can begin. All restrictions encountered in the gathering of facts must be taken into account at this time. After the layout has been completed and the facilities layout engineer is satisfied with the final form, the layout should be checked out in the area. This may save much adjusting of the layout after its approval by a higher authority and the embarrassment of having to seek approval again after changes.

The final layout should be reviewed with and signed by representatives of the operating and service departments. Only after these departments have given their approval should the layout be submitted to the plant manager for his approval.

The facilities layout engineer has the responsibility to follow up as the equipment is being installed and during the initial operations in the newly laid out area. The importance of the follow-up is emphasized.

Plant Layout for Better Materials Handling

INTRODUCTION

One very important factor affecting handling costs is the physical layout of the plant. Every time parts or materials move, it costs you money. And, if parts and materials must travel back and forth unnecessarily during processing, costs can rise to alarming heights. Any steps that can be taken to minimize such travel are worth considering.

PLANT LAYOUT

In the ideal plant, raw materials would enter at one end, go through the various processing steps in order, and emerge at the other end without any backtracking or side trips. Obviously, this is not possible in most plants. It could be achieved only by a company that produced a single type of product, and that could start from the ground up to build a one-story plant in a straight line. For most companies, actual plant layout represents a compromise between this ideal and the actual space available, location of departments that cannot be moved, and the processing needs of a variety of items.

Yet, practically every company will find worthwhile opportunities to reduce handling costs by studying layout and processing sequences and by rearranging the ground plan to achieve minimum total travel for each part and material. In addition, it's possible to speed the flow of materials, reduce accident hazards, and eliminate handling bottlenecks. And, in planning a new plant, it's possible to avoid built-in handling costs by considering layout long before construction starts. Future headaches can be eased by making the new plant as flexible as possible from the handling point of view. In other words, plan the plant not only for the processing system you now expect to use, but also for possible future changes.

If you're planning a new multistory plant to process bulk material, you'll want to provide holes through the floors to allow passage of chutes and tubes. But you'll be wise to have bracing members arranged in such a way that new holes can be put through at almost any spot you may desire in the future. Otherwise, if you later move equipment and cut new holes, you may seriously weaken the floor.

If your plant is already built, there is not much you can do about the location of girders or of certain special equipment (in the example in Figure 8–7, for instance, the heat-treat department is considered immobile), but you will still want to keep next year's needs in mind when planning tomorrow's changes. Perhaps it might be better to spend a little more for portable, rather than fixed, conveyors so that when methods change, you'll be able to rearrange the conveyors easily. Or perhaps you should think twice about putting that hole through the north wing's ceiling. Maybe you'll want to use the second story for storage later on and won't be able to because the floor has been weakened too much.

Naturally, there are occasions when permanent installations should be made. But they should be studied from all angles before actual installation starts. It's often worth paying a premium—in actual money or in a slightly-less-than-perfect setup—to keep your layout flexible and ready for future changes.

methods study.

PLANNING SPATIAL RELATIONSHIPS

What steps should you take in finding the best possible compromise between the space you have available and the ideal layout? The first step is the same whether you are planning a new plant or rearranging an old one: without reference to present physical layout, make up a flow-process chart, listing the operations involved in making *each* of your products. Start with the delivery of the raw material, and carry the list right through to final shipping. A partial list of this type is shown in Figure 8–8. In addition to noting operations, it's important to indicate the approximate *amount* of material that must be moved—per hour, day, or week—and the frequency of movement.

Now, if you were planning a new plant and expected to make only a single item, you could simply draw a map of your floor

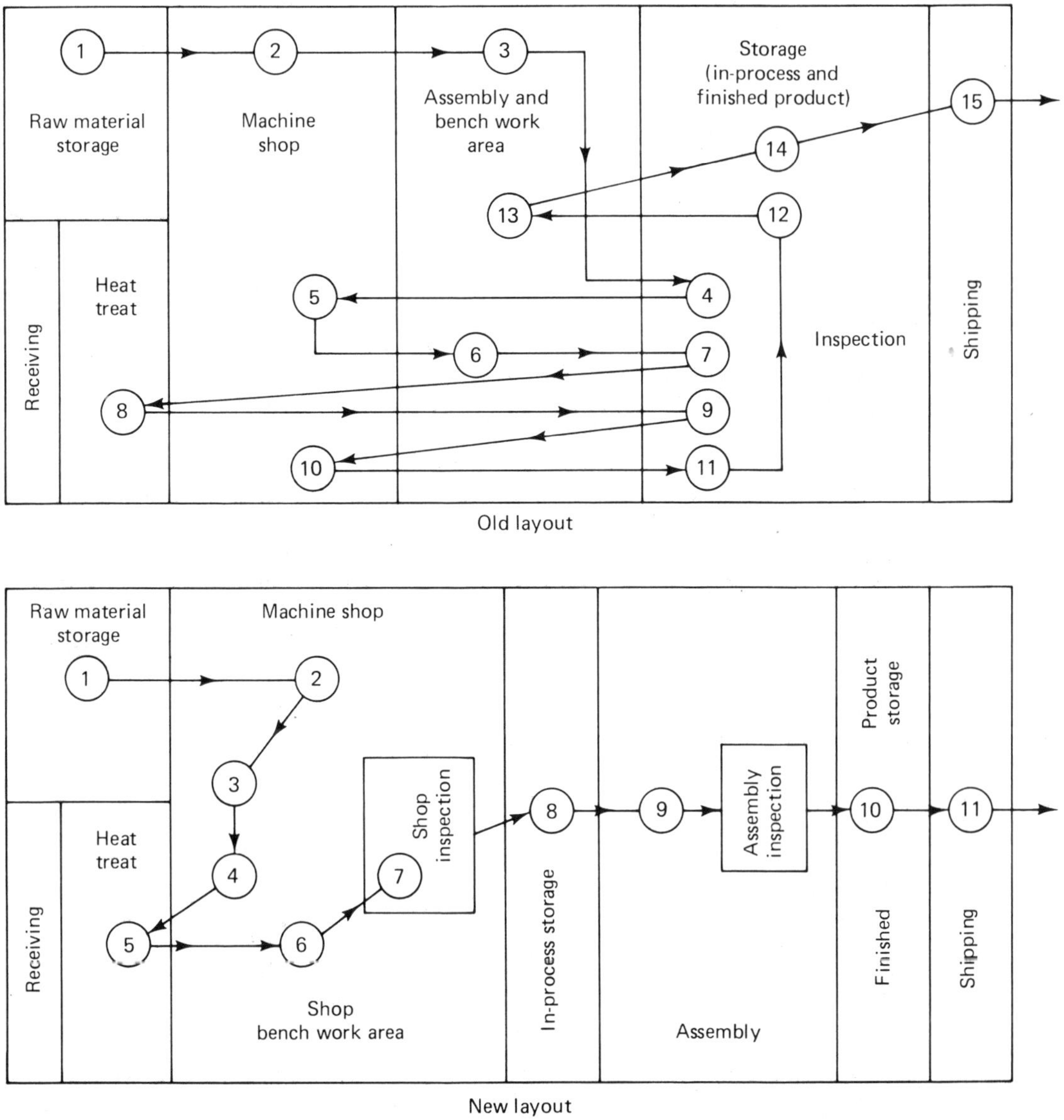

FIGURE 8–7. Plant Layout.

space, and set the operations down one after another in proper sequence, starting at one end of the plant and finishing at the other. You would, of course, have to decide how much space should be alloted to each operation, and consider other factors like aisle width, but it would be a fairly straightforward job.

Name: Donald R. Herzog, Ph.D., P.E., Consulting Industrial Engineer

Date: 2. Sept. 1982 Score ______

Product name	Flow begins	Flow ends	Date
Threaded insert	Raw material Storage	Shipping	3. Sept. 1982

Prepared by: D.R. Herzog	Section: Ind. Engineering	Approved by: K. Cizek

Process symbols and no. used: ○ Operations 7 □ Inspections 4 ⇨ Transportations ___ D Delays ___ ▽ Storages 2

Task no.	Process symbols	Description of task	Place	Machine or tools required
1	○ ➡ □ D ▽	Deliver raw material	Raw material Storage	
2	● ⇨ □ D ▽	Turn, thread on end, cut off	Machine shop	✓
3	● ⇨ □ D ▽	Clean and burr	Assembly area	✓
4	○ ⇨ ■ D ▽	Inspect	Inspection	
5	● ⇨ □ D ▽	Turn, thread, drill other end	Machine shop	✓
6	● ⇨ □ D ▽	Clean	Assembly area	✓
7	○ ⇨ ■ D ▽	Inspect	Inspection	
8	● ⇨ □ D ▽	Heat-treat	Heat-treat	✓
9	○ ⇨ ■ D ▽	Inspect	Inspection	
10	● ⇨ □ D ▽	Grind shoulder	Machine shop	✓
11	○ ⇨ ■ D ▽	Inspect	Inspection	
12	○ ⇨ □ D ▼	Store	Storage area	
13	● ⇨ □ D ▽	Assemble	Assembly area	✓
14	○ ⇨ □ D ▼	Store	Storage area	
15	○ ➡ □ D ▽	Ship	Shipping	

FIGURE 8–8. Flow-Process Chart, Old Method.

Name: Donald R. Herzog, Ph.D., P.E., Consulting Industrial Engineer

Date: 2 Sept. 1982 Score: ______

Product name	Flow begins	Flow ends	Date
Threaded insert	Raw material storage	Shipping	3. Sept. 1982

Prepared by: D. R. Herzog Section: Ind. Engineering Approved by: K. Cizek

Process symbols and no. used: ○ Operations 6 □ Inspections 1 ⇨ Transportations 2 D Delays ______ ▽ Storages 2

Task no.	Process symbols	Description of task	Place	Machine or tools required
1	○ ➡ □ D ▽	Deliver raw material	Raw material Storage	
2	● ⇨ □ D ▽	Turn, thread on end, cut off	Machine shop	✓
3	● ⇨ □ D ▽	Turn other end, thread, drill	Machine shop	✓
4	● ⇨ □ D ▽	Clean and inspect	Shop area	
5	● ⇨ □ D ▽	Heat-treat	Heat-treat	✓
6	● ⇨ □ D ▽	Grind shoulder	Shop area	✓
7	○ ⇨ ■ D ▽	Inspect	Shop inspection	
8	○ ⇨ □ D ▼	In-process storage	Storage	
9	● ⇨ □ D ▽	Assemble	Assembly inspection	✓
10	○ ⇨ □ D ▼	Store	Product storage	
11	○ ➡ □ D ▽	Ship	Shipping	
	○ ⇨ □ D ▽			
	○ ⇨ □ D ▽			
	○ ⇨ □ D ▽			
	○ ⇨ □ D ▽			

FIGURE 8–9. Flow-Process Chart, New Method

Unfortunately, few companies are in that enviable position. Most companies make more than one part or product, and most have a far-from-ideal physical plant in which to work. Plant layout then becomes a process of compromise, not only in terms of materials handling problems, but also in terms of lighting, location of plant services, servicing equipment, and so on.

Often, materials handling problems can be simplified by combining process improvement with plant rearrangement. Suppose, for instance, you produce a part that must be heat-treated twice during fabrication, and at present it moves from a production area to the heat-treating department on two occasions. One way to hold handling to a minimum might be to place the heat-treating department midway between the two production departments. If, however, travel between the first production operation and heat-treating is considerably longer, overall, than travel between the second production operation and heat-treating, the most practicable solution might well be to locate the heat-treating department right next to the first production operation, and leave a greater distance on the less-traveled route.

That's one type of solution, but there are, of course, several others. It might be possible, for instance, to eliminate one or both heat treatments by redesigning the part. It might also be possible to simplify handling by installing an induction or flame heater right on the production line. Every possible solution should be considered before a final decision is made.

Thus, the process of study, measurement, and compromise goes on. Figures 8–7 to 8–9 show a simplified example of layouts and process charts before and after rearrangement. Note that just by rearranging the plant layout, it would be possible to reduce handling a great deal. When, at the same time, unnecessary cleaning and inspections are eliminated, and the remaining bench work and inspections are performed at departmental stations, rather than in a separate area, the number of operations and the distance of travel are greatly reduced. Although this is an armchair example, it shows the methods used and the savings that can be achieved when layout, handling, and production methods are studied as a whole.

OTHER FACTORS TO CONSIDER

Spatial location is only one of the factors to be considered in planning plant layout to reduce materials handling costs. Another—and a very important—consideration is the type of handling equipment that is to be used. It works both ways: The type of equipment affects the layout; and the layout affects the type of equipment that is chosen.

Obviously, forklift trucks can't climb stairs, and cranes won't hang from skyhooks. But there are other, less obvious, factors to consider. If, for example, forklift trucks are to be used, it is good to have aisles wide enough to permit easy passage of two fully loaded trucks, without danger of bumping. Crossroads should be avoided as far as possible (a circular road around the outside of the plant or midway between the center and the walls is good, provided it is practical from other points of view). Where aisles cross, it's important to make sure there is good visibility in both directions for truck operators on both roads. Blind intersections are extremely hazardous. Therefore, it is not a good idea to locate a large, bulky machine at the corner of such an intersection. Doors, too, must be wide enough to accommodate fully loaded trucks, and provision of a separate pedestrian exit is a good safety precaution. Lighting above aisles rates special consideration. Even if no machine work is performed along aisles, a rather high level of lighting is required for safe truck operation. Floors, too, should be checked for smoothness, as well as for ability to stand constant travel by fully loaded trucks.

If cranes are to be used for handling, floor smoothness is less important, but it's still necessary to leave enough aisle space for maneuvering loads, to make sure there are no tall machines projecting into the freeway, and, of course, to make sure that the ceiling will bear the largest possible load that might be handled. Overhead conveyors, if placed close to work areas, should be well above head height and should be arranged so that they can be screened to prevent parts from dropping on workers' heads (something that happens far more often than many people realize).

Materials handling affects plant layout in still another way—as a limited factor. One company, for instance, decided to shift department locations so that one area, originally used for light assembly work, would be converted to storage. Only after all the related shifts had been made did they discover that the floor in this area could hold only one pallet-load, instead of the three-high piles they had planned. That meant they'd need three times as much storage space—or would almost have to rebuilt the plant to reinforce the floor. In the end, the change had to be abandoned and everything had to be moved back to its former location. Thus, a plant layout that does not consider materials handling problems is likely to be unsatisfactory. But when handling and layout are planned together, real savings can be achieved.

A manufacturer of fractional horsepower motors, for instance, cut travel in assembly alone from 14 to 9 miles by revising layout of the assembly department. (The mileage figures represent the total distance traveled by all parts making up a single motor as they went from one workbench and inspection station to another. Parts may move only a few feet at a time, but the distances may add up to a staggering total, as this example shows.)

In a metalworking plant, better layout improved handling efficiency so much that overtime—which previously accounted for 30 percent of labor costs—was eliminated entirely. In a plastics plant, product damage dropped to a fraction of its former cost when layout was simplified and handling reduced. Those are just a few of many examples that might be cited. Experts agree that there is always room for improvement in plant layout. The best layout becomes obsolete as new manufacturing methods are adopted and new products developed. The only way for any plant to keep on its toes is by constant study of materials handling and plant layout problems and by changes to meet new needs as they develop.

Computerized Facilities Design

No two fields are so closely related as materials handling and plant layout. When these two fields are combined, the result is called facilities design. If a problem exists in one of the areas, both of the areas must be analyzed. There exist a few traditional graphical techniques that do not directly consider materials handling but are concerned with the layout of a facility.

Several analytical plant layout techniques may be used in resolving material handling problems. Although none of these techniques results in an optimal facilities design, they consist of systematic procedures that allow the generation and evaluation of alternative plant layouts and materials handling systems. These techniques aid in the process of developing a final solution.

Travel charting, for example, is a manual improvement technique that allows the generation and evaluation of plant layouts by minimizing the volume-distance product. The most common goal in designing layouts is to minimize transportation costs or distance traveled. The volume-distance product is defined as the product of the from–to chart and the distance matrix, where the distance matrix usually consists of the rectilinear distance between department centroids. Even though the travel charting technique offers ingenious solutions, it is extremely tedious to use.

COMPUTERIZED PLANT LAYOUT

The problems of coping with the complexity of process layout have decreased since the development of a number of computerized methods during the late 1960s. Each of these methods is described briefly below. The first three computerized models cope with the complexity of the process layout problems and use heuristics—that is, common sense rules—for generating alternatives and then evaluating them.

Automated Layout Design program (ALDEP)

ALDEP (automatic layout design program) was developed by IBM in 1967. It handles only qualitative-criteria layout problems. The inputs to ALDEP include a relationship matrix and constraints such as building dimensions (size), fixed location of departments, stairways, and so on. This program begins by randomly selecting a department and placing it in the layout plan. In the next step, all remaining departments are scanned and one with a high closeness relationship rating (A-E-I-O-U-X format) is selected and placed in the layout next to the first department. If a high closeness rating cannot be found, a department is selected at random and placed in the layout. This selection process continues until all departments have been placed in the layout plan. A total score for the layout is then calculated by converting each closeness relationship to a numerical scale and adding the values of those relationships in the layout. The entire process is then repeated by starting with a different random department as the first step. This method is well suited to revisions of existing layouts.

This program is a heuristic technique for generating good layouts for examination. It can be used in an interactive mode by a facilities planning engineer who may adjust the layout as it evolves. The program is designed to manipulate up to sixty-three departments and a three-story building.

Computerized Relationship Layout Planning (CORELAP)

CORELAP (computerized relationship layout planning) is a quantitative-criteria layout program similar to ALDEP. It was developed by R. C. Lee and J. M. Moore in 1967, and later improved by R. Sepponen in 1969. It handles up to seventy departments. The inputs to CORELAP include a relationship matrix and restrictions on layout such as the building description given in length-to-width ratio and the fixed department locations. The departments can be formed by combining area modules of specific size. The relationship matrix is connected to numerical values for closeness ratios.

The computer printout is in the form of a numerical layout matrix, which must be later smoothed out by hand to produce an acceptable solution. It is interesting to note that if CORELAP were run a second time, it would derive the same solution. Unlike ALDEP, the CORELAP procedure is completely deterministic.

Computerized Relative Allocation of Facilities (CRAFT)

CRAFT (computerized relative allocation of facilities technique) was developed by G. C. Armour and Elwood S. Buffa in 1963, and refined in 1964. It uses a quantitative-criteria layout formultion and can handle up to forty departments or activity centers. It is a computerized improved heuristic technique used to develop a layout that will approach the minimal transportation cost, where the transportation cost is defined as the product of the volume-distance product and the move costs.

CRAFT is frequently used as a computerized travel charting technique. It is relatively easy to apply and offers considerable flexibility in analyzing plant layout and material handling problems. It has proved to be a valuable technique for generating and evaluating alternative facilities designs when properly applied by an engineer who understands its assumptions, shortcomings, and technical aspects. This computer program is available through the IBM Share Library.

Computerized Facilities Design (COFAD)

COFAD (computerized facilities design) is a computerized improvement heuristic technique that realistically may be used to jointly resolve the plant layout and materials handling system selection problem. COFAD consists of a plant layout solution procedure and a materials handling solution procedure. It determines, for the layout resulting from CRAFT, the costs of performing each move via each of the alternative materials handling equipment types. These costs are the input of the materials handling solution procedure. The minimal cost materials handling system that evolves from the routine is the basis for the determination of the move costs that are cycled back through the CRAFT routine. This iterative procedure continues until steady-state is reached. Although the use of COFAB is somewhat complex, it offers excellent flexibility in generating and evaluating problems and allows realistic experimentation with alternative facilities designs. COFAD, if used by someone familiar with its shortcomings, assumptions, and mechanics, can be a tremendous aid in developing a facilities design.

Plant Layout Analysis and Evaluation Technique (PLANET)

PLANET (plant layout analysis and evaluation technique) is a computerized construction heuristic technique having input and objectives similar to those of CRAFT. On the basis of interdepartment flow data, it computes the penalty cost associated with separating departments. Three heuristic algorithms are available for generating alternative configurations to be manually evaluated and adjusted by the user. The selection methods determine, via common sense evaluations of the flow data, the order in which the departments should enter the layout. Once this order is determined for each of the selection methods, a placement routine is entered which, via a trial and error procedure, determines the location for entering departments which minimizes the increase in handling costs. Different solutions may result from the placement routine for different results from the selection methods. It is very useful for generating alternative layouts when properly used by one who understands its assumptions, shortcomings, and the theoretical and practical knowledge of its construction.

STATE OF THE ART IN FACILITIES DESIGN

Over the years many principles have been developed to guide the facilities design engineer. Even so, considerable art is still involved in materials handling and plant layout problems. Application of these principles requires more of an experimentation approach than quantitative measurements and evaluation. On the other hands, considerable research has been and is being conducted with a view to achieving a more scientific approach to the solution of facilities design problems.

Applications of Industrial Robots

Another significant step toward increased automation of handling is the use of industrial robots.[2] Robotics, the science of designing and applying robots, is growing quickly. Applications of industrial robots are proliferating throughout the world.

Robots vary widely in complexity and capability. However, all have several basic components in common—a mechanical manipulator, a controller that stores data and directs movement of the manipulator, and a power supply. In a sophisticated robot, control is effected by a minicomputer.

Some robots are relatively simple devices with fixed programs designed for very specific, limited tasks. Others are easily reprogrammable and can manipulate over many axes of freedom. They have built-in memories and can be led through work sequences in the field. Mechanical arms of manipulating elements of robots can be fitted with various types of tooling, such as grasping fingers, welding heads, power tools, and paint-spraying heads. Figure 8–10 shows examples of robot applications. The following are some applications in which industrial robots are being used:

Palletizing
Die casting
Stamping
Machine loading
Welding
Plastic molding
Forging
Assembly
Hazardous environments

Industrial robots are excellent tools in hazardous applications where humans should be kept away from the operating environment. They are also well suited for rote tasks that are tedious, boring, or degrading to humans. In many cases, the introduction of robots to assembly, sorting, or manufacturing operations can provide significant jumps in productivity. As with any item of industrial equipment, robots must be carefully cost-justified for the tasks at hand, except for situations where they provide obvious safety or social benefits.

Newer generation robots are being equipped with optical sensors and TV cameras to provide visual inspection and analysis capabilities. Other types of sensors can be used to provide robots with tactile or touch-and-feel capability. Feedback systems can then be tied in with sensors to permit alterations in operating programs to be made automatically. The logical extension of such developments is an integrated system of operations involving sensors, actuators, manipulators, computers, and teaching and diagnostic equipment used in performing automated batch manufacturing.

The science of robotics has been called by some the "second industrial revolution." The first industrial revolution involved the development of machines to perform mechanical work that previously had been done only by humans. The second revolution—in its infancy but growing—has to do with incorporating intelli-

[2]This section is taken from *Basics of Material Handling,* April 1981, pp. 60–62, by permission of the Material Handling Institute, Inc. Pittsburgh, Pa.

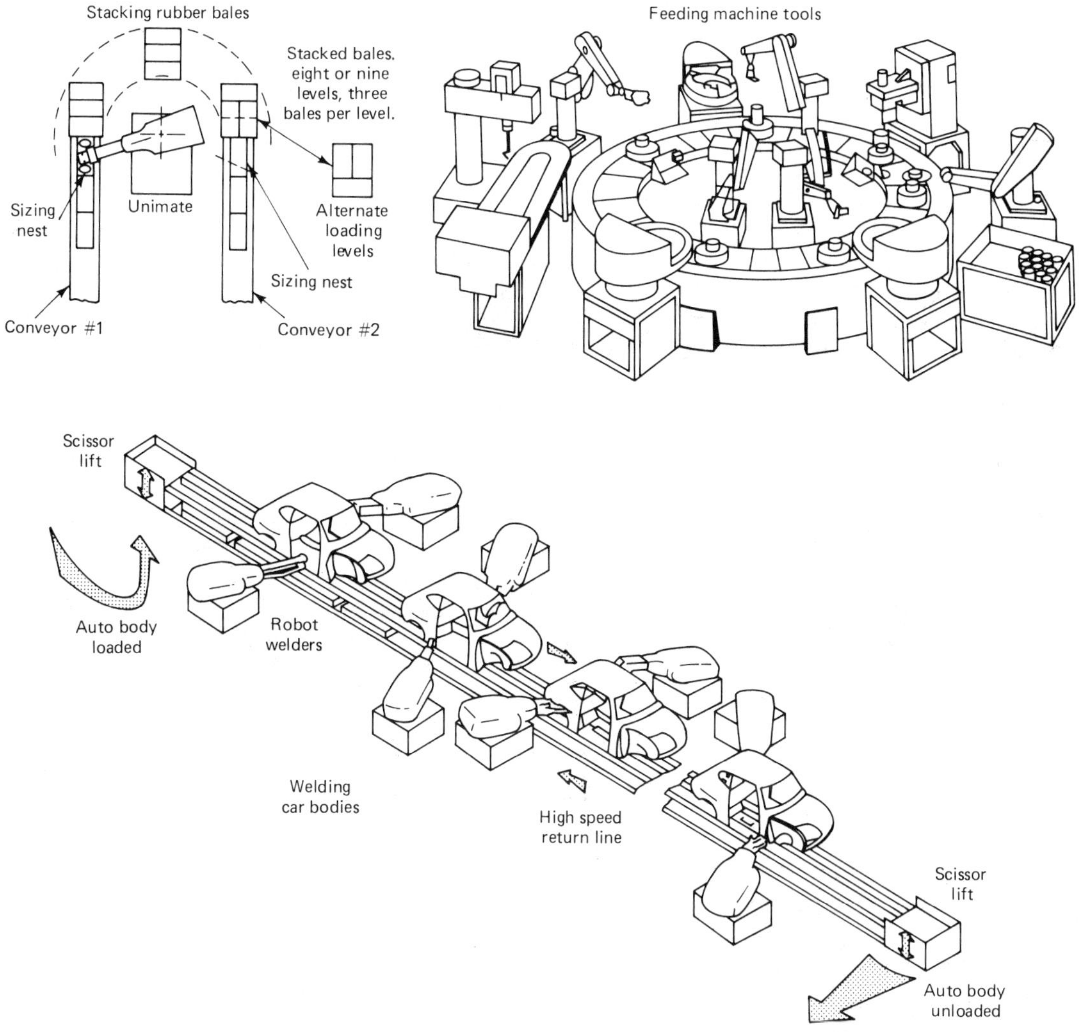

FIGURE 8–10. Examples of Industrial Robot Applications.

gence functions into these working machines. (A familiar example is the use of numerically controlled—NC—machines in place of older units that required manual turning of hand cranks to control removal of metal or wood.) There is little doubt that robots will be widely used as handling tools in the future.

IBM PROGRAMMABLE ROBOT UNIT

International Business Machines Corp. entered the infant robotics market in 1982 with a one-armed programmable robot system that can be attached to the IBM personal computer. Standards have not yet been established in the industry.

IBM's robot, the 7535 Manufacturing System, is designed for operations such as automatic assembly and insertion of automotive and electrical parts. In consists of a controller with an operator panel and a jointed arm capable of moving in four directions. The control unit can store as many as five types of routines for picking up, assembling, or loading parts found in automotive, appliance, electronic, and other manufacturing operations.

Many 7535s can be programmed with a single IBM personal computer, using a special version of IBM's new robotics language called AML (A Manufacturing Language). IBM's 7535 is being built by Sankyo Seiki Manufacturing Co., Ltd., of Japan, following IBM design specifications.

IBM is expanding its test marketing of an advanced robotics system, the IBM RS I. This system has a hydraulically powered arm that can move in six directions and ends in a two-fingered gripper. The gripper can be equipped with tactile and infrared optical sensors. When programmed with IBM's new robotic language, AML, the robot can respond to such English-language commands as "grasp and transport."

The optical sensing unit tells the robot machine whether an object is between the fingers of its gripper. If the machine is being used to put parts on a keyboard, for example, as it is used in IBM factories today, the sensor can tell if a feeder box is empty and signal the operator. The machine can also be programmed to go on to another job rather than just stop when its feeder is empty. Tactile sensors enable the robot to jiggle a part into place if the part is improperly aligned.

IBM has been testing its advanced robot in about fifteen customer locations and at IBM manufacturing facilities. IBM's entry into robotics gives credibility to the industry. From now on, robotics is going to be more than a concept or a gimmick. It's going to be an industrial phenomenon.

OTHER ROBOT MAKERS

The robot industry in the United States is currently dominated by Unimation Inc., a Condec Corp. subsidiary, and Cincinnati Milacron Inc., which together have about 80 percent of the market. Other major makers are Prab Robots Inc., and Asea Inc. But large companies are finding the area increasingly attractive.

Others already involved in robot manufacturing include General Electric Co., which licenses technology from DEA of Italy and Hitachi Ltd. of Japan, and Westinghouse Electric Corp., which licenses technology from Olivetti Group. General Motors Corp. makes robots for internal use. American Telephone & Telegraph Co. recently opened up a corporate robotics center to evaluate capabilities of twelve commercial robots, and says it is working on developing its own.

Operations Analysis Techniques

MANAGEMENT

In materials handling and storage operations, management includes, among other things, the proper utilization of materials handling equipment and storage space, the logical grouping of activities to provide for a straight-line flow, and the integration of effort to insure the maximum productivity of all personnel. This section explains some of the management techniques that are particularly appropriate to materials handling operations and storage facilities and that experience has proved to be most effective.

A good manager will operate according to the capabilities of his work force and the facilities placed at their disposal. He must know the "how" and "why" of what he is asking and must be able to evaluate what he is getting. Likewise, his work force must understand his directions in order to be able to obtain his objectives.

The successful manager will operate with a high degree of flexibility. He will meet sudden and large impacts on one activity by shifting personnel and equipment from another that is less pressingly engaged. Operations of low priority will be set up as standby projects to be accomplished when the high priority work load drops temporarily. The balance between work load and men and materials begins with the smallest operation and ends with the total production from the entire activity.

Organization is the structure by which these responsibilities are carried out and management is the planning, directing, coordinating, and controlling mechanism by which the organization is made to function. Certain underlying principles apply to effective organization, which, when coupled with the application of sound management techniques, will contribute immeasurably to achieving maximum efficiency, economy, and safety in operations.

PRODUCTION CRITERIA

The productivity of every operation is contingent upon the establishment of a standard of performance. The following basic criteria, essential to the achievement of maximum productivity of any operation, should be observed:

1. Select qualified workers.
2. Train all workers.
3. Inform all workers of established production standards.
4. Provide adequate supervision for every operation. Each supervisor should know the job and should know how to instruct others on the job.
5. Use standard methods. The best way to accomplish a job is to use the simplest, easiest, and most economical method from the standpoint of man-hours and equipment.
6. Reduce operations to routine, where practicable.
7. Use statistics, charts, and graphs to show daily work accomplishment, operational trends, and work goals. Such aids give information quickly, foster competition, and point out weak spots and deficiencies that require attention.

Adequate records of production are essential as management tools and should be provided in order that all major data on work load may be accumulated accurately.

ANALYSIS OF METHODS

Materials handling equipment should not be selected or requisitioned for an operation until a thorough analysis has been made of the materials to be handled, the conditions and environment in which the work must be performed, and the method to be employed. The equipment may be suitable for the method suggested; but if there is a better method, maximum utilization of the equipment will not be achieved. There are several ways by which the method to be employed can be analyzed.

Operation Lists

In any handling problem, several specific operations must be performed. A list of these operations, in the sequence in which performed, should be made. This listing may be sufficient to indicate the method to be employed, and, in any case, it will serve as a valuable guide and check to more detailed analyses that may be made at a later date.

Work Simplification

The purpose of work simplification is to make the work easier to perform by eliminating unnecessary steps and by developing or finding simpler methods of doing the necessary steps. This is accomplished by questioning each step in the process, changing the sequence, or by combining some of the operations. Its tools are flow charts (Figures 8–11 A and B), operation analysis charts, and flow diagrams (Figure 8–12).

Motion Study

Motion study refers to the study of the motions made by the worker in performing assigned tasks. This study may be merely visual observation of the worker. Things to observe include the distance the operator reaches for his tools and supplies, the number of steps he takes, the repetition of tasks, and the smoothness of the motion pattern. Uncertain and irregular motions on the part of the operator indicate a lack of familiarity with the job and a lack of skill in performance. Often, a list of the specific tasks carried out by a worker in connection with the performance of an operation can help to eliminate unnecessary steps and excessive movements by the worker. The operation analysis chart may simplify the analysis during a motion study.

Flow Chart and Flow Diagram

The flow chart and the flow diagram should be used for the study of the flow of materials from one work area to another. The completed flow chart will show the operation involved, including distances and the number of times the procedure is repeated (see Figure 8–11A, B). The completed flow diagram, a picture of the operation, will indicate the distance and other physical conditions. The flow chart makes use of the following standard symbols:

Operations: ○
Transportations: ⇨
Inspections: □
Delays: D
Storages: ∇

After recording the present method and other pertinent data, the flow chart should be studied with consideration for the following:

What?
How?
Why?
Where?
When?
Frequency?
Total time per year?

This study should show the possibilities for improvement and the steps in the operation that may be eliminated. In studying the steps of the operation, consider the following:

Can I eliminate?
Can I simplify?
Can I combine several steps?
Can I change the sequence of steps?

On the basis of this study, a proposed method that utilizes available equipment should be developed. This proposed new method should be tested for practicability and anticipated savings.

Time Study

Time study is an analysis of an operation that is based upon the determination of the time required to perform each part of the

Identification			
Project no.	Chart no. 1	Operation charted: Unloading Cartons from box cars and Storing	
Type of chart: Men and Equipment		Activity (name and location): Railroad Siding	
Charted by: Dr. R. Singer (Date) 8/25/82		Exact point at which operation begins: Box bar	Exact point at which operation ends: Box bar
Approved by: [illegible] (Date)			
Yearly production: 60,000 Cartons.	Cost unit		

Quantity information			Equipment	Code	Equipment	Code
Unit: Cartons	Units per hour: 133	Units per year: 60,000	Manual Labor	1	Tractor and Trailer	
Cubic feet per unit: 6	Weight per unit: 25 lb		Fork Lift Truck @ 5 mph	2	Train @ 15 mph	4
Cubic feet per hour: 800	Weight per hour: 3325		Quantity Roller	3		

Present method

Quantity unit charted	Symbols	Description	No. of emp	Equipment code	Distance moved	Unit time in Minutes: Oper.	Trans.	Inspec.	Delay	Stor.
1 quantity roller	①	Position quantity roller conveyors in box bar	2	1	—					
25 cartons	⇨2	Transport cartons to conveyors 2 at a time	2	1	250					
25 cartons	③	Position cartons on conveyor	2	1	0	0.98				
25 Cartons	⇨4	Transport cartons on conveyor	0	3	20					
25 Cartons	⑤	Pick up cartons from conveyor	2	1	0	0.98				
25 cartons 1 pallet	⑥	Position cartons on Pallet	2	1	0	0.79				
1 Pallet	⑦	Pick up each pallet	1	2	0	0.17				
1 Pallet	⇨8	Transport to storage	1	2	1000					
1 Pallet	⇨9	Transport vertically (elevate)	1	2	9					
1 Pallet	⑩	Position pallet	1	2	0	0.08				
	⑪	Back away and lower	1	2	0	0.30				
	⇨12	Transport empty	1	2	1000					
		Summary for 100 cartons								
		(Time in man minutes)								
100 Cartons or	①		2	1	—	3.00				
4 Pallets	⇨2		2	1	1000		8.00			
	③		2	1	0	3.92				
	⇨4		2	3	—		1.00			
	⑤		2	1	0	3.92				
	⑥		2	1	0	3.16				
	⑦		4	2	0	0.68				
	⇨8		4	2	4000		9.08			
	⇨9		4	2	36		1.20			
	⑩		4	2	0	0.32				
	⑪		4	2	0	1.20				
4 Pallets	⇨12		4	2	4000		9.08			
		Total quanity rollers	2	1	1000	14.0	9.00			
		Total fork lift Trucks	4	2	8036	2.20	19.36			
		Grand Total.			9036	16.20	28.36			

(a)

FIGURE 8–11A. Flow Chart.

Cross Reference

Summary	Present method		Proposed method		Difference		
Direct labor unit cost							Total yearly saving in cost of direct labor
Distance traveled (in feet)	9036		2196		6870		
	Number	Time in	Number	Time in	Number	Time in	Cost of installing proposed method
○ Operations	7	16.20	6	6.00	-1	-10.20	
⇨ Transportations	5	28.36	5	10.72	0	-17.64	Estimated net saving in first year
□ Inspections	0		0				
D Delays	0		1	4.84	+1	4.84	
▽ Storages	0		0				Net savings in time per unit 23.00

Proposed method

Quantity unit charted	Symbols	Description	No. of emp	Equipment code	Distance moved	Oper.	Trans.	Inspec	Delay	Stor.
25 Cartons	① ⇨ □ D ▽	Palletize in box car	1	1	0	0.79				
	○ ② □ D ▽	Transport empty - fork truck enters box car	1	2	20		1.00			
1 pallet	③ ⇨ □ D ▽	Pick up pallet	1	2		0.08				
1 pallet	○ ⇨ □ D ▽	Transfer pallet to trailers	1	2	20		1.00			
1 pallet	○ ⇨ □ D ▽	Load one pallet on each of four trailers	1	2	0	0.08				
4 pallets	○ ⇨ □ D ▽	Tractor trailer waiting time	1	4	0				4.84	
4 pallets	○ ⇨ □ D ▽	Transfer to storage	1	4	1000		0.76			
1 pallet	○ ⇨ □ D ▽	Unload pallets from trailers	1	2	0	0.17				
1 pallet	○ ⇨ □ D ▽	Transport vertially (elevate)	1	2	9		0.30			
1 pallet	○ ⇨ □ D ▽	Position pallet	1	2	0	0.08				
	○ ⇨ □ D ▽	Back away and lower	1	2	0	0.30				
	○ ⇨ □ D ▽	Transport empty tractor trailer	1	4	1000		0.76			
	○ ⇨ □ D ▽									
	○ ⇨ □ D ▽									
	○ ⇨ □ D ▽									
	○ ⇨ □ D ▽	Summary for 100 cartons								
	○ ⇨ □ D ▽	(Time in man minutes)								
	○ ⇨ □ D ▽		1	1	0	3.16				
	○ ⇨ □ D ▽		4	2	80		4.00			
	○ ⇨ □ D ▽		4	2	0	0.32				
	○ ⇨ □ D ▽		4	2	80		4.00			
	○ ⇨ □ D ▽		4	2	1	0.32				
	○ ⇨ □ D ▽		1	4	0				4.84	
	○ ⇨ □ D ▽		1	4	1000		0.76			
	○ ⇨ □ D ▽		4	2	0	0.68				
	○ ⇨ □ D ▽		4	2	36		1.20			
	○ ⇨ □ D ▽		4	2	0	0.32				
	○ ⇨ □ D ▽		4	2	0	1.20				
	○ ⇨ □ D ▽		1	4	1000		0.76			
	○ ⇨ □ D ▽	Total fork lift trucks			196	6.00	9.20			
	○ ⇨ □ D ▽	Total tractor trailers			2000	0	1.52		4.84	
	○ ⇨ □ D ▽	Grand total.			2196	6.00	10.72			
	○ ⇨ □ D ▽									

Flow Process Chart of Handling Problem

(b)

FIGURE 8–11B. Flow Chart.

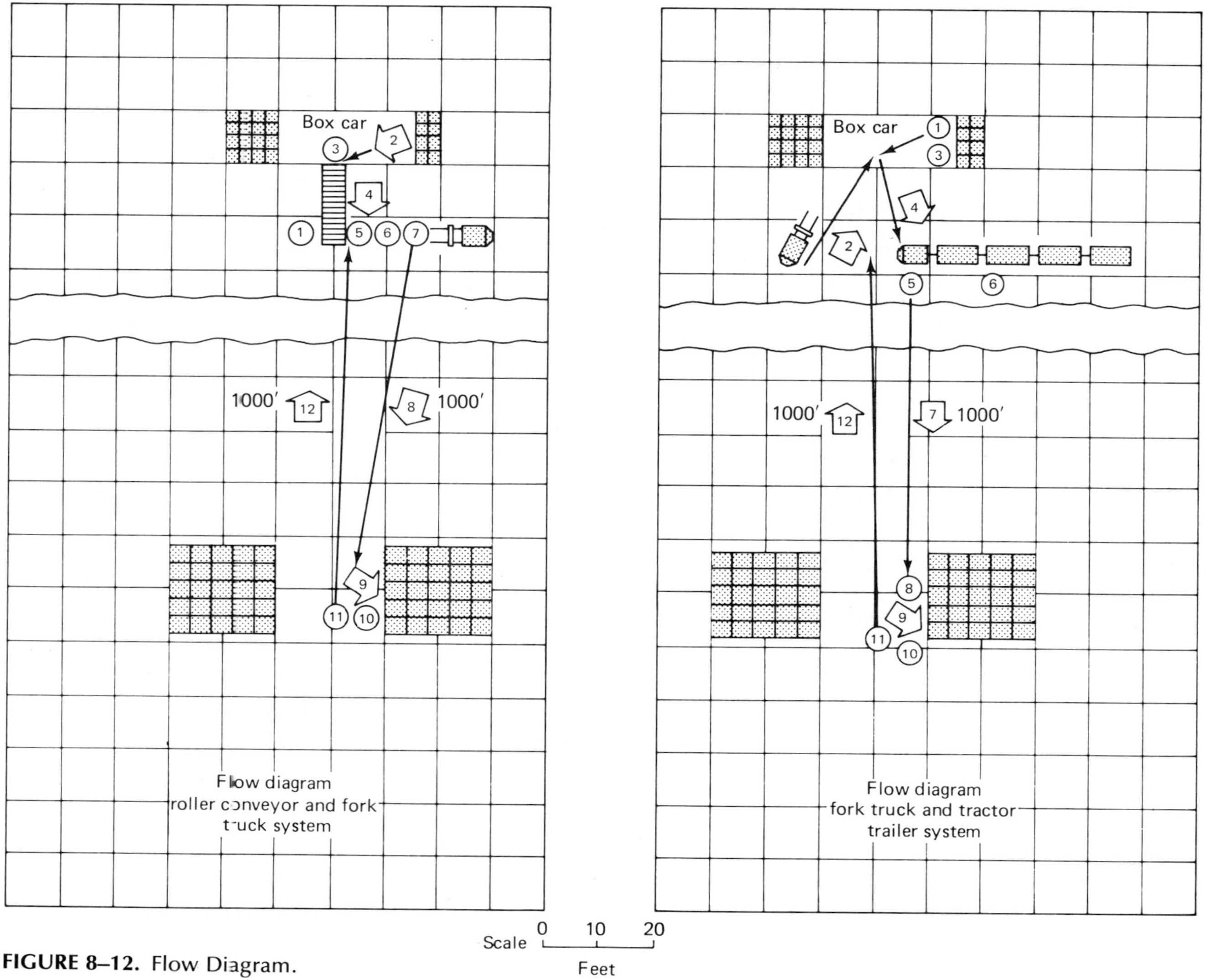

FIGURE 8–12. Flow Diagram.

operation. The operation must be divided so that performance of each part can be timed. The actual timing of each performance should be relatively easy; the difficulty will be to ensure that the timing reflects normal operations under normal conditions. The timing of an operation may be used as a basis for comparing performance of the proposed new method with the old method. The timing standards will be valid only as long as changes are not made in the operation, the system, condition of the operating equipment, and the number of personnel assigned to the job.

Sample Study

With Additional Equipment. In the facility under study, highway trailers and boxcars have been unloaded by gravity conveyors and forklift trucks. Because of increased activity at the facility, it was proposed to add two forklift trucks to the three already in operation. However, use of a tractor-trailer system may be a better solution of the problem. The flow chart and flow diagram for this operation are shown by Figures 8–11A,B, and 8–12. An overall study shows that the average operation involved in unloading a boxcar by this method, summarized from Figure 8–12, is shown in Table 8–1. The total man-minutes for unloading 100 cartons is shown in Table 8–2.

Without Additional Equipment. After studying the method of operation and determining what savings could be made without using any additional equipment, you should consider eliminating the double handling required by the roller conveyor. If the roller conveyor is eliminated and the fork truck worked directly into the freight car, (11.50 × 2) 23.00 man-minutes will be saved per 100 cartons; but an additional time of 1.87 minutes, for travel of 20 feet and maneuvering into boxcar, will be involved.

The net saving on this is 23.00 man-minutes less 4 × 1.87 or 7.48 man-minutes per 100 cartons, or (15.52 × 600) 9,312 man-minutes, or 155 man-hours per year. Justifying the cost of additional equipment will not be involved; but the forklift trucks and operators will be required for an additional 4 × 1.87 × 600, or 4,488 man-

TABLE 8-1.

Operation	*No. of Minutes*	*No. of Men*
Position gravity roller or wheel conveyor in boxcar or trailer	1.50	2
Unload 100 cartons using conveyor and positioning on four general purpose pallets	10.00	2
Pick up each pallet	0.17	1
Transport 1,000 feet at 5 mph	2.27	1
Transport vertically (elevate) 108 inches	0.30	1
Position load	0.08	1
Back away and lower	0.30	1
Transport empty 1,000 feet	2.27	1
Total gravity conveyor time	11.50	2
Total forklift truck time	5.39	1

TABLE 8-2.

Operation	*Total Man-minutes*
Position gravity roller	1.50 x 2 = 3.00
Unload 100 cartons	10.00 x 2 = 20.00
Pallet and forklift	5.39 x 4 = 21.56
Total man-minutes	44.56
Total cartons unloaded in a year: 60,000, requiring (600 x 44.56) 26,736 man-minutes, or 446 man-hours.	

minutes, or 75 man-hours per year, and charges for both will offset part of the saving. The 44.56 man-minutes for 100 cartons will be reduced by 23 man-minutes, because of eliminating the roller conveyor, and increased by 7.48 man-minutes, for the additional use of the forklift truck, which will result in a net saving of 15.52 man-minutes, and an adjusted figure of 29.04 man-minutes. Substituting a tractor-trailer train for the direct travel of the forklift truck will adjust the operation, which is summarized from Figure 8–12 in Table 8–3.

This, compared with 29.04 man-minutes shows a saving of 7.48 man-minutes per 100 cartons, or 4,488 man-minutes per year, or 75 man-hours per year. The tractor-trailer train will be engaged 6.36 minutes for every 100 cartons, which totals 3,816 minutes or 64 hours per year. The use of this equipment may be justified when

TABLE 8-3.

Operation	*Labor Time (One Man)*	*Trailer Time*
Enter boxcar and pick up each pallet	1.87	
Transport 20 feet	1.00	
Load each trailer	0.08	
Tractor-trailer time four cars travel at 15 mph	—	0.76
Unload each trailer	0.17	
Trailer waiting time	—	4.84
Transport vertically (elevated) 108 inches	0.30	
Position load	0.08	
Back away and lower	0.30	
Empty trailer—return to boxcar	—	0.76
Total man-minutes	3.80 x 4 = 15.20 per 100 cartons	

Labor Time	*Trailer Time*	*Total man-hours*
15.20	6.36	21.56

D = Define E = Evaluate
A = Analyze S = Select
G = Generate I = Implement

Problems		Graphical: Motion analysis	Assembly diagramming	Process diagramming	Shipping and receiving analysis	Storage analysis	Spatial planning	Material handling audit	ABC analysis	Plant layout	Analytical: Scheduling	Work sampling	Line balancing	Plant layout	Simulation	Conveyor analysis	Waiting line	Linear programming	Cash flow analysis
Design or redesign of	Workstations	D A S I					G	E											
	General area	E		D A			E	E I	A S	A G	I	A		G E	E	E			E S
	Assembly area	A	D G I				G	E					G S				E		
	Receiving and shipping area	E			D A I		G	E I	A	G S		A		G S	E		E		
	Dock and siding area	E			D A I		G	E I	A					G S	E		E		
	Storage and warehouse area				A	D A I	G	E I	A	G S	I	A E		G S	E				E S
	In-process storage area			D A		D A I	E	E	A S	G		A	A G	G	E	E	E		E S
	Total facilities	E		D A	D A I	D A I	G E	D E I	A S	A G	I	D	E	G E	E	E			E S
Operational problems regarding	Maintenance	D G						D E I	A	G	E S I	A		G	E			S	E S
	Damaged materials	G		A G	G	G		D E I	A			A							E S
	Pilferage							D E I	A G			A							E S
	Safety	S						D E I	A G			A E							
	Supervision and control			D				D A I	S		E I	A	G			E	E	S	
	Space utilization			D	A	A	G E	D I	G	A G E S		A E		G E S				S	E S
	Excessive labor costs	A G E	A	A				D E I	A S		E	A E	G		E		E		E S
	Excessive equipment costs	E		A G				D E I	A S		E	A E			E				E S
	Excessive in-process material costs			D A		A		D E I	A S		G E	A	A		E	E	E		E S

SOURCE: James A. Tompkins, "Quantitative Methods in the Design, Analysis and Implementation of Material Handling Systems" (Paper delivered at the 1979 Institite for Material Handling Instructors, Ames, Iowa,

FIGURE 8–13. Materials Handling Problem Solving.

other work will occupy the residual time of the tractor-trailer train, and when the operating cost for the train and tractor is less than the cost of the 75 man-hours saved. The trailers may be uncoupled when there is another load for the tractor to handle and waiting time for the tractor and tractor operator eliminated. By eliminating the waiting time of 4.84 man-minutes, the savings will be increased from 7.48 to 12.31 man-minutes per 100 cartons, or 7,392 man-minutes per year, or 123 man-hours per year. The cost of tractor-trailer train operation can be calculated on a basis of:

$$\frac{1.52}{\text{man-minutes per travel cycle}} \times \frac{600}{\text{cycles per year}} \times \frac{1/60}{\text{hours per minute}},$$

which equals 15 man-hours per year. (Since the total time of 6.36 minutes includes 4.84 minutes for delay, then for continuous operations a net of 1.52 minutes [6.36 minus 4.84 equals 1.52] would be required for one cycle of tractor travel time.)

MATERIALS HANDLING PROBLEM SOLVING

Figure 8–13 is a matrix representing the most applicable pragmatic quantitative methods that may be used as aids for the various steps of the problems addressed in this chapter. The letters within the matrix represent the steps (D = Define the problem, A = Analyze the problem, and so on) in resolving the given problem by means of the indicated technique.

IMPROVING EFFICIENCY

Each materials handling operation should be studied now and then to obtain improved efficiency. Figure 8–14 illustrates a sequence of graduated improvements over time.

IMPROVING TECHNIQUES

Regardless of the apparent acceptability of a materials handling method, the possibility of further improvement should always be considered. As a technique is improved, the opportunities for reducing labor and equipment requirements are proportionately enhanced. Operations should be continually appraised for possible improvement. Acknowledging experience to be a factor of considerable magnitude to a storage operator, adoption of an attitude such as "let's do it this way because we always have" can only penalize the ability to improve. An open-minded attitude regarding operational change is therefore a "must." Apparent benefits in progression as shown in Figure 8–14 are obvious. As each stage is implemented, the complications of operations balancing have been simplified and the production potential and operational costs have been considerably affected.

Computing Capacities of Forklifts

Manufacturers rate forklift trucks according to their ability to lift materials with a 24-inch load center. The term *load center* refers to the distance from the heel of the fork to the center of the load. For the safe load capacity at any given load center to be computed, the inch-pound capacity of the truck must first be computed. The inch-pound capacity of forklift trucks is based on the distance in inches from the center of the drive axle to the center of the load. Under no circumstances may this inch-pound capacity be exceeded, because the truck will tip forward if the load on the forks is greater than the inch-pound capacity. The method of computation is shown in Figure 8–15.

When a load with a length other than that specified by the manufacturer is calculated, or when one truck is compared with another of a different rating, the inch-pound rating must be computed. The inch-pound rating is W, the rated load; multiplied by C, the distance from the center of the front axle to the center of the load:

$$\text{Inch-Pound Rating} = W \times C.$$

The inch-pound rating becomes a constant for that particular truck. Then, in order to

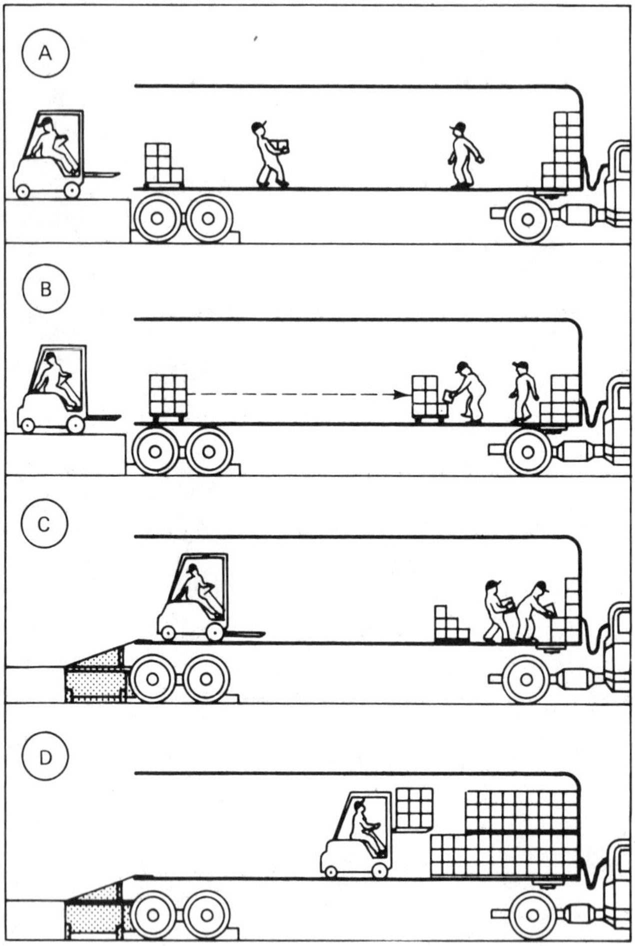

FIGURE 8–14. Graduated Sequence of Experienced Operations Improvement.

figure (1) the maximum load length for any given load; or (2) the maximum load for any given load length, the formula can be reversed to give this information:

$$(1) \quad C = \frac{\text{Inch-Pound Rating}}{W}$$

$$(2) \quad W = \frac{\text{Inch-Pound Rating}}{C}.$$

Example: A truck has a rating of 4,000# @ 24"—which means a 4,000-pound load has its center 24 inches from the heel of the fork. The specifications show that the distance from the center of the axle to the heel of the fork is 15 inches. By applying the formulas, the inch-pound rating may be arrived at:

$$C = A + B, \text{ or } 15 + 24 = 39 \text{ in.}$$

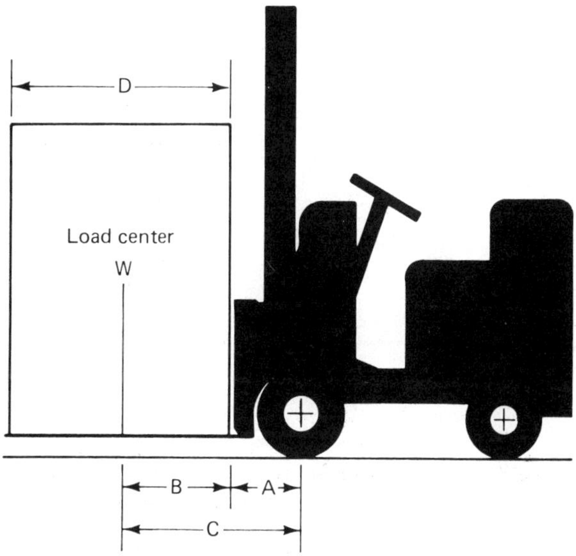

A = Distance from center of front axle to heel of fork measured in inches
B = D/2 = Distance fron heel of fork to center of load measured in inches
C = A + B = Distance from center of front axle to center of load measured in inches
D = 2 X B length of load
W = Weight of load measured in pounds

FIGURE 8–15. Computing Inch-pound Rating of a Forklift Truck.

Inch-Pound Rating = $W \times C$, or
4,000 × 39 = 156,000 inch-pounds.

The rating of 156,000 inch-pounds then becomes a constant for the truck in question. Then, the length of a pallet or skid having a gross weight of 2,500 pounds can be determined by applying the formulas:

$$C = \frac{\text{Inch-Pound Rating}}{W} \text{ or } \frac{156{,}000}{2{,}500} = 62 \text{ in.}$$

$$B = C - A \text{ or } 62 \text{ in.} - 15 \text{ in.} = 47 \text{ in.}$$

$$D = 2 \times B \text{ or } 2 \times 47 \text{ in.} = 94 \text{ in. allowable load length.}$$

Or, as another example, it is desired to know the maximum weight limit for a load 84 inches long, by applying the formulas:

$$B = \frac{D}{2} \text{ or } \frac{84}{2} = 42 \text{ in.}$$

$$C = A + B \text{ or } 15 \text{ in.} + 42 \text{ in.} = 57 \text{ in.}$$

$$W = \frac{\text{Inch-Pound Rating}}{C} \text{ or } \frac{156{,}000}{57''} =$$

2,737 pounds gross weight allowed.

If the load center is longer than the manufacturer's rated load center, the capability is reduced. The inch-pound capacity of the truck is the constant factor from which capabilities at varous load centers may be computed.

Glossary

The following is a glossary of selected words and terms making up some of the language of materials handling and storage personnel:

Aisle: Any passageway within a storage area.

Cross aisle: A passageway at right angles to main aisles, used for the movement of supplies, equipment, and personnel.

Fire aisle: A passageway established to aid in fighting or preventing the spread of fire, or for access to fire fighting equipment.

Main aisle: A passageway wide enough to permit the easy flow of equipment, supplies, and personnel; generally runs the length of the building.

Allocated space: A definite number of net square feet of a specific type of storage space formally apportioned for use.

Assignment of space: Designation of specific space within the installation for storage purposes.

Bay: Designated area within a section of a warehouse or depot shop, usually outlined or bounded by posts, pillars, columns, or painted lines.

Bin area: An area for the storage of supply items that are binnable by nature.

Box: A rigid container having closed faces, usually constructed of wood, metal, paperboard, fiberboard, plywood, plastic, or a combination of such materials; strength and stability depend upon the material of the faces and the fastening of faces in assembling the box.

Bulk storage: (1) Any large quantity of supplies usually in original containers. (2) Storage of liquids or solids such as coal, lumber, rubber bales, petroleum products, or ores in tanks or piles.

Bursting strength: The pressure required to rupture a container when it is tested in a specified instrument under specified conditions.

Carrier: A commercial transportation media providing railroad cars, motor trucks, ships, airplanes, or other conveyances for transporting supplies.

Chute: Usually an inclined trough, sometimes a tube, used to convey supplies from an upper to a lower level.

Container: A receptacle such as a bag, barrel, drum, box, crate, or package used to hold and to protect contents.

Crate: A rigid shipping container constructed of structural members fastened together to hold and protect the contents. It may be sheathed or unsheathed.

Cross stacking: The placing of one layer of containers at right angles to those just below to increase the stability of the stack.

Cross tie: Cross layers of supplies as in cross stacking, except that only an occasional layer is crossed, and not every other one.

Cube: The product of length by width by depth.

Drum: Round, straight-sided, and flat-ended cylindrical storage or shipping container; made of metal, plywood, fiberboard, or polyethylene, or a combination thereof.

Dunnage: Any material (boards, planks, blocks, pneumatic pillows) used to support or secure supplies in storage or in transit.

Floor load: Weight that can safely be supported by a floor, expressed in pounds per square foot of floor space.

Floor plan: A scale drawing of the floor area, a building showing columns, stair wells, elevator shafts, offices, washrooms, doors, and other structural features.

Gross weight: The weight of the container plus its contents.

Honeycombing: The storing or withdrawing of supplies in a manner that results in vacant space that is not usable for storage of other items.

Inventory: A physical count performed to determine the on-hand quantity of an item or group of items.

Labor pool: A centrally controlled group of workers who are assigned to particular jobs or areas when needed.

Large-lot storage: A quantity of supplies, four or more stacks, stored to maximum height.

Layout: A floor plan showing assignment of gross space for storage operations and supporting functions.

Loading platform: A flat surface to facilitate loading or unloading, usually erected alongside a warehouse at the approximate level of a rail car or truck floor.

Materials handling: Movement of supplies from one place or operation to another.

Materials handling equipment: Any devices, mechanically or manually operated, used for movement or handling of supplies.

Net weight: The weight of the contents, not including the container.

Nomenclature: A noun and any adjectives required to describe and identify an item of supply.

Pallet: A low portable platform of wood, metal, or fiberboard to facilitate the act of moving, storing and transporting of materials as a unit.

Palletized unit load: Quantity of any item, packaged or unpackaged, arranged on a pallet and securely fastened thereto, so that the whole is handled as a unit.

Ramp: An inclined plane serving as a way between different levels.

Receiving: The receipt of inbound supplies; includes preplanning, handling, and document processing incident to inbound supplies.

Shipping: Actions necessary to deliver material to a carrier for movement to a consignee.

Shipping container: Any suitable exterior container used for shipment of supplies.

Space:

Aisle in storage: Any passageway in the storage area.

Assembly: Area used for collecting and combining material components.

Bin storage: Area in which bins have been erected; includes the aisles and working space between bins.

Gross space for storage: The amount of gross space for storage operations less those areas used in support of storage functions; that is, assembly area, packing and crating area, elbow room, and so on.

Gross space used in support of storage functions: That area used for preservation and packaging, assembly, packing and crating, container manufacturing, receiving, shipping, inspection and identification, administrative storage offices, rest areas, tool rooms, and other similar support areas.

Gross storage: Gross area regardless of its location or the purpose for which the space was designed or designated that is assigned or used for any operation involving storage or the support of storage functions.

Spot: The placing of a truck or freight car in a desired function preparatory to loading or unloading.

Stack: A quantity of supplies stored vertically, occupying approximately one pallet space on the floor, utilizing necessary storage aids to assure stability.

Storage: The keeping or placing of property in a warehouse, shed, or open area; or the state of being stored.

Storing: The orderly arranging of supplies in storage.

Supplies: All items necessary for the equipment, maintenance, and operation of a materials handling and storage facility.

Tier: A horizontal layer of a column, row, or stack.

Transportation: Media for the movement of personnel and material.

Unit Load: A number of items, or bulk material, so arranged or restrained so that the load can be picked up and moved as a single object too large or bulky for manual handling, and which upon being released will retain its initial arrangement for later movement. Single objects too large for manual handling are also considered unit loads.

Utilities: Facilities constructed for the service of the depot, such as boiler rooms, power plants, and the like.

Warehousing: The performance of physical functions incident to receipt, storage, and issue of supplies.

Questions

1. What is materials handling?
2. List the principles, and briefly discuss the importance of each.
3. What are the five main principles of materials handling?
4. What are the factors considered in the selection of conveyors?
5. What are the rules for the economic utilization of industrial trucks in warehousing activities?
6. What new technology has most recently been integrated in AS/RS manufacturing activities?
7. List the factors that are often included in the economic justification for AS/RS.
8. What is the primary objective of facilities layout?
9. List some appropriate criteria for use in determining whether a process or product layout should be employed in facilities design.
10. What data and/or information does an industrial engineer need to solve facilities layout projects?
11. What type of layout material do you suggest for use when laying out:
    a. a machine shop for a vocational school
    b. an appliance warehouse
    c. a legal office for nine partners
    d. a university chemical engineering laboratory
    e. a group psychiatric practice
    f. an aircraft carrier.

    State your reasons.
12. For facilities design and layout to reach maximum efficiency, is it necessary for both materials handling and plant layout be organized under one department? Support your answer.
13. If you were developing a computer program to evaluate alternative layouts, what variable would you consider necessary?
14. List some of the most commonly used computerized layout methods utilized by industrial engineers today.
15. List the several common basic components in all industrial robots.

16. Three important dimensions of the growth of robotics are subject to economic analysis. They are (1) the determinants of the magnitude of the growth of the robotics industry; (2) the impact of robots on unemployment; and (3) the impact that robots will have on wages, profits, and prices. What is your view on each?
17. Explain the part that operations analysis plays in the solution of materials-handling problems.
18. List some of the commonly used techniques in solving materials-handling problems.
19. What are the essential differences between graphical and analytical techniques used in materials-handling analyses.
20. A four-wheel gasoline-powered fork-lift truck has a rating of 3,825 lbs. (1,735 kg) at 24 inches (61 cm). The specifications state that the distance from the center of the front axle to the fork is 14.5 inches. What is the meter-kilogram rating? What is the maximum weight limit for a load 2.1 meters long?
21. What is a palletized unit load?

Bibliography

MATERIALS HANDLING

Apple, James M. *Plant Layout and Materials Handling.* New York: Ronald Press, 1963.

Bolz, H., and Hageman, G. E. *Materials Handling Handbook.* New York: Ronald Press, 1958.

Carson, G. B. *Production Handbook.* New York: Ronald Press, 1972.

Footlik, I. M., and Carle, J. F. *Industrial Material Handling.* Cleveland: Lincoln Extension Institute, 1968.

Immer, John R. *Material Handling.* New York: McGraw-Hill, 1961.

Kulwiec, Raymond A. *Basics of Material Handling.* Pittsburgh, Pa.: The Material Handling Institute, 1981.

Sims, E. Ralph, Jr. *Planning and Managing Materials Flow.* Boston: Industrial Education Institute, 1968.

Stocker, Harry E. *Materials Handling.* 2nd ed. Englewood Cliffs, N.J.: Prentice-Hall, 1951.

Tyler, E. S. *Materials Handling.* 2 Vols. New York: McGraw-Hill, 1970.

Woodley, D. R. *Encyclopedia of Material Handling.* 2 Vols. New York: Pergamon Press, 1964.

MATERIALS HANDLING EQUIPMENT

Apple, James. *Material Handling Systems Design.* New York: Ronald Press, 1972.

Bowman, Daniel. *Lift Trucks—A Practical Guide for Buyers and Users.* Boston: Cahners, 1972.

Conveyor Equipment Manufacturers' Association. *Conveyors Terms and Definitions.* Washington, D.C.: 1966.

Haynes, D. O. *Material Handling Equipment.* Philadelphia, Pa.: Chilton, 1957.

———. *Material Handling Applications.* Philadelphia, Pa.: Chilton, 1957.

Hudson, W. G. *Conveyors and Related Equipment.* New York: John Wiley and Sons, 1954.

Keller, H. C. *Unit Load and Package Conveyors.* New York: Ronald Press, 1967.

The Material Handling Institute. *The Emerging Impact of Automatic Identification Systems, Automatic Identification Manufacturers.* Pittsburgh, Pa.: Author, 1974.

Stoess, H. A., Jr. *Pneumatic Conveying.* New York: John Wiley and Sons, 1970.

MATERIAL HANDLING ANALYSIS

Morris, W. T. *Analysis for Material Handling Management.* Homewood, Ill.: Richard D. Irwin, 1962.

Muther, Richard. *Systematic Handling Analysis.* Kansas City, Mo.: Management & Industrial Publishers, 1969.

Sims, Eugene R. *Planning and Managing Material Flow.* Boston: Cahners, 1968.

PLANT LAYOUT

Francis, R. L., and White, J. A. *Facility Layout and Location: An Analytical Approach.* Englewood Cliffs, N.J.: Prentice-Hall, 1974.

Immer, John R. *Layout Planning Techniques.* New York: McGraw-Hill, 1953.

Moore, James M. *Plant Layout and Design.* New York: Macmillan, 1962.

Muther, Richard. *Practical Plant Layout.* New York: McGraw-Hill, 1955.

———. *Systematic Plant Layout.* Boston: Industrial Education Institute, 1972.

Reed, Ruddell, Jr. *Plant Layout.* Homewood, Ill.: Richard D. Irwin, 1967.

———. *Plant Location, Layout and Maintenance.* Homewood, Ill.: Richard D. Irwin, 1967.

PHYSICAL DISTRIBUTION AND LOGISTICS MANAGEMENT

Ballow, R. H. *Business Logistics Management.* Englewood Cliffs, N.J.: Prentice-Hall, 1973.

Bowersox, D. J. *Logistical Management.* New York: Macmillan, 1978.

Bowersox, D. J., Smykay, E. W., and LaLonde, B. J. *Physical Distribution Management.* Rev. New York: Macmillan, 1968.

Davis, G. M., and Brown, S. W. *Logistics Management.* Lexington, Mass.: Lexington Books, 1974.

Heskett, J. L., et al. *Business Logistics.* 2nd ed. New York: Ronald Press, 1973.

Magee, J. F. *Industrial Logistics: Analysis and Management of Physical Supply and Distribution Systems.* New York: McGraw-Hill, 1968.

Sussames, J. E. *Industrial Logistics.* Boston: Cahners, 1972.

STORAGE, WAREHOUSING, AND PACKAGING

Briggs, Andrew J. *Warehouse Operations, Planning and Management.* New York: John Wiley and Sons, 1960.

Brown, Kenneth. *Packaging Design Engineering.* New York: John Wiley and Sons, 1959.

Friedman, W. F., and Kepness, J. J. *Industrial Packaging.* New York: John Wiley and Sons, 1960.

Jenkins, Creed H. *Modern Warehouse Management.* New York: McGraw-Hill, 1968.

U.S. Department of Air Force. *Storage and Material Handling.* Air Force Manual 67–3. Washington, D.C.: U.S. Government Printing Office, 1969.

Part IV
Work Methods

Chapter 9

Work Scheduling

INTRODUCTION

This chapter is designed to illustrate how and where work scheduling techniques can be used in the management process. It is also designed to develop a more comprehensive understanding of these techniques by those persons who are in a position to use or direct the use of these basic management aids and who should be obtaining the benefits that application of these techniques can provide.

The application of work scheduling is for planning and controlling the use of men, material, and equipment, and for planning and controlling the generation of management data for decisionmaking.

The Scheduling Process

Scheduling is merely deciding when work will be performed—a time decision. It is a timetable of projected operations and events. Scheduling governs the start and completion of work and the expenditures of resources on each activity in a plan. For scheduling to be effective it must be concerned with the following considerations:

1. Work to be done—operations involved.
2. Time to do work.
3. Resource availability (people, equipment, facilities, money).

In addition to time decisions, the scheduling process involves process decisions and place decisions. To arrive at the initial schedules, these decisions may be made by planners, schedulers, and supervisors. Progress reporting, the next aspect of the scheduling process, occurs after the schedule has been dispatched and work has begun. Incorporating data in the scheduling process does not involve decisions. It is more a mechanical step that provides information for the final aspect of the scheduling process—that of updating the schedule. This process recycles continuously until the work project is finished. There is considerable variation in how often the schedule is updated. The progress reporting and updating aspects are the controlling features of the scheduling process. When we speak of a scheduling system, we are really referring to a scheduling and controlling system. Planning, controlling, and scheduling techniques run the gamut from a duty roster or a simple calendar maintained by a secretary to the complex program evaluation and review technique (PERT) for major projects or production efforts.

Criteria for Comparison of Alternative Scheduling Techniques

It is difficult to assess the usefulness of a given scheduling technique. To facilitate such evaluation, a list of features that are desirable in any scheduling technique is given below. No value weights have been assigned to these features because that step is inherently subjective.

1. *Accuracy.* The system should provide accurate information.
2. *Reliability.* Progress data should be consistent regardless of who collects it or when it is collected.

Parts of this chapter have been taken from Department of the Army, *Work Scheduling Handbook,* DOA Pamphlet No. 5-4-6, Washington, D.C., January 1974.

3. *Simplicity.* The technique should be easy to explain and understand and simple to operate.
4. *Universality of project coverage.* All levels of management should be able to use the information in the system, and all relevant factors to be controlled should be encompassed by the one system.
5. *Decision analysis.* A system that enables management to simulate the impacts of alternative courses of action can simplify and improve decisionmaking.
6. *Updating.* The scheduling technique should rapidly and easily incorporate information on project progress.
7. *Flexibility.* The scheduling technique should easily adapt to changes in the project.
8. *Cost.* The scheduling system should provide the required information at the lowest cost. Cost is difficult to measure for several reasons:
   a. Total scheduling costs are needed to compare techniques, but there is no agreement as to what costs should be included.
   b. Systems that are most useful in terms of the above criteria generally cost more to operate. The proper cost statistic is not total dollar cost but cost per unit of utility or benefit. This cannot, as yet, be precisely measured.
   c. Cost depends largely on the size of the program and involves both fixed and variable cost. Scheduling techniques with high fixed costs tend to be more economical in large-scale than in small-scale applications.

BASIC SCHEDULING CHARTS

The basic charts described in this section may serve as the core of a simple scheduling system or as part of a larger, more complex scheduling system. These charts visually show task relationships, task schedules, and progress on tasks scheduled. The five techniques described in this chapter are: the process chart, the lead time chart, the Gantt chart, the milestone chart, and the man-hour load chart.

Process Charts

Process charts give a description of a process or work cycle. These charts help one to visualize the current procedures and operations. Although they do not have a time scale, they can provide a good idea of necessary time relationships. The term *process chart* is given to a group of charts that includes the flow process chart, the operation chart, the procedure chart, the process chart-product analysis, and the process chart-man analysis. The differences in the charts are in form and in application. All, however, use symbols (circles, squares, triangles, and so on) to present tasks, and straight lines to connect symbols for tasks done in sequence. The symbols are those usually used by industrial engineers. An example of a flow process chart is shown in Figure 9–1. Examples of other kinds of process charts are not included in this chapter, but may be found in any book on work measurement, methods study, time and motion, and so on. There is some disagreement among authors as to what the different charts are called and what symbols are used.

Lead Time Charts

The lead time chart is simply a process chart with a time scale added. If the time scale is marked off in calendar dates, the lead time chart will indicate the schedule for each task. However, since it does not show where the work is done, the lead time chart is usually considered a process planning tool rather than a scheduling tool. It is used to show plans and operation schedules visually, and it is also a basic

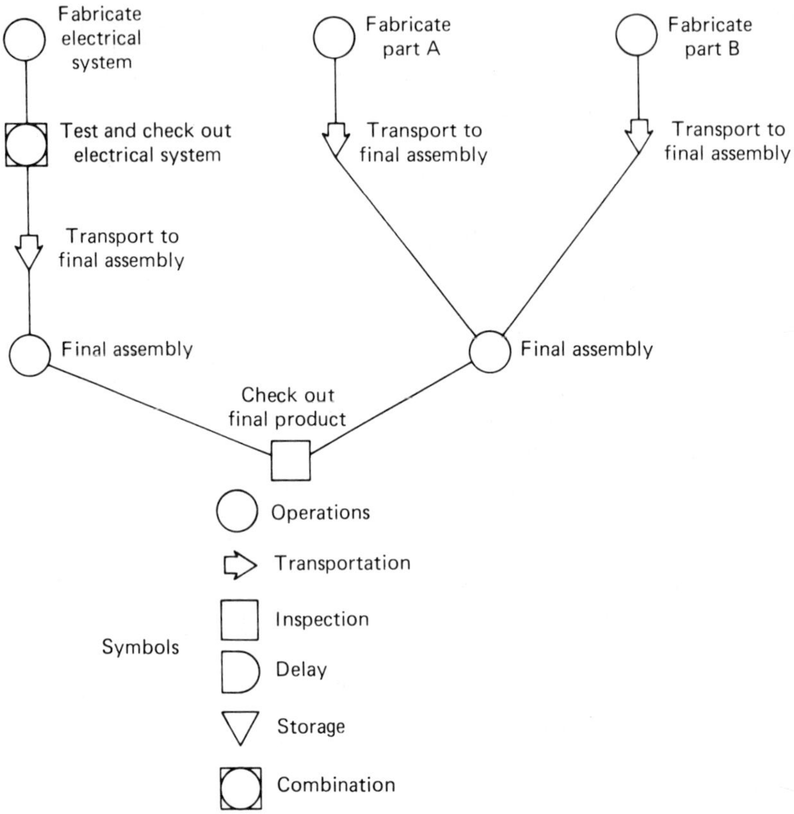

FIGURE 9–1. Flow Process Chart.

step in the line-of-balance scheduling technique described later in this chapter. The chief characteristic of the lead time chart is that it shows the latest possible start times for tasks.

Figure 9–2 is an example of a lead time chart. Note that circles are used for all points instead of the flow process symbols. The reason is that the lines between the circles represent the process, and each circle represents completion or start of a process. (Circles are called control points.) In the flow process chart, representing both processes and process completions is unnecessary; for the lead time chart, however, both must be represented in order to show the time durations of tasks.

Lead time means the time from a given point until project completion. Thus, the lead time for control point 5 is 16 days. The activity at control point 5 should start at least 16 days prior to the project finish, or the project will be delayed. Similarly, the task following control point 7 should start at least 12 days prior to project finish. Because great care is needed to assure that tasks tie together at the proper time, lead time charts are more difficult to construct than process charts.

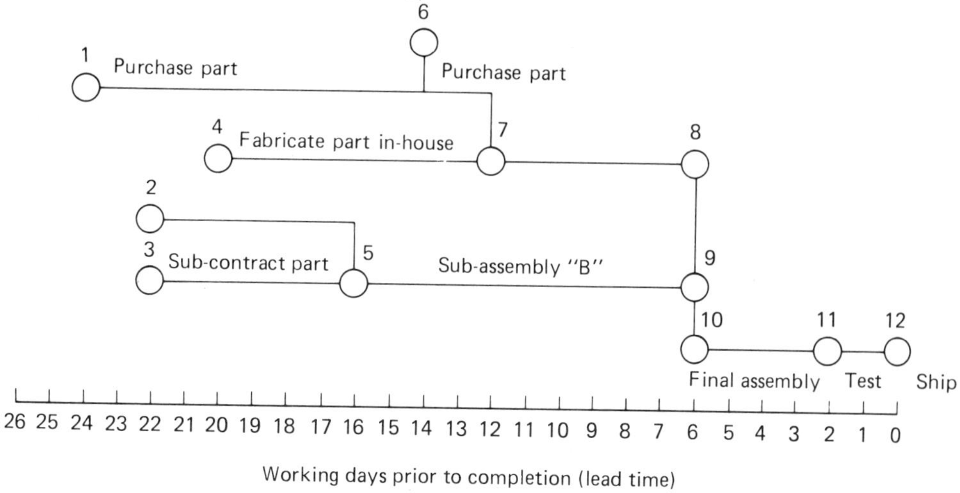

FIGURE 9–2. Lead Time Chart.

Gantt Charts

The Gantt chart is basically a bar chart or line chart with time graduations shown along the horizontal and people, organizations, machines, or tasks shown along the vertical. The bars (or lines) show the time units of work that are scheduled for each person, organization, machine, or task. The Gantt chart can be used to control the schedule as well as to portray the initial schedule; progress on scheduled work is entered periodically; reasons for being ahead of or behind schedule may be shown, in coded form, on the chart; and from this the schedule may be updated. The Gantt chart is an effective planning and scheduling tool for operations involving a minimum of interrelationships but not for large-scale research and development projects. Table 9–1 summarizes the strengths and weaknesses of the Gantt technique and its variations. All of the variations of the Gantt technique use a form of the basic chart described above. Two examples will be discussed here, one for nonrepetitive production and the other for repetitive production.

Application to Nonrepetitive Production. Figure 9–3 is a Gantt chart showing the scheduled activities for a hypothetical missile system development example.

Each activity that is in a series cannot begin until the preceding activity is completed. Characteristically, the Gantt chart shows each activity at its earliest starting time. For example, consider activities 9–11 and 11–13: "Install missile at site" (11–13) obviously can't begin until "transport missile to site" (9–11) has been completed. The kind of Gantt chart in Figure 9–3 is a very useful visual device for the manager, but it does not show who is responsible for performing the activities. Figure 9–4 shows the same data and schedule as the preceding figure, but rearranged to show what organization is responsible for each activity.

As mentioned earlier, the Gantt chart may also be constructed so that people or kinds of machines are listed in the left-hand column. A machine-oriented Gantt

TABLE 9-1.
Gantt Technique—Strengths and Weaknesses

Criteria	*Strengths*	*Weaknesses*
1. Accuracy	Good in repetitive work—time estimates likely to be good and production is easy to count.	In nonrepetitive work accuracy of estimate of task completion percentage is subject to error.
2. Reliability	Simplicity of technique helps project manager to set up consistent progressing system.	In repetitive work production count can be "doctored." Large nonrepetitive projects involve many different progress estimators which tend to hurt consistency.
3. Simplicity	Easy to understand, to accept, and to implement.	Requires good time estimates or standards, which are not simple to develop.
4. Universality of Project Coverage	Effective at work center levels. Can cover well a given phase of a life cycle.	Not effective for large, complex projects.
5. Decision Analysis		No capability to simulate alternatives.
6. Forecasting	Shows clearly ability to meet schedules in repetitive work.	Does not readily show ability to meet schedule if many interrelated tasks are involved.
7. Updating	Easy to update if program is static.	
8. Flexibility		Much chart reconstruction needed to show program changes.
9. Cost	Data gathering and display are relatively inexpensive.	Frequent program changes cause costly redrafting of charts.

chart would be useful, for example, in scheduling a computer and auxiliary equipment in a data processing center. Being very expensive, the computer would probably be fully scheduled with work for three shifts first. Other machines—sorter, collator, printer, card punch, and the like—would then be scheduled with any work needed to support the computer schedule. The Gantt chart and lead time chart are related. Both have a horizontal time scale and both sequence tasks in a similar manner. There are obvious minor differences in the way the time scale is numbered and in the task symbols used. A more significant difference is that the lead time chart omits the left-hand column that classifies the tasks in some way. The main difference is that lead time charts must show latest possible start times for tasks, whereas Gantt charts need not do this.

Application to Repetitive Production. The Gantt technique was originally developed to schedule and control repetitive production. Its application to nonrepetitive production was presented first since project management often involves single-unit production. Frequently, however, a project will involve a repetitive task. An example of repetitive packing of cartons will be used to demonstrate this Gantt application. The object will be to compare the actual rate that a packing section is packing cartons, with a normal or standard rate.

If we assume this comparison is made weekly, it is necessary, in order to arrive at the actual packing rate, to count the number of cartons packed for the week and divide it by the number of hours the packing section worked. For example, if 800 cartons were packed last week by five packers working a 40-hour week, the rate

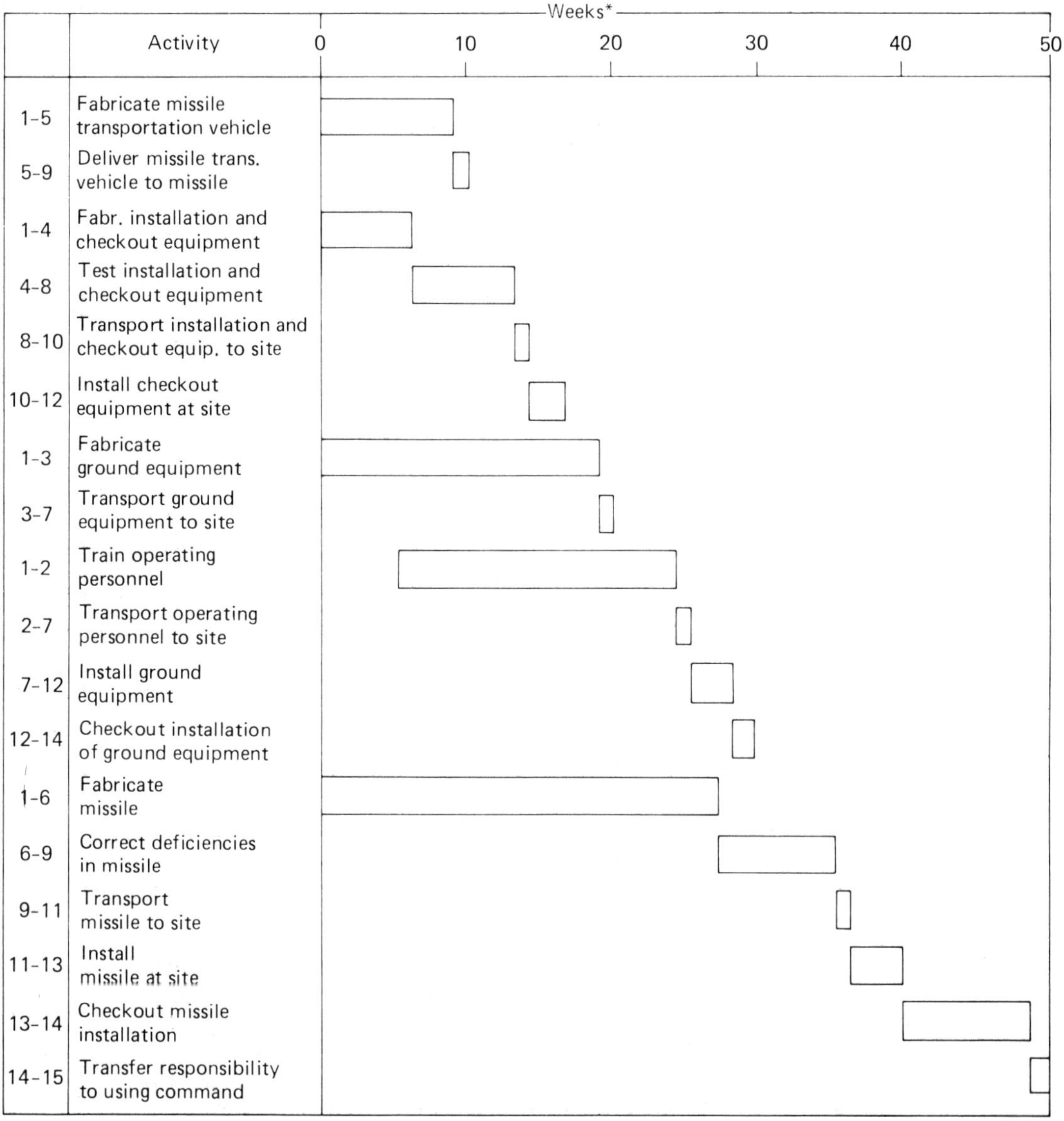

*Time scale may be in calendar time

FIGURE 9–3. Gantt Chart: Nonrepetitive Production, Activities Schedule.

is 200 hours ÷ 800 cartons = 0.25 hours per carton. Assume that the standard time for a man to pack a carton is 0.20 hours per carton. The packers have actually taken 0.05 hours too long per carton. Stated another way, they have packed only 800 per week instead of the standard of 1,000 per week (0.20 hr per carton × 200 hr per week).

The manager would use this information to judge what the effects will be on other work and on final completion date(s).

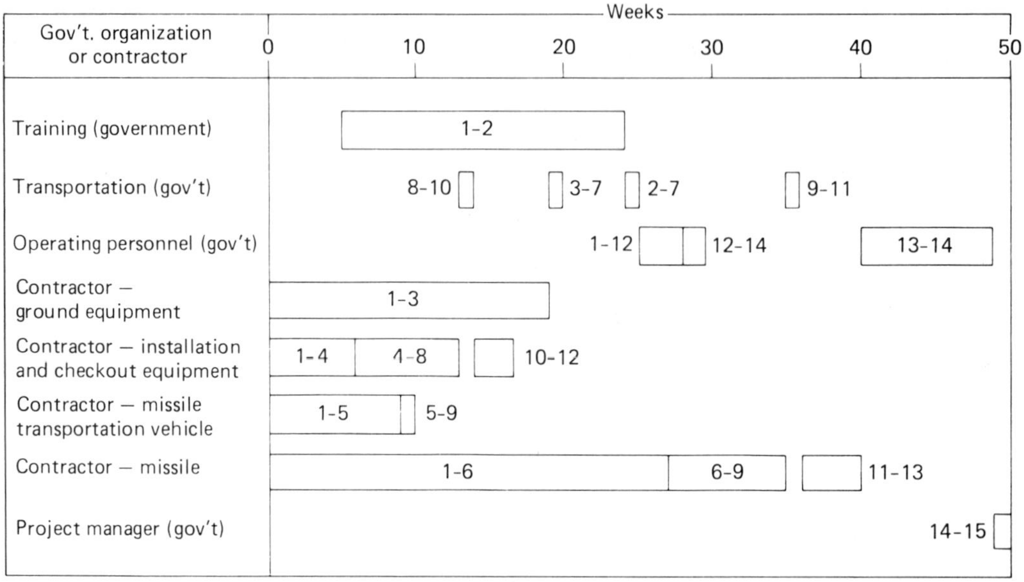

FIGURE 9–4. Gantt Chart: Nonrepetitive Production, Organization Schedule.

This would point out any need for corrective action, for example, putting the packers on overtime.

If packing is the only repetitive task in the project, it would probably not be worthwhile for the manager to display the information on a Gantt chart. If there are several such tasks, however, the Gantt chart can save time in recording progress information and in analyzing it for possible corrective action. Figure 9–5 shows the data for the packing section plus two other hypothetical sections. The legend explains all of the progress information that is entered on the chart. In keeping with the management-by-exception principle, there are no symbols to explain ahead-of-schedule status—only the problems. Note that the bars and solid lines do not indicate the schedule. They indicate progress. The schedule is simply 200 cartons per day, day in and day out. Whereas the Gantt chart for nonrepetitive production is useful for display of related task and progress, the chart for repetitive production is useful only for progress purposes.

Figure 9–5 may provide all the information the manager needs to control schedules. If the section gets far behind schedule, however, he may want more detailed information on what is happening within the sections. Figure 9–6 gives a detailed breakdown of the summary data in Figure 9–5. It shows what manpower problems or machine problems contribute to behind-schedule status. Gantt charts for repetitive tasks can be constructed with different degrees of detail for use by different levels of management.

Milestone Charts

The milestone chart is an outgrowth of the Gantt chart. A milestone may be described as an important event in the path of project completion. All milestones are not equally significant. A milestone may be the com-

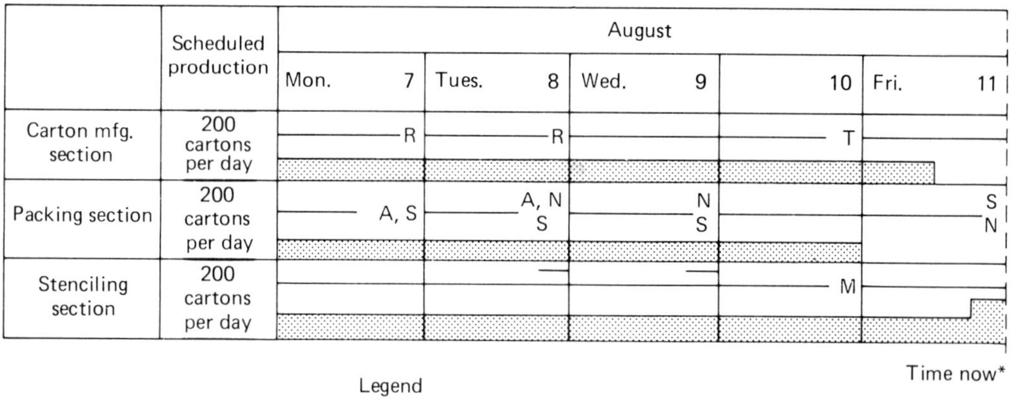
Scheduled production
August
Mon. 7
Tues. 8
Wed. 9
10
Fri. 11
Carton mfg. section
200 cartons per day
R
R
T
Packing section
200 cartons per day
A, S
A, N S
N S
S N
Stenciling section
200 cartons per day
M
Time now*

Legend

1 —— Amount of work actually done in a day.

2 [shaded box] Weekly total for section.

3 Reasons for falling behind:

A = Absent
N = New operator
S = Slow operator
R = Repairs needed
T = Tool trouble
M = Material delay

FIGURE 9–5. Gantt Chart: Repetitive Production.

pletion of an entire short activity or a part of a longer activity. When milestone charts are used, progress reports are made when the milestones are scheduled for completion. If applicable, progress reports should present analyses as to why the milestones were not reached on schedule.

Figure 9–7 is an example of a milestone chart. It is like Figure 9–4 except that in Figure 9–7 the arrows showing when progress will be checked are at selected milestones. Progress is checked twice for activity 1–3, three times for activity 1–6, and only at scheduled completion for all the others.

The total number of activity progress reports is 20 in Figure 9–7; in Figure 9–4 checking progress on each activity every week totals 120 activity reports. Each time progress is reported, many people must take time to check out and estimate percentage of completions. Thus, the milestone techniques saves a great deal of time and money by reporting progress when it is most needed—provided the milestones have been carefully selected.

Man-hour Load Charts

Man-hour load scheduling is a more flexible version of the Gantt application to nonrepetitive work: In manpower loading, task completion dates are specified but task start dates are not. Those responsible may work on the task any time they wish, as long as it is completed at the end of the

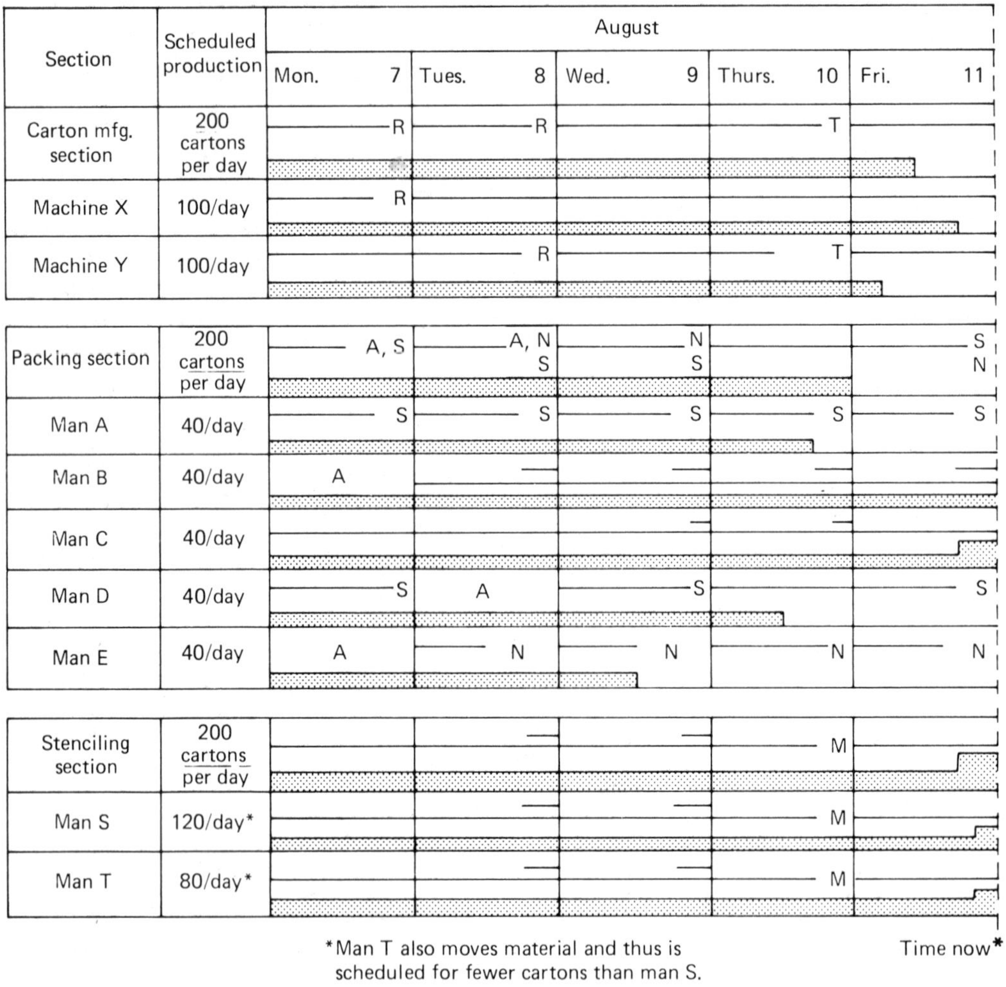
Section
Scheduled production
August
Mon. 7
Tues. 8
Wed. 9
Thurs. 10
Fri. 11
Carton mfg. section
200 cartons per day
Machine X
100/day
Machine Y
100/day
Packing section
200 cartons per day
Man A
40/day
Man B
40/day
Man C
40/day
Man D
40/day
Man E
40/day
Stenciling section
200 cartons per day
Man S
120/day*
Man T
80/day*
*Man T also moves material and thus is scheduled for fewer cartons than man S.
Time now*

FIGURE 9–6. Gantt Chart: Repetitive Production (Detail).

load period. In Figure 9–4 activities 1–5 and 5–9 are scheduled to start at week 0 and finish at week 10. If these activities do not need to be completed until week 35, the man-hour load technique can be used. In this, the schedule would indicate the due date (week 35) and the number of weeks of work involved (10), but not the start date. The work could then be done as it best fits in with other scheduled work and capabilities. It is sometimes necessary to maintain tight scheduling and tight control in order to meet deadlines. This applies to complex and uncertain projects in which many blocks of work tie in closely with one another. However, when task due dates are less critical and task time estimates are more certain, it is often better to schedule more flexibility using man-hour loading.

The charting of man-hour load schedules

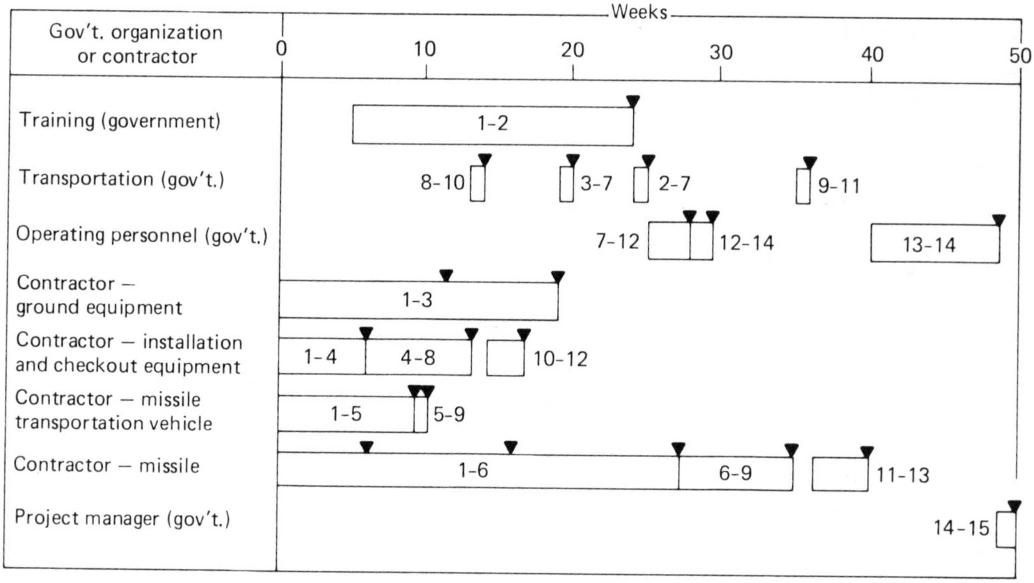

FIGURE 9–7. Milestone Chart: Nonrepetitive Production, Organization Schedule.

can be done in a number of ways, two of which are presented here. Figure 9–8 is like Figure 9–4, except some of the activities have been man-hour loaded. For example, activity 1–3 is man-hour loaded. It is shown as a shaded bar between weeks 10 and 29. This means that it should take 19 weeks to do the work, and it must be finished by the 29th week. It need not begin at week 10, but may start anytime between weeks 0 and 10. Activity 3–7 following 1–3 is shown unshaded, which means it will start precisely at week 29 and finish at week 30. Then the next activity, 7–12, is again man-hour loaded. It is shown between weeks 33 and 36, but it may start anytime between weeks 30 and 33.

Progress reports for man-hour loaded activities would be in accord with the location of bars on the chart. Thus, for activity 1–3 progress would not be checked until after the 10th week. If the activity actually begins at week 0, the first progress report would occur at week 11—if we assume weekly reporting—and would show ahead-of-schedule status.

A more rigid variation of the man-hour loading is one that is sometimes called load-by-schedule technique. It is commonly used by contractors or government industrial installations in scheduling routed work—work done in support shops such as the wood shop, sheet metal shop, and welding shop. Figure 9–9 is a simplified chart showing three job orders scheduled into two shops by this technique. In this example, the schedule period is one week. It could be two weeks, a month, or any other convenient time frame. In the load-by-schedule period technique, any operations shown within a schedule period must be done by the end of that period. They can start any time as long as that completion date is met. In Figure 9–9 the sheet metal shop has one week to do the first operation of job orders 101 and 102; in that same week the welding shop has to do the first operation of job

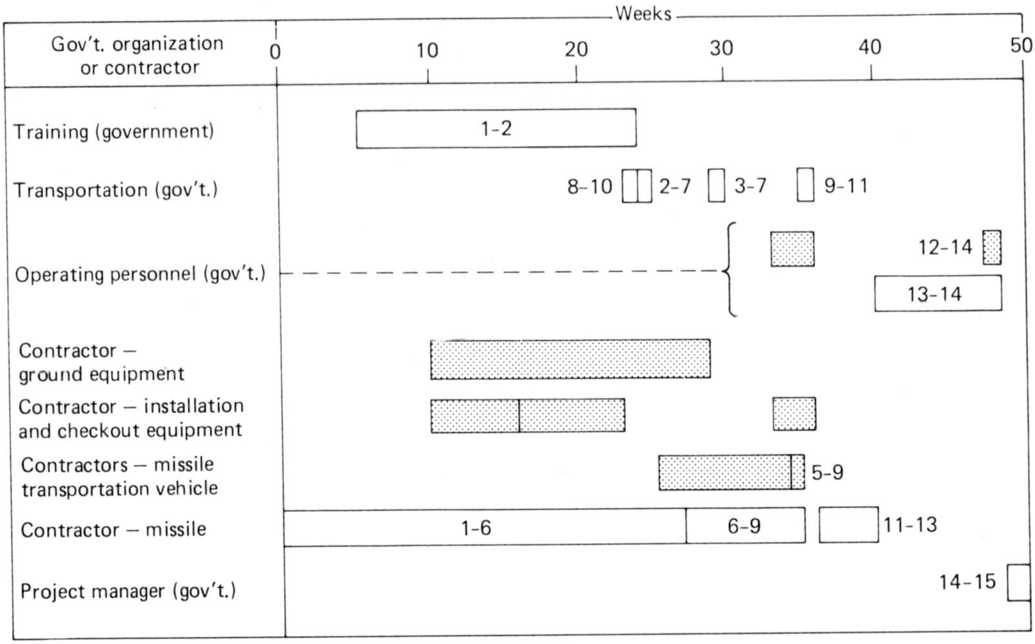

Note: Shaded bars represent manhour loading.
Nonshaded bars represent ordinary Gantt scheduling.

FIGURE 9–8. Gantt Man-hour Load Chart: Nonrepetitive Production, Organization Schedule.

order 103. In the second week, the sheet metal shop does the second operation of job order 103, and the welding shop does the second operation of job orders 101 and 102.

For job orders with many operations, the material is routed from shop to shop in this manner, each shop getting one week to accomplish its operation. Rush jobs, of course, would not be scheduled this way. The technique is useful for normal routed job-order production in that it allows the shop foreman a great deal of flexibility in assigning work most economically. Unscheduled time remaining in a schedule period is available for last-minute

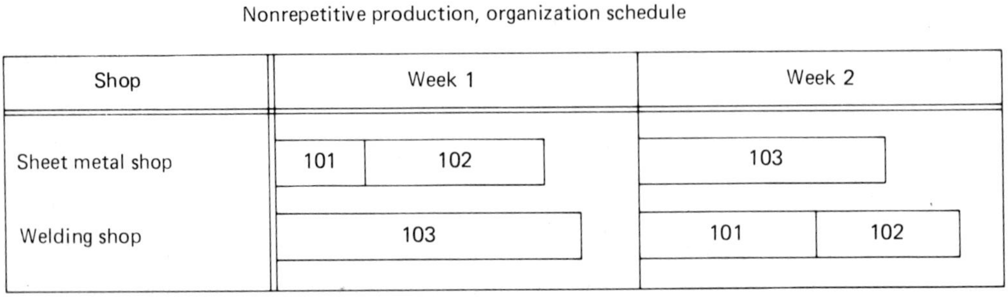

Nonrepetitive production, organization schedule
Shop
Week 1
Week 2
Sheet metal shop
101
102
103
Welding shop
103
101
102

FIGURE 9–9. Gantt Load-by-Schedule-Period Chart.

rush jobs or for such things as internal shop maintenance.

The strengths and weaknesses for the man-hour load techniques are the same as those shown in Table 9–1, except that the man-hour load techniques provide greater flexibility at a sacrifice in forecasting ability.

LINE-OF-BALANCE (LOB) TECHNIQUE

The line-of-balance (LOB) technique is useful in controlling complex repetitive production projects with a number of interrelated activities. It employs the lead time chart and the project delivery schedule in analyzing progress data for each control point. The line of balance shows what control points need attention now, in order to maintain schedules in the future.

Although there is also a version of LOB for nonrepetitive production, it is rarely used. The networking techniques have been found to be simpler and to provide more complete control of complex nonrepetitive production. The LOB technique is product oriented. Its key feature is that bottlenecks in the production process are brought out. Management must then take proper action, generally increasing the resources at the bottlenecks. Consequently, Gantt and LOB are complementary techniques. The various steps of the LOB technique are explained below.

Objectives

The first step is to draw the contract delivery schedule or what is called the "objective" chart (Figure 9–10). The purpose of this chart is to give the cumulative units to be delivered and the dates for delivery. This information is charted by the contract schedule line. The term *contract schedule* should be interpreted broadly to include in-house and contracted production. This chart (Figure 9–10) shows the actual delivery as of the end of April.

Program

The second step is to chart the program. The program or production plan is merely a lead time chart. Only the most meaningful events should be selected as control points for the lead time chart.

The lead time chart for this example is shown in Figure 9–11. The twelve control points represent the key tasks in manufacturing one unit of a hypothetical product. The program tells us that initial purchasing (control point 1) must begin 24 working days prior to any scheduled delivery. In order to meet the first scheduled delivery of five units by the last day of December (see contract schedule in objective chart) purchasing must begin 24 working days prior to 1 January. The lead time for the other control points can be related to the delivery schedule in a similar manner.

Progress and Line of Balance

The third step, the progress chart (Figure 9–12), shows the status of the twelve control points. The bar for control point 4 shows that 60 units have been fabricated, the bar for control point 9 shows 40 units assembled. Other control points can be interpreted similarly.

Next, the line of balance is constructed to analyze how present progress will affect future schedules. The line of balance represents the number of units that should have passed through each control point so that future deliveries can be met. The line of balance is drawn on top of the bars on the progress chart in order to show status of control points. The difference between the line and the top of a bar for a control point is the number of units behind or ahead of schedule.

The technique for constructing the line of balance is as follows:

1. Select a control point, say 7.
2. Using the program chart (Figure 9–11) determine the lead time, that is, the

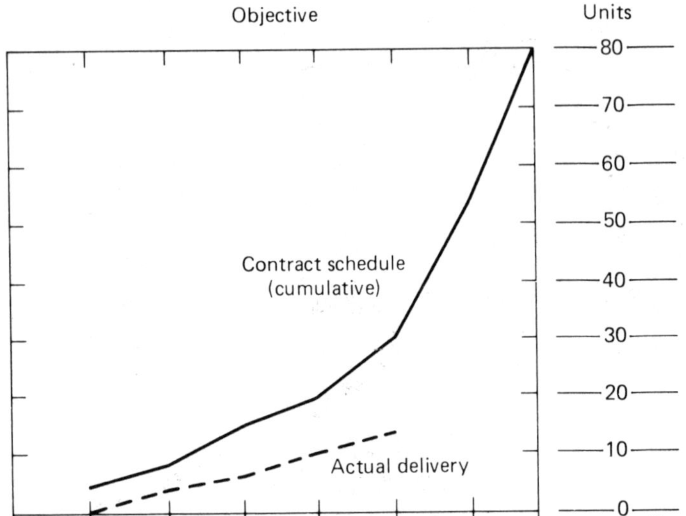

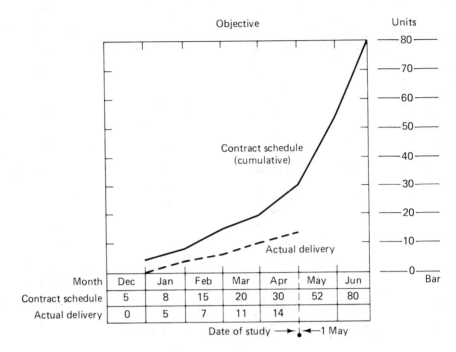

Month	Dec	Jan	Feb	Mar	Apr	May	Jun
Contract schedule	5	8	15	20	30	52	80
Actual delivery	0	5	7	11	14		

Date of study → ← 1 May

FIGURE 9–10. Objective Chart.

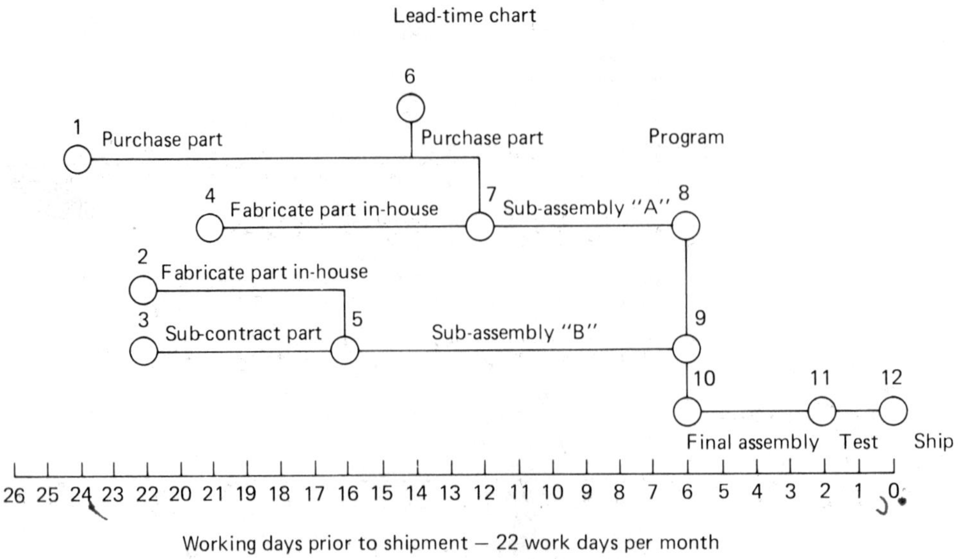

FIGURE 9–11. Lead-time Chart.

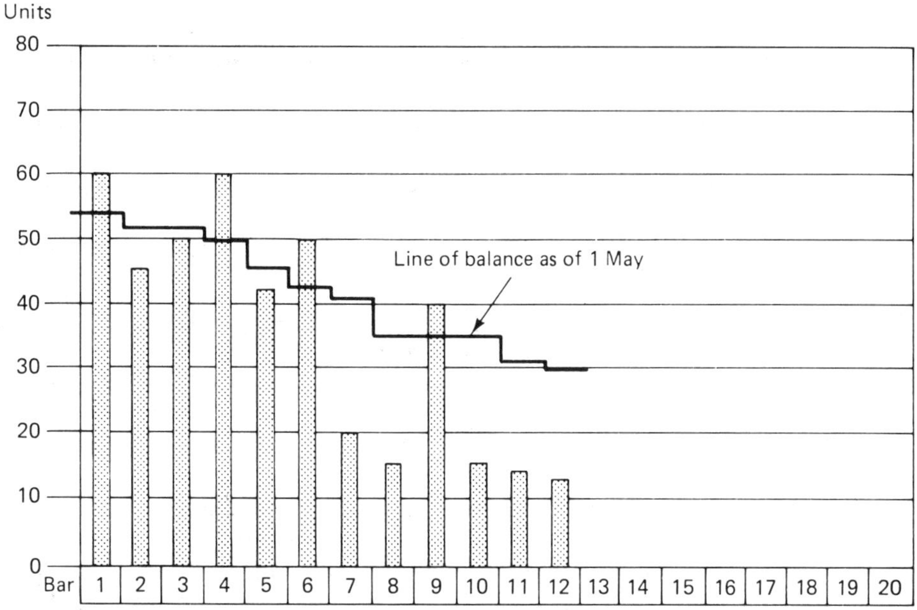

FIGURE 9–12. Progress Chart.

time from the control point to shipment. In this case the lead time is 12 working days.

3. Using this number determine the date that the units now at this control point should be ready for shipment (May 1 plus 12 working days lead time is May 16).
4. On the contract schedule line (Figure 9–10), find the point corresponding to this date (May 16) and determine how many units are scheduled for completion at that time (41).
5. Draw a line on the progress chart at that level (41) over control point 7.
6. Repeat these procedures for all the control points and connect the horizontal lines. The resulting line is the line of balance. It indicates the number of units that should have passed through each control point on the date of the study (May 1) if the delivery schedule is to be met.

With the LOB charts shown in this chapter, management can tell at a glance how actual progress compares with planned progress. Analysis of the charts can pinpoint problem areas. Updating the charts requires a good status reporting system, which can be mechanized if the project is large and complex. A computer program has been developed by the Army Management Engineering Training Agency, Rock Island, Illinois, that will provide printouts of all the information required on the LOB charts. Actually, since the program provides all the information, the printouts could be used by themselves without the need for charts. Graphic display of the information is, however, usually desirable.

Table 9–2 summarizes the strengths and weaknesses of the LOB technique.

TABLE 9-2.
LOB Technique–Strengths and Weaknesses (In Repetitive Production)

Criteria	*Strengths*	*Weaknesses*
1. Accuracy	Completion time estimates are good, since work is repetitive.	
2. Reliability	Compares favorably with Gantt technique.	
3. Simplicity		How the line of balance is constructed is not always understood.
4. Universality of Project Coverage		Well suited only for production phase of life cycle. Does not emphasize resource allocation directly.
5. Decision Analysis		No capability to simulate alternatives.
6. Forecasting	Very good for indicating whether or not schedules can be met.	
7. Updating		Considerable clerical effort needed to update graphs. Computer processing can reduce this effort.
8. Flexibility		Inflexible. When major program changes occur, all LOB phases must be redesigned.
9. Cost	Data gathering and computations can be handled routinely and at moderate expense.	

Program Evaluation and Review Technique (PERT)

INTRODUCTION

Much has been written about the role of a manager, his functions, and environment. The manager must use the latest available tools to overcome obstacles produced by rapid changes in technology. Through the use of current management tools he can be more effective. Just as effective managers are made, not born, improvements in the management process are developed. They do not just happen. A manager has the inherent responsibility to develop the main and supporting objectives of his organization, and to ensure the accomplishment thereof through the continuous direction of others. This responsibility includes planning, scheduling, and controlling. The manner in which this responsibility is carried out has become known as the work management process cycle. The framework of this cycle follows:

1. The objective must be established. Management decides the goal it desires and must work toward.
2. Plans must be developed. Estimates of resources required are made. The routes for traveling toward the goal are outlined in detail.
3. The timetables for traveling specific distances in the route are set. Scheduling of activities along all routes must be completed.
4. After the operation begins, evaluation of progress on all routes against the timetables (schedules) and cost esti-

mates are essential. Problems must be detected on a timely basis and the facts related thereto assembled for review. Only significant problems and deviations from the plan or schedule along with remedial action being taken and results to be expected are reported to top management (the management by exception principle).

5. On the basis of the circumstances, the facts, and the impact on the total program objective, decisions must be made by management. Changes in assignment of resources (manpower, supplies, equipment, dollars) may be necessary to get the program back on schedule. Other actions must be taken as necessary.
6. It may be necessary, after decisions to act are made, to recycle the process—change the scheduled plan. It is through this recycling method that management achieves and maintains control of the objective oriented effort.

New management devices, techniques, or tools have emerged with each new development and improvement in the management process cycle.

PERT DEVELOPMENT AND APPLICATION

Although the actual emergence of PERT, per se, into the inventory of management tools occurred since World War II, the search for a solution to the problems it solves began years ago. There is, therefore, no doubt that some aspects of the PERT system have been used in some form for many years. It may be said that, as a rule, top-level management has always striven to find a better way of doing things and, if possible, at a lower cost. The degree to which effort was applied to this goal varied in organizations. However, uniformity of need that produced the effort existed as follows:

1. Lack of a method or technique for establishing objectives, selecting routes to travel, schedules to follow, controlling while en route, and communicating to all concerned.
2. Lack of a way of gathering information and analyzing en route progress on total program.
3. Lack of an accurate means of predicting accomplishment as scheduled.

With the technological advances made during and after World War II, the problems of management increased. Time and cost took on increased significance. Formerly, industry had produced requirements with relatively simple manufacturing processes. This technological revolution brought on greatly increased complexity. The management tools were no longer adequate to cope with the many difficult problems of control in both industry and government. The methods used to control production sequencing and scheduling were inadequate owing to the many possible combinations and variations of complex production.

PERT embraces a group of management concepts, each of which can be used effectively by itself; but when grouped together into an integrated system, they ensure the optimum use of time and resources available to accomplish a known goal. Among these concepts are: (1) the use of a network to represent plans, (2) the prediction of time needed to complete each phase of the project, (3) the recognizing and measuring of uncertainty, and (4) the continual revision of plans and operations to meet unpredictable situations and environment. By combining these time-tested management procedures in one overall approach, PERT provides a means of defining, interrelating, and integrating what must be done to accomplish project objectives on time. PERT, then, is a detailed and interrelated master plan that has sufficient built-in flexibility to serve as a stable guide for a complex project through its many steps to completion.

Many techniques, procedures, and systems have been developed to aid the manager in the fulfillment of his responsibilities. Traditionally, these aids have been most effective in a manufacturing or continuous type of production application. Among these techniques are the flow process chart, the Gantt chart, the milestone chart, and the line-of-balance chart. These techniques are not by any means obsolete; in fact, each has a place in production applications. However, management found that these existing techniques did not completely meet their needs in the special project area. Therefore, using these previously developed techniques as a point of departure, managers of special projects selected the appropriate procedures from these formerly successful techniques, adding their own unique methods, and devised this relatively new and integrated means of planning, called PERT. PERT, then, was not developed by a revolutionary process; instead, it could be better described as a product of evolution.

In late 1956, a step toward positive results in improving the inventory of management tools was begun by James E. Kelly, Jr., of Remington Rand, and Morgan R. Walker of E. I. Du Pont de Nemours. Their work on a planning and scheduling technique to assist in the management of a project to overhaul a large chemical plant and keep downtime of production to a minimum resulted in the development of the Critical Path Method (CPM). This technique involved reducing the amount of time required to overhaul the plant, which in turn would reduce the direct and indirect cost normally lost during periods of production downtime. CPM utilized networks as does PERT.

The actual development of PERT is attributed to the U.S. Navy's Special Projects Office. In 1956, this office began searching for management control ideas for use in the Navy's missile development program. The search took Special Projects Office personnel throughout private industry; the U.S. Air Force, which already had a missile program; and the Navy. Because of similarities in problems, the Navy adopted many of the management control techniques used by the Air Force. Later, these ideas were combined with others—some were new, some were already in use, and some had been used for centuries. From this combination of ideas, PERT was developed early in 1958. However, it was not until late 1958 that the Navy began using PERT on its Polaris missile program. PERT proved highly successful on the project; in fact, much of the success for the rapid development of the Polaris missile was attributed to this new management tool. Shortly after the Navy began using PERT, the Air Force became interested in it and was so impressed that in 1959 it applied PERT to its missile development programs. Since its initial success on the Polaris program, the use of PERT on other government projects has resulted in the saving of time and money.

PERT weathered the usual criticism that follows the introduction of a new management tool and, through increased application, improvements have been made, thereby increasing its usefulness. Some examples of known programs or project applications in government and industry are:

1. Weapon and space systems acquisition.
2. Atomic energy programs.
3. Support equipment management.
4. Maintenance planning.
5. Construction operations.
6. Installing and debugging a computer system.
7. Military operations.
8. New product development.

9. Planning and launching a new product.

Striking examples of profit improvement and time saving have been attributed to the use of PERT. The Catalytic Construction Company has reported an average time reduction of 22 percent along with a 15 percent reduction in "expediting costs" on almost fifty projects. Du Pont reported a 37 percent reduction in downtime of production during the repair of a chemical plant in Louisville. Department of Defense (DOD) agencies have successfully used PERT in the Polaris acquisition program, the Atlas E and F, Titan I and II, and the Minuteman Site Activation programs, and in others that have greatly improved the ability of the agency to control the program and to manage "by exception." Where time or cost is of importance—regardless of the size of the program, project, or task—PERT can be applied with success. The cost of using computers for computing estimated time and reporting status may limit applicability on some tasks. However, consideration should be given in those cases for a manual application to offset the cost of computers. Where computer costs are prohibitive or when computers are not available, PERT can be implemented on a manual basis. The usefulness of PERT will undoubtedly continue to grow as government and industry become increasingly aware of areas in which such a management tool can produce a savings of time and costs.

PERT does nothing by itself. It must be used by management as a tool. The success of any organization depends upon establishment of objectives and detailed planning for their accomplishment. Broadly speaking, PERT helps the manager provide a better disciplined and more complete planning device; a more accurate approximation of time and cost requirements of a program; and a more efficient control technique for viewing program progress, making decisions, and communicating changes required. Although PERT may not be considered the solution to all problems, it does provide an excellent tool for:

1. Coordinating and integrating effort, thus enabling management to view the total program, project, or task with the interrelationships of its activities, regardless of organizational lines.
2. Developing a logical and adequate plan that reflects interrelationships of activities and reduces the possibility of excluding activities or improper scheduling by the use of networks.
3. Estimating realistic target dates (time requirements) through the use of acceptable statistical methods.
4. Predicting the probability of meeting deadlines and staying within budgets through the use of acceptable mathematical formulas.
5. Identifying problem or potential problem areas in time for preventive action.
6. Improving communication between line and staff personnel (between the operators, technicians, planners, and management).
7. Measuring accomplishment of actual time and cost against schedules, budgets, and objectives. Continuous en route measurements provide the opportunity for considering on a timely basis trade-offs in funds, manpower, performance, and time between critical and noncritical areas in order to improve schedule plans for one or more programs or the total program.
8. Relating the progress of effort, for each activity, in making scheduled dates and projected costs as they pertain to the activity and the total program, project, or task.
9. Testing and evaluating the effects of a management decision by a simulation technique prior to implementation of the decision.

Management benefits from the common use of PERT. All levels make up a team that serves as an aid to communication in all phases of the program. PERT has been found to be especially useful in construction, system development, and production projects.

PERT NETWORK

PERT is but one of the operational tools developed to aid management in planning and scheduling work. This tool, which is based upon the network theory, is a powerful but simple technique that is particularly useful in analyzing, planning, and scheduling large complex projects. It also provides a means of determining which jobs or activities comprising a project are critical in their effect on the total project time and how best to schedule all jobs in a project to meet a target date at minimum cost.

PERT is specific and is based primarily upon goals. Figure 9–13 illustrates A PERT network. Each event from A through N is a goal. Event A is the goal to begin the project, event N is the goal of the project's completion, and all the events in between are intermediate goals that must be met along the road. The lines connecting these

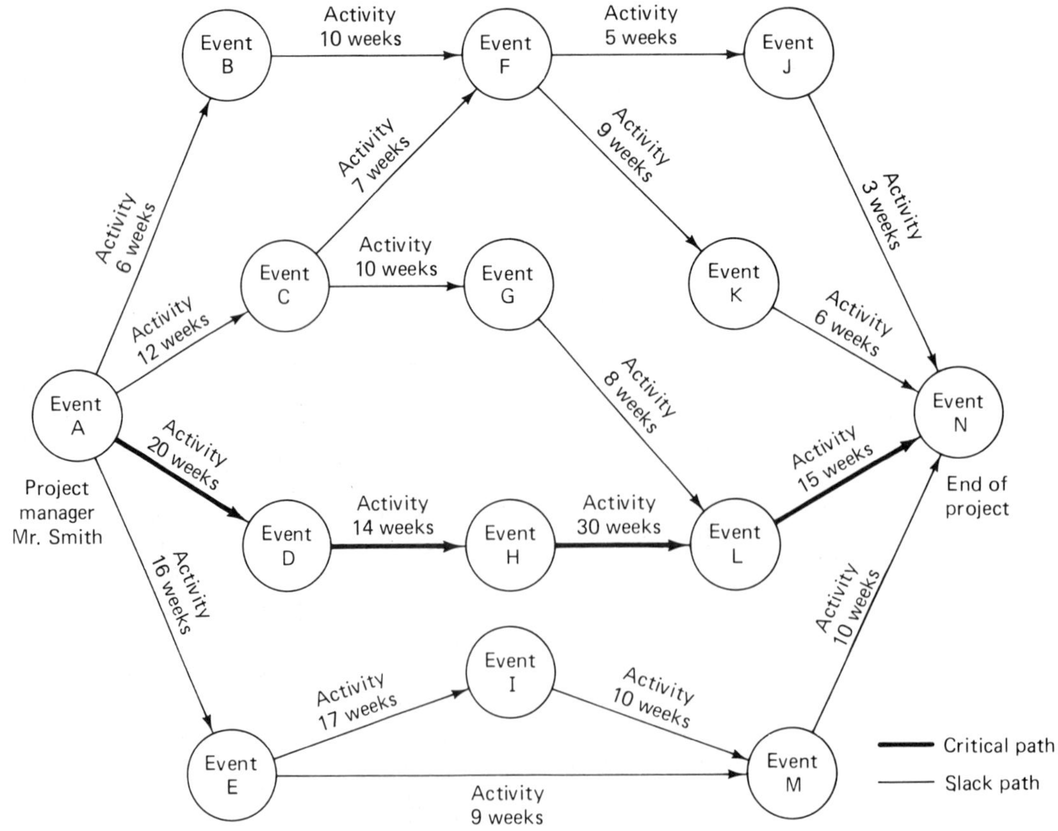

FIGURE 9–13. PERT Network.

events or goals represent the work or the activities necessary to reach the next goal.

PERT can be a valuable tool for the work systems analyst as well as the manager. Both are vitally concerned with planning, and whenever any plan is of sufficient complexity to justify putting it on paper, PERT will provide a better way to do it.

Before beginning to use the PERT network to plan a major project in detail, the manager or work systems analyst should organize his thoughts concerning the project by defining his objectives and dividing his large project into its major work areas. In developing program objectives, the manager's first job is to define the project. Before using PERT to aid in the planning of a complex project, a person must know exactly what he hopes to accomplish. Two specific procedures are of great help in defining the objectives of a project:

1. The large, complex project must first be broken down into manageable subdivisions. When this is done, the manager must define the objective for each subdivision in sufficient detail to enable a person unfamiliar with the project to know specifically what must be accomplished before that section of the overall project is completed.
2. In defining the objectives for each subdivision, the manager should begin with the ultimate objective of the entire project and work back toward the beginning of the project. This is called a top-down approach. By this procedure, the entire project is totally related to the final objective of the entire project, and the manager can easily recognize any area that does not in any way help achieve the ultimate goal. Furthermore, by developing goals on the basis of the end product, we are assured that all parts of the program are integrated into the total program. In this way, we can see the interdependencies and interrelationships of all the program objectives.

WORK BREAKDOWN

At this point, the manager must itemize the various tasks that need to be accomplished to meet the final objective. These tasks should be arranged in the order that they will occur and should be assigned to managers who will have primary responsibility for their completion. To do this, the top manager uses a work breakdown structure in which he takes the final, intermediate, and initial objectives and converts them into work areas.

In any integrated time-resource management system, it is imperative that both resources and time are planned and controlled from a common framework or structure that defines the major areas of work effort and their interrelationships. Such a common framework provides a master plan whereby all aspects of the project may be managed. Using the top-down approach, the manager starts from the highest level of management that will use PERT as a vehicle for controlling the progress of the project, and progressively breaks down each component part of the project into orderly subdivisions until the least significant subdivision becomes the smallest manageable unit for planning and control purposes. These smallest manageable units are called end-item subdivisions. They represent the hardware, equipment, or facilities that are used, and the services that are to be performed. Each of these end items could be further subdivided into functional phases.

The number of subdivisions of a project depends upon several factors:

1. How large and how complex is the project? A small project will have a limited number of levels, and a large or complex project will have many levels.
2. What is the degree of certainty in the work? As the degree of uncertainty increases, more levels will be required.
3. How familiar are the people with the work to be performed? The less familiar the operating personnel are with the

work to be done, the larger will be the number of levels required.

4. How much time is available? The more time we have available, the more levels we can use.
5. How many participating organizations are involved, and how complex are their structures?
6. Who is responsible for each phase of the work?

Sections of the work breakdown structure can vary in the number of levels into which they are divided. Certain areas, such as major phases of work effort that represent significant expenditures of time or resources, warrant the establishment of several levels. Other areas such as test operations will not necessarily warrant as many levels. For each level in the work breakdown structure, objectives and plans for meeting the objectives must be formulated. There are several advantages in developing a work breakdown structure: it defines the tasks involved in a project through an exhaustive analysis of the entire project; it establishes a framework for planning and controlling the schedule and performance objectives for all levels of management; and it establishes the basis for constructing the PERT network diagram and facilities defining project tasks and activities.

NETWORKING

After the manager has completed his work breakdown structure to determine the basic administrative and physical task involved in the project, the actual construction of a PERT network is not difficult. This network is a visual presentation of the flow plan of the project objectives and is based upon the Gantt charting technique developed by Henry Gantt prior to World War I.

Explanation of Terms

The following terms are unique to the concept of PERT. Before discussing the network diagram in detail, we must understand the meaning of these terms.

Event: An event is an identifiable point in time at which something is accomplished. There may be work and, therefore, time involved in bringing about this accomplishment. However, the fact that the event is accomplished in no way requires either work or time. In the PERT network, an event is shown as a circle, square, or some other similar symbol. The event labeled within a circle merely means that this action is completed. There is neither work nor time involved at the moment this action is completed. Thus, the completion of each basic task of a project is shown on a network as an event.

Activity: On the PERT network shown in Figure 9–13, you undoubtedly noticed the term *activity*. You also noted that an activity is represented on a PERT network by an arrow and that an activity separates one event from another. An activity is a clearly defined task to which a known quantity of manpower and other resources is applied. Each activity represents effort and resources applied over a period of time. An activity is always bounded by two events. An activity cannot be started until the preceding event has been completed. In contrast to an event, an activity represents both time and work.

Network: The term *network* has already been introduced here. Let's examine this concept a little further. The network shows the interdependencies among the tasks or activities and illustrates the sequence in which they are planned. For each step of the plan it shows the work that must precede the other steps and the activities that may be carried on simultaneously or independently. Through the use of detail nets (which show the project plan in complete detail); summary nets (which depict the major events and activities of the plan), and subnets (which portray sections of the master plan), subordinate participants may clearly see what parts they must carry out and how their work relates with the work of others; they will also better understand their responsibility toward securing the goal. In this way the manager may design the level of detail to be consistent with the level of management, and higher levels of management can also be quickly informed of a proposal for their consideration or approval.

Developing the Network

One question that should always be asked during the construction of a PERT network is, "Does this network show the truth—the real way the project will be accomplished?" The way it should be done is a problem that should be resolved long before the actual construction of the PERT network. In depicting the truth on the PERT network, you must accurately show the interrelationship. To determine this interrelationship and interdependency of events and activities is the most difficult task of the PERT analyst. Some managers who are experienced with this procedure believe that the best way to accurately construct the network is to start with the end event and work backwards. others maintain that it is better to start at the beginning event. Whichever way the user finds easier is the best way for him to build his PERT network. In either case, the analyst must know how to correctly express activities and events if he is to design a workable network.

In developing a PERT network, the manager can simplify his task if he has established a set of rules to guide him.

FIGURE 9–14. Beginning Event.

These rules will vary with the individual, the project, and the methods used. The following is one suggested set of rules or procedures for expressing the events within the PERT network:

1. Define the beginning event with a title which describes the project. For example, note Figure 9–14.
2. Establish and define events that are significant to the beginning. For example, note that Figure 9–15, depicts the beginning of a network defining a computer installation project. The chain or connection of these events should not be started until after all significant events are determined. Once all events significant to the beginning have been established and defined, a line is drawn between these events and event A, as shown in Figure 9–15, and to other events to which it is related. For example, the site selection affects the installation plans. Therefore, the interrelationship of the site selection event and the plan development is clear. Thus, a line would be drawn between event D and event C with the arrow pointing toward event C. The direction of the arrow is determined by which event must be completed first. In the preceding case, installation plans are usually developed after the site selection has been made.
3. Establish and define all significant events involved in completing events B, C, and D (Figure 9–16). Again, no attempt should be made to connect these events or make the chain until it

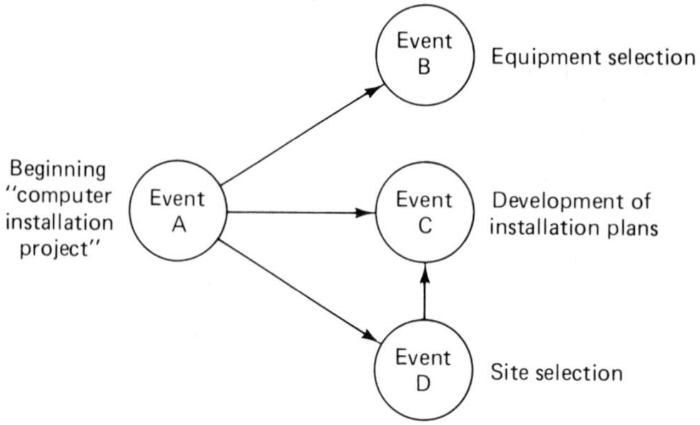

FIGURE 9–15. Beginning of a Network.

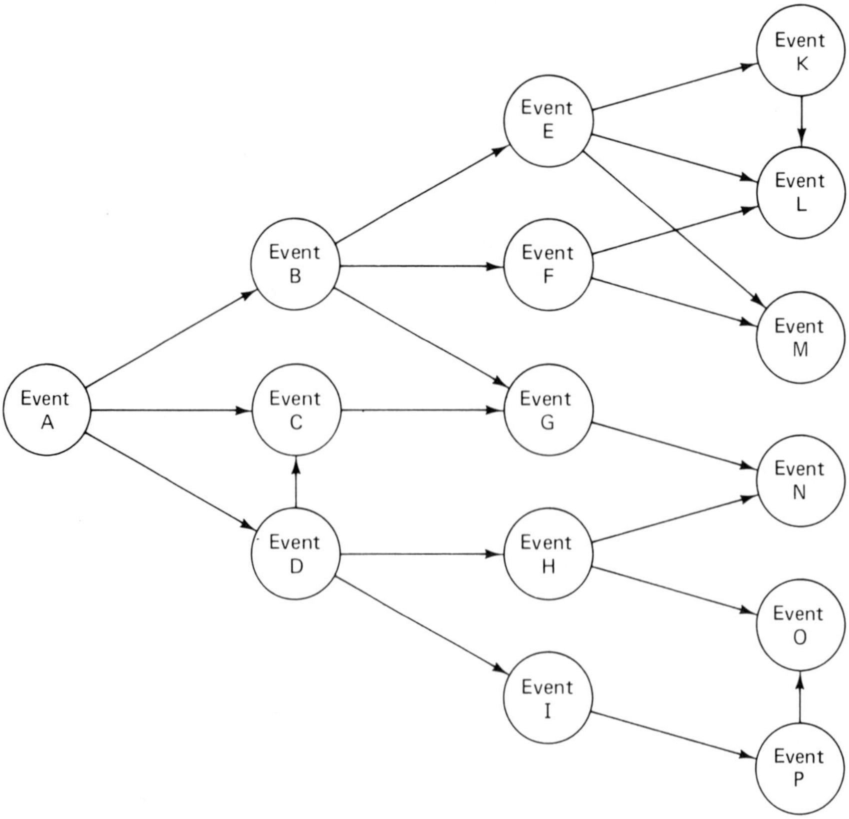

FIGURE 9–16. Continuation of a Network.

is certain that all events involved in completing events B, C, and D have been established, defined, and recorded on the PERT network (See Figure 9–15). Then, the chain or connecting lines establishing the relationship of events can be drawn.

4. To complete the network construction, continue in a similar manner with all other events. By working forward, a level at a time, you will establish and define all significant events involved in the project. After the events portion of the network is completed, a thorough study should be made of it. All significant events except the beginning and ending ones should have at least one connecting event on each end. When a significant event does not have a connecting event on each end, an event has been omitted. The omitted event must be defined and a determination must be made as to whether or not it is covered by the scope of the project. If it is covered by the scope of the project, it must be included in the network; if not, it may be omitted.

Three basic concepts are involved in expressing activities on a PERT network. First, the correct method must be used in expressing activities in which one activity precedes another. Second, the correct method must be used to express activities that are occurring at the same time. Third, each activity must be shown as having a unique pair of events.

1. When one activity precedes another, the two activities are separated by an event.
2. When several activities occur at the same time in order to approach a particular event, all of them are expressed on a PERT network.
3. Each activity expressed on a PERT network must be described or bounded by a unique pair of events so that managers are able to explicitly identify each activity. But two activities cannot be bounded by the same pair of events. For example, in Figure 9–17 two activities emerge from the event entitled "counselors." One activity is entitled "dean of students orients counselors"; the other, "counselors prepare for new students." As shown in Figure 9–17, these activities are bounded by the same pair of events, "counselors arrive" and "new students arrive." Since two activities cannot be bounded by the same pair of events, the activities are shown incorrectly in Figure 9–17. Figure 9–18 illustrates how these activities should be shown. The activities "dean of students orients counselors" and "counselors prepare for new students" must be completed prior to the beginning of the next activity. Furthermore, both activities must be completed before the event "new students arrive," is accomplished. To depict this situation correctly on a PERT network, a dummy activity must be used. Dummy activities are used to

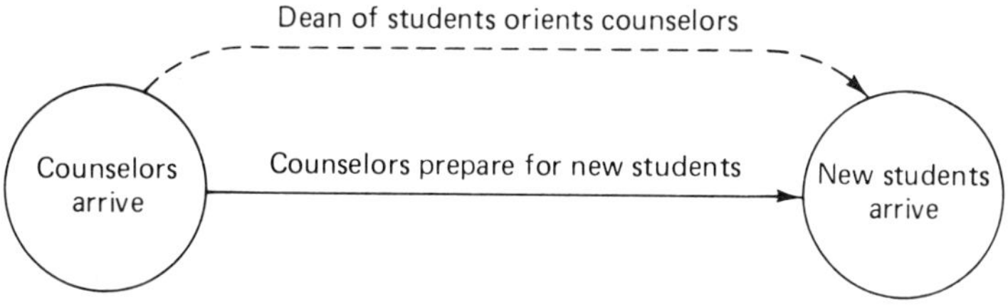

FIGURE 9–17. Incorrect Representation of Activities.

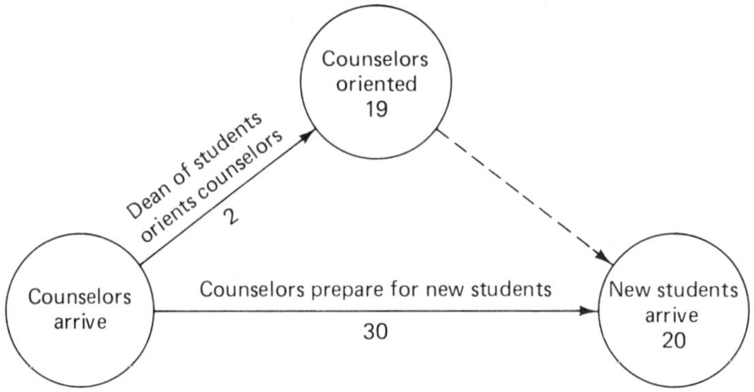

FIGURE 9–18. Correct Representation of Activities.

comply with the principles of network construction, which specify that each activity must have a unique pair of events. A dummy activity does not represent the expenditure of time or other resources. It is represented on a PERT network by a dotted line similar to the one between events 19 and 20 in Figure 9–18. It is used only to show relationships and dependencies activities and to add clarity to the network diagram.

4. When completed, the network diagram will show a unique identification for each activity, significant points needed for reporting purposes, all activities leading to the completion of an event, and all restrictive relationships between events.
5. Once the PERT network is constructed, one can start to see the power of this technique. Managers can see how the status of a single event or activity could affect subsequent events and activities. Other advantages of the PERT diagram are as follows:
   a. It is an excellent vehicle for communication.
   b. It identifies interrelationships and interdependencies.
   c. It forces detailed planning.
   d. It provides a basis for making changes.
   e. It uncovers difficult areas.
   f. It relates the various parts to the whole.

Determining Expected Time

One of the tasks of the PERT analyst is to obtain time estimates for completion of each activity shown on the network. This is necessary because PERT associates an elapsed time with an activity. Elapsed time is the amount of time that it takes from start to completion of an activity. In order to determine what this elapsed time is likely to be, it is necessary to estimate. This estimated procedure is one of the basic concepts of PERT and is designed to recognize the uncertainty in an activity and to arrive at more precision in planning figures.

Time Estimates. To determine the estimated elapsed time for each activity, the analyst must obtain three time estimates, which are initially entered for each activity on the network. These estimates are obtained from the individuals who are responsible for performing the various activities in question or those with the greatest knowledge of the activity that is to be performed.

1. *Optimistic time.* Optimistic time is the minimum time required to complete a given activity. This time estimate is based upon the expectation that everything involved in accomplishing the activity will go perfectly, or will be accomplished under the best possible conditions.
2. *Pessimistic time.* Obviously, pessimistic time is the opposite of optimistic time. This time estimate is based upon the expectation that everything involved in accomplishing the activity that could go wrong will go wrong. Thus, this time estimate is the maximum time in which this activity could be accomplished.
3. *Most likely time.* This time estimate is defined as the time allowed for the completion of an activity based upon the past experience of the estimator. This allows for both good and bad circumstances to enter into the completion of the activity. It is the time that would occur if the activity were repeated many times under exactly the same conditions. This is the best "honest time" estimate that the estimator can make.

Expected Time. Expected time is the time in which the department responsible for completing the activity will have a 50 percent chance of completing it in that time or less. This is done by combining the three time estimates mathematically. One formula for finding the expected time, sometimes referred to as mean time, is:

$$t_e = \frac{a + b + 4m}{6}.$$

In this formula t_e means expected time, a is optimistic time, b is pessimistic time, and m is most likely time. For example, the optimistic time for a specific activity is 50 days. The pessimistic time for this activity is 100 days, while the most likely time is estimated at 75 days. Using our formula, we calculate expected time as follows:

$$t_e = \frac{50 + 100 + 300}{6}$$

$$t_e = \frac{450}{6}$$

$$t_e = 75.$$

If we knew the probability function for completing the activity, we would use this in computing activity time rather than the formula just discussed. (Probability function is beyond the scope of this discussion.)

Earliest Time, Latest Time, and Slack Time

The critical path consists of the sequence of events and activities that ultimately determines the earliest possible time for completion of the project. In other words, the critical path is the longest time path through the network and will thus control the completion schedule of the entire project. In order to determine the critical path, we must have a completed network diagram that includes proper logic and all events and activities with their interrelationships. Furthermore, the expected time for each activity must be recorded on the network. Note in Figure 9–19 the number 1 between events 0 and 1, the number 25 between events 1 and 10, and the number 10 between events 1 and 5. The cited numbers indicate the expected time required to complete the activities between the events indicated, and serve as the basis for computing earliest time, latest time, and slack time.

Step 1. The first step in the procedure used to determine the critical path is to determine the *earliest possible time* (called earliest time) for the completion of each event in its proper sequence along one or more

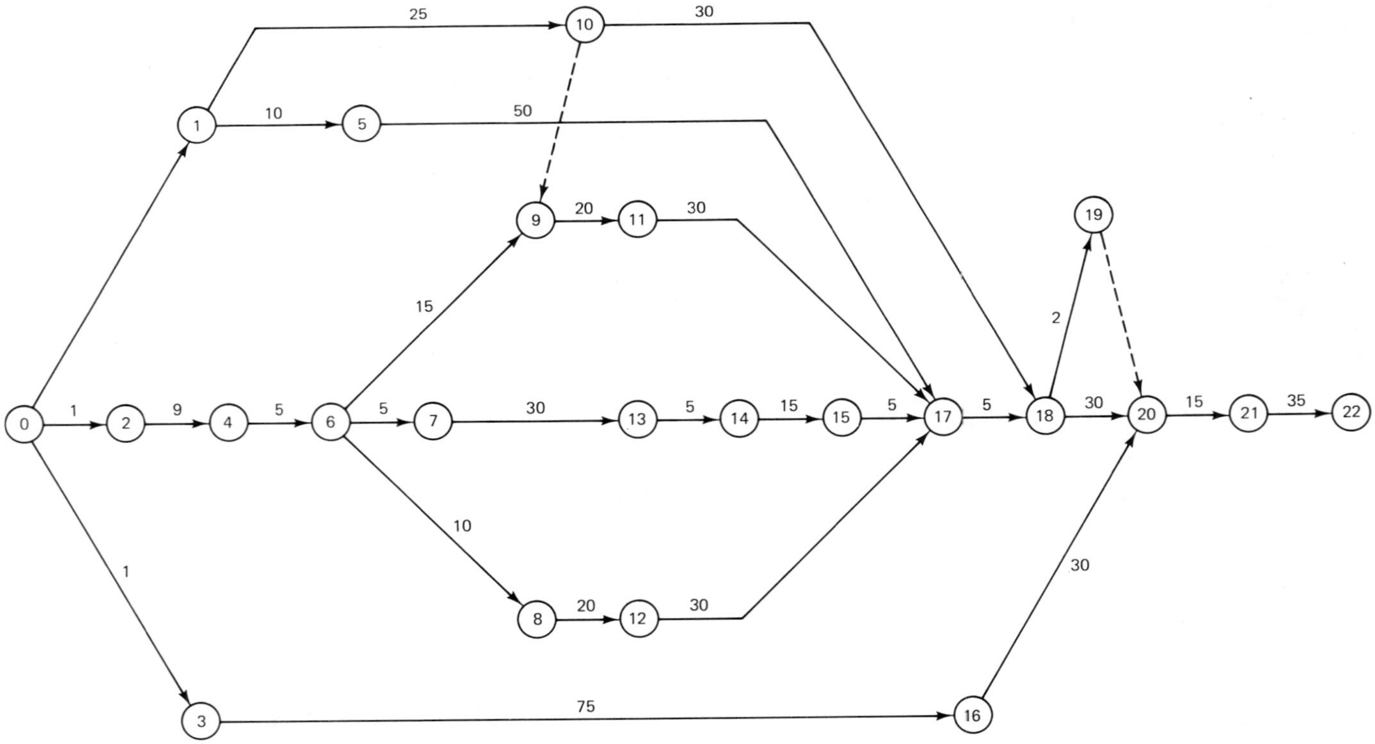

FIGURE 9–19. PERT Network Displaying Activity Times.

paths. In calculating the earliest time for each event, start with the first event or the starting event of the PERT network and proceed from left to right across the network. From this starting point, note the determined expected time along each path to the next event. For the first event on each path, this involves merely noting the expected time for the intervening activity; in Figure 9–19, the earliest time for events 1, 2, and 3 is 1. Determining the earliest time for the subsequent events along a path requires addition; one must add the expected time for each event to the earliest time (TE) for the preceding event. For example, in Figure 9–20, event 6 has an earliest time (TE) of 15: this is determined by adding the expected time between events 4 and 6 to the TE determined for event 4(10). When two or more activities come together at a specific event, we call the event a merge point. To determine the earliest time at a merge point, all paths leading to that event must be considered and the one with the longest time value should be selected. For example, note event 9 of Figure 9–20. Two activities come together at this merge point: one activity stems from event 10; it is made up of the path connecting events 0, 1, 10, and 9; and it has an earliest time count of 26. Another activity stems from event 6; is made up of the path connecting events 0, 2, 4, 6, and 9; and has an earliest time count of 30. Obviously, the longest path in terms of time value would be the path stemming from event 6 with a time value of 30; this is the path used to determine the earliest time of event 9.

Step 2. The next step of the procedure used to determine the critical path is to determine the *latest possible time* (called latest time) by which each event in the network must be completed to meet the established completion date. The procedure for counting the latest time is the reverse of the method for counting the earliest time since the calculating begins with the final event of the network and proceeds back across the network from right to left.

The first factor that must be determined in calculating latest time is the point in time when the final event must be completed. In other words, when must the entire project be finished? Because of emergency conditions, a project such as site activation may need to be completed within 150 days. On the other hand, because of the activation of other sites, the activation of the sites used as our example may be given 180 days for completion. In such instances, the 150 or 180 days that have been established for the completion of the project would also be the latest time (TL) for the final event of the project.

However, the latest time (TL) is usually the earliest completion time of the network. For example, we determined in Figure 9–20 that the earliest time for the completion of event 22 is 165; hence, the most logical latest time (TL) for this network is 165. Therefore, for purposes of illustration, we will use 165 as the established point in time for the completion of the project. Then 165 becomes the TL for event 22.

The second factor to be determined in computing the latest time for an event is the amount of time involved in completing the activities on the appropriate path between the final event and the event in question. To determine this, we must subtract the intervening activity time from the latest time established for each event in its proper sequence along a path of the network. For example, in Figure 9–21, to determine the latest time for event 21, we merely subtract the activity time between event 21 and event 22 (35) from the established latest time of 165. Hence, the latest time for event 21 is 130.

The next event for which we must compute latest time (TL) is event 20. This is done by subtracting the intervening activity time between event 20 and event

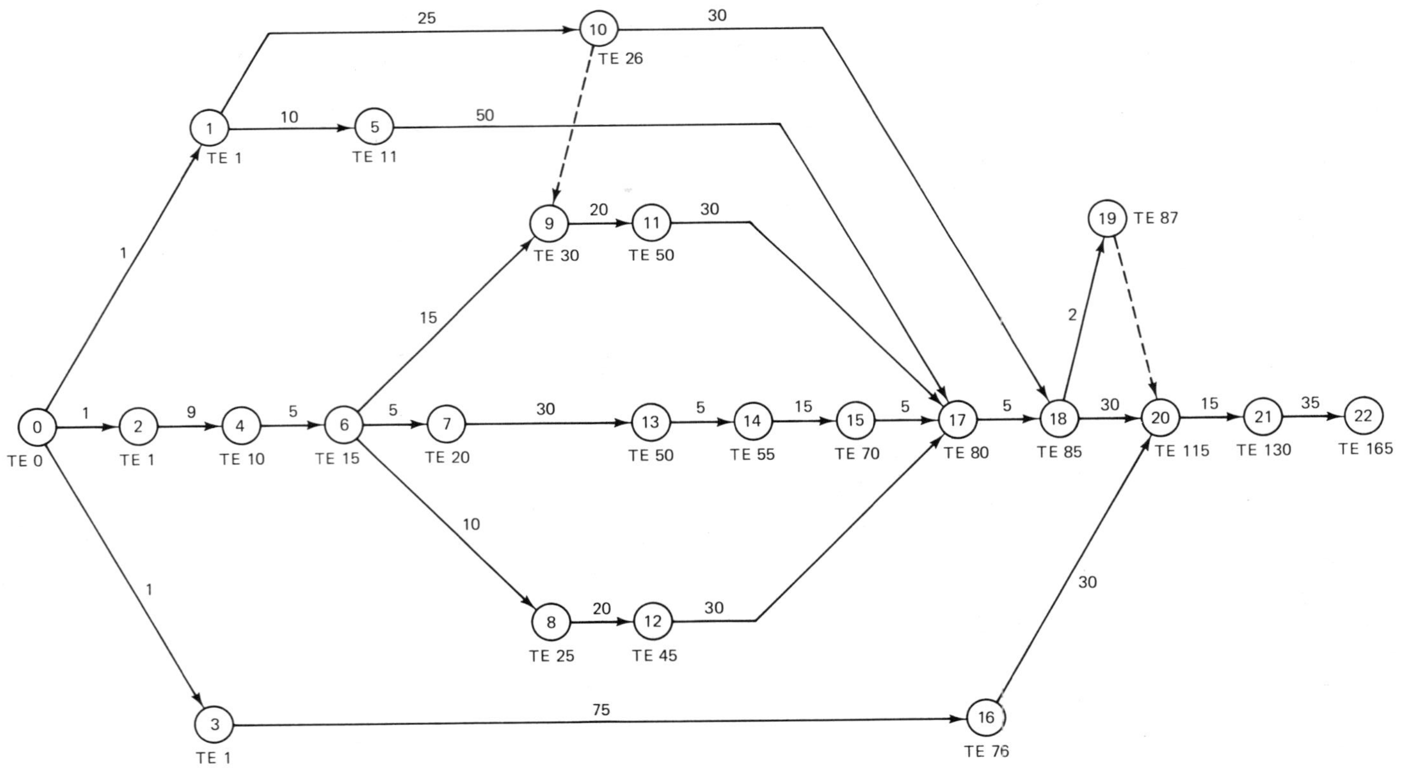

FIGURE 9–20. PERT Network Displaying Earliest Time (TE) for Each Event.

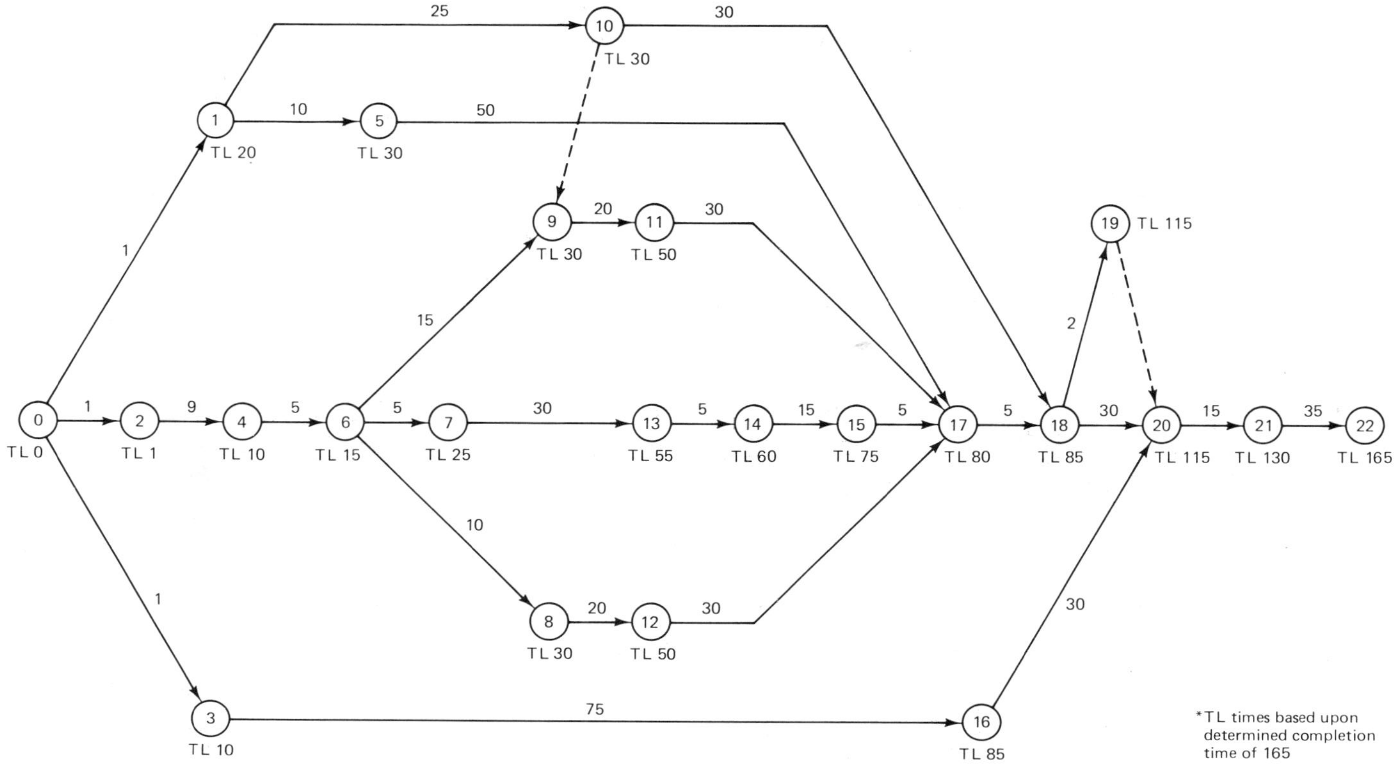

FIGURE 9–21. PERT Network Displaying Time Latest (TL) for Each Event.

21 from the TL for event 21 (130). Hence, the TL for event 20 is 115. Since no activity time is involved in the dummy activity between 19 and 20, the TL for 19 is also 115.

Event 18 presents a new problem. When two or more activities stem from an event, we call that event a burst point. Two activities stem from the burst point at event 18; these activities are the activity between 18 and 19 and the activity between 18 and 20. In such a case the latest time (TL) must be computed for both paths and the one with the lowest time value should be selected. In the case of event 18, the computation from the path leading from event 19 results in a TL of 113 (115 minus 2), whereas the computation for the path leading from event 20 gives a TL of 85 (115 minus 30). The lowest time value of the two TLs is that of 85; therefore, the TL of event 18 is 85.

By backtracing on each path, the latest time for each event is computed in order of occurrence, subtracting the intervening activity time between the event in question from the TL for the preceding event. The TL for event 17 is 80 (85 minus the intervening activity of 5). From this merge point at event 17, the TL for all events on each of the separate paths are calculated in the order of their occurrence.

Step 3. The third step in the procedure for determining the critical path is to determine the *slack time* for each event on the network diagram. This is determined by simply subtracting the earliest time (TE) value from the latest time (TL) value for each event. For example, in Figure 9–20 we determined that the earliest time (TE) for the completion of event 3 was 1, and in Figure 9–21 we determined that the latest time (TL) for the completion of event 3 was 10; the slack time, therefore, for event 3 would be 9 (Figure 9–22). It is possible to get a plus (+), a zero (0), or a minus (−) result. A plus result indicates excessive time. A zero indicates that there is just enough time. A minus condition shows that there is not enough time. The formula for computing slack time in any of these cases for a particular event is: $TL - TE = S$ (slack time).

Notice the significant value that this computed slack time has for the managers involved. The resources for all events that have an excess slack time could be reallocated to other activities that are in danger of falling behind schedule.

Events that have a slack value of zero will usually be on the critical path. However, if the time for the entire project is reduced, events on the critical path will have minus slack value. In such cases, events with a slack value of zero could well be on a slack path. Likewise, if the time for the entire project is extended, all events will have a plus slack time.

DETERMINING THE CRITICAL PATH

Upon completing the time calculations for a PERT network, we are ready to determine the critical path. The critical path is made up of all the events with a minimum event slack time (*S*) on one specific path through the network. These events and their connecting activities represent the longest path between the beginning event and the final event. If the estimated time for any of the activities along the critical path is extended, the time for the entire project will be extended by a corresponding amount. Conversely, if the time for any event along the critical path is shortened, one of two things can happen. The critical path may remain the same and the time for the entire project shortened by a corresponding amount. A new critical path with the same or shortened completion time than the original completion time may be developed. Usually on a large network diagram, only 10 percent of the activities in the network are on the critical path. From an analysis of the critical path, the

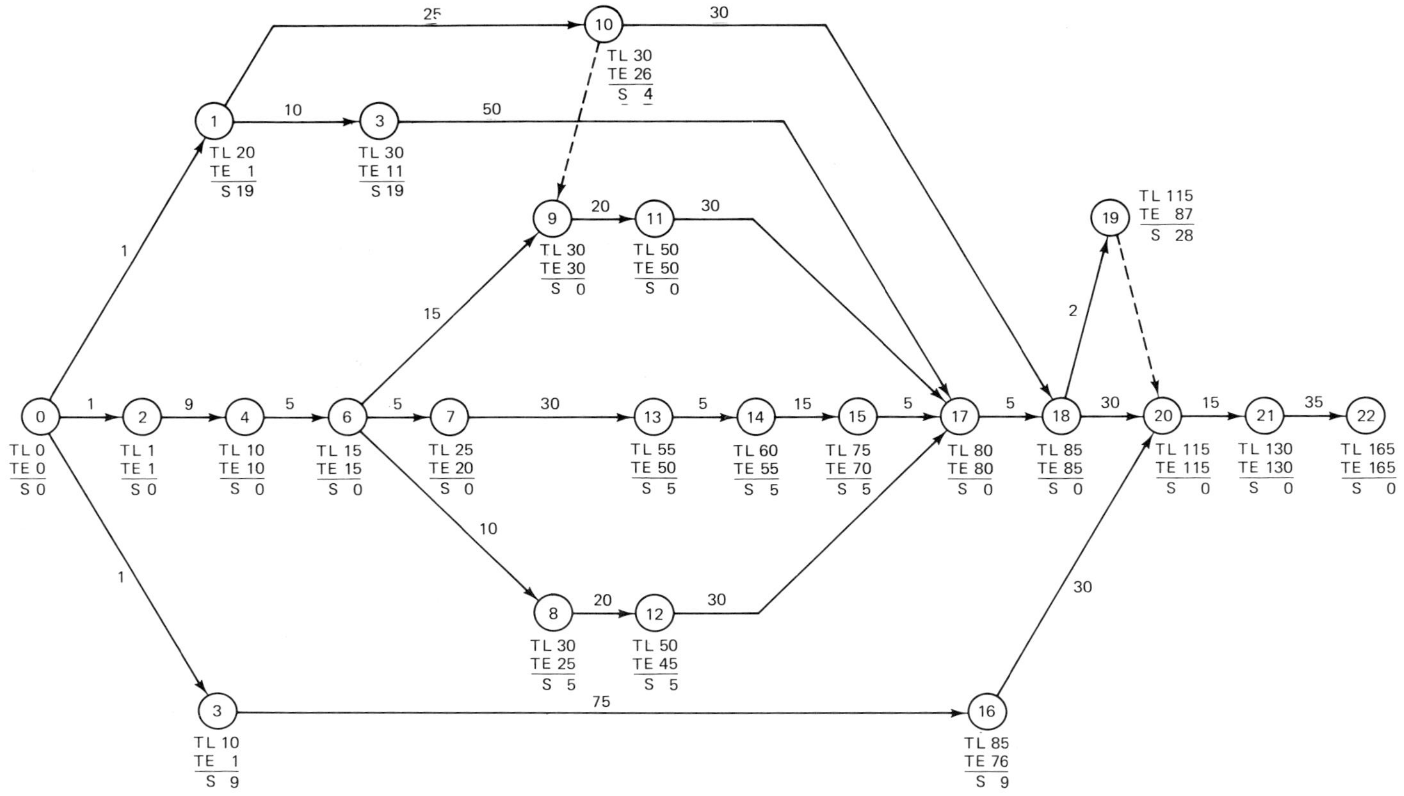

FIGURE 9–22. PERT Network Displaying Computed Slack Time (S) for Each Event.

manager can tell which activities and events must be completed on time to ensure that the projected completion date of the project is met.

Furthermore, the determination of the critical path enables the manager to use his critical resources more effectively. All other paths through the network except the critical path are slack paths. These indicate to the manager where excess resources or time in the form of slack exist. An analysis of these slack paths helps ensure that the project is being executed in the most efficient manner. Slack paths may have resources that can possibly be applied to activities on the critical path to shorten the critical path and, thus, shorten the time for the completion of the entire project. When a manager moves resources from activities on slack paths to activities on the critical path, we have a trade-off of resources. These resources could consist of manpower, equipment, or money. In order for resources to be traded off, the resources must be interchangeable. Of course, the one resource that is always interchangeable is money.

The center of any large PERT system is the computer. It constantly computes any alterations and thus maintains the position of the current program's progress with emphasis upon slack times and critical paths. By processing the PERT statistics, the computer provides management with a timely, as well as accurate, series of reports that pinpoint the progress to date and predict the future of the project being planned.

There is nothing stable about the critical path of a PERT network. As the project progresses, the expected time will be replaced by the actual completion time for each activity. As discussed earlier, the critical path may also be changed by the reallocation of resources. As the critical path changes, the attention of management becomes focused on new events and activities. Thus, the great advantage of PERT is that it enables management to focus its attention on the activities and events that are the most critical for the completion of the project at any time during the actual work on the project (Figures 9–19 through 9–22).

The final component of the PERT system is the dynamic nature of its progress reporting system. Progress reports must be made to reflect any deviation from the original plans. As a result, those who manage the project will always be in a better position to correct problem areas before they threaten the achievement of the final completion date. The format of reports and the frequency of reporting will vary according to the nature of the project, but a definite system of reporting must be established before implementing PERT. The original and all subsequent PERT reports dealing with the progress of the project should indicate the specific points at which corrective action should be taken by event, by activity, and by the total system.

One important advantage that PERT has over other management control techniques is its adaptability for use with the computer. The computer can calculate and print out critical and slack paths. The significant point is that it can do this at any time during the progress of the project, taking into consideration changes in activity times and project completion times which may have been revised. Consequently, within a few minutes, the computer can provide management with updated earliest time (TE), latest time (TL), and slack time (S), as well as the critical path. A graphic portrayal of a system that could be established to maintain an efficient computer-controlled PERT network operation is shown in Figure 9–23.

PERT TIME SYSTEM

Earlier we defined PERT for the purposes of this chapter as a management tool for planning and control of time, cost, and technical performance in the achievement of objectives. During the early stages of

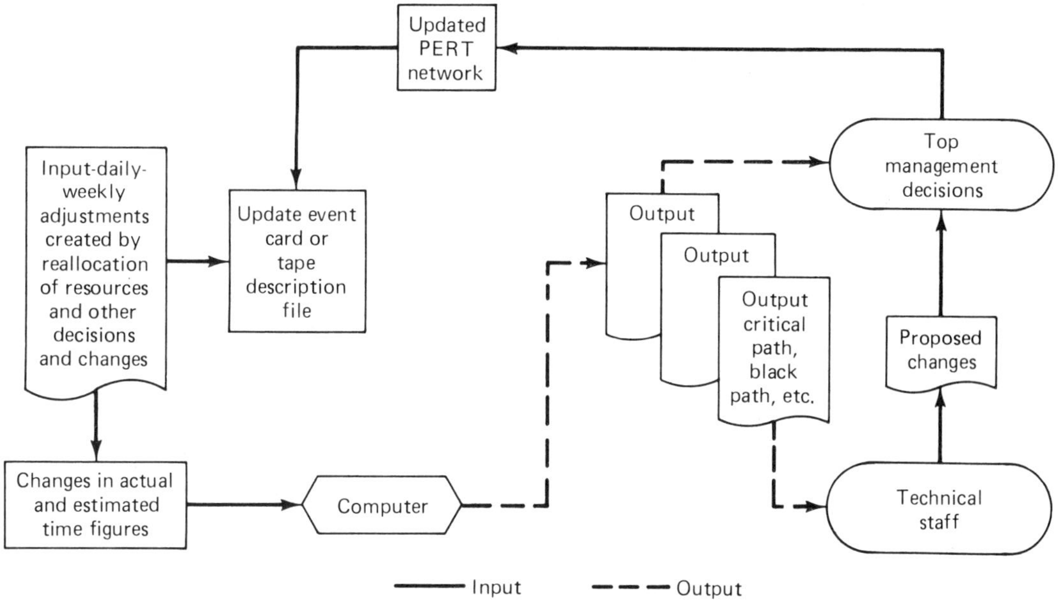

FIGURE 9–23. Computerized PERT System.

development, the control of cost was not a feature of PERT. Therefore, you will find many articles that refer to PERT as it originally was developed—a basic time control tool. With the inclusion of costs, the separate titles of PERT time and PERT cost came into being. PERT time, as used in this chapter, is applicable to the technique without cost controls.

PERT time is utilized in programs, projects, or tasks where control of time is the major factor. Control of costs is, to be sure, important in any government or industry program, project, or task. However, there are situations where control of time will inherently invoke the needed control of cost without the necessity of the added cost of implementing PERT cost. As an example, a high-priority, one-time project with or without an assigned deadline for completion might be assigned to an existing organization already having adequately assigned resources. Such resources, manpower, materials, facilities, and equipment would not have to be procured especially for the project nor would there be contractual services involved. Therefore, PERT time would be adequate in controlling achievement of the project objective.

The purpose of this section is to highlight the essentials of PERT time. The concepts of PERT as previously discussed included both PERT time and PERT cost. Discussion of these two systems individually will acquaint you with the peculiarities of each. Figure 9–24 depicts PERT time and the major steps in the system.

Among the qualities of an effective manager is the ability to plan and make decisions. Although the manager cannot delegate planning or decisionmaking, he can make use of certain tools that will help in the performance of these functions. PERT (time and cost) forces detailed planning and provides adequate data for the decisionmaking process. The planning phase of PERT (time or cost) is of extreme importance. All levels of management

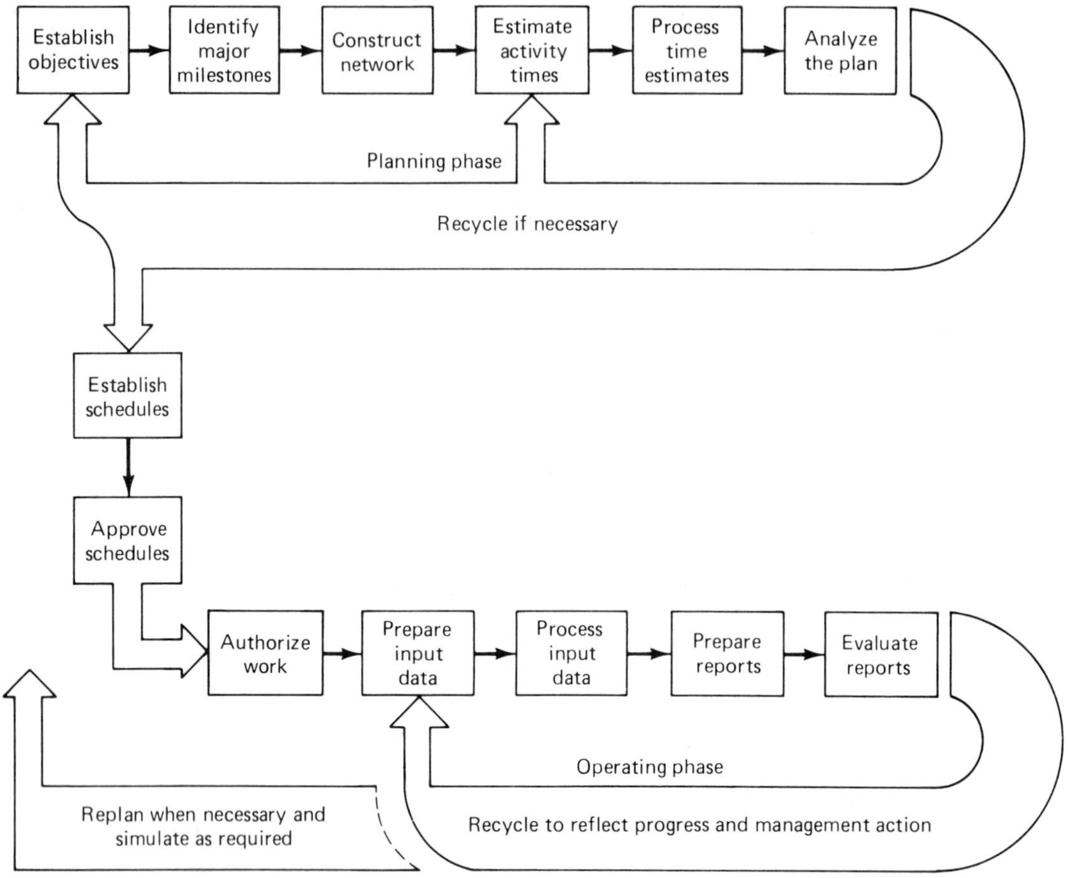

FIGURE 9–24. PERT Time—Planning and Operating Phases.

benefit by application of the planning technique. Whether PERT is being utilized or not, the lowest level supervisor can apply the initial steps of the planning process to any task to be accomplished and, by so doing, can enhance his chances of a timely and successful accomplishment. The work breakdown structure provides the framework for planning and control and is becoming a tool of management within itself. Management today has three basic needs: a better coordinated scheme of production; a procedure to predict accomplishment more accurately; and a standard for measuring progress. PERT satisfies the requirement for all three in almost any task that requires a systematic or planned approach to reach a designated objective or goal.

Planning Phase

In PERT time, attainment of the goals of the planning phase will produce end items as follows:

Master Time Plan. This is expressed in the form of a network that includes: identifying and defining the primary and supporting objectives; establishing the work breakdown structure; identifying the major milestones; building of the network, and making time estimates.

Schedule. It is based on the master time plan and includes establishment of the timetable that actually governs the start and completion of work and resource expenditures required by individual activities of the network or plan.

The importance of detailed coverage in the planning phase cannot be overemphasized. There must be a valid schedule, or resources will be erroneously committed. Prior to obtaining approval of the entire plan, network, and schedule, the plan may be tested for validity by simulation. Also, following approval, refinements are made and alternate plans developed. These may also be tested prior to implementation by simulation. Calculations and simulations are produced mechanically where computers are available. In discussing time calculations, we earlier introduced the formula

$$t_e = \frac{a + 4m + b}{6}.$$

The expected elapsed time, t_e, is a statistically weighted average of the three time estimates: optimistic, most likely, and pessimistic. The use of this formula presupposes that the expected activity time, where three estimates are involved, is best represented by a distribution of values. Therefore, a Beta distribution formula is used as the vehicle to distribute activity time values. If the times were distributed on a curve, it would resemble the normal bell curve used in statistics. The most likely time (m) would be in the mode of the curve and its range is between the optimistic (a) and pessimistic (b) times. The wider the range between a and b (optimistic and pessimistic time estimates), the greater the degree of uncertainty associated with t_e. The degree of uncertainty or variance associated with t_e for each activity is of concern to users of PERT. To assist in the program analysis, the following formula is used to determine statistically the variance in each t_e:

$$\sigma^2 = \left(\frac{b - a}{6}\right)^2.$$

If you are familiar with statistics, you recognize that σ^2 (sigma squared) stands for variance and that one-sixth of the range of estimates is being used as an estimate of the standard deviation which, when squared, equals the variance. Highlighting activities with a high variance assists management in controlling. Revisions to plans may be necessary to produce greater reliability. Once the schedule had been developed and applied to the network, its feasibility may be questioned. This is particularly true if an analysis reveals excessive quantities of slack time ($T_L - T_E$). This condition will most likely require calculations to determine the probability of the schedule being met. The scheduled date, T_S, for an event can be compared statistically with the T_E of the same event and its associated standard deviation to obtain the probability of meeting the scheduled date. A special formula is used for the calculation that is, as are most calculations, performed by the computer. If a low probability of meeting the scheduled date exists, it may be necessary to revise the plan and schedule. Once all changes which were found necessary during development of the schedule are made to the plan, and any required rescheduling accomplished, the program plan is ready for approval by top management.

Operating Phase

Approval of the program plan provides the signal to authorize work and commence the program effort. The PERT time implementing team will have already established a reporting and program evaluation procedure. Basically, the informational needs of the various levels of management must be considered in determining reporting requirements. Managers at any level, as a rule, require (by exception) only that information from PERT (time or cost) that concerns their activities and responsibilities. Objectives become more detailed as they are communicated downward through the organization structure.

The reverse is true of progress reporting and evaluations that must be communicated upward through the organizational structure and conform to the management by exception principle. PERT time reporting must be in understandable form, easy to use, and qualitative rather than quantitative. The fact that problem solving decisions will be based upon reported data demands timely, factual, and reliable information. The flow of information up and down the organizational structure must be maintained throughout the operational phase of PERT time.

Briefings and displays based on analytical results are used to inform top levels of management of the program status. Data portrayed will include historical, current, as well as predictive information. The success of the program evaluation and decisionmaking process depends upon the products of analyses being concise, accurate, and significant for the level of management using them. Narrative reports may be used to portray significant problem areas.

As a rule, decisions made from the results of analyses will require action in one, or a combination of the following forms:

1. Trade-off resources from noncritical or less critical elements to elements in a critical status with respect to overall program effectiveness in relation to the schedule.
2. Increase or decrease the resources allocated to the program element.
3. Revise planned work sequence.
4. Change scheduled completion date.

Decisions made during the top-level briefings are recorded and then communicated, as official changes to the program plan, to the organizational elements responsible for implementing action. The overriding objective of briefings is to correlate and ensure that all efforts are continuously moving toward the program goals. In this manner effective and efficient controls are maintained. Regularly scheduled meetings for briefing top management are desirable. Additionally, an established PERT information center with display and conference rooms for conducting briefings enhances the system by keeping participants aware of their responsibility to review and control the program.

PERT/COST

There are many versions of PERT. One of these versions is PERT/cost. This version was developed by the U.S. Armed Services and various businesses for weapon systems development projects contracted for by the U.S. Government. This version adds the consideration of resources costs to PERT. PERT/cost assists managers by providing information at the level of detail needed for planning schedules and costs, evaluating schedules and cost performance, and predicting and controlling time and cost overruns.

The PERT/cost technique, an extension of the basic PERT/time technique, has been developed to meet planning and control costs of each level of management. The usefulness of PERT/cost can be shown most easily by the following abbreviated description of the way the system operates.

Both cost and schedule are planned and controlled on a common framework or structure. This integration, a significant feature of the PERT/cost technique, permits more accurate measurement of progress and enables managers to appraise more realistically the consequences of alternative courses of action.

The accuracy of the system depends upon the clarity and completion of the original statement of work. The program is first defined and then broken down into end item subdivisions and then into the work packages to be assigned to first-line supervisors.

The second step in applying the PERT/cost technique is the construction of a network consisting of the activities (program tasks) to be performed and the events or milestones to be attained. The sequence in which the activities are planned to be performed creates various paths from the beginning to the end of the program network. The time required by a path is determined by totaling the time for the longest time path through the network, which will control the schedule for the entire program. This is called the critical path. Any delay in completing the activities or this path will create a potential schedule slippage for the program as a whole.

After the schedule has been prepared, the responsible operating engineers and management personnel develop cost estimates for each work package, basing the costs on the manpower and other resources required to perform the program on schedule. They then analyze the estimates to eliminate unnecessary manpower, materials, and services cost. By this technique, cost estimates are applied at the lowest level of work assignment in the program and may be progressively summarized at each level of the work breakdown structure. Components, subassemblies, or major assemblies costs are generated in this manner. The technique also provides for direct integration of time (schedule) and cost at any level of the work breakdown structure. A company may use its existing accounting procedures for accumulating estimates and actual cost information used by the PERT/cost technique. Figure 9–25 depicts the PERT/cost of work for one new develop-

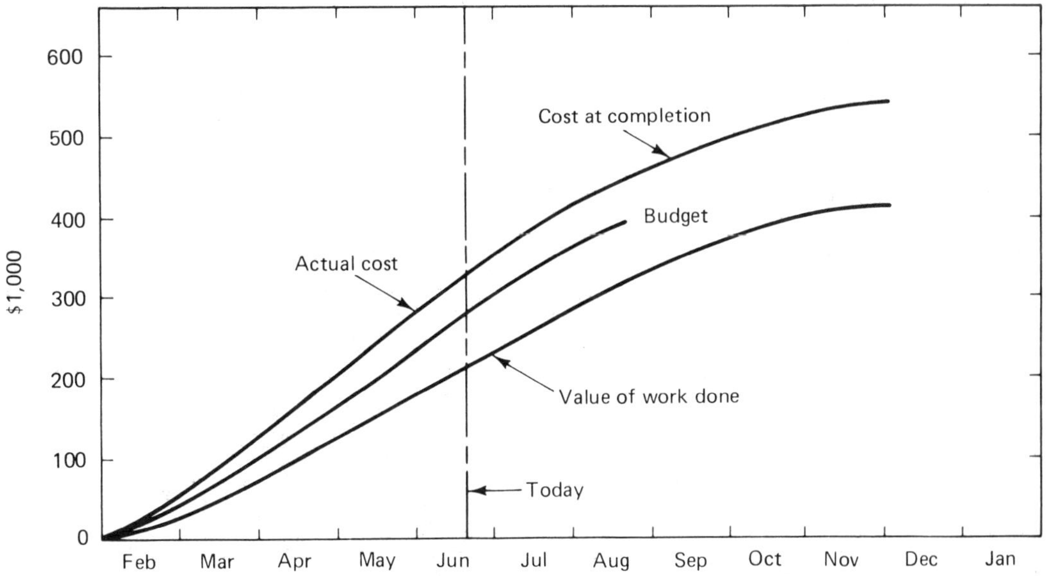

FIGURE 9–25. PERT/Cost of Work.

ment project of a commercial chemical company.

The PERT/cost technique requires periodic comparisons of the actual costs incurred for each work package and the actual time observed by each activity with their original estimates. This comparison significantly improves cost and schedule control by establishing the cost and time status of the program and identifying any potential cost overruns and schedule slippages. Concurrent estimates of the cost and time needed to complete work not yet performed are also obtained in order to predict future schedule slippages and cost overruns and to identify difficulties in the performance of critical work packages early enough to take constructive management action. As the program progresses, actual costs and times are collected at the work package level and progressively summarized. These actual time and cost inputs are compared with estimates to indicate the program status.

PERT COST SYSTEM

The PERT cost system is a complement to the original and basic PERT time system. Because development programs have become increasingly complex in recent years, program managers have needed a tool to more effectively plan and control both schedules and cost of the required work. PERT cost added to PERT time techniques provides the manager at each level with information that will enable him to determine:

1. Whether estimated cost for completing the total program is realistic.
2. Whether program costs of elements of the total program are within committed cost estimates, and, if not, the amount of the difference.
3. Whether requirements for other resources (for example, manpower) have been adequately planned and assigned to minimize premium costs and idle time.
4. How to best reassign or trade off manpower and other resources to improve a lagging element of the schedule.
5. How to best reassign manpower and other resources made available by changes in program activities.
6. The impact of alternative courses of action on the program elements prior to the implementation.

Summary

The networking concept required by the PERT/cost technique that defines activities and interrelationships between activities is a vast improvement over the Gantt chart, which shows activities but does not indicate their relationships or, at best, indicates only a vague relationship in time. They are also an improvement over the milestone charts that describe points in time when various items are complete or available, but not the interrelationships among these items. These charts usually fail to identify the progress that must be made in one task before subsequent tasks can begin. PERT networks, unlike milestone charts, recognize the progress that must be made in one task before subsequent tasks can begin. The identification of activities and their points of interaction is an essential of networking. Figure 9–26 shows a summary comparison of the Gantt chart, the milestone chart, and the PERT network, clearly identifying the advantages of PERT/cost.

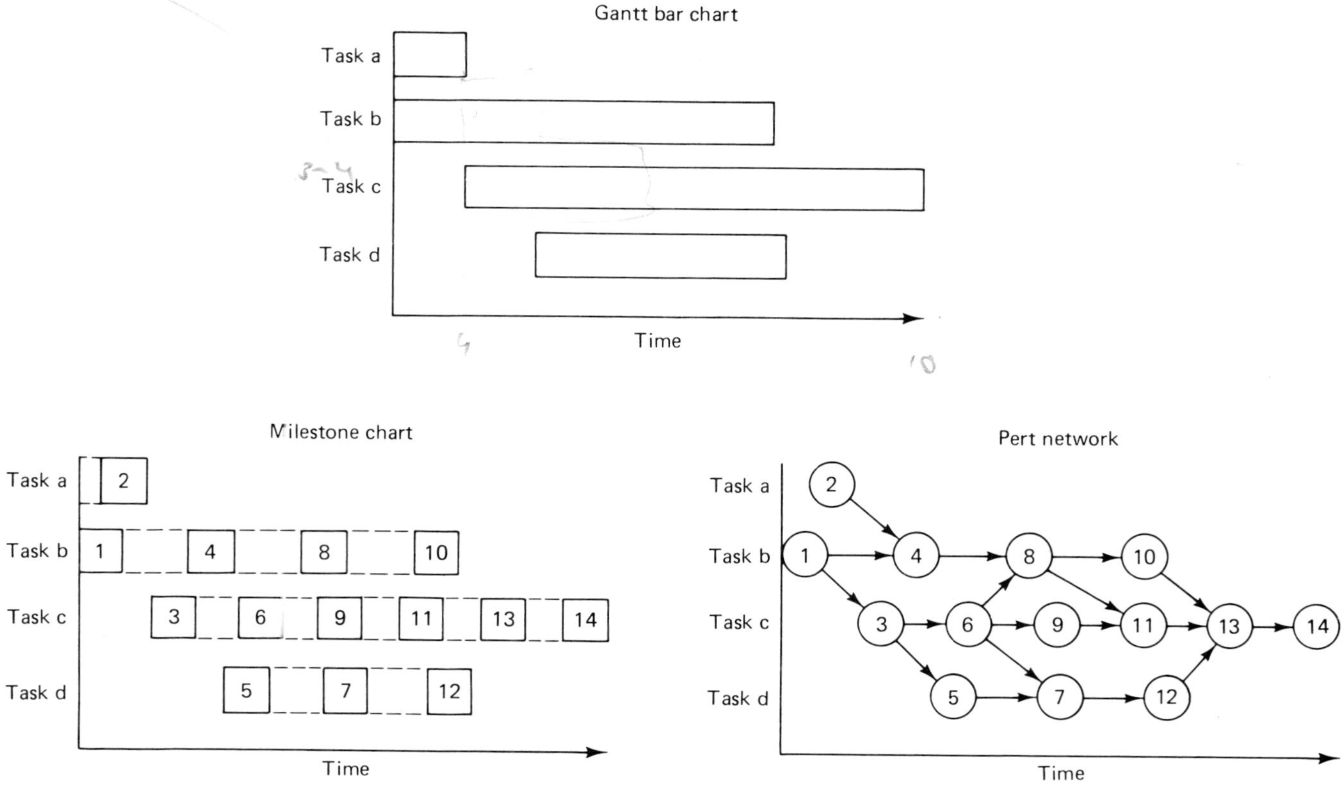

FIGURE 9–26. Summary Comparison of Schedule Planning Techniques.

Glossary

Activity: The work required to accomplish an event. Depicted on the PERT network by an arrow and identified by the numbers of the events at either end of that arrow (that is, activity 20–30 is represented by an arrow connecting event bubbles 20 and 30).

Arrow: Used to depict an activity.

Bar chart: A pictorial representation of the work required to complete a project; shows work either in parallel or in series, a predecessor of the PERT network.

Bubble: A circle or other shape representing an event on PERT network.

CPM: A project planning and control technique that deals with both the time and cost constraints.

Critical path: The longest path through a network.

Dummy activity: An activity that represents no work or expenditure of time—inserted to maintain the logic of the network.

Event: A specific instant of time, either the start or completion of a mental or physical task; represented on the PERT network by a bubble within which is the event number and a brief description beginning either with S (start) or C (complete).

Lead times: Times assigned to activities in order to give the entire network the desired time relationships. Lead times are preceded by the initials LT.

Milestone: An important or key section of a project.

Milestone chart: An evolutionary step between the bar chart in which each long-term job is represented by a bar, and the PERT network in which each small component of a long-term job is represented by a related event bubble; in the milestone chart, bars were broken up into sections (milestones), but were not related to milestones in other bars.

Most likely time: The length of time in which an activity could probably be completed.

Network: The PERT project planning device—a pictorial description of the interrelationships of all required events and activities making up a project.

Optimistic time: The length of time required for an activity if everything goes perfectly.

Path: A way through the network identified by the event numbers falling on the path chosen. (See also *critical, semicritical,* and *slack.*)

PERT: Program evaluation and review technique—a quantitative planning and control device.

PERT/cost: A project planning and control technique that deals with both the time and cost constraints.

Pessimistic time: The length of time required for an activity if everything possible goes wrong and holds up completion as much as possible.

Predecessor event: The event immediately preceding the one in question.

Printout: English language output of a computer printer.

Probability: A measure of uncertainty—as used in PERT, an approximation of the likelihood of meeting the schedule date.

S: Slack time.

Scheduled completion date: The date by which the entire project is scheduled to be finished. The date of the end event if no specific scheduled completion time has been established.

Semicritical path: A path through the network shorter than the critical path but longer than the slack (shortest) path.

Skeleton network: A complete but undetailed network showing only the main parts of the total project and used as a base for drawing detailed network.

Slack for any path: The difference between the latest allowable time and the earliest completion date.

Slack for the critical path: The difference in time between the scheduled completion time (or latest allowable time of the end event) of the entire project and the time of the longest path.

Slack path: The shortest path through the network.

Successor event: The event immediately following the one in question.

Time estimate: The approximation of the length of time required to complete an activity.

t_e: Expected time.

TE: Earliest expected time.

TL: Latest allowable time.

TM: Most likely time.

TO: Optimistic time.

TP: Pessimistic time.

TS: Scheduled time (scheduled completion date).

Practical Exercises

Problem 1.
Situation:

PERT/time reference diagram (Figure 9–27).

Requirements:

a. Compute t_e for activity BD on the diagram below, using the formula

$$t_e = \frac{a + 4m + b}{6}.$$

t_e for activity BD = ______________

b. Compute the TE and TL for events G and C on the diagram below.

(1) TE for G ______________

(2) TL for G ______________

(3) TE for C ______________

(4) TL for C ______________

c. Compute the length of time to complete the following network paths, calculate

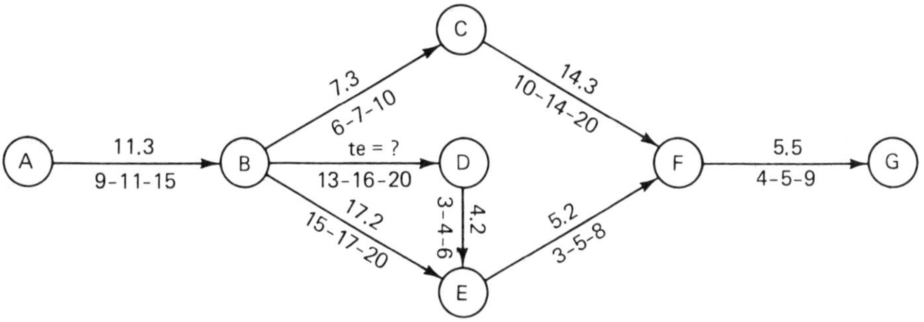

FIGURE 9–27. PERT/Time Reference Diagram.

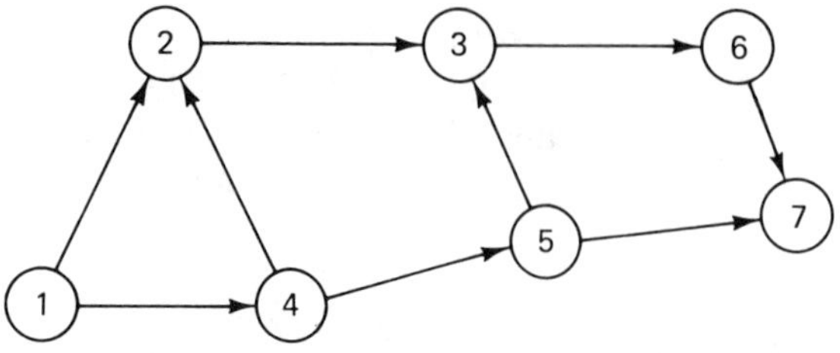

FIGURE 9–28. Diagram of PERT Problem.

the slack on each path, and mark the critical path on the diagram:

	Time	Slack
(1) ABCFG	________	(4)________
(2) ABDEFG	________	(5)________
(3) ABEFG	________	(6)________

(7) Mark CP on diagram.

Situation:

You have just been informed that activity BC required 12.7 weeks to finish instead of the planned 7.3 weeks. Therefore, as project manager, you must determine the effect this delay will have on the scheduled project completion date.

Requirement:

Recompute the length of time to compute each path and calculate the slack on each path.

	Time		Slack
a. ABCFG	________	d.	________
b. ABDEFG	________	e.	________
c. ABEFG	________	f.	________

Problem 2.

Situation:

a. You are a project officer whose mission is to modify certain components of an existing vehicle.

b. You may shorten the length of time the project takes but you will incur increased overtime costs by the factor shown in the last column of Table 9–3. Conversely, overtime costs can be saved by lengthening the time of the project by the same change factor. However, the range column shows the limits within which an activity must be performed.

c. Costs of $5,000/week are incurred when the project deadline is not met.

TABLE 9-3.
PERT/Cost Reference Table*

Activity	*Description*	*TE*	*Range*	*Activity Cost*	*Change Factor*
MN	Hire people	11	9-15	$13,200	$1,200
NO	Complete engine	7	6-10	6,650	950
NP	Complete transm.	16	13-20	14,720	920
NQ	Complete frame	17	15-20	15,810	930
OR	Test engine	14	10-20	8,960	640
PR	Test transm.	9	6-13	6,390	710
QR	Test frame	5	3-8	2,350	470
RS	Final assembly	6	4-9	1,260	210
		Total cost		$69,340	

*Figures in table are purely for instructional purposes and do not correspond to any project.

TABLE 9-4.

Activity	Description	New TE	Range	New Activity Cost	Change Factor
MN	Hire people		9-15		$1,200
NO	Complete engine		6-10		950
NP	Complete transm.		13-20		920
NQ	Complete frame		15-20		930
OR	Test engine		10-20		640
PR	Test transm.		6-13		710
QR	Test frame		3-8		470
RS	Final assembly		4-9		210
		New total cost			

Requirements:

a. Construct a new network diagram showing the relationship between the activities. Label the diagram with the appropriate given information.

b. Complete the system in 35 weeks and at a cost of not more than $76,000. Place the new values in Table 9–4:

Problem 3.

Compute the probability, P_r, of meeting the scheduled date, T_s, of 54 days for Event 6 of the following PERT network. The time estimates are shown in Table 9–5. Hint: Determine the critical path, then figure the variance for each activity on the critical path. Use

$$Z = \frac{Ts - Te}{\sqrt{\Sigma\sigma^2_{TE}}}$$

to find the value of Z. Then, enter a table of values of the standard normal distribution function, that can be found in most statistics handbooks, for the probability (P_r).

TABLE 9-5.

Predecessor Event	Successor Event	*a*	*m*	*b*
1	2	5	12	17
1	4	8	10	13
4	2	9	11	12
2	3	2	7	10
4	5	5	8	9
5	3	21	23	31
6	7	14	18	22
5	7	6	9	12
3	6	8	13	17

IF NOAH BUILT THE ARK TODAY[1]

The story is told in the Book of Genesis about a man named Noah. Noah was a simple, uncomplicated man who had a great deal of faith. In his day and age that was an exceedingly rare quality. His neighbors, in fact, thought him downright odd.

Noah was asked by the Lord to complete an unusual task—build a ship of gigantic size on dry land. The Lord gave Noah the specifications and a deadline for completing the work. Noah probably had some misgivings about such a project. This feeling undoubtedly was heightened by the fact that Noah had no formal marine architectural training and little experience in this line of work.

[1]Reprinted by permission of Procurement Associates, Inc., © 1980, Covina, California.

But being a simple, faithful man, Noah set to work. You can imagine the shock when the Lord asked him to fill the three stories of the ark with animals, birds, and bugs of all kinds—two by two—until all earthly creatures were aboard. Then Noah, his three sons, and their wives boarded the ark while the Lord caused it to rain.

Little detail is given in the Bible but we do know that: "Thus did Noah, according to all that God commanded him, so he did."

Now, let's assume that Noah lived in the 20th century. By 1980 Noah is a successful businessman. He's a little odd. He seems to have some faith (which is a rare quality in this day and age).

Our modern Noah is asked by the Lord to build a large ship and fill it with animals, two by two. The Lord gives Noah the specifications and a deadline for the work. This is how the weekly progress reports to the Lord might read:

Progress Report No. 1

A marine architect was located. He feels that while the original design of the vessel is sound, it lacks esthetic qualities. The architect is now preparing design modifications. A planning team has been organized and the project is being converted to PERT (Program Evaluation and Review Technique), a method of critical path scheduling. An engineering team has been formed and is studying utilization of space within the ark.

Progress Report No. 2

A computer was purchased and work progress will be controlled by the computer. As engineering and technical data will be put on the computer, the Joint Subcommittee for Planning, Engineering, and Management has selected Fortran as the machine language.

Progress Report No. 3

The availability, price, and physical characteristics of gopher wood were statistically compared to other woods. While gopher wood is acceptable and available locally, the Joint Management Committee decided that balsa wood is cheaper and provides optimum buoyancy. The import time from South American jungles is critical, but there are firm commitments from a Brazilian vendor.

Progress Report No. 4

Problems have delayed construction. Our engineers have discovered that pitch, the sealant called for in the original specifications will not work on balsa wood. They are investigating other sealers. They are also reconsidering and reevaluating gopher wood. The Brazilian vendor's first delivery of balsa was a week late, but future deliveries should be within estimates and will allow sufficient construction time.

Progress Report No. 5

Construction was delayed again this week. The engineers recommended that balsa wood be used and a new epoxy resin be used as the sealant. However, it was later discovered that the sealant manufacturer had lost his approved vendor rating because of a security violation. Two government inspectors at our construction site insist that all suppliers be on the approved vendor list. The Joint Management Committee accordingly has decided to use gopher wood and pitch as originally specified.

Progress Report No. 6

Computer reports indicate that animal gathering should begin and that construction should be half complete. Actual construction began after a short delay while the computer underwent modification for Fortran. Full overtime schedules have been ordered to meet the revised revision of the revised schedule. The Joint Committee on Animal Gathering is being formed.

Progress Report No. 7

In answer to the Lord's inquiry about the gathering of elephants, giraffes, and kangaroos, the following memo was sent:

To: The Lord
From: Father Noah
Subject: Gathering of elephants, giraffes, and kangaroos.

Gathering procedures for elephants and giraffes is not critical, for they do not lie on the critical path. Gathering of kangaroos lies along the critical path, and this phase will begin after the slow-footed sloth has been collected. Every effort will be made to ensure the prompt gathering of kangaroos.

Father Noah
Project Administrator

cc: Austral Animal Gathering Committee

Animal gathering is being handicapped by the Society for the Prevention of Cruelty to Animals. They insist that it would be inhuman to coop animals up in such tight quarters for any extended period.

Progress Report No. 8

Construction is in full phase. The Joint Management Committee has decided that the architect's design will have to be modified from two stories with French balconies to the original three stories without balconies. The architect miscalculated the required square footage required per animal. This change will require additional time, but it has appeased the Society for the Prevention of Cruelty to Animals. They have stopped picketing the project.

Smithsonian Institution and Audubon Society experts have arrived to help catalog the animals.

The most pressing problem is the presence of the two government inspectors who insist on inspecting all materials used in constructing the ark.

Progress Report No. 9

Work is handicapped by the lack of storage space for animals. This storage was caused by the arrival of 700 kangaroos. Apparently, there was some mixup in approvals by the Australian committee.

However, one major breakthrough in the project has been achieved. The two government inspectors discovered they were working on the wrong project. They have since departed Project Ark.

Progress Report No. 10

Construction is going on around the clock, but animal gathering has ceased. The Personnel Department has refused to hire any more animal gatherers until job descriptions for all the gathering classifications have been completed. Father Noah and his sons also have undergone extensive physical and mental examinations to determine their fitness for the project.

Progress Report No. 11

Father Noah and the Joint Committee have been holding round-the-clock meetings. Noah has asked the Lord for a delayed completion date. Construction is almost complete, but animal gathering is lagging. The chief of animal gathering has been fired. Experts from the Smithsonian Institution, using computer reports, estimate that animal gathering will take another three weeks. Concentrated effort is being made to reduce this to two weeks.

Progress Report No. 12

Construction of the ark was stopped for two days by a court injunction obtained by a Brazilian, who has brought suit for breach of contract for delivery of 5 million board feet of balsa wood. Father Noah was rejected as a crew member. It was felt that his age would add to the generation gap at the completion of the project. One of the Smithsonian consultants has been selected to take Noah's place. He knows the animals' feeding habits, has a Ph.D. degree in Agronomy, and is the son of the gopher wood supplier.

Progress Report No. 13

The following correspondence has been noted:

To: Father Noah
From: The Lord
Subject: Request for time extension for Project Ark.

Unfortunately, Project Ark lies on the critical path of Project Deluge.

REQUEST DENIED

The Lord

Questions

1. Work planning, scheduling, and controlling techniques run the gamut from a simple calendar with notes on it for activities to be done to the complex PERT methods for large-scale projects. What other techniques are used in American industries today?
2. What is the Gantt chart? Describe its application to nonrepetitive production.
3. How does a milestone chart differ from a Gantt chart?
4. What is the key feature of the line-of-balance (LOB) technique? What are its weaknesses?
5. Describe the information requirements and the objective of the line-of-balance technique.
6. Which scheduling technique is aimed at improving (a) resource allocation, (b) customer service, (c) a commercial airline, (d) a medical clinic, and (e) a government agency such as the Social Security Administration?
7. Describe the development of the critical path method (CPM) and PERT/cost system.
8. Under what circumstances is the use of a probablistic approach, for example, PERT, most appropriate?
9. Describe in your own words the meaning of the following terms related to the critical path network:

   a. event
   b. activity
   c. most likely time
   d. expected time
   e. latest time
   f. milestone
   g. predecessor event
   h. critical path
   i. scheduled time
   j. slack time

10. Give the formula for the determination of the expected time (t_e), and explain each term. Give the formula to determine the variance in each t_e.
11. How is the critical path drawn through a network?

12. How does the industrial engineer or project analyst determine the probability of being at a given event on time?
13. Of what use is the formula

$$Z = \frac{T_s - T_E}{\sqrt{\Sigma\sigma^2_{TE}}}$$

used in PERT?
14. What are some of the conceptual and practical problems encountered in critical path applications?

Bibliography

Antil, J. M., and Woodhead, R. W. *Critical Path Methods in Construction Practice.* New York: John Wiley and Sons, 1970.

Archibald, R. D., and Victoria, R. L. *Network-Based Management System* (PERT/CPM). New York: John Wiley and Sons, 1967.

Baker, K. R. *Introduction to Sequencing and Scheduling.* New York: John Wiley and Sons, 1974.

Coffman, E. G., Jr. *Computer and Job-Shop Scheduling Theory.* New York: John Wiley and Sons, 1976.

Department of the Army. "Work Scheduling Handbook." DOA Pamphlet No. 5–4–6. Washington, D.C.: Hdqs. DOA, January 1974.

Department of Defense. *PERT/COST System Design.* DOD/NASA Guide. Washington, D.C., June 1962.

Department of the Navy. *Line of Balance Technology.* NAVMAT P-1851. Washington, D.C., November 1966.

Federal Electric Corporation. *A Programmed Introduction to PERT.* New York: John Wiley and Sons, 1963.

Johnson, R. A., Kast, F. E., and Rosenzweig, J. E. *The Theory and Management of Systems.* New York: McGraw-Hill, 1967.

Kavenaugh, Thomas C. *Construction Management: A Professional Approach.* New York: McGraw-Hill, 1978.

Levin, Richard L., and Kirkpatrick, C. A. *Planning and Control with CPM/PERT.* New York: McGraw-Hill, 1966.

Malcom, Donald G., Rosenboom, C. E., Clark, C. E., and Fazar, W. "Application of a Technique for Research and Development Program Evaluation." *Operations Research,* Vol. 7, No. 5 (September–October 1959).

Maynard, H. B. *Industrial Engineering Handbook.* New York: McGraw-Hill, 1971.

Martino, R. L. *Critical Path Networks.* New York: McGraw-Hill, 1970.

O'Brien, J. *CPM in Construction Management.* New York: McGraw-Hill, 1971.

U.S. Army Management Engineering Training Agency. *A Line of Balance Computer Program.* Rock Island, Ill., May 1967.

———. *Work Planning and Control Systems.* Course Book. Rock Island, Ill., 197?

U.S. Army Ordnance Center and School. "Program Evaluation Review and Technique/Cost (PERT/COST)". Pamphlet 901–2. Aberdeen Proving Ground, Md., March 1970.

Chapter 10

Work Measurement

INTRODUCTION

The five basic functions of management are planning, organizing, directing, coordinating, and controlling the available resources to achieve defined objectives and programmed goals. One of the most challenging problems of management is to give authority to those capable of exercising it and yet retain control in the hands of those ultimately responsible. If management is to function effectively, devoting its major attention to planning, directing, and coordinating activities, it must be free at every level of all unnecessary burden of detail. The function of control is a basic process of top management.

In this text we are concerned with the control function of management and, in particular, the development of work measurement data, the establishment of standards, and the determination of professional effectiveness.

There is one self-evident and overriding purpose in review and analysis; namely, to measure accomplishments against related goals, standards, or what we have programmed. In turn, this appraisal is designed to point up the need for corrective action in programs, in performance, or in the distribution of resources.

What Is Work Measurement?

Work measurement is designed to determine the productivity of manpower. It does this by relating the number of man-hours that should have been spent (according to a preestablished standard) to the number of productive man-hours actually expended to produce the number of units of work completed during the reporting period. This relationship is expressed as a percentage of effectiveness. In other words, work measurement is a technique for evaluating the performance of personnel; also for relating this performance to fund utilization. Through work measurement, we aim to establish an equitable relationship between the volume of work performed and the manpower, time, and costs used in the performance of that volume. The prime use of work measurement data is at the first-line supervisory level.

Work measurement is an interrelated group of techniques for measuring the amount or quantity of work accomplished or to be accomplished and for developing a time standard for performing work of acceptable quality. Work measurement tells how long it has taken, and how long it should take, to do a piece of work or perform a service or task. The question of how long is one of three questions, whether expressed or not, that arise for any person when given a new assignment or job to perform. Answers are customarily supplied to the first two questions (what is to be done, and how well it is to be done), but often reliable answers are not given for the third (how long it should take). The more specific the answers to these questions, the fewer the possibilities for misunderstanding, friction, ill will, and for waste of various kinds. In being specific about what is to be done, a statement of method is involved. For this reason, one cannot divorce methods study from work measurement, but must be concerned with both methods and measurement in a given situation. In being specific about how long it has taken or should take to produce a product or service, a statement of work measurement is involved. These three answers are required whether a supervisor is instructing a worker, a chief is planning a project, or a plant superintendent is managing a factory.

It would be folly for management to attempt to manage without the knowledge of how long it should take to perform work, whether it is producing a product, such as farm tractors, or providing support activity, such as maintenance or administration. Therefore, considerations concerning the application of work measurement as a management tool should not be *if* work measurement should be used, but rather *what type* of work measurement should be used and *to what extent* it should be applied.

Even the simplest type of activity requires a knowledge of how long it takes to do a job in order to plan and control the work load. As an organization increases in size and complexity, this basic information becomes more important to management.

Determination of the type of work measurement and the extent of application might better be expressed as an evaluation of two factors:

1. How effective will the standards be in increasing economy, providing data for planning purposes, and developing methods control?
2. What kind of standards are to be used, considering their cost in time, money, and skills required?

The Department of Defense DIMES Program

In 1963 the Department of Defense (DOD) initiated the Defense Integrated Management Engineering Systems (DIMES). The initial purpose of Project DIMES was to assure the availability to managers of the generally accepted industrial management techniques used by their counterparts in private industry for the decisionmaking process. To achieve this purpose, a five-year time frame was established for attaining substantial and technically acceptable adoption of industrial management techniques. It was immediately apparent that the total task involved was tremendously large as well as complex. Additionally, the technical talent available (standards technicians, industrial engineers), or that could be made available, was inadequate to achieve the objectives of the project at one point in time. The obvious answer was to divide the total task into categories and establish pilot installations that would permit the assignment and training of sufficient technical talent, and provide technical data and experience for other similar installations as they were brought into the program.

Project DIMES was divided into three phases: Phase I, work measurement; Phase II, work planning and control; and Phase III, standard cost accounting. Phasing was keyed to the basic objectives of Project DIMES and provided for their orderly attainment. In Phase I emphasis was placed upon methods improvements and performance standards. As the standards coverage was increased, emphasis was to be placed upon formalizing a system for productivity planning and manpower assignment (Phase II). Phase III envisioned translating the results of the first two phases into a standard cost accounting system. None of these techniques was new. DOD installations have been using them on and off since 1950, when the use of performance standards was legalized by statute. However, for the first time top-level support was being given to the program from the White House and the Bureau of the Budget, down through the secretary of defense to the secretaries of the Army, Navy, and Air Force, and the director of the Defense Logistics Agency.

Staffing for Work Measurement

In accordance with current industrial usage, the following guidance is provided for planning and determining the number of personnel required for the work measurement program:

1. For areas susceptible to engineered (performance) standards, a ratio of 1 analyst (work measurement specialist) will be used for each 100 individuals whose work is to be covered by standards.
2. For areas susceptible to nonengineered standards, that is, statistical standards or technical estimates, a ratio of 1 analyst (work measurement specialist) will be used for each 400 individuals whose work is to be covered by the standards.
3. Consultants or contractual assistance may also be used.

Definition of Terms

Certain terms used in this text are peculiar to work measurement. Other terms used are in accordance with current glossaries and dictionaries of terminology. Terms are listed and defined in the glossary at the end of this chapter.

FUNDAMENTALS OF WORK MEASUREMENT

Work measurement produces maximum benefits at the supervisory level of operational activities. It is here that basic statistics on work load, production, personnel, and costs originate. It is also at this level that standards can be applied to specific units of work in order to schedule and control work, to transfer personnel within the organization, to foster a spirit of competition between individuals and groups, to prevent bottlenecks from developing, and to reduce the backlog of work. Plainly, it is at this level that standards can be most efficiently applied to specific units of work in order to schedule and control the consumption of a manager's resources.

The basic performance data of activities are carried forward by feeder reports. These data become an integral and vital tool with which the manager and his staff manage the operations of the firm. Performance data may play a useful role at higher levels above the level when properly adjusted, integrated with, and related to reported information on financial management, production management, and manpower.

Under this concept, the percentage of effectiveness of personnel when used alone and without other data does not measure the effectiveness of an organization, oganizational element, or an activity in accomplishing its total work load or its programs or schedules of work within prescribed periods of time.

The objectives of work measurement are to promote increased effectiveness and economy in the use of resources, such as facilities, manpower, materials, and equipment, by improving methods, distribution, conditions, layout, and procedures. In addition, work measurement provides current and reliable reference data with which: (1) staffing requirements for current and projected work load may be determined; (2) the execution of programs may be reviewed and analyzed more readily by each successive level of management; (3) standard cost accounting systems may be developed and used; (4) work may be scheduled and controlled; and (5) budgets may be developed.

Another objective is to develop a labor and production reporting system that will help to evaluate and analyze organizational performance.

Standards of Measurement[1]

Throughout industry, key management personnel are asking themselves the question, "Do performance standards really

[1]Parts of this section and the next two sections have been taken from *Work Measurement*, Special Text 14-199, June 1973 edition, by permission of the U.S. Army Training Support Center and the U.S. Army Institute of Administration, Fort Harrison, IN.

enable us to control and plan our operations better?" Those who lack knowledge of exactly what standards are, their characteristics, limitations, and advantages, frequently answer negatively. They distrust the system and question its validity. Others with both a clear understanding of the principles involved and an insight of the working applications of the system answer yes. These people have learned how to use the system to serve their management needs. Recognizing what it will and will not do for them, they have made work measurement an invaluable management tool.

TECHNIQUES OF WORK MEASUREMENT

Work measurement can be performed using a variety of techniques and procedures. Some of these techniques require specialized knowledge and training and are, therefore, applied by those possessing this capability, such as management analysts or industrial engineers. Other techniques do not require special skills and therefore can be applied by any reasonably intelligent person after brief instruction.

Some of the techniques of work measurement such as engineered standards require more effort, time, and money to establish than do others. In return, these techniques produce standards of greater validity and reliability. The degree of validity and reliability required will depend upon the intended use of the work measurement data.

An appreciation of each of the various techniques is necessary before one can decide what type and to what extent work measurement should be applied. These techniques are described next.

Technical Estimate

This technique is concerned with the time (man-hours) it should take an individual or group possessing required skills to produce a work unit at a normal pace forecasted by technically qualified individuals. The estimate is based upon a detailed analysis of the components of a work unit. This technique depends solely upon the judgment of the person making the estimate. (A technical estimate can be obtained in a matter of minutes from the mechanic or supervisor for the repair of a particular part.) Technical estimates are nonengineered standards developed usually without the aid of a timing device or sampling technique. Technical estimates should be made by a person technically qualified in a given area and are generally based upon a procedure that breaks the estimate into a series of small individual estimates summarized to obtain a standard time.

Statistical/Historical Standard

The time (man-hours) it should take an individual or group to complete a work unit can be determined from a statistical analysis of past performance data. In its simplest form, this represents the time it has taken on the average to do the work.

Engineered Standard

This standard refers to the time (man-hours) it should take an individual or a group to complete a work unit working at a normal pace according to a specified method, as determined by a detailed study of the job. In essence, this represents the time the average trained or skilled person should take to do the work. Engineered standards usually are determined by one of the following techniques:

Direct time study.

Work sampling (rated for pace).

Predetermined time systems (compilation from basic time data).

Standard data (compilation from standard elemental data).

Time and Motion Study Chronometers
1/100 minute (decimal)

HEUER

Say "Hoy-er"

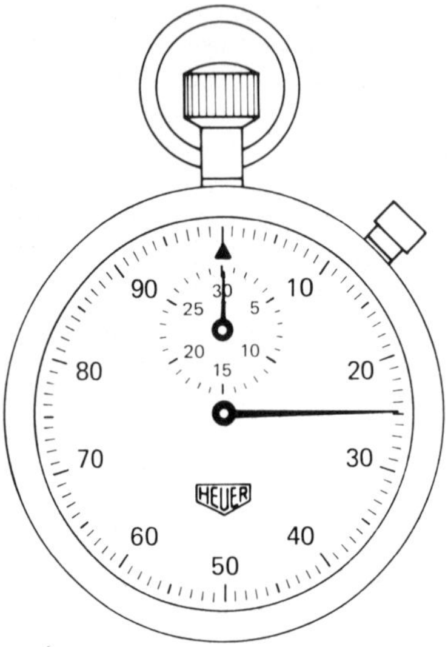

1

1
Ref. 408.213 – Ø53 mm

1/100 minute (decimal-) recorder, 0–30 minute register. 2 crown functions with time-out and fly-back return. Precision lever movement, 7 jewels, shockprotected.

2
Ref. 508.213 – Ø53 mm

1/100 minute (decimal-) recorder, central 0–60 minute register. 2 crown functions with time-out and fly-back return. Precision lever movement, 7 jewels, shockprotected.

3
Ref. 512.413 – Ø58.5 mm

1/100 minute (decimal-) recorder with split action, central 0–60 minute register. 2 crown functions with time-out and locked return. Control of split action by left side push button. Precision lever movement, 7 jewels, shock-protected.

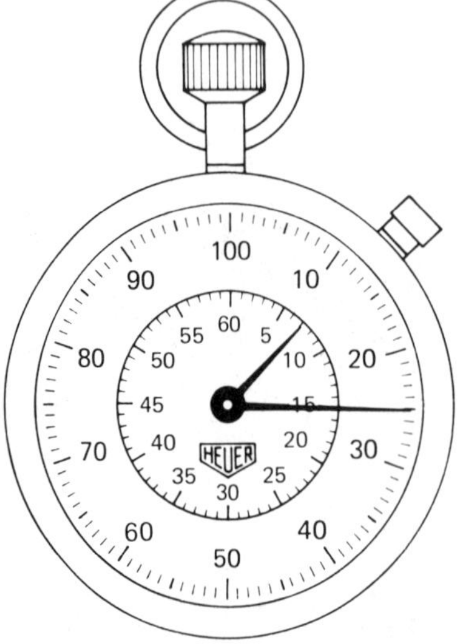

2

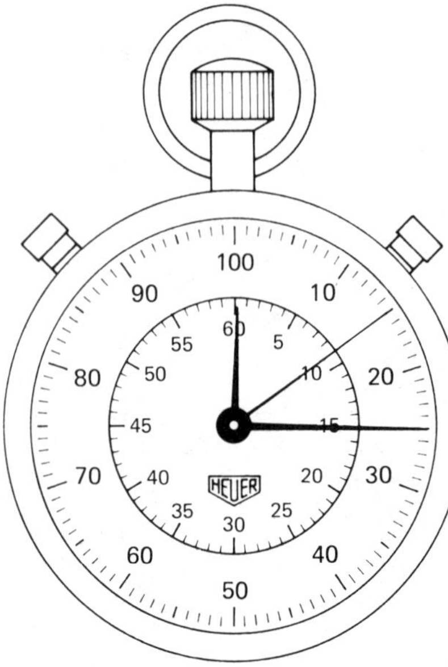

3

FIGURE 10–1. Time and Motion Study Chronometers.

Direct Time Study. This term refers to studies conducted at the work site in which the recorded time values are obtained from direct observation with the aid of a stopwatch, wristwatch, or other timing devices such as motion picture analysis or a time-study machine. Instruments for measuring time precisely are shown in Figure 10-1. There are several types of time studies. They may be classified as short cycle or long cycle, which refers to the length of the work cycle under observation. Also, there are one-cycle time studies and studies involving many cycles.

Time study using a stopwatch or clock is perhaps the oldest of the work measurement techniques. It lends itself well to the development of engineered standards since the direct observation aspect enables the analyst to record all necessary information. Figure 10-2 depicts a time study observation form.

Work Sampling. Standard times may readily be derived from sampling studies that involve recording a series of randomly spaced observations of task and then synthesizing the data obtained into a standard time.

Predetermined Time Systems. This group of techniques refers to an entire series of specific techniques. They are all based upon a detailed breakdown of fundamental hand and body motions to which time values have been assigned. Thus, if the motion pattern for a job can be described in terms of fundamental hand and body motions, the time for completion can be synthesized from the predetermined times. This technique produces an engineered standard.

Standard Data. This technique employs the same principles as predetermined time systems only and is concerned with data of a more gross nature. The standard time for a task is described in terms of elemental times and then synthesized into a total standard time for the task or job. Both predetermined time systems and elemental standard data systems will yield engineered standards.

Many contend that one of the most accurate means of measuring elemental motions, called *therbligs,* is by motion picture. (See the glossary for a definition of therbligs.) Figure 10-3 depicts the use of three stopwatches to obtain an accurate and practical method of measuring therbligs.

Staffing Patterns

Several procedures frequently used by the analyst may be classified in this category. They do not result in a work standard in the sense that the other techniques do since no work unit is involved. Staffing patterns are manning ratios, expressions of manpower, or spaces required to support a certain level of activity (population served) in an organization. They may be developed from:

Standard times compiled by any of the above-mentioned techniques.

Simulation or waiting line theory.

Directed requirements.

Historical data.

From the above description it should be apparent that the right technique needs to be selected for each use of work measurement. An engineered time standard established by a time and methods study is the proper technique for janitorial work—not a statistical standard based on the present work methods of the janitor. But an engineered time standard derived from predetermined time is not the appropriate technique to use for secretarial work—rather, work sampling with a pace rating would be better. Table 10-1 provides comparative information needed for the selection of the right work measurement technique for different kinds of activities.

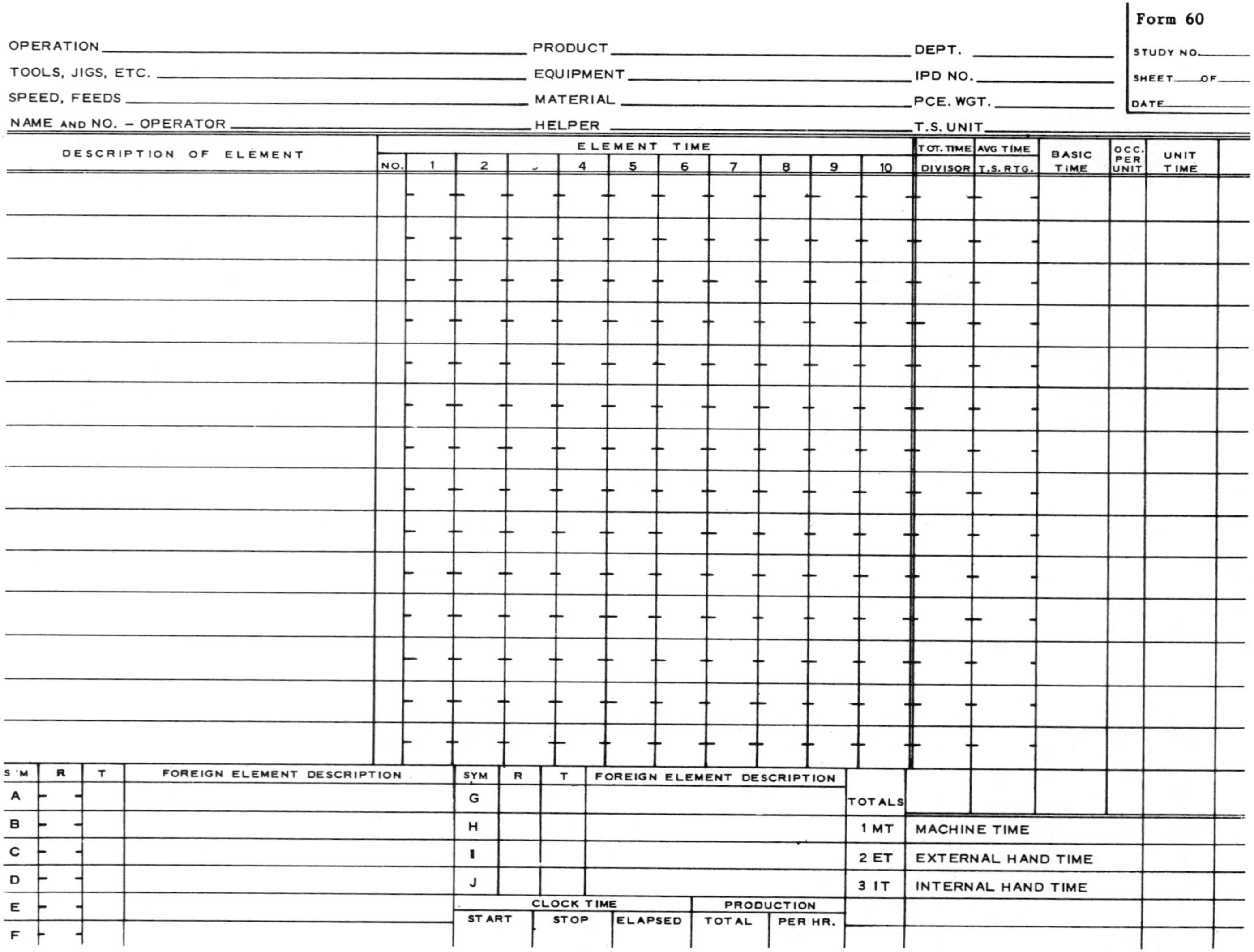

Form 60

STUDY NO.____
SHEET____OF____
DATE____

OPERATION ____ PRODUCT ____ DEPT. ____
TOOLS, JIGS, ETC. ____ EQUIPMENT ____ IPD NO. ____
SPEED, FEEDS ____ MATERIAL ____ PCE. WGT. ____
NAME AND NO. – OPERATOR ____ HELPER ____ T.S. UNIT ____

DESCRIPTION OF ELEMENT	ELEMENT TIME NO.	1	2	[illegible]	4	5	6	7	8	9	10	TOT. TIME / DIVISOR	AVG TIME / T.S. RTG.	BASIC TIME	OCC. PER UNIT	UNIT TIME

SYM	R	T	FOREIGN ELEMENT DESCRIPTION	SYM	R	T	FOREIGN ELEMENT DESCRIPTION
A				G			
B				H			
C				I			
D				J			
E							
F							

CLOCK TIME			PRODUCTION	
START	STOP	ELAPSED	TOTAL	PER HR.

TOTALS
1 MT MACHINE TIME
2 ET EXTERNAL HAND TIME
3 IT INTERNAL HAND TIME

FIGURE 10–2. Repetitive Time Study Record.

CALCULATIONS

		CYCLIC TASK TIME		MIN./UNIT
1	MT	Machine Time		
2	EHT	External Hand Time		
3	IHT	Internal Hand Time		
4	THT	Total Hand Time	(2) + (3)	
5	PA	Process Control Standby	(1) − (3)	
6	NT	Necessary Time	(1) + (2)	
7	Pn	Prod./Hr. @ N.T.	60 ÷ (6)	
		ALLOWANCE TO CYCLIC TASK TIME		
a	M	Material Supply Delay: Code___, ______Min./______Pcs. Code___, ______Min./______Pcs.		
b	F	Fatigue: Code__________, ______% of ( ) ________ Refer to (4) and (5) ______% of ( ) ________		
c		Sub-Total	(6) + (a) + (b)	
d	T	Trouble Delays: Code______	/480 Min.	%
e	P	Personal	/480 Min.	%
f	L	Lunch	/480 Min.	%
g	C	Prep. and Cleanup	/480 Min.	%
			/480 Min.	%
h		Sub-Total (d) + (e) + (f) + (g)	/480 Min.	%
k	AT	Allowed Time: (c) ÷ (1.00 − h) = (c) ÷ (__________)		
8	Pa	Prod./Hr. @ A.T.	60 ÷ (k)	
m	I	Incentive Allowance: ________ % of (k)		
		STANDARD ALLOWED TASK TIME		
9	ST	Std. Time $= \frac{NT + M + (F \times NT)}{1.00 - (T + P + L + C)} (1.00 \times 1)$	(k) + (m)	

Date Effective ______________

Observer ______________

Std. Hrs./C, $(9) \times \frac{100}{60}$ =

Std. Pieces/Hr., $\frac{100}{\text{Std.Hrs./C}}$ =

DESCRIPTION OF OPERATION

REASON FOR STUDY – APPLICATION – DISPOSITION

CHECKED ______________ DEPT. ______________ DIV. ______________

FIGURE 10–2 (continued).

TABLE 10–1.
Work Measurement Techniques and Their Application

Techniques	*Types of Operations*	*Examples of Operations*	*Application of Techniques*
Time study	Repetitive, short cycle work performed at essentially one work station.	Parts assembly, machining, packaging, typing, filing, editing, packing.	Conduct detailed methods study. Establish elements to be timed. Record time with stop watch or camera (micromotion). Establish statistical reliability. Rate performance. Determine and apply allowances.
	Irregular, medium to long cycle work, frequently performed by moving about several work stations.	Janitorial, clerical, rebuild, repair, warehousing.	Conduct methods study. Establish gross elements to be timed. Record time with stop watch or camera (memo-motion). Establish statistical reliability. Rate performance. Determine and apply allowances. *Note:* This type of work is frequently highly irregular before analysis, but is susceptible to a reasonable amount of standardization of method.
Work sampling	Irregular work where a work unit is highly correlated to work input.	Clerical, rebuild, repair, warehousing, facility maintenance, indirect labor.	Prepare gross description of method. Define elements and end point. Choose level of accuracy desired. Establish number of observations required for statistical reliability. Set up random schedule. Make instantaneous observations and tally. Obtain production count during study. Rate performance (random sampling). Determine and apply allowance.
	Development of management information. *Note:* Not used to establish work measurement standards.	Determination of delays, utilization of people and equipment, work distribution, feasibility studies, performance checks.	Define elements and end points. Establish number of observations required. Set up random schedule. Make instantaneous observations and tally. Determine percentage of total time spent on various categories of work and non-work.
Predetermined time	Repetitive short cycle work where volume is high.	Assembly, machining, packaging, packing, shipping, stock picking, editing.	Standardize method (break down into basic motions). (therbligs). Make precise measurement of all variables, such as distance. Determine time values from tables. Determine and apply allowances.
	Check as to consistency of direct time study standards.	Assembly, machining, machine operations.	Same as in predetermined time first type of operation.

TABLE 10–1 (continued).
Work Measurement Techniques and Their Application

Techniques	*Types of Operations*	*Examples of Operations*	*Application of Techniques*
Standard data	Repetitive work and medium cycle work where volume is high.	Assembly, machining, packaging, typing, filing, editing.	Determine and define motion patterns (elements). Average the variables into small categories. Determine time values from predetermined time standard tables (in some instances from direct time studies). Arrange in one of following forms for rapid and economical use: tables, curves, nomographs, alignment charts, multivariable charts, formula.
	Repetitive work where volume is low, or long irregular cycle work where work volume is high.	Assembly, machining, packaging, rebuild, repair, maintenance, clerical, warehousing.	Determine and define motion patterns. Average the variables into gross categories. Determine time values from direct time studies or predetermined time standard tables. Arrange as in standard data, first type of operations listed.
Technical estimate	Highly technical or irregular work.	Maintenance, rebuilding, repair of complex items.	Break down operation into elements. Estimate time it should take to perform work (est. made by supervisor, inspector, analyst). Use historical reports, standard data, time study, experience, etc. for each element. Record data and evaluate. Determine and apply allowances to estimate.
	Scheduling and controlling projects for priority, status, evaluation and costing.	Technical, engineering, and research projects.	Same as in technical estimate, first type of operation listed, except the estimate is made by supervisor.
Historical	Irregular work where a work unit may be determined.	Administrative, indirect labor, warehousing.	Develop and/or analyze records of man-hours expended and related output of units produced. Measure central tendency (mean, median, mode, quartile, regression, etc.). Select realistic work unit and correlate input to output.
Staffing pattern	Highly irregular for which no work may be determined.	Administrative, Support activities.	Analyze historical records of similar activities. Determine staffing ratios of number of support personnel to supported personnel.

SOURCE: U.S. Army Management Engineering Training Agency, *Work Measurement* (Course Books, Rock Island, Il., 1971, pp. 3.5–3.8

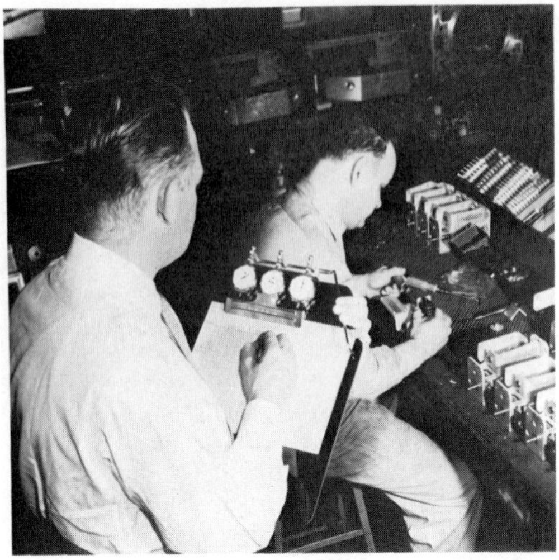

FIGURE 10–3. Method of Measuring Therbligs. By using three Meylan stopwatches at once and reading the one that has "stopped" after each element, the observer has an accurate and practical method of measuring therbligs. (Courtesy of Meylan Stopwatch Corp., New York, N.Y.)

The selection of the proper technique for establishing standards is essentially the choice of the individual analyst. His decision is based on the nature of the work—repetitive or nonrepetitive, length of the work cycle, frequency of typical jobs, and so on. Time study, work sampling, and statistical standards are particularly appropriate for installation application. Technical estimates, synthesized systems, and staffing patterns may be used, if required.

EFFECTIVENESS OF EACH WORK MEASUREMENT TECHNIQUE

How effective will the standards be in increasing efficiency, providing data for planning purposes, and developing methods of control? The expected answer would be, "very effective." A better answer would be, "it depends." One of the determining factors is the selection of: (1) the right tool for the job, and (2) the right technique for the desired use of work measurement.

A carpenter would certainly select a wood chisel rather than a screwdriver to cut a recess for a lock in a new door. Similarly, the selection of the proper technique of work measurement will depend upon the intended use of the work measurement data.

A technique of work measurement is often associated with a particular type of activity. However, work measurement in any of its types is not limited to any specific activity. Whether a job occurs in the office, shop, or in a research activity, does not, in itself, determine the best method of establishing standards. It might be economically desirable, for example, to set engineered standards for several jobs in an office, provided the use of the standards justified their cost.

Many organizations point with pride to their engineered standards in the shop, but are willing to accept the gross control of statistical standards in administrative and maintenance work. However, many of the larger industries are seeking the increased accuracy of engineered standards in these areas and are finding auxiliary benefits accruing as a result.

The first benefit is the increased use of standardized and usually more effective methods than were in use prior to the setting of engineered standards. The second benefit is derived from the fact that the time allowed for the job by the engineered standard is adjusted to compensate only for recognized allowances such as personal time, official break periods, cleanup time, machine maintenance, and similar factors. The effects of all other lost time occurring in actual operation because of lack of material, failure to assign work properly, inadequate training and other management or supervisory errors will immediately be reflected in the performance report. Once these time-wasters are identified, action can be taken by management to reduce or eliminate the causes.

Where To Use Work Measurement

Most activites are measurable. Many are easy to measure and the cost is low. But some activities are very difficult to measure satisfactorily and the cost may be high compared to the benefts. Many activities can be readily measured today that were considered unmeasurable three decades ago. Repetitive kinds of work are usually the easiest and least costly to measure. However, techniques for measuring nonrepetitive work are now widely used and the cost has dropped sharply. Much of the work in offices and job shops is nonrepetitive yet is being successfully measured in many organizations. Today it is not a question of whether an activity can be measured—the question is, Is it profitable to measure it?

Thus, a manager needs to weigh the cost of installing and maintaining a work measurement program against the anticipated benefits before starting any comprehensive plan to apply this management tool to all activities. Good practice is to select first those activities that can be measured quickly, with the least cost, and with the best prospect of benefit, and later on to measure the more difficult areas.

The following list identifies some of the most difficult activities to measure. These should be avoided as it is clearly unprofitable to assign time standards to them with today's techniques. This compilation is presented on the assumption that most activities can be profitably measured; only the exceptions are listed. It is anticipated that this list will grow shorter as work measurement techniques improve. The exceptions are:

1. Corporate officers and division administrators, together with their immediate and personal staffs.
2. Supervisors, activity chiefs, foremen, and managerial heads of organizations and their immediate personal staffs.
3. Members of study and fact finding groups; members of analytical and interpretative groups; members of inspection and audit teams.
4. Members of staffs developing policy, and staffs providing advice and coordinating of operations.
5. Students and trainees.
6. Personnel conducting applied and basic research (other than technicians and subprofessional employees doing repetitive work).
7. Speech writers and public relations personnel.
8. Planners and programmers (other than automated data processing personnel).
9. Doctors and nurses assigned to first aid units; and others who are in similar standby activities.
10. And others where the production or the output of the personnel is not readily identified or measurable in quantitative terms.

Notwithstanding the advice to avoid measuring the work of personnel listed above, work sampling is an excellent technique for identifying working and nonworking time of individuals. In can be used on many of the personnel in the list and might be profitable to try. The time spent by personnel on activities that do not support or pertain to the assigned job is lost or wasted time. Work sampling is useful in revealing this loss.

Development and Analysis of Work Measurement Data

One of the basic problems of any operating manager is to know how much work his organization is accomplishing in relation to the amount it should accomplish within available resources. Such knowledge is vital for appraising performance of subordinates, for planning and scheduling work, and for allocating manpower and other resources.

Various procedures have been and are being devised to provide this information. Essentially the procedures or systems involve bringing together data as to work performed by employees or equipment in quantity measures, costs incurred, and standards of performance for analysis. The systems generally employ the techniques similar to those used in standard cost systems in which standards or targets are established and actual performance is periodically compared with standards.

Work measurement systems are devoted to relating units of work produced to man-hours expended. Data produced by work measurement systems are expressed in man-hours rather than dollars. Data expressed in such a manner are often easiest for first-line supervisors and others to understand and use. Most first-line supervisors are in a position to control only the quantity of labor applied to their operations. Since manpower (or labor) costs constitute the bulk of the total cost of many operations in a production activity, controlling the quantity of labor applied to operations will go far toward controlling the total cost of the operations.

The comptroller can assist operating managers by designing the procedures that will provide them with information as to the work performed and manhours applied. He can render additional service, if required, by helping them develop equitable standards of performance and by providing periodic analyses of actual performance in relation to the standards developed.

PRELIMINARY STEPS IN DEVELOPMENT OF ENGINEERED WORK MEASUREMENT STANDARDS

Thus far, we have considered what work measurement is, its objective, where it is used, and who is responsible for it. But just how does it work? How do we develop it and put it to work for us? The following is a suggested procedure or method for realistically applying work measurement. This method may be deviated from or several of the steps may be undertaken simultaneously, depending upon the circumstances. Essentially the task of developing a work measurement system includes the following steps.

Indoctrination of Personnel

Indoctrinate all management personnel in the purposes and uses of work measurement. This indoctrination should also cover the relationship of work measurement to scheduling work, budgeting, programming, accounting, and manpower activities.

Preliminary Study

Work measurement studies will normally be conducted by teams assigned to activities of varying size. Teams will vary in number due to the size and complexity of the activity being studied.

A written communication should be prepared by the work measurement department for the signature of the works manager or comparable official announcing each work measurement study. This should be sent to each interested level of management as to the schedule of studies.

Prior to entrance into the work area all available reference material should be received by each team member. Applicable portions of the following documents should be studied:

1. Organization and functions manual.
2. Latest manpower survey.
3. Local management or operating regulations.
4. Management studies.

5. Internal audits and reviews.
6. Performance information.

The team members, having familiarized themselves with background information, are ready for an entrance review with the operating official. The entrance interview is normally held in the office of the operating official. It is attended by the chief of the activity being studied, personnel of his selection, the work measurement chief, and all members of the team. At this time the operating official will normally discuss the mission, organization, and work load of the activity. He may cover problem areas and items of particular interest. This interview is followed by a walkthrough of the work site and an introduction to the supervisors. During this walkthrough the team should acquaint themselves with the general layout and the work flow.

The team should thoroughly review plant regulations, standing operating procedures (SOP), work distribution charts, task lists, flow charts, operational reports, job descriptions, and organizational charts. Copies of reviews, inspections, and audits by outside organizations should be requested and carefully studied. The analyst should not consider any of these documents as an absolute reflection of what is being done in the activity.

Select and Define Measurable Work Areas

The activity must be broken down into work areas. Work areas may identify a single operation such as filing, but they will usually identify a function such as mail and records. Work areas generally conform to organization, a grouping of related activities, or to a function. A useful work area includes the following characteristics.

1. The work area should be well defined. If it conforms to an organizational element, it should include all the individuals assigned to the element, unless the definition clearly indicates that it does not. For example, in a pay section composed of six pay clerks, one file clerk, and one supervisor, the pay clerks will produce a tangible work unit, such as vouchers processed. The file clerk and the supervisor do not produce any vouchers, but their work efforts are directly related to the production of vouchers. The number of vouchers processed may serve as a convenient measure for the total pay section.
2. All of the individuals in a work area should be doing related work.
3. A good work area should be manageable:
   a. If a work area is too large:
      (i) Fluctuations in performance go unnoticed. Shortfalls in one element will be compensated for by output in other elements.
      (ii) Data generated through the reporting system are meaningless. If the performance effectiveness should indicate a need for corrective action, the area is too large to suggest what action is necessary or where the action should be taken.
   b. If a work area is too small:
      (i) The reporting system may be burdensome for the amount of potential benefit.
      (ii) Minor fluctuations in work load may create distortions in reporting.
4. An accurate strength figure should be obtained from a reliable source. This strength figure should be broken down into the work areas to ensure full coverage of the activity. All personnel working in the activity who are subject to work measurement study coverage should be included.
5. Measured work is generally routine and repetitive in nature. In this type of work

area, there is a reasonably constant relationship between the amount of work produced and the time expended. Examples of measured work areas are:

a. Receiving of material.

b. Unit assembly.

c. A communication center.

6. Unmeasured work is generally diverse in nature, and is not routine, repetitive, or recurring. There are likely to be wide variations in the ratios of work produced to time expended. An example of an unmeasured work area is staff work (certain portions of staff operations may be easily measured because a unit of measure can be selected which will accurately and readily describe the quantity of work produced, that is, cards punched, claims processed). In this type of work area, there may not be a direct relationship between the amount of work produced and the personnel required.

Improve Work Methods, Conditions, Tools, and Equipment

In work measurement, we define work areas and measure how much work is done in these areas through the use of work units. However, before such a system is established, we should be certain that work methods, conditions, tools, and equipment are in good shape. There is no sense in measuring how much work is inefficiently done under poor working conditions. Industrial engineers should make a careful analysis of the organizational structure, work relationships, conditions, procedures, systems, methods, tools, and equipment and make any needed improvements in these areas before a work measurement system is set up. If needed improvements are not made prior to setting up a work measurement system and historical data are used to set the performance standard, operations can go on in their same inefficient way without being noticed. Work measurement is without meaning unless the performance standard is accurate. The performance standard must represent the amount of work an individual should accomplish if he does his work in the most efficient manner. Likewise, a performance standard for a group or the entire organization must represent the amount of work the organization accomplishes if the organization operates efficiently. The worker as well as the supervisor must agree on the work methods. The analyst must insure that the method is being followed.

Forms should be available to the analyst for use in making a methods study. Generally speaking, methods improvement forms are completed for two reasons: (1) to show conditions before and after improvement; and (2) to document a method or procedure. The following methods improvement forms should be considered for use in a methods study.

1. Physical layout sketch sheet.
2. Activity list.
3. Work distribution chart is used to show the breakdown of activities in a work area and each employee's contributions to each activity in terms of man-hours. This aids the analyst in evaluating the organization and in isolating improper use of skills, uneven distribution of work, misdirected effort, and the like.
4. Flow process chart is used to show the present and proposed flow of men and material.
5. Procedures chart is used primarily for recording the flow of paper work through multiple work areas or sections.
6. Cutout template for space planning is a form to be used in conjunction with floor plans for planning layout.

Simplify and Stabilize the Work Methods in Use

A performance standard becomes invalid each time a significant change in methods or procedures is made. There is no point in developing a performance standard for any operation that is not stabilized in terms of work methods or machines. It is often found, however, that the attempt to develop a performance standard will reveal inefficient procedures that can be corrected. When this happens, the performance standard must be redeveloped from data obtained under the revised procedures.

Selection of Work Units

For each measured work area, a work unit that represents the quantity of work performed must be selected and defined:

1. Work units should be representative of the work effort in the work area. They should denote actual accomplishment.
2. Work units should be expressed in terms that simplify, as far as possible, the recording, compiling, and use of performance data. For example, if there is already a requirement to measure work in a given work area and the unit of measure being used meets the criteria for a good work unit, this item should be adopted as the work unit for that work area. Following are some other guidelines on the selection of work units:
   a. If the volume of work is large, work units should be expressed in hundreds or thousands to simplify recordkeeping. If 25 miles of road must be resurfaced, we would not measure the accomplishment of work in units of square inches. More likely, we would use a unit of "thousands of square feet (yards) or miles of road" to measure performance.
   b. Use only one work unit for each work area whenever possible. Unfortunately, this is not always possible. It may be necessary in a particular work area to select more than one work unit. Thus, we have what are commonly referred to as multiple work units.
   c. Multiple work units are used in those instances where more than one work unit is designated, both of which together express the total work in a given work area.
   d. Where a work area is common to subordinate activities, the same work unit definition should be used by all subactivities.
   e. Performance factors and work units should not become confused. Performance factors are ordinarily associated with work loads (number of trainees) and staffing patterns (population served), but their use is for relating work load to dollar cost rather than for analyzing performance. Many performance factors do not necessarily reflect time and effort; therefore, they are not always a true measure of work performance. A performance factor is a selected indicator used as a barometer, gauge, or a gross measurement to express the relationship of the projected work level, work level in being, or the work accomplished in relation to the level of resource requirements and utilization. An example of a performance factor is square yards of surfaced areas. A work unit is an item of measurement selected to express, quantitatively, the work accomplished in a given measurable work area. An example of a work unit is square yards of surfaced area maintained or

square yards of surfaced area repaired (a completed action). A performance factor includes a broad spectrum of activities while a work unit includes only a specific definitive area of responsibility. Thus, performance factors are not always good work units, but work units can always pass as performance factors.

Choose a Work Unit That Fits the Work Being Done. This is as important as stabilizing the work method, because any change in what is being counted immediately invalidates the past measurements. The work unit must relate itself to the work being done by the activity being measured. Work load designations, such as population or population served, and noncumulative, fixed-type work load factors, such as square footage of buildings, boiler horsepower capacity, acreage, fixtures, and so on, are not valid work units for determining a meaningful performance standard and should not be used. In some cases, the work being done is not readily measurable and may be of such a nature that measurement is not even indicative of the importance of the work.

The work unit chosen represents output; therefore, it must be countable. It is easy to make a count of the number of documents filed, number of work orders completed, and similar tangible items. It is more difficult to determine a proper work unit where varying work is done, as in medical treatments. In such cases, the number of examinations performed may be more easily counted than the number of individuals who appear for treatment, since the same person may appear more than once. A count by individual might require identification of each visitor by name, and a consequent laborious tally of rosters.

Select Work Units for Measurable Work Areas

A work unit is a description of the work performed by an individual or a group of people. For example, in a machine shop the work unit for one of the workers might be the number of items manufactured. Another worker might have a work unit described as number of items assembled. The work unit for the entire shop, however, might better be described as number of jobs completed.

Work units may be selected that describe a simple individual operation such as number of envelopes opened, or a complex procedure such as number of applications processed, during which each application passes through numerous operations by many individuals.

The term *work unit* is used in this text to designate accountable work produced, as differentiated from the term *work load factor*, which may represent a programming factor not necessarily useful in performance analysis, such as a population.

A well-chosen work unit should be:

1. Directly related to the time and effort spent on the activity.
2. Related to the mission of the organization and the budget process.
3. Economical to use.
4. Convenient to report.
5. Mutually exclusive so that an item or act will not tend to be counted under more than one work unit.
6. Subject to audit so that the accuracy of a work count can be verified.
7. Readily understood by those who plan, schedule, and control the work.
8. Such as to readily permit a workload to be translated into an anticipated work count prior to the performance of the activity.

9. Related to overall productivity so as to assist in measuring progress toward top-level goals.
10. Helpful in indicating specific opportunities for management improvement.
11. Of such a nature that once started it may be completed.
12. Readily separable from the total work with a definite beginning and end.
13. Identifiable when it is seen being performed.
14. Suitable for use with the most feasible work measurement technique.
15. Sufficiently common so as to appear in the activity for a reasonable period of time.
16. Have a correlation coefficient of 0.7. Normally, when a figure of less than 0.7 is attained, the work center should be reexamined to determine if a more valid work unit should be used.

Design a Simple and Practical Method for Counting Work Units and Time Expended (Man-hours). It is preferable to use existing records to obtain work count and man-hours expended. Counts should be made of man-hours expended in both productive and nonproductive time.

Productive Time. Productive man-hours are those expended on the job by personnel subject to formal personnel authorization vouchers issued by personnel or higher authorities. Ordinarily, productive time is that time during which the employee is in a work status. This would include overtime and standby time. Other productive man-hours are those expended on the job by personnel not subject to formal personnel authorization vouches issued by higher authority to the using organization.

Nonproductive Time. Nonproductive man-hours are those such as vacation and sick leave, special orientations, and training. Holidays not worked will be treated in the same manner as Sundays not worked (that is, they will be considered outside of the normal work schedule and will not be reported for performance analysis purposes). Holidays will be accounted for as required for cost accounting or payroll purposes.

DEVELOPMENT OF STATISTICAL PERFORMANCE STANDARDS

Performance standards are to be developed for each work area determined to be measurable; they may be either engineered or statistical. Engineered standards are more precise than statistical standards and also more expensive to establish, requiring a higher degree of technical skill in the personnel who set the standards. Statistical standards are less precise than engineered standards, and nontechnically trained personnel may be used to establish them under qualified supervision. There are two basic steps in the development of statistical standards—accumulating performance data and establishing the standard.

1. *Accumulate Performance Data.* This step may be accomplished in several ways. Figure 10–4 illustrates one method by which this may be done. It records work units produced and man-hours expended within each area for which we wish a quantitative measurement. Monthly postings may be made to this form as soon as the information becomes available. From the collected statistics illustrated in Figure 10–4, a performance ratio (man-hours per work unit) may be calculated for each month by dividing the productive man-hours expended by the number of work units

Work area ______	Work unit ______		
Month (1)	Work units produced (2)	Man-hours expended (3)	(Performance ratio) man-hours per work unit (4)
January 1981	4,252	3,781	0.889
February	3,756	3,508	0.934
March	4,915	4,025	0.819
April	4,093	3,520	0.860
May	4,350	3,480	0.800
June	5,304	3,750	0.707
July	4,458	3,700	0.830
August	5,053	3,901	0.772
September	5,001	3,726	0.745
October	4,330	3,698	0.854
November	4,031	3,600	0.893
December	4,300	3,939	0.916
January 1982 ______	(Add monthly postings as data becomes available)		

Data to be entered in column (2) and column (3) are derived from feeder reports.

The ratios in column (4) are computed by dividing column (3) by column (2).

NOTE: The data used in this figure should not be considered typical of any work area. They are used for illustrative purposes only.

FIGURE 10–4. Recording of Performance Data.

actually produced. Note that man-hours are always expressed in decimal form, that is, 30 minutes is 0.5; one and one-quarter hours is 1.25.

2. *Establish the Standard.* The data shown in Figure 10–4 may then be rearranged in a manner illustrated in Figure 10–5. Note that the information relating to each month is arranged in ascending order of numerical values of the performance ratios. In this way, the best ratio will appear at the top and the worst ratio at the bottom of the listed items. The standard may then be computed from this array by means of a uniform method referred to as the average of the upper half. The average of the upper half is obtained by dividing the total man-hours expended in the upper half by the total work units produced in the upper half of the arrayed ratios. This process is illustrated in Figure 10–5.

Work area ______________________ Work units ______________________

Work units produced		Man-hours expended		(Performance ratio) man-hours per work unit		
5,304	Upper half of array	3,750		0.707		Array in ascending order ↓
5,001		3,726		0.745		
5,053		3,901		0.772		
4,350		3,480		0.800		
4,915		4,025		0.819		
4,458		3,700		0.830		
4,330	29,081	3,698	22,582	0.854	0.777	
4,093	(1)	3,520	(2)	0.860	(3)	
4,252		3,781		0.889		
4,031		3,600		0.893		
4,300		3,939		0.916		
3,756		3,508		0.934		

(1) Total work units produced in upper half of array.

(2) Total man-hours expended in upper half of array.

(3) Statistical performance standard obtained by dividing (2) by (1).

NOTE: The data used in this figure are those shown in Figure 10-4 and should not be considered typical. They are used for illustrative purposes only.

FIGURE 10–5. Establishing the Statistical Standard.

Consideration should be given to the following factors when establishing statistical standards:

a. Express statistical standards of measurement in terms of man-hours per unit of work performed for measured work areas.

b. To achieve uniformity, statistical standards of measurement should normally be limited to no more than three significant figures. For example: 123., 12.3, 1.23, .123, and 0.0123. When the computation of a standard results in an insignificant fraction, the work unit should be changed so that a more significant figure will result, for example, square inches to square feet or square yards.

c. Performance data should not include periods during which exceptional circumstances or conditions occurred.

d. Where an odd number of ratios appear in an array, drop the worst ratio and then divide the remaining ratios into two equal parts for computation of the average of the upper half.

Why average the upper half of our performance data? One of the methods for statistically computing a performance standard averages only the upper half of the basic performance data. This results in an ambitious standard that is perhaps difficult to meet. To allow a slight oversimplification, it has been attained only 25 percent of the time upon which the standard was based. How then can we justify this method as fair? Standards are used for different purposes, of course. The degree of validity and reliability required will depend upon the intended use of the work measurement data. If straight unadjusted production data (average) are used as the basis of a standard, that standard will be whatever the operators on the job want it to be. The standard is simply what has been and, therefore, permits people to create the basis on which they will be evaluated. Such a standard might well be appropriate and useful for planning purposes, but not necessarily so for evaluation, particularly if it is to be used as a basis for wage payment. It is quite possible that the level of performance embodied in average production data is not the desired norm so that an adjustment may be desirable. Similarly, since changes in methods and conditions may well have occurred over the period covered by production data used, a correction for this may also be desirable. Averaging the upper half is a recognized method for attempting to accomplish a correction for some of the unknowns with respect to such things as conditions existing, level of employee application, and method used for the data period. When used as goals, standards should be realistic, though reasonably difficult to achieve. They should motivate and inspire workers to an optimistic, positive attitude toward their work. They should be reasonably high, yet attainable. As such, this method presents an excellent challenge. At the same time, supervisors must be ready to accept the fact that difficult goals will not be reached on every attempt. Standard performance of 90 percent or less may be a frequent occurrence. Planners and programmers should know how standards are computed and, where and when appropriate, anticipate less than 100 percent effectiveness by the labor force.

Advantages and Disadvantages of a Statistical Standard

Advantages.

1. More economical (effort, time, cost).
2. Requires a minimum of skill to establish.
3. Sometimes the only technique available.

Disadvantages.

1. Reflects the time it actually took, not the time it should take.
2. Accepts past performance as satisfactory. (Poor control device.)
3. No way of knowing if past and present methods are the same.

Statistical standards are, in effect, a history of past performance and indicate the effectiveness achieved under certain conditions. Standards developed under inefficient operations cannot be distinguished from standards derived from good working methods. There is no way to determine the reasons for such poor performance from statistical standards. However, discrepancies in data revealed during the development of standards may identify or isolate problem areas for specific investigation. Statistical standards are useful for measuring performance where strict accuracy is not essential. Such standards, however, are no more useful than the degree of accuracy of any of the measurements made. Care should be taken to record work count and time with as much accuracy as possible.

DEVELOPMENT OF ENGINEERED STANDARDS

An engineered performance standard is a measure of how long a job should take using a specified method, under specified conditions, working at a normal pace for a qualified employee. Elements of an engineered standard are:

1. Standardized method. A record of the standard practice or method followed when the standard was developed. This should contain specific statements describing the work situation and method which provides the basis for the standard time and also clearly identifies the work unit being measured.
2. A definition of standard time. A written definition of what is considered as standard.
3. A record of the observed or synthesized time values used in determining the final standard time. These time values may have been derived from stopwatch study, film analysis, sampling study or standard data tables.
4. A record of computations used to determine the statistical reliability of the standard and a statement of what the statistical reliability is.
5. A record of the rating or leveling observed during performance while the time values were recorded. This is basically a comparison of observed operator pace compared with the analyst's concept of normal as described in the definitions of standard time.
6. An explanation of what personal, fatigue, and delay allowances were used in the final computation of standard time.
7. A record of how the standard time was computed showing each computation step by step.

The formula for establishing an ETS (engineered time standard) is:

$$\text{ETS (per work unit)} = \frac{\text{working man hours} \times \text{pace} \times \text{allowances factor}}{\text{work units}}$$

Definition of Standard Time

The standard time is the amount of time necessary to accomplish a unit of work, using a given method and equipment, under given conditions of work, when worked on by an operator possessing a specified amount of skill and aptitude, with sufficient training to perform the job properly, and working at a normal pace for a given period of time.

Pace-rating Procedure

Pace rating is a procedure in which the rating analyst observes the rate (speed) of work pace (performance) and compares it against his concept of standard (normal) performance for the job. The rating analyst uses percentages to express the performance rate that he sees. Normal performance is usually expressed as 100 percent; higher or lower rates of performance are similarly expressed as percentages above or below 100 percent. The analyst in his comparison mentally computes the rating percentage that applies to the performance he observes, be it normal or above or below normal. Synonymous terms are effort rating, pace rating, leveling, performance rating, and speed rating.

The normal pace may be defined as some fraction of the maximum pace that can be maintained on the job, day after day, without physical harmful effects to the operator. In establishing what is normal performance for a job (prior to pace rating) the analyst is forced to relate the activity he sees to the performance of a task for which there is a well established concept of normal. Some common established concepts of normal are: walking three miles per hour on level ground; dealing a deck of fifty-two playing cards into four equal piles in 0.50 minute; or filling a standard pegboard with thirty pins using a two-handed method in 0.41 minute. The main limitation of the analyst is in applying these established concepts of normal to a large variety of operations. In actuality, the supervisor of the work area should assist by conveying verbally or showing the analyst his concept of the normal work rate for his area, that is, level of performance the supervisor believes the standards should represent. The analyst must then develop the ability to satisfactorily compare the observed rate of work to his mental image of the normal rate for that operation, then convert this to a numerical rating factor.

Training an analyst to pace rate involves the use of a series of films developed by the Society for Advancement of Management (SAM) to instill a common concept of normal. During the orientation phase the analyst observes scenes of individuals performing various technical and clerical jobs at a normal pace (100 percent). On the basis of their exposure to these films, the participants will employ their concept of normal in the evaluation of subsequent films that show individuals performing jobs at predetermined speeds above and below normal. During the rating sessions, care must be taken to ensure that the projector is operating at the prescribed speed. Proper speed is 960 frames per minute for SAM films. A standard deviation of 12 percent or less between the actual performance rating shown in the film and the analyst's estimated rating is acceptable if the errors are random, that is, sometimes a little high, sometimes a little low. Analysts should participate in film sessions every two weeks to maintain rating ability.

Procedures for Setting Personal, Fatigue, and Delay Allowances

Engineered standards must take into consideration not only those periods of time in which the operator is able to work at the job, but also those periods in which he is prevented from working by such things as equipment failures, stoppage of material flow, and defective parts. In addition, personal needs and the effects of fatigue must be considered. In other words, allowances must be made in the time standard to provide for such delaying and retarding factors that are beyond the worker's control.

Many methods are used to determine the allowances for personal, fatigue, and delay (PF&D) allowances. A given percentage is sometimes used for all three allowances. In other cases a given percentage is used for personal needs, then a sliding scale is used to compute fatigue and unavoidable delay allowances. Another approach, shown later, requires that all three allowances be computed according to working conditions and variables encountered. Allowances are converted to an allowance factor, which is incorporated into the formula for computing an engineered performance standard. Since the percentage allowed has a direct bearing on the final standard, it should be arrived at in the most scientific manner possible. Before a percentage allowance is determined, the following factors must be taken into consideration.

1. Time allowed to take care of personal needs.

2. Working conditions such as extreme heat, cold, exposure, fumes, and so on, must be considered since they increase the time required to do the job.
2. Heavy physical effort must be considered because it will affect the time required to do the job. Fatigue will cause the employee to slow his pace in order to continue his work for the day.

Consider only those delays that cannot be controlled by the employee or management (unavoidable delay). If delay is classified as avoidable it is the responsibility of the supervisor or management to take steps to eliminate such delays, that is, shortage of parts or supplies, failure to assign work, inadequate training, and supervisory errors. Avoidable delay will be reflected in the percentage of effectiveness of the operation (to be discussed later). The three types of allowances are as follows: personal time, fatigue, and delay.

Determining Allowances for Personal Time. When an operation allows two 10-minute breaks during an 8-hour (480 minutes) day, a basic allowance of 4 percent would be used (Table 10–2).

TABLE 10-2.
Allowances

	Allowances	*Percent Allowed*
1	Basic allowance.	4
2	Add the percentage allowance according to the following classification:	
a	Normal office conditions.	0
b	Normal shop, central heat, slightly dirty or greasy.	1
c	Slightly disagreeable. Exposed to weather part of time, poor heating, etc.	3
d	Exposed to extremely disagreeable conditions most of time. Proximity to hot objects, continuous exposure to disagreeable odors and fumes, etc.	6
3	Add the following allowances where applicable:	
a	For areas where smoking is prohibited.	2
b	Where 5 minutes is allowed at end of the day to return tools to storage or to clean up work area.	1

Determination of Allowances for Fatigue.

Allowances for Physical Requirements of the Job.

1. Consider the average weight handled per man and the percentage of time that the man is under load. Also, consider the height that load must be lifted.
2. Allowances. The percent allowed given in Table 10–3 is based on handling from a stock at a height of from knee-level to chest-level and placing on a skid at a height from floor-level to chest-level. For picking up load from floor, multiply basic allowance by 1.10. For placing load above chest-high, multiply basic allowance by 1.10. For pushing the load along the floor, multiply basic allowance by 0.50. (For pushing, in order to determine pounds handled, estimate pounds of effort required to push the load, not the weight of the load itself.)

Mental Concentration Allowances.

1. Consider the degree of concentration necessary to perform the job and the amount of variety in the tasks. Highly repetitive jobs should be low in this factor.
2. Allowances would be given according to the classifications given in Table 10–4, using the percent allowance stated.

Operator's Position Allowances.

1. Consider the position that the employees must assume to perform the operation.

TABLE 10-3.

Pounds Handled	*Percentage of Time Under Load*			
	25	50	75	100
0-1	1	1	1	1
1-10	1	2	3	4
11-20	3	5	7	10
21-30	4	9	13	17
31-40	6	13	19	25
41-50	9	17	25	34
51-60	11	22	33	44
61-70	14	28	41	55
71-80	17	34	51	68
81-90	21	42	62	83
91 and over	25	50	75	100

TABLE 10-4.

Class	*Percent Allowed*
a. Work largely committed to habit: simple calculations on paper; reading easily understood material such as routine or familiar instructions; counting, and recording; simple inspection requiring attention but little discretion, arranging papers by letters or numbers.	0
b. Work requiring full attention: copying numbers, addresses or instructions; memory of number or part name while checking stock or parts list. Simple division of attention between work at hand and jobs of others, conveyor or time schedule, simple calculations in head, filing papers by subject of familiar nature.	2
c. Work requiring concentrated attention: reading of non-routine instructions; routine calculations on paper such as long division and four-place multiplication, checking number, parts, papers, etc. Requiring crosscheck or doublecheck; division of attention between three components such as counting, inspecting, and grading; or driving over unfamiliar route, watching vehicle traffic, and route signs.	4
d. Work requiring deep concentration: complicated or swift mental calculations; unfamiliar calculations on paper; memorizing; inspection work requiring interpretation and discretion of unfamiliar nature, as when working against nonroutine specifications; highly divided attention between phases of work, operations of others, hazards, etc.	8

Use the classification that best describes the average condition if it is assumed that the job would be less tiresome if the position can be varied frequently.

2. Classify allowances as shown in Table 10–5.

TABLE 10-5.

Class	Percent Allowed
Sitting or standing	0
Sitting	1
Walking	1
Standing	2
Climbing or descending ramp, stairs or ladder	4
Working in close, cramped position	7

Allowances for Monotony.

1. Consider the fatigue resulting from fast, highly repetitive operations. The cycle time is the time elapsed from starting one element until the same element is started again.
2. Classify according to cycle time and give the percentage of allowance (see Table 10–6).

TABLE 10-6.

Cycle Time	Percent Allowed
0.0-0.20 minutes	4
0.21-0.40 minutes	3
0.41-0.80 minutes	2
0.81-2.50 minutes	1
2.50 minutes or more	0

Allowances for Restrictive Safety Devices. Consider devices that are required by the job and that cause fatigue when worn. Allowance should be made here only if it is necessary to move the devices occasionally for relief, or if wearing them causes fatigue. If more than one device is required, add the allowances (see Table 10–7).

TABLE 10-7.

Class	Percent Allowed
Face shield	2
Rubber boots	2
Goggles or welding mask	3
Tight, heavy protective clothing	4
Filter mask	5
Safety glasses	0

Determining Allowance for Delay.

1. Consider the job in relation to adjacent jobs. How long can any adjacent job be shut down before the job being studied is affected? Also, consider other delays inherent in the job, such as moving from one work station to another, waiting for cranes, etc. No delays that can be prevented by the employee should be considered here (see Table 10–8).

TABLE 10-8.

Class	Percent Allowed
Isolated job. Little coordination with adjacent jobs.	1
Fairly close coordination with adjacent jobs.	2

2. Where employees are required to move from one work station to another to balance adjacent stations, add the allowances indicated in Table 10–9.

TABLE 10-9.

Move	*Percent Allowed*
Move once each 5 minutes	5
Move once each 30 minutes	3
Move once each 60 minutes	2
Move once each 2 hours	0

3. For crane waits (where overhead cranes are used to handle material) add 0.10 percent per crane lift per day. Where work is performed on a complicated machine, an allowance for machine down time should be added. This allowance may be arrived at by calculating the normal down time by ratio-delay (work sampling) studies or other means.

Examples of Application. An example of the application of the allowance factors can be seen in an operation where an employee is unloading boxes from a truck and placing them on an adjacent pallet. The following conditions are in effect:

1. The operation is performed outside a warehouse, in an area where smoking is prohibited.
2. The boxes weigh 25 pounds each and the employee is under load 75 percent of the time. The boxes are being taken from a stack slightly higher than the employee's head and being placed on a pallet 4 inches above the floor.
3. The work is purely routine.
4. The employee walks approximately 5 feet with each box.
5. The cycle time (per box) is 0.50 minutes (30 seconds).
6. No restrictive safety devices are required.
7. If the pallets were not removed from the work area within 30 minutes after being loaded, the area would become so congested that it would be necessary to stop unloading the boxes until the pallets were removed.

Table 10–10 shows the three main types of allowances and their percentages under these conditions.

TABLE 10-10.

Computation of Allowance	*Percent Allowed*
Personal	
Base	4.0
Class C; slightly disagreeable, exposed to weather	3.0
Add for No Smoking area	2.0
Fatigue	
Physical—25 pounds handled 75 percent of time; boxes are obtained from level above chest-high, 9 percent × 1.10	9.9
Mental: Class A	0.0
Position: Class C (walking)	1.0
Monotony: Class C (0.50 minutes)	2.0
Restrictive safety devices: none	0.0
Delays	
Class C: fairly close coordination (30 minutes)	2.0
Total allowance	23.9

The formula for computing the allowance factor is:

$$AF = 1 + \frac{\text{minutes/day allowance}}{480 - \text{minutes/day allowance}}.$$

The percentage of allowance factor must be converted to minutes and applied to the above formula to determine allowance factor:

$$480 \times 23.9 = 114.72 = 115 \text{ minutes/day}$$

$$AF = 1 + \frac{115}{480 - 115} = 1.31.$$

If this operation is studied and the cycle time is determined to be 0.555 minutes and the leveling factor (pace rating) is 90 percent, the standard time would be computed as follows: 0.555 × 0.90 × 1.31 = 0.654 standard minutes (39.2 seconds).

Another Example. Consider a simple clerical operation where papers are being filed numerically. Assume the following conditions:

1. Work is performed in an office.
2. Employee must be standing while performing the work.
3. The cycle time (per paper filed) is 0.30 minutes (18 seconds).
4. The work is in fairly close coordination with the operation which supplies the papers to be filed. That the operation could be shut down approximately 25 minutes before a delay would occur in the filing operation.

Table 10–11 shows the allowance percentages under these conditions.

If this operation is studied and the cycle time is determined to be 0.30 minutes with a leveling factor of 100 percent, the standard time would be computed as follows: 0.30 × 1.00 × 1.14 = 0.342 standard minutes.

TABLE 10-11.

Computation of Allowance	*Percent Allowed*
Personal	
Base	4.0
Class A	0.0
Fatigue	
Physical: less than 1 pound handled	1.0
Mental: Class B	2.0
Position: Class D (standing)	2.0
Monotony: Class B (0.30 minutes)	3.0
Restrictive safety devices: none	0.0
Delays	
Class A: fairly close coordination	2.0
Total allowance	14.0

THEORY OF WORK SAMPLING

The theory of work sampling is based upon the laws of probability and boils down to the assumption that if you make a sufficient number of observations of a work area at random times, you can accurately describe the work pattern. For example, if you make 10,000 observations of a work area and observe employees filing 1,000 times, you may safely conclude that 10 percent of the time is spent on filing in that work area.

Only competent work measurement analysts should attempt to establish production standards with the work sampling technique. Validity of standards developed will depend upon the observer's thorough understanding of sampling procedures and ability to pace rate.

Procedure for Conducting a Work Sampling Study

The general procedure for conducting a work sampling study to determine areas in need of methods improvement may be described as follows.

Determine the Purpose of the Study. Prior to planning the details and actually conducting a work sampling study, it is important that careful consideration be given to the purpose of the study or the use that will be made of the information derived from the study. With work sampling, it is relatively easy to establish a subjective relationship between the accuracy needed in the data to be provided by the study and the potential value or benefit to be derived from the data. Since accuracy is mathematically related to the number of observations, costs can be controlled by stating the accuracy requirements desired after considering the potential use of the data provided. A typical accuracy requirement for purposes of determining possible areas in need of a methods study would range from ±3 percent to ±5 percent at a confidence level of 95 percent. Thus, if ±5 percent accuracy requirements were stated for a study and the subsequent sampling showed that 20 percent of an engineer's time was spent on clerical jobs, we would be 95 percent sure that the actual or true time spent on clerical jobs was between 15 and 25 percent (20 ± 5 percent).

To summarize, the first step in any work sampling study is to determine realistic accuracy requirements after considering the intended use of the information that the study will provide.

Obtain the Cooperation of the Supervisor. The second step in the study is to obtain the cooperation of the supervisor of the area in which the study is to be conducted. Even though he may be the one who requested assistance to solve a method problem, it is important that he be apprised of your plans to use the work sampling technique. Therefore, a careful explanation of the theory, concepts, purpose, application, and results to be expected from such a study is necessary.

Select Categories for Observation. This step involves an evaluation of the work performed in the work area to be studied. Subsequent to this, the activities of the area must be subdivided into categories or tasks, which collectively represent every function that is performed. The categories selected are a direct function of the purpose or objective of the study. For example, if we were only interested in determining the amount of idle time, one of the categories might be idle. On the other hand, if we were interested in determining the causes of idle time, we might elect to use categories such as idle-personal time, idle-lack of work, idle-receiving instructions, and so on. Thus, the activity of a work area may be subdivided in any manner desired, provided that all observable activities are included in one of the defined categories.

Design the Study. This step can be divided into several parts:

Determine the Length of the Study. In many work areas, certain cyclic patterns can be observed. For example, in a budget office or in a mail and records function, the pattern of work varies throughout definite time periods on a recurring basis. Thus, although the effort devoted to each of the categories may vary considerably from day to day, the same general pattern can be observed between successive time periods. Thus, to gain valid results from work sampling, at least one complete cycle (or some multiple) must be included in the study. If the area to be observed does not have a work cycle, it is desirable that the study continue for a period of at least one week.

Determine the number of observations required. The procedure here is as follows:

1. The number of observations that are needed for the study can be determined by use of a chart, Table 10–12. To use this chart, an estimate of the percentage of occurrence (p) for each of the categories to be observed in the study is required plus a statement of accuracy requirements (as discussed above). The category estimated to take the most time is the controlling factor in using the chart. If it is estimated that one of the functions in a work area takes approximately 40 percent of the worker's time then the other functions combined would take the remaining 60 percent of the worker's time. We would check the left-hand column of the chart under "% Occurrence" for the .40/.60 combination. If we accept an error rate of ± .04, the table will show that 600 observations are required.

TABLE 10-12.
Sample Size Required for p Values, 95% Confidence Limits

% Occurrence (in Decimal)	% Acceptable Error Expressed in Decimals ± 0.01	± 0.02	± 0.03	± 0.04	± 0.05
0.01/0.99	396	99	44	25	16
0.02/0.98	784	196	87	49	31
0.03/0.97	1164	291	129	73	47
0.04/0.96	1536	384	171	96	61
0.05/0.95	1900	475	211	119	76
0.06/0.94	2256	564	251	141	90
0.07/0.93	2604	651	289	163	104
0.08/0.92	2944	736	327	184	118
0.09/0.91	3276	819	364	205	131
0.10/0.90	3600	900	400	225	144
0.11/0.89	3916	979	435	245	157
0.12/0.88	4224	1056	469	264	169
0.13/0.87	4524	1131	503	283	181
0.14/0.86	4816	1204	535	301	193
0.15/0.85	5100	1275	567	319	204
0.16/0.84	5376	1344	597	336	215
0.17/0.83	5644	1411	627	353	226
0.18/0.82	5904	1476	656	369	236
0.19/0.81	6156	1539	684	385	246
0.20/0.80	6400	1600	711	400	256
0.21/0.79	6636	1659	737	415	265
0.22/0.78	6864	1716	763	429	275
0.23/0.77	7084	1771	787	443	283
0.24/0.76	7296	1824	811	456	292
0.25/0.75	7500	1875	833	469	300
0.26/0.74	7696	1924	855	481	308
0.27/0.73	7884	1971	876	493	315
0.28/0.72	8064	2016	896	504	323
0.29/0.71	8236	2059	915	515	329
0.30/0.70	8400	2100	933	525	336
0.31/0.69	8556	2139	951	535	342
0.32/0.68	8704	2176	967	544	348
0.33/0.67	8844	2211	983	553	354
0.34/0.66	8976	2244	997	561	359
0.35/0.65	9100	2275	1011	569	364
0.36/0.64	9216	2304	1024	576	369
0.37/0.63	9324	2331	1036	583	373
0.38/0.62	9424	2356	1047	589	379
0.39/0.61	9516	2379	1057	595	381
0.40/0.60	9600	2400	1067	600	384
0.41/0.59	9676	2419	1075	605	387
0.42/0.58	9744	2436	1083	609	390
0.43/0.57	9804	2451	1089	613	392
0.44/0.56	9856	2464	1095	616	394
0.45/0.55	9900	2475	1100	619	396
0.46/0.54	9936	2484	1104	621	397
0.47/0.53	9964	2491	1107	623	399
0.48/0.52	9984	2496	1109	624	399
0.49/0.51	9996	2499	1111	625	400
0.50	10000	2500	1111	625	400

% Occurrence = Estimated or Observed Frequency of Category or Element
% Acceptable Error = Acceptable Deviation from True Percentage.

2. The number of observation trips required each day of the study is now determined by:

$$\text{trips/day} = \frac{\text{observations required}}{\text{(study days)(observations/trip)}}$$

3. A preliminary work sampling is usually made to determine the percentage of time spent in the various categories and to suggest necessary refinement in categories. Usually three days is sufficient time for a preliminary. The number of observations taken during the preliminary is based on an estimate of each category percentage applied to the formula,

$$N = \frac{4P\,(1-P)}{S^2},$$

where N = number of observations; P = percent occurrence; S = percentage of acceptable error.

Example: If we use a confidence level of 95 percent and a P value of .90/.10 (90 or 10 percent), then:

$$N = \frac{4(.90)(.10)}{(.05)^2} = \frac{4(.0900)}{.0025} = \frac{.3600}{.0025} = \begin{array}{l}144\\ \text{observations.}\end{array}$$

In Table 10–12 the same line is used for .90/.10 or .10/.90.

4. It is sometimes necessary to add 20 percent to the number of daily observations to compensate for absence from work and other factors that affect observations. Observation intervals should be based on two considerations:
   a. The number of daily observations required.
   b. The time frame required by the analyst to complete one observation cycle. This will depend on the number of people in the work area, probable dispersion of employees, difficulty in establishing work categories, and so on.

5. The length of the study is determined by the work cycle and the number of observations required. Care should be exercised to ensure equitable coverage of all the activities in the work area. Coverage must be in terms of full cycles.

6. Select random times of observation. Since observations must be made on a random basis, the analyst must pick his times for making observation of the activity on a random basis. There are numerous methods of doing this. These range from the use of random number tables to the drawing times of observation from a hat containing slips of paper that cover each minute of the day. Whatever procedure is used, it is essential that the times ultimately selected will allow opportunity for observation of the activity under study without any bias on the part of the observer.

7. Design study forms. This is usually best accomplished by custom designing a suitable format for your requirements. The form used for making observations should be kept as simple as possible. Data summary sheets may also be designed for use in summarizing the data collecting on the observation forms.

Study Forms. Experience has shown that the following forms are helpful in making a work sampling:

1. Work measurement preliminary study data sheet. A form that serves to:
   a. Document conditions in the work area at time of entrance.
   b. Estimate the potential labor dollar coverage.
   c. Estimate the total amount of time to be spent in each work area.
   d. Determine potential usefulness of standards.
2. Work measurement study schedule. A planning document that lists all work areas, measured and unmeasured, in

the study—physical location of work areas, hours of work, work cycle, population, and required number of observations.

3. Unmeasured work area documentation. A form for documenting all the considerations of the analyst when determining a work area unmeasurable.
4. Work unit documentation. A form to be completed by the analyst when he begins the study of a particular work area. It should include all the work units that the analyst considered during the course of study.
5. Random observation time schedule. A form showing the date, work area, name of analyst, random time selected for observations, number of observations, and number of trips.
6. Work sampling observations. A form to be used as a working paper by the analyst. It can be completed by listing the employees in the work area across the top of the form and the categories down the left margin. A line should be skipped for times designated for pace rating and the word *pace* substituted for time. Observations will be made by inserting the function category number in the space opposite the observation time and under the employee's name, as shown in Table 10–13.

TABLE 10-13.

Category	*Time*	*Smith*	*Black*	*Bell*
1. Typing	0805	3	4	1
2. Filing	1115	3	1	2
3. Preparing reports	Pace	100	95	110
4. Supervision	1355	4	6	2
5. Unavoidable delay	1550	5	2	1
6. Personal Time	1625	2	1	1

7. Work sampling observation recap sheet. A form used to summarize category data from the work sampling observation forms.
8. Work sampling pace rating recap sheet. A form used to summarize pace rating data from the work sampling observation forms.
9. Work sampling standard computation sheet. A form used for the actual computation of the performance standard. Allowances should be reflected in terms of minutes per individual per day. Categories should be listed at the left of the page. Computations should be shown in the format of the formula. Figure 10–6 is a work sampling record and Figure 10–7 is a work sampling computation sheet.

Conduct the Study. The procedure here is as follows:

Make Observations. At the specified times, the analyst should walk to a preselected point and observe the worker. The analyst classifies the activity of the worker, at the instant of observation, into one of the predefined categories on his work sampling observation sheet. Each worker is observed each trip and is counted as one observation. Each worker should be pace-rated at least 25 percent of the observations.

Calculations. The percentage occurrence (P) for each day of each category is determined by dividing the number of observations of the category by the total number of observations for the day. For example, if a category, "perform clerical work," was observed 10 times a day in which 100 observations were made, the P value would be: 10/100 or .10 (10 percent). The same relationship is used on a cumulative basis at the end of the study.

Control Charts. A useful device to use during a study is a control chart on one or two of the study categories. Each control chart consists of three elements:

Work sampling record	Dates: Started	Dates: Completed
	26 Apr 81	14 May 81

Dept:	Function and subfunction
Flight Instrument Training Center	Operations 3100 Synthetic Trainers 3130, Instrument Trainer 3130B

Summary

Data: Sampling days	1	2	3	4	5	6	7	8	9	10	11	12	13	14	15	16
Data: Day of month	26	27	28	29	30	3	4	5	6	7	10	11	12	13	14	
Assigned time	64.0	64.0	64.0	64.0	64.0	64.0	64.0	64.0	64.0	64.0	64.0	64.0	64.0	64.0	64.0	
Sampled time	64.0	64.0	71.0	56.0	56.0	64.0	64.0	64.0	56.0	56.0	64.0	64.0	72.0	72.0	64.0	
Number samplings	64	64	71	56	56	64	64	64	56	56	64	64	72	72	64	
Average leveling factor	1.04	1.02	0.98	1.00	1.05	0.94	0.96	1.04	1.04	1.06	0.94	0.96	0.98	0.98	0.96	
Work load volume	32	28	25	14	16	30	26	19	26	28	16	32	30	32	30	
Productivity	0.62	0.60	0.59	0.63	0.62	0.61	0.63	0.61	0.60	0.60	0.62	0.61	0.63	0.61	0.59	

Data: Sampling days	17	18	19	20	21	22	23	24	25	26	27	28	29	Total	Average
Data: Day of month															
Assigned time														960.00	64.0
Sampled time														951.00	63.4
Number samplings														951	63.4
Average leveling factor														14.95	1.00
Work load volume														384	25.60
Productivity															0.61

Work center statistics

Work load factor	Productive time	Leveling factor	Leveled time
Monthly Instrument Training Hours	582.96	1.00	582.96
	Allowance factor	Allowed time	Standard time
	1.196 (1.139)	697.22	1.8157

Form # 1DD1 D-38555

FIGURE 10–6. Work Sampling Record.

Record of computations								
Category			Samples	Actual percentage $\bar{p}$	Accuracy	Productive time	Leveled time
A.			B.	C.	D.	E.	F.
Productive	Direct	Briefing and debriefing	88	0.0925		87.97	
		Instruction	147	0.1546		147.02	
		Maintenance and repair	204	0.2145	0.0266	203.99	
	Indirect	Clerical	56	0.0589		56.01	
		Plans and preparation	30	0.0315		29.96	
		Supervision	58	0.0610		58.01	
Special categories							
Clean-up			40	0.0421			
Absent			102	0.1072			
Delay			17	0.0179			
Personal and rest			74	0.0778			
Idle			135	0.1420			
Total			N = 951	1.0000		582.96	582.96
			$\sqrt{N}$ = 30.84				

FIGURE 10–7. Work Sampling Computation.

1. A horizontal line scaled for successive days of the study period (time series).
2. A value assigned to this line which is equal to the estimate of the percentage occurrence (P) for the category being plotted.
3. Two horizontal limit lines scaled vertically in percentages above and below the middle horizontal line described in 1 above.

The results of each day's observations (percentage occurrence, P, for the category) are plotted on this chart against the time scale. According to whether or not the plotting falls within the range of the control (limit) lines or whether successive plottings show certain patterns of behavior (for example, trend) the analyst has a means of determining if the activity under measurement is changing. The control chart provides a means of determining if the study is in control (if the data collected each day are representative of what is happening in the activity); it also provides useful information on the nature of activity being observed.

An alignment chart for determining control limits for a study is illustrated in Figure 10–8.

Evaluate and Summarize the Results. The final step in conducting a work sampling study is to compile all the data collected into a meaningful format. This final summarization, plus analysis of the data collected, must be done in view of the original or revised objective of the study. Although several methods problem areas may have been uncovered by the study, the analyst must exercise caution in giving out information without the approval of the supervisor. A decision to solve the problems discovered with a formal methods study may follow where the problems cannot be solved with informal means:

$$\text{standard time/unit} = \frac{\text{working man-hours} \times \text{pace} \times \text{allowance factor}}{\text{work units}}$$

Example:
Data: See Table 10–14.

1. Compute available hours (covered by sampling period):

   5 workers × 3 weeks × 40 hrs/week
   = 600 man-hours
   3 workers × 1 week × 40 hrs/week
   = $\frac{120}{720}$ man-hours.

2. Compute leveled productive time (Table 10–15).

TABLE 10-14.

Category	*No. of Observations*	*Average Leveling or Rating Factor (Pace)*
Time stamping	500	0.75
Recording the order	300	0.90
Filing the order	400	0.80
Routing the order	400	1.00
Unavoidable delay	100	—
Idle	300	—
Total observations	2,000	

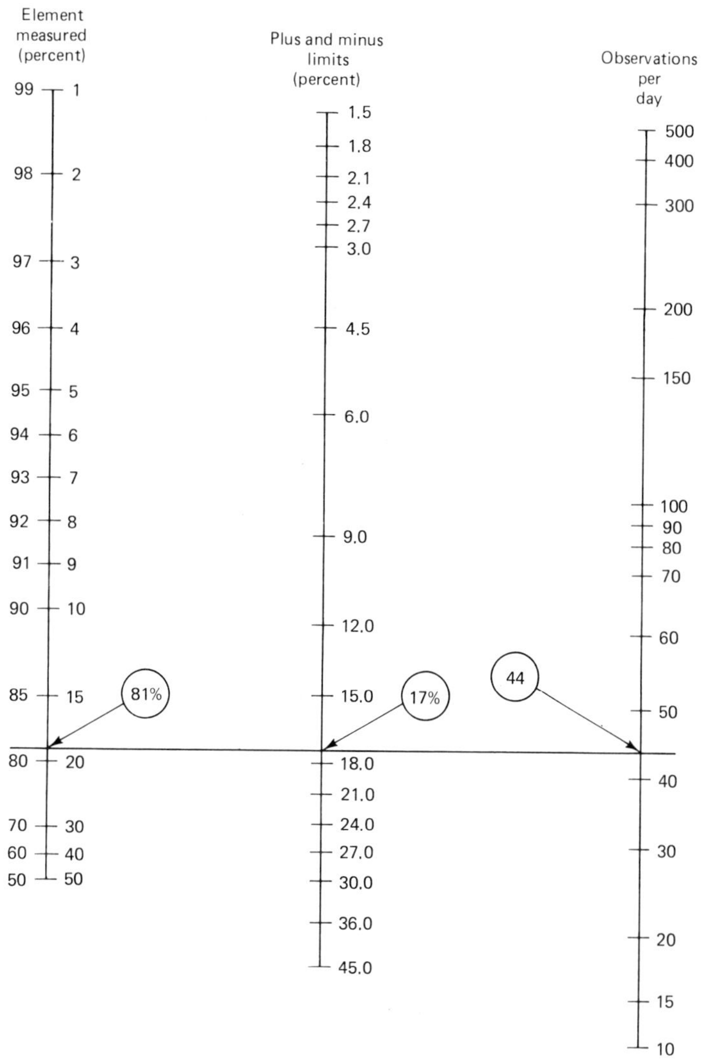

Control limits for your work sampling study results are found in this chart. 1. Mark on left hand line the observed percentage of the element measured. 2. On the right-hand line mark the total number of observations made each day of the study. 3. Connect the two points by a straight line. 4. Read the allowable variation (control limits) on the center line.

Example: If the element measured during a 10-day study is 81%, and the number of daily observations is 44, then each day's percent activity should be between 64% and 98% (81% ± 17%) to be statistically stable. Find the cause for any day that is outside limits. Data connected with that cause should be thrown out in order to achieve the statistical reliability you're looking for.

FIGURE 10–8. Alignment Chart for Determining Control Limits.

TABLE 10-15.

Category	P (%)	*Avail. Time*	*Prod. Time*	*Level Factor*	*Leveled Prod. Time*
Time stamping	25%	720 hrs.	180 hrs.	0.75	135.0 hrs.
Recording the order	15%	720	108	0.90	97.2
Filing	20%	720	144	0.80	115.2
Routing	20%	720	144	1.00	144.0

Total 491.4 hrs.

3. Compute allowance factor (allowances = 50 min/day):

$$AF = 1 + \frac{\text{min/day}}{\text{480-min/day}}$$

$$= 1 + \frac{50}{430} = 1 + 0.116 = 1.12.$$

Allowance of 50 minutes must be expressed as a percentage of work time of the day. When work day is 480 minutes (8 hours × 60 minutes) and we have a 50-minute allowance per person, then 480 − 50, or 430 minutes is available for production: 50 ÷ 430 = .116 = 12% of work time. This is expressed as 1.12 in the formula.

4. Compute standard time unit

std. time/unit

$$= \frac{\text{leveled prod. time} \times AF}{\text{number of units prod.}}$$

$$= \frac{491.4 \times 1.12}{1{,}000}$$

$$= .550 \text{ hrs/unit.}$$

Application and Review of Work Measurement Standards

USE OF PERFORMANCE STANDARDS

There is no reason to develop performance standards unless they are to be used. Historically, performance standards developed in business and industrial operations were designed to determine "a fair day's work for a fair day's pay." Workers who were paid at piece rates or on the basis of output objected to time and motion studies and the setting of standards because they feared the resulting speedup of work created by increasingly stricter standards. This attitude still exists in the minds of some workers. Experience has proved, however, that once reasonable standards are set, they are an advantage to the worker because he is protected from speedups that may result from the lack of any standard defining a fair day's work. Because of this problem, a supervisor should not initiate time studies or record data for development of a performance standard until the purpose for setting a standard has been carefully explained to each person involved.

In industry, performance standards generally are used to:

1. Establish individual production goals as a means of evaluating individual performance in terms of established standards. This may ultimately result in the retention, promotion, or reassignment of individuals.
2. Revise work methods (work simplification) to eliminate inefficient or uneconomical operations.
3. Determine manpower requirements to accomplish a given work load and thus establish personnel space and fund requirements for cost-of-performance budgeting.

Properly developed and properly used performance standards are essential to good management at every level of operation. Inaccurate standards, developed from poorly defined work units, incorrect data, or inefficient work methods, represent wasted time and effort. Furthermore, poor standards may be worse than none at all, particularly if they create personnel problems through unfair demands. On the other hand, good standards become a solid justification for needed personnel actions, fund requirements, or personnel spaces. Of great importance is the use of performance standards by management to determine the effectiveness of operations.

Using the principles outlined above, each supervisor should review his operation with the following objectives:

1. To establish a performance standard for each measurable operation that can be used for proper management.
2. To periodically review each existing performance standard and bring it up to date.
3. To use performance standards as a basis for justifying personnel and funds and determining the efficiency of operations.

In addition to the guidance furnished previously in this text regarding the mechanics of developing, using, and recording performance data, the following points relating to the development and use of performance standards should be given careful consideration.

It will likely be noted that many of the major organization groups will contain work units of fairly broad scope suitable for measuring operations of groups of people rather than individuals. These are measurable mainly in terms of man-hours spent on the particular work unit. Where several persons are engaged in an operation, such as number of items fabricated, it is important that accurate work records be maintained both on work output and on actual man-hours expended by each individual concerned. It may be advisable that a performance standard be developed first for each individual before the entire operation is measured. Thus, in a field maintenance shop, it may be better to first set separate performance standards for mechanics and standards for clerical personnel handling job orders before attempting to establish a shop-wide performance standard based on jobs completed. The resulting performance standard can be no more accurate than the time and work load data recorded. Records based on memory, such as "put down 3 or 4 hours," make the data useless. Data must be recorded hourly or daily as needed and must be the most accurate measurements possible under the circumstances.

If proper time and work load records are kept and the work methods are properly stabilized, the resulting data should be free of wide deviations. Regardless of sudden sharp and large increases in work load, the time required by one person or the group to perform one work unit should not materially change since, for practical purposes, normal efficiency should have been achieved. When sudden heavy increases in work load are accomplished in normal time and without increase in personnel, it may indicate that the original performance standard was too loose.

A good performance standard should be sufficient proof of adequacy of work methods and justification for increases or decreases in manpower. A poor performance standard provides no benefits either to the operator, supervisor, or higher managers. A poor standard represents only time and effort wasted in recording useless data. The recording of time and work load data should be performed by supervisors or persons not engaged in the actual work in order to ensure objective quantitative measurements.

In repetitive operations, such as putting heels on shoes, it is not necessary to make continuous time records of performance or work load. An observer can make individual random time studies of the time necessary to put heels on one pair of shoes. Time studies of this nature should cover periods of about a half hour at a time. A sufficient number of separate readings should be taken in individual time studies in order that sufficient statistical data are available to indicate reliability. Care must be taken to eliminate data where operators appear to be working exceptionally fast merely because of the fact that they are aware that their work is being timed. This tendency is reduced by taking a number of readings at one time until the operator eventually returns to normal speed when he becomes accustomed to being timed.

Every effort should be made to accurately record nonproductive time so that the performance standard is developed only from that time needed to do the particular piece of work. Similarly, borrowed labor time and overtime must be carefully included in the man-hours spent to perform the work.

Sometimes, so-called work units are developed that do not represent the work performed by the operation to which the accounts pertain, but are based on what more properly can be termed an area of responsibility, such as number of pieces of equipment assigned. Because only man-hours expended by the operating unit are recorded, there is no countable measure of output. A work load designation of this type should be reviewed and revised, wherever possible, to one which more specifically and clearly defines what the operating activity does.

PERIODIC REVIEW OF PERFORMANCE STANDARDS

Performance standards developed by activities for work areas for which a quantitative measurement is desired will be reviewed by the managers having jurisdiction over the work area concerned. However, this should not be construed to delay the use of a standard, pending review by the managers. It is incumbent upon the manager to advise the activity promptly of the results of any critical review of proposed standards. The requirement for review does not mean that standards must be changed solely because they are reviewed. Changes in standards should be based upon cogent reasons, such as changes in methods or equipment, so that the change in the standard can be explained to and understood by all personnel concerned. Units concerned will specify the procedures and frequency of reviews according to their own needs and experience. It is emphasized that performance standards are developed, changed, or discarded as time goes on, depending on their ultimate usefulness to management. There should be no hesitation to revise the definitions pertaining to work areas or work units or to revise performance standards whenever circumstances dictate. Review of performance standards by management is useful to determine that:

Standards are realistic, equitable, and present a challenge but, at the same time, are attainable.

Activities or units are applying the principles of work measurement properly.

Satisfactory progress in establishing standards is being maintained.

COMPUTATION AND USE OF PERCENTAGE OF EFFECTIVENESS

Percentage of effectiveness is computed to show how the actual amount of work accomplished compared with the established standard of performance. This computation highlights work areas where additional managerial effort is required or where outstanding performance may be identified. Percentage of effectiveness is also used to adjust personnel requirements, schedules of work, and budgets when they are based upon work measurement standards. If the number of productive man-hours actually used equals the number established as the standard for a measured amount of work, the effectiveness of the labor used to accomplish this work load is 100 percent. If the number of productive man-hours actually used is greater than the number established by the standard, the effectiveness is below 100 percent. If the converse is true, the effectiveness is above 100 percent. In order to compute percentage of effectiveness, we must first arrive at the number of standard man-hours, or the hours which should have been used with a given work load and standard of measurement, and the number of man-hours actually spent in accomplishing this work load. An explanation of each of these items follows:

Measured productive man-hours. Measured productive man-hours are the actual number of hours spent accomplishing a given work load during a particular period of time.

Standard man-hours. Standard man-hours are computed to show the number of hours it should have taken to perform a given volume of work. It is based on work performed at the rate of the selected performance standard. Standard man-hours are computed by multiplying the actual number of work units produced by the standard of measurement. For example, 1,806 actual work units and a standard of measure is 15.1. Computation: 1,806 × 15.1 = 27,270 standard man-hours.

Computation of percentage of effectiveness. Percentage of effectiveness is computed to show how work performed compares with the established standard of performance. It is determined by dividing the standard man-hours by the total productive man-hours and multiplying the quotient by 100. The answer is expressed in percent. The usually allowable deviation in this area is 20 percent below or above normal of 100 percent. The deviation is also referred to as the range of tolerance. When you use the range of tolerance as a means of comparison, any percentage of effectiveness between 80–120 is considered to be in the zone or range of tolerance. For example, 3,435 standard man-hours and 3,600 actual man-hours. Computation: 3,435 ÷ 3,600 = .9541 × 100 = 95.41 percent effectiveness.

Range of acceptable performance. In analyzing performance, the common practice is to focus attention *first* upon work areas where percentage of effectiveness is less than 80; next, in areas where percentage of effectiveness is more than 120; and lastly, in areas where percentage of effectiveness is between 80 and 120. However, this common practice should not influence managers and supervisors to ignore completely those work areas in which the percentage of effectiveness is between 80 and 120, as a sharp rise or fall in the percentage of effectiveness in a work area might highlight an incipient problem that deserves management attention.

A percentage of effectiveness of less than 80 or more than 120 ordinarily is an indication that a study should be made to determine the causes. Incomplete planning, poor scheduling, inadequate supplies of material, or improper tools or equipment may be contributing to poor performance. Performances may be exceptionally high because of inadequate staffing, rush orders, or peak loads for which exceptional effort is required to complete projects. In either case, management should determine the cause so that the conditions can be corrected as soon as possible. Lastly, work areas or work units may need clarification, performance data may be incorrectly reported, the time standard may need adjustment, or other factors may be responsible for the apparent unusual percent effectiveness. Repeated performance above or below the acceptable range indicates the need for a survey of the operations, including study of procedures, work flow, layout, and manpower utilization.

Fluctuations in percentage of effectiveness are to be anticipated. However, where percentage of effectiveness fluctuates within the range of 80 to 120, it is customary to consider such fluctuations acceptable variations. Generally speaking, percentage of effectiveness between 80 and 120 is considered acceptable and thus justifies lower priority of attention as outlined above.

As dictated by subsequent experience, the range of 80 to 120 percent may be narrowed down; for example, 90 to 110 percent. Analyses of feeder report data at more frequent intervals than monthly, offer an early opportunity to detect unsatisfactory performance and to initiate action to effect improvement.

Improving Performance Effectiveness

When the percentage of effectiveness of a particular measured work area is continually low or high, it can likely be attributed to one or more of the following factors:

Staffing
Deviation from standard policies
Quality of work
Improper scheduling
Equipment
Supplies
Plant layout
Leave
Low individual productivity
Morale problems

Why Disregard Nonproductive Time in Computation of Effectiveness?

Percentage of effectiveness is only one index of the efficiency of a work area. As such, it is descriptive of just one relationship: the ability of workers to produce during the time they are actually on the job. The usefulness of this tool lies in its purity. We can analyze a work area over a span of time or compare the indexes of several work areas at one point in time. Any exceptional variances can be immediately traced back to the raw data of the ratio: standard man-hours divided by actual productive man-hours. To include another variable, such as nonproductive time, would mask the cause of the variance and weaken the validity of the index.

Percentage of effectiveness cannot be used alone to evaluate an activity. To do so would encourage charging excess amounts of time as nonproductive in order to earn a higher index rating. Percentage of effectiveness should be used with at least one other measure showing the percentage of total time that is productive. A third good performance index would be an expression of total programmed man-hours divided by total actual man-hours.

Integration of Work Measurement with Other Management Systems

Work measurement may be correlated with other managerial procedures as follows:

Programming. Data may be used to assist in scheduling work to be accomplished. The computation of the performance ratio and standard performance can be used for this purpose:

1. Performance ratio:

$$\frac{\text{Man-hours expended}}{\text{Work units produced}} = \text{Performance ratio.}$$

2. Standard performance:

   Work units required multiplied by the performance standard = standard performance (required man-hours).

For example, application of the formula in 1 above gives the average time to complete one work unit; the formula in 2 above gives the required job time based on a performance standard. Programmed work load computed by use of either formula will give a more accurate estimate of total output for any given period of time.

Budgeting. The standard unit cost—that is, what it should cost to produce a product or service—can be used in the budget estimating procedure when standards have been established. Given a standard unit cost and a programmed work load, dollar budgeting figures can be developed on the basis of these quantitative factors. A significant portion of standard cost may be labor. Work measurement standards specify required man-hours (labor) input to produce a product or service. By using average labor cost per man-hour within a work area, we can convert these to a dollar figure. The addition of other cost factors such as material and overhead results in total unit standard cost for use in budget estimating:

> Labor (average cost per man-hour × work measurement standard) + material cost per work unit + overhead = standard unit cost.
>
> Standard unit cost × programmed workload = estimated budget requirement.

Other performance data—for example, percentage of effectiveness—when based on approved performance standards and reflecting desired results will provide valid support to future requirement or budget requests.

Percentage of Effectiveness

$$\frac{\text{Standard man-hours}}{\text{Actual man-hours}} \times 100 = \begin{matrix}\text{Percentage of} \\ \text{effectiveness.}\end{matrix}$$

Assume: 27,500 units are produced in 3,600 man-hours. The performance standard has been established as .125. Compute the percentage of effectiveness.

$$.125 \times 27{,}500 = 3{,}437.5$$

$$\frac{3{,}437.5}{3{,}600} \times 100 = 95.4\%.$$

Management Improvement. Keeping a daily record of work accomplishment is, in itself, an incentive for improved performance. Comparing work accomplished with appropriate standards developed by the installation will assist in locating areas in need of improvement.

Manpower Control. Standards are employed in evaluating operations in the control phase of managing. The statistical standard, based on experience data, is often used because it is relatively expedient to develop and maintain and yet specific and accurate enough to provide meaningful guidance. Control of manpower entails the development and application of standards, known as yardsticks, which provide a point of reference in the determination of manpower requirements. In the development and maintenance of such statistical standards, it is necessary to continually scrutinize the effort expended to ensure that it is not excessive in view of the benefits realized. Work load and man-hour data collected at operating levels under the requirements for control of manpower serve two purposes:

1. Provide a significant basis for the manager, through his analysts, to evaluate personnel requirements of specific activities.
2. Provide a basis to develop and refine yardsticks, the standards essential to effective and equitable manpower control.

There is no intent that effort be spent in maintaining work load and man-hour data that does not directly serve these two purposes.

Formula for the Determination of Manpower Requirements.

$$\text{Manpower requirements}^* = \frac{\text{Average work units/day} \times \text{Standard} \times 1.11 \text{ leave factor}}{8 \text{ (standard hours/work day)}}$$

*Personnel requirements for the period if the standards were met. Above formula can be adjusted whereby data applied to formula is for a one week period or a one month period. In effect, the answer is the number of man-days, man-weeks, or man-months, including a leave factor.

Estimating and Planning. To determine the number of man-hours required to eliminate a backlog of 500 work units with a standard of 1.88:

$$500 \times 1.88 = 940 \text{ man-hours.}$$

ANALYSES OF WORK MEASUREMENT DATA AND THEIR MANAGEMENT USE

The benefits that accrue from certain types of analyses are obvious, such as comparison of planned work load for the reporting period against the work load actually accomplished during that period. Using such an analysis, the manager or his designated representative can decide whether some changes in operations need to be made because of a failure to adhere to the programmed work load.

Another analysis could be a comparison of the costs programmed against the costs actually incurred. Such information makes it possible for the manager and his staff to determine whether plans can be accomplished at their present cost or whether there should be a reprogramming of future plans.

BASIC CONSIDERATIONS IN DEVELOPING STANDARDS OF MEASUREMENT

The following considerations will assist in establishing and maintaining realistic, equitable, and attainable standards of measurement.

Before establishing a standard, analyze the operations thoroughly and improve methods and procedures wherever practicable to obtain the most efficient and effective operations.

The participation of operating supervisors and other key individuals in the development of standards of measurement is essential and vital. Such participation fosters the active support and acceptance of a standard by those whose operations are being measured.

Repeated performances above or below the acceptable range of variation is one indication of a need for reexamination of the standard. This reexamination should verify basic data and disclose whether or not the standard was established on erroneous data or what other conditions have changed. Periodic reviews of standards of measurement are essential to identify those that are outmoded and are in need of change. Reviews and changes in standards should be made as changes in methods or equipment, plant layout, or other reasons make previous standards invalid.

The development of standards is closely related to the selection of good work units and definitions. A poor work unit sometimes allows one to manipulate the percentage of effectiveness at will by exercising control over the amount of time expended or the type of work performed in a given work area. With good work units, the amount of work produced will vary directly with the number of productive man-hours expended. Therefore, the percentage of effectiveness is not subject to manipulation, since the basic ratio of man-hours per work unit should not vary except when reflecting genuine increase or decrease in effectiveness.

SUMMARY OF WORK MEASUREMENT STANDARDS

Time Study

What Is Required? An opportunity for a trained observer to time an individual job actually being performed by a definite method (preferably the improved and standardized method).

What Must Be Done? The job method must be completely described, the cycle or elemental times must be obtained by use of stopwatch or motion picture camera, the performance of the operator or operators compared to concept of normal, and allowances made for personal and unavoidable delays. With the above information, the allowed time for the various units of production can be determined.

How Long Will It Take? From two to three hours for simple, short-cycle jobs to days or weeks for complex, long-cycle jobs.

What Are the Characteristics? This type of standard is generally considered a valid and reliable basis for establishing time standards. The job content and the standard time are specifically defined. Because the method, quality, working conditions, and operator performance are standardized (highly), it is easy to identify a deviation from standard and to assign a cause for the deviation.

Advantages

1. Detailed methods description (good for control purposes).
2. Relatively accurate work measurement technique.
3. Obtain actual time values for jobs being observed.

Disadvantages

1. Each job must be observed and the performance pace rated.
2. Not economically applicable to all jobs.

Work Sampling

What Is Required? An opportunity for an observer to note which categories of work or nonwork the operator or operators are engaged in at the random times he makes his observations.

What Must Be Done? The job must be broken down into categories of work and nonwork and these categories described; at random intervals, the activity must be observed and the observations classified into the proper categories with sufficient observations taken to get a reliable sample; the performance of the operator or operators is compared to the concept of normal; and allowances are made for personal and unavoidable delays. During the period the job is being observed, a production count must be obtained (unit of measure) and the total time of the study must be recorded. With the above information, the allowed time for the various units of production can be determined.

How Long Will It Take? From one week to several months, depending upon the number of different types of work and nonwork being observed (complexity of the activities being observed).

What Are the Characteristics? This type of standard will give substantially the same results as time study standards where there is a clear distinction between working time and idle time. In establishing a work sampling standard, the observers must be alert for slight methods changes on the part of the operators. This type of study does not allow as fine a breakdown of activities and delays as time study. The job content and the standard time are specified in general terms. Because job conditions (such as method, quality, and operator performance) are standardized, it is relatively easy to identify a deviation from standard and to assign a cause for the deviation.

Advantages

1. Can be used to measure activities that are impractical or costly to measure by other means.
2. Requires less time (can study several operators or machines at once).
3. Generally less costly than time study.

Disadvantages

1. Not generally economical for studying a single operator.
2. Methods control may not be as precise as time study.
3. Operator may change work pattern without being observed.

Predetermined Time Systems

What Is Required? Dimensional sketch of workplace layout and product along with information about other features of the job. Requires that the person applying the predetermined time system be completely familiar with the system and able to identify the basic motions pertinent to the job being studied.

What Must Be Done? The method for performing the job must first be described in terms of elements, then the elements broken down into basic motions pertinent to the particular predetermined time system, time values for the various basic motions chosen from tables and allowances made for personal and unavoidable delays. With the above information, the allowed time for the various units of production can be determined.

How Long Will It Take? From two to three hours for simple, short-cycle jobs to days for complex, long-cycle jobs.

What Are the Characteristics? This type of standard is as valid and reliable as time study for setting time standards. Where predetermined time system time values are used to set standards on all the activities, the various standard times will be more consistent for all the standards. Good work measurement technique to use to establish standard time on manual jobs before the jobs are begun. Can be used for control purposes where all or most of the activities are covered by similar standards.

Advantages

1. More consistency between time values.
2. Eliminates performance rating by analyst.
3. Can be used to compare methods (provided there is no machine time).
4. Can set standard time for job prior to performing the job.
5. Provides a sound basis for engineered standard data.

Disadvantages

1. Judgment is required to identify basic motions.
2. Not applicable to process-controlled, machine-controlled, and long or irregular cycle jobs.
3. Detailed type of analysis, costly.

Standard Data

What Is Required? Time values in the form of tables, curves, charts or formulae for units of work (elements) small enough to permit determining the step-by-step time required by any method involving these job elements. A person technically qualified to break the job down into its various elements and able to apply the correct time values to those job steps.

What Must Be Done? The method for performing the job must be broken down into elements, time values for the various elements selected from tables, curves, charts, or formulas, and allowances made for personal and unavoidable delays. With the above information, the allowed time for the various units of production can be determined. If time values are not available for each element, the data must first be obtained by either time study, use of predetermined time system, work sampling, or possible historical data. Preferably the elemental time values should have been obtained by observing the element being performed in several different jobs.

How Long Will It Take? Minutes to hours to determine time values for jobs, depending upon the complexity of the job, and sometimes weeks to months, depending upon the amount of data necessary to set up the elemental standard data source documents.

What Are the Characteristics? This type of standard is generally considered to be a valid and reliable basis for establishing standards. However, when all activities are covered by elemental standard data, the various standard times will be more consistent for all the standards. It is a very good work measurement technique to use to establish standard time on jobs before the jobs are begun. Because job conditions are standardized, it is easy to identify a deviation standard and to assign a cause for the deviation.

Advantages

1. More consistency between time values.
2. Can be used to compare methods.
3. Can set standard time for a job prior to performing the job.

Disadvantages

1. Requires time to build up standard data.
2. Costly to build up standard data.

Technical Estimate

What Is Required? A person technically qualified to recognize the various phases of the work to be accomplished.

What Must Be Done? Job broken down into phases and time estimated for each phase. Experience or past performance data will form the basis for the time estimates.

How Long Will It Take? From minutes to days, depending upon the complexity of the job.

What Are the Characteristics? This type of standard is based upon the personal judgment of the person making the estimate. His technical estimate of how long it should take to do the job may vary greatly from how long it actually takes to do the job. Thus, it is difficult to accurately assign a cause to deviations from standard.

Advantages

1. May be the only technique available to establish time limits on certain types of jobs (technical projects, research projects, and so on)
2. Relatively cheap (in relationship to time).

Disadvantages

1. Time to do the job is an estimate; thus, worker's actual time may show wide variance (poor control device).
2. No way of knowing what methods are used to do the job.

Historical Standards (Statistical)

What Is Required? Data on past performance of individual jobs, producing like product, expressed in man-hours expended, and units produced.

What Must Be Done? A relationship between units of product and man-hours expended must be found and statistically validated.

How Long Will It Take? From days to weeks to months, depending upon the amount of data required or available.

What Are the Characteristics? This type of standard is based upon the assumption that what has happened in the past is good practice and that what will happen in the future will not alter the relationship between units of product and man-hours expended. As a result, it is difficult to identify a significant deviation from standard and more difficult to accurately assign a cause.

Advantages

1. Sometimes it is the only technique available for limited coverage in a hurry.

Disadvantages

1. Accepts past performance as satisfactory (poor control device).
2. No way of knowing if past and present methods are the same.

Staffing Pattern

What Is Required? A person with a semibroad management background technically qualified to recognize the various phases of the work to be accomplished. Person must have appreciation of management process so as to be able to determine various relationships and effects of support and supported functions.

What Must Be Done? The job must be broken down into and identified as major functional areas. It must also be identified as major and minor for support. Relationships, direct and indirect, among areas must be identified. Each job is compared to similar functional areas and relationships which seem to be working in a satisfactory manner.

How Long Will It Take? From minutes to days, depending upon the complexity of the job.

What Are the Characteristics? This type of standard is based upon the personal background and judgment of the person(s) making the estimate. His estimate of the situation depends greatly upon his ability to infer, draw analogies and conclusions based on other similar situations. It is difficult to determine the cause of deviations from those anticipated—cannot tell whether poor performance, poor conditions, or incorrect original determination is the cause.

Advantages

1. May be only technique available to establish manpower requirements.
2. Relatively quick and cheap.

Disadvantages

1. Accepts past relationship as being sound.
2. No real way of knowing validity.

Glossary

Activity: A function or a group of related functions that may be carried on at a location that has been designated as a unit, department, or division.

Allowance: A time increment added to the normal work time, for production loss due to fatigue, personal necessities, and unavoidable delays.

Average of upper half: The quotient obtained by dividing the total man-hours expended by the total work units produced in the upper half of an array of monthly performance ratios for a work area. This array generally covers a base period of at least twelve months.

Basic performance data: The basic data used in work measurement are man-hours expended and work units produced.

Correlation coefficient: Correlation analysis measures the degree of relationship between two variables, that is, between work units produced and time required to complete those work units. Ideally, this comparison would require a summary of work units produced and man-hours expended each month for a twelve-month period (examples: items issued vs. customers served; line items processed vs. documents processed).

Engineered standard: The time (usually man-hours) it should taken an individual or a group to complete a work unit working at a normal pace according to a specified method as determined by a detailed study of the job.

Fair day's work: The amount of work that can be produced during a working day by a qualified worker possessing average skill who follows a prescribed method, and who works under specific conditions at a normal pace.

Method study: A detailed examination made for the purpose of improving the procedures and sequence of motions followed by workmen or machines to accomplish a given operation or work task.

Nonproductive man-hours: Nonproductive man-hours are hours that are nonproductive, such as vacation time, sick leave, special orientation, and training.

Normal pace: The work rate of workmen performing under capable supervision but without the stimulus of an incentive wage payment plan. This pace can easily be maintained day in and day out without undue physical or mental fatigue and is characterized by fairly steady exertion of reasonable effort. Sometimes represented by the effort involved in walking 3 miles per hour on level ground.

Percentage of effectiveness: The ratio, expressed as a percent, obtained by dividing the number of standard man-hours by the actual number of measured man-hours expended and muliplying the quotient by 100.

Performance effectiveness: The ratio obtained by dividing the number of standard man-hours by the actual number of man-hours consumed and multiplied by 100 to obtain a percentage.

Performance ratio: A performance ratio is the average number of actual man-hours taken to complete one work unit in a given measured work area. The ratio is obtained by dividing the actual productive man-hours expended by the number of work units produced.

Performance standards: A performance standard is a measure of how much time it should normally take for one individual to do a particular job under the particular working conditions in effect. A performance standard does not set the fastest nor the slowest time in which an operation may be performed—it represents the desirable time required. The conditions under which work is performed affect the resulting standard.

Predetermined time system(s): A method for determining the standard time for a job; involves analyzing an operation and assigning to each motion of the operators a time value which has been previously determined for the basic motions that are used in doing work (sometimes referred to as therbligs). Typical systems are:

BMT: Basic motion times

MTM: Methods time measurement

WF: Work factor

MOST: Maynard operation sequence technique

Productive man-hours: Productive man-hours are those spent on the job by personnel subject to formal personnel vouchers. Other productive man-hours are those spent on the job by personnel not subject to formal personnel allocation vouchers.

Rating (leveling): Involves comparing the performance or effective effort of the workman to the effort exerted in normal pace. This involves the pace a workman is working, that is, 110 percent, 80 percent, and so on, of normal pace. Synonymous terms are effort rating, pace rating, leveling, performance rating, and speed rating.

Standard man-hours: The computed man-hours that should be or should have been expended to produce a given number of work units based upon an established standard.

Standard man-hours (earned man-hours): Computed man-hours within which a given number of work units can be produced on the basis of an established standard (number of work units produced times the standard equals standard man-hours).

Statistical standard (historical standard): The time (man-hours) it should taken an individual or group to perform a work unit based upon statistical analysis of past performance data.

Subactivity: A breakdown of an activity into subfunctions or one group of related functions for purposes of organization, supervision, accounting, or physical control.

Supervisory level: That level of any organization in which one supervisor is responsible for the scheduling of day-to-day work, the assigning of tasks to individual workers or groups of workers engaged in homogenous types of work, and the direct supervision of two or more individuals. In connection with performance analysis, the term *supervisory level* is commonly used in referring to subactivities or lower echelons.

Therblig: Any one of a number of basic elements devised by Gilbreth to afford analysis of working methods. The elements include physical movements and mental processes associated with movement. Gilbreth spelled backwards.

Time standard: Also called performance standard, standard time, or simply, standard. An established number of man-hours for the accomplishment of a unit of work.

Time study: Upon completion of the methods study, a time study is made of the procedure to determine the time required to perform the operations or elements thereof using a suitable timing device and recording the observations. The observed times are adjusted by the rating against normal pace to derive the standard time which should be required to perform the operation. Includes determination of allowances and the establishment of a standard or prescribed method.

Technical estimate: The time (man-hours) it should take an individual or group possessing required skills to produce a work unit at a normal pace as forecasted by technically qualified individuals and based upon a detailed analysis of its components.

Work area: (1) A group of closely related work processes within a specific functional area for which man-hours are charged; (2) the category of work for which quantitative measurement is desired; a subdivision of the organization for management control purposes; (3) sometimes called work or cost center.

Work measurement: (1) Measures the amount or quantity of work accomplished or to be accomplished by an individual or group; (2) provides a time standard for performing work of an acceptable quality; (3) informs management of the performance effectiveness of the work force.

Work sampling: A procedure similar to time study except that the conclusions are based on intermittent observations in place of continuous observations.

Work unit: An item of work or unit of measure selected to express quantitatively the work accomplished in a work area (for example, 1 pound of laundry washed, 1 door hung, 1 voucher audited).

Practical Exercises

To insure a more thorough understanding of the principles of work measurement, three practical exercises are furnished for your benefit.

EXERCISE 1: EVALUATING PERFORMANCE

A supervisor has ten clerks engaged in completing work-in-file inquiries. The machine record system consolidates the clerks' individual production tallies and issues a weekly production report. The supervisor looks at the information relative to his ten clerks and notes the following:

Clerk	*Inquiries*	*Standard Time*	*Actual Time*
1	92	18 hours	40 hours
2	118	22 hours	40 hours
3	215	42 hours	40 hours
4	130	28 hours	40 hours
5	171	36 hours	40 hours
6	227	44 hours	40 hours
7	128	24 hours	40 hours
8	239	46 hours	40 hours
9	191	40 hours	40 hours
10	154	34 hours	40 hours

Problem

1. What is the efficiency of each clerk?
2. What action should the supervisor take relative to each clerk?

EXERCISE 2: COMPUTATION OF PERCENT OF EFFECTIVENESS

Problem: Using the table below:

1. Compute percentage of effectiveness.
2. Indicate by asterisk (*) those work areas to be reported under the "Management by Exception" principle, if allowable deviation in performance is 15 percent.

Performance Standard	*Work Units Completed*	*Standard Man-hours*	*Actual Man-hours*	*Percentage Effectiveness*
(1)	(2)	(3)	(4)	(5)
.125	27,500		3,600	
1.70	3,750		7,900	
18.1	250		4,400	
.013	35,450		400	
.250	1,850		500	
.075	28,460		2,200	

EXERCISE 3: WORK SAMPLING STANDARD COMPUTATION

A work sampling study was conducted for the purchase order typing section of Gee Whiz Corporation over a ten-day period. The work area was authorized for four employees. The results of the study were as follows:

1. The employees devoted 49 percent of their time to the typing of purchase orders.
2. Personal needs, including authorized breaks, occupied 67 minutes of each employee's time.
3. Based upon a pace rating of each employee each time an observation was

made, the clerks were adjudged to be working 80 percent of efficiency as a group throughout the course of the study.

4. All four employees were available for work eight hours each day.
5. During the course of the study, 1,560 purchase orders were written by the four employees.

Problem:

Using the above results, calculate a performance standard for purchase order typing.

Questions

1. Define work measurement. What are the objectives of work measurement?
2. What is the DIMES program and its three phases?
3. List and briefly explain each of the techniques of work measurement.
4. Which of the work measurement techniques produce standards of greater validity and reliability?
5. What are the predetermined time systems? What are the two most popular systems?
6. What is the purpose of work sampling? The number of observations to take depends upon what three things?
7. How are standard data obtained to apply to an application to be measured?
8. Give criteria on which a work study analyst selects the proper work measurement technique for different kinds of activities.
9. List work activities that are often exempt from work measurement techniques.
10. What tasks are undertaken prior to the development of engineered work measurement standards?
11. Explain why a methods study should precede a time study.
12. What is a work unit and how is it selected?
13. Define the following terms:
    a. method study
    b. productive time
    c. nonproductive time
    d. productive man-hours
    e. work area
    f. a fair day's work
    g. performance ratio
    h. performance effectiveness
14. Under what condition is a statistical standard useful in measuring performance?
15. List the elements necessary to develop engineered standards.
16. Define standard time. What are the elements in the formula for determining the standard time to accomplish a unit of work.
17. What main factors must be considered in determining the overall allowance? Given the allowance factor formula.
18. Give the formula for determining the standard time from a work sampling study of a task.
19. Define pace rating or leveling. How is it determined by the work study analyst?
20. A work measurement study was undertaken, using the continuous method of timing, of an operator using a machine to pierce two 3/16″ hexagon holes in each end of a link of 16 gauge metal (Table 10–16). Times are in 100ths of minutes (Table 10–17). Omit unavoidable delays to determine average time for each element. Allowances per 8-hour shift are clothes change 10 minutes, unavoidable delays 15 min-

TABLE 10-16.

No.	*Elements*	*Ending Points*
1.	Pickup piece (LH), to die (11″) and position to die.	Release piece.
2.	Close cam clamp, trip press [pierce (1) 3/16″ hex. hole, open clamp].	Release clamp lever.
3.	Remove piece, turn 180°, reposition in die.	Release piece.
4.	Close cam clamp, trip press [pierce (1) 3/16″ hex. hole, open clamp].	Release clamp lever.
5.	Remove piece from die and position on skid at left.	Release piece.

TABLE 10-17.

Element	*Cycle Number and Time*															*Performance*
	1	*2*	*3*	*4*	*5*	*6*	*7*	*8*	*9*	*10*	*11*	*12*	*13*	*14*	*15*	*%*
1	08	37	173	202	287	17	49A	78	12	58B	84	13	819	47	85	98
2	12	41	76	06	91	22	53	83	16	62	87	17	23	51	89	100
3	18	48	82	13	98	28	59	90	23	67	95	23	28	67C	96	102
4	22	52	86	18	303	32	63	94	427/	70	99	28	32	71	900	100
5	28	60/	192	225/	10	338	70	402	543	576	605	634/	839	877	906	102

/used to indicate start of noncyclical element.

TABLE 10-18.

Noncyclical elements		
1.66 personal	A. Straighten stock	Included in allowances as unavoidable delays.
2.54 wipe die 1/14 pieces	B. Oily stock-sticks	
5.36 inspections 1/20 pieces	C. Drop piece	
8.11 wait for load change 1/1000 pieces		

utes, rest periods 24 minutes, area clean-up 10 minutes, and shower out 18 minutes. Labor is $9.10 per hour.

a. Compute the labor standard for this operation.

b. What is the standard labor cost for piercing each piece?

c. How many pieces per operator should be expected per 8-hour shift?

21. Using the alignment chart and the formula given above, determine the control limits for this set of conditions. A 10-day work sample observed that the operator was idle 84 out of 820 observations. What is the control limit for p? Is there much difference in the control limits determined by each method?

Control limit for

$$p = p \pm 3\sqrt{\frac{p(1-p)}{n}}$$

N = total number of observations.

n = number of daily observations.

p = number of "operator idle" observations.

Bibliography

Backman, J. *Wage Determination: An Analysis of Wage Criteria*. Princeton, N.J.: Van Nostrand, 1960.

Barnes, Ralph M. *Motion and Time Study: Design and Measurement of Work*. 7th ed. New York: John Wiley and Sons, 1980.

———. *Motion and Time Study*. 2nd ed. New York: John Wiley and Sons, 1940.

———. *Work Sampling*. 2nd ed. New York: John Wiley and Sons, 1957.

Belcher, D. W. *Wage and Salary Administration*. Englewood Cliffs, N.J.: Prentice-Hall, 1955.

Brenna, C. W. *Wage Administration*. Homewood, Ill.: Richard D. Irwin, 1957.

Carroll, P. *Better Wage Incentives*. New York: McGraw-Hill, 1957.

Carter, A. *Theory of Wages and Employment*. Homewood, Ill.: Richard D. Irwin, 1959.

Eliot, J. *Equitable Payment*. New York: John Wiley and Sons, 1961.

Gantt, H. L. *Work, Wages and Profits*. New York: Engineering Management, 1913.

Gilbreth, F. B., and Gilbreth, L. M. *Fatigue Study*. 2nd ed. New York: Macmillan, 1919.

Gomberg, W. A. *A Trade Union Analysis of Time Study*. 2nd ed. Englewood Cliffs, N.J.: Prentice-Hall, 1955.

Hansen, B. L. *Work Sampling: For Modern Management*. Englewood Cliffs, N.J.: Prentice-Hall, 1960.

Hutchinson, R. Dale. *New Horizons for Human Factors in Design*. New York: McGraw-Hill, 1981.

Johnson, F. H. *Job Evaluation*. New York: John Wiley and Sons, 1949.

Karger, D. W., and Bayha, F. H. *Engineered Work Measurement*. New York: Industrial Press, 1977.

Konz, Stephen. *Work Design*. Columbus, Oh.: Grid Publishing, 1979.

Krick, E. V. *Methods Engineering*. New York: John Wiley and Sons, 1960.

Lantham, E. *Job Evaluation*. New York: McGraw-Hill, 1955.

Lovejoy, L. C. *Wage and Salary Administration*. New York: Ronald Press, 1959.

Maynard, H. B., and Stegemerten, G. J. *Guide to Methods Improvement*. New York: McGraw-Hill, 1944.

———. *Industrial Engineering Handbook*. New York: McGraw-Hill, 1963.

Maynard, H. B., et al. *Methods Time Measurement*. New York: McGraw-Hill, 1946.

Mundel, Marvin E. *Motion and Time Study: Improving Productivity*. 5th ed. Englewood Cliffs, N.J.: Prentice-Hall, 1978.

McCormick, E. J. *Human Factors in Engineering and Design*. 4th ed. New York: McGraw-Hill, 1976.

Nadler, Gerald. *Work Design: A Systems Concept*. Rev. ed. Homewood, Ill.: Richard D. Irwin, 1970.

Neibel, Benjamin W. *Motion and Time Study*. 7th ed. Homewood, Ill.: Richard D. Irwin, 1976.

Patton, J. A., Littlefield, C. L., and Self, S. A., *Job Evaluation, Text and Cases*. Homewood, Ill.: Richard D. Irwin, 1964.

Presgrave, R. and Bailey, G. B. *Basic Motion Timestudy*. New York: McGraw-Hill, 1957.

Quick, J. H., Duncan, J. H., and Malcolm, J. A. *Work Factor Time Standards*. New York: McGraw-Hill, 1962.

U.S. Army Institute of Administration. *Work Measurement*. ST 14-199. Fort Benjamin Harrison, Ind., February 1975.

U.S. Army Management Engineering Training Agency. *Methods Study*. Defense Management Joint Course Book. Rock Island, Ill., Rev. 1971.

———. *Work Measurement.* Defense Management Joint Course Book. Rev. Rock Island, Ill., 1971.

———. *Work Planning and Control Systems.* Defense Management Joint Course Book. Rock Island, Ill., Rev. 1971.

Whisler, T. L., and Harper, S. F. *Performance Appraisal.* New York: Holt, Rinehart & Winston, 1962.

Zander, Kjell B. *Work Measurement Systems.* New York: Marcel Dekker, 1980.

Part V
Operations Control

Chapter 11

Production Control

INTRODUCTION

With the widespread development of production systems during the last century, production control has evolved into a complex activity. Of particular significance in this evolutionary process has been the reactive nature of new developments. That is, contrary to many other disciplines, production control techniques have grown and changed to meet the needs of the specific types of systems in which they are used. No single, all-encompassing theory will provide complete control over all productive systems. In order to function effectively, each type of production system must be specifically planned and must have a control system that meets that particular production system's needs. Unless these requirements are fulfilled, some if not all aspects of the production system will be ineffective or, more likely, will fail.

The objective of this chapter is to provide an understanding of the various types of production systems, the procedures necessary to properly plan for effective utilization of these production systems, and the methods that are appropriate to control the production system. The chapter also presents a discussion of how the production system and its planning and method of control should be coordinated with long-range strategic policies of the organization in which they exist (see Figure 11–1).

As indicated in Figure 11–1, long-range corporate strategy forms the basis for overall policy for marketing, production, and financial objectives. In addition, finance and marketing provide parameters to assist in the definition of the production system. Once the production system has been defined, the appropriate, specific system can be identified and its details can then be developed.

The directional flows indicated in Figure 11–1 are significant. Although flow is bidirectional in the majority of relations, there is only unidirectional flow between production control and the marketing and finance functions. There must be no direct interaction in the opposite direction in these two instances if unnecessary static that could result in an ineffective production control system is to be avoided.

Strategic Policy

The strategic policy of a firm defines the mission of the organization by addressing the following questions: what is the organization's purpose, what market will it serve, and what position will it take within its particular industry. Of additional consideration is how suppliers, governmental agencies, stockholders, and other entities will be served by the organization.

Unfortunately, determination of strategic policy for an organization often evolves without specific effort on the part of management. This evolution without proper direction can lead a firm into deadends from which recovery may be impossible. Thus, it is important for the organization to formally establish long-range strategic policy, contingent on its capabilities and its environment.

This chapter was written by Emil Albert, D.B.A., Associate Professor of Finance, Western Michigan University, Kalamazoo, Michigan.

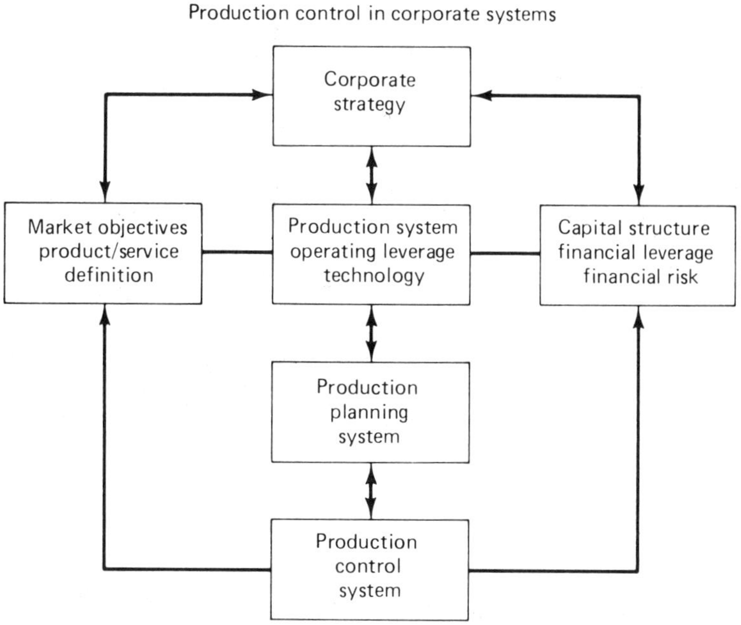

FIGURE 11–1. Production Control in Corporate Systems

Determinants of Strategic Policy. Factors that will affect the strategic policy of an organization can be divided into those external to the firm and those that are internal:

1. *External factors* include all aspects of the environment such as the market, domestic and foreign competition, government regulation, and industry structure.
2. *Internal factors* include such elements as technical capabilities of the firm, technology used, research and design efforts, management talent, and personal desires of the organization members.

Strategic policy determination is an extensive field in its own right and is beyond the scope of this chapter. It is important that strategic policy be properly formulated and communicated throughout the organization so that the planning and control process enhances strategic policy rather than operating contrary to policy.

Strategic policy, once defined, is carried into the functional areas of marketing, finance, and production to generate operating policies in these areas commensurate with the firm's objectives. Functional policies are carried out by such activities as selling stock, establishing the marketing organization, selecting plant sites and equipment, and other activities, all of a long-range nature. Once these activities are carried out, they are not easily changed and, consequently, they determine the direction of the organization over an extended time period.

The production function is responsible for the selection of a production system, made up of facilities and equipment, that will provide a product or service, and thus will carry out the organization's strategic policy. The production system is normally the most permanent and least flexible part of the total organization. It is critical that the organization's strategic policy be reflected in the specific decisions that are made regarding the selection of a production system. Such a decision requires knowledge of the various types of production systems that can be used. These systems are described in a later section of the chapter.

The Product Life Cycle. The concept of a life cycle for a product or service is an important component of theories relating to the selection of production systems, and production planning and control procedures. Very briefly, the concept of a product life cycle states that each product goes through a series of stages from its inception to its ultimate decline in the marketplace. As the product proceeds through the stages of its life cycle, characteristics of the product must change to satisfy the customer, these characteristics are summarized in Table 11–1.

Consideration of these characteristics assists in determining the appropriate production system to produce a product or service that can successfully satisfy market conditions.

PRODUCTION SYSTEMS

Three criteria must be defined before a specific production system can be developed:

1. *Product/service parameters.* As discussed in the previous section, corporate strategy, along with marketing policy, establishes the product or service specifications and the size of the intended market, which in turn determine volume.
2. *Working capital resources.* The financial function provides working capital for inventories, accounts receivable and accounts payable, and the purchase of facilities and equipment. Although the relationship is less obvious, working capital resources affect the implementation of the production system. Lack of working capital to finance inventories can preclude operation of the production system according to the production plan.
3. *Production/service technology.* The choice of facilities, equipment, materials, and labor used in the production system will be determined primarily by the technology employed by the system.

Types of Production Systems

Production systems are generally classified according to their physical characteristics, such as the layout of equipment and the size of the facility relative to the target market. The common names given to the classifications are project, job shop, intermittent shop, assembly line, and flow process system. Each of these is described briefly below.

TABLE 11-1.
Life Cycle Characteristics of a Product or Service

Life Cycle Stage	*Volume*	*Design*	*Price*	*Profit Margin*
Introduction	Very low	Unique	Very high	Loss
Growth	Low	Variable	High	High
Maturity	Medium	Limited	Medium	Medium
Saturation	High	Rigid	Low	Low
Decline	Medium to low	Variable	Medium	High

Project System. A project system is one that is normally set up to produce a single item such as a high rise building, a missile site, and the like. It is unique in that the system is moved to the product rather than the product being produced at the system site. Also, it is temporary in nature since completion of the product or service terminates the need for the system in that location. The system must then be dismantled and removed to a new site, where it is rebuilt in a new configuration.

Inputs for a project tend to have particular characteristics. Materials are specifically designed for the project so volume is very low. Also, little storage is provided at the project site because of security and location problems. The labor force on a project consists primarily of craftsmen who must be highly skilled and have the ability to perform independently, often under adverse conditions. Facilities and equipment are usually general purpose.

Job Shop System. The second production system, the job shop, is particularly suited to products or services with a low demand and varying characteristics in the early stages of the life cycle. Because of these product or service characteristics, job shop facilities are physically organized by activities called a process layout, wherein like activities are grouped together in a single physically defined area.

The characteristics of the inputs in a job shop are somewhat similar to the project. Labor is highly skilled, and facilities and equipment are general purpose. However, the materials used differ in that they are usually readily available in the marketplace in small volume, rather than being of a specialized nature.

Intermittent Shop System. The intermittent shop is very similar to the job shop. It is also physically organized by activities as in process layout. But it differs from the job shop in that it is designed to provide a product or service that is specified in greater detail and is in higher demand early in the product life cycle. These characteristics provide increased stability for the system.

Although inputs to the intermittent shop are similar to the job shop, there is a tendency to use some specialized facilities, equipment, and material, along with somewhat less skilled labor.

Assembly Line System. A production system that is made up of assembly lines is designed to produce products and services of a very high relative volume and well-defined, stable product or service characteristics. This system differs from the previously described systems in that it is physically laid out to provide efficient product flow. The assembly line is typically characterized as a product-oriented layout wherein the flow through the system is a well-defined, rigid path.

The disadvantages associated with an assembly line arise from the difficulties associated with making changes to the product and the system and the problem of balancing the rates of production at the various work stations in the system. For these reasons, an assembly line is most effective where the major characteristics of the product or service are maturity and large relative volume.

The characteristics of inputs to an assembly line are substantially different from the previously described systems. Facilities and equipment used in the system are specialized and require extensive tooling; consequently, labor can be less skilled. Materials can be, and often are, especially developed for a particular system in order to provide increased efficiency.

Flow Process System. This type of production system is a refinement of assembly lines. The refinements are designed to overcome the problem of product design change and work load balance through the use of quick changeover tooling and rigid controls on production rates and material flows. This improvement is achieved by sacrificing flexibility in the overall rate of production of the system. A flow process system must operate at a constant daily rate of production for an extended period in order to amortize a substantial investment with relatively small per unit savings over a large number of units.

System input characteristics are similar to those of the assembly line, except for the quick-change tooling and the higher skill level of workers.

The current emphasis placed on the use of industrial robots is an example of the facilities and equipment being placed into use in flow process systems. These robots can easily be reprogrammed by highly trained personnel to perform different activities, thus providing a way of overcoming some of the rigidity problems in the system.

Selection of Production System

No single production system can perform efficiently in a changing market as a product or service moves through the stages of its life cycle. As the product moves from very low volume and unclear specifications to high volume with well defined specifications, and ultimately to extinction, the appropriate production system changes. This is illustrated in Figure 11–2.

Initially, a project system is most appropriate for preproduction or single-item production. However, as volume increases and specifications are clarified, the job shop, intermittent shop, assembly line, and flow process systems, respectively, become most efficient. At the end of the product's life cycle, an intermittent or job shop may again be most appropriate.

At this point, the question must be raised as to whether the product life cycle is dictated by the production system or is independent of the production system.

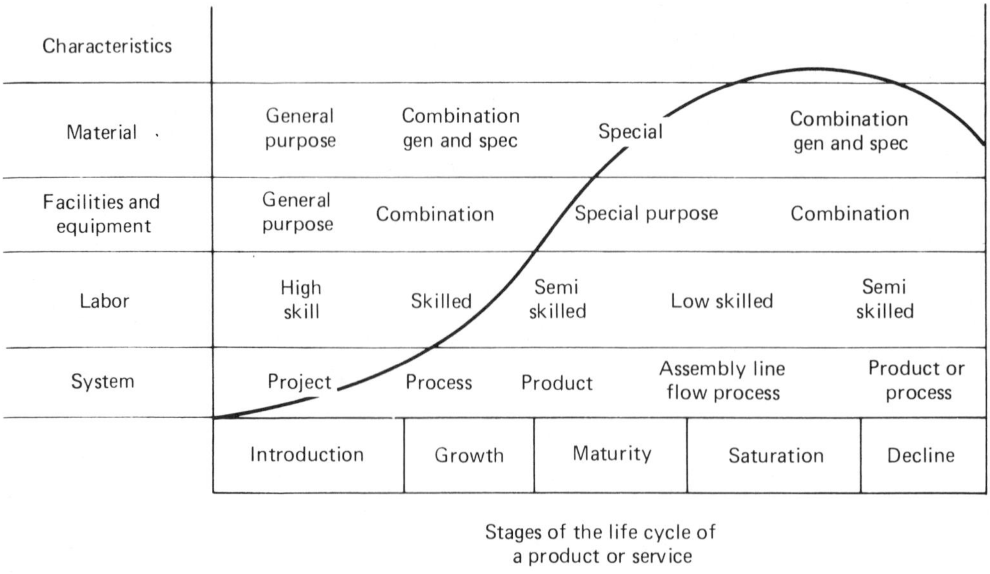
Characteristics
Material
General purpose
Combination gen and spec
Special
Combination gen and spec
Facilities and equipment
General purpose
Combination
Special purpose
Combination
Labor
High skill
Skilled
Semi skilled
Low skilled
Semi skilled
System
Project
Process
Product
Assembly line flow process
Product or process
Introduction
Growth
Maturity
Saturation
Decline
Stages of the life cycle of a product or service

FIGURE 11–2. Production System Characteristics Related to a Product Life Cycle

Recent trends in world industrial activity tend to favor the latter. If this is the case, as product life cycles become shorter, the life of efficient production systems must become shorter and more vulnerable to sudden obsolescence. This suggests that a major criterion in selecting a production system should be its flexibility in adapting to change, which will increase the life of the production facility and consequently its economic value. This is substantiated to some extent by the large number of facility changes that have taken place in recent years.

Production Planning

Production planning is the process of converting corporate strategy along with market and financial policy into details for the efficient utilization of the production system. This procedure is illustrated in Figure 11–3. The production planning process itself deals with the conversion of generalities of strategy and policy to specifics that are required to efficiently utilize the production system.

Strategy and Policy Inputs. Corporate strategy, marketing policy, and financial policy provide parameters within which the production planning process is carried out. These include:

1. *Product/service definition.* Production planning must be provided with a complete definition of the product or service in terms of appropriate engineering data. These usually take the form of drawings, bills of material, and process specifications.
2. *Marketing policy.* The marketing policy should include data on sales volume, terms of sales, seasonal and cyclical sales patterns, warehousing requirements, and any special marketing plans.

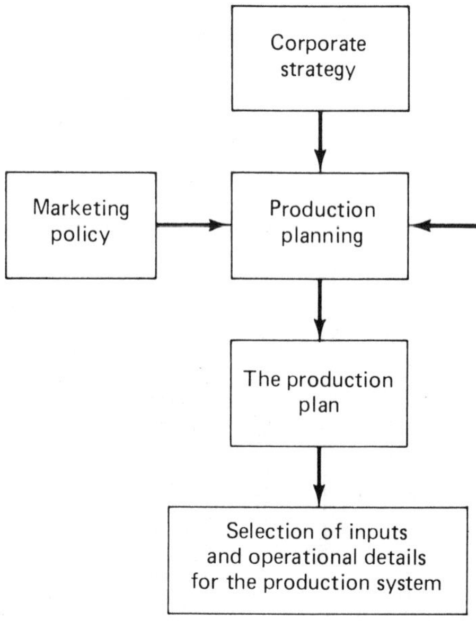

FIGURE 11–3. The Production Planning System

3. *Financial Policy*. The availability of working capital should be provided in the financial policy so that purchases of material, input of labor, and inventory plans can be accurately coordinated in the production plan.

Production Planning Activities. Production planning is concerned with the efficient use of a production system that is operating under constraints of the technology installed when the production system was established. The effectiveness of the production planning process is directly related to how well the production system in existence is able to function under the parameters established by the corporate strategy and policies. This production planning process is carried out on an aggregate basis, an intermediate basis, and a detail basis:

1. *Aggregate planning*. Aggregate planning is concerned with detail plans over extended time periods of up to a year or more. Figure 11–4 illustrates the relationships between sales, inventories, and aggregate production plans. Examples of extreme types of production plans, discussed in detail later in the chapter, are the chase policy and the level production plan. The chase policy increases or decreases production to coincide with fluctuating sales. At the opposite end of the continuum is the level production plan wherein production is maintained at a constant level over the aggregate planning period. These extreme plans, along with variations, are appropriate under particular strategies and policies.

2. *Intermediate planning*. Intermediate planning is concerned with the stocks and flows of the product over the production cycle defined as that period beginning with a commitment to obtain inputs of labor and material and ending with delivery of the product to the consumer. In intermediate planning, requirements for all sectors of the facility must be established and a determination made as to whether or not sufficient capacity is available to accommodate the production plan. If sufficient capacity is available, intermediate planning can proceed with the determination of the flow demands on the part of the production system by like groups of products or services. If sufficient capacity is not available, aggregate production planning will need to be revised until requirements are less than or equal to available capacity.

3. *Detail production planning*. Detail production planning, often called scheduling

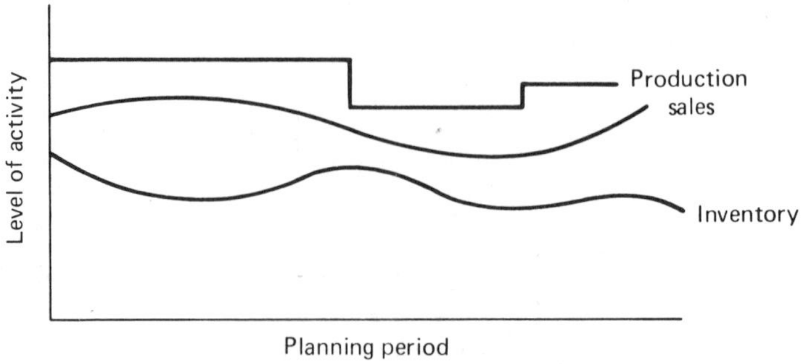

FIGURE 11–4. Diagram of Production, Sales, and Inventory Activity During the Aggregate Planning Period

and loading, is concerned with the determination of which specific products and services are to be produced on a short-term basis, usually a week in the job and intermediate shop, and daily in the flow process system. Detail scheduling and loading can be accomplished by working from the present time into the future, specifying when material is to be available and when sequential activity is to be performed, and, finally, arriving at the time the product or service will be completed. Conversely, the details can be carried from a future time backward to the present time, thus indicating when various activities need to be started.

There is no single approach to production planning appropriate in all types of production systems. Rather, a fragmented approach has developed over past years wherein specialized production planning techniques have been developed to fit particular needs. Nevertheless, some general characteristics of production planning approaches are more appropriate in some production systems than others. Criteria for decisionmaking in this area are discussed in more detail later.

Production Control

PRODUCTION CONTROL ACTIVITIES

Having defined production systems and production planning, we can now discuss the subject of production control. Although there are as many different specific definitions of production control as there are authors writing about the subject, the consensus seems to lean toward defining production control as creating action in the production system and monitoring that action. These activities are more commonly labeled dispatching and expediting, respectively.

At this point it is important to emphasize that production control cannot be carried out without concurrent activity in inventory control, although, of necessity, the two subjects are being treated separately in this book (inventory control is discussed in Chapter 13). In actual operations, the two activities are inseparable.

Specific production control activities and their normal sequence of events are summarized in Table 11–2. These activities do not all exist formally in all types of production systems, but they are control activities that must be performed if system efficiency is to be maintained. Likewise, they are not all carried out by a production control department as such. The important point is that the control activity must be carried out somewhere in the organization.

All of the production control activities are concerned with ensuring compliance with the production plan in the most efficient manner and with taking any necessary corrective action at the earliest possible time.

Production control can be viewed as a servo system. In its simpler version, a plan is established, production is begun, and control monitors activity. As deviations from the plan enter the system, corrective action is taken to make necessary adjustments so that actual activity is brought into compliance with the plan. If actual conditions exceed specific limits established, the production plan may require revision by complete replanning. Corrections are made after the system deviations are detected; thus the system reacts to actual activity.

More advanced versions of production control systems attempt to anticipate deviations so that corrective action can be taken to maintain the production system in compliance with the plan.

TABLE 11-2.
Production Control Activities

Activity	*Description*
Order preparation	Prepare necessary orders, authorization work tickets, move tickets, etc., so that all production activities receive complete and correct information identifying what is to be done and when.
Loading	Assign work to be performed to specific machine and work centers, including time and quantity information.
Issue requisition	Release information to purchasing and inventory control relative to what materials are required, how much, and when.
Dispatch	Release work orders to assigned machine and work centers.
Engineering data control	Obtain current product data for machine and work center usage regarding detail product specifications.
Tool control	Provide data concerning tools and their location.
Expediting	Establish priorities on specific jobs that need to proceed faster or slower than plan.
Floor control	Provide feedback to production planning, cost accounting, and sales relative to actual activity.
Order closeout	Control the physical movement of product to either inventory or the customer and terminate the production order.

PRODUCTION PLANNING AND CONTROL TECHNIQUES

Up to this point in the discussion, the emphasis has been on production systems and production planning and control activities. We now turn to various techniques used in the production planning and production control functions. Later in the chapter, the various types of techniques are correlated with the production systems discussed in a previous section.

A wide variety of planning and control techniques are currently in use in world industrial organizations. These range from the detailed just-in-time systems, currently receiving wide attention, to the simple yet effective manual systems that have been in use for decades. Between these two extremes are a number of general types. These include Gantt systems, PERT/CPM systems, and material requirement planning systems.

The individuals concerned with production planning and control, regardless of their level in an organization, must keep one fact in mind at all times: there is theoretically no method of effectively controlling all the activities in a production facility at the same time. At best, results will be suboptimum and often only acceptable.

A simple illustration should clarify the tyical problem faced by a production planner. If 18 jobs need to be planned at one time, there will be $|18|$ or 6.4×10^{15} possible combinations. If a computer could check 100,000 combinations per second, it would require over 200 years to check all the possible combinations. Very few systems or customers are able to wait that long for an effective plan and for delivery of a product or service. In reality, of course, all combinations need not be checked, but the example does illustrate the nature of the problem that production planning and control techniques must address. Possible alternatives must be identified and reduced to a manageable number in a short period of time. An acceptable single alternative, then, has to be selected and implemented.

Manual Control Systems

Manual control systems are not normally given extensive consideration in the literature. One reason for this is that they exist in so many varieties that it would be an insurmountable project to try to describe all of them. Therefore, our discussion here is limited to only a few aspects of manual control systems.

It is important to recognize that all production planning and control systems are concerned with the conversion of policy and strategy into details for the efficient utilization of the production system. In some instances, the memory of an efficient production planner can do this better than any mechanical device, as long as the volume of data is limited. Consequently, in some cases an individual can carry out production planning and control with very simple instructions and records, often of a verbal nature.

Little-Black-Book-in-the-Back-Pocket of-the-Supervisor Technique

This technique originated at about the same time as the first production activity began, and we would be remiss if we did not recognize its existence and importance. This technique meets all the criteria of an effective system. It provides information regarding:

1. How to produce an item.
2. How to set up equipment.
3. Which workers perform best on which jobs.
4. What material to use and where it is stored.
5. When the customer needs delivery.

For additional detailed information regarding manual planning and control systems, the reader is referred to James H. Greene's *Production and Inventory Control* (see bibliography at the end of the chapter). This is an excellent source of information on specific systems and techniques. In addition, control systems equipment suppliers can provide data and assistance on special control needs.

Gantt Chart Systems

Gantt systems, developed by Henry L. Gantt early in this century, are applicable for production planning and control in (simpler) production systems and can be used for layout and sequencing of activities, loading activities on machines and work centers, and evaluating performance against a plan.

As an illustration, the construction of a door hinge requires the stamping of two leaves, the cutting of the hinge pin, and finally, the assembly of the three components into a completed assembly. These activities are summarized in Figure 11–5.

In addition to the production activity information provided in Figure 11–5, before production planning can be carried out, it is necessary to determine the number of assemblies to be produced and the amount of lead time for each activity, including purchase of material and queue time (waiting time). In the preceding example let us assume that lead time for the leaves is two weeks each, while the hinge pin and assembly each require one week. Let us also assume that the quantity required is 1,000 assemblies. This informa-

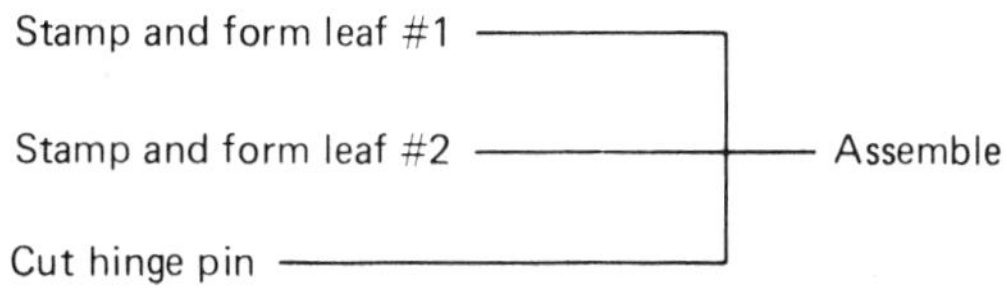

FIGURE 11–5. Door Hinge Production Activities

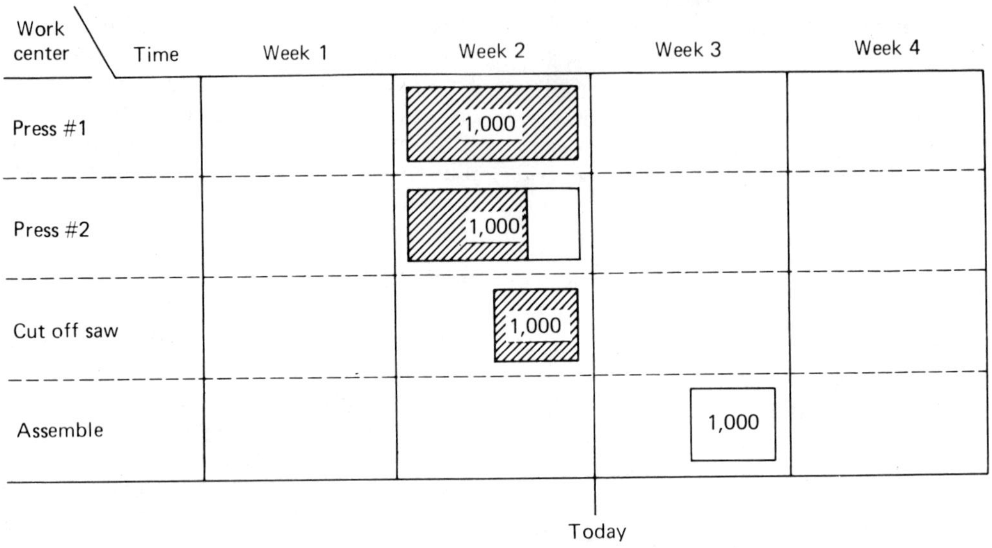

FIGURE 11–6. Gantt Chart for Door Hinge Production Schedule

tion would be displayed on a Gantt chart as shown in Figure 11–6. The vertical axis displays the activities and the horizontal axis, time.

As time progresses and activities are completed, actual performance is recorded on the chart by blocking out completed activities. As shown in Figure 11–6, at the end of week 2, all of one leaf and the pin are complete, but the other leaf is only partly completed. Corrective action is now indicated to rectify the delay or to replan the job.

Gantt charts allow production planning and control to be carried out and displayed graphically. This provides for easier understanding of what was intended and what has actually occurred. Gantt charts require supplemental reports and activities, in some form, in order to function effectively. These activities are summarized in Table 11–2. In addition, the user must recognize that Gantt charts are not easily changed; consequently, a production system that is susceptible to continuous deviations in activity cannot be effectively planned and controlled by the use of Gantt-type charts. The charts soon become obsolete, after which they are usually ignored until the next planning cycle.

PERT/CPM Planning and Control Systems

The program evaluation and review technique and the critical path method of directed graphs are excellent techniques for planning and controlling single-item production. For details as to the use of PERT/CPM techniques, see Chapter 9.

Implementation of PERT/CPM Systems. A directed graph type of planning and control provides definitive start and end dates for all activities to be performed. The technique indicates critical areas where management effort needs to be concentrated in order to avoid delays in the project. It also reveals where trade-offs can be made to maintain plan.

Directed graphs are relatively easy to keep current and, consequently, are superior to Gantt charts in this aspect. This advantage can become a problem, though, if variations in performance cause oversensitive shifts in plans and result in costly revisions in activities. Because perfect planning is impossible, each activity should be allowed a reasonable degree of variance before replanning is undertaken.

Material Requirement Planning (MRP)) Systems

With the availability of computers having large storage capacity at relatively low cost, it has become possible to design material requirements planning systems. These systems were developed to overcome problems with which prior systems were unable to cope. The first problem that earlier systems, particularly economic order quantity (EOQ) systems, failed to consider was the problem of independent and dependent demand. While EOQ systems operated on the assumption that demand for each item was independent and its use determined directly by customer demand, in reality only end items are demanded by customers. The demand for subassemblies, components, and materials depends on how each of these is used in the end item. This dependent demand is a function of strategy and policy as culminated in the production plan, and is only indirectly a function of customer demand.

A second problem area dealt with in MRP systems is the maintenance of accurate and current records. Only computers are able to manipulate data with sufficient speed to keep records current. Computers are also able to adjust records as production planning and control generate changes. But a word of caution is appropriate at this point: computers can generate data quickly, but they can also compound errors quickly, with consequent dire results.

Material requirements planning systems can be used to accomplish planning and control at various levels of complexity and detail. A simple version can be used to maintain inventory records, release production and purchase orders, and establish due dates. More advanced versions also formulate the detail scheduling of work centers, develop engineering data control, and have rescheduling features. Some advanced versions, known as MRPII, coordinate data from various functions including engineering, marketing, finance, cash management, and other major areas to provide complete system planning and control. The following discussion is limited to the simpler MRP systems, since indepth discussion of the advanced versions is beyond the scope of this chapter.

Objective of MRP systems. All versions of MRP systems have several basic objectives:

1. To reduce inventory to current needs for customer demand or planned schedules.
2. To determine quantities of items or materials to produce or purchase on a required basis or a least-cost program.
3. To accept changes into the system in order to generate appropriate revisions to schedules, quantities, and due dates.
4. To provide the capability to plan ahead and to replan.

Inputs to an MRP System. Computers can only work with the information they have. Therefore, it is imperative that current, accurate data be provided to the production planning and control system. A first requirement is an accurate product structure, normally referred to as a bill of material.

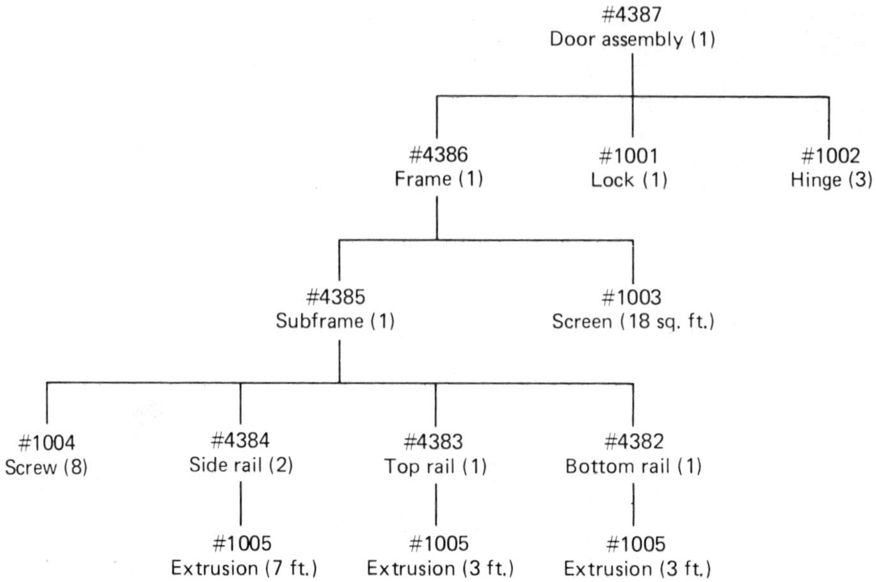

FIGURE 11–7. Product Structure for Part Number 4387 Screen Door Assembly

Bill of Material. An example of a bill of material for a screen door as illustrated in Figure 11–7.

According to this product structure, four rails are fabricated from extrusions and are then joined with eight screws, after which screening is added. Next, three hinges and a lock are assembled to the frame to complete the unit.

The various items in the product structure are associated with different levels in the bill of material. The final assembly is normally considered to be the zero (0) level. In the example in Figure 11–7, this would be part #4387 screen door. Level-one (1) items, which are assembled into the level-zero (0) item, are the #4386 frame, the #1001 lock, and three #1002 hinges. Level-three (3) items are the #4385 subframe and the #1003 screen. Continuing on, level four (4) consists of eight #1004 screws, two #4384 siderails, a #4383 top rail, and a #4382 bottom rail. Finally, level five (5) consists of the #1005 extrusion.

Accurate Inventory Records. A key element of a well-functioning MRP system is accurate information as to what is available in inventory and what is to be produced. These data will be available if proper inventory control procedures are instituted, as discussed in detail in Chapter 13.

Because of their vital importance to an effective MRP system, the functions that need to be performed are reviewed below to further emphasize their importance.

First, statistically accurate data on each inventory item must be maintained through physical security of inventory and through audit control of inventory transactions. This control should provide accurate record such as the:

Issues: The physical removal of inventory from controlled stock areas.

Receipts: The physical movement of inventory into controlled stock areas.

Open orders: Production and purchase orders in various stages of completion.

Commitments: Material assigned to open orders but not removed from controlled stock areas.

On-hand balances: Physical inventory on hand in controlled areas.

Availability: Excess inventory that can be used for future commitments.

Second, inventory records should provide appropriate planning data. These data are necessary in order to be able to perform detail scheduling activities as explained in a previous section. The specific items that should be included are:

Lead time for purchase or production: Total time from commitment to receipt.

Cost per unit: Inventoriable costs including material, labor, and burden.

Method of ordering: System aspects of determining order procedure.

Method of determining order quantity: See Chapter 13.

Safety stock levels: Amount of inventory reserved for coverage of usage variance.

The third type of information that accurate inventory records provide is data on production planning and control reports and action reports. These include:

Stock status report: A complete inventory report covering data described above.

Production orders: A complete package of instructions for producing a specified quantity of product or service.

Purchase orders: A legal commitment to a supplier.

Late order report: A list of production and purchase orders behind planned completion.

Inventory level report: A financial report indicating the amount of inventory on hand.

The three areas that inventory records cover, as discussed above, provide data for a basic MRP system. More elaborate systems would have additional information beyond the scope of this discussion. These data must be properly maintained, as previously noted, so that accuracy and timeliness are within statistically acceptable confidence limits.

Customer Requirements. A material requirement planning system is a proactive system. It uses aggregate, intermediate, and detail planning criteria to determine what will be produced and when, in order to satisfy the independent demand of the market.

Beginning with projected sales over the planning period, a forecast must be made of the expected independent demand for all items to be produced during that planning period. The quantities to be produced may differ from the quantities expected to be sold, depending on the aggregate production planning method selected for the production system. It is very important to establish an aggregate plan that is as accurate as market conditions will allow. Once the plan is implemented and material and labor are committed, changes become difficult and costly. For this reason, MRP systems operate more effectively under stable aggregate plans.

It is important to reemphasize that MRP systems are proactive. The planning system causes action in the production system and generates benefits previously prescribed to an effective MRP system. Being proactive, planning must be based on projected future customer demand, which is always subject to some degree of variation. The planning system will not remove this variability from the customer demand; actually, the planning system may mask market variability and lead management to assume stability when it does not exist. One possible result could be excessive inventories, which cause working capital problems, in some cases leading to bankruptcy, as many large firms discovered in 1982. The other possible result could be excessive shortages and loss of business. Both of these problems must be considered when the firm's strategy and policies are being coordinated with the production system and the planning system.

Operation of an MRP System. The functions of an MRP system can best be illustrated by a simple example, the screen door in Figure 11–7, which provides one set of required information as outlined in the bill of material discussed earlier.

The inventory record information required for the MRP example is summarized in Table 11–3 as a typical inventory stock status report. In the left-hand column are listed part numbers followed by descriptions. Each row across the table contains data relative to the item. The first column, "On Hand," provides information on the amount of inventory in stock. The second column, "On Order," is the amount previously ordered, either through a purchase order or production order. "Required" is the amount committed for existing detail plans, and "Available" is the balance that can be used for new plans. The "available" figure is calculated by combining "on hand" plus "on order" minus "required". The last column provides information on when to order. For the sake of simplicity, data included in this example have been limited to essentials. In most systems, additional information would be included.

Another type of data necessary in an MRP system is intermediate planning of number of units to be produced and when. These data are given in Table 11–4. For our purposes, we will assume a level production policy.

Three sets of data, the bill of material, the inventory stock status, and the intermediate forecast, provide the necessary information to develop a detail production plan using material requirement planning.

A net material requirement is projected for each item by working backward from independent demand for completed screen doors and service locks and hinges taken from Table 11–4. The independent demand is projected into dependent demand for all parts and material according to bill-of-material information from Figure 11–7. The amount of each component required for 100 units is summarized in Table 11–5. The net material requirement plan for each item is determined by working backward from the last time period, in this case week 10 in Table 11–6. The gross requirement of 100 each of part #4387 screen door (Table

TABLE 11-3.
Inventory Stock Status Report—Screen Doors

Part #	*Description*	*On Hand*	*On Order*	*Required*	*Available*	*Lead Time*
4387	Screen door	50	150	250	0	1
4386	Door frame	10	140	150	0	1
1001	Door lock	50	250	250	50	4
1002	Door hinge	100	600	650	50	3
1003	Screen	1,000	3,000	3,600	400	2
4385	Sub frame	20	170	190	0	1
4384	Side rails	0	340	340	0	2
4383	Top rail	0	170	170	0	2
4382	Bottom rail	0	170	170	0	2
1004	Screws	1,000	1,000	1,360	640	2
1005	Extrusion	0	3,500	3,400	100	3

TABLE 11-4.
Intermediate Forecast for Screen Doors and Service Parts

Item	Time Required			
	Week			
	7	8	9	10
Screen doors			100	100
Locks for service			100	
Hinges for service				200

11–5) is entered in week 10, and in week 9 in the net material requirement plan (Table 11–6). From the inventory stock status report it can be determined that there are 50 part #4387 screen doors available over and above current needs; these will be applied against the 100 required in week 9, leaving a net requirement of 100 in week 10, and 50 in week 9. If the plan is to be met, orders of 50 and 100 need to be released in weeks 8 and 9, respectively, to allow for the one week of lead time required. These data are entered in "Order Due" and "Order Release" rows in Table 11–6 for part #4387 screen doors and in the "On Order" column in Table 11–3.

TABLE 11-5.
Gross Requirements for 100 Screen Doors

Part #	Description	Quantity Per Assembly	Quantity for 100 Doors
4387	Screen door	1	100
4386	Door frame	1	100
1001	Door lock	1	100
1002	Door hinge	3	300
1003	Screen	18 sq. ft.	1800 sq. ft.
4385	Sub frame	1	100
4384	Side rail	2	200
4383	Top rail	1	100
4382	Bottom rail	1	100
1005	Extrusion	20 ft.	2000 ft.
1004	Screw	8	800

To start 50 screen doors in week 8 and 100 in week 9, the corresponding numbers of components of frames, locks, and hinges must be available in weeks 8 and 9, respectively. Note that 100 locks in week 9 and 200 hinges in week 10 are added to cover service requirements from Table 11–4.

The same procedure is continued backward until the dependent demand for all items is netted. As can be seen in this example, the #4387 screen door and some of the #1001 locks and #1002 hinges are independent because their demand is determined by the market. The rest of the item's demand is determined by the production policy and production plan. Therefore, forecasts of economic activity should be only indirectly related to consumer demand and directly related to production plans.

Once a detail net material requirement plan is completed, it is initialized by the release of purchase orders and production orders according to the "Order Release" rows. Once the plan is initialized, physical activity commences as materials are purchased and received, and labor is assigned to work centers. Having been activated at a level established in the aggregate production plan, the net material requirement plan becomes very difficult to change over the intermediate planning period of the production cycle.

In this example only eleven different items were included in the bill of material. It is easy to see that a manual application of MRP becomes quite cumbersome for even relatively simple products. For all but a very few cases, MRP needs the assistance of a computer and appropriate software, both of which are commercially available from a number of excellent sources. Computers provide the capability to replan frequently as changes become necessary in the production plan. However, a word of caution is necessary concerning changes. Adjustments within the production cycle should be limited to only very critical

TABLE 11-6.
Net Material Requirements Plan

			Week									
Part #		*Qty.*	*1*	*2*	*3*	*4*	*5*	*6*	*7*	*8*	*9*	*10*
4387	Required										100	100
Door	Available	50										
Lead time	Net required										50	100
1 week	Order due										50	100
	Order release									50	100	
4386	Required									50	100	
Frame	Available	20										
Lead time	Net required									30	100	
1 week	Order due									30	100	
	Order release								30	100		
1001	Required								30	100	100	
Lock	Available	10										
Lead time	Net required								20	100		
4 weeks	Order due								20	100	100	
	Order release				20	100	100					
1002	Required								90	300	200	
Hinge	Available	50										
Lead time	Net required								40	300	200	
3 weeks	Order due								40	300	200	
	Order release					40	300	200				
1003 *etc.*												

changes in order to avoid creating chaos. The magnitude of the problems that can be created by attempting to make changes during the production cycle can be illustrated in a simple example. If the production cycle is five weeks long, the activity for the following four weeks depends on what happens in the first week. The total expected variance is the sum of the expected variance in each of the five weeks. Any change in the production plan in week one will also be experienced in week five and all the weeks between. It is not difficult to visualize the impact that relatively small production planning changes can have because of the dependency from week to week in the production cycle.

Flow Process Control

Flow process control techniques are limited in application to special production systems. In their purest form, these systems are relatively large, are limited to a single product group, and operate for long periods at a constant rate.

Obviously, such a system can function effectively only if there is a constant demand to absorb this continued production or if artificial methods are used to stabilize demand and supply. Monopolies and oligopolies can best control supply to limit the amount of production relative to demand and thereby create conditions that satisfy the need for operation over long periods at a constant rate. Some Japanese manufacturers have been very successful in using flow control procedures in the manufacture of automobiles, televisions, and other high-volume consumer items. Their success results from their strong emphasis on export markets and the use of Japanese domestic demand to absorb fluctuations in export demand.

Flow process control, often referred to as just-in-time production, must begin with a production plan designed to maintain a constant rate of production over an extended time period of an intermediate range or longer. During this time period, production is locked in as to quantities of specific models to be produced. As an example, let us assume that our production system calls for the production of 1,000 television units per day to provide the most efficient level of production. Our intermediate planning and control will be based on the production of 1,000 units per day, thus the burden of absorbing market fluctuations must fall on the marketing and distribution segments of the overall system.

Objectives of a Flow Process Control System. The objectives of a flow process control system are:

1. A reduction of in-process inventory and raw material inventory.
2. A minimization of manufacturing costs by increasing productivity and reducing setup time to achieve the most efficient trade-off.
3. An increase in the use of the capacity of the production system to near optimum levels to provide economies of scale.
4. A capability to plan ahead.

Significantly absent in the objectives stated above is a reduction in finished goods inventory and the ability to accept changes in the short run.

Inputs to a Flow Process Control System. Unlike MRP, a flow process control system can function effectively without the use of a computer because of a minimum number of product changes and planning changes. Even so, current, accurate data are imperative if a flow process control system is to operate successfully.

Bill of Material. A first requirement is an accurate product structure bill of material similar to that for the screen door in Figure 11–7. In order to provide variations of products to satisfy consumer demand, product design should be viewed as a grouping of like products made up of a number like components called families. These like components are joined together in various combinations to produce variety in the end product, while at the same time minimizing the number of diffferent components that need to be produced.

As an example, if our objective is to produce television sets, we might start with three cabinets, two different receivers, and two different picture tubes, one black and white and one colored. These can be combined into $3 \times 2 \times 2$ or twelve (12) sets from only 7 different components. This same concept is carried back into the parts that make up the component. This provides the capabilities to produce a variety of end products and yet minimize setup changes and improve productivity in component production. The benefits of this concept increase geometrically as the number of components increases arithmetically.

Inventory Records. These are of less concern in a flow process control system because inventory is controlled through an elaborate physical storage and movement system rather than a record system.

Rigid Aggregate and Intermediate Plans. Such plans are necessary to provide for material and labor inputs to the system at a specific and constant level.

TABLE 11-7.
Television Set Market Forecast

Model Identification	*Daily Demand*
A	100 units
B	200
C	300
D	100
E	100
F	50
G	50
H	50
I	20
J	10
K	10
L	10

Operational Requirements of a Flow Process Control System. The operation of a flow process control system begins with an aggregate and intermediate plan designed to achieve stability and level production. Using the previous example of television sets to be produced at a rate of 1,000 units per day, we find that production planning would need to break down the 1,000 units into specific models in the product family. In our example, we would have to produce 12 different models to arrive at the total production figure of 1,000 per day. Market forecasting provides information as to how total production should be broken down for detail planning (as shown in Table 11–7).

A second step in the operation of a flow process control system requires a basic change in the production system itself; more specifically, the development of the ability to make setup changes in a very short period of time to provide production flexibility. This flexibility, and its advantages, can be better understood if we consider the following example and illustration.

Assume a machine normally requires 4 hours to change over. Using the trade-off analysis approach, it would require a relatively large production run to affect the

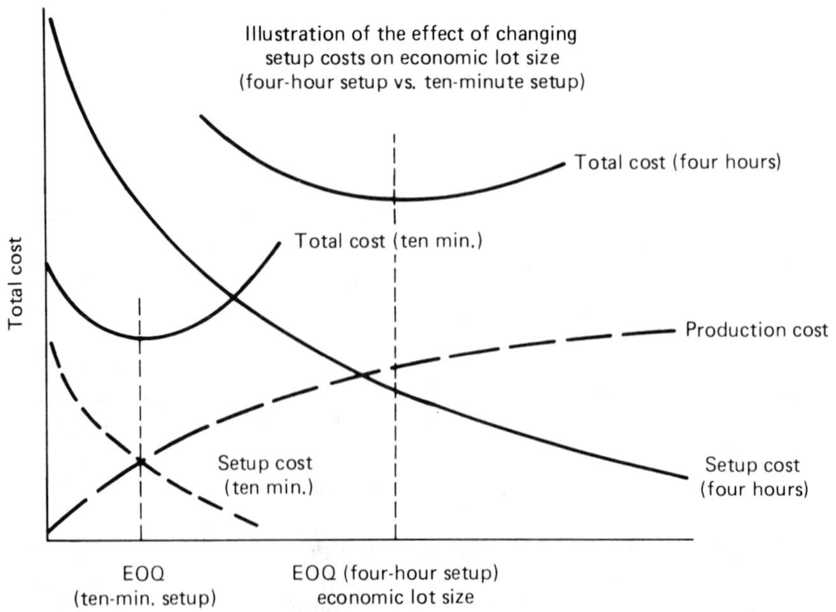

FIGURE 11–8. Illustration of the Effect of Changing Setup Costs on Economic Lot Size (four-hour setup vs. ten-minute setup)

fixed setup costs as illustrated in Figure 11–8.

By developing techniques that drastically reduce setup time, the changeover time might be reduced to 10 minutes, thereby decreasing lot size at a much lower setup cost and only a small sacrifice in production cost per unit. In actual practice, Japanese firms and a few U.S. firms have reduced lot sizes to a fraction of the daily demand for a component.

The third requirement in establishing a flow process control system is to establish an effective supplier network. The network must meet three objectives:

1. *Quick, reliable delivery.* The supplier network must be able to deliver in a short time period with 100 percent reliability. This requires that the suppliers be geographically concentrated so that delivery time does not exceed one day.
2. *Dependable quality.* Only acceptable components must be supplied since a reduction in in-process inventory due to material rejects could cause a production shutdown. Suppliers must provide assurance that only quality material is delivered to the user.
3. *Long-term supplier relations.* By establishing sources of supply that continue over extended periods, an understanding relationship can be developed to minimize problems between the supplier and the user.

Implementation of a Flow Process Control System. Flow process control begins with the development of the smallest lot size of production that can be produced efficiently. In our example, let us assume that lots of 50 or 100 television sets and components are the most economical lot sizes to produce. The daily demand shown in Table 11–7 might then be converted into a detail production plan as shown in Table 11–8.

Several significant factors are revealed in Table 11–8. First, even though a total of 300 model C television sets are required per day, they are produced three times per day in lots of 100 each time. Second, the low volume items are produced on alternative days in lots of 50. And finally, the schedule covers an extended period of 12 weeks.

In the next phase in implementing the system, we must determine how many of each component should be in the system at any time on the basis of production and

TABLE 11-8.
Daily Production Plan for One Week*

Model/Day	*Monday*	*Tuesday*	*Wednesday*	*Thursday*	*Friday*
A	100	100	100	100	100
B	100	100	100	100	100
C	100	100	100	100	100
D	100	100	100	100	100
B	100	100	100	100	100
C	100	100	100	100	100
E	100	100	100	100	100
F	50	50	50	50	50
G	50	50	50	50	50
H	50	50	50	50	50
C	100	100	100	100	100
I	50			50	
J		50			
K			50		
L					50
Daily Total	1,000	1,000	1,000	1,000	1,000

*NOTE: Plan to be repeated for twelve weeks

delivery time constraints. For example, if conditions require two days of production in the system, then only two days of cabinets, tubes, and chassis are all the system will allow to be produced ahead of schedule. If a two-day supply of cabinets consists of 1,000 of model 1, 600 of model 2, and 400 of model 3, then this is all a supplier will be allowed to produce.

Control of component production is achieved through the use of cards that authorize production of 10 lots of 100 each of model 1 cabinet. As assembly uses up a lot of 100, an empty bin and a production card authorizes the cabinet producer to refill the bin with 100 good cabinets within a given time period. The detail production plan for the final product then becomes the authority for component production on a just-in-time basis, with a minimum of paper work and no inventory stock status record.

A flow process control production system with appropriate planning and control techniques is not a system that can be easily instituted in a wide variety of facilities. Rigid plans over extended periods are necessary. This means some other part of the corporate system, usually the distribution system, must absorb fluctuations in demand. Acceptable quality on a continuous basis is also imperative as there is no inventory to absorb rejects. In addition, a geographically concentrated supplier system is necessary to minimize delivery time.

Coordination of Systems

Success in implementing and operating an efficient production planning and control system depends on the degree to which all the systems in the organization are coordinated. Beginning with an assumption that correct corporate strategy has been selected and a correspondingly appropriate production system has been established, we can proceed with the selection of production planning and control systems and techniques.

TABLE 11-9.
Comparison of Production Systems and Characteristics of Planning and Control Techniques

	Characteristic		
System	*Flexible*	*Computer Required*	*Ease of Replanning*
Manual	Yes	No	Yes
Gantt chart	Limited	No	Limited
PERT/CPM	Limited	Usually	Yes
MRP	Limited	Yes	Limited
Flow process	No	No	No

Characteristics of various techniques have been discussed in previous sections of the chapter. They are now summarized in Table 11–9. The review of the characteristics of various approaches of production planning and control illustrated in Table 11–9 clearly indicates that methods in current use are not of universal application. Rather, the systems in use are only applicable to specific production systems and must be carefully selected to achieve effective results.

Production systems are generally rated on their efficiency relative to cost, rate of output, quality, flexibility, and complexity. The five production systems discussed in this chapter, when measured according to the above criteria, form a continuum. As an example, a project system is characterized by very low volume, comparatively high cost, extreme quality variation, inflexibility relative to the project under construction, and a high level of complexity. At the other end of the spectrum, the flow process system is known for its very high volume, relatively low cost, usually high quality, inflexibility, and relative simplicity. When one considers that we are only measuring five different systems on five basic criteria, it is not difficult to understand why production planning and control systems do not have universal application. Instead, each production system if it

TABLE 11-10.
Guidelines for Coordination of Production Systems and Planning and Control Systems

	Planning and Control System		
Production System	*Aggregate Plan*	*Intermediate Plan*	*Detail Plan*
Project	Chase	PERT/CPM	Manual
Job shop	Chase	Gantt	Manual
Intermittent	Modified chase	Basic MRP	Computer and manual
Assembly line	Modified level	Advanced MRP	Weekly computer
Flow process	Level	Just in time	Daily manual

is to be effective, requires some degree of adaptation of the planning and control system.

Given an understanding of the complexity of the production systems and the adaptability of the production planning and control system, some general guidelines for selection of coordinated systems are in order. These guidelines are summarized in Table 11–10.

Aggregate Planning. As the product volume grows from very low volume to mass production, the type of production system changes from a project system to a process layout and then to a product layout. In this transition, cost structures change from low fixed-high variable at the project end, to high fixed-low variable at the flow process end of the spectrum. Profitability hinges on maintaining continuous use of the facilities; consequently, a level aggregate production plan is most logical and efficient at the flow process end. At the same time, the flow process end of the production system is less adaptable to change; therefore, some phase of the organization other than the production system itself must compensate for fluctuations in demand.

Intermediate Planning and Control. As far as intermediate planning is concerned, the most important aspect is the selection of a planning and control system that will be compatible with both the production system itself and the aggregate planning system that is in use.

Project systems and job shop systems normally have a demand that fluctuates extensively. The planning and control systems in use are designed to accommodate demand fluctuations within the production system itself. The intermediate planning and control system must be able to track these demand fluctuations and respond to the changes. PERT/CPM planning and control systems, when used in conjunction with a computer, are adaptable to change. Gantt systems are only partly successful; consequently, when a job shop is subjected to extensive demand fluctuations, the Gantt system will require additional intermediate planning and control techniques. One approach is to use a gross manual technique, or a PERT/CPM system modified for job shop application in conjunction with a small computer. In any case, a primary criterion of the planning and control system should be flexibility.

Intermediate planning and control at the flow process end of the continuum are less complicated because the production system should not be subjected to the same degree of change as the project system. The intermediate planning and control system that is selected for a high-volume production system should be designed to achieve efficient use of the production system and the system's inputs.

This efficiency can best be achieved if the planning and control system's objectives are to minimize inventories, downtime, and rejects, and to maximize output, utilization of labor, and utilization of facilities. In the United States, MRP, with its many versions, will best serve the intermediate production planning and control needs for intermittent and assembly line production systems, if the MRP system is adapted to fit the specific production system's need and the firm's strategy and policy.

Very few production systems are in existence today in the United States that meet the conditions for successful intermediate planning and control of a flow process production system. The problem is with the production system itself, rather than with just-in-time planning and control techniques. It is too early to establish the degree of success to be expected in the application of just-in-time planning and control systems. They are designed to meet specific needs of a flow process system, and in order to be successful, at least two conditions are necessary. First, the production system must be a true flow process production system, as described earlier in this chapter. Second, the just-in-time planning and control system must be designed to fit the production system specifically and in complete detail.

Detail Planning and Control. The detail planning and control system is concerned more with control than planning at the project end of the production system continuum. Manual systems of PERT/CPM systems in conjunction with a computer provide control that is proportional to the amount of effort expended. The details of a very simple project can be maintained easily by an individual either by memory or on a simple record. Nothing more is needed, nor should more effort be expended.

As the size of the system is increased and the volume of production is enlarged, details must be recorded for comparison beween plan and performance. The point at which a detail system should be converted from manual to computer-based is the point at which cost trade-offs are equal. Manual systems are low fixed-high variable cost systems with a relatively high degree of flexibility. Computer systems are medium to high fixed-low to medium-variable cost systems with much less flexibility than manual systems. A high-volume assembly line using MRP can be most efficiently operated by a computer for detail planning and control to continually return status information through the use of a shop floor control, (the feeding of performance information from the production system to the planning and control system on an on-line basis). Again, as in intermediate planning and control, the detail system must be designed to fit the specific needs of the production system and the strategy and policy of the firm.

Detail planning and control in a flow process system can function well with a manual system. This is because detail information regarding available inventory is built into the previously described card and bin system. Also, the production system does not tolerate change; replanning is virtually unknown to the system. Each day's plan must be completed that day. No allowance is made for variations. If the daily production rate exceeds plan, production is terminated early in the day. If daily production is not met, overtime is expended immediately to complete the daily plan. In this way, plan and performance are the same each day. No variation exists; consequently, no replanning is necessary and recordkeeping is minimized. Only when the production system is designed to function in this manner and strategy and policy are established accordingly, will a flow process production system function effectively in accordance with detail planning and control.

Summary

Production control is concerned with the creation and monitoring of action in the production system. Production control can best achieve its objectives if appropriate production planning has been accomplished. Production planning is the process of converting corporate strategy and policy into details so that the production system can be efficiently utilized.

Strategy and policy formulation is the responsibility of top management of the organization with specific contributions being provided by the various functional areas:

Engineering: Detail product or service definition.

Marketing: General specifications and volume forecast.

Finance: Funds for facilities and working capital.

Production: Selection of facilities, inputs and operation of the system.

In the selection of a production system, the position of the product or service in its life cycle is the determinant of the type of system that will be most effective in meeting corporate strategy and policy.

Production planning is carried out on three levels: aggregate planning involves extended time periods necessary for making capacity changes; intermediate planning covers the time period associated with system inputs; and detail planning usually covers a short time period such as a day or a week.

The techniques by which production control is achieved are:

Manual systems

Gantt charts

PERT/CPM directed graphs

Material requirements planning

Flow process control ("just in time")

There are no free lunches in doing an effective job in production planning and control. The functions cannot be carried out on the basis of generalities. The production systems must be matched with the strategy and policies of the organization and with the life cycle of the product or service. Planning must be carried out on all three levels. Finally, appropriate control techniques must be utilized that match the specific production system and the organizational strategy and policy.

Questions

1. What is the production cycle in weeks for the screen door assembly discussed in the chapter?
2. What is the dependent variable and the independent variable in a chase production planning policy?
3. In using a just-in-time production control system, how are fluctuations in demand absorbed by the total system?
4. What purposes do accurate inventory data serve in an MRP system?

5. On the basis of a life cycle approach, what type of production system would be appropriate for:
   a. Automobile assembly line?
   b. Robot manufacturer?
   c. Tobacco farm?
6. Complete the net requirements plan in Table 11–6.
7. Explore the use of PERT/CPM production control procedures in the recommission of the battleship *Wisconsin*.
8. Give explicit reasons why an MRP system might be unsuccessful in a job shop?
9. How many different variations could be made from a series of families of 4, 4, 5, and 3 variations in each of four components? If a family approach were not used, how many models would have to be set up?
10. Identify the theoretical characteristics of inputs for each of the following businesses.
    a. Steel mill
    b. Grocery store
    c. Personal computer manufacturer

Bibliography

Chase, Richard B., and Nicholas J. Aquilano. *Production and Operations Management*. 3rd ed. Homewood, Ill.: Richard D. Irwin, 1981.

Christensen, C. Roland, Kenneth R. Andrews, and Joseph L. Bower. *Business Policy*. 4th ed. Homewood, Ill.: Richard D. Irwin, 1978.

Greene, James H. *Production and Inventory Control, Systems and Decisions*. Rev. ed. Homewood, Ill.: Richard D. Irwin, 1974.

Laufer, Arthur C. *Operations Management*. 2nd ed. Cincinnati: South-Western, 1979.

Schroeder, Roger G. *Operations Management*. New York: McGraw Hill, 1981.

Stair, Jr., Ralph M., and Barry Render. *Production and Operations Management*. Boston: Allyn and Bacon, 1980.

Starr, Martin K. *Production Management Systems and Synthesis*. 2nd ed. Englewood Cliffs, N.J.: Prentice-Hall, 1972.

Stone, Robert B. "GM Tries "Just-in-Time" System for Inventory/Production Control." *Michigan Purchasing Management* 67 (April 1982): 6–10.

Wheelwright, Steven C. "Reflecting Corporate Strategy in Manufacturing Decisions." *Business Horizons*. (February 1978): 57–66.

CMS Production Control System 1. Bill of Material Module. Detroit, Mich.: Burroughs Corporation, April 1979.

CMS Production Control System 1. Material Requirements Planning Module. Detroit, Mich.: Burroughs Corporation, September 1979.

CMS Production Control System 1. Stock Status Module. Detroit, Mich.: Burroughs Corporation, March 1979.

COPICS Advanced Function Material Requirements Planning—II. Program Number: 5785-GBF. International Business Machine Corporation, 1980.

COPICS Bill of Material Online—II. Program Number: 5785-GBA. International Business Machine Corporation, 1980.

COPICS Shop Order Release—II. Program Number: 5798-DCQ. International Business Machines Corporation, 1980.

Chapter 12

Statistical Quality Control

INTRODUCTION

In Chapter 2, you have worked with the frequency distribution, the average, the standard deviation, and the normal curve for both grouped and ungrouped data. As indicated, the average or mean is a measure of central tendency of the data, whereas the range and standard deviation are measures of dispersion, and the standard deviation is the most efficient measure of spread in the sense that it gives a more precise estimate of the standard deviation of the larger group or universe from which the sample of observation is drawn.

One of the central problems in statistics is to estimate population values from sample values. It turns out (you may have some difficulty understanding this at first) that the sample average or mean is itself an unbiased estimate of the population mean or true mean. However, the sample range and sample standard deviation need correction factors, depending on the sample size, in order to make them unbiased estimates of the true standard deviation of the lot or universe. This will become clearer as you proceed. You should now be knowledgeable in the basic statistical methods that you will need for work in SQC. The basic tools of SQC are control charts and acceptance sampling inspections. Both of these tools depend on a knowledge of the use of frequency distributions, frequency curves, measures of central tendency and dispersion, and the ability to compute relationships of items within a frequency distribution. Statistical quality control (SQC) has been defined as the application of statistical techniques to the collection and analysis of data obtained by sampling in order to achieve maximum economy in the manufacturing operations of design, production, and inspection.

Although quality control is as old as the first attempt to manufacture items, statistical quality control was first used in 1924 at the Bell Telephone Laboratories by Walter A. Shewhart. These techniques seemed radical to many industrial manufacturers, and it was not until 1940–1942 that the use of statistical quality control was standardized for use by manufacturers of defense material.

Today, most of our larger corporations are using statistical quality control methods extensively, and many others are in the process of instituting them. Some of these corporations are General Electric Company, General Motors Corporation, Ford Motor Company, Westinghouse Corporation, and North American Rockwell Corporation.

Statistical quality control is important in the metalworking industries. Almost all of our major industries are active users of statistical quality control, and those that are not are introducing its use whenever possible. If you ever have anything to do with procurement, you will find that acceptance sampling, which is an integral part of statistical quality control, is written into the contracts for material. Statistical quality control is a powerful tool that is used to reduce cost and waste and to increase quality in manufacturing process. It needs to be understood by design and inspection personnel, as well as production person-

---

This material has been revised and updated from *Statistical Quality Control*, Ordnance Subcourse 522, 1967, by permission of the U.S. Army Ordnance Center and School, Aberdeen Proving Ground, Md.

nel. Finally, it can be used in the field in such activities as maintenance and spot-check inspections and reconditioning operations.

This chapter is not designed to make you an expert in quality control. Many men have spent a lifetime of work on the subject of one of the areas of quality assurance. Several formulas and tables are used in this chapter; for our purposes, we will accept them as fact without explanation.

A good textbook on statistics will be an invaluable aid. If this subject interests you beyond the scope of this chapter, refer to textbooks on statistical quality control and continue your study. This is a relatively new field and has a bright and promising future.

HISTORY OF STATISTICAL QUALITY CONTROL

The use of statistical methods as a means of controlling the quality of manufacturing products is a relatively new industrial development. The system proved to be a success from the beginning, resulting in reduction of defective parts and assemblies, improvement of product uniformity, and better service in the field.

As we noted earlier, the principles of statistical quality control were developed, beginning in 1923, by Walter A. Shewhart, in the Bell Telephone Laboratories. During 1924, the first practical applications were begun in the manufacture of components for telephone equipment. Later the system was introduced in the electrical, metalworking, and ordnance industries.

The first quality control text, *Economic Control of Quality of Manufactured Product,* was published in 1931 by Shewhart. This work spread information about statistical quality control to colleges and universities and to industrial companies. It also stimulated an interest in quality control outside the United States. At the invitation of the British Standards Institute, Shewhart visited England in 1932 to discuss with English statisticians and manufacturers the work being done in the United States. This visit resulted in appointment of a British Standards Institute committee on quality control, which in 1935 published E. S. Pearson's monograph on quality control, entitled *The Application of Statistical Methods to Industrial Standardization and Quality Control.*

Meanwhile, in the United States, several industrial companies were experimenting with the methods, and successful application had been made at Picatinny Arsenal in ordnance manufacture. On the basis of the experience at Picatinny, the system of quality control was adapted to many uses in ordnance manufacture and surveillance of ammunition. In 1940, the U.S. War Department requested the American Standards Association to standardize quality control techniques, where possible, so as to make them generally available to all manufacturers of defense material. The American War Standards on control chart analysis were prepared by this committee. These standards were widely distributed in the United States during World War II.

In many colleges and universities, evening courses on statistical quality control were given as war training courses under the sponsorship of the U.S. Office of Education. In addition to these, intensive quality control courses were offered to representatives of industry and the armed forces.

At the conclusion of World War II, a number of quality control groups were meeting regularly in widely separated parts of the country. Several of these groups requested the National Research Council to make a survey to determine what kind of national organization was needed for further advancement and application of quality control methods. The conclusion of this investigation was that a national quality control society appeared essential to further expansion in the field. On February 16, 1946, the American Society for Quality Control was formed with

George D. Edwards of the Bell Telephone System as president.

BASIC CONCEPTS OF STATISTICAL QUALITY CONTROL

Statistical quality control (SQC) is a management tool aimed at insuring product uniformity. Statistical methods are techniques for collecting, presenting, analyzing, and interpreting numerical data. In statistical quality control, these techniques are applied to inspection and test data for setting standards and checking adherence to them so as to achieve maximum economy in manufacturing operations. In its broadest sense, quality control must be concerned with all of the steps taken to regulate variables encountered in manufacturing operations that affect the excellence of the end product. These variables are men, materials, machines, and manufacturing conditions.

Probability

In mass production of products, it is impractical, if not impossible, to make each unit of a product exactly the same as every other unit. Variations in dimensions and other quality characteristics of industrial-products are related directly to probability principles. The laws of probability operate in manufacturing processes just as much as they do in insurance rates or in games of chance. Whenever we use samples to estimate the characteristics of a phenomenon, we run the risk of being wrong. A powerful technique in statistics for determining risk is known as the theory of probability. With it, we can determine the chances of an event occurring or not occurring, provided statistics are available on the number of items or measurements that exist in that phenomenon. For example, what are the chances of drawing an ace of spades from a conventional deck of 52 cards? The answer is 1 in 52, because there is only one ace of spades in the deck of 52 cards. What are the chances of picking any ace from such a deck? The answer is 4 in 52 or 1 in 13, because there are 4 aces in the deck of 52 cards. By inference, it can be seen that probability is defined by the simple formula:

$$\text{Probability } (P) = \frac{\text{Number of successful items } (S)}{\text{Total number of items } (T)}$$

$$P = \frac{S}{T}$$

With this formula, the chances of an event happening can be readily computed once the numerator and denominator are known or can be approximated.

Example 1: If there are 18 balls in a bag, 3 white, 6 red, and 9 black, what is the probability of drawing a white ball from the bag:

P = Probability

S = Number of successful events = 3

T = Total number of items or events = 18

Substituting for S and T we get: $P = 3/18$. The probability of drawing a white ball, therefore, is 3/18 or 1/6. By the same procedure, the probability of drawing a red ball is 6/18 or 1/3. The probability of drawing a black ball is 9/18 or 1/2.

Example 2: If a lot contains 10,000 parts and 100 are found to be defective, what is the probability of a defective part in the lot?

S = 100

T = 10,000, we get:

$$P = \frac{100}{10{,}000} = \frac{1}{100}$$

The probability of a defective part is 1/100 or .01. In general, if a set of objects is classified in a particular way, such that the classes are mutually exclusive and exhaustive, the probability of an object belonging to a given class is the relative frequency of that class in the set. Probability pertains to a given set of things, physical or abstract, classified in a particular way. In working with probabilities, you must understand what probability sets are involved.

Probability as a Predictor of Variations.

If a penny is tossed and allowed to fall, the penny will come to rest with either a head or tail showing. Accordingly, the probability of a head is 1/2. The probability of a given attribute is defined as the relative frequency of that attribute in a specified set. This definition becomes useful when coupled with the axiom that "in a long series generated from the given set by a random operation, the probability becomes a good forecast of the relative frequency of the given attribute." Thus, if the coin is well balanced, we may predict on the basis of this axiom that, when the coin is shaken or tossed in a random manner, the relative frequency of a head in many tossings will be close to 1/2. Probability is thus a mathematical parameter that may be used to make good predictions of relative frequency in mass phenomena, provided these phenomena are random.

Product Quality Variations

At the basis of the theory of control charts is a differentiation of the causes of variation in quality. From a statistical point of view, it is recognized that certain variations in the quality of a product belong to the category of chance variations, about which little can be done other than to revise the process. This chance variation is the sum of the effects of the whole complex of chance causes. The set of chance causes that produces variation in the quality of a manufactured product is like the set of forces that causes a penny to turn up heads or tails when it is tossed in a random manner. Besides chance causes of variation in quality, assignable causes can produce variations. These are fairly large variations that are attributable to special causes that can be identified and removed. For the most part, assignable causes consist of:

1. Differences among machines.
2. Differences among workers.
3. Differences among materials.
4. Differences in each of these factors over time.
5. Differences in their relationships to one another.

CONTROL CHART

According to Walter A. Shewhart in his book, *Statistical Method from the Viewpoint of Quality Control,* a control chart is a statistical device used principally for the study and control of a repetitive process. It may serve to define the goal or standard for a process that the management might strive to attain; it may be used as an instrument for attaining that goal; or it may serve as a means of judging whether the goal has been reached. Therefore, it is an instrument to be used in specification, production, and inspection.

Theory

Knowledge of the behavior of chance variations is the foundation on which control chart analysis rests. If a group of data is studied and it is found that their variation conforms to a statistical pattern that might reasonably be produced by chance causes, then it is assumed that no assignable causes are present. The conditions that produced this variation are, accordingly, said to be under control. They are under control in the sense that, if chance causes alone are at work, then the amount and character of the variation may be predicted for large numbers. Now, if the variations in the data do not conform to a pattern that might reasonably be produced by chance causes, then it is concluded that one or more assignable causes are at work. In this case, the conditions producing the variation are said to be out of control.

Example. Suppose samples of a given size are taken from a process at more or less regular intervals and suppose that for each sample some statistic X is computed. Being a sample result, X will be subject to sampling fluctuations. If no assignable causes are present, these sampling fluctuations in X will be distributed in a definite statistical pattern, such as that pictured in Figure 12–1. If enough samples are taken, it is possible to estimate the average point and certain extreme points on the tail of this distribution. Assuming the distribution to be normal in form, then, from the samples on hand, it is possible to estimate the average and the standard deviation of the distribution of X.

If the vertical scale of a chart is calibrated in units of X and the horizontal scale marked with respect to time or some other basis for ordering X, and if horizontal lines are drawn through the estimated means of X and through an extreme value on the upper and lower end of the distribution of X (Figure 12–2), the result is a control chart for X. If sample values of X are plotted for a significant range of output and time, and if these values all fall within the control limits and conform to a pattern of random variation, the process is in a state of statistical control at the level designated with respect to a given measure of quality. In the use of control charts, it is the goal of management to reduce fluctuations in a process until they are in a state of statistical control at the level desired.

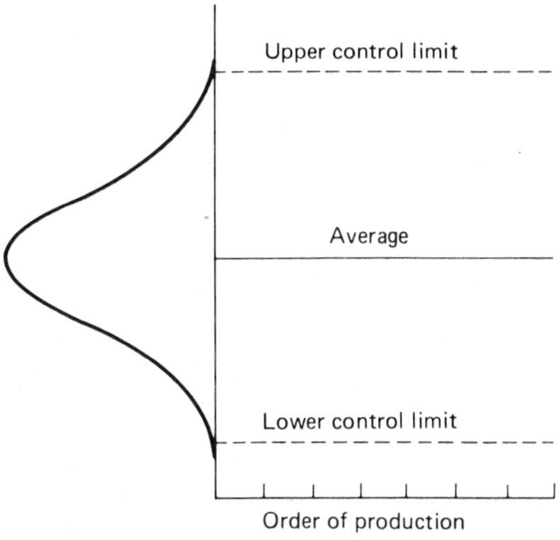

FIGURE 12–2. An Illustration of the Theoretical Basis for a Control Chart.

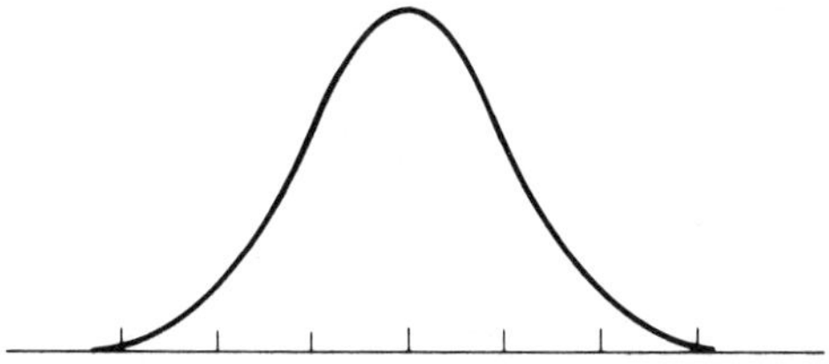

FIGURE 12–1. Distribution of Chance Variations in a Sample Measure of Quality.

ACCEPTANCE SAMPLING

It is to be emphasized that the purpose of acceptance sampling is to determine a course of action, not to estimate lot quality. Acceptance sampling prescribes a procedure that, if applied to a series of lots, will give a specified risk of accepting lots of given quality. The indirect effects of acceptance sampling on quality are likely to be much more important than the direct effects. When a supplier's product is being rejected at a high rate, he takes steps to improve his production methods. Acceptance sampling is likely to be used under the following conditions:

1. When cost of inspection is high.
2. When 100 percent inspection of all items is time-consuming, and a carefully worked out sampling plan will produce as good a result.
3. When inspection is destructive. In this case, sampling must be used. It should be recognized that, although modern sampling acceptance procedures are generally superior to traditional sampling methods established without reference to the laws of probability, anyone who uses acceptance sampling must face the fact that whenever a portion of the stream of product submitted for acceptance is defective, some defective items are likely to be passed by any sampling acceptance scheme. The statistical approach to acceptance sampling frankly faces this fact. It attempts to evaluate the risks assumed with alternative sampling procedures and to make a decision as to the degree of protection needed in any instance. It is then possible to choose a sampling acceptance scheme that gives a desired degree of protection with due consideration for the various costs involved.

THE TOOLS OF STATISTICAL QUALITY CONTROL

Statistical quality control techniques are generally applied in several fields. Two of them are process control and acceptance techniques.

Process Control

As material is processed, samples are taken and inspected. From the results of these inspections, the process is either judged to be operating in a normal fashion or subject to unusual conditions. This decision is based upon the interpretation of a quality control chart. The control charts may be divided into two categories:

1. Control chart for a variable. Whenever the inspections involve a numerical classification of a quality characteristic, the data are said to involve variables. When a diameter is recorded in inches, hardness in Rockwell units, chemical contents in percentages, or an angle in degrees, the data are recorded as a variable.
2. Control chart for an attribute. If a part is simply judged good or bad, the reason is recorded in terms of attributes. The material either is of the proper hardness or it isn't, the chemical content is either acceptable or it isn't, the finish is either smooth or it isn't. These classifications provide data in attribute form.

   The $\bar{X}$ and R charts are for variables data, and the p, np, and c charts are for attribute data. These charts are useful in detecting, at the earliest possible time, conditions that cause defective material. Thus, a process may be corrected before it produces large quantities of defective material.

Acceptance Techniques

Acceptance sampling techniques are designed to permit valid decisions to be based upon a relatively small sample of material. This permits us to inspect a sample of the parts and to decide upon this evidence whether or not the entire group of parts is satisfactory. Most of the acceptance sampling plans are based upon attribute inspection. The most widely used plans at the present time are the Joint Army and Navy (JAN) Standards and their successor, Military Standards 105A.

DEFINITIONS

Some terms used in quality control are defined below.

Attribute: A property either possessed or not possessed by a unit of product. It is a characteristic measurement of quality, not on a continuous scale, but simply by the presence or absence of some desired property (attribute) or the conformance or nonconformance of the property to a standard. The method of attributes in statistical quality control consists simply of noting the presence or absence of some characteristic (attribute) in each of the units of a group under examination and counting how many do or do not possess it. Example: GO/NO-GO gauging of a dimension (measurement).

Distribution: A frequency diagram, curve, or law, that describes the random or uncontrollable variability of a statistical variable.

Inspection: The process of gauging or measuring against a standard or a specification.

Lot (universe): These terms are used synonymously and mean a collection of units of product.

Measure of dispersion: The measure of dispersion is the value that tells us about the consistency of other values and their spread or locations in a distribution. Two of these measures are the range (R), a simple measure of dispersion, and the standard deviation (σ).

Measure of central tendency: The measure of central tendency is the value that is considered the middle or central point about which most other values or points are centered. The average or mean ($\bar{X}$), mode, and median are all measures of central tendency.

Normal curve: The normal curve is a widely used bell-shaped curve of distribution which describes adequately the variation of many measurable characteristics; for example, the length or diameter of a part from a controlled production process. The normal curve is of great importance in quality control work.

Poor quality: Condition that results when an item fails to meet the specification or fails to conform to intended use.

Quality: The dictionary defines quality as an attribute, characteristic, class, kind, or grade. For the purpose of statistical quality control, quality is based on whether or not the item meets the specifications and whether or not it is economically produced for the purpose intended.

Quality control: Methods or techniques used in manufacturing processes to regulate or control quality variations that may affect the economical production of a usable item.

Sample: A sample is a group of units or items taken from a larger collection of units. This group of items serves to provide information that can be used as a basis for judging the quality of the larger volume of material or for furnishing information on the production process. Sampling consists of selecting a group of units from a larger lot (universe).

Specification: A document, usually legal in character, that specifies the requirement or requirements that the quality of the item must satisfy.

Statistics: In a popular sense, statistics are facts stated in terms of numbers; for example, vital statistics. In the sense of this text, the term refers to a scientific method that can be used to great advantage to draw accurate or valid conclusions from numerical data; that is, for judging the whole from a part or estimating characteristics of the lot or universe from a sample drawn from it.

Statistical quality control: The application of statistical techniques or methods to the collection and analysis of data from a production process in order to detect assignable causes of variation and to achieve maximum efficiency and economy in manufacturing operations, production, design, and inspection.

Tolerance: The allowable deviation from the standard. Example: ± 0.0002 of an inch.

Variable: A quantity such as weight in pounds or ounces, height in inches, a dimension in inches, temperature in degrees, and so on, which is subject to variation and measured on a continuous scale. The method of variables in statistical quality control consists of measuring and recording the numerical magnitude of a quality characteristic for each of the units in the group or sample under consideration. This generally involves reading a scale of some kind.

Symbols used in Statistical Quality Control.

$>$ Greater than.

$<$ Less than.

$\geqslant$ Equal to or greater than.

$\leqslant$ Equal to or less than.

N The number of units in a lot.

n The number of observed values in the sample.

X The observed value of a quality characteristic; individual specific values are designed X_1, X_2, X_3, X_4, and so on.

$\bar{X}$ The average (arithmetic mean) of a series of observed values, computed from the formula:

$$\bar{X} = \frac{X_1 + X_2 + X_3 + X_4 + \ldots\ldots + X_n}{n}$$

σ The standard deviation, computed as the root-mean-square deviation of observed values about their average:

$$\sigma = \sqrt{\frac{(X_1 - \bar{X})^2 + (X_2 - \bar{X})^2 + \ldots\ldots + (X_n - \bar{X})^2}{n}}$$

The following equivalent formula may also be used:

$$\sigma = \sqrt{\frac{X_1^2 + X_2^2 + X_3^2 + \ldots\ldots + X_n^2}{n} - \bar{X}^2}$$

R The range, computed as the difference between the largest observed value and the smallest observed value.

P The fraction defective, computed as the number of defective units divided by the total number of units inspected.

pn The number of defective units in a sample of n units.

c The number of defects in a sample of stated size.

$\bar{\bar{X}}, \bar{\sigma}, \bar{R}, \bar{p}, \overline{pn}, \bar{c}$ The average of a set of subgroup values of $\bar{X}$, σ, R, p, pn, or c.

$\bar{X}', \sigma', \bar{p}', p'n, c'$ The selected standard values of $\bar{X}$, σ, p, pn, or c for use in computing control limits.

d_2 The constant used to relate average range ($\bar{R}$) to the standard deviation of the universe (σ') by the formula: $\sigma' = \bar{R}/d_2$.

A_2 Factor for computing control limits for averages.

D_3 and D_4 Factors for computing control limits for ranges.

Introduction to Data Analysis

It is customary to start a discussion of statistics with a discussion of frequency distributions. Getting numbers into the form of a frequency distribution is the first step toward getting them into manageable form. It also facilitates further statistical treatment as well as subsequent analysis and interpretation. In analysis data, one of the first steps is to count the number of times a given variation occurs. If we list the various values of a variable in order of size and give the frequencies with which each size occurs, we have what is called a frequency distribution.

FREQUENCY DISTRIBUTION

In making a frequency distribution of continuous data, it is almost always necessary to group the data into classes or intervals. In grouping data into classes or intervals, it is simplest to keep the size of the interval constant.

Construction of a Frequency Distribution

The procedure to be followed in constructing a frequency distribution may be outlined as follows: (Consider the data in Table 12–1 on page 398.)

1. Determining the range (the difference between the highest measurement and the lowest measurement). The highest measurement in the table is 67.0, and the lowest is 63.5; hence, the range (R) is 67.0 minus 63.5, or 3.5. You will note that this also establishes the end points of the distribution.
2. The next step is to tabulate and classify the individual measurements into groups. This involved tallying and counting the frequencies of occurrence of different observations. Table 12–2 shows the tally of these 200 thickness measurements in the form of a frequency distribution. If you plot the frequency against the measurements, you will develop a graphical representation of the frequency distribution (Figure 12–3). Other graphical representations can be developed from the same data, such as the histogram, frequency bar chart, and the frequency polygon (Figure 12–4 on page 400).

Average and Standard Deviation

In presenting data, it often happens that showing a series of frequency distributions will require too much space. Some more precise form of presentation must be found, such as the average and standard deviation (SD).

The Average for Ungrouped Data. The average $\bar{X}$ for ungrouped data is defined as the sum of all the measures (of the quality characteristic) divided by the number of measures (N). For the general case, if X_1, X_2, X_3, X_4 . . . . X_N are measures of a quality characteristic, the average, $\bar{X}$, is given by the relationship:

$$\bar{X} = \frac{X_1 + X_2 + X_3 + X_4 + \ldots . X_N}{N}.$$

This relationship may be written in short form as follows:

$$\bar{X} = \frac{\Sigma X}{N}.$$

This is read, "If X is a measure of a quality characteristic, the average $\bar{X}$ is equal to the

TABLE 12-1.
Thickness Measurements in Meters

64.5	64.5	66.5	64.5	65.5	65.5							
65.5	65	65.5	66	66	65							
64.5	64.5	67	65	64.5	64.5							
65	65	66.5	65.5	65	64.5							
66	65	65	65	65.5	66							
65.5	64.5	65	64	65	65							
66	65	65.5	64.5	65	65							
65.5	65.5	65	64.5	65	65.5							
65	64.5	65	65.5	65.5	65.5							
65	64.5	64.5	65	66	65.5							
65	64	66	64.5	65.5								
65.5	65	65	65	66								
65	65.5	64	65	65								
64.5	65	65.5	64.5	64.5								
66	66	65.5	65	65.5								
65.5	64.5	65.5	64.5	64.5								
65.5	65.5	65	64.5	64.5								
65	66	66.5	65	64								
65.5	65.5	64	65	66								
64	66	64.5	65	65.5								
65.5	65	64.5	65.5	64.5								
66	65.5	64	65	65.5								
64.5	65	65	65.5	65								
63.5	64.5	65	66	65.5								
64.5	65	64.5	65.5	65.5								
66	65	65.5	66	67								
65.5	65	65.5	65	64.5								
65	65.5	65	65.5	65								
66	65.5	65	66	65								
65.5	64.5	65	64.5	65.5								
66	65	64.5	63.5	65								
65.5	65	65	64.5	65.5								
65	64	65	66	66								
65.5	64.5	65	65.5	66								
65	65	66	64	65.5								
65	66	65.5	65.5	66								
65	65	66	65	65.5								
64.5	65	65.5	65.5	65								

RANGE (R) = 67.0–63.5 = 3.5

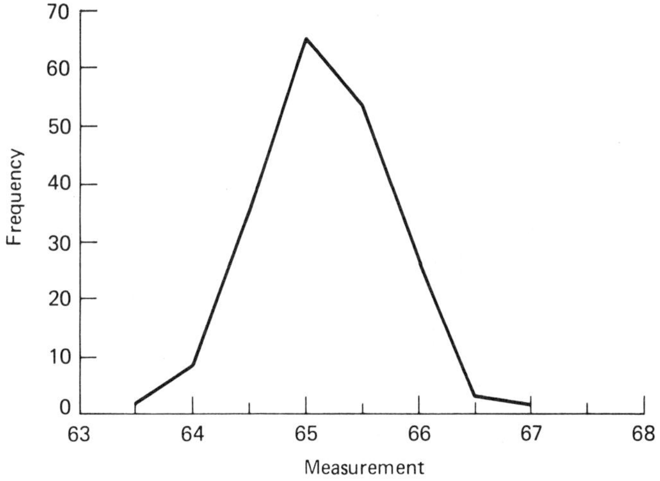

FIGURE 12–3. Frequency Distribution.

TABLE 12-2.
Frequency Distribution for Thickness Measurements

Measurement	*Tally*	*Frequency* *f*
67.0	//	2
66.5	///	3
66.0	𝍸 𝍸 𝍸 𝍸 𝍸 //	27
65.5	𝍸 𝍸 𝍸 𝍸 𝍸 𝍸 𝍸 𝍸 𝍸 𝍸 ////	54
65.0	𝍸 𝍸 𝍸 𝍸 𝍸 𝍸 𝍸 𝍸 𝍸 𝍸 𝍸 𝍸 𝍸 /	66
64.5	𝍸 𝍸 𝍸 𝍸 𝍸 𝍸 𝍸 //	37
64.0	𝍸 ////	9
63.5	//	2
		Total 200

sum of all the measures (ΣX) divided by number of measures (N)."

Example: What is the average score achieved on an arithmetic test by ten 10-year-old boys? The scores are as follows: 80, 76, 42, 92, 70, 68, 84, 76, 68, 70.

$$\bar{X} = \frac{80 + 76 + 42 + 92 + 70 + 68 + 84 + 76 + 68 + 70}{10}$$

Adding the scores and dividing by 10, we get

$$\bar{X} = \frac{726}{10} = 72.6.$$

The Standard Deviation (σ). The standard deviation of a set of observed data is a measure of the variation of individual observations about their average. The symbol for the standard deviation is the Greek letter σ (sigma) and is computed as the root-mean-square deviation about the average value. To compute the standard deviation for ungrouped data, subtract the average from each measurement; square the differences; find the average of the squares; take the square root of the quantity found. Expressed as a formula for n (number of), measurements, X_1, X_2, X_3, X_4, X_5 . . . . X_n,

$$\sigma = \sqrt{\frac{(X_1 - \bar{X})^2 + (X_2 - \bar{X})^2 + (X_3 - \bar{X})^2 + \ldots + (X_n - \bar{X})^2}{n}},$$

or simply

$$\sigma = \sqrt{\frac{\Sigma(X - \bar{X})^2}{n}}.$$

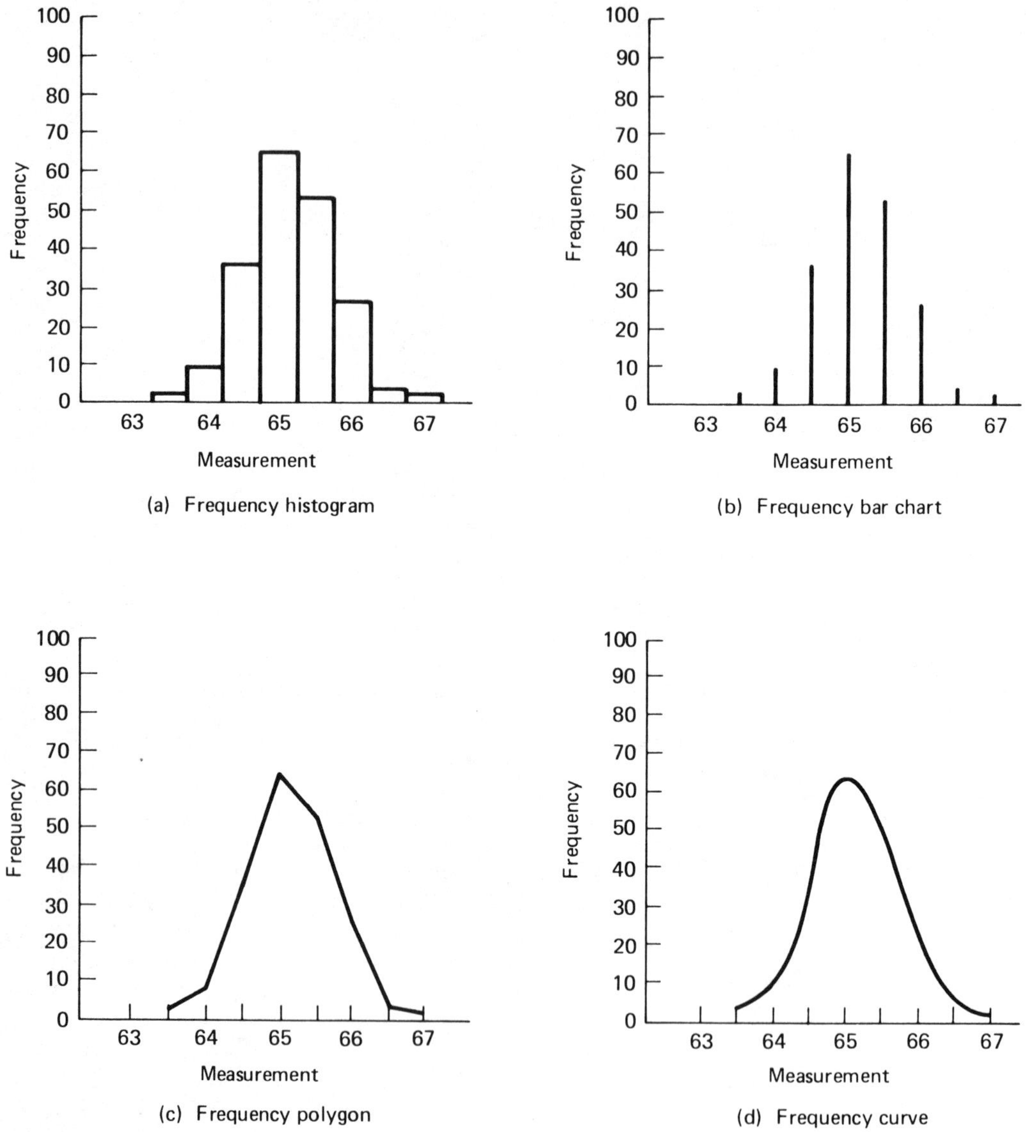

FIGURE 12–4. Graphical Representation of Frequency Distribution for 200 Thickness Measurements.

TABLE 12-3.
Scores

Scores	$(X - \overline{X})$	$(X - \overline{X})^2$
$X_1 = 80$	$80 - 72.6 = +7.4$	$(+7.4)^2 = 54.76$
$X_2 = 76$	$76 - 72.6 = +3.4$	$(+3.4)^2 = 11.56$
$X_3 = 42$	$42 - 72.6 = -30.6$	$(-30.6)^2 = 936.36$
$X_4 = 92$	$92 - 72.6 = +19.4$	$(+19.4)^2 = 376.36$
$X_5 = 70$	$70 - 72.6 = -2.6$	$(-2.6)^2 = 6.76$
$X_6 = 68$	$68 - 72.6 = -4.6$	$(-4.6)^2 = 21.16$
$X_7 = 84$	$84 - 72.6 = +11.4$	$(+11.4)^2 = 129.96$
$X_8 = 76$	$76 - 72.6 = +3.4$	$(+3.4)^2 = 11.56$
$X_9 = 68$	$68 - 72.6 = -4.6$	$(-4.6)^2 = 21.16$
$X_{10} = 70$	$70 - 72.6 = -2.6$	$(-2.6)^2 = 6.76$

In industrial applications of statistical methods, the standard deviation is around 1/6 of the range for a sufficiently large number of observations (over 100).

Example: Find the standard deviation of the 10 scores on the arithmetic test for 10-year-olds. We found the average to be $\overline{X} = 72.6$. The scores are shown in Table 12–3.

Adding $(X - \overline{X})^2$, we get $\Sigma(X - \overline{X})^2 =$ 1,576.40

$$\sigma - \sqrt{\frac{\Sigma(X - \overline{X})^2}{N}}$$

where

$$\Sigma(X - \overline{X})^2 = 1{,}576.40$$

$$N = 10$$

$$\sigma = \sqrt{\frac{1{,}576.40}{10}} = \sqrt{157.640 = 12.55}$$

The Average for Grouped Data. The average for grouped data is given by the relationship:

$$\text{Average } (\overline{X}) = \frac{\text{sum of the frequencies times the measures } (\Sigma fX)}{\text{total number of measures } (N)}$$

or

$$\overline{X} = \frac{\Sigma fX}{N}$$

TABLE 12-4.
Length Measurements in Meters for a Group of Steel Beams

64.5	65.5	64.0	66.0	66.0	64.0	65.0
66.5	65.0	63.5	64.5	65.5	66.5	65.0
64.5	65.0	64.0	63.5	66.0	67.0	64.5
65.0	63.0	65.0	64.5	63.5	66.5	66.0
64.0	64.5	65.5	66.0	64.5	65.0	65.0
65.5	65.0	64.0	65.5	65.0	65.0	64.0
66.0	64.5	65.5	65.0	65.5	65.5	65.5

Example: Make a frequency distribution and compute the average for data in Table 12–4.

Table 12–5 shows the measurements organized in a frequency distribution.

$$\overline{X} = \frac{\Sigma fX}{N}.$$

Adding the fX column, we get $\Sigma fX =$ 3,185.5; adding the frequency column, we get $N = 49$; and substituting these values in the formula, we get:

TABLE 12-5.
Frequency Distribution of the Data in Table 12-4.

X *Measures*	*Tally*	*f* *Frequency*	*fX*
67.0	/	1	67.0
66.5	///	3	199.5
66.0	卌 /	6	396.0
65.5	卌 ////	9	589.5
65.0	卌 卌 //	12	780.0
64.5	卌 ///	8	516.0
64.0	卌 /	6	384.0
63.5	///	3	190.5
63.0	/	1	63.0

$$\bar{X} = \frac{3{,}185.5}{49} = 65.$$

The average length of the beams is 65.0 meters.

The Standard Deviation for Grouped Data. The standard deviation for grouped data is given by the relationship:

$$\sigma = \sqrt{\frac{\Sigma fX^2}{N} - \bar{X}^2},$$

where σ = standard deviation, f = frequency, N = total number of measures, and $\bar{X}$ = average.

Example: Consider Table 12–6 and compute the standard deviation.

$N = 200$

$$\text{The average } (\bar{X}) = \frac{\Sigma fX}{n} = \frac{13{,}032.0}{200} = 65.16.$$

The standard deviation

$$(\sigma) = \sqrt{\frac{\Sigma fX^2}{n} - \bar{X}^2} = \sqrt{\frac{849{,}238}{200} - (65.16)^2}$$

$$\sigma = \sqrt{4{,}246.19 - 4{,}245.8256} = \sqrt{.3644}$$

$$\sigma = .60.$$

THE NORMAL CURVE

The normal curve is generally assumed to represent the frequency distributions whose control charts for average and range are in control. Thus, we have a powerful tool to predict the variations encountered in controlled manufacturing processes.

Consider the problem of estimating the number of cases between two specifications in a normal distribution. If we have a process under control, we can estimate the percentage of a product that falls between a lower specification limit, X_L, and an upper specification limit, X_u. In order to do this, we must know the specification limits, the average ($\bar{X}$), and the standard deviation (σ). For the example under consideration, the data are as follows:

X_L = Lower specification limit = 134.3
X_u = upper specification limit = 145.1
$\bar{X}$ = average = 140.6
σ = standard deviation = 3.6

The problem is to predict the percentage of the product that falls between the two specification limits. The procedures follow:

1. The upper limit of 145.1 lies at a distance of 4.5 points from the average. This is

TABLE 12-6.
Statistical Calculations from Frequency Distribution for 200 Thickness Measurements

Measurements (X)	*Frequencies f*	*First Product (f X)*	*Second Product (f X²)*
67.0	2	134.0	8,978.00
66.5	3	199.5	13,266.75
66.0	27	1,782.0	117,612.00
65.5	54	3,537.0	231,673.50
65.0	66	4,290.0	278,850.00
64.5	37	2,386.5	153,929.25
64.0	9	576.0	36,864.00
63.5	2	127.0	8,064.50
Totals	200	13,032.0	849,238.00

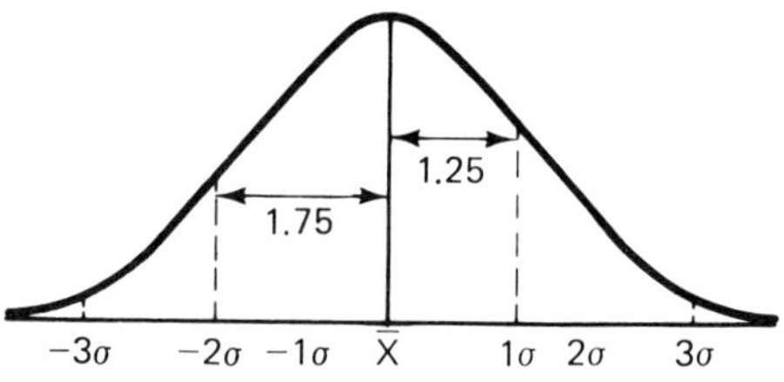

FIGURE 12–5. Normal Distribution.

determined from the relationship, $X_u - \bar{X}$(145.10 − 140.60 = 4.50). Dividing this difference from the mean by the standard deviation (4.5/3.6), we get 1.25 as the distance that 145.1 lies to the right of the average (Figure 12–5). From Table 12–7, we find, opposite to 1.25, the percent of distribution area under the normal curve between X_u *and* $\bar{X}$, which is 39.44 percent.

2. Similarly, taking the lower limit, we compute the value of $\bar{X} - X_L$ (140.60 − 134.30 = 6.30). Dividing this deviation from the mean by standard deviation (6.30/3.60), we get 1.75 as the distance that 134.3 lies to the left of the average (Figure 12–6). From Table 12–7, we find opposite 1.75, the percent area under the normal curve between X_L and $\bar{X}$, which is 45.99.

3. By adding the two values (39.44 + 45.99 = 85.43), we obtain the approximate percentage of the distribution falling between the upper and lower specification limits.

TABLE 12-7.
Percentage of Total Area Under the Normal Curve Between the Average and Varying Distances from the Average

X/σ, where X = $\bar{X} - X_L$ or $X_u - \bar{X}$	*Percent of Total Area*	*X/σ, where X = $\bar{X} - X_L$ or $X_u - \bar{X}$*	*Percent of Total Area*
0.0	00.000	2.0	47.725
0.1	03.983	2.1	48.214
0.2	07.926	2.2	48.610
0.3	11.791	2.23	48.710
0.4	15.542	2.3	48.928
0.5	19.146	2.4	49.180
0.6	22.575	2.5	49.379
0.7	25.804	2.5758	49.500
0.8	28.814	2.6	49.534
0.9	31.594	2.7	49.653
1.0	34.134	2.8	49.744
1.1	36.433	2.9	49.813
1.2	38.493	3.0	49.865
1.25	39.44	3.1	49.903
1.3	40.320	3.2	49.931
1.4	41.924	3.3	49.952
1.5	43.319	3.4	49.966
1.6	44.520	3.5	49.977
1.7	45.543	3.6	49.984
1.75	45.99	3.7	49.989
1.8	46.407	3.8	49.993
1.9	47.128	3.9	49.995
1.96	47.500	4.0	49.997

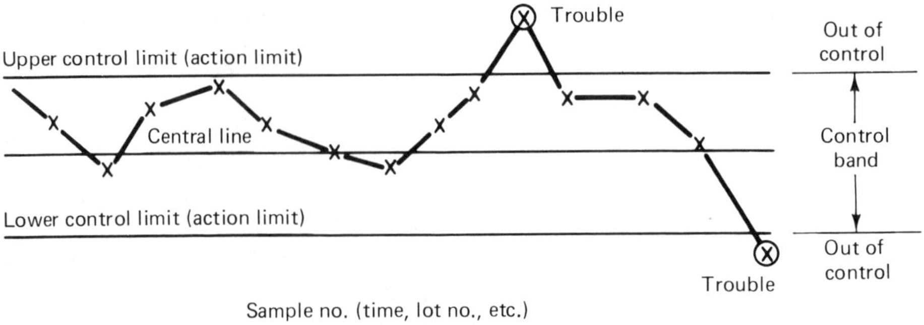

FIGURE 12–6. Sample Control Chart with Limits.

Statistical Control Charts

We have seen how graphic and numerical presentation of frequency distributions can indicate the overall spread of a distribution and its general shape relative to the normal curve. Before we get into the subject of the standard control charts most frequently used, we should mention two other charts that are sometimes made from the data obtained by sampling. The first one is a chart for individual measurements, consisting of the tolerance limits and the individual values. The second chart is a chart of average measurements of samples, consisting of the tolerance limits and the average sample measurements. They may be of interest to the production supervisor, but they do not give the basis for action that the statistical control charts do.

Frequency distributions are primarily useful in giving a picture of product quality at a given instant of time or in summarizing quality results for a fairly long period of time. When it is necessary to measure quality variations on an hourly or daily basis, it is desirable to compute the average and range of percent defective every hour or every day. In following such regular checks on variations, we are concerned not so much with the individuals as with getting a picture of the process or product as a whole from inspection of the samples selected. Variation is inherent in all natural phenomena. Variations in the quality of manufactured articles are inevitable. The idea of an exact repetitive operation is unrealistic. No two objects are made exactly alike, and we must think in terms of the chance that a quality characteristic does not differ from the standard quality by more than a certain amount.

As stated earlier, the sources of variations in manufactured products are men, materials, machines, and manufacturing conditions. By means of statistical quality control methods, these variations may be separated into two types of causes:

1. Chance variations due to random variations in the process.
2. Nonchance variations for which a cause is assignable. The separation of these two types of variations is the special province of the *control chart.*

Chance causes of variations are always present, inherent in the nature of the process, neither identifiable nor removable, and not within our power to regulate. If a stable system of chance causes alone is operating in a process and causing the variations in quality, then:

1. The product cannot be improved except by basically changing or redesigning the process.
2. The process exhibits its natural variability.
3. The magnitude of quality variations in the product can be predicted.

Accurate predictions and sound decisions can be made only from data that come from a stable system of chance causes. Such a stable system of chance causes may be illustrated using a drum containing a quantity of numbered disks. Rotate the drum so the disks are well mixed. Withdraw one disk, record the number, and replace. Repeat the operation. If the disks are essentially alike and if the drum, the method, and conditions of drawing do not change, the drawings exemplify a constant system of chance causes. A process is said to be in a state of statistical control or in statistical control, or in control when a stable system of chance causes only seems to be operating to effect the observed quality variations. The magnitude of the quality variations of a statistically controlled process is due to the process itself and cannot be altered except by basically changing the process. It is important to understand constant-cause systems, because some such stable system of chance causes is inherent in any particular scheme of production and inspection. The effects of such a constant-cause system are visible when no assignable causes of variation are present.

Assignable causes arise from specific maladies of the process and are potentially identifiable. Since these causes are identifiable, they can be removed. They are within our power to regulate and, when they occur, they merit prompt investigation. If these assignable causes are at work (in addition to the ever present chance causes) there is no way to predict the variability of the product. The product can be improved by detecting, identifying, and eliminating these assignable causes. The presence of assignable causes of variation can be detected by comparing the pattern of variation we actually have with the pattern we would expect to have if chance causes alone were operating. The control chart is the tool used for this purpose. The assignable cause of variation is identified and removed by an engineering investigation, when it is considered economical to do so. Best results are obtained by cooperation between the engineer who knows statistics and the statistician who knows the process.

1. The control chart is a graphical record of the quality of current production showing quality variations by a series of points plotted in order of production.
2. A control chart generally has the features indicated in Figure 12–6. The central line indicates what is to be expected; the points tend to vary above and below this line. The control limits assist in judging the significance of the quality variations from the central level. When only chance causes of variation are operating, the points fall inside the control band, and the process is then said to be in control. Statistical control is established by the construction of control or action limits, such that the occurrence of points outside these limits is regarded as equivalent to the following:
    a. Assignable causes of variation are present.
    b. The process is out of control.
    c. Production personnel must take action to identify and eliminate assignable causes.

The control chart is a device of the statistician to detect the presence of assignable causes of variation. The actual deviation and elimination of the assignable cause(s) are tasks for production and engineering personnel. The chart shows *when* you're in trouble, not *what* the trouble is. The fact that we know *when* assists in the determination of *what*. Knowing the time trouble occurred often helps in the diagnosis, that is, in the identification of the trouble. In addition, the control chart often gives a warning of impending difficulty. Steps can be taken to investigate the situation and prevent the actual occurrence of trouble. Thus, since the control chart gives a pictorial record of what is happening *while* it is happening, it aids in building quality into the product at the machine—where it belongs. Quality cannot be obtained by screening or gauging inspections, when it is too late.

CONTROL LIMITS

Control chart theory supplies simple formulas and tables for computing the central and control limit lines. The control limits are set to strike an economic balance, based on experience, between two kinds of errors: looking for assignable causes when they are present. The control limits assist judgment on whether or not a state of control exists. They assist in attaining and maintaining control. When a control chart is first applied to a manufacturing process, a state of control is not usually found. However, control must be established at a satisfactory level by the elimination of all assignable causes of variation from the process before maximum efficiency in the operation can be obtained. Quality must be built into the product; it can't be inspected into it. Control limits further enable us to detect assignable causes of variation by providing criteria for discriminating between causes of variation that may reasonably be attributed to chance from those causes of variation that may not be reasonably attributed to chance. Finally, action limits tell us when it pays to take action on the process (assignable causes) and when it would be a waste of time (chance causes). Certain advantages arise when a process is in a state of control:

1. The variation between individual items is at a minimum.
2. The quality of the product can be reliably judged by samples.
3. The percentage of product whose quality lies within any given limits can be accurately predicted.
4. The amount of sampling inspection can be reduced, and acceptance can be based on facts of control chart.
5. There is a basis for comparing the specifications with the product coming from the controlled process.

The consistency or regularity of performance is indicated by the position of points with respect to the control band (sometimes with respect to runs above and below the central line). A succession of points inside the control band indicates a consistent process. In addition, it represents uniformity of product in terms of its basic variability and the average quality level of production.

TYPES OF CONTROL CHARTS

There are two main types of control charts, depending on the two principal types of inspection, control charts for variables (inspection by variables) and control charts for attributes (inspection by attributes). Inspection is said to be by variables when a quality characteristic of the item is measured; an actual measurement is made and recorded in pounds, feet, seconds, ohms, feet per second, and so on. Inspection is said to be by attributes when the unit of product is classified simply as defective or nondefective with respect to a given specification or set of specifications.

The common control charts for variables are:

(1) Chart for averages . . . . chart for $\bar{X}$.
(2) Chart for ranges . . . . chart for R.

(3) Chart for standard deviation . chart for σ.
(4) Chart for individual values . . chart for X.

The common control charts for attributes are:

(1) Chart for fraction defective . . chart for p.
(2) Chart for number defective . chart for pn.
(3) Chart for number of defects per unit (or per 100 units) . . . chart for c.

CONTROL CHART FOR VARIABLES

In a given manufactured product, certain quality characteristics may be measured in the form of a length, weight, time, resistance, and so on. These measured characteristics define how closely the individual units of product approach standard quality. After a number of like units of the product have been measured for the same quality characteristic, a control chart for variables can be constructed from these measurements. Such a control chart for variables is designed to answer three important questions: Is the process consistent? What is the average quality of product? How variable is the quality? The control chart for averages provides information on the average quality. The control chart for ranges provides information on the variability. The process is consistent, in statistical control, only if points consistently fall inside the control limits on both charts.

The steps in constructing control charts for variables may be listed as follows:

1. Select a dimension or other characteristic, X, which investigation has indicated it would be economical to control.
2. Choose a suitable measuring device. All gauges and measuring instruments used should be checked for accuracy.
3. Decide on a sample size, n. This may be a number from 2 up; samples of 4 or 5 are commonly used.
4. Take a random sample of size n from the machine. Measure each specimen in the sample. Record the measurements on an appropriate form. The samples should be chosen so that variation within a subgroup tends to be minimum and variation between subgroups, maximum.
5. Find the average, $\bar{X}$, of the n measurements. If $n = 5$, this is done by adding the five measurements and dividing by 5. This gives us our first sample average, $\bar{X}_1$.

$$\bar{X} = \text{the sample average}$$
$$= \frac{\text{sum of } n \text{ sample measurements}}{\text{the sample size } (n)}.$$

6. Find the range, R, of the five measurements. This is done by subtracting the smallest measurement in the subgroup of 5 from the largest, that is,

$$R = X(\max) - X(\min).$$

7. Repeat the operations in (4), (5), and (6) until about 25 samples have been measured. We now have 25 averages (25 $\bar{X}$s) and 25 ranges (25Rs).
8. Find the average of the means, or grand average, $\bar{\bar{X}}$.

$$\bar{\bar{X}} = \frac{\text{sum of all the } \bar{X}\text{s (sample averages)}}{\text{number of samples}}.$$

9. Find the average of the ranges, $\bar{R}$. This is done by adding the 25 ranges and dividing by 25.

$$\bar{R} = \frac{\text{sum of all the } R\text{s (sample ranges)}}{\text{number of samples}}.$$

10. Corresponding to the sample size n used, select the appropriate numbers A_2, D_3, and D_4, from Table 12–8.

TABLE 12-8.

Factors for Determining from $\bar{R}$ the 3 σ Central Limits for $\bar{X}$ and R Charts.

n	A_2	D_3	D_4
2	1.88	0	3.27
3	1.02	0	2.57
4	0.73	0	2.28
5	0.58	0	2.11
6	0.48	0	2.00
7	0.42	0.08	1.92
8	0.37	0.14	1.86
9	0.34	0.18	1.82
10	0.31	0.22	1.78
11	0.29	0.26	1.74
12	0.27	0.28	1.72
13	0.25	0.31	1.69
14	0.23	0.33	1.67
15	0.22	0.35	1.65

11. Calculate the upper and lower control limits for averages, using the following formulas:

Upper control limit for $\bar{X}$ = $UCL\bar{X} = \bar{\bar{X}} + A_2\bar{R}$

Lower control limit for $\bar{X}$ = $LCL\bar{X} = \quad - A_2\bar{R}$

Central line = $\bar{\bar{X}}$.

12. Calculate the upper and lower control limits for ranges, using the following formulas:

Upper control limit for R = $UCLR = D_4\bar{R}$

Lower control limit for R = $LCLR = D_3\bar{R}$ (this is zero for n = 6 or less)

Central Line = $\bar{R}$.

13. Prepare two charts, one for $\bar{X}$ and the other for R, on suitable graph paper. The vertical scales at the left are for $\bar{X}$ and R; the horizontal scale identifies the samples, taken in order as the first, second, third, and so on.

14. On the charts, draw the three lines for $\bar{\bar{X}}$, $UCL\bar{X}$, and $LCL\bar{X}$ on the chart for $\bar{X}$. Then draw the three lines for $\bar{R}$, $UCLR$, and $LCLR$ on the chart for R.

15. Plot, in order, the values of $\bar{X}$ found in step 7 on the chart for $\bar{X}$ and the values of R on the chart for R. We now have two control charts, one for averages ($\bar{X}$), the other for ranges (R).

16. Any value of $\bar{X}$ or R falling outside the respective control limits is an indication of assignable causes of variation; that is, lack of control. Such causes should be identified and eliminated by an engineering investigation.

17. Continue taking samples as desired, plotting the additional $\bar{X}$s and Rs, extending the control limits and central lines, and noting where the new points lie on the chart. Investigate out-of-control points.

18. Lack of control may be indicated by extreme runs, even though none of the points is outside the control bands. Such lack of control is indicated by seven successive points on the same side of the central line.

19. When the process exhibits control, the process is consistent. The average quality of the process can now be estimated from $\bar{\bar{X}}$. The variation, that is, the standard deviation of the individual items turned out by the process, may be estimated from $\bar{R}/d_2$ where d_2 depends on n as shown in Table 12–9.

From this calculation, we can determine the process capability or normal variability. The estimated average $\bar{X}'$ and the estimated standard deviation σ' may conflict with the specifications. The specification limits specify the average value of a quality characteristic and the extreme permissible values for the individual item. It is essential to know the differences between specification (or tolerance) limits and control limits. This will be covered later.

TABLE 12-9.

n	2	3	4	5	6	7	8
d_2	1.128	1.693	2.059	2.326	2.534	2.704	2.847
n	9	10	11	12	13	14	15
d_2	2.970	3.078	3.173	3.258	3.336	3.407	3.472

20. When the process is in statistical control and it is found that individual items do not meet specifications, we must make basic changes in the process to bring the product in line with the specifications, or adjust the specification limits to the existing level of control, or sort out nonconforming units from all lots.

Example. Consider the data given in Table 12–10, which shows 10 samples of 5 units each taken from a machine at hourly intervals. The machine turns out 2,000 units per hour, so that the 10 samples of 5 or 50 units represent some 20,000 piece parts. Follow the steps just outlined in the construction of a control chart for variables, and construct a control chart for the variables, averages ($\bar{X}$), and ranges (R). Start computations at step 5.

---

1. Find the sample average:

$$\bar{X} = \frac{.24580 + .24680 + .24650 + .24640 + .24630}{5}$$

$$= \frac{1.231.80}{5}$$

$$\bar{X} = .24636$$

2. Find the sample range: $R = .24680 - .24580 = .00100$.

3. Find the sample standard deviation:

$$\sigma = \sqrt{\frac{(X_1 - \bar{X})^2 + (X_2 - \bar{X})^2 + (X_3 - \bar{X})^2 \ + (X_4 - \bar{X})^2 + (X_5 - \bar{X})^2}{N}}$$

$$\sigma = \sqrt{\frac{(.2458-.24636)^2+(.2468-.24636)^2+(.24650-.24636)^2+(.24640-.24636)^2+(.24630-.24636)^2}{5}}$$

$$\sigma = \sqrt{\frac{(-.00056)^2 + (.00044)^2 + (.00014)^2 + (.00004)^2 + (-.00006)^2}{5}}$$

$$\sigma = \sqrt{\frac{.0000005320}{5}} = \sqrt{.0000001064} = .000326$$

Extracting the square root we get $\sigma = .000326$.

TABLE 12-10.

Time	Measurements	Sample Average $\bar{X}$	Sample Range R	Sample Standard Deviation σ
0900	0.2458			
	68			
	65			
	64			
	63	0.24636	0.0010	0.000326
1000	0.2463			
	66			
	68			
	65			
	71	0.24666	0.0008	0.000273
1100	0.2463			
	67			
	67			
	71			
	65	0.24666	0.0008	0.000265
1200	0.2463			
	67			
	66			
	68			
	69	0.24666	0.0006	0.000206
1400	0.2472			
	65			
	68			
	69			
	70	0.24688	0.0007	0.000232
1500	0.2469			
	77			
	72			
	68			
	67	0.24706	0.0010	0.000361
1600	0.2468			
	72			
	66			
	65			
	76	0.24694	0.0011	0.000408
1700	0.2465			
	67			
	70			
	80			
	73	0.24710	0.0015	0.000525

TABLE 12·10. *(Continued)*.

Time	Measurements	Sample Average $\bar{X}$	Sample Range R	Sample Standard Deviation σ
0900	0.2467			
	73			
	70			
	69			
	71	0.24700	0.0006	0.000200
1000	0.2465			
	71			
	67			
	68			
	67	0.24676	0.0006	0.000196
		Grand Average	Average Range	Average Standard Deviation
		$\bar{\bar{X}} = 0.24681$	$\bar{R} = 0.00087$	$\bar{\sigma} = 0.000299$

4. By the same procedure, compute the sample average, range, and standard deviation for each sample. The results of these calculations are shown in Table 12–10.
5. Find the grand average $\bar{\bar{X}}$:

$$\bar{\bar{X}} = \frac{\text{sum of all the } \bar{X}\text{s}}{\text{number of averages}} = \frac{2.46808}{10}$$

$$\bar{\bar{X}} = .24681$$

6. Find the average of the ranges, $\bar{R}$.

$$\bar{R} = \frac{\text{sum of all the ranges } (\bar{R})}{\text{number of ranges}}$$

$$\bar{R} = \frac{.0087}{10} = .00087$$

7. Find the upper and lower control limits for averages:

($UCL\bar{X}$) upper control limit for $\bar{X} = \bar{\bar{X}} + A_2\bar{R}$

$$UCL\bar{X} = .24681 + A_2\,(.00087)$$

A_2 is obtained from Table 12–8. For sample size 5, $A_2 = .58$; therefore,

$$UCL\bar{X} = .24681 + (.58)\,(.00087)$$
$$= .24681 + .00050$$
$$= .24731$$

($LCL\bar{X}$) lower control limit for $\bar{X} = \bar{\bar{X}} - A_2\bar{R}$

$$LCL\bar{X} = .24681 - (.58)\,(.00087)$$
$$LCL\bar{X} = .24681 - .00050$$
$$= .24631$$

8. Find the upper and lower control limits for range (R):

($UCLR$) upper control limit for $R = D_4\bar{R}$

$D_4 = 2.11$ (for sample size 5, $D_4 = 2.11$; see Table 12–8).

$\bar{R} = .00087$;

therefore,

UCLR = 2.11 (.00087)

= .0018

(LCLR) lower control limit for $R = D_3\bar{R}$

$D = 0$ (for sample size 5, $D_3 = 0$; see Table 12–8).

$\bar{R} = .00087$

hence: LCLR = 0 (0.00087) = 0

9. Prepare a chart for averages. This is accomplished by constructing lines representing the grand average, upper control limit $\bar{X}$, and the lower control limit $\bar{X}$ (Figure 12–7) and then plotting the sample averages against time.

10. Prepare a chart for ranges. This is done by constructing lines representing the average R, upper control limit for range

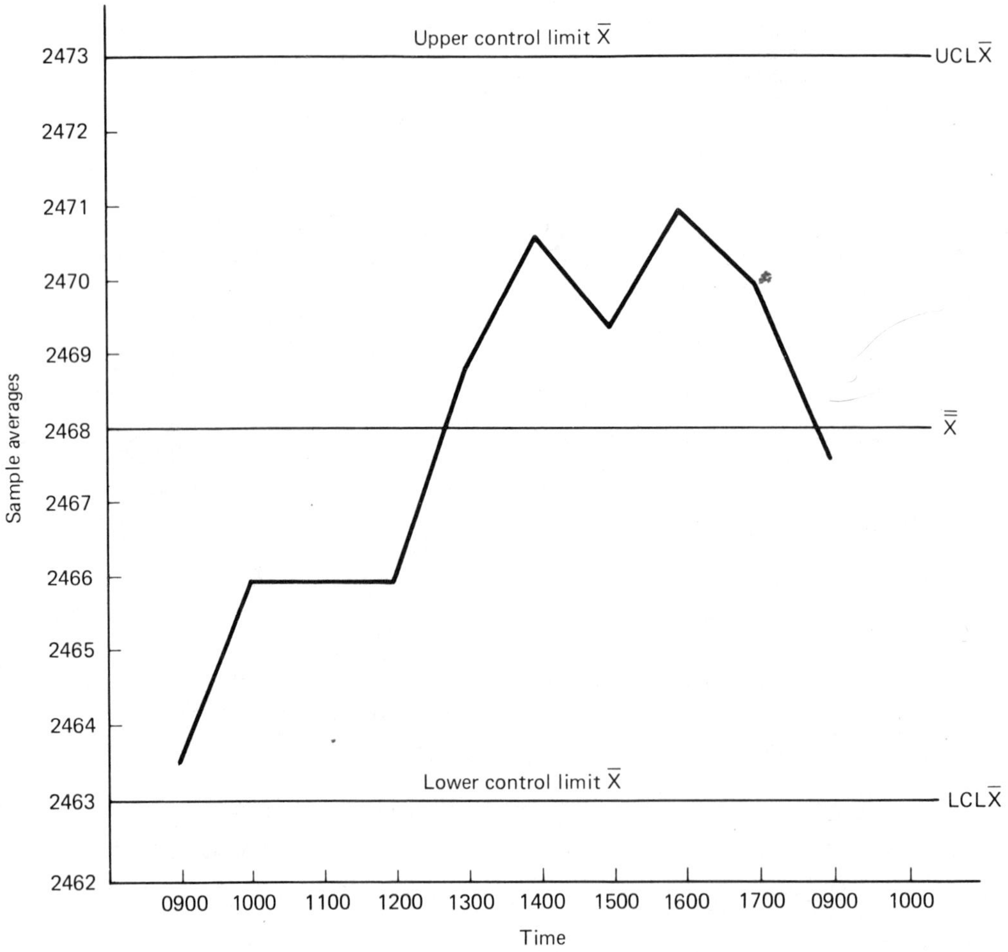

FIGURE 12–7. Control Chart for Averages.

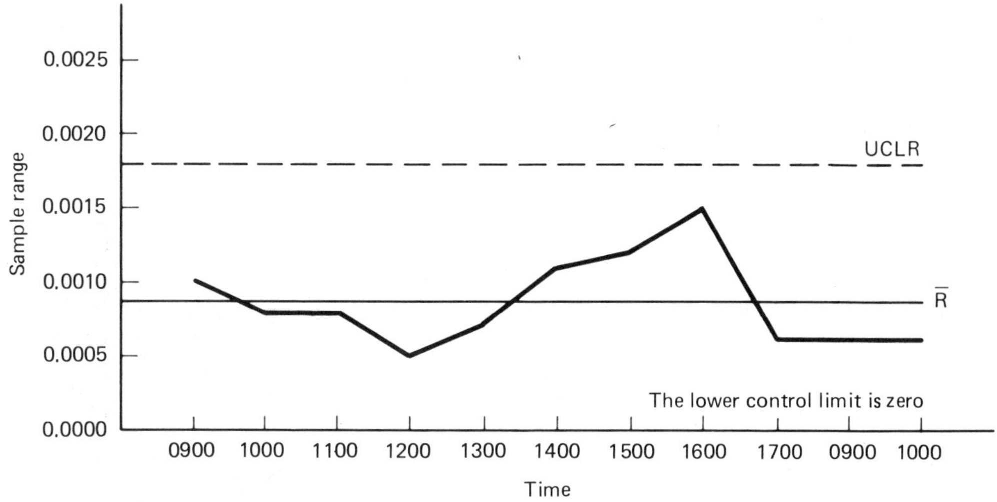

FIGURE 12–8. Control Chart for Range.

(UCLR), and lower control limit for range (LCLR) (if one exists). See Figure 12–8. Now, plot the sample ranges against time.

In Figures 12–7 and 12–8, control charts are constructed for sample averages and sample ranges, respectively. The central line is $\bar{X}$ = .24681. Control limits for averages are placed at .24631 and .24731. Since there are no points outside the control limits, the process appears to be in control. The upper control limit for sample ranges is .00184. The lower control limit for range is 00. Since there are no points outside the control limits, the process appears to be in control. Viewing the two charts together, we may tentatively conclude that the process is in a state of statistical quality control. However, there is some indication that trouble may be expected soon since there appears to be an upward trend, from left to right (order of production), in the same average.

When there are no points outside the control limits, we can be fairly sure that no assignable causes are operating. But we cannot be completely sure. We must, in fact, take a closer look at the chart. A process can be out of control; that is, assignable causes could be operating, even when no points are outside of the limits. This will happen in cases of extreme runs. When, for instance, seven successive points are on the same side of the central line, we should suspect that the process is out of control. We might hold the same suspicion in the case of other extreme runs, such as a case where 12 of 14 successive points are on the same side of the central line. When we see an extreme run approaching one of these, we should be ready for trouble.

When we see a point outside the control limits, we know, of course, that an assignable cause or causes are operating. Just knowing that the causes are operating is helpful. But we can find out even more information about the assignable causes operating from a careful study of the control chart. The chart will tell us, for instance, when the assignable causes first appeared. Knowing when a cause first appeared can help us speculate what the cause is and thereby help us detect the cause.

SPECIFICATIONS AND CONTROL LIMITS

Thus far, we have been concerned with determining whether a process is in statistical control. The problem we must now solve is whether a process that is in control meets specifications. It must be remembered that analysis of control limits only tells us whether or not the process is operating in a consistent manner. Specification limits, however, tell us what is wanted, and they refer to individual units of product. Specification limits are set by man, often arbitrarily. Control limits are based on averages; specifications are based on individual items.

It must be emphasized at the beginning that if the process is operating in a consistent manner, the chart should show a state of control. The plottings on the $\bar{X}$ and R charts should be within their control limits and randomly dispersed about the center lines. When this is true, we say the process is in control. This observation must be based on the $\bar{X}$ and R charts. If the process is meeting specifications, the control limits for the separate items must fall inside the specification limits. This observation must be based upon the comparison of the control limits for single items with the specification.

Control Limits for Single Items

When quality variations in individual items are the result of a constant system of chance causes, industrial experience indicates that such measurements often have a pattern of variation which can be approximated with sufficient accuracy by the normal curve. In a controlled process where single items follow a normal pattern, the average for single items $\bar{X}'$ and the standard deviation for single items σ' are usually estimated from data computed in connection with the control chart. Thus, $\bar{X}' = \bar{\bar{X}}$, and $\sigma' = \bar{R}/d_2$.

Experience shows that, as long as the process continues in a state of statistical control, approximately 68 percent of the item measurements will fall within standard deviation to the left of the average plus one standard deviation to the right of the average ($\bar{X} \pm 1\sigma'$) (Figure 12–9).

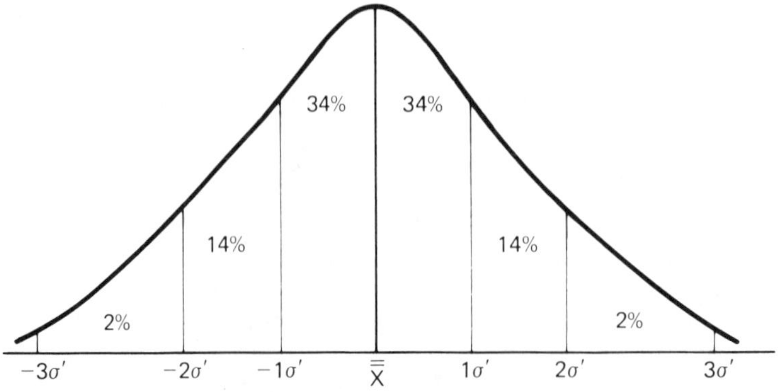

FIGURE 12–9. A Normal Distribution Showing Standard Deviations.

Approximately 96 percent of the items fall within ($\bar{\bar{X}} \pm 2\sigma'$) and approximately 100 percent, or all the items, fall within ($\bar{\bar{X}} \pm 3\sigma'$). For such a controlled process, it is customary to say that:

the upper control limit for items (UCLI) is $\bar{X}' + 3\sigma'$.

the lower control limit for items (LCLI) is $\bar{X}' - 3\sigma'$.

Since $\bar{X}' = \bar{\bar{X}}$ for a controlled process, the working formulas for the control limits are:

$$\text{UCLI} = \bar{\bar{X}} + 3\sigma'$$

$$\text{LCLI} = \bar{\bar{X}} - 3\sigma'$$

where $\sigma' = \bar{R}/d_2$.

Substituting for sigma prime (σ'), we get:

$$\text{UCLI} = \bar{\bar{X}} + \frac{3\bar{R}}{d_2}$$

$$\text{LCLI} = \bar{\bar{X}} - \frac{3\bar{R}}{d_2}$$

where $\bar{R}$ = average range, and d_2 = a factor based on sample size.

Sample size	d_2
2	1.128
3	1.693
4	2.059
5	2.326

Example: Given the average range = 7.58; $d_2 = 2.326$; and the grand average $\bar{\bar{X}}$ = 141.55; compute the upper and lower control limits for items.

$$\text{UCLI} = \bar{\bar{X}} + \frac{3\bar{R}}{d_2}$$

$$= 141.55 + \frac{3(7.58)}{2.326}$$

$$= 141.55 + 9.75$$

$$= 151.30$$

$$\text{LCLI} = \bar{\bar{X}} - \frac{3\bar{R}}{d_2}$$

$$= 141.55 - 9.75$$

$$= 131.80$$

Specification (Tolerance) Limits

Specification limits and tolerance limits are used interchangeably in this text. It is fundamental that the basis of all specification limits is the service need of the part or article being produced. When specifications are set, it is important to make certain that the process can turn out a product that meets specifications. It becomes necessary, therefore, to compare the process with specifications or tolerances.

Example: Consider the process with an average range of 7.58, $d_2 = 2.326$, $\bar{\bar{X}}$ = 141.55, and specification limits of 141.55 ± 3. The metric unit of measure for the product produced is the millimeter. The upper control limit for single items is 151.30. The lower control limit is 131.80. The questions to be answered are as follows: Are parts being produced that are above the upper specification? Are parts being produced that are below the lower specification? How does the process average compare with the middle of the specifications? How does the process spread compare with the allowable tolerance?

Specification	Process
Upper specification = 144.55	151.30 = Upper control limit for single items
Lower specification = 138.55	131.80 = Lower control limit for single items
Middle specification = 141.55	141.55 = Process average
Total tolerance = 6, i.e., ±3	19.50 = Process spread (UCLI − LCLI)

In an analysis of the above data, the values are compared horizontally. For instance, the upper specification limit, 144.55, is compared with the upper control limit single items, 151.30. This indicates the process is expected to produce parts that are above the upper specification and are therefore defective. The second row indicates that the process is expected to produce parts that are below the lower specification and are therefore defective. The third row shows the process average to be right on. The fourth row indicates that the process spread is greater than the allowable tolerance; thus, the process exhibits too much variation.

From our comparison, we have discovered that the process is producing defective parts. We are likely to ask, how bad is it? The answer to this question may be found by applying what we learned previously about the area under the normal curve:

$$X_u = T_u = \text{upper specification limit} = 144.55$$

$$\bar{X}' = \bar{\bar{X}} = 141.55$$

$$X_L = T_L = \text{lower specification limit} = 138.55$$

$$\sigma' = \text{standard deviation for items} = \frac{\bar{R}}{d_2} = \frac{7.58}{2.326} = 3.25$$

$$\frac{X_u - \bar{\bar{X}}}{\sigma'} = \frac{144.55 - 141.55}{3.25} = \frac{3.00}{3.25} = .92.$$

This represents the distance in standard deviation units that the upper specification limit is from the average. From Table 12–11, we see that .92 corresponds to 32.12 percent. By the same process, we find that the lower specification limit is 32.12 percent. These two numbers, when added together, equal 64.24 and represent the percentage of the area under the normal curve. This tells us that 64.24 percent of the items produced by the process will meet specifications.

For this process, the percentage of defective parts is 35.76. Whether this percentage of defective parts is important or not must be a decision made by production management and engineering design personnel. It is obvious from the comparison that although the process is in statistical control, some individual items do not meet specifi-

TABLE 12-11.
Percentage of Total Area under the Normal Curve

$\frac{X_u - \bar{\bar{X}}}{\sigma'}$	00	01	02	03
0.0	00.00	00.40	00.80	01.20
0.1	03.98	04.38	04.78	05.17
0.2	07.93	08.32	08.71	09.10
0.3	11.79	12.17	12.55	12.93
0.4	15.54	15.91	16.28	16.64
0.5	19.15	19.50	19.85	20.19
0.6	22.57	22.91	23.24	23.57
0.7	25.80	26.11	26.42	26.73
0.8	28.81	29.10	29.39	29.67
0.9	31.59	31.86	32.12	32.38
1.0	34.13	34.38	34.61	34.85
1.1	36.43	36.65	36.86	37.08
1.2	38.49	38.69	38.88	39.07
1.3	40.32	40.49	40.66	40.82
1.4	41.92	42.07	42.22	42.36
1.5	43.32	43.45	43.57	43.70

cations. This situation requires a decision by the appropriate person. One of three decisions may be made. It may be decided to make basic changes to bring the process in line with specifications, or to adjust the specifications limits to the existing level of control, or to sort out nonconforming units from all lots.

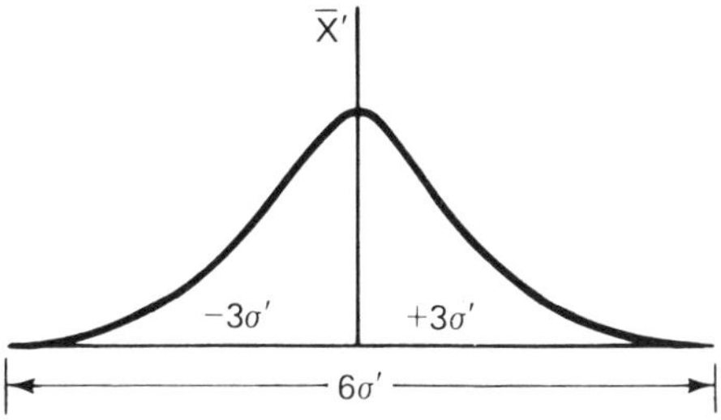

FIGURE 12–10. Three Standard Deviations Under a Normal Curve.

RULES FOR EVALUATION OF A CONTROL CHART

Process capability may be defined from control chart data when the process is in control. These process capability limits (natural tolerances) may be related in individual units of product, using the formulas:

1. Process capability = $\bar{\bar{X}} \pm 3\sigma'$.
2. Process capability =

$$\bar{\bar{X}} \pm \frac{3\bar{R}}{d_2} \text{ where } \sigma' = \frac{\bar{R}}{d_2}.$$

3. It is thus evident that the process capability range must be less than the specification range if the process is to produce good units of product at all times. This requires that: Process capability ≤ upper specification limit (T_u) minus lower specification limit (T_L) or

$$(6\frac{\bar{R}}{d_2} \leq T_u - T_L).$$

   Similarly, the process average must be satisfactorily located in the specification range, if finished units are to conform to the specification limits as well as control limits.

Rule 1: The average range, $\bar{R}$, must be equal to or less than $d_2/6$ (the upper tolerance limit T_u minus the lower tolerance limit T_L) if the product is to completely meet tolerances. Thus, even though the process is in control,

$$\bar{R} \leq \frac{d_2}{6}(T_u - T_L)$$

for a good control chart.

The basis for this rule is as follows: If σ' is the standard deviation of an approximately normal distribution, the individuals of the distribution will spread out a distance of $3\sigma'$ on either side of the population average ($\bar{X}'$); that is, the single items will vary between $\bar{X}' \pm 3\sigma'$. In other words, the single items will be found in a band centered at $\bar{X}'$ and $6\sigma'$ units wide. If the product is to meet specifications, it is necessary that the band not be wider than the tolerance or specification range (Figure 12–10); that is: $6\sigma'$ must not be greater than $T_u - T_L$. Since $\sigma' = \bar{R}/d_2$, then

$$6 \times \frac{R}{d_2} \leq (T_u - T_L) \text{ or } \bar{R} \leq \frac{d_2}{6}(T_u - T_L)$$

which is the formula given above.

Rule 2: Assuming the condition for Rule 1 is satisfied, then both control limits for X must be within the band obtained by measuring a distance $(3/d_2 - A_2)\,\bar{R}$ in from each specification limit. This means that ULC$\bar{X}$ cannot be closer to T_u than $(3/d_2 - A_2)\bar{R}$, and LCL$\bar{X}$ cannot be closer to T_L than

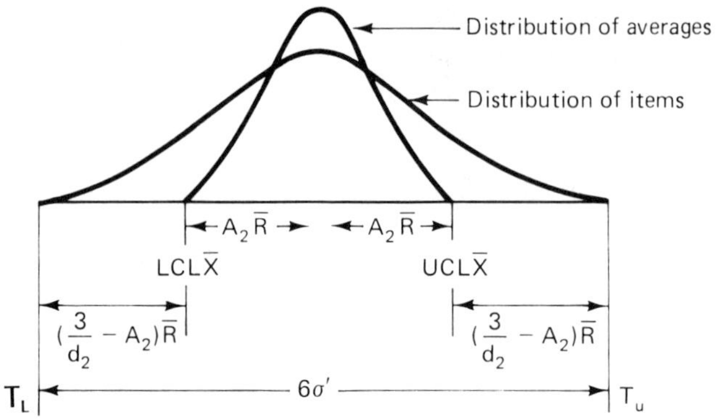

FIGURE 12–11. A Distribution of Averages and of Items.

$(3/d_2 + A_2)\bar{R}$, if the product is to meet specifications, as illustrated in Figure 12–11.

Individuals of an approximately normal population lie within $3\sigma'$ of the population average $\bar{X}$. Averages will then lie within $A_2\bar{R}$ of the grand average. From the diagram it is clear that UCL$\bar{X}$ must not be closer to a tolerance limit than $(3/d_2 + A_2)\bar{R}$. If a control limit is closer than $3/d_2 + A_2)\bar{R}$ to a tolerance limit, the product will not completely fall within the tolerances.

Features of Production That a Control Chart Is Designed To Control

There are three distinct features in the production of a component. Faults arising in these three different ways manifest themselves quite differently on the control chart and require different types of action.

Regularity or Consistency of Performance—Control. This is the first and most essential feature to be checked. It is mandatory that erratic behavior be eliminated. We must have some assurance that what is being done today can be done again tomorrow, and that our estimate of the quality of a product (good or poor) is a reliable estimate and one not likely to be upset by the introduction of assignable causes of variation, which can and ought to be tracked down and eliminated. Faults under this heading are shown up by the repeated presence of points outside their control limits, either on the chart for averages or for ranges, or both. The process of getting rid of these out-of-control points is the process of bringing about statistical control. This is quite independent of the tolerance or specification limits and is simply concerned with stabilizing the production at its natural level. Whether or not this natural level is good enough to meet the man-imposed specification is dealt with below.

Uniformity of Product—Dispersion, Variability. No machine, however good, can produce all components exactly alike even when all assignable causes of variation have been detected and removed; there will still remain a certain amount of variability owing to chance causes of variation. This natural and basic variability is measured by the average sample range, $\bar{R}$, after the process has been brought under control. If the product is to meet specifications, it is essential that the natural variability of the process should not exceed a certain value. In other words, there is a limit to the size of the average sample range, $\bar{R}$, if the product is to meet specifications. This limit is given in Rule 1 above as:

$$\bar{R} \leq \frac{d_2}{6} X(T_u - T_L).$$

Average Level of Production—Average of Process and Blueprint Average. Even though a process shows statistical control and $\bar{R}$ satisfies Rule 1, the control chart may still be poor because $\bar{\bar{X}}$ is too far away from the blueprint average. This is usually a matter of tool setting and is generally the easiest of the three types of fault to correct. Rule 2, concerning the position of the control limits on the chart $\bar{X}$, is a mixture of the features of process capability and $\bar{R}$, because we can see that Rule 2 may be broken either because $\bar{R}$ is too large, and $\bar{\bar{X}}$ is close to the blueprint average, or because $\bar{\bar{X}}$ is not close enough to the blueprint average and the size of $\bar{R}$ is satisfactory. It is for this reason that Rule 1 is put first, as the more essential, so that the fault of having too large an average range (or variability) can be quickly picked up and distinguished from mere setting troubles. When a control chart is running satisfactorily, with its limits in their correct positions, we see that the action to be taken in the event of a point falling outside a control limit is different according to whether the offending point is on the average $\bar{X}$ chart or range R chart. A drift of points toward a control limit on the $\bar{X}$ chart, or a point outside it, is an indication that the machine needs resetting. A point above the upper control limit on the range chart, however, is a matter requiring more fundamental attention to the machine or operation and cannot be corrected by resetting alone.

MODIFIED CONTROL LIMITS

It is a characteristic of many processes that the average level of a given quality characteristic cannot be maintained at a given point over any considerable period of time. This is frequently due to process changes that come with time, such as the wearing down of a cutting tool, or the gradual change in process temperatures with continued operation, and so on. In such situations, it is often the case that the process capability at a given instant of time is much closer than required by the specification limits. Thus, the process capability range may use only a small portion of the specification range. When working with such a process, the changes in level must be accepted as inevitable (at least for the time being), and modified control limits must be set so as to assure the maximum length of production runs, while still preventing the manufacture of defective product. This can usually best be done by setting the modified control limits a distance up from the lower specification limit and the same distance down from the upper specification limit. This distance is $(3/d_2 - A_2)\bar{R}$.

As long as the process operates within these modified control limits, the product turned out will meet specification limits, and the process need not be shut down. Table 12–12 gives the factors for such modified control limits as computed from $(3/d_2 - A_2)$ for various sample sizes:

1. Upper modified control limit = upper specification limit − control limit factor $\bar{R}$.
2. Lower modified control limit = lower specification limit + control limit factor $\bar{R}$.

Modified control limits are used when the process capability range is less than the specification range. This keeps you from unnecessarily resetting the machine or tool when you are still making a satisfactory product. When using modified limits, you must remember that only the average chart is modified and that the range chart must be maintained as is and must be constantly

TABLE 12-12.

Sample Size	Control Limit Factor $\frac{3}{d_2} - A_2$
2	0.78
3	0.75
4	0.73
5	0.71
6	0.70
7	0.69
8	0.68
9	0.67
10	0.66
11	0.66
12	0.65
13	0.65
14	0.64
15	0.64

checked. If by using Rule 1 you find that your process is far superior to what is needed, you should apply modified control limits. In certain cases, modified control limits apply to dimensions that must be held even more closely than by using the factors above. Frequently, these modified control limits are set by the formula

$$\left(\frac{3}{d_2} - \frac{2}{3A_2}\right) \bar{R},$$

reflecting the allowed variation in samples corresponding to 2σ limits.

Example: Given the following data for a process that is in statistical control, compute the modified control limits. $\bar{\bar{X}}$ = .24680; $\bar{R}$ = .00087; UCL$\bar{X}$ = .24730; LCL$\bar{X}$ = .24630.

Specification limits = .24680 ± .0020

Sample size = 5

UMCL = upper modified control limit

LMCL = lower modified control limit

T_u = upper specification limit = .24880

T_L = lower specification limit = .24480

$\left(\frac{3}{d_2} - A_2\right)$ = control limit factor = .71 (for sample size 5)

$\bar{R}$ = average range = .00087.

In symbols, the modified control limits are given by:

$$(1)\ \text{UMCL} = T_u - \left(\frac{3}{d_2} - A_2\right)\bar{R}$$

$$(2)\ \text{LMCL} = T_L + \left(\frac{3}{d_2} - A_2\right)\bar{R}$$

Hence:

$$\text{UMCL} = .24880 - .71\ (.00087) = .24880 - .0006 = .24820.$$

$$\text{LMCL} = .24480 + .71\ (.00087) = .24480 + .0006 = .24540.$$

Figure 12–12 gives a picture of the process, showing the upper and lower control limits for averages and the upper and lower modified control limits for averages. The specification limits are not shown. The upper and lower control limits may be computed using the following formulas:

$$(1)\ \text{UCL}\bar{X} = \bar{\bar{X}} + A_2\bar{R}.$$

$$(2)\ \text{LCL}\bar{X} = \bar{\bar{X}} - A_2\bar{R}.$$

Table 12–13 is used in estimating the standard deviation (σ'). An estimate of the standard deviation (σ') of a population may be obtained by multiplying the average sample range ($\bar{R}$) of a number of samples, each of n individuals, by the factor $1/d_2$ given below.

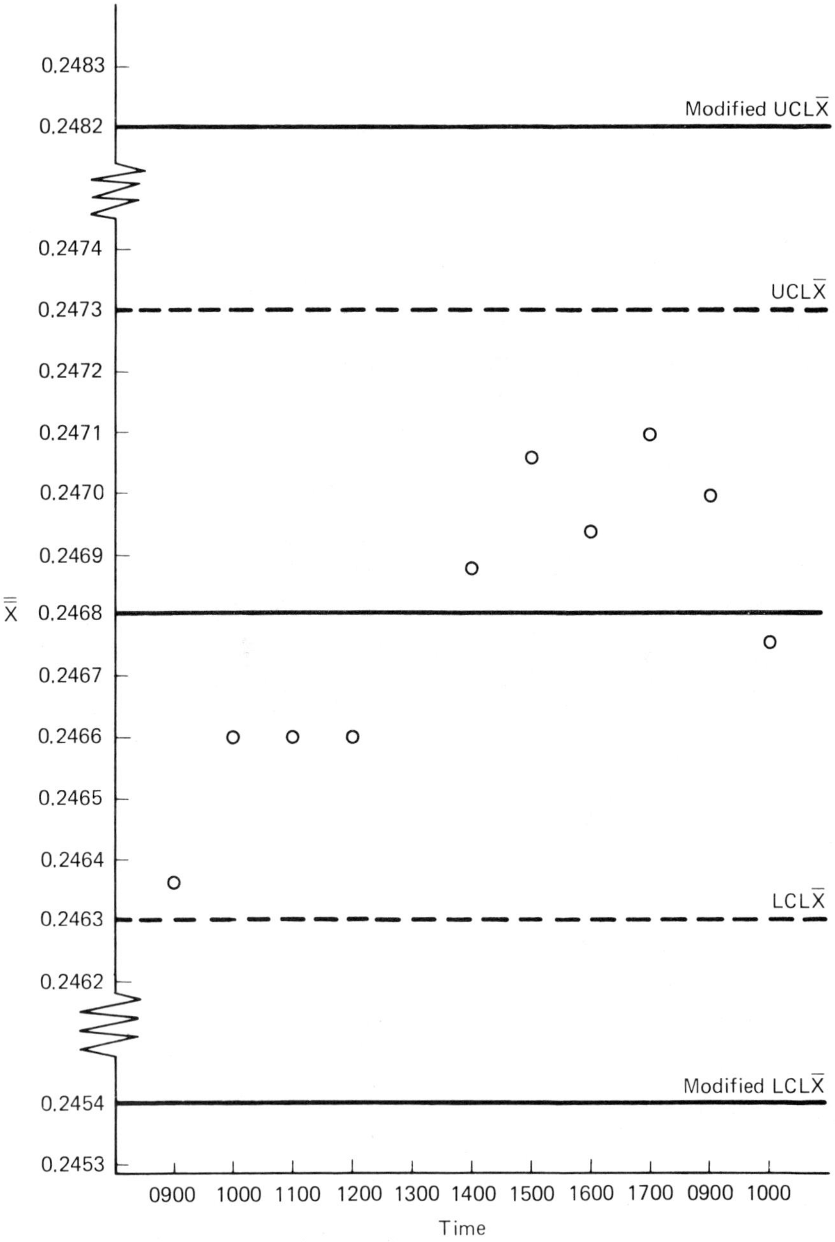

FIGURE 12–12. Control Limits and Modified Control Limits.

TABLE 12-13.
Estimating the Standard Deviation (σ)

No in Sample (n)	2	3	4	5	6	7	8	9	10
$\frac{1}{d_2}$ =	0.8862	0.5908	0.4857	0.4299	0.3946	0.3698	0.3512	0.3367	0.3249
d_2 =	1.128	1.693	2.059	2.326	2.534	2.704	2.847	2.970	3.078

$$\sigma' = \frac{\bar{R}}{d_2} = \bar{R} \times \frac{1}{d_2}.$$

Table 12–14 gives the factors for critical examination of a control chart. The average sample range, $\bar{R}$, over a period must never be greater than L times the drawing tolerance ($L = d_2/6$).

$$\bar{R} \leqslant L(T_u - T_L).$$

Both control limits for averages must lie between the lines drawn at

$$T_u - M\bar{R} \text{ and } T_1 + M\bar{R}. \quad M\bar{R} = (\bar{R} - A_2).$$

$$L = \frac{d_2}{6}. \; M = \frac{3}{d_2} A_2.$$

TABLE 12-14.
Factors for Critical Examination of a Control Chart

No in Sample	*L*	*M*
2	0.19	0.78
3	0.28	0.75
4	0.34	0.73
5	0.39	0.71
6	0.42	0.70
7	0.45	0.69
8	0.47	0.68
9	0.49	0.67
10	0.51	0.66

Table 12–15 is used to modify the central limits for sample. Draw modified limits on the average chart at $T_u - K\bar{R}$ and $T_1 + K\bar{R}$.

$$K = \frac{3}{d_2} - \frac{2}{d_2 \sqrt{n}}.$$

Table 12–16 gives A_2 and D_4 values for control limits for sample averages and ranges. Draw control limits on the average chart at $\bar{\bar{X}} \pm A_2 2\bar{R}$. Draw a control limit on the range chart at $D_4\bar{R}$.

$$A_2 = \frac{3}{d_2 \sqrt{n}}.$$

CONTROL CHARTS FOR ATTRIBUTES

Thus far, we have discussed the control charts used in process control. In this section, we are primarily concerned with the charts that are used mostly at the end of the production line but that can also be used to advantage to control the process. These charts are very often the first to be made and used when statistical quality control is instituted, because data of the attribute (inherent quality of item) type may be more readily available. Here, again, we will take figures from case histories instead of making an experiment in drawing samples ourselves. This is the phase of

TABLE 12-15.
Modified Control Limits for Sample

No in Sample	2	3	4	5	6	7	8	9	10
K =	1.41	1.09	0.97	0.91	0.86	0.83	0.81	0.79	0.77

Sample Size	*Control Limit Factor* $\frac{3}{d_2} - A_2$
2	0.78
3	0.75
4	0.73
5	0.71
6	0.70
7	0.69
8	0.68
9	0.67
10	0.66
11	0.66
12	0.65
13	0.65
14	0.64
15	0.64

statistical quality control that is concerned with judging whether the product is defective or not defective relative to a standard or specification requirement.

TABLE 12-16.
Control Limits for Sample Averages and Ranges

No in Sample	A_2	D_4
2	1.88	3.27
3	1.02	2.57
4	0.73	2.28
5	0.58	2.11
6	0.48	2.00
7	0.42	1.92
8	0.37	1.86
9	0.34	1.82
10	0.31	1.78

INSPECTION BY ATTRIBUTES

When a record shows only the number of articles conforming and the number of articles failing to conform to any specified requirements, it is said to be a record by attributes.

Our preceding discussion of control charts covered their application to measured values of a quality characteristic; this section will deal with inspection data from classification of units as good or bad, as an "attribute." For example, the item inspected conforms or does not conform to a given standard (visual or otherwise), passes or fails, a go/no-go gauge application.

The results of such attribute inspections may be effectively used for the analysis of control. The quality of the process or product may be judged in terms of failure to meet the required standard called *defects* or *defectives*. Such analysis can be used in connection with results of acceptance inspection of sublots by the inspector. The primary value, however, concerns manufacturing operations in the shop or on the assembly line.

All control charts provide a graphical record of quality in that they plot the results of each inspection performed on a single quality characteristic or group of characteristics. Attributes control charts record values of quality as fraction or percent defective (p), or number defective (pn), or number of defects per unit (c). The abscissa scale is divided according to order: time, subgroup, lot, and so on.

The control limits on the chart are of assistance in judging the significance of variations in quality of the product in terms of its fraction defective, number defective, or defects per unit. As for measurements charts, such limits are so placed that a plotted point falling outside them during production may be taken as an indication of a cause of variation that is worth identifying.

The common control charts for attributes are:

(1) Chart for fraction defective . . chart for p.
(2) Chart for number defective . chart for pn.
(3) Chart for number of defects per unit (or per 100 units) . . . chart for c.

CONTROL CHARTS FOR FRACTION OR PERCENTAGE DEFECTIVE

Listed below are important details about control charts:

1. The p type charts must always be used for inspection of critical defects.
2. In any one inspection process, p and pn charts are never both used—only one or the other is used.
3. Normally, it is incorrect to average the values of p when the subgroup size is not constant. When the number of pieces (size of subgroup) inspected during a period or per day is not constant, it is somewhat time-consuming and involves considerable work to compute the periodic or daily control limits. Therefore, when the size of the subgroup is not more than 10 percent away from the average daily production, it is permissible to establish a single set of control limits based on an expected average period or daily production.
4. We do not permit negative values for control limits; so, if the value for LCLp is negative, it is plotted as zero. In our formula, n will, in many cases, equal the average daily production.
5. When we compute new control limits for the fraction defective by using the previous week's data, isolated instances of out-of-control averages are not considered—they are subtracted from both the total production and the number of days.

Fraction defective (p) is defined as the ratio of the number of defective items found in any particular inspection (or series of inspections) to the total number of items actually inspected. Percentage defective (100 p) is merely 100 times the fraction defective. For charting and for general presentation, the fraction defective is generally converted to percentage defective.

Consider the case of a producer's 100 percent inspection for a serious defect or group of defects where daily production is 500 items; $n = 500$. The result of inspection for the first day is 50 defectives; $c = 50$. We, therefore, may calculate the fraction defective:

$$P_1 = \frac{50}{500} = .10$$

For percentage defective, we have $100p_1 = 100(.10) = 10.0\%$.

Although this result represents the actual observed quality of production for this day, any 100 percent inspection may be considered a sample of an infinite, or very large, population of probable production. The results of such a sample are, therefore, affected by a multitude of chance causes of variation.

The result of inspection for the second day is 70 defectives; $c = 70$. We calculate, as before, the fraction defective: $P_2 = 70/500 = .14$ or 14.0 percent defective. A comparison of the results of inspection for the first and second days might bring forth some reaction from the plant supervision and the production foreman. Supervision's opinion may be that production the second day is worse than the first day. On the other hand, the foreman may shrug it off as just a bad day or, in reasoning from some known events of the second day, blame such a result on a change in personnel, use of different raw material, change of tools, and so on. In order that we may study the results of such a daily 100 percent inspection, let us tabulate the results in a convenient form as shown in Table 12–17. These daily percentage defective results are plotted on the control chart with proper sequence as to time.

There may be many possible reasons advanced for such daily shifts in quality. However, just as two manufactured items can never be produced exactly alike in all respects, so production from day to day cannot be expected to be identified in fraction defective. Whatever the reasons for such differences in results, explainable or unexplainable, they are the sources of variation in the process. It is important at the outset of any attempt to improve or control the quality of a process that all of the known assignable causes of variation be removed or corrected where this is practicable.

To summarize our results for the week, we find the total number inspected is 2,500, $n = 2{,}500$; and the total number defective is 250, $c = 250$. Computing, as before, $\bar{p} = 250/2{,}500 = .10$. Note that we use the symbol $\bar{p}$ to express the "average fraction defective." Likewise, $100\,\bar{p} = 10.0$ percent, the "average percent defective."

Referring to the daily results, we may now say that the average daily fraction defective over this period has been .10. We now draw a line on our chart at the value .10 to represent the value $\bar{p}$ (Figure 12–13). Such a calculated value of $\bar{p}$ is often referred to as the process average or quality level.

If the sources of variation that affect the production process are considered to be inherent in the process, that is, chance variation, a logical question may now be asked. Has there been any significant day-to-day change in quality? The answer to

TABLE 12-17.
Fraction or Percent Defective

Date	*Number Inspected* *n*	*Number of Defectives* *c*	*Fraction Defective* *p*	*Percent Defective* *100 p*
Oct 10	500	50	0.10	10.0
11	500	70	0.14	14.0
12	500	40	0.08	8.0
13	500	60	0.12	12.0
14	500	30	0.06	6.0
	2,500	250		

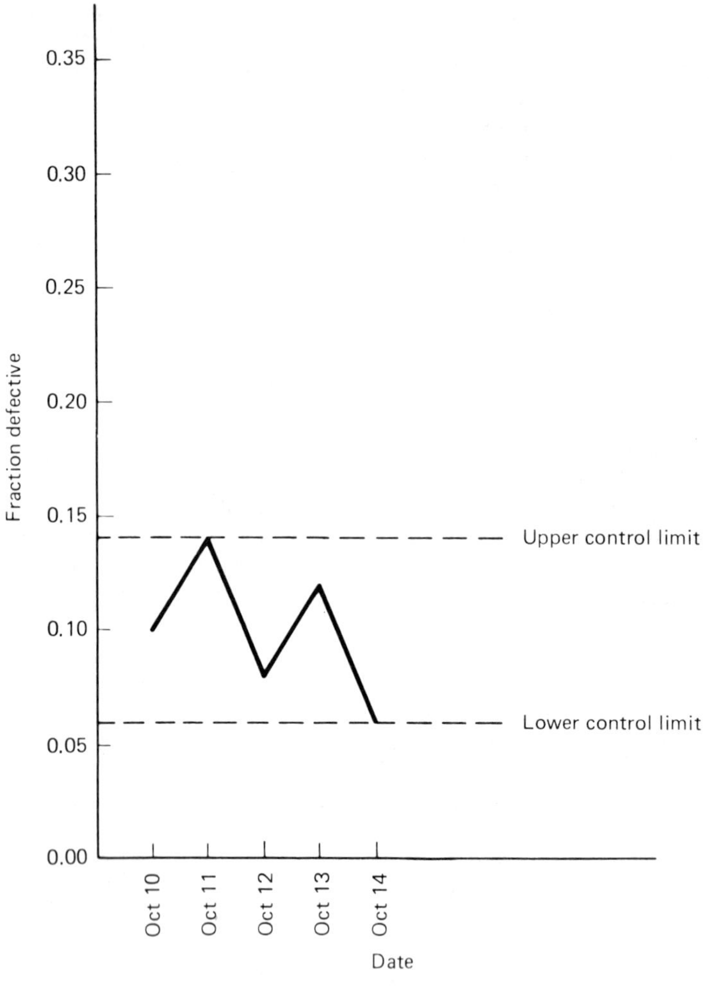

FIGURE 12–13. Control Chart for Fraction Defective.

this important question is provided by the techniques of statistical quality control. The procedures are based on sound mathematical theory, which removes the guesswork of subjective reasoning. The statistical reasoning involved in answering this question goes like this: If the probability of obtaining a fraction defective a given amount greater or less than the expected average fraction defective, $\bar{p}$, is sufficiently rare, than we shall conclude that a significant change has occurred in the process.

By the use of the point binomial formula, we can obtain a very good approximation of the probability of the occurrence of any number of defectives in a given sample selected from a population of known fraction defective. However, the calculation of exact probabilities is burdensome and is seldom needed in control chart application.

Assuming any given probability of occurrence of defectives, we can express it as so many standard deviations from the value of $\bar{p}$. The formula for standard deviation of the binomial for percent defective is:

$$\sigma_p = \sqrt{\frac{\bar{p}(1-\bar{p})}{n}}.$$

If we are willing to adopt the rule that we shall consider a change in fraction defective to be significant if it would occur only 1 time in approximately 370 by chance alone, we would then use the well-known 3 sigma limits.

To calculate the limits within which daily fraction defective values may be expected to fall by chance alone (unassignable causes), we shall use the formulas:

$$\text{UCL}p = \bar{p} + 3\sqrt{\frac{\bar{p}(1-\bar{p})}{n}}$$

$$\text{LCL}p = \bar{p} - 3\sqrt{\frac{\bar{p}(1-\bar{p})}{n}}.$$

In this problem, $n = 500$, and we have found $\bar{p} = .10$. Substituting these values in the formulas above we obtain:

$$\text{UCL}p = .10 + 3\sqrt{\frac{(.10)(.90)}{500}}$$

$$= .100 + .040 = .140$$

$$\text{LCL}p = .10 - 3\sqrt{\frac{(.10)(.90)}{500}}$$

$$= .100 - .040 = .060.$$

In terms of percent defective, the formula for the control limits becomes

$$\bar{p}\,\% \pm 3\sqrt{\frac{\bar{p}\%\,(100-\bar{p}\%)}{n}}\ \%.$$

By placing the calculated limits on the chart (see Figure 12–13), we have now created a control chart that can be used to advantage in analyzing the condition of the process. On the basis of the 3 sigma control limits, our hypothesis is that no fraction defective shall be considered unusually large, unless it is greater than $\bar{p} + 3\sigma_p$ or considered unusually small unless lower than $\bar{p} - 3\sigma_p$. None of the daily fraction defective values obtained was outside these control limits. Thus, the changes in fraction defective that did occur may be considered due to chance causes of variation. From the quality control point of view, we say that the process exhibits a state of control. We have calculated limits on the basis of only five values for the purpose of illustration; ordinarily, in practice we would not do so until at least 20 or 25 individual values have been obtained.

In the control chart, it will be noted that on the second and fifth days the fraction defective is at the upper (UCLp) and lower (LCLp) limits, respectively. Additional daily inspection results might very well show the process to be out of control.

The question of where to set control limits depends on what risks we are willing to take looking for trouble when it does not exist, and not looking for trouble when it does exist. Generally, the 3-sigma limits are used as a basis for positive action. Using the 3-sigma limits as our criterion for control, we now continue our limit lines on the chart for another period, say one week, and if all of the daily fraction defective values fall within the control limits, we can make use of this added information to recalculate the process average fraction defective ($\bar{p}$), recalculate the limits, and project them on the chart for the next period of production. In projecting limits ahead, we are assuming the p value to be our standard average fraction defective. Such a standard value is given the symbol p'.

The standard average fraction defective (p') adopted may be a continuously adjusted value based on accumulated data, or it may be an assumed or desired standard. If it is an assumed value, the effect of the limits based thereon will be to attempt to bring the process within control at a desired quality level. However, to do this may require major changes in the process. For any standard really to be accepted by production personnel as a basis for action, there needs to be evidence that the standard is attainable.

To return to our illustration, suppose that, during the second week, a daily fraction defective value of .15 were to be obtained. Should this value, which exceeds our upper control limit of .14, be used in the recalculation of the average fraction defective $\bar{p}$? It must be remembered that when a single fraction defective value falls outside of the 3 sigma control limits, there is small chance of obtaining such a value when the level of quality actually has not changed. However, unless a reason is found for this out-of-control value of p, we should use the value .15 in the subsequent recalculations of $\bar{p}$ and the new control limits. If, however, a value appreciably beyond the limits is obtained (say .25 in our illustration), it may be safely considered that this is due to some unidentified cause, and we would disregard the value for purposes of recomputing $\bar{p}$.

If a control chart indicates that the process is not in control, as shown by a fair proportion of values beyond the calculated control limits, then such control limits should not be used in the plant. For control limits to be respected, there needs to be evidence that it is possible to stay within the control limits most of the time. Until such evidence exists, the drawing of control limits on a chart can be of little help and may hurt the control chart program by creating a state of mind antagonistic to control limits.

Interpretation or Lack of Control

Individual points beyond control limits are evidence of assignable causes of variation.

1. Definite shifts of average fraction defective, either better or worse, will almost invariably occur if the p chart is used over any considerable length of time. Such shifts in level are often evident merely from inspection of the control chart.
2. Slight shifts in level of quality *may* be detected by observation of extreme runs above or below the p value, as well as points out of control.
3. If a shift in level is suspected, any group of consecutive results may be combined to calculate a new $\bar{p}$. With n equal to the number inspected in the new set of results and p' equal to the original standard average fraction defective, compute the upper or lower control limits, depending on the direction of the suspected shift of level, and compare these computed limit values with the new $\bar{p}$ to detect any assignable shift.

Calculation of Control Limits When Sample Size Is Variable

In the illustration discussed above, the sample size was constant, $n = 500$.

1. More often in practice, however, it is impossible to maintain a constant sample size. If control charts are being kept on the results of 100 percent inspection of daily or weekly production, such production is almost certain to vary. Furthermore, the size of samples from lots of varying size will also differ. Because chance sampling fluctuations decrease as sample size increases, it is necessary to calculate new control limits for each point on the chart if the sample size is not constant. Limits are closer together for large samples than for small ones.
2. Where the sample size does not vary too much, the average sample size may

be used as a constant size. If a sample p value falls near the control limit, whether inside or outside of limits, the actual control limits for that particular value should be computed to determine whether or not the value is really in or out of control.

3. Another possible procedure is to use three sets of limits, one for the expected average sample size, one close to the expected minimum, and one close to the expected maximum. This scheme is not satisfactory unless the data are shown on the same sheet with the control chart, with the figures for each sample on the same line with the plotted point for the sample, so that the sample size may be seen at a glance.

Charts for Number Defective

If the sample size is constant, a number defective (pn) chart may be more convenient to use than a fraction defective (p) chart.

The central line $\overline{pn}$ is equal to the average fraction defective times the number of items inspected in the sample and represents the expected number of defectives to be found in a sample of size n.

The formulas for the control limits are:

$$\text{UCL}pn = \bar{p}n + 3\sqrt{n\bar{p}(1-\bar{p})}$$
$$\text{LCL}pn = \bar{p}n - 3\sqrt{n\bar{p}(1-\bar{p})}.$$

These limits determine the maximum and minimum number of defectives that might be found in any sample size n as a result of chance sampling variation alone, if the process is controlled at an average quality level of $\bar{p}\,n$.

Fraction defective charts can be converted to number defective merely by altering the scale and multiplying the central line value and the control limits by n.

CONTROL CHARTS FOR DEFECTS

Although somewhat more limited in use than fraction defective or number defective control charts, there are charts in terms of number of defects, called c charts. These charts are particularly valuable in cases where we cannot fix a definite sample size n.

In many different kinds of manufactured articles, the opportunities for defects are numerous, even though the chance of a defect occurring in any one spot is small. Whenever this is true, it is correct to base control limits on the assumption that the Poisson distribution is applicable. The limits on the control chart for defects are based on this assumption. A Poisson chart is illustrated in Figure 12–14.

Small c has two meanings, and we should clearly understand both meanings so that we can use each one correctly.

1. We first define c as the number of defects in a sample of stated size.
2. We also use c to represent the acceptance number in acceptance sampling schemes. This is discussed later.

The Poisson distribution, or Poisson law, is the basis for charts on the number of defects. An entire book could be written on it and its use by mathematical statisticians and engineers in industry.

The Poisson form of distribution represents a family of curves, the shape of each depending on the average value or the single parameter, pn, or the distribution. This law can be applied to quality control only when (1) the probability of an event happening is very small, less than about 1 in 10, and (2) the sample size compared with the total distribution or lot size is less than 10 percent.

The standard deviation of the Poisson distribution is simply the square root of the

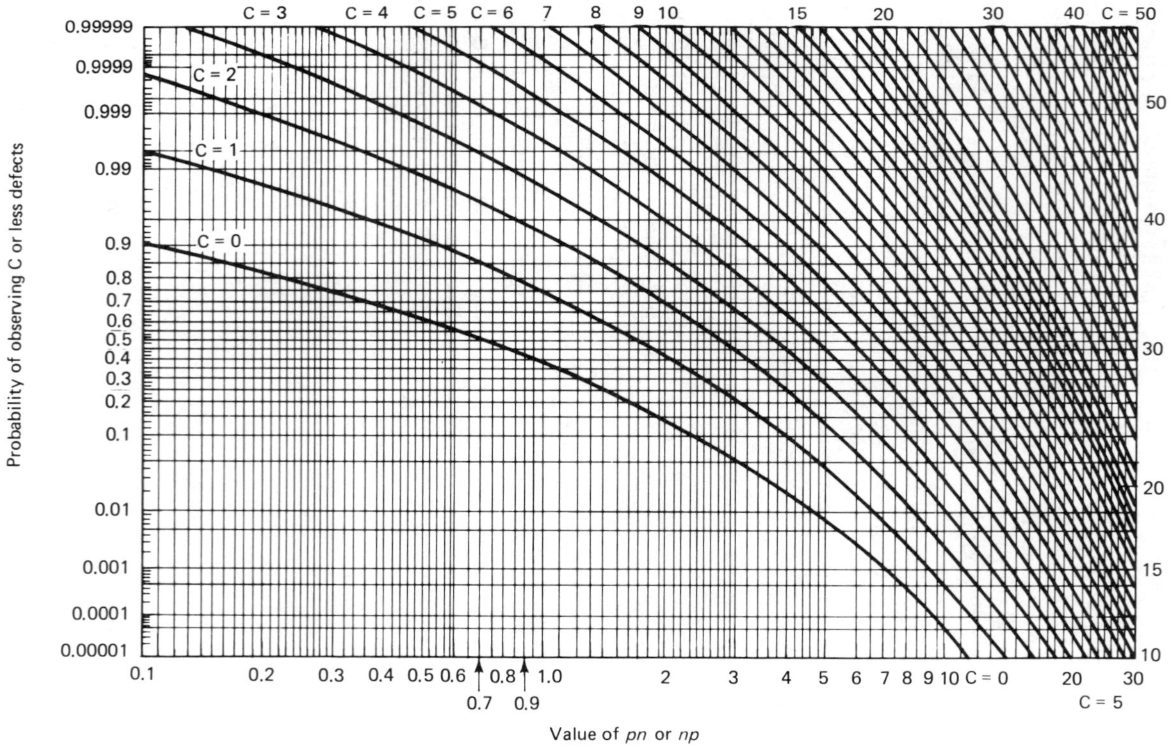

Curves for determining probability of observing *c* or fewer defects in a sample of *n* articles selected from product in which the fraction defective is *p*. Curves apply when *p* is 0.10 or less, 2% is <.

FIGURE 12–14. Poisson Chart.

expected number of occurrences. This makes the computation of control limits very easy. It is important to remember that the Poisson distribution is skewed and that, when 3σ limits are used, equal probability levels of significance are not represented by the upper and lower levels. Also, the larger the value of n and the smaller the value of p, the more accurate will be the Poisson approximation.

In inspection for defects, it is important that the unit size be reasonably constant, whether it be an item, a length, an area, and so on. However, slight variations up to ± 5 percent may be allowed. Some representative types of defects to which c charts may be applied are as follows:

1. The number of defects found in final inspection of an electrical appliance.
2. The number of defects in a plated or painted surface of a given area.
3. The number of insulation breakdowns in voltage tests of wire or cable.
4. The number of imperfections in a plastic sheet.
5. The number of defects observed in inspection of a roll of paper.

To compute control limits, we again make use of the standard deviation. The standard deviation of the Poisson distribution is $\sqrt{\bar{c}}$. Because the Poisson is not a symmetrical distribution, the upper and lower 3-sigma limits do not correspond exactly to equal probabilities of a point on the control chart falling outside limits even though there has been no change in the process. For practical use, however, 3-sigma limits are satisfactory. The formulas for control limits are:

$$\text{UCL}c = \bar{c} + 3\sqrt{\bar{c}}$$

$$\text{LCL}c = \bar{c} - 3\sqrt{\bar{c}}.$$

Sampling Inspection

Sampling inspection may be defined as the process of measuring, examining, testing, or otherwise comparing the unit of product with the requirements. Inspection by attributes is inspection whereby either the unit of product is classified simply as defective or nondefective, or the number of defects in the unit of product is counted, with respect to a given requirement or set of requirements.

The unit of product is the thing inspected in order to determine its classification as defective or nondefective, or to count the number of defects. It may be a single article, a pair, a set, a length, an area, an operation, a volume, a component of an end product, or the end product itself. The unit of product may or may not be the same as the unit of purchase, production, or shipment.

When some of the product submitted for inspection does not conform to specifications, even 100 percent inspection will seldom eliminate all of the deficiencies. The best protection against the acceptance of a defective product is having the product made right in the first place. The greatest contribution that statistical quality control makes to better quality lies not in what it contributes to sampling inspection but in the way it helps produce a better product.

Nevertheless, acceptance inspection of raw materials, manufactured parts, and final product is a necessary part of manufacturing. It is often necessary, or at least economical, to conduct this inspection on a sampling basis. In fact, sampling inspection also has a psychological advantage over 100 percent inspection.

Any plan of sampling inspection implies a willingness to take a chance on accepting some nonconforming product. Although this hazard is always present in every sampling procedure, the chance may not consciously be faced by those who specify the sampling schemes. The statistical approach to acceptance procedures faces the fact that some defective items may be passed by any sampling plan. It attempts to evaluate the risk assumed with alternative sampling inspection procedures and to make a decision as to the degree of protection needed in any instance. It is then possible to choose a sampling acceptance plan that gives a desired degree of protection with a minimum total amount of inspection.

Need for Sampling

When sampling inspection for acceptance purposes is carried out without the benefit of formal rules regarding size and frequency of sample, the inspector often uses an informal rule. This is not good from a statistical standpoint. This informal rule permits his current decisions on acceptance to be influenced by the knowledge of the past quality history of the product being sampled. Although the same item may be produced by different firms to be submitted for the same inspection, the inspector might check only a few items from a firm that he considers reliable, and he may critically examine many pieces from another firm because he considers it an unreliable source. There are several drawbacks to this practice. An inspector's memory of the past quality history is sometimes inaccurate. He may transfer to another job or die. Sometimes the inspector's confidence in a certain product may disarm him to the extent that he will become lax. These limitations indicate the need for a definite system regarding sample size and frequency of sampling, as well as a basis for acceptance and rejection. Here again, definite systems many times favor the product in cycles and give us a false promise of quality.

Straight percentage plans of sampling are very poor, statistically. This is due to the fact that precision in estimating quality of the lot sampled. This lesson deals with some of the methods and types of acceptance sampling programs.

Types of Defects Encountered in an Inspection

Before an inspector can fulfill his duties, he must be aware of the various types of defects. This will permit a smooth production operation and allow for the most thorough inspection in a minimum of time.

A classification of defects is the enumeration of possible defects of the unit of product classified according to their seriousness. A defect is any nonconformance of the unit of product with specified requirements. Defects will normally be grouped into one or more of the following classes; however, defects may be grouped into other classes or into subclasses within these classes:

1. *Critical defect.* A critical defect is one that judgment and experience indicate is likely to result in hazardous or unsafe conditions for individuals using, maintaining, or depending upon the product or defect that judgment and experience indicate is likely to prevent satisfactory performance of the function of a major end item, such as an aircraft, automobile or electrical apparatus.
2. *Major defect.* A major defect is one, other than critical, that is likely to result in failure, or to reduce materially the usability of the unit of product for its intended purpose.
3. *Minor defect.* A minor defect is one that is not likely to reduce materially the usability of the unit of product for its intended purpose, or is a departure from established standards having little

bearing on the effective use or operation of the item.

Types of Defectives

A defective is a unit of product that contains one or more defects. Defectives will usually be classified as follows:

1. *Critical defective.* A critical defective contains one or more critical defects and may also contain major and/or minor defects.
2. *Major defective.* A major defective contains one or more major defects and may also contain minor defects but contains no critical defect.
3. *Minor defective.* A minor defective contains one or more minor defects but contains no critical or major defect.

OBJECTIVES IN ACCEPTANCE SAMPLING INSPECTION

After a number of units of a product are contracted for by the purchaser, the producer makes these units subject to specifications and submits them to the purchaser for acceptance. It is likely that some of the units submitted are defective, although how many and which ones are defective are not known. The purchaser is faced with the problem of deciding which units to accept and which to reject. A perfect acceptance program would enable the purchaser to accept all nondefective units and to reject all defective ones; such a program would encourage and assist the producer to improve the quality of his product; the program would be easy to administer and economical in cost. This ideal will seldom, if ever, be achieved in practice. It does serve to illustrate, however, the objectives in terms of which any acceptance program should be judged.

The objective of acceptance inspection is twofold. First, the acceptance inspection must assure that each producer establishes and maintains a production process (including the manufacturer's inspection), which normally will present for acceptance material of satisfactory quality. Second, it must afford adequate assurance against the acceptance of any definitely inferior sublots of material that may be presented.

Sampling inspection is widely applicable as a method for determining the quality and acceptability of a product. It is almost always possible to use sampling inspection for this purpose; if inspection is destructive or costly, sampling inspection may be the only feasible method. The four principal uses of sampling inspection in industry are:

1. To determine the quality and acceptability of incoming raw materials, the incoming semifinished product, and incoming finished product.
2. To determine the acceptability for further processing within the plant of semifinished product made in the plant.
3. To determine the quality and acceptability of the outgoing product.
4. To improve and control the quality of product.

SAMPLING PLAN AND TYPES OF SAMPLING

A sampling plan indicates the number of units of a product from each lot or batch that are to be inspected (sample size or series of sample sizes) and the criteria for determining the acceptability of the lot or batch (acceptance and rejection numbers). Examples of single, double, and multiple sampling (selected from MIL-STD-105D, "Acceptance Sampling Inspection by Attributes" for AQL = 2.5 percent on Inspection Level II) are shown in Table 12–18.

TABLE 12-18.
Examples of Lot-by-lot Sampling Inspection Plans

Inspection Lot Size: 3,400

Type of Sampling	*Sample Size*	*Acceptance Number*	*Rejection Number*
Single	225	11	12

Inspection Lot Size: 3,400

Type of Sampling	*Sample*	*Sample Size*	*Combined Samples*		
			Size	*Acceptance Number*	*Rejection Number*
Double	First	150	150	7	19
	Second	300	450	18	19

Inspection Lot Size: 3,400

Type of Sampling	*Sample*	*Sample Size*	*Combined Samples*		
			Size	*Acceptance Number*	*Rejection Number*
Multiple	First	50	50	0	5
	Second	50	100	3	8
	Third	50	150	5	11
	Fourth	50	200	8	13
	Fifth	50	250	10	15
	Sixth	50	300	13	18
	Seventh	50	350	15	20
	Eighth	50	400	19	20

Single Sampling

A procedure in which one sample is inspected before a decision is reached regarding the disposition of the sublot or inspection lot. Inspection lots of 3,400 items are formed and, from each inspection lot, the inspector draws a sample of 225 items. Each of the 225 items is subjected to a quality test. If 11 or fewer items fail the test, the inspection lot is accepted; if 12 or more items fail the test, the inspection lot is rejected. The acceptance or rejection of the inspection lot depends on the number of defective items in the single sample. Such a single-sampling plan is completely described by its inspection lot size, sample size, acceptance number, and rejection number. In the above example, the inspection lot size is 3,400, the sample size is 225, the acceptance number is 11, and the rejection number is 12. In single-sampling plans, the acceptance number is always one less than the rejection number; thus, a definite decision on the inspection lot is always reached by the time all items in the sample have been inspected.

Double Sampling

A procedure in which a second sample is inspected if the results obtained from the first sample are inconclusive. For example, inspection lots of 3,400 items are formed and the inspector draws a first sample of 150 items and inspects each of them. If the first sample contains 7 or fewer defective items, the inspection lot is accepted; if it contains 19 or more defective items, the inspection lot is rejected, no decision is reached, and the inspector draws a second sample of 300 items. If the total of 450 items inspected in both samples contains 18 or fewer defective items, the inspection lot is accepted; if it contains 19 or more, the inspection lot is rejected. The acceptance and rejection numbers for the first sample in double sampling lead to three possibilities, rather than two as in single sampling. The inspection lot may be rejected, it may be accepted, or the decision may be deferred until evidence from a second sample is gathered. If the inspection lot is neither accepted nor rejected on the basis of the evidence of the first sample, it is sure to be accepted or rejected after the second sample has been inspected, since in double sampling, the second acceptance number is always one less than the second rejection number.

Multiple Sampling

A multiple sampling plan is a grouped and truncated sequential sampling plan.

Some of the terms used in the above definition also need defining. Sequential analysis applies strictly when one item is inspected at a time; a decision to accept the inspection lot, reject the inspection lot, or continue inspection is made after every item; and no definite upper limit is set on the number of items inspected. Item-by-item sequential plans do not, however, seem desirable or feasible for a large-scale inspection program. It is preferable to use a grouped sequential; that is, a multiple sampling plan in which a group of items is selected at random and inspected. On the basis of the results for this group, the inspection lot is accepted or rejected, or an additional group of items is selected and inspected, and so forth. Also, it is preferable to truncate the sequential plan, that is, to set a definite upper limit on the number of items inspected.

In the example in Table 12–18 the inspector selects from an inspection lot of 3,400 items a first sample of 50 items and inspects each of them. If the first sample contains no defective items, the inspection lot is accepted then and there. If it contains 5 or more defective items, the inspection lot is rejected then and there. If it contains 1, 2, 3, or 4 defective items, no decision is reached, and the inspector draws a second sample of 50 items and inspects each of them. If the total number of defective items in the 100 items examined is 3 or fewer, the inspection lot is now accepted; if the total number of defective items is 8 or more, the inspection lot is now rejected; if the total number of defective items is more than 3 but less than 8, he takes a third sample of 50 items; and so on. This process is continued until a decision is reached, which will be after the eighth sample at the latest, since, for the eighth sample, the acceptance number is one less than the rejection number.

The single, double, and multiple sampling plans shown in Table 12–18 provide similar protection against accepting inferior products. Or, more exactly, they have similar operating characteristic curves.

MIL-STD-105D

Both the old standard sampling inspection plan and the new MIL-STD-105D were developed to provide military/defense inspectors with a method of acceptance inspection that will be uniform throughout the country, will provide assurance that material accepted is actually satisfactory to the Department of Defense, and will provide this assurance with a minimum of inspection effort. These plans are based on a clear recognition of the relative responsibilities of the contractor, as producer, and the government, as consumer, with respect to quality.

TYPES OF ACCEPTANCE PROGRAMS

A method of procuring high-quality product is to purchase only from suppliers who have in the past consistently supplied high-quality products. Clearly, this does not constitute a complete acceptance program in itself. There are almost as many methods of acceptance inspection as there are inspection problems. In examining the methods used at one time or another for the go/no-go types of defects, it has been found that only three types have seen extensive use: 100 percent screening inspection, lot-by-lot inspection, and spot-check inspection.

Screening

It is sometimes necessary to inspect each submitted item of a product, and to reject all defective items. This type of inspection is required for critical defects whenever there is the slightest danger that such defects may occur. Such 100 percent inspection accompanied by rejection of all defective items is called screening. Screening is the only program that could possibly guarantee the rejection of all defective items and only defective items. Furthermore, such perfection can be approached only if suitable automatic machines are available to do the inspecting, or the inspector is not subjected to a load so excessive as to impair his accuracy. Suitable automatic machines are rarely available, so screening is ordinarily expensive in personnel and time; moreover, screening will rarely, in practice, eliminate all defective items. Obviously, if the quality test for each item is destructive, screening is out of the question. Screening, by itself, is not likely to contribute much to the improvement of the quality of product submitted in the future; this is particularly true when the producer and consumer are independent parties, and the consumer is carrying out acceptance inspection. Under screening, the producer has only defective items returned to him; all nondefective items are accepted. He, therefore, has little incentive to improve the quality of the product or to cull out defective items himself. In effect, the consumer is doing part of the producer's work for him, since it is the responsibility of the producer to deliver satisfactory product.

Lot-by-Lot Inspection

In many cases, it is not necessary to screen the product, and an adequate control of quality may be attained by subjecting the product to lot-by-lot sampling inspection. In screening, all submitted items of product are inspected, and each item is accepted or rejected; in lot-by-lot sampling inspection, only some of the submitted items of product are inspected, and groups of submitted items, called inspection lots, are accepted or rejected as a whole. In lot-by-lot sampling inspection, the product is divided into appropriate inspection lots; one sample (that is, a collection of items) or several samples are drawn from the inspection lot, and the inspection lot is accepted or rejected according to the number of defective items found in the sample or samples.

Spot-check Inspection

It is practically impossible to state a simple definition for spot-check inspection. This is not because the methods are complicated, but rather because the methods are so variable. In many cases, there is no formal or routine inspection procedure, and even the inspector himself finds it difficult to describe his procedure or to pass it along to a new man. As used to describe such cases, the term *spot check* covers everything from very little inspection to no inspection at all. In the better instances, a method does exist and it has been observed in such cases that the method involves a sampling procedure that differs from lot-by-lot inspection only in that samples are much smaller and that, in general, no formal attempt is made to identify or group a lot or sublot.

SPOT-CHECK VS. LOT-BY-LOT INSPECTION

Spot-check inspection was used long before the advent of lot-by-lot inspection. Even today, many inspectors charged with responsibility for acceptance inspection think that spot-check inspection is preferable to, or at least as good as, lot-by-lot inspection. It will be shown that this view is erroneous.

The primary purpose of inspection is to control the quality of accepted material. The effectiveness of inspection, therefore, must be measured in terms of how well it acts to prevent the acceptance of defective material. We will examine the effectiveness of spot-check inspection and compare its effectiveness with that of other methods.

In the case of 100 percent inspection, where every piece is inspected, the only way in which a defective piece can be accepted is through human error on the part of the inspector. To maintain effectiveness, conditions that lead to human error must be eliminated or minimized. Thus, if fatigue is a factor, then the schedule of inspection must be arranged to minimize fatigue. This may involve an increase in personnel but, if 100 percent inspection is necessary, then it is necessary to provide sufficient personnel to do the job adequately.

In the case of sampling inspections, only a portion of the accepted material is inspected. Although every defective in the sample may be discovered and rejected, nevertheless, the remainder of the material may contain defectives that are neither discovered nor rejected. The effectiveness of sampling inspection depends upon how well the sampling procedures, and the action taken upon the basis of the sample, act to control the quality of the material that is accepted without further inspection.

The spot-check inspection frequently consists of inspecting a piece selected at certain intervals from the production line. This inspection is termed a percentage check. In a 10 percent check, every tenth piece is inspected; in a 1 percent check, every hundredth piece is selected for inspection. The action taken after inspection varies, but it has been found that all methods that have been observed are one of three basic types. These three types vary only in the action that is taken when a defective is discovered:

Type A: Here the only action is to reject any pieces that are discovered to be defective. No action is taken with respect to the uninspected pieces on the production line.

Type B: Whenever a defective piece is found, all the pieces between that piece and the next preceding, or next succeeding, piece normally inspected are inspected.

Type C: Whenever a defective piece is found, all the pieces between the next preceding and next succeeding piece normally inspected are inspected.

These three types include practically all cases in which pieces are selected with any regularity. It is not necessary that the procedure be rigid. In the 20 percent check, for example, it is not essential that exactly every fifth piece be inspected. The effectiveness will be the same as long as, on the average, one piece out of every five is inspected.

When quality is good, it makes no difference which type of spot check is used, and even the lot-by-lot inspection is no better than the spot check. This is a rather obvious conclusion. When quality is satisfactory, there is no need for inspection, and so the manner of inspection is immaterial. If the manufacturer could be depended upon to produce or submit only satisfactory material at all times, industry and government could dispense with inspection entirely.

As the average incoming quality becomes worse, the method of inspection becomes increasingly important. It is apparent that type C is the best type of spot check, type B the next best, and type A the poorest. But, in fact, none of these methods is materially better than no inspection at all. When the average incoming quality is 10 percent defective, the average outgoing quality, with no inspection at all, remains 10 percent defective. If we use the type C spot check, examining one unit out of every five produced, we find the average outgoing quality is improved to 7.5 percent defective. However, if the effect on an acceptance inspection is as small as this, it can hardly be called worthwhile. In contrast, the curve for lot-by-lot inspection shows that when the average incoming quality is 10 percent, the average outgoing quality is only 0.4 percent, under standard sampling for a sublot of 500 pieces and an acceptable quality level of 1.0 percent. The first sample size was 50, giving a nominal inspection of 10 percent, equal to that shown for the spot-check inspections.

It may be argued that no good inspector relies solely on the spot check and that a good inspector would stop production entirely if he discovered that the quality produced was as bad as 10 percent defective. This may be entirely true. However, in order to discover that quality is poor, the inspector must accumulate data. Having inspected 50 pieces, for example, during his spot-check inspection and found 5 of them defective, he realizes that quality is excessively poor and stops production. This prevents the further production and acceptance of poor material. Meanwhile, he must determine what to do with the material already inspected. If this is accepted without further ado, then it is quite probable that it still contains most of the defective pieces that were originally present. However, if the inspector is thorough, he will demand that all of this material be reinspected. If he does that, he is actually doing a lot-by-lot inspection. He is basing his action on an accumulated sample of 50 pieces, and he is rejecting for reinspection the entire sublot (or inspection lot) from which that sample was taken. The only remaining distinction will be that, since he was depending on a spot check, he made no effort to identify the sublot, and he will now find it difficult to isolate it for purposes of rejection. The argument that a good inspector relies on more than the mere spot check, therefore resolves itself into a statement that a good inspector actually, and perhaps without realizing it, operates on a form of lot-by-lot inspection. If that be true, it would be far better for him to recognize the fact and to organize his inspection procedure accordingly.

Although the spot check is normally identified with a given percentage of inspection, this percentage is not necessarily the total amount of inspection, performed. In the type A spot check, where the discovering of a defective piece does not result in any further action with respect to the remaining material, this percentage is actually the total inspection performed. However, in the type B and type C spot checks, the discovery of a defective piece means that additional pieces must be inspected. Therefore, in these types, the total amount of inspection depends on the number of defective pieces discovered.

It is apparent that as the quality of the incoming material becomes worse, the amount of inspection increases for type B and type C spot checks. Thus, in a 10 percent spot check, the actual amount of inspection is 10 percent only when the incoming material is perfect. When the incoming material contains 10 percent defective pieces, the plans automatically lead to more inspection. For the type A spot check, the amount of inspection is always 10 percent; for the type B, the amount of inspection increases as quality becomes worse; for the type C, the amount of inspection increases even more rapidly. Contrast this with the amount of inspection involved in the lot-by-lot inspection plan. When quality is good, the amount of inspection is less than that required by the type C spot check. As quality becomes worse, the amount of inspection becomes less than that of type B and approaches that of type A. At the same time, this lot-by-lot plan provides a tremendous advantage with respect to the control of quality.

To explain this peculiar behavior of the lot-by-lot plan, it should be remembered that, under a double-sampling plan, second samples are not necessary when quality is good, so that only the sample of 50 pieces (10 percent of the sublot of 500) is inspected. When quality becomes somewhat poor, second samples are sometimes required, and the amount of inspection increases. When quality becomes quite poor, either the first sample alone suffices to show that the sublot should be rejected and second samples are not necessary or, if a second sample is required, only a portion of it has to be inspected to discover that the sublot should be rejected.

As a final comment on the quantity of inspection, it should be noted that when the production process produces defective material, the only way of improving the quality is to inspect, to discover the defective pieces, and to remove them. In the lot-by-lot method, the inspector merely measures the quality. If the quality is satisfactory, he accepts all the material. If the quality is unsatisfactory, he rejects all of it, leaving the task of discovering and removing the defective pieces to the contractor, who is responsible for their being there. In fact, it is precisely because a lot-by-lot inspection causes the contractor to reinspect defective sublots that it provides such good control of quality with so little inspection. In the spot-check method, the plan of inspection combines the operations of measuring quality and removing defective pieces (and does both operations poorly). The result is that the inspector performs the extra inspection necessary for discovering and removing defective pieces. This is the reason the spot check involves more inspection than the lot-by-lot method.

As an acceptance inspection, the spot check involves both more inspection and less control over the quality of accepted material than does the lot-by-lot method of inspection. Consequently, the spot check is seldom used by industries producing technical products.

EFFECT OF LOT-BY-LOT SAMPLING INSPECTION ON QUALITY OF PRODUCT

The acceptance or rejection of an entire inspection lot on the basis of the quality of a sample drawn from that inspection lot provides a strong incentive for the producer to improve the quality of his product. If large inspection lots are even occasionally rejected, the producer may find much of his profit eaten up in screening, reworking, or in scrap. The way to reduce the number of inspection lots rejected, and thereby reduce these costs, is to submit a product of higher quality.

Both sampling and screening provide information that, if properly acted upon, helps to improve the quality of the submitted product. The recording and processing of this information are neither difficult nor unduly time-consuming, and it is the experience of those who have used sampling inspection plans that such recording and processing pay dividends.

RISKS IN LOT-BY-LOT SAMPLING INSPECTION, PRODUCER AND CONSUMER

In any sampling acceptance procedure, there are two risks involved: (1) the risk of accepting material of unsatisfactory quality, which is the consumer's risk; and (2) the risk of rejecting material of satisfactory quality, which is the producer's risk. One of the most important problems in planning sampling inspection procedures is to keep each of these risks down to a satisfactory value. Unfortunately, a provision that tends to lower one of these risks will, in general, tend to increase the other. One can determine the size of these two risks from the operating characteristic curve for the particular sampling plan under consideration. One must avoid adopting a sampling plan that may be perfectly satisfactory with respect to one risk, yet wholly impractical with respect to the other.

No sampling plan can assure the complete separation of defectives from nondefectives among the submitted items, for not all of the items are inspected. Thus, accepted inspection lots may contain some defective items, and rejected inspection lots may contain some nondefective items. Moreover, sometimes a low-quality inspection lot (that is, an inspection lot containing many defective items) will be accepted, and sometimes a high-quality inspection lot will be rejected. While good sampling plans prevent such errors from being made often, it must be remembered that samples obey the laws of chance and, therefore, will occasionally be of a quality that is far out of line with the quality of the inspection lots from which they were drawn. When these risks are balanced against the great saving in cost, sampling inspection will generally be preferred to screening. If the product can be tested only destructively, sampling inspection is necessary and will provide protection against accepting more than a small number of low-quality inspection lots and against rejecting more than a small number of high-quality lots.

Acceptance inspection risks are due to many factors such as faulty gauges or testing equipment, careless inspection, sampling errors, and so on. All such factors must, of course, be taken into consideration in the planning and supervision of acceptance inspection. Risks due to faulty gauges, careless inspection, poor judgment, and so on, are very real, and they must be eliminated as far as practicable by administrative and supervisory control. Risks due to sampling errors, however, cannot be eliminated by administrative or supervisory control and must, therefore, be controlled through inspection planning. Statistical methods have been developed that permit the evaluation of the risks due to sampling and, hence, provide the possibility of fixing these risks at a satisfactory value through inspection planning.

Summary

One hundred percent inspections for acceptance do not materially improve the quality of a product. They only remove some of the defects. They do not change the process, nor do they alone provide any incentive for the manufacturer to improve the quality of his product.

Acceptance sampling principles can be applied to all the phases of manufacturing or production, that is, to the inflow of raw material, the actual process, final inspection, and customer acceptance. The use of statistical techniques to change the process, however, is really process control.

Single-sampling plans base all the judgment on one sample, and a resultant advantage is that we have a constant work load on inspection. In double sampling, we always inspect the first sample and may or may not have to inspect the second sample. Double sampling has a psychological advantage, in a way, as it appears to give the product a second chance. A single-sampling and a double-sampling inspection plan may involve the same amount of risk in accepting poor quality; the one selected, therefore, depends on administrative grounds or the inspection load. If quality is very good or very bad, fewer items will be inspected on the average for the double-sampling procedure than in single sampling.

The multiple-sampling plan may be ideal from many standpoints, although the inspection load varies. With it, we can do less inspecting on the average—with the same protection—than with any of the other systems.

In devising sampling procedures, we may try to reach a perfect plan, but this is next to impossible. Our goal is to reject the maximum number of poor lots and accept the maximum number of good lots.

Inspection by screening is not possible if the testing is destructive; for nondestructive testing, it is good when mechanical or automatic means may be used for inspection. There is little incentive for the producer to improve his quality. A screening inspection of 100 percent must be made for all critical defects. This system is seldom used by producers of technical products.

In a lot-by-lot inspection plan the product is divided into lots, and a sample must be taken from each lot. The entire lot is accepted or rejected on the basis of the number of defects found in the sample. This type of program provides incentive for the manufacturer to produce good quality items.

Spot-check inspections are not considered good from the standpoint of statistical quality control. There is no definite standard operating procedure involved. In comparison to lot-by-lot inspections, very small samples may be taken, with no particular reference being made to specific lots of the product. There is no incentive for the manufacturer to ship quality products and an opportunity exists for attempting to push poor-quality products through the inspection, thereby taking a calculated risk on acceptance.

Glossary

Certain terms require definition in order to promote a better understanding of the uses of sampling inspection:

Acceptance number: A number associated with each sample of a sampling plan. An inspection lot is passed for a class of defects after inspection of a particular sample, if the total number of defectives of that class found in that and all preceding samples combined is equal to, or less than, the acceptance number associated with that sample.

A defective: Any article, unit, or specimen containing one or more defects with respect to the quality characteristic(s) under consideration.

Defect: Any deviation of a dimension, finish, or other quality characteristic of an article or unit from specification or drawing requirements, or from accepted standards of good workmanship.

Defects per unit: A measure of quality obtained by dividing the number of defects of the units of material under consideration by the total number of such units. Thus, the defects per unit in a sublot of electrical detectors is the ratio of the total number of defects in all the electrical detectors in the sublot to the total number of electrical detectors in the sublot.

Fraction defective: A measure of quality expressed by the ratio of the number of defective articles to the total number of articles under consideration. Thus, the fraction defective in a sublot is the ratio of the total number of defective articles in the sublot to the total number of articles in the sublot.

Inspection by attributes: Inspection that merely determines whether the article or unit does or does not conform to the specified requirement(s) for the quality characteristic(s) under consideration (for example, go/no-go gauging.) In inspection by attributes, quality is usually measured in terms of percent defective or defects per unit.

Inspection by variables: Inspection in which actual measurement on a continuous scale is made on the article, specimen, and so on, for the quality characteristic under consideration (for example, tensile testing of steel). In inspection by variables, quality is usually measured in terms of the average, or the average and the dispersion.

Lot: Applies to any collection of articles, units, or quantity of material that would be assigned a separate lot number.

Lot-by-Lot sampling inspection: In lot-by-lot sampling inspection, only some of the submitted items of the product are inspected, and groups of submitted items, called sublots or inspection lots, are accepted or rejected as a whole according to the number of defective items or defects found in the sample or samples.

100 percent inspection: Inspection in which every article or unit is inspected for the quality characteristic(s) under consideration.

Percent defective: Fraction defective multiplied by 100.

Producer and consumer: Producer may refer to a plant furnishing new material, semifinished, or finished product to another plant or user (this plant or user is the consumer); or producer may refer to one division of a plant furnishing semifinished product to another division (consumer) that will use this project at the next stage of manufacture.

Quality characteristics: Any property for which material is subject to inspection.

Quality of a lot: Sampling plans are used in inspection to accept or reject products submitted in batches or groups, called sublots or inspection lots; efficient sampling plans will generally accept lots of high quality and reject lots of low quality. Whenever sampling plans are used to reach decisions on lots of a product, it is clearly necessary to decide what is meant by high quality and low quality or, more generally, to decide how the quality of a lot shall be described. There are many ways of describing the quality of a lot with respect to the product's characteristic or characteristics being inspected. The following are perhaps the most common:

The average of the characteristic among the items in a lot, the characteristic being measured along a scale (arithmetic mean).

The variability of the characteristic among the items in a lot, the characteristic being measured along a scale (standard deviation).

The ratio of the variability to the average of the characteristic of the items in a lot (this ratio multiplied by 100 equals coefficient of variation).

The average number of defects per unit or item in a lot (defects per unit or item).

The percentage of defective items in a lot (percentage defective).

Each of these methods give a gradation of quality. The line between lot quality that is considered high and lot quality that is considered low depends largely on the intended use of the product.

Quality of an item: The problem of describing the quality of an item (unit) or product is somewhat independent of the problem of describing the quality of a lot. The most common methods of describing the quality of an item are:

By variables, that is, by measurement of some characteristic of an item along a continuous scale. Examples: hardness in Rockwell units; strength in pounds; length in centimeters.

By counting along a discrete scale. Examples: number of loose connections per electric motor; number of flaws per linear yard of textiles.

By attributes; that is, by classification of the quality of an item into one of two classes. Example: correctly or incorrectly assembled, strong or weak, within or without tolerances.

Rejection number: Number associated with each sample of a sampling plan. An inspection lot is rejected for a class of defectives after inspection of a particular sample, if the total number of defectives of that class found in that and all preceding samples combined is equal to, or greater than, the rejection number associated with that sample.

Sample: A number of articles, units, specimens, or a portion of material selected from a lot or sublot for purposes of inspection or testing.

Sampling inspection: Inspection in which only sample portions of the total number of articles or units of the total quantity of material are inspected for the quality characteristic(s) under consideration. Quality of the product is evaluated by inspecting some, but not all, of the product.

Sublot: Ordinarily, a sublot is defined as a fractional part of a lot. However, in the standard sampling inspection plan, the definition of a sublot is any collection of articles, units, or quantity of material that is inspected for acceptance or rejection as a group. A sublot is really an inspection lot and the sublot can be an entire lot, if the entire lot is inspected for acceptance or rejection as a group.

Acceptance Sampling

Inspection for acceptance purposes is carried out at many stages in manufacturing. There may be inspection of incoming materials and parts, process inspection at various points in the manufacturing operations, final inspection by a manufacturer of his own product, and, ultimately, inspection of the finished product by one or more purchasers.

Much of this acceptance inspection is necessarily on a sampling basis. All acceptance tests that are destructive of the item tested must inevitably be done by sampling. In many instances, sampling inspection is used because the cost of 100 percent inspection is prohibitive. In still other cases, because of the effect of fatigue involved in 100 percent inspection, a good sampling inspection plan may actually give better quality assurance than 100 percent inspection.

Any sampling inspection plan involves certain risks because of possible sampling errors. Such errors arise because of the fact that the quality of the sample selected from an inspection lot may differ somewhat from the quality of that total lot. The lot or sublot may consist of from ten to thousands of articles. Most of these articles may be satisfactory, but some may be defective. If a sample is selected from a lot or sublot containing a certain fraction of defective articles and, if the sample is inspected on an attributes basis, then the sample may be found to contain zero, one, two, or more defectives. The smaller the sample, the greater may be the difference between the fraction defective in the sample and the fraction defective in the lot. Hence, having observed a certain fraction defective in a sample, one may not be certain whether the fraction defective of the lot is equal to, greater than, or less than the fraction defective in the sample and, therefore, some risk is necessarily involved in the sampling procedure.

It is the purpose of this section to describe how such risks can be computed for simple inspection plans involving inspections on an attributes basis. A method for presenting such computations in the form of a graph is known as an operating characteristic curve (OC), and the effect upon such curves of changes in either sample size or acceptance criterion is discussed below.

ACCEPTANCE SAMPLING TERMINOLOGY

This terminology is given to promote a better understanding of acceptance sampling. The overall application of tables and graphs is included in MIL-STD-105D. This publication provides data for inspectors, etc. (MIL-STD-105D is not furnished with this text.)

Acceptable Quality Level (AQL)

The AQL is the maximum percentage defective (or the maximum number of defects per hundred units) that, for purposes of sampling inspection, can be considered satisfactory as a process average.

When a customer designates some specific value of AQL for a certain defect or group of defects, he indicates to the supplier that his acceptance sampling plan will accept the great majority of the lots or batches that the supplier submits, provided that the process average level of percentage defective (or defects per hundred units) in these lots or batches are no greater than the designated value of AQL. Thus, the AQL is a designated value of percentage defective (or defects per hundred units) that the customer indicates will be accepted most of the time by the acceptance sampling procedure to be used. The sampling plans provided herein are so arranged that the probability of acceptance at the designated AQL value depends upon the sample size, being generally higher for large samples than for small ones, for a given AQL. The AQL alone does not describe the protection to the customer for individual lots or batches but more directly relates to what might be expected from a series of lots or batches, provided the steps indicated in this section are taken. It is necessary to refer to the operating characteristic curve of the plan, to determine what protection the customer will have.

The designation of an AQL shall not imply that the supplier has the right to supply knowingly any defective unit of product.

The AQL to be used will be designated in the contract or by the responsible authority. Different AQLs may be designated for groups of defects considered collectively or for individual defects. An AQL for a group of defects may be designated in addition to AQLs for individual defects, or subgroups, within that group. AQL values of 10.0 or less may be expressed either in percentage defective or in defects per hundred units; those over 10.0 shall be expressed in defects per hundred units only.

Initiation of Inspection

Normal inspection will be used at the start of inspection unless otherwise directed by the responsible authority:

1. Normal, tightened, or reduced inspection shall continue unchanged for each class of defects or defectives on successive lots or batches, except where the switching procedures given below require a change. The switching procedures shall be applied to each class of defects or defectives independently.
2. When normal inspection is in effect, tightened inspection shall be instituted when two out of five consecutive lots or batches have been rejected on original inspection (that is, resubmitted lots or batches are ignored for this procedure).
3. When tightened inspection is in effect, normal inspection shall be instituted when five consecutive lots or batches have been considered acceptable on original inspection.
4. When normal inspection is in effect, reduced inspection shall be instituted, provided that all of the following conditions are satisfied:
   a. The preceding ten lots or batches have been on normal inspection and none has been rejected on original inspection.
   b. If double or multiple sampling is in use, all samples inspected should be included, not first samples only.
   c. Production is at a steady rate.
   d. Reduced inspection is considered desirable by the responsible authority.
5. When reduced inspection is in effect, normal inspection shall be instituted if any of the following occurs on original inspection.
   a. A lot or batch is rejected.
   b. A lot or batch is considered acceptable.
   c. Production becomes irregular or delayed.
   d. Other conditions warrant that normal inspection shall be instituted.
6. In the event that ten consecutive lots or batches remain on tightened inspection (or such other number as may be designated by the responsible authority), inspection under the provisions of this document should be discontinued pending action to improve the quality of submitted material.

Sampling Plans

A sampling plan that indicates the number of units of product from each lot or batch that are to be inspected (sample size or series of sample sizes) and the criteria for determining the acceptability of the lot or batch (acceptance and rejection numbers).

1. The inspection level determines the relationship between the lot or batch size and the sample size. The inspection level to be used for any particular requirement will be prescribed by the responsible authority. Three inspection levels, I, II, and III, are given in Table 12–19 for general use. Unless otherwise specified, inspection level II will normally be used. However, inspection level I may be specified when less discrimination is needed, or level III may be specified for greater discrimination. Four additional special levels: S-1, S-2, S-3, and S-4, are given in the same table and may be used when relatively small sample sizes are necessary and large sampling risks can or must be tolerated. In the designation of inspection levels S1 to S4, care must be exercised to avoid AQLs inconsistent with these inspection levels.
2. Sample sizes are designated by code letters. Table 12–20 is used to find the applicable code letter for the particular

TABLE 12-19.
Sample Size Code Letters

Lot or Batch Size			Special Inspection Levels				General Inspection Levels		
			S-1	S-2	S-3	S-4	I	II	III
2	to	8	A	A	A	A	A	A	B
9	to	15	A	A	A	A	A	B	C
16	to	25	A	A	B	B	B	C	D
26	to	50	A	B	B	C	C	D	E
51	to	90	B	B	C	C	C	E	F
91	to	150	B	B	C	D	D	F	G
151	to	280	B	C	D	E	E	G	H
281	to	500	B	C	D	E	F	H	J
501	to	1200	C	C	E	F	G	J	K
1201	to	3200	C	D	E	G	H	K	L
3201	to	10000	C	D	F	G	J	L	M
10001	to	35000	C	D	F	H	K	M	N
35001	to	150000	D	E	G	J	L	N	P
150001	to	500000	D	E	G	J	M	P	Q
500001	and over		D	E	H	K	N	Q	R

lot or batch size and the prescribed inspection level.

3. The AQL and the code letter shall be used to obtain the sampling plan from Tables 12–20 to 12–29. When no sampling plan is available for a given combination of AQL and code letter, the tables direct the user to a different letter. The sample size to be used is given by the new code letter, not by the original letter. If this procedure leads to different sample sizes for different classes of defects, the code letter corresponding to the largest sample size derived may be used for all classes of defects when designated or approved by the responsible authority. As an alternative to a single plan with an acceptance number of 0, the plan with an acceptance number of 1, with its correspondingly larger sample size for a designated AQL (where available), may be used when designated or approved by the responsible authority.

4. Three types of sampling plans—single, double, and multiple—are given in Tables 12–20 to 12–29, respectively. When several types of plans are available for a given AQL and code letter, any one may be used. A decision as to type of plan, either single, double, or multiple, when available for a given AQL and code letter, will usually be based upon the comparison between the administrative difficulty and the average sample sizes of the available plans. The average sample size of multiple plans is less than for double (except in the case corresponding to single acceptance number 1), and both of these are always less than a single sample size. Usually, the administrative difficulty for single sampling and the cost per unit of the sample are less than for double or multiple.

5. The percentage defective of any given quantity of units of product is one

hundred times the number of defective units of product contained therein divided by the total number of units of product:

Defects per hundred units

$$\text{Percentage defective} = \frac{\text{Number of defectives}}{\text{Number of units inspected}} \times 100.$$

Determination of Acceptability

Single Sampling Plan. The number of sample units inspected shall be equal to the sample size given by the plan. If the number of defectives found in the sample is equal to, or less than, the acceptance number, the lot or batch shall be considered acceptable. If the number of defectives found in the first sample is equal to, or greater than, the first rejection number, the lot or batch shall be rejected.

Double Sampling Plan. The number of sample units inspected shall be equal to the first sample size given by the plan. If the number of defectives found in the first sample is equal to, or less than the first acceptable number, the lot or batch shall be considered acceptable. If the number of defectives found in the first sample is equal to, or greater than, the first rejection number, the lot or batch shall be rejected. If the number of defectives found in the first sample is between the first acceptance and rejection numbers, a second sample of the size given by the plan shall be inspected. The number of defectives found in the first and second samples shall be accumulated. If the cumulative number of defectives is equal to or less than the second acceptance number, the lot or batch shall be considered acceptable. If the cumulative number of defectives is equal to, or greater than the second rejection number, the lot or batch shall be rejected.

Multiple Sample Plan. Under multiple sampling, the procedure shall be similar to that specified in the double sampling plan except successive samples required to reach a decision may be more than two.

Special Procedure for Reduced Inspection. Under reduced inspection, the sampling procedure may terminate without either acceptance or rejection criteria having been met. In these circumstances, the lot or batch will be considered acceptable, but normal inspection will be reinstated starting with the next lot or batch.

Defects per Hundred Units Inspection. To determine the acceptability of a lot or batch under defects per hundred units inspection, the procedure specified for percentage defective inspection above shall be used, except that the word defects shall be substituted for defectives.

Operating Characteristic (OC) Curves. The operating characteristic curves for normal inspection indicate the percentage of lots or batches that may be expected to be accepted under the various sampling plans for a given process quality. The OC curves shown for AQLs greater than 10.0 are based on the Poisson distribution and are applicable for defects per hundred units inspection; those for AQLs of 10.0 or less and sample sizes of 80 or less are based on the binomial distribution and are applicable for percentage defective inspection: those for AQLs of 10.0 or less and sample sizes larger than 80 are based on the Poisson distribution and are applicable either for defects per hundred units inspection, or for percentage defective inspection (the Poisson distribution being an adequate approximation to the binomial distribution under these conditions). Tabulated values, corresponding to selected values of probabilities of acceptance (P_a in percent), are given for each of the curves shown, and, in addition, for tightened inspection, and

SINGLE
NORMAL

TABLE 12-20.
Single Sampling Plans for Normal Inspection (Master Table)

Sample Size Code Letter	Sample Size	*Acceptable Quality Levels (Normal Inspection)* 0.010	0.015	0.025	0.040	0.065	0.10	0.15	0.25	0.40	0.65	1.0	1.5	2.5	4.0	6.5	10	15	25	40	65	100	150	250	400	650	1000
		Ac Re	Ac Re	Ac Re	Ac Re	Ac Re	Ac Re	Ac Re	Ac Re	Ac Re	Ac Re	Ac Re	Ac Re	Ac Re	Ac Re	Ac Re	Ac Re	Ac Re	Ac Re	Ac Re	Ac Re	Ac Re	Ac Re	Ac Re	Ac Re	Ac Re	Ac Re
A	2	↓	↓	↓	↓	↓	↓	↓	↓	↓	↓	↓	↓	↓	↓	0 1	↓	↓	1 2	2 3	3 4	5 6	7 8	10 11	14 15	21 22	30 31
B	3	↓	↓	↓	↓	↓	↓	↓	↓	↓	↓	↓	↓	↓	0 1	↑	↓	1 2	2 3	3 4	5 6	7 8	10 11	14 15	21 22	30 31	44 45
C	5	↓	↓	↓	↓	↓	↓	↓	↓	↓	↓	↓	↓	0 1	↑	↓	1 2	2 3	3 4	5 6	7 8	10 11	14 15	21 22	30 31	44 45	↑
D	8	↓	↓	↓	↓	↓	↓	↓	↓	↓	↓	↓	0 1	↑	↓	1 2	2 3	3 4	5 6	7 8	10 11	14 15	21 22	30 31	44 45	↑	↑
E	13	↓	↓	↓	↓	↓	↓	↓	↓	↓	↓	0 1	↑	↓	1 2	2 3	3 4	5 6	7 8	10 11	14 15	21 22	30 31	44 45	↑	↑	↑
F	20	↓	↓	↓	↓	↓	↓	↓	↓	↓	0 1	↑	↓	1 2	2 3	3 4	5 6	7 8	10 11	14 15	21 22	↑	↑	↑	↑	↑	↑
G	32	↓	↓	↓	↓	↓	↓	↓	↓	0 1	↑	↓	1 2	2 3	3 4	5 6	7 8	10 11	14 15	21 22	↑	↑	↑	↑	↑	↑	↑
H	50	↓	↓	↓	↓	↓	↓	↓	0 1	↑	↓	1 2	2 3	3 4	5 6	7 8	10 11	14 15	21 22	↑	↑	↑	↑	↑	↑	↑	↑
J	80	↓	↓	↓	↓	↓	↓	0 1	↑	↓	1 2	2 3	3 4	5 6	7 8	10 11	14 15	21 22	↑	↑	↑	↑	↑	↑	↑	↑	↑
K	125	↓	↓	↓	↓	↓	0 1	↑	↓	1 2	2 3	3 4	5 6	7 8	10 11	14 15	21 22	↑	↑	↑	↑	↑	↑	↑	↑	↑	↑
L	200	↓	↓	↓	↓	0 1	↑	↓	1 2	2 3	3 4	5 6	7 8	10 11	14 15	21 22	↑	↑	↑	↑	↑	↑	↑	↑	↑	↑	↑
M	315	↓	↓	↓	0 1	↑	↓	1 2	2 3	3 4	5 6	7 8	10 11	14 15	21 22	↑	↑	↑	↑	↑	↑	↑	↑	↑	↑	↑	↑
N	500	↓	↓	0 1	↑	↓	1 2	2 3	3 4	5 6	7 8	10 11	14 15	21 22	↑	↑	↑	↑	↑	↑	↑	↑	↑	↑	↑	↑	↑
P	800	↓	0 1	↑	↓	1 2	2 3	3 4	5 6	7 8	10 11	14 15	21 22	↑	↑	↑	↑	↑	↑	↑	↑	↑	↑	↑	↑	↑	↑
Q	1250	0 1	↑	↓	1 2	2 3	3 4	5 6	7 8	10 11	14 15	21 22	↑	↑	↑	↑	↑	↑	↑	↑	↑	↑	↑	↑	↑	↑	↑
R	2000	↑	↑	1 2	2 3	3 4	5 6	7 8	10 11	14 15	21 22	↑	↑	↑	↑	↑	↑	↑	↑	↑	↑	↑	↑	↑	↑	↑	↑

↓ = Use first sampling plan below arrow. If sample size equals, or exceeds, lot or batch size, do 100% inspection.

↑ = Use first sampling plan above arrow.

Ac = Acceptance number.

Re = Rejection number.

SINGLE
TIGHTENED

TABLE 12-21.
Single Sampling Plans for Tightened Inspection (Master Table)

Sample Size Code Letter	Sample Size	0.010	0.015	0.025	0.040	0.065	0.10	0.15	0.25	0.40	0.65	1.0	1.5	2.5	4.0	6.5	10	15	25	40	65	100	150	250	400	650	1000
		Acceptable Quality Levels (Tightened Inspection)																									
		Ac Re	Ac Re	Ac Re	Ac Re	Ac Re	Ac Re	Ac Re	Ac Re	Ac Re	Ac Re	Ac Re	Ac Re	Ac Re	Ac Re	Ac Re	Ac Re	Ac Re	Ac Re	Ac Re	Ac Re	Ac Re	Ac Re	Ac Re	Ac Re	Ac Re	Ac Re
A	2	↓	↓	↓	↓	↓	↓	↓	↓	↓	↓	↓	↓	↓	↓	↓	↓	↓	↓	1 2	2 3	3 4	5 6	8 9	12 13	18 19	27 28
B	3	↓	↓	↓	↓	↓	↓	↓	↓	↓	↓	↓	↓	↓	↓	0 1	↓	↓	1 2	2 3	3 4	5 6	8 9	12 13	18 19	27 28	41 42
C	5	↓	↓	↓	↓	↓	↓	↓	↓	↓	↓	↓	↓	↓	0 1	↓	↓	1 2	2 3	3 4	5 6	8 9	12 13	18 19	27 28	41 42	↑
D	8	↓	↓	↓	↓	↓	↓	↓	↓	↓	↓	↓	↓	0 1	↓	↓	1 2	2 3	3 4	5 6	8 9	12 13	18 19	27 28	41 42	↑	↑
E	13	↓	↓	↓	↓	↓	↓	↓	↓	↓	↓	↓	0 1	↓	↓	1 2	2 3	3 4	5 6	8 9	12 13	18 19	27 28	41 42	↑	↑	↑
F	20	↓	↓	↓	↓	↓	↓	↓	↓	↓	↓	0 1	↓	↓	1 2	2 3	3 4	5 6	8 9	12 13	18 19	↑	↑	↑	↑	↑	↑
G	32	↓	↓	↓	↓	↓	↓	↓	↓	↓	0 1	↓	↓	1 2	2 3	3 4	5 6	8 9	12 13	18 19	↑	↑	↑	↑	↑	↑	↑
H	50	↓	↓	↓	↓	↓	↓	↓	↓	0 1	↓	↓	1 2	2 3	3 4	5 6	8 9	12 13	18 19	↑	↑	↑	↑	↑	↑	↑	↑
J	80	↓	↓	↓	↓	↓	↓	↓	0 1	↓	↓	1 2	2 3	3 4	5 6	8 9	12 13	18 19	↑	↑	↑	↑	↑	↑	↑	↑	↑
K	125	↓	↓	↓	↓	↓	↓	0 1	↓	↓	1 2	2 3	3 4	5 6	8 9	12 13	18 19	↑	↑	↑	↑	↑	↑	↑	↑	↑	↑
L	200	↓	↓	↓	↓	↓	0 1	↓	↓	1 2	2 3	3 4	5 6	8 9	12 13	18 19	↑	↑	↑	↑	↑	↑	↑	↑	↑	↑	↑
M	315	↓	↓	↓	↓	0 1	↓	↓	1 2	2 3	3 4	5 6	8 9	12 13	18 19	↑	↑	↑	↑	↑	↑	↑	↑	↑	↑	↑	↑
N	500	↓	↓	↓	0 1	↓	↓	1 2	2 3	3 4	5 6	8 9	12 13	18 19	↑	↑	↑	↑	↑	↑	↑	↑	↑	↑	↑	↑	↑
P	800	↓	↓	0 1	↓	↓	1 2	2 3	3 4	5 6	8 9	12 13	18 19	↑	↑	↑	↑	↑	↑	↑	↑	↑	↑	↑	↑	↑	↑
Q	1250	↓	0 1	↓	↓	1 2	2 3	3 4	5 6	8 9	12 13	18 19	↑	↑	↑	↑	↑	↑	↑	↑	↑	↑	↑	↑	↑	↑	↑
R	2000	0 1	↑	↓	1 2	2 3	3 4	5 6	8 9	12 13	18 19	↑	↑	↑	↑	↑	↑	↑	↑	↑	↑	↑	↑	↑	↑	↑	↑
S	3150			1 2																							

↓ = Use first sampling plan below arrow. If sample size equals, or exceeds, lot or batch size, do 100% inspection.

↑ = Use first sampling plan above arrow.

Ac = Acceptance number.

Re = Rejection number.

SINGLE
REDUCED

TABLE 12-22.
Single Sampling Plans for Reduced Inspection (Master Table)

Sample Size Code Letter	*Sample Size*	0.010	0.015	0.025	0.040	0.065	0.10	0.15	0.25	0.40	0.65	1.0	1.5	2.5	4.0	6.5	10	15	25	40	65	100	150	250	400	650	1000
		Acceptable Quality Levels (Reduced Inspection)																									
		Ac Re	Ac Re	Ac Re	Ac Re	Ac Re	Ac Re	Ac Re	Ac Re	Ac Re	Ac Re	Ac Re	Ac Re	Ac Re	Ac Re	Ac Re	Ac Re	Ac Re	Ac Re	Ac Re	Ac Re	Ac Re	Ac Re	Ac Re	Ac Re	Ac Re	Ac Re
A	2	↓	↓	↓	↓	↓	↓	↓	↓	↓	↓	↓	↓	↓	↓	0 1	↓	↓	1 2	2 3	3 4	5 6	7 8	10 11	14 15	21 22	30 31
B	2	↓	↓	↓	↓	↓	↓	↓	↓	↓	↓	↓	↓	↓	0 1	↑	↓	0 2	1 3	2 4	3 5	5 6	7 8	10 11	14 15	21 22	30 31
C	2	↓	↓	↓	↓	↓	↓	↓	↓	↓	↓	↓	↓	0 1	↑	↓	0 2	1 3	1 4	2 5	3 6	5 8	7 10	10 13	14 17	21 24	↑
D	3	↓	↓	↓	↓	↓	↓	↓	↓	↓	↓	↓	0 1	↑	↓	0 2	1 3	1 4	2 5	3 6	5 8	7 10	10 13	14 17	21 24	↑	↑
E	5	↓	↓	↓	↓	↓	↓	↓	↓	↓	↓	0 1	↑	↓	0 2	1 3	1 4	2 5	3 6	5 8	7 10	10 13	14 17	21 24	↑	↑	↑
F	8	↓	↓	↓	↓	↓	↓	↓	↓	↓	0 1	↑	↓	0 2	1 3	1 4	2 5	3 6	5 8	7 10	10 13	↑	↑	↑	↑	↑	↑
G	13	↓	↓	↓	↓	↓	↓	↓	↓	0 1	↑	↓	0 2	1 3	1 4	2 5	3 6	5 8	7 10	10 13	↑	↑	↑	↑	↑	↑	↑
H	20	↓	↓	↓	↓	↓	↓	↓	0 1	↑	↓	0 2	1 3	1 4	2 5	3 6	5 8	7 10	10 13	↑	↑	↑	↑	↑	↑	↑	↑
J	32	↓	↓	↓	↓	↓	↓	0 1	↑	↓	0 2	1 3	1 4	2 5	3 6	5 8	7 10	10 13	↑	↑	↑	↑	↑	↑	↑	↑	↑
K	50	↓	↓	↓	↓	↓	0 1	↑	↓	0 2	1 3	1 4	2 5	3 6	5 8	7 10	10 13	↑	↑	↑	↑	↑	↑	↑	↑	↑	↑
L	80	↓	↓	↓	↓	0 1	↑	↓	0 2	1 3	1 4	2 5	3 6	5 8	7 10	10 13	↑	↑	↑	↑	↑	↑	↑	↑	↑	↑	↑
M	125	↓	↓	↓	0 1	↑	↓	0 2	1 3	1 4	2 5	3 6	5 8	7 10	10 13	↑	↑	↑	↑	↑	↑	↑	↑	↑	↑	↑	↑
N	200	↓	↓	0 1	↑	↓	0 2	1 3	1 4	2 5	3 6	5 8	7 10	10 13	↑	↑	↑	↑	↑	↑	↑	↑	↑	↑	↑	↑	↑
P	315	↓	0 1	↑	↑	0 2	1 3	1 4	2 5	3 6	5 8	7 10	10 13	↑	↑	↑	↑	↑	↑	↑	↑	↑	↑	↑	↑	↑	↑
Q	500	0 1	↑	↓	0 2	1 3	1 4	2 5	3 6	5 8	7 10	10 13	↑	↑	↑	↑	↑	↑	↑	↑	↑	↑	↑	↑	↑	↑	↑
R	800	↑	↑	0 2	1 3	1 4	2 5	3 6	5 8	7 10	10 13	↑	↑	↑	↑	↑	↑	↑	↑	↑	↑	↑	↑	↑	↑	↑	↑

↓ = Use first sampling plan below arrow. If sample size equals, or exceeds, lot or batch size, do 100% inspection.

↑ = Use first sampling plan above arrow.

Ac = Acceptance number.

Re = Rejection number.

† = If the acceptance number has been exceeded, but the rejection number has not been reached, accept the lot, but reinstate normal inspection (see 10.1.4).

DOUBLE
NORMAL

TABLE 12-23.
Double Sampling Plans for Normal Inspection (Master Table)

Sample Size Code Letter	Sample	Sample Size	Cumulative Sample Size	*Acceptable Quality Levels (Normal Inspection)*																									
				0.010	0.015	0.025	0.040	0.065	0.10	0.15	0.25	0.40	0.65	1.0	1.5	2.5	4.0	6.5	10	15	25	40	65	100	150	250	400	650	1000
				Ac Re	Ac Re	Ac Re	Ac Re	Ac Re	Ac Re	Ac Re	Ac Re	Ac Re	Ac Re	Ac Re	Ac Re	Ac Re	Ac Re	Ac Re	Ac Re	Ac Re	Ac Re	Ac Re	Ac Re	Ac Re	Ac Re	Ac Re	Ac Re	Ac Re	Ac Re
A				↓	↓	↓	↓	↓	↓	↓	↓	↓	↓	↓	↓	↓	↓	↓	↓	↓	•	•	•	•	•	•	•	•	•
B	First	2	2	↓	↓	↓	↓	↓	↓	↓	↓	↓	↓	↓	↓	↓	•	↑	↓	0 2	0 3	1 4	2 5	3 7	5 9	7 11	11 16	17 22	25 31
	Second	2	4																	1 2	3 4	4 5	6 7	8 9	12 13	18 19	26 27	37 38	56 57
C	First	3	3	↓	↓	↓	↓	↓	↓	↓	↓	↓	↓	↓	↓	•	↑	↓	0 2	0 3	1 4	2 5	3 7	5 9	7 11	11 16	17 22	25 31	↑
	Second	3	6																1 2	3 4	4 5	6 7	8 9	12 13	18 19	26 27	37 38	56 57	
D	First	5	5	↓	↓	↓	↓	↓	↓	↓	↓	↓	↓	↓	•	↑	↓	0 2	0 3	1 4	2 5	3 7	5 9	7 11	11 16	17 22	25 31	↑	↑
	Second	5	10															1 2	3 4	4 5	6 7	8 9	12 13	18 19	26 27	37 38	56 57		
E	First	8	8	↓	↓	↓	↓	↓	↓	↓	↓	↓	↓	•	↑	↓	0 2	0 3	1 4	2 5	3 7	5 9	7 11	11 16	17 22	25 31	↑	↑	↑
	Second	8	16														1 2	3 4	4 5	6 7	8 9	12 13	18 19	26 27	37 38	56 57			
F	First	13	13	↓	↓	↓	↓	↓	↓	↓	↓	↓	•	↑	↓	0 2	0 3	1 4	2 5	3 7	5 9	7 11	11 16	↑	↑	↑	↑	↑	↑
	Second	13	26													1 2	3 4	4 5	6 7	8 9	12 13	18 19	26 27						
G	First	20	20	↓	↓	↓	↓	↓	↓	↓	↓	•	↑	↓	0 2	0 3	1 4	2 5	3 7	5 9	7 11	11 16	↑	↑	↑	↑	↑	↑	↑
	Second	20	40												1 2	3 4	4 5	6 7	8 9	12 13	18 19	26 27							
H	First	32	32	↓	↓	↓	↓	↓	↓	↓	•	↑	↓	0 2	0 3	1 4	2 5	3 7	5 9	7 11	11 16	↑	↑	↑	↑	↑	↑	↑	↑
	Second	32	64											1 2	3 4	4 5	6 7	8 9	12 13	18 19	26 27								
J	First	50	50	↓	↓	↓	↓	↓	↓	•	↑	↓	0 2	0 3	1 4	2 5	3 7	5 9	7 11	11 16	↑	↑	↑	↑	↑	↑	↑	↑	↑
	Second	50	100										1 2	3 4	4 5	6 7	8 9	12 13	18 19	26 27									
K	First	80	80	↓	↓	↓	↓	↓	•	↑	↓	0 2	0 3	1 4	2 5	3 7	5 9	7 11	11 16	↑	↑	↑	↑	↑	↑	↑	↑	↑	↑
	Second	80	160									1 2	3 4	4 5	6 7	8 9	12 13	18 19	26 27										
L	First	125	125	↓	↓	↓	↓	•	↑	↓	0 2	0 3	1 4	2 5	3 7	5 9	7 11	11 16	↑	↑	↑	↑	↑	↑	↑	↑	↑	↑	↑
	Second	125	250								1 2	3 4	4 5	6 7	8 9	12 13	18 19	26 27											
M	First	200	200	↓	↓	↓	•	↑	↓	0 2	0 3	1 4	2 5	3 7	5 9	7 11	11 16	↑	↑	↑	↑	↑	↑	↑	↑	↑	↑	↑	↑
	Second	200	400							1 2	3 4	4 5	6 7	8 9	12 13	18 19	26 27												
N	First	315	315	↓	↓	•	↑	↓	0 2	0 3	1 4	2 5	3 7	5 9	7 11	11 16	↑	↑	↑	↑	↑	↑	↑	↑	↑	↑	↑	↑	↑
	Second	315	630						1 2	3 4	4 5	6 7	8 9	12 13	18 19	26 27													
P	First	500	500	↓	•	↑	↓	0 2	0 3	1 4	2 5	3 7	5 9	7 11	11 16	↑	↑	↑	↑	↑	↑	↑	↑	↑	↑	↑	↑	↑	↑
	Second	500	1000					1 2	3 4	4 5	6 7	8 9	12 13	18 19	26 27														
Q	First	800	800	•	↑	↓	0 2	0 3	1 4	2 5	3 7	5 9	7 11	11 16	↑	↑	↑	↑	↑	↑	↑	↑	↑	↑	↑	↑	↑	↑	↑
	Second	800	1600				1 2	3 4	4 5	6 7	8 9	12 13	18 19	26 27															
R	First	1250	1250	↑	↑	0 2	0 3	1 4	2 5	3 7	5 9	7 11	11 16	↑	↑	↑	↑	↑	↑	↑	↑	↑	↑	↑	↑	↑	↑	↑	↑
	Second	1250	2500			1 2	3 4	4 5	6 7	8 9	12 13	18 19	26 27																

↓ = Use first sampling plan below arrow. If sample size equals, or exceeds, lot or batch size, do 100% inspection.
↑ = Use first sampling plan above arrow.
Ac = Acceptance number.
Re = Rejection number.

DOUBLE
TIGHTENED

TABLE 12-24.
Double Sampling Plans for Tightened Inspection (Master Table)

Sample Size Code Letter	Sample	Sample Size	Cumulative Sample Size	0.010	0.015	0.025	0.040	0.065	0.10	0.15	0.25	0.40	0.65	1.0	1.5	2.5	4.0	6.5	10	15	25	40	65	100	150	250	400	650	1000
				Ac Re	Ac Re	Ac Re	Ac Re	Ac Re	Ac Re	Ac Re	Ac Re	Ac Re	Ac Re	Ac Re	Ac Re	Ac Re	Ac Re	Ac Re	Ac Re	Ac Re	Ac Re	Ac Re	Ac Re	Ac Re	Ac Re	Ac Re	Ac Re	Ac Re	Ac Re
A				↓	↓	↓	↓	↓	↓	↓	↓	↓	↓	↓	↓	↓	↓	↓	↓	↓	↓	•	•	•	•	•	•	•	•
B	First	2	2	↓	↓	↓	↓	↓	↓	↓	↓	↓	↓	↓	↓	↓	↓	•	↓	↓	0 2	0 3	1 4	2 5	3 7	6 10	9 14	15 20	28 29
	Second	2	4	↓	↓	↓	↓	↓	↓	↓	↓	↓	↓	↓	↓	↓	↓		↓	↓	1 2	3 4	4 5	6 7	11 12	15 16	23 24	34 35	52 54
C	First	3	3	↓	↓	↓	↓	↓	↓	↓	↓	↓	↓	↓	↓	↓	•	↓	↓	0 2	0 3	1 4	2 5	3 7	6 10	9 14	15 20	28 29	↑
	Second	3	6	↓	↓	↓	↓	↓	↓	↓	↓	↓	↓	↓	↓	↓		↓	↓	1 2	3 4	4 5	6 7	11 12	15 16	23 24	34 35	52 54	↑
D	First	5	5	↓	↓	↓	↓	↓	↓	↓	↓	↓	↓	↓	↓	•	↓	↓	0 2	0 3	1 4	2 5	3 7	6 10	9 14	15 20	28 29	↑	↑
	Second	5	10	↓	↓	↓	↓	↓	↓	↓	↓	↓	↓	↓	↓		↓	↓	1 2	3 4	4 5	6 7	11 12	15 16	23 24	34 35	52 54	↑	↑
E	First	8	8	↓	↓	↓	↓	↓	↓	↓	↓	↓	↓	↓	•	↓	↓	0 2	0 3	1 4	2 5	3 7	6 10	9 14	15 20	28 29	↑	↑	↑
	Second	8	16	↓	↓	↓	↓	↓	↓	↓	↓	↓	↓	↓		↓	↓	1 2	3 4	4 5	6 7	11 12	15 16	23 24	34 35	52 54	↑	↑	↑
F	First	13	13	↓	↓	↓	↓	↓	↓	↓	↓	↓	↓	•	↓	↓	0 2	0 3	1 4	2 5	3 7	6 10	9 14	↑	↑	↑	↑	↑	↑
	Second	13	26	↓	↓	↓	↓	↓	↓	↓	↓	↓	↓		↓	↓	1 2	3 4	4 5	6 7	11 12	15 16	23 24	↑	↑	↑	↑	↑	↑
G	First	20	20	↓	↓	↓	↓	↓	↓	↓	↓	↓	•	↓	↓	0 2	0 3	1 4	2 5	3 7	6 10	9 14	↑	↑	↑	↑	↑	↑	↑
	Second	20	40	↓	↓	↓	↓	↓	↓	↓	↓	↓		↓	↓	1 2	3 4	4 5	6 7	11 12	15 16	23 24	↑	↑	↑	↑	↑	↑	↑
H	First	32	32	↓	↓	↓	↓	↓	↓	↓	↓	•	↓	↓	0 2	0 3	1 4	2 5	3 7	6 10	9 14	↑	↑	↑	↑	↑	↑	↑	↑
	Second	32	64	↓	↓	↓	↓	↓	↓	↓	↓		↓	↓	1 2	3 4	4 5	6 7	11 12	15 16	23 24	↑	↑	↑	↑	↑	↑	↑	↑
J	First	50	50	↓	↓	↓	↓	↓	↓	↓	•	↓	↓	0 2	0 3	1 4	2 5	3 7	6 10	9 14	↑	↑	↑	↑	↑	↑	↑	↑	↑
	Second	50	100	↓	↓	↓	↓	↓	↓	↓		↓	↓	1 2	3 4	4 5	6 7	11 12	15 16	23 24	↑	↑	↑	↑	↑	↑	↑	↑	↑
K	First	80	80	↓	↓	↓	↓	↓	↓	•	↓	↓	0 2	0 3	1 4	2 5	3 7	6 10	9 14	↑	↑	↑	↑	↑	↑	↑	↑	↑	↑
	Second	80	160	↓	↓	↓	↓	↓	↓		↓	↓	1 2	3 4	4 5	6 7	11 12	15 16	23 24	↑	↑	↑	↑	↑	↑	↑	↑	↑	↑
L	First	125	125	↓	↓	↓	↓	↓	•	↓	↓	0 2	0 3	1 4	2 5	3 7	6 10	9 14	↑	↑	↑	↑	↑	↑	↑	↑	↑	↑	↑
	Second	125	250	↓	↓	↓	↓	↓		↓	↓	1 2	3 4	4 5	6 7	11 12	15 16	23 24	↑	↑	↑	↑	↑	↑	↑	↑	↑	↑	↑
M	First	200	200	↓	↓	↓	↓	•	↓	↓	0 2	0 3	1 4	2 5	3 7	6 10	9 14	↑	↑	↑	↑	↑	↑	↑	↑	↑	↑	↑	↑
	Second	200	400	↓	↓	↓	↓		↓	↓	1 2	3 4	4 5	6 7	11 12	15 16	23 24	↑	↑	↑	↑	↑	↑	↑	↑	↑	↑	↑	↑
N	First	315	315	↓	↓	↓	•	↓	↓	0 2	0 3	1 4	2 5	3 7	6 10	9 14	↑	↑	↑	↑	↑	↑	↑	↑	↑	↑	↑	↑	↑
	Second	315	630	↓	↓	↓		↓	↓	1 2	3 4	4 5	6 7	11 12	15 16	23 24	↑	↑	↑	↑	↑	↑	↑	↑	↑	↑	↑	↑	↑
P	First	500	500	↓	↓	•	↓	↓	0 2	0 3	1 4	2 5	3 7	6 10	9 14	↑	↑	↑	↑	↑	↑	↑	↑	↑	↑	↑	↑	↑	↑
	Second	500	1000	↓	↓		↓	↓	1 2	3 4	4 5	6 7	11 12	15 16	23 24	↑	↑	↑	↑	↑	↑	↑	↑	↑	↑	↑	↑	↑	↑
Q	First	800	800	↓	•	↓	↓	0 2	0 3	1 4	2 5	3 7	6 10	9 14	↑	↑	↑	↑	↑	↑	↑	↑	↑	↑	↑	↑	↑	↑	↑
	Second	800	1600	↓		↓	↓	1 2	3 4	4 5	6 7	11 12	15 16	23 24	↑	↑	↑	↑	↑	↑	↑	↑	↑	↑	↑	↑	↑	↑	↑
R	First	1250	1250	•	↑	↓	0 2	0 3	1 4	2 5	3 7	6 10	9 14	↑	↑	↑	↑	↑	↑	↑	↑	↑	↑	↑	↑	↑	↑	↑	↑
	Second	1250	2500		↑	↓	1 2	3 4	4 5	6 7	11 12	15 16	23 24	↑	↑	↑	↑	↑	↑	↑	↑	↑	↑	↑	↑	↑	↑	↑	↑
S	First	2000	2000			0 2																							
	Second	2000	4000			1 2																							

(Column headings 0.010–1000: Acceptable Quality Levels (Tightened Inspection))

↓ = Use first sampling plan below arrow. If sample size equals, or exceeds, lot or batch size, do 100% inspection.

↑ = Use first sampling plan above arrow.

Ac = Acceptance number.

Re = Rejection number.

• = Use corresponding single sampling plan (or alternatively, use double sampling plan below, when available).

DOUBLE
REDUCED

TABLE 12-25.
Double Sampling Plans for Reduced Inspection (Master Table)

Sample Size Code Letter	Sample	Sample Size	Cumulative Sample Size	*Acceptable Quality Levels (Reduced Inspection)†*																									
				0.010	0.015	0.025	0.040	0.065	0.10	0.15	0.25	0.40	0.65	1.0	1.5	2.5	4.0	6.5	10	15	25	40	65	100	150	250	400	650	1000
				Ac Re	Ac Re	Ac Re	Ac Re	Ac Re	Ac Re	Ac Re	Ac Re	Ac Re	Ac Re	Ac Re	Ac Re	Ac Re	Ac Re	Ac Re	Ac Re	Ac Re	Ac Re	Ac Re	Ac Re	Ac Re	Ac Re	Ac Re	Ac Re	Ac Re	Ac Re
A				↓	↓	↓	↓	↓	↓	↓	↓	↓	↓	↓	↓	↓	↓	•	↓	↓	•	•	•	•	•	•	•	•	•
B				↓	↓	↓	↓	↓	↓	↓	↓	↓	↓	↓	↓	↓	•	↑	↓	•	•	•	•	•	•	•	•	•	•
C				↓	↓	↓	↓	↓	↓	↓	↓	↓	↓	↓	↓	•	↑	↓	•	•	•	•	•	•	•	•	•	•	↑
D	First	2	2	↓	↓	↓	↓	↓	↓	↓	↓	↓	↓	↓	•	↑	↓	0 2	0 3	0 4	0 4	1 5	2 7	3 8	5 10	7 12	11 17	↑	↑
	Second	2	4															0 2	0 4	1 5	3 6	4 7	6 9	8 12	12 16	18 22	26 30		
E	First	3	3	↓	↓	↓	↓	↓	↓	↓	↓	↓	↓	•	↑	↓	0 2	0 3	0 4	0 4	1 5	2 7	3 8	5 10	7 12	11 17	↑	↑	↑
	Second	3	6														0 2	0 4	1 5	3 6	4 7	6 9	8 12	12 16	18 22	26 30			
F	First	5	5	↓	↓	↓	↓	↓	↓	↓	↓	↓	•	↑	↓	0 2	0 3	0 4	0 4	1 5	2 7	3 8	5 10	↑	↑	↑	↑	↑	↑
	Second	5	10													0 2	0 4	1 5	3 6	4 7	6 9	8 12	12 16						
G	First	8	8	↓	↓	↓	↓	↓	↓	↓	↓	•	↑	↓	0 2	0 3	0 4	0 4	1 5	2 7	3 8	5 10	↑	↑	↑	↑	↑	↑	↑
	Second	8	16												0 2	0 4	1 5	3 6	4 7	6 9	8 12	12 16							
H	First	13	13	↓	↓	↓	↓	↓	↓	↓	•	↑	↓	0 2	0 3	0 4	0 4	1 5	2 7	3 8	5 10	↑	↑	↑	↑	↑	↑	↑	↑
	Second	13	26											0 2	0 4	1 5	3 6	4 7	6 9	8 12	12 16								
J	First	20	20	↓	↓	↓	↓	↓	↓	•	↑	↓	0 2	0 3	0 4	0 4	1 5	2 7	3 8	5 10	↑	↑	↑	↑	↑	↑	↑	↑	↑
	Second	20	40										0 2	0 4	1 5	3 6	4 7	6 9	8 12	12 16									
K	First	32	32	↓	↓	↓	↓	↓	•	↑	↓	0 2	0 3	0 4	0 4	1 5	2 7	3 8	5 10	↑	↑	↑	↑	↑	↑	↑	↑	↑	↑
	Second	32	64									0 2	0 4	1 5	3 6	4 7	6 9	8 12	12 16										
L	First	50	50	↓	↓	↓	↓	•	↑	↓	0 2	0 3	0 4	0 4	1 5	2 7	3 8	5 10	↑	↑	↑	↑	↑	↑	↑	↑	↑	↑	↑
	Second	50	100								0 2	0 4	1 5	3 6	4 7	6 9	8 12	12 16											
M	First	80	80	↓	↓	↓	•	↑	↓	0 2	0 3	0 4	0 4	1 5	2 7	3 8	5 10	↑	↑	↑	↑	↑	↑	↑	↑	↑	↑	↑	↑
	Second	80	160							0 2	0 4	1 5	3 6	4 7	6 9	8 12	12 16												
N	First	125	125	↓	↓	•	↑	↓	0 2	0 3	0 4	0 4	1 5	2 7	3 8	5 10	↑	↑	↑	↑	↑	↑	↑	↑	↑	↑	↑	↑	↑
	Second	125	250						0 2	0 4	1 5	3 6	4 7	6 9	8 12	12 16													
P	First	200	200	↓	•	↑	↓	0 2	0 3	0 4	0 4	1 5	2 7	3 8	5 10	↑	↑	↑	↑	↑	↑	↑	↑	↑	↑	↑	↑	↑	↑
	Second	200	400					0 2	0 4	1 5	3 6	4 7	6 9	8 12	12 16														
Q	First	315	315	•	↑	↓	0 2	0 3	0 4	0 4	1 5	2 7	3 8	5 10	↑	↑	↑	↑	↑	↑	↑	↑	↑	↑	↑	↑	↑	↑	↑
	Second	315	630				0 2	0 4	1 5	3 6	4 7	6 9	8 12	12 16															
R	First	500	500	↑	↑	0 2	0 3	0 4	0 4	1 5	2 7	3 8	5 10	↑	↑	↑	↑	↑	↑	↑	↑	↑	↑	↑	↑	↑	↑	↑	↑
	Second	500	1000			0 2	0 4	1 5	3 6	4 7	6 9	8 12	12 16																

↓ = Use first sampling plan below arrow. If sample size equals, or exceeds, lot or batch size, do 100% inspection.

↑ = Use first sampling plan above arrow.

Ac = Acceptance number.

Re = Rejection number.

• = Use corresponding single sampling plan (or alternatively, use double sampling plan below, when available).

† = If, after the second sample, the acceptance number has been exceeded, but the rejection number has not been reached, accept the lot, but reinstate normal inspection (see 10.1 4).

MULTIPLE
NORMAL

TABLE 12-26.
Multiple Sampling Plans for Normal Inspection (Master Table)

Acceptable Quality Levels (Normal Inspection)

Sample Size Code Letter	Sample	Sample Size	Cumulative Sample Size	0.010	0.015	0.025	0.040	0.065	0.10	0.15	0.25	0.40	0.65	1.0	1.5	2.5	4.0	6.5	10	15	25	40	65	100	150	250	400	650	1000
				Ac Re	Ac Re	Ac Re	Ac Re	Ac Re	Ac Re	Ac Re	Ac Re	Ac Re	Ac Re	Ac Re	Ac Re	Ac Re	Ac Re	Ac Re	Ac Re	Ac Re	Ac Re	Ac Re	Ac Re	Ac Re	Ac Re	Ac Re	Ac Re	Ac Re	Ac Re
A				⇩	⇩	⇩	⇩	⇩	⇩	⇩	⇩	⇩	⇩	⇩	⇩	⇩	⇩	•	⇩	⇩	•	•	•	•	•	•	•	•	•
B				⇩	⇩	⇩	⇩	⇩	⇩	⇩	⇩	⇩	⇩	⇩	⇩	⇩	•	⇧	⇩	‡	‡	‡	‡	‡	‡	‡	‡	‡	‡
C				⇩	⇩	⇩	⇩	⇩	⇩	⇩	⇩	⇩	⇩	⇩	⇩	•	⇧	⇩	‡	‡	‡	‡	‡	‡	‡	‡	‡	‡	⇧
D	First	2	2	⇩	⇩	⇩	⇩	⇩	⇩	⇩	⇩	⇩	⇩	⇩	•	⇧	⇩	# 2	# 2	# 3	# 4	0 4	0 5	1 7	2 9	4 12	6 16	⇧	⇧
	Second	2	4															# 2	0 3	0 3	1 5	1 6	3 8	4 10	7 14	11 19	17 27		
	Third	2	6															0 2	0 3	1 4	2 6	3 8	6 10	8 13	13 19	19 27	29 39		
	Fourth	2	8															0 3	1 4	2 5	3 7	5 10	8 13	12 17	19 25	37 34	40 49		
	Fifth	2	10															1 3	2 4	3 6	5 8	7 11	11 15	17 20	25 29	36 40	53 58		
	Sixth	2	12															1 3	3 5	4 6	7 9	10 12	14 17	21 23	31 33	45 47	65 68		
	Seventh	2	14															2 3	4 5	6 7	9 10	13 14	18 19	25 26	37 38	53 54	77 78		
E	First	3	3	⇩	⇩	⇩	⇩	⇩	⇩	⇩	⇩	⇩	⇩	•	⇧	⇩	# 2	# 2	# 3	# 4	0 4	0 5	1 7	2 9	4 12	6 16	⇧	⇧	⇧
	Second	3	6														# 2	0 3	0 3	1 5	1 6	3 8	4 10	7 14	11 19	17 27			
	Third	3	9														0 2	0 3	1 4	2 6	3 8	6 10	8 13	13 19	19 27	29 39			
	Fourth	3	12														0 3	1 4	2 5	3 7	5 10	8 13	12 17	19 25	37 34	40 49			
	Fifth	3	15														1 3	2 4	3 6	5 8	7 11	11 15	17 20	25 29	36 40	53 58			
	Sixth	3	18														1 3	3 5	4 6	7 9	10 12	14 17	21 23	31 33	45 47	65 68			
	Seventh	3	21														2 3	4 5	6 7	9 10	13 14	18 19	25 26	37 38	53 54	77 78			
F	First	5	5	⇩	⇩	⇩	⇩	⇩	⇩	⇩	⇩	⇩	•	⇧	⇩	# 2	# 2	# 3	# 4	0 4	0 5	1 7	2 9	⇧	⇧	⇧	⇧	⇧	⇧
	Second	5	10													# 2	0 3	0 3	1 5	1 6	3 8	4 10	7 14						
	Third	5	15													0 2	0 3	1 4	2 6	3 8	6 10	8 13	13 19						
	Fourth	5	20													0 3	1 4	2 5	3 7	5 10	8 13	12 17	19 25						
	Fifth	5	25													1 3	2 4	3 6	5 8	7 11	11 15	17 20	25 29						
	Sixth	5	30													1 3	3 5	4 6	7 9	10 12	14 17	21 23	31 33						
	Seventh	5	35													2 3	4 5	6 7	9 10	13 14	18 19	25 26	37 38						
G	First	8	8	⇩	⇩	⇩	⇩	⇩	⇩	⇩	⇩	•	⇧	⇩	# 2	# 2	# 3	# 4	0 4	0 5	1 7	2 9	⇧	⇧	⇧	⇧	⇧	⇧	⇧
	Second	8	16												# 2	0 3	0 3	1 5	1 6	3 8	4 10	7 14							
	Third	8	24												0 2	0 3	1 4	2 6	3 8	6 10	8 13	13 19							
	Fourth	8	32												0 3	1 4	2 5	3 7	5 10	8 13	12 17	19 25							
	Fith	8	40												1 3	2 4	3 6	5 8	7 11	11 15	17 20	25 29							
	Sixth	8	48												1 3	3 5	4 6	7 9	10 12	14 17	21 23	31 33							
	Seventh	8	56												2 3	4 5	6 7	9 10	13 14	18 19	25 26	37 38							
H	First	13	13	⇩	⇩	⇩	⇩	⇩	⇩	⇩	•	⇧	⇩	# 2	# 2	# 3	# 4	0 4	0 5	1 7	2 9	⇧	⇧	⇧	⇧	⇧	⇧	⇧	⇧
	Second	13	26											# 2	0 3	0 3	1 5	1 6	3 8	4 10	7 14								
	Third	13	39											0 2	0 3	1 4	2 6	3 8	6 10	8 13	13 19								
	Fourth	13	52											0 3	1 4	2 5	3 7	5 10	8 13	12 17	19 25								
	Fifth	13	65											1 3	2 4	3 6	5 8	7 11	11 15	17 20	25 29								
	Sixth	13	78											1 3	3 5	4 6	7 9	10 12	14 17	21 23	31 33								
	Seventh	13	91											2 3	4 5	6 7	9 10	13 14	18 19	25 26	37 38								
J	First	20	20	⇩	⇩	⇩	⇩	⇩	⇩	•	⇧	⇩	# 2	# 2	# 3	# 4	0 4	0 5	1 7	2 9	⇧	⇧	⇧	⇧	⇧	⇧	⇧	⇧	⇧
	Second	20	40										# 2	0 3	0 3	1 5	1 6	3 8	4 10	7 14									
	Third	20	60										0 2	0 3	1 4	2 6	3 8	6 10	8 13	13 19									
	Fourth	20	80										0 3	1 4	2 5	3 7	5 10	8 13	12 17	19 25									
	Fifth	20	100										1 3	2 4	3 6	5 8	7 11	11 15	17 20	25 29									
	Sixth	20	120										1 3	3 5	4 6	7 9	10 12	14 17	21 23	31 33									
	Seventh	20	140										2 3	4 5	6 7	9 10	13 14	18 19	25 26	37 38									

⇩ = Use first sampling plan below arrow. If sample size equals, or exceeds, lot or batch size, do 100% inspection.

⇧ = Use first sampling plan above arrow.

Ac = Acceptance number.

Re = Rejection number.

• = Use corresponding single sampling plan (or alternatively, use double sampling plan below, when available).

‡ = Use corresponding double sampling plan (or alternatively, use double sampling plan below, when available).

= Acceptance not permitted at this sample size.

MULTIPLE
NORMAL

TABLE 12-27.
Multiple Sampling Plans for Normal Inspection (Master Table Continued))

Sample Size Code Letter	Sample	Sample Size	Cumulative Sample Size	Acceptable Quality Levels (Normal Inspection)																									
				0.010	0.015	0.025	0.040	0.065	0.10	0.15	0.25	0.40	0.65	1.0	1.5	2.5	4.0	6.5	10	15	25	40	65	100	150	250	400	650	1000
				Ac Re	Ac Re	Ac Re	Ac Re	Ac Re	Ac Re	Ac Re	Ac Re	Ac Re	Ac Re	Ac Re	Ac Re	Ac Re	Ac Re	Ac Re	Ac Re	Ac Re	Ac Re	Ac Re	Ac Re	Ac Re	Ac Re	Ac Re	Ac Re	Ac Re	Ac Re
K	First	32	32	↓	↓	↓	↓	↓	•	↑	↓	# 2	# 2	# 3	# 4	0 4	0 5	1 7	2 9	↑	↑	↑	↑	↑	↑	↑	↑	↑	↑
	Second	32	64									# 2	0 3	0 3	1 5	1 6	3 8	4 10	7 14										
	Third	32	96									0 2	0 3	1 4	2 6	3 8	6 10	8 13	13 19										
	Fourth	32	128									0 3	1 4	2 5	3 7	5 10	8 13	12 17	19 25										
	Fifth	32	160									1 3	2 4	3 6	5 8	7 11	11 15	17 20	25 29										
	Sixth	32	192									1 3	3 5	4 6	7 9	10 12	14 17	21 23	31 33										
	Seventh	32	224									2 3	4 5	6 7	9 10	13 14	18 19	25 26	37 38										
L	First	50	50					•	↑	↓	# 2	# 2	# 3	# 4	0 4	0 5	1 7	2 9	↑										
	Second	50	100								# 2	0 3	0 3	1 5	1 6	3 8	4 10	7 14											
	Third	50	150								0 2	0 3	1 4	2 6	3 8	6 10	8 13	13 19											
	Fourth	50	200								0 3	1 4	2 5	3 7	5 10	8 13	12 17	19 25											
	Fifth	50	250								1 3	2 4	3 6	5 8	7 11	11 15	17 20	25 29											
	Sixth	50	300								1 3	3 5	4 6	7 9	10 12	14 17	21 23	31 33											
	Seventh	50	350								2 3	4 5	6 7	9 10	13 14	18 19	25 26	37 38											
M	First	80	80				•	↑	↓	# 2	# 2	# 3	# 4	0 4	0 5	1 7	2 9	↑											
	Second	80	160							# 2	0 3	0 3	1 5	1 6	3 8	4 10	7 14												
	Third	80	240							0 2	0 3	1 4	2 6	3 8	6 10	8 13	13 19												
	Fourth	80	320							0 3	1 4	2 5	3 7	5 10	8 13	12 17	19 25												
	Fifth	80	400							1 3	2 4	3 6	5 8	7 11	11 15	17 20	25 29												
	Sixth	80	480							1 3	3 5	4 6	7 9	10 12	14 17	21 23	31 33												
	Seventh	80	560							2 3	4 5	6 7	9 10	13 14	18 19	25 26	37 38												
N	First	125	125			•	↑	↓	# 2	# 2	# 3	# 4	0 4	0 5	1 7	2 9	↑												
	Second	125	250						# 2	0 3	0 3	1 5	1 6	3 8	4 10	7 14													
	Third	125	375						0 2	0 3	1 4	2 6	3 8	6 10	8 13	13 19													
	Fourth	125	500						0 3	1 4	2 5	3 7	5 10	8 13	12 17	19 25													
	Fifth	125	625						1 3	2 4	3 6	5 8	7 11	11 15	17 20	25 29													
	Sixth	125	750						1 3	3 5	4 6	7 9	10 12	14 17	21 23	31 33													
	Seventh	125	875						2 3	4 5	6 7	9 10	13 14	18 19	25 26	37 38													
P	First	200	200		•	↑	↓	# 2	# 2	# 3	# 4	0 4	0 5	1 7	2 9	↑													
	Second	200	400					# 2	0 3	0 3	1 5	1 6	3 8	4 10	7 14														
	Third	200	600					0 2	0 3	1 4	2 6	3 8	6 10	8 13	13 19														
	Fourth	200	800					0 3	1 4	2 5	3 7	5 10	8 13	12 17	19 25														
	Fifth	200	1000					1 3	2 4	3 6	5 8	7 11	11 15	17 20	25 29														
	Sixth	200	1200					1 3	3 5	4 6	7 9	10 12	14 17	21 23	31 33														
	Seventh	200	1400					2 3	4 5	6 7	9 10	13 14	18 19	25 26	37 38														
Q	First	315	315	•	↑	↓	# 2	# 2	# 3	# 4	0 4	0 5	1 7	2 9	↑														
	Second	315	630				# 2	0 3	0 3	1 5	1 6	3 8	4 10	7 14															
	Third	315	945				0 2	0 3	1 4	2 6	3 8	6 10	8 13	13 19															
	Fourth	315	1260				0 3	1 4	2 5	3 7	5 10	8 13	12 17	19 25															
	Fifth	315	1575				1 3	2 4	3 6	5 8	7 11	11 15	17 20	25 29															
	Sixth	315	1890				1 3	3 5	4 6	7 9	10 12	14 17	21 23	31 33															
	Seventh	315	2205				2 3	4 5	6 7	9 10	13 14	18 19	25 26	37 38															
R	First	500	500	↑		# 2	# 2	# 3	# 4	0 4	0 5	1 7	2 9	↑															
	Second	500	1000			# 2	0 3	0 3	1 5	1 6	3 8	4 10	7 14																
	Third	500	1500			0 2	0 3	1 4	2 6	3 8	6 10	8 13	13 19																
	Fourth	500	2000			0 3	1 4	2 5	3 7	5 10	8 13	12 17	19 25																
	Fifth	500	2500			1 3	2 4	3 6	5 8	7 11	11 15	17 20	25 29																
	Sixth	500	3000			1 3	3 5	4 6	7 9	10 12	14 17	21 23	31 33																
	Seventh	500	3500			2 3	4 5	6 7	9 10	13 14	18 19	25 26	37 38																

↓ = Use first sampling plan below arrow. If sample size equals, or exceeds, lot or batch size, do 100% inspection.

↑ = Use first sampling plan above arrow (refer to preceding page, when necessary).

Ac = Acceptance number.

Re = Rejection number.

• = Use corresponding single sampling plan (or alternatively, use multiple plan below, when available).

\# = Acceptance not permitted at this sample size.

MULTIPLE
TIGHTENED

TABLE 12-28.
Multiple Sampling Plans for Tightened Inspection (Master Table)

Sample Size Code Letter	Sample	Sample Size	Cumulative Sample Size	0.010	0.015	0.025	0.040	0.065	0.10	0.15	0.25	0.40	0.65	1.0	1.5	2.5	4.0	6.5	10	15	25	40	65	100	150	250	400	650	1000
				Ac Re	Ac Re	Ac Re	Ac Re	Ac Re	Ac Re	Ac Re	Ac Re	Ac Re	Ac Re	Ac Re	Ac Re	Ac Re	Ac Re	Ac Re	Ac Re	Ac Re	Ac Re	Ac Re	Ac Re	Ac Re	Ac Re	Ac Re	Ac Re	Ac Re	Ac Re
A				↓	↓	↓	↓	↓	↓	↓	↓	↓	↓	↓	↓	↓	↓	↓	↓	↓	↓	•	•	•	•	•	•	•	•
B																		•			++	++	++	++	++	++	++	++	++
C																	•	↓		++	++	++	++	++	++	++	++	++	↑
D	First	2	2	↓	↓	↓	↓	↓	↓	↓	↓	↓	↓	↓	↓	•	↓	↓	# 2	# 2	# 3	# 4	0 4	0 6	1 8	3 10	6 15	↑	↑
	Second	2	4																# 2	0 3	0 3	1 5	2 7	3 9	6 12	10 17	16 27		
	Third	2	6																0 2	0 3	1 4	2 6	4 9	7 12	11 17	17 24	26 36		
	Fourth	2	8																0 3	1 4	2 5	3 7	6 11	10 15	16 22	24 31	37 46		
	Fifth	2	10																1 3	2 4	3 6	5 8	9 12	14 17	22 25	32 37	49 55		
	Sixth	2	12																1 3	3 5	4 6	7 9	12 14	18 20	27 29	40 43	61 64		
	Seventh	2	14																2 3	4 5	6 7	9 10	14 15	21 22	32 33	48 49	72 73		
E	First	3	3	↓	↓	↓	↓	↓	↓	↓	↓	↓	↓	↓	•	↓	↓	# 2	# 2	# 3	# 4	0 4	0 6	1 8	3 10	6 15	↑	↑	↑
	Second	3	6															# 2	0 3	0 3	1 5	2 7	3 9	6 12	10 17	16 25			
	Third	3	9															0 2	0 3	1 4	2 6	4 9	7 12	11 17	17 24	26 36			
	Fourth	3	12															0 3	1 4	2 5	3 7	6 11	10 15	16 22	24 31	37 46			
	Fifth	3	15															1 3	2 4	3 6	5 8	9 12	14 17	22 25	32 37	49 55			
	Sixth	3	18															1 3	3 5	4 6	7 9	12 14	18 20	27 29	40 43	61 64			
	Seventh	3	21															2 3	4 5	6 7	9 10	14 15	21 22	32 33	48 49	72 73			
F	First	5	5	↓	↓	↓	↓	↓	↓	↓	↓	↓	↓	•	↓	↓	# 2	# 2	# 3	# 4	0 4	0 6	1 8	↑	↑	↑	↑	↑	↑
	Second	5	10														# 2	0 3	0 3	1 5	2 7	3 9	6 12						
	Third	5	15														0 2	0 3	1 4	2 6	4 9	7 12	11 17						
	Fourth	5	20														0 3	1 4	2 5	3 7	6 11	10 15	16 22						
	Fifth	5	25														1 3	2 4	3 6	5 8	9 12	14 17	22 25						
	Sixth	5	30														1 3	3 5	4 6	7 9	12 14	18 20	27 29						
	Seventh	5	35														2 3	4 5	6 7	9 10	14 15	21 22	32 33						
G	First	8	8	↓	↓	↓	↓	↓	↓	↓	↓	↓	•	↓	↓	# 2	# 2	# 3	# 4	0 4	0 6	1 8	↑	↑	↑	↑	↑	↑	↑
	Second	8	16												# 2	0 3	0 3	1 5	2 7	3 9	6 12								
	Third	8	24												0 2	0 3	1 4	2 6	4 9	7 12	11 17								
	Fourth	8	32												0 3	1 4	2 5	3 7	6 11	10 15	16 22								
	Fifth	8	40												1 3	2 4	3 6	5 8	9 12	14 17	22 25								
	Sixth	8	48												1 3	3 5	4 6	7 9	12 14	18 20	27 29								
	Seventh	8	56												2 3	4 5	6 7	9 10	14 15	21 22	32 33								
H	First	13	13	↓	↓	↓	↓	↓	↓	↓	↓	•	↓	↓	# 2	# 2	# 3	# 4	0 4	0 6	1 8	↑	↑	↑	↑	↑	↑	↑	↑
	Second	13	26											# 2	0 3	0 3	1 5	2 7	3 9	6 12									
	Third	13	39											0 2	0 3	1 4	2 6	4 9	7 12	11 17									
	Fourth	13	52											0 3	1 4	2 5	3 7	6 11	10 15	16 22									
	Fifth	13	65											1 3	2 4	3 6	5 8	9 12	14 17	22 25									
	Sixth	13	78											1 3	3 5	4 6	7 9	12 14	18 20	27 29									
	Seventh	13	91											2 3	4 5	6 7	9 10	14 15	21 22	32 33									
J	First	20	20	↓	↓	↓	↓	↓	↓	↓	•	↓	↓	# 2	# 2	# 3	# 4	0 4	0 6	1 8	↑	↑	↑	↑	↑	↑	↑	↑	↑
	Second	20	40										# 2	0 3	0 3	1 5	2 7	3 9	6 12										
	Third	20	60										0 2	0 3	1 4	2 6	4 9	7 12	11 17										
	Fourth	20	80										0 3	1 4	2 5	3 7	6 11	10 15	16 22										
	Fifth	20	100										1 3	2 4	3 6	5 8	9 12	14 17	22 25										
	Sixth	20	120										1 3	3 5	4 6	7 9	12 14	18 20	27 29										
	Seventh	20	140										2 3	4 5	6 7	9 10	14 15	21 22	32 33										

↓ = Use first sampling plan below arrow. If sample size equals, or exceeds, lot or batch size, do 100% inspection.
↑ = Use first sampling plan above arrow.
Ac = Acceptance number.
Re = Rejection number.
• = Use corresponding single sampling plan (or alternatively, use multiple sampling plan below, where available).
++ = Use corresponding double sampling plan (or alternatively, use multiple sampling plan below, where available).
# = Acceptance not permitted at this sample size.

MULTIPLE
REDUCED

TABLE 12-29.
Multiple Sampling Plans for Reduced Inspection (Master Table)

Sample Size Code Letter	Sample	Sample Size	Cumulative Sample Size	Acceptable Quality Levels (Reduced Inspection)†																									
				0.010	0.015	0.025	0.040	0.065	0.10	0.15	0.25	0.40	0.65	1.0	1.5	2.5	4.0	6.5	10	15	25	40	65	100	150	250	400	650	1000
				Ac Re	Ac Re	Ac Re	Ac Re	Ac Re	Ac Re	Ac Re	Ac Re	Ac Re	Ac Re	Ac Re	Ac Re	Ac Re	Ac Re	Ac Re	Ac Re	Ac Re	Ac Re	Ac Re	Ac Re	Ac Re	Ac Re	Ac Re	Ac Re	Ac Re	Ac Re
A				↓	↓	↓	↓	↓	↓	↓	↓	↓	↓	↓	↓	↓	↓	•	↓	↓	•	•	•	•	•	•	•	•	•
B				↓	↓	↓	↓	↓	↓	↓	↓	↓	↓	↓	↓	↓	•	↑	↓	•	•	•	•	•	•	•	•	•	•
C				↓	↓	↓	↓	↓	↓	↓	↓	↓	↓	↓	↓	•	↑	↓	•	•	•	•	•	•	•	•	•	•	↑
D				↓	↓	↓	↓	↓	↓	↓	↓	↓	↓	↓	•	↑	↓	‡	‡	‡	‡	‡	‡	‡	‡	‡	‡	↑	↑
E				↓	↓	↓	↓	↓	↓	↓	↓	↓	↓	•	↑	↓	‡	‡	‡	‡	‡	‡	‡	‡	‡	‡	↑	↑	↑
F	First	2	2	↓	↓	↓	↓	↓	↓	↓	↓	↓	•	↑	↓	# 2	# 2	# 3	# 3	# 4	# 4	0 5	0 6	↑	↑	↑	↑	↑	↑
	Second	2	4													# 2	# 3	# 3	0 4	0 5	1 6	1 7	3 9						
	Third	2	6													0 2	0 3	0 4	0 5	1 6	2 8	3 9	6 12						
	Fourth	2	8													0 3	0 4	0 5	1 6	2 7	3 10	5 12	8 15						
	Fifth	2	10													0 3	0 4	1 6	2 7	3 8	5 11	7 13	11 17						
	Sixth	2	12													0 3	1 5	1 6	3 7	4 9	7 12	10 15	14 20						
	Seventh	2	14													1 3	1 5	2 7	4 8	6 10	9 14	13 17	18 22						
G	First	3	3	↓	↓	↓	↓	↓	↓	↓	↓	•	↑	↓	# 2	# 2	# 3	# 3	# 4	# 4	0 5	0 6	↑	↑	↑	↑	↑	↑	↑
	Second	3	6												# 2	# 3	# 3	0 4	0 5	1 6	1 7	3 9							
	Third	3	9												0 2	0 3	0 4	0 5	1 6	2 8	3 9	6 12							
	Fourth	3	12												0 3	0 4	0 5	1 6	2 7	3 10	5 12	8 15							
	Fifth	3	15												0 3	0 4	1 6	2 7	3 8	5 11	7 13	11 17							
	Sixth	3	18												0 3	1 5	1 6	3 7	4 9	7 12	10 15	14 20							
	Seventh	3	21												1 3	1 5	2 7	4 8	6 10	9 14	13 17	18 22							
H	First	5	5	↓	↓	↓	↓	↓	↓	↓	•	↑	↓	# 2	# 2	# 3	# 3	# 4	# 4	0 5	0 6	↑	↑	↑	↑	↑	↑	↑	↑
	Second	5	10											# 2	# 3	# 3	0 4	0 5	1 6	1 7	3 9								
	Third	5	15											0 2	0 3	0 4	0 5	6	2 8	3 9	6 12								
	Fourth	5	20											0 3	0 4	0 5	1 6	2 7	3 10	5 12	8 15								
	Fifth	5	25											0 3	0 4	1 6	2 7	3 8	5 11	7 13	11 17								
	Sixth	5	30											0 3	1 5	1 6	3 7	4 9	7 12	10 15	14 20								
	Seventh	5	35											1 3	1 5	2 7	4 8	6 10	9 14	13 17	18 22								
J	First	8	8	↓	↓	↓	↓	↓	↓	•	↑	↓	# 2	# 2	# 3	# 3	# 4	# 4	0 5	0 6	↑	↑	↑	↑	↑	↑	↑	↑	↑
	Second	8	16										# 2	# 3	# 3	0 4	0 5	1 6	1 7	3 9									
	Third	8	24										0 2	0 3	0 4	0 5	1 6	2 8	3 9	6 12									
	Fourth	8	32										0 3	0 4	0 5	1 6	2 7	3 10	5 12	8 15									
	Fifth	8	40										0 3	0 4	1 6	2 7	3 8	5 11	7 13	11 17									
	Sixth	8	48										0 3	1 5	1 6	3 7	4 9	7 12	10 15	14 20									
	Seventh	8	56										1 3	1 5	2 7	4 8	6 10	9 14	13 17	18 22									
K	First	13	13	↓	↓	↓	↓	↓	•	↑	↓	# 2	# 2	# 3	# 3	# 4	# 4	0 5	0 6	↑	↑	↑	↑	↑	↑	↑	↑	↑	↑
	Second	13	26									# 2	# 3	# 3	0 4	0 5	1 6	1 7	3 9										
	Third	13	39									0 2	0 3	0 4	0 5	1 6	2 8	3 9	6 12										
	Fourth	13	52									0 3	0 4	0 5	1 6	2 7	3 10	5 12	8 15										
	Fifth	13	65									0 3	0 4	1 6	2 7	3 8	5 11	7 13	11 17										
	Sixth	13	78									0 3	1 5	1 6	3 7	4 9	7 12	10 15	14 20										
	Seventh	13	91									1 3	1 5	2 7	4 8	6 10	9 14	13 17	18 22										

↓ = Use first sampling plan below arrow. If sample size equals, or exceeds, lot or batch size, do 100% inspection.

↑ = Use first sampling plan above arrow.

Ac = Acceptance number.

Re = Rejection number.

• = Use corresponding single sampling plan (or alternatively, use multiple sampling plan below, where available).

‡ = Use corresponding double sampling plan (or alternatively, use multiple sampling plan below, where available).

= Acceptance not permitted at this sample size.

† = If, after the second sample, the acceptance number has been exceeded, but the rejection number has not been reached, accept the lot, but reinstate normal inspection (see 10.1 4).

for defects per hundred units for AQLs of 10.0 or less and sample sizes of 80 or less.

The process average is the average percentage defective or average number of defects per hundred units (whichever is applicable) of product submitted by the supplier for original inspection. Original inspection is the first inspection of a particular quantity of product as distinguished from the inspection of a product that has been resubmitted after prior rejection.

The average outgoing quality (AOQ) is the average quality of an outgoing product including all accepted lots or batches plus all rejected lots or batches after the rejected lots or batches have been effectively 100-percent inspected and all defectives replaced by nondefectives. The average outgoing quality limit (AOQL) is the maximum of the AOQs for all possible incoming qualities for a given acceptance sampling plan. AOQL values are given in Table 12–30 for each of the single sampling plans for normal inspection and in Table 12–31 for each of the single sampling plans for tightened inspection.

Average sample size curves for double and multiple sampling show the average sample sizes that may be expected to occur under the various sampling plans for a given process quality. The curves assume no curtailment of inspection and are approximate to the extent that they are based upon the Poisson distribution, and that the sample sizes for double and multiple sampling are assumed to be $0.631n$ and $0.25n$, respectively, where n is the equivalent single sample size.

The sampling plans and associated procedures given in this book were designed for use where the units of product are produced in a continuing series of lots or

AOQL
NORMAL

TABLE
Average Outgoing Quality Limit Factors

Code Letter	Sample Size	Acceptable											
		0.010	0.015	0.025	0.040	0.065	0.10	0.15	0.25	0.40	0.65	1.0	1.5
A	2												
B	3												
C	5												
D	8												4.6
E	13											2.8	
F	20										1.8		
G	32									1.2			2.6
H	50								0.74			1.7	2.7
J	80							0.46			1.1	1.7	2.4
K	125						0.29			0.67	1.1	1.6	2.5
L	200					0.18			0.42	0.69	0.97	1.6	2.2
M	315				0.12			0.27	0.44	0.62	1.00	1.4	2.1
N	500			0.074			0.17	0.27	0.39	0.63	0.90	1.3	1.9
P	800		0.046			0.11	0.17	0.24	0.40	0.56	0.82	1.2	1.8
Q	1250	0.029			0.067	0.11	0.16	0.25	0.36	0.52	0.75	1.2	
R	2000			0.042	0.069	0.097	0.16	0.22	0.33	0.47	0.73		

Note: For the exact AOQL, the above values must be multiplied by $\left(1 - \frac{\text{Sample size}}{\text{Lot or Batch size}}\right)$

batches over a period of time. However, if the lot or batch is of an isolated nature, it is desirable to limit the selection of sampling plans to those, associated with a designated AQL value, that provide not less than a specified limiting quality protection. Sampling plans for this purpose can be selected by choosing a limiting quality (LQ) and a consumer's risk to be associated with it. If a different value of consumer's risk is required, the OC curves and their tabulated values may be used. The concept of LQ may also be useful in specifying the AQL and inspection levels for a series of lots or batches, thus fixing minimum sample size where there is some reason for avoiding (with more than a given consumer's risk) more than a limited proportion of defectives (or defects) in any single lot or batch.

PROBABILITIES OF OCCURRENCE

Suppose we have a lot consisting of a very large number of articles that are 10 percent defective and, hence, 90 percent good. Further, suppose that the defective articles and good articles are thoroughly mixed, and we consider drawing (at random) samples of one, two, three, and so on, articles. If we draw a single article, it will either be a defective article or a good article. Now, since there are 10 percent defective articles in the large lot, the chance that in a single drawing we will obtain a defective article is .1, and hence the probability that the article will be a good article is .9.

To take another case, if our sample is to consist of two articles and we draw at random a sample of two, then we may

12-30.
for Normal Inspection (Single Sampling)

Quality Level													
2.5	4.0	6.5	10	15	25	40	65	100	150	250	400	650	1000
		18			42	69	97	160	220	330	470	730	1100
	12			28	46	65	110	150	220	310	490	720	1100
7.4			17	27	39	63	90	130	190	290	430	660	
		11	17	24	40	56	82	120	180	270	410		
	6.5	11	15	24	34	50	72	110	170	250			
4.2	6.9	9.7	16	22	33	47	73						
4.3	6.1	9.9	14	21	29	46							
3.9	6.3	9.0	13	19	29								
4.0	5.6	8.2	12	18									
3.6	5.2	7.5	12										
3.3	4.7	7.3											
3.0	4.7												
2.9													

AOQL
TIGHTENED

TABLE
Average Outgoing Quality Limit Factors

Code Letter	Sample Size	Acceptable											
		0.010	0.015	0.025	0.040	0.065	0.10	0.15	0.25	0.40	0.65	1.0	1.5
A	2												
B	3												
C	5												
D	8												
E	13												2.8
F	20											1.8	
G	32										1.2		
H	50									0.74			1.7
J	80								0.46			1.1	1.7
K	125							0.29			0.67	1.1	1.6
L	200						0.18			0.42	0.69	0.97	1.6
M	315					0.12			0.27	0.44	0.62	1.0	1.6
N	500				0.074			0.17	0.27	0.39	0.63	1.0	1.6
P	800			0.046			0.11	0.17	0.24	0.40	0.64	0.99	1.6
Q	1250		0.029			0.067	0.11	0.16	0.25	0.41	0.64	0.99	
R	2000	0.018			0.042	0.069	0.097	0.16	0.26	0.40	0.62		
S	3150			0.027									

Note: For the exact AOQL, the above values must be multiplied by $\left(1 - \frac{\text{Sample size}}{\text{Lot or Batch size}}\right)$

obtain no defective articles in the sample of two, we may obtain exactly one defective article, or we may obtain two defective articles. There are no other possibilities. If we consider the order of drawing the sample of two articles, we obtain two defective articles only when both the first and second articles drawn are defective. This may be represented as *dd*. The chance of this occurrence (assuming independent drawings) is (.1) (.1) = .01.

In order to obtain one defective in a sample of two, then only the first item drawn can be defective or only the second item drawn can be defective. These occurrences may be represented as *dg* or *gd*. The chance of *dg* is (.1)(.9) = .09, and the chance of *gd* is (.9)(.1) = .09. Hence, the total chance of obtaining exactly one defective in a sample of two is .09 + .09 = .18.

The occurrence of two good articles in a sample of two is represented by *gg*, and the chance of this is (.9) (.9) = .81. It will be noted that the sum of the chances of drawing no defectives, one defective, or two defectives in a sample of two is

$$(gg) + (dg + gd) + (dd)$$
$$.81 + .18 + .01 = 1.00,$$

as it should be, since the events are mutually exclusive.

The events and chances involved in drawing a sample of two articles can be represented schematically as

$$(.9 + .1)^2 = (.9)^2 + 2(.9)(.1) + (.1)^2$$
$$= .81 + 2(.09) + .01 = 1.00.$$

This is in the form of the binomial expan-

12-31.
for Tightened Inspection (Single Sampling)

Quality Level													
2.5	4.0	6.5	10	15	25	40	65	100	150	250	400	650	1000
						42	69	97	160	260	400	620	970
		12			28	46	65	110	170	270	410	650	1100
	7.4			17	27	39	63	100	160	250	390	610	
4.6			11	17	24	40	64	99	160	240	380		
		6.5	11	15	24	40	61	95	150	240			
	4.2	6.9	9.7	16	26	40	62						
2.6	4.3	6.1	9.9	14	25	39							
2.7	3.9	6.3	10	16	25								
2.4	4.0	6.4	9.9	16									
2.5	4.1	6.4	9.9										
2.6	4.0	6.2											
2.5	3.9												
2.5													

sion, the first term giving the chance of no defectives in two, the second term giving the chance of exactly one defective in two (that is, either the first article or the second article being defective), and the last term represents the chance of two defectives in two.

1. In the expansion

$$(.9 + .1)^2 = (.9)^2 + 2(.9)(.1) + (.1)^2$$

the chance of zero or one defective in two is the sum of the first and second terms; that is, $(.9)^2 + 2(.9)(.1) = .99$. The chance of one or two defectives is the sum of the second and third terms; i.e., $2(.9)(.1) + (.1)^2 = .19$.

2. In drawing a sample of three items, there are the following possibilities:

ggg	(.9)(.9)(.9)	=	.729
ggd	(.9)(.9)(.1)	=	.081
gdg	(.9)(.1)(.9)	=	.081
dgg	(.1)(.9)(.9)	=	.081
			.243
gdd	(.9)(.1)(.1)	=	.009
dgd	(.1)(.9)(.1)	=	.009
ddg	(.1)(.1)(.9)	=	.009
			.027
ddd	(.1)(.1)(.1)	=	.001

Total = No defectives + 1 defective + 2 defectives + 3 defectives.

Chance = .729 + .243 + .027 + .001 = 1.000.

3. In terms of the binomial expansion, the chance of 0, 1, 2, or 3 defectives is given by

$$(.9 + .1)^3 = (.9)^3 + 3(.9)^2(.1) + 3(.9)(.1)^2 + (.1)^3$$

0	1	2	3
def	def	def	def.

The chance of not more than one defective in three is given by the sum of the first and second terms, that is, $(9)^3 + 3(.9)^2(.1) = .972$. The chance of not more than two defectives is the sum of the first, second, and third terms; that is, $(.9)^3 + 3(.9)^2 (.1) + 3(.9) (.1)^2 = .999$.

Using the above steps, we thus have a general method of finding chances of exactly 0, 1, 2, and so on, defectives in samples of various sizes from a lot of given percent defective and also the chances of zero, not more than one defective, not more than two defectives, and so on. In addition, we can use any proportion of defectives in the lot we care to for the above procedure.

THE POISSON DISTRIBUTION

From your introduction to sampling inspection, you realize the need for having sampling plans available that have been previously constructed. It is desirable, however, for you to know how some of these tables can be constructed. For our use, a rather simplified law, known as the Poisson distribution, is sufficiently accurate for most of our sampling inspection problems or plans and the associated probabilities. The Poisson law, which is an approximation to a more exact law that applies in sampling inspection, can be used to save labor in calculating sampling inspection tables. Moreover, the Poisson type distribution itself occurs rather frequently in nature and in sampling inspection problems, in addition to being a sufficiently close approximation to more complicated types of distributions. In most cases, it is not necessary to calculate the values for the Poisson law, as these values can be taken directly from prepared tables or charts (see Figure 12–14).

There are three rules that should be satisfied, however, before you can use the Poisson distribution approximation. These rules are:

1. $p \leq 0.10$. This fraction defective, p, must be very small because the Poisson law is based on this assumption. The larger p is, the more inaccurate our computations become.
2. $n \leq 50$. The sample size or number, n, should be fairly large for a good approximation. We will cover this factor more fully in the discussion of sample size.
3. $n/N \leq 0.20$. The Poisson tables assume the lot size N to be infinity, and, the closer we come to a small fraction for n/N, the nearer we come to approximating an N of infinity.

Fortunately, we do not have to make computations as above (which will be very cumbersome for larger sample sizes) to obtain probabilities of occurrences of 0, 1, 2, and so on, defectives since such probabilities are tabulated or obtainable more easily by other means. When the fraction defective of the lot sampled is not greater than about .10 or 10 percent (which is the region we are primarily concerned with in practice), the Poisson chart in Figure 12–14 is very useful. This chart can be used to find the chance of obtaining not more than $c = 0, 1, 2$, and so on, defectives in any sample of size n for lots of fraction defective p not greater than .10 (we assume also here that the lot is about 10 or more times as large as the sample). As an example, consider the case of a lot containing 1 percent defective articles, and we want to find the chance of obtaining not more than two defective articles in a sample of 50 drawn from the lot. In this case $n = 50$, $np = (50)(.01) = .5$. We enter the bottom of the chart with $np = 5$ and go upward until we come to the curve $c = 2$. From this point, we go horizontally to the left and read .986 on the percent probability of acceptance scale. Thus, if the lot is 1 percent defective, the chance of obtaining not more than two defectives in a random sample of 50 items is .986, or 98.6 percent. Similarly, the chance of not more than one defective is about .913, so that the chance of exactly two defectives for the case considered here is .986 − .913 = .073.

ESTABLISHING A SAMPLING PLAN

Three elements are necessary in defining or determining the appropriate single sampling plan: lot size N (from which the sample is drawn); sample size n; and the acceptance number c (the maximum allowable number of defects in the sample).

1. If the Poisson assumption is nearly satisfied, one can compute the probability of observing c or fewer defects by use of the chart shown in Figure 12–14 on page 430.
2. To plot the operating characteristic (OC) curve for a particular sampling plan, (1) assume a value for p, (2) find the value of p multiplied by n, which is the expected number of defectives in the sample, (3) read Pa (probability of acceptance) from the appropriate table or graph, and (4) plot the value for Pa on your graph paper corresponding to the appropriate value of p. (*Caution:* use extreme care when reading the vertical scale of this chart to avoid errors in Pa.)
3. When assuming a set of values for p, we normally do not exceed $p = .10$. Suggested values to be used are shown in the following illustration of how to plot an OC curve in Figure 12–15, and Table 12–32.

Plotting the above values of Pa percent against $100p$, we get the operating characteristic curve (shown in Figure 12–15). The purpose of the OC curve is to analyze the performance of a particular sampling plan on many different quality levels for lots of various fractions defective which may be submitted for inspection. OC curves picture the ability of any sampling plan to discriminate between good and bad lots. For any given fraction defective, the OC curve gives the probability that a lot will be accepted by the sampling plan. For example, the single sampling plan, $n = 45$, $c = 0$, will accept about 41 percent (and reject

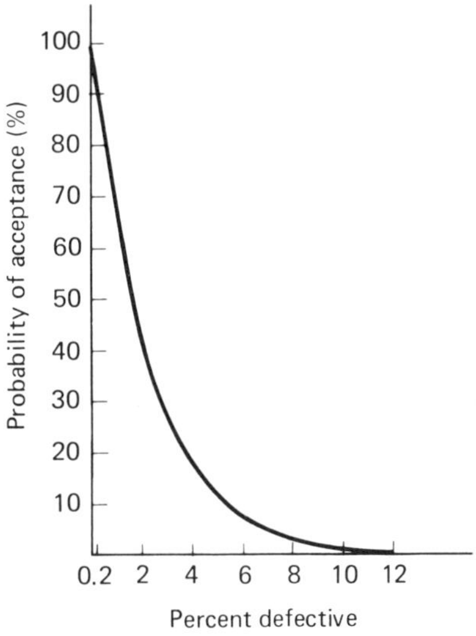

FIGURE 12–15. Operating Characteristic Curve.

TABLE 12-32.
Sampling Plan

Sampling Plan	Computations			
	p	*pn*	*Pa*	*Pa%*
$N = \infty$	0.002	0.09	0.914	91.4%
$n = 45$	0.02	0.9	0.407	40.7%
$c = 0$	0.04	1.8	0.165	16.5%
	0.06	2.7	0.068	6.8%
	0.08	3.6	0.027	2.7%
	0.10	4.5	0.011	1.1%

59 percent) of the lots submitted that contain 2 percent defective articles.

Many times, it is important to know the probability of accepting a lot with a certain percentage defective using a particular sampling plan. This is possible by defining the sampling plan and then plotting the probability of acceptance against the various percent defectives of lots which may be presented for acceptance inspection. The resulting curve is known as an operating characteristic curve or an OC curve.

THE OPERATING CHARACTERISTIC CURVE

For the single sampling plan were $c = 0$ and $n = 5$, we can plot the graph of the chance of obtaining no defectives in five against the fraction defective of the lot sampled. Such a graph is called the operating characteristic curve of the sampling plan and is exhibited in Figure 12–16 for the sampling plan $c = 0$ and $n = 5$. If p represents the fraction defective of the lot sampled, then the probabilities of acceptance on the attached graph for the plan $c = 0$ and $n = 5$ may be obtained from the formula

$$P_a = (1 - p)^5$$

The OC curve for the plan $c = 0$, $n = 5$ was obtained in this way (from tables actually), since the graph covers fractions defective greater than $p = .10$ and the sample size $n = 5$ is quite small.

It can be seen that the OC curve is of considerable importance since it depicts the chance that a submitted lot of any given fraction defective will be accepted under the sampling inspection plan. (This is also the proportion of submitted lots of a given fraction defective which will pass the acceptance criteria of the sample.)

In Figure 12–16, there is plotted the OC curve of the sampling plan, $c = 2$, $n = 80$. This OC curve may be obtained rather accurately by using the Poisson chart. For example, let us check the probability of acceptance at the lot quality of $p = .05$ or 5 percent defective. For this case, $pn = (.05)(80) = 4.0$. Hence, entering the Poisson chart (Figure 12–14) with $pn = 4.0$ and $c = 2$, we find that the probability of acceptance is .231, which checked with the chart.

Efficiency of Large Samples

The OC curves for the above two plans illustrate a very important point concerning sampling inspection. Suppose the acceptable quality level (AQL) = .01 or 1 percent defective, and we have the job of performing acceptance on 8,000,000 items that are to be split up into lots. Consider two procedures for inspection. Plan A would call for dividing the 8,000,000 articles into 16,000 lots of 500 articles each and inspecting 5 items from each lot of 500 items, using an acceptance number of 0. On the other hand, Plan B would call for dividing the 8,000,000 items into 1,000 lots of size 8,000 each, using the inspection plan $n = 80$, $c = 2$. Note that the amount of inspection called for by Plan A ($5 \times 16{,}000 = 80{,}000$) is the same as that called for by Plan B ($80 \times 1{,}000 = 80{,}000$). For the AQL of 1 percent defective, both sampling plans will accept 95 percent of the lots of quality 1 percent defective and reject 5 percent of such lots. However, Plan B is considerably more effective than Plan A, because it will accept more lots of fraction defective less than 1 percent and will reject considerably more lots of fraction defective greater than 1 percent. As a matter of fact, Plan A will accept about 44 percent of lots presented for inspection which are 15 percent defective, whereas Plan B will accept none of these! This illustrates the importance of grouping material into large lots in order to use large sample sizes and thereby gain power of discrimination. The above also illustrates the fact that acceptance numbers other than 0 can be used to advantage provided the sample size is chosen properly.

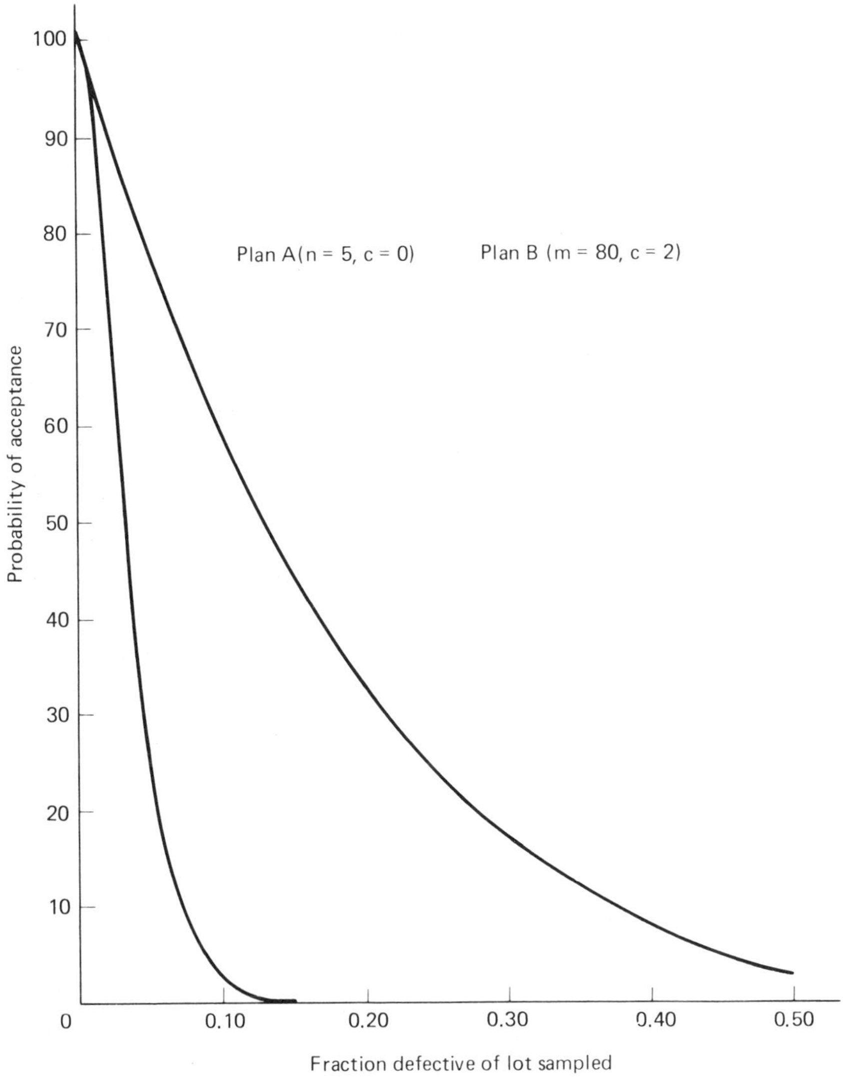

FIGURE 12–16. Operating Characteristic Curve.

Effect of Inspection Lot Size on Curve

In Figure 12–16, we have also depicted the OC curve of the single sampling plan $n = 5$, $c = 0$, where it was assumed that the lot was very large in size. Suppose, however, that we consider taking samples of size 5 from an inspection lot of size 50. In this case, the chance of obtaining no defectives in 5 for a lot of fraction defective .06 or 6 percent turns out to be .724, whereas for a very large lot this probability is .734. There is thus very little practical difference. This is somewhat of a critical example as the sample size (5) is 10 percent of the rather small lot size (50). This indicates, as is true generally, the inspection lot size has little effect on the percentage of inspection lots accepted.

Effect of Sample Size on OC Curve

As indicated in Figure 12–16, the plan $n = 80$, $c = 2$ will accept more of the good lots (of fraction defective not greater than 1 percent) and will reject more of the poor lots (of fraction defective greater than 1 percent) than the plan $n = 5$, $c = 0$. In this connection, the use of large sample sizes will lead to efficient discriminating power or a more powerful OC curve. The OC curves for small sample sizes, on the other hand, will not in general curve downward as sharply as OC curves for large samples, and hence the small sample sizes cannot control errors in rejecting good lots and accepting poor lots to as low a figure as that resulting from the use of the large sample sizes.

Effect of Acceptance Numbers on OC Curves

For a given sample size n, an increase in the acceptance number c will result in moving the OC curve (to the right) toward a position of allowing more and more lots of poorer quality to pass. This effect is illustrated in Figure 12–16. Basically, as the acceptance number increases, the sample size must also increase in order to keep the LTPD equal. LTPD (lot tolerance percent defective) is that value of percent defective for which it is desirable to accept practically no lots or, at most, say 10 percent. In other words, it is a value of p that can barely be accepted. Hence, the larger the c (with its correspondingly larger n), the more discriminating the curve will be. An increase in c without an increase in n will result in allowing more and more lots of poorer quality to pass.

Effect on OC Curves of Percent Inspection Plans As Lot Size Varies

In order to point out the importance of sample size as compared to percentage inspection and the importance of acceptance number, consider the following very common practice. A usual custom in inspection has been to specify a fixed percentage of the lot to be inspected as a sample and to require that no defectives be allowed in the sample. Suppose that a manufacturer presents lots that vary in size (from 100 to 2,000) and that his quality level is equivalent to 6 percent of defective material. Consider a sampling plan involving a 5 percent sample and no defectives in the sample. Table 12–33 illustrates the point.

Hence, for $n = 5$, we accept 73.4 percent and reject 26.6 percent of the lots submitted; for $n = 10$, we accept on the average about 60 in 100 lots and reject about 40 in 100, and so on. For a sample of size 50, we only accept about 8 in 100 lots and reject about 92 in 100. Yet, for all the sampling plans, the presented lots are of the same quality. This weakness can be overcome by allowing the acceptance number c to be greater than 0 for the larger sample sizes.

An undesirable result connected with the above is that whereas for $N = 200$, $n = 10$, $c = 0$, 40 percent of lots which are 6 percent defective are rejected, we have for the plan $N = 1{,}000$, $n = 50$, $c = 0$, that 63 percent of lots only 2 percent are rejected!

A common practice has been to set up a plan that uses a constant percentage of the lot as the sample size (Figure 12–17). The user of such a plan believes that it gives a constant protection against defective lots, but it doesn't. The acceptance number used is usually required to be

TABLE 12-33.
Percent Inspection Table

Lot Size N	*Sample Size* n	*Probability of Obtaining No Defectives*
100	5	0.734
200	10	0.599
400	20	0.358
800	40	0.129
1,000	50	0.077
2,000	100	0.006

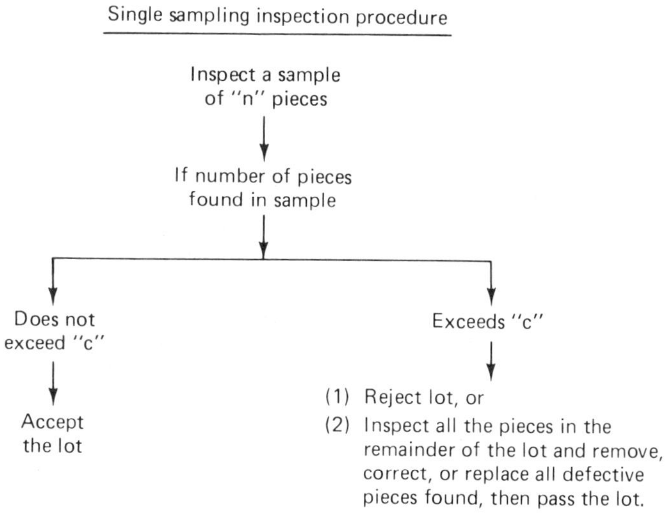

FIGURE 12–17. Single Sampling Inspection Procedures.

zero. The lot size has little or no effect on the discriminating ability of the curve. If the third rule for the Poisson assumption is satisfied, we can disregard the size of N and then, of course, the difference in the OC curves for different lot sizes is very slight.

CONSUMER'S RISK AND PRODUCER'S RISK

Consumer risk is the risk of accepting material of unsatisfactory quality. For any specified quality level, that is, any fraction defective, consumer's risk is given as the percentage below the OC curve. Producer's risk occurs in rejecting material of a satisfactory quality. More specifically, it is the risk of the producer that, if he submits a lot of a specified quality, it will be rejected. (It is 100 percent minus the *Pa* percent.) Ordinarily, the producer's risk is associated with an acceptable quality level (AQL). Normally, it is about 10 percent or less, and for any specified quality it is the percentage above the OC curve.

In our discussion of the producer's risk, we introduced the term AQL (acceptable quality level). The AQL is a nominal value expressed in terms of percentage defective or defects per hundred numbered units, whichever is applicable, specified for a given type product. For most sampling inspection problems, it turns out in practice to be that fraction defective for which 90 to 95 percent of the product submitted will be accepted.

AVERAGE OUTGOING QUALITY LEVEL (AOQL)

If lots rejected by a particular sampling plan are 100 percent inspected and removed of all defectives, then AOQL is the worst average quality of the lots after inspection and screening of rejected lots for removal of all defective articles. This outgoing quality depends, of course, on the incoming quality; if the product submitted for inspection is perfect, then the outgoing product is also perfect. If the product submitted for inspection is so bad that all of the lots are rejected and all of the defectives are found in 100 percent inspection, then outgoing quality is also perfect. Between these two extremes lies a range of incoming quality through which the outgoing quality will have varying degrees of imperfection. The maximum possible value of the average percentage defective of the outgoing product is called the AOQL. If a sampling plan involves 100 percent inspection of all rejected lots, regardless of the incoming quality submitted, the average outgoing quality will not be worse than the AOQL.

GOVERNMENT INSPECTION

In U.S. Department of Defense inspections, it is not necessary to calculate tables or set up new sampling procedures, because there is a publication prepared for use in military inspections by attributes. Military Standard 105D sets forth sampling procedures and tables for inspection by attributes. Before one can use MIL-STD-105D, certain information is necessary. One must have a classification of defects, an AQL for each class of defects, the process average percent defective of the supplier (estimated by an arithmetic mean computed from the results of sampling inspection of the preceding 10 lots), the inspection level to be used, and the size of the lot to be submitted.

Military Standard 105D is approved by the Departments of the Army, the Navy, and the Air Force, and the Defense Logistics Agency for use in establishing sampling plans and for inspection by attributes. This standard is mandatory for use by the services when applicable.

SAMPLING PROCEDURES IN PROCUREMENT

An important step in carrying out any established sampling plan is the sampling procedure. The inspector should attempt to draw items from an inspection lot so that these items constitute a sample that fairly represents the quality of the entire inspection lot. Experience clearly shows that human beings, unaided by special devices for selection of a random sample, are unable to avoid some bias in selection of samples. However, some of the more obvious biased practices in selection of samples, such as taking items from the top of a container every day, taking no items from the top of a container, taking items that appear to be defective, and taking the output of certain machines and not others, can readily be avoided by an inspector and will be a great step toward selection of a sample that fairly represents the inspection lot.

The operating characteristic curves of the military standard sampling plans are calculated on the assumption that random sampling is achieved. Randomness cannot be exactly defined. In general, for random sampling, the selection of an item must be unrelated to its properties (the drawing of a major defective might be unrelated to its being a major defective) and the various selections must occur in complete disorder unpredictable by formula. These, of course, are negative criteria, and the positive content of randomness must remain undefined.

Random Sampling Plans

The only way to guarantee the random selection of a sample is by special devices that eliminate personal discretion in the selection of items. As a hypothetical sample, the particular items to be selected for a random sample could be determined as follows:

1. Number consecutively the items in the inspection lot.
2. Number cards or a wheel of chance correspondingly.
3. Where cards are being used, shuffle cards and select blindly from the shuffled deck as many cards as there are items in the proposed sample.

4. Where a wheel is being used, spin the wheel and select the item corresponding to the number the wheel stops on. Repeat until the sample is completely selected.
5. Select items from the inspection lot corresponding to the numbers determined from the cards or wheels.
6. It is obvious that the numbering of items in an inspection lot is usually impracticable and the finding of the item having a given number is also usually difficult. However, practical plans can often be devised for a particular inspection operation. Presentation of lots for inspection often involves fixed racks, trays, containers, or some geometric pattern. Suppose, for example, that an inspection lot of 500 shells is presented in 20 columns of 25 each in a rectangular pattern as shown in Figure 12–18. If a single sample of 50 is to be selected, a series of 50 code designations such as 5–25 (designating the 25th item in the 5th column) can be prepared in such a way that the first part of the code number is equally likely to be any number from 1 to 20, and the second part of the code any number from 1 to 25. The code numbers could be made up in advance by a special device (wheel, cards, or the like). The codes would be determined randomly, but they could be listed in a convenient manner for drawing (all those in column 1, all those in column 2, and so on).

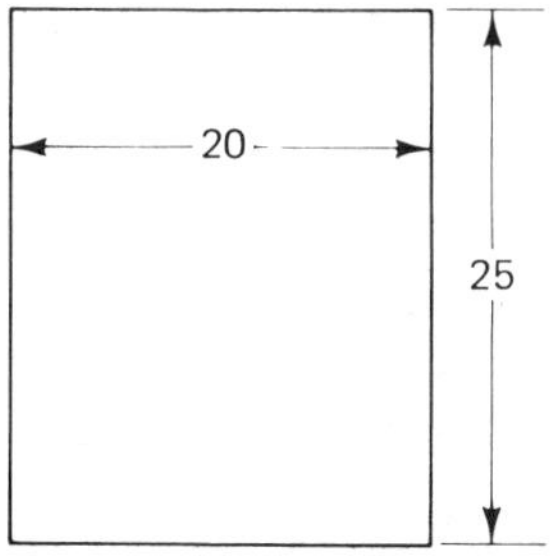

FIGURE 12–18. Rectangular Pattern Shell Lot.

The Sampling Rules

Since the use of the random sampling plans described are not ordinarily practicable in inspection, several rules have been devised to increase likelihood that a sample will fairly represent the inspection lot from which it is drawn.

Rule 1: Draw proportional samples.

Example a. Suppose an inspection lot of 2,000 items is presented in 20 containers of 100 items each, and the sampling plan calls for a sample of 100. According to Rule 1, five items should be selected from each of 20 trays.

Example b. Suppose that inspection is done as items move along a conveyor belt, and an inspection lot consists of 2,000 items, and the sampling plan calls for a sample of 100. Since 2,000 divided by 100 equals 20, then one item should be selected from every 20 pieces that pass by on the belt. Care should be taken not to draw every twentieth item nor follow any specific plan in selection of this one item out of each 20 items.

Rule 2: Draw sample items from all parts of each division of the inspection lot.

Example: In Example a under Rule 1, the location from which the five items are drawn should be varied from container to container.

Rule 3: Draw sample items without regard to quality.

Example: The inspector should not make an inspection of the lot before beginning to draw a sample or make any attempt to find defectives. Obvious defectives that catch the eye should be removed from the inspection lot and excluded from the sample.

Relation of the Sampling Rules to Randomness. From a strictly technical viewpoint, sampling Rules 1 and 2 contradict the principle of randomness since we follow a definite pattern. However, in practice, the results approach those of randomness closer than any other method except those employing gambling devices.

Effect of Sampling Rules on OC Curves. As has been previously mentioned, the OC curves are calculated with the assumption that sampling is random. However, the use of the sampling rules approaches the results of randomness, and the effect on the OC curve is negligible from a practical standpoint. The theoretical effect of the sampling rules is a steepening of the OC curve so that good inspection lots are accepted more often while bad ones are accepted less often than if random sampling were used. This is a desirable effect from the standpoint of the consumer. Of course, if some trays have all defective items and the rest all nondefective items, there will be a decided difference in the OC curves under the sampling rules and the OC curve for random sampling. However, such situations are unlikely to arise under normal industrial conditions. In all cases, the tendency exists for the OC curve to steepen under the sampling rule.

Inspection of Resubmitted Material. When a rejected inspection lot is screened for any major defectives, it is important for the inspector to assure himself that the resubmitted lot is free of major defectives and the number of minors has not increased. When supervision of the contractor's screening or reworking is practicable, it may be appropriate to inspect the resubmitted lot only for the class of defects or even a particular defect for which the lot was rejected. Where supervision of screening or reworking is not practical and it is possible to increase the minors while correcting the major, it may be appropriate to sample for both classes of defects. Ordinarily, it is customary to use normal acceptance criteria on resubmitted lots for the class or classes being checked. However, in some cases where supervision of screening and reworking is not practical, a more severe acceptance criteria may be in order.

Questions

1. If there are 50 chips in a bowl, 10 white and 40 black, what is the probability of drawing a white chip from the bowl?
2. In the normal distribution, what percentage of measurement will fall between $\mu \pm \sigma$?
3. If a lot contains 100,000 parts and 200 are found to be defective, what is the probability of a defective part in the lot?
4. The process capability of a key operation has been determined to be as follows: average = 41.8, standard deviation = 4. What portion of the product will be between the specification limits of 35 to 45?
5. Twenty samples of five each of an aircraft fitting are taken at the rate of one sample per hour. The total (sum) of the sample averages is .0671. The total (sum) of the sample range is .0124. A_2 = .58 for sample size 5. Round off to four decimal places. D_4 = 2.11, and D_3 = 0. What is the grand average ($\bar{X}$) of the samples? What is the

average sample range ($\bar{R}$)? What is the upper control limit for $\bar{X}$)? What is the lower control limit for ($\bar{X}$)? What is the upper control limit for R? *What is the lower control limit for R*?

6. Given the average range of 8.62, and a UCLR of 18.04, previous $\bar{R}$ was 8.63 and UCLR was 18.20. What conclusion may be drawn from these data?
7. What are the three important aspects of production that a control chart is designed to control?
8. A component is being produced with a nominal dimension of 1.5000 and a drawing tolerance of ± 0.0040. Twenty-five samples of size 4 are taken. $\bar{R}$ = 0.0011; $\bar{X}$ = 1.5490. What is the upper modified control limit? What is the lower modified control limit?
9. What charts are used for inspection by attributes?
10. When does the Poisson distribution apply to a population or universe in SQC?
11. What is the percentage defective if pn = 5.4 and n = 90?
12. What two types of risk are involved in any sampling acceptance inspection? Define each.
13. What is the producer's risk if the AQL is 0.01 (1 percent) in a sampling plan in which N = 10,000; n = 150; and c = 3?
14. What is the acceptance number in a single sample plan if the lot is 3,000, sample size is 200, and rejection number is 11?
15. Lots of size 1,000 are coming into the inspection department. You are considering sampling plans which could be used to accept 90 percent of the lots which are presented for acceptance. The acceptance quality for each lot is 2 percent defective. What is the sample size when c = 0? What is the sample size when c = 2?

Bibliography

STATISTICAL QUALITY CONTROL

Besterfield, Dale H. *Quality Control: A Practical Approach.* Englewood Cliffs, N. J.: Prentice-Hall, 1979.

Burr, Irving. *Elementary Statistical Quality Control.* New York: Marcel Dekker, 1978.

Burr, Irving. *Statistical Quality Control Methods.* New York: Marcel Dekker, 1976.

Carrubba, Eugene R., et al. *Assuring Product Integrity.* Lexington, Mass.: Lexington Books, 1975.

Caves, Richard E., and Roberts, Marc J., eds. *Regulating the Product: Quality and Variety.* Cambridge, Mass.: Ballinger, 1975.

Charbonneau, Harvey C., and Webster, Gordon L. *Industrial Quality Control.* Englewood Cliffs, N. J.: Prentice-Hall, 1978.

Feigenbaum, Armand V. *Total Quality Control: Engineering and Management.* New York: McGraw-Hill, 1961.

Grant, Eugene L., and Leavenworth, Richard. *Statistical Quality Control.* 5th ed. New York: McGraw-Hill, 1980.

Guenther, William C. *Scientific Sampling for Statistical Quality Control.* New York: Macmillan, 1977.

Halpern, S. *The Assurance Sciences: An Introduction to Quality Control and Reliability.* Englewood Cliffs, N. J.: Prentice-Hall, 1978.

Hansen, Bertrand. *Quality Control: Theory and Applications.* Englewood Cliffs, N. J.: Prentice-Hall, 1963.

Hayes, Glenn E., and Romig, Harry G. *Modern Quality Control.* Encino, Calif.: Glencoe Press, 1977.

Juran, Joseph M. *Quality Control Handbook.* 3rd ed. New York: McGraw-Hill, 1974.

Juran, Joseph M., and Gyma, Frank M., Jr. *Quality Planning and Analysis.* 2nd ed. New York: McGraw-Hill, 1980.

Knowler, L. A., et al. *Quality Control by Statistical Methods.* New York: McGraw-Hill, 1969.

Lester, Ronald H., and Enrick, Norbert Lloyd. *Quality Control for Profit.* New York: Industrial Press, 1977.

Ott, Ellis R. *Process Quality Control.* New York: McGraw-Hill, 1975.

Sarkadi, K., and Vincze, I. *Mathematical Methods of Statistical Quality Control.* New York: Academic Press, 1974.

U.S. Army Material Command. *Quality Assurance—Reliability Handbook.* AMCP 702-3, October 1968.

RELIABILITY ENGINEERING

Amstadter, Bertram L. *Reliability Mathematics Fundamental Practical Procedures.* Hightstown, N. J.: McGraw-Hill, 1971.

Arinc Research Corporation. *Reliability Engineering.* Englewood Cliffs, N. J.: Prentice-Hall, 1964.

Bompas-Smith, J. *Mechanical Survival: The Use of Reliability Data.* Hightstown, N. J.: McGraw-Hill, 1973.

Buckland, W. R. *Statistical Assessment of the Life Characteristic.* New York: Hafner Press, 1964.

Calabro, S. R. *Reliability Principles and Practices.* Hightstown, N. J.: McGraw-Hill, 1962.

Gertsbakh, I. B., and Kordonskly, K. B. *Models of Failure.* New York: Springer-Verlag, 1969.

Green, A. E., and Bourne, A. J. *Reliability Technology.* New York: John Wiley and Sons, 1972.

Grouchko, Daniel, ed. *Operations Research and Reliability.* New York: Gordon and Breach, 1971.

Halpern, S. *The Assurance Sciences: An Introduction to Quality Control and Reliability.* Englewood Cliffs, N. J.: Prentice-Hall, 1978.

Haviland, Robert P. *Engineering Reliability and Long Life Design.* New York: Van Nostrand Reinhold, 1964.

Ireson, William G. *Reliability Handbook.* Hightstown, N. J.: McGraw-Hill, 1966.

Kapur, K. C., and Lamberson, L. K. *Reliability in Engineering Design.* New York: John Wiley and Sons, 1977.

Polovko, A. M. *Fundamentals of Reliability Theory.* Nashville, Tenn.: Academic Press, 1968.

Shooman, Martin L. *Probabilistic Reliability: An Engineering Approach.* Hightstown, N. J.: McGraw-Hill, 1968.

Siddall, James. *Analytical Decision Making in Engineering Design.* Englewood Cliffs, N. J.: Prentice-Hall, 1972.

Smith, Charles O. *Introduction to Reliability in Design.* Hightstown, N. J.: McGraw-Hill, 1976.

Tsokos, C. P., and Shimi, I. N., eds. *The Theory and Applications of Reliability: With Emphasis on Bayesian and Nonparametric Methods.* Nashville, Tenn.: Academic Press, 1977.

Zelen, Marvin, ed. *Statistical Theory of Reliability.* Madison: University of Wisconsin Press, 1963.

Chapter 13

Inventory Control

INTRODUCTION

One of the most expensive and difficult logistical tasks is that of maintaining an inventory of goods. A logistics system involves ordering, storing, and distributing billions of dollars worth of items that have a significant impact on our economy. It is an area in which good management can have far-reaching effects.

The inventory problem resolves itself into three basic questions, the answers to which constitute inventory policy:

1. What to order.
2. When to replenish.
3. What quantity to order.

Because of the nature of the inventory problem, it is particularly suited for quantitative analysis. One of the most successful applications of operations research in industry has been in analyzing inventory systems in an effort to determine optimum inventory policy. In this chapter, we look at some of the elements of inventory policy that are most amenable to quantitative analysis and explore some of the approaches being used.

INVENTORY THEORY

The inventory process is the retention of material or manpower in order to facilitate a smooth-flowing efficient operation (that is, a blacklog of men, machines, or goods is maintained so that when the system or operation approaches the point of exhausting its supply, the backlog may be used to ensure its continuous functioning). The problem involved in the inventory process hovers around the cost of first maintaining an inventory and secondly of not having sufficient inventory to satisfy the commitments of the operation. Ackoff and Rivett[1] suggest an associated cost is (1) "A cost which increases as inventory increases," and (2) "A cost which decreases as inventory increases."

Costs that increase as inventory increases are:

1. Storage costs.
2. Obsolescence.
3. Spoilage.
4. Taxes.
5. Insurance.
6. Depreciation.
7. Interest of invested capital.
8. Tie-up of invested capital.
9. Space utilization.
10. Physical handling.
11. Accounting.

According to Ackoff and Rivett, costs that decrease as inventory increases include:

1. "Shortage or outage cost—inability to meet demand or delays. As inventory increases the likelihood of delays in meeting demand decreases."
2. "Setup and takedown costs—preparing, processing, and closing out a purchase or production order, in production, adjusting the equipment for new manufacturing operations." The greater the

[1] Ackoff, Russel L. and Rivett, Patrick, *A Manager's Guide to Operations Research.* (New York: John Wiley and Sons, 1963), pp. 35–36.

Parts of this chapter have been taken and revised by permission from *Operations Research Application in Supply.* Pamphlet 901,U.S. Army Ordnance Center and School, Aberdeen Proving Ground, Md., March 1970.

production or purchase quantity, the less frequently orders need to be processed and so this cost will decrease as inventory increases.

3. "Purchase price or direct production—quantity discounts reduce price but if used lead to larger purchases and larger inventories." Larger production runs generally lead to greater efficiency and hence lower unit cost but higher inventory.
4. "Labor stabilization costs if demand fluctuates and one wishes to minimize inventory, it is necessary to vary the production rate and increase costs of hiring, firing, and training personnel."

Another cost that can be considered in the inventory area is the cost resulting from production. Increasing production increases inventory. Also, an inventory must be maintained to ensure smooth operation of production.

The importance of proper inventory control as a prerequisite for the successful operation of any organization is as follows. First, the inventory problem is a classic example of an executive-type problem wherein the different functional departments of a manufacturing enterprise have conflicting objectives. The marketing department of a company, for example, would like to have a large inventory of different items to achieve uninterrupted and satisfactory customer service. This requirement of the marketing department, however, clashes with the objectives of the finance department, which would like to see the inventory investment as low as possible. Similarly, the production department may wish to manufacture in large lot sizes to minimize production costs and to level off production. But, this will give rise to increased in-process inventories, which may violate the working capital limitations of the organization. Thus, the inventory policy of an organization must be developed and designed in view of all these considerations, and it must be operated to simultaneously achieve satisfactory customer service, stable production rates, and minimum possible total costs of operations. By its very nature and extent of influence, the inventory problem deserves attention at very high levels of management hierarchy.

Secondly, in terms of financial magnitude, the inventory problem is of imposing proportions. The amount of capital tied up in the inventories of a number of large business enterprises is of such a dimension that even a small reduction of inventories obtained through proper control can result in substantial savings.

Thirdly, poor inventory control has been cited as the culprit in a large number of business failures on the American business scene. This is especially true for business enterprises still in their infancy. The inexperienced businessman may not fully appreciate the complexities of the inventory problem, the fluctuations of the required inventory levels created by changes in demand, and the ultimate effect of the inventory forces in deciding the fate of his young enterprise. Furthermore, the question of inventories is closely tied to the phenomenon of business cycles and thus deserves more attention by economic theorists in developing a more realistic theory of the firm.[2]

It is widely believed that an inventory problem is a situation in which management has to decide on the level of raw materials and purchased parts stock to meet production demands, determine the length of production runs to satisfy a given demand rate, maintain a certain supply of finished goods to satisfy customer demand, and so on. The problem is essentially one of how much to store per unit of time to meet future demand. In short, the

---

[2]See Whitin, Thomson M. *The Theory of Inventory Management.* (Westport, Conn.: Greenwood Press, 1970).

problem of inventories pervades all operations concerned with the matter of storage versus time through all the stages of procurement, production, and distribution.

The very nature of the problem under discussion suggests that both sides of the inventory question must be examined in order to develop a sound inventory policy. First, since inventories are kept to meet future demand, the analyst must predict the nature of this demand. Is it the type of demand that can be reasonably assumed to occur with certainty? Such, for example, would be the case while production plans are being made to fulfill contractual obligations. Or is it the type of demand that must be classified as a probabilistic demand? In such cases, firms are faced with future demands that must be predicted in terms of probabilities. Depending on the nature of the products, discrete as well as continuous probability density functions can be employed to approximate such demands. Demand predictions should also take note of such factors as seasonality, trends, introduction of new competitive items, and the like. In short, the analyst must consider all relevant factors before assuming a particular demand function.

On the other side of the inventory coin, the questions to be asked are: What is to be stored or produced? How much is to be stored or produced per unit of time? If we assume the existence of a given demand function, the objective of the inventory policy is to answer these questions in view of certain criteria such as minimum total costs, minimum expected total costs, or maximum average level of profit per period.

SYSTEMS OF INVENTORY CONTROL

It is extremely difficult to classify all the possible inventory control systems that are being used or that could be used in business and industry. Most of these systems, however, can be grouped under one or two basic systems: the *two-bin system* or the *ordering cycle system*, or some variation or combination of these basic systems.

In the two-bin system, which is perhaps the oldest system of inventory control, each item is stored in two bins. One of the bins contains sufficient stock to meet the demand between the arrival of one order and the placement of the next order. The second bin contains sufficient supply to meet the expected demands during the purchasing lead time plus a safety reserve. In this system, a purchasing order is issued as soon as the supply in the first bin falls to a predetermined level. In its simplest form, the order quantity in this system for a particular item is fixed while the time between ordering fluctuates depending upon the rate of depletion. In other words, the "when" fluctuates with the rate of usage but the "how much" remains constant. Often referred to as the fixed order system, perhaps its greatest advantage lies in its ease of operation. On the other side of the balance sheet, many operational complications can arise. For example, if several items are purchased from the same source, a rigid adherence to the system may result in loss of opportunities for price and freight discounts. Then, too, if the item must be stored at different locations in the plant, much of the automaticity of the fixed order system is lost. The determination of optimum ordering quantity and the decision on the amount to be stored in the second bin are, of course, the analytical aspects of this system.

The ordering cycle system, sometimes called periodic reordering, fixes the time of reordering, while the amount ordered is allowed to fluctuate depending on the expected demand during the next reordering period. At the end of each reordering cycle, the items are ordered to bring the stocks up to some specific supply control level. The amount ordered is usually sufficient to cover the demand for the purchasing lead time plus one reorder cycle. The order quantities are usually specified in terms of a certain number of day's requirements. The most important advantage of this type of inventory control system lies in its adaptability for exercising tighter control on high-value items. The main disadvantage results from the necessity of determining different reordering cycles, ordering quantities, and safety allowances in a multi-item organization having different demand distributions, different carrying charges, and so on, for various inventory items. In practice, in designing a particular system of inventory control, the planner can take elements from both systems, depending upon the nature of the operations, demand for the different items, and other related factors pertinent to an economical inventory control.

As a check on the operational efficiency of a particular control system, most firms keep records of what is called inventory turnover ratio. For all inventory items, these ratios are calculated by dividing average monthly or yearly inventories into monthly or annual sales. For the most part, inventory turnover ratios are optimized in terms of historical comparisons available from the firm or industry records. Thus, the inventory turnover ratios may be thought of only as a supplementary tool of control, because they are essentially determined by the prior decisions of how much to store per unit of time.

Any system of inventory control needs an information feedback mechanism in order to operate successfully. This is accomplished either by taking a physical inventory at the end of a specific time interval, or by instituting perpetual inventory procedures. Most large organizations maintain perpetual inventory records. This is especially feasible where the volume of business is large enough to justify the installation of a computer. As long as consistency is practiced in inventory valuations, the perpetual inventory method is usually recommended for operating a system of inventory control.

Inventory Models

INVENTORY CONTROL MODELS

The analytical approach to decisionmaking emphasizes the importance of describing the problem, building a suitable model, solving the model, and then applying the solution to the problem at hand. During the stage of model building, if pertinent variables are amenable to measurement and quantification, the analyst can employ mathematical expressions to approximate reality. Such models, since they employ mathematical symbolism, are called symbolic models. The solution of the model is obtained by manipulation of assumed relationships of different variables by the rules and laws of mathematics.

Since model building is a process of abstraction, the resulting model is rarely a complete and faithful representation of reality. However, the testing of a model will usually reveal if it is good enough to predict the future, explain the effects of changes in the variables, and explain the phenomenon to be examined with a certain degree of reliability. It is with these considerations in mind that inventory models should be built and solved. Assumptions must be carefully stated and before a particular model is applied in solving an inventory problem, the suitability of the model must be thoroughly examined.

It is extremely difficult to give an exhaustive classification of the characteristics of inventory problems since they can exist in virtually innumerable combinations. Hence, in the discussion that follows, an attempt will be made to present only some of the basic models of inventory control dealing with inventory problems having a specific set of characteristics.

In considering the inventory situation, the operations research approach found it necessary to treat the cost simultaneously. This is necessary in order to develop optimum inventory policies to meet specific objectives such as minimum out-of-stock conditions, minimum inventory cost, best reorder cycle, and so on.

Among the types of inventory models to meet a variety of conditions are:

1. Elementary inventory models.
2. Inventory models with price breaks.
3. Inventory models with restrictions.
4. Probabilistic demand.
5. Probabilistic demand with production lead time.

These models are concerned with the frequency of ordering items, number of items to be ordered, and ascertaining the future demand. The purpose of the studies is to minimize total inventory cost, which is a function of holding cost per item per time period, shortage costs per item per time period, setup cost per production run, and ordering cost per item. A simple graphic analysis of total cost as a function of inventory and reorder cost would look like that in Figure 13–1. Note that the problem is to select the point where total cost is minimum.

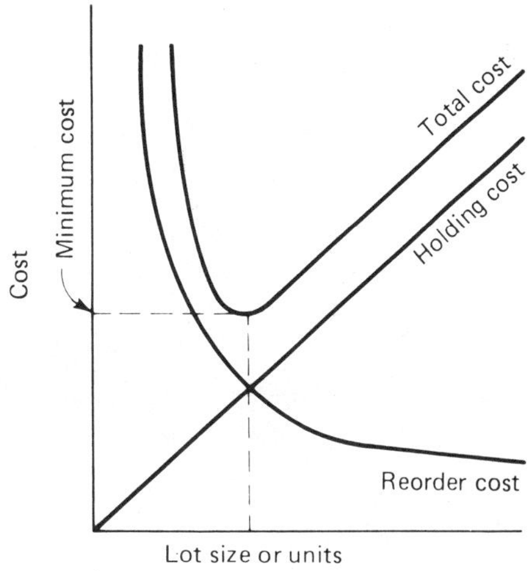

FIGURE 13–1. A Graphic Model of a Single Inventory Problem.

DETERMINISTIC MODELS

EPQ Model

The basic economic purchasing quantity (EPQ) model assumes that:

1. The demand rate is known with certainty.
2. Depletion of stock is linear and constant.
3. Price per unit of inventory item is constant; that is, no discount is available for quantity purchases.
4. Carrying costs vary linearly with the level of an average inventory.
5. Cost of processing a purchase order is constant per order.
6. Lead time is a constant; that is, stockout is not possible.

Let us adopt the following symbolic representation:

D = demand rate expressed in physical units per time period (for example, units/year).

Q = quantity per order.

C = price per unit of inventory item ($/unit).

I = carrying cost per unit time expressed as a fraction of average inventory value ($) for the demand period.

S = cost of processing a purchase order ($/order).

Then, assuming a safety reserve of zero, the total costs (TC) for the demand period are:

Total costs = costs of the inventory items + carrying costs + costs of processing purchase orders.

$$TC = DC + \frac{ICQ}{2} + \frac{D}{Q} S.$$

The economic purchasing quantity (*EPQ*) is obtained when this total cost function assumes its minimum value. Thus, taking its first derivative with respect to Q and equating it to zero we obtain:

$$\frac{dTC}{dQ} = \frac{IC}{2} - \frac{DS}{Q^2} = 0$$

$$\text{i.e., } EPQ = Q = \sqrt{\frac{2DS}{IC}}.$$

Under the assumptions of this model, the formula for *EPQ* remains the same even if we have a safety reserve. For example, with a constant safety reserve of K units:

$$TC = CD + IC\left(\frac{Q}{2} + K\right) + \frac{DS}{Q}.$$

Taking the first derivative of this function with respect to Q and equating it to zero again yields:

$$EPQ = \sqrt{\frac{2DS}{IC}}.$$

The basic *EPQ* formula can also be derived by noting that the total cost curve (under the assumptions of this model) has a minimum point determined by the intersection of the carrying costs line and the ordering costs curve. This is due to the fact that the carrying costs are represented by a straight line having a positive slope, and the ordering costs take the form of a rectangular hyperbola. Thus, the optimum order quantity can be obtained by equating these two costs:

$$IC\left(\frac{Q}{2}\right) = \frac{D}{Q} S \text{ or } \frac{ICQ}{2} = \frac{DS}{Q}$$

$$\text{so } EPQ = Q = \sqrt{\frac{2DS}{IC}}.$$

The same results can be obtained if an incremental type of analysis is employed to solve this problem.[3]

If discounts for quantity purchases are not available, the decision on order quantity will not affect the yearly costs of the required supply. However, whereas a positive change in the order quantity will result in added carrying costs, it will reduce the costs for processing purchase orders. It stands to reason, then, that the optimum order quantity will be obtained when, for any addition to the order quantity, the positive change in the carrying costs equals the negative change in the ordering costs. In other words, *EPQ* is determined from the following equations (when a small quantity ΔQ is added to the order quantity Q); changes in carrying costs = changes in ordering costs.

$$CI\left(\frac{Q + \Delta Q}{2} - \frac{Q}{2}\right) = S\left(\frac{D}{Q} - \frac{D}{Q + \Delta Q}\right)$$

$$\text{or } CI\left(\frac{\Delta Q}{2}\right) = SD\left(\frac{\Delta Q}{Q^2 + Q\Delta Q}\right)$$

$$\text{or } Q^2 + Q\Delta Q = \frac{2DS}{IC}$$

as ΔQ approaches zero,

$$EPQ = Q = \sqrt{\frac{2DS}{IC}}.$$

The basic *EPQ* formula has now been derived by taking three different routes of analysis. In general, inventory problems can be solved by employing either the total value type of analysis or the incremental

[3]Edward H. Bowman, and Fetter, Robert B. *Analysis for Production Management* (Homewood, Ill.: Richard D. Irwin, 1961), Chapter 10.

approach. An illustrative example for *EPQ* would be:

Let D = 1,500 units per year

C = \$5,00 per unit

I = 15 percent per year

S = \$10.00 per order.

Under the assumptions of this model,

$$EPQ = \sqrt{\frac{2DS}{IC}} = \sqrt{\frac{2(1500)(10)}{(0.15)(5)}} = 200 \text{ units.}$$

EMQ Model

The basic economic manufacturing quantity (EMQ) model assumptions are the same as in the EPQ model discussed above, except that inventories do not build instantaneously. On the other hand, inventories accumulate at a rate equal to the difference between the production rate (P) and the consumption rate (D). Here, the analyst must choose the manufacturing lot size that will balance the setup costs versus the carrying charges. Let S represent the setup cost per order in this case. The other symbols have the same meaning as given in the EPQ model. Then:

Total costs = costs of the inventory items + setup costs + carrying costs.

Setup cost per setup cycle $= S$

Setup cost per unit of time $= \frac{S}{t} = \frac{DS}{Q}$

Physical inventory per setup cycle =

$$\frac{1}{2^t} \cdot \frac{Q}{P} (P - D)$$

Average physical inventory per unit of time

$$\frac{1}{t} \cdot \frac{1}{2}t \; \frac{Q}{P} \; (P-D) = \frac{1}{2} \; \frac{Q}{P} (P-D)$$

Hence, carrying costs per unit of time

$$= IC \cdot \frac{Q}{2P} (P-D)$$

$$TC = CD + \frac{DS}{Q} + \frac{ICQ}{2P} (P-D)$$

$$\frac{dTC}{dQ} = DSQ^{-2} + \frac{IC}{2P} (P-D) = 0$$

or $EMQ = Q = \sqrt{\frac{2DS}{IC} \cdot \left(\frac{P}{P-D}\right)}$

As in the case of the EPQ model, the basic EMQ model can also be derived by equating carrying costs and setup costs. In other words, the equation of condition for EMQ (under the stated assumption) is:

Carrying costs = setup costs

or $IC \cdot \frac{Q}{2P} (P-D) = \frac{DS}{Q}$

or $\text{EMQ} = Q = \sqrt{\frac{2DS}{IC} \cdot \left(\frac{P}{P-D}\right)}$

The EPQ and EMQ models derived above assume, among other things, that the demand rate is known with certainty. However, in a number of situations the analyst may at best be able to forecast future demand only in terms of probabilities.

Management Applications

DETERMINATION OF A REORDER POINT

Reorder points are determined for many reasons. For example, the reorder point may be determined in consideration of the investment to be made in inventory to reduce the effect of variations in usage during procurement lead time. As well, usage during lead time can vary. The time

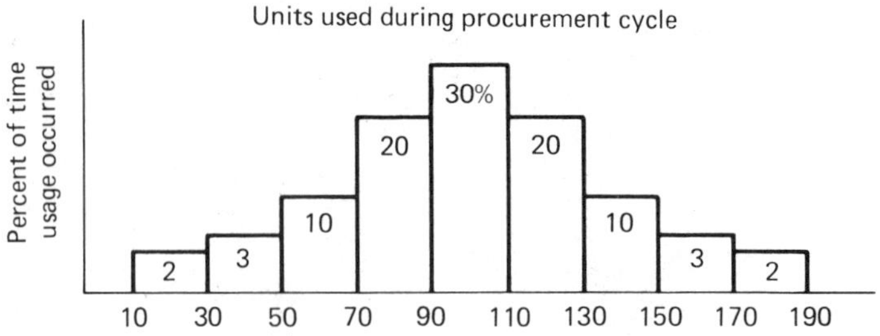

FIGURE 13–2. A Simplified Model of the Determination of a Reorder POint.

required for a procurement action may vary, or the usage rate may vary for a particular procurement period. It is necessary to collect information on the probability of usage during procurement. As an example, let us consider data presented in Figure 13–2.

On the average, 100 units will be used. If management is willing to be out of stock on this item 2 percent of the time, the reorder formula will be:

$$\text{Reorder point} = 100 + 70$$

(See Figure 13–3.) Seventy units will be carried to protect against the expected variation from the usual usage during procurement.

If they are willing to be out of stock 5 percent of the time, they need carry only 50 units as a cushion. The amount of the cushion can be optimized if the cost of carrying a specific cushion can be compared to the cost of being out of stock with a certain frequency.

Frequently, the distribution of usage during lead time is normal or Poisson; in these cases, tables are available to simplify the data collection and calculation of the reorder point.

Inventory Problems and Solutions

Typical inventory problems are:

1. The demand for a product called Zag is constant and amounts to 60,000 units per year. Order costs are $60 per order. Inventory carrying costs are 60 percent of average inventory value per year. The unit price of Zag is $4. Determine the economic purchasing quantity if shortages are not permitted.

2. The EPQ model can be modified to incorporate a penalty for being out of stock:

$$Q = \sqrt{\frac{2DS}{IC}} \cdot \sqrt{\frac{IC + C_s}{C_s}}.$$

where C_s is the cost per unit for being out of stock. For example, assume that in problem 1 if a requirement for Zag cannot be satisfied, there is shortage cost of $1.00 per unit per year.

3. A newspaper boy buys papers for 12 cents each and sells them for 17 cents each. He cannot return unsold newspapers. Daily demand has the following distribution:

Number of Customers:	23	24	25	26	27	28	29	30	31	32
Probability:	0.01	0.03	0.06	0.10	0.20	0.25	0.15	0.10	0.05	0.05

If each day's demand is independent of the previous day's, how many papers should he order each day to maximize expected profits?

Solutions to inventory problems can be solved by well-known standard formulas.

Example: Economic purchasing quantity can be calculated from:

$$Q = \sqrt{\frac{2DS}{IC}},$$

where: D = 60,000 units per year, S = \$60 per order, I = 16% of average inventory value, and C = \$4 per unit.

$$Q = \sqrt{\frac{2(60{,}000)(60)}{0.16\,(4)}} = \sqrt{11{,}250{,}000} = 3{,}354 \text{ units.}$$

The economic purchasing quantity is 3,354 units of Zag per order. Orders should be placed 60,000 ÷ 3,354 ≃ 18 times per year.

Example: Economic purchasing quantity with shortages allowed can be calculated from:

$$Q = \sqrt{\frac{2DS}{IC}} \cdot \sqrt{\frac{IC + C_s}{C_s}},$$

where: D = 60,000 units per year, S = \$60 per order, I = 16% of average inventory value, C = \$4 per unit, and C_s = \$1.00 per unit short.

$$Q = \sqrt{\frac{2(60{,}000)(60)}{0.16\,(4)}} \cdot \sqrt{\frac{0.16\,(4) + 1.00}{1.00}}$$

$$Q = \sqrt{11{,}250{,}000} \cdot \sqrt{1.64} = \sqrt{18{,}450{,}000}$$

$$Q = 4{,}295 \text{ units.}$$

The economic purchasing quantity is 4,295 units of Zag per order. Orders should be placed 60,000 ÷ 4,295 ≃ 14 times per year.

Example: Profit = revenue − cost. Let X = number of papers purchased and D = demand (see Table 13–1).

The optimal number of papers to purchase is 27. Expected (average) daily profit will be \$1.29.

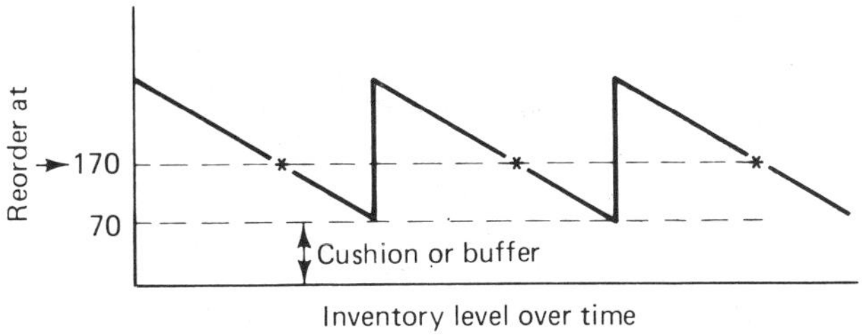

FIGURE 13–3. An Illustration of a Reorder Point.

TABLE 13-1.

X	$P(D \geqslant X)$	Expected Revenue (17 ¢ Each)	12 ¢ Each Cost	Expected Profit
23	1.00	3.91 (1.00) = 3.91	2.76	\$1.15
24	0.99	3.91 (0.01) + 4.08 (0.99) = 4.08	2.88	1.20
25	0.96	3.91 (0.01) + 4.08 (0.03) + 4.25 (0.96) = 4.24	3.00	1.24
26	0.90	3.91 (0.01) + 4.08 (0.03) + 4.25 (0.06) + 4.42 (0.90) = 4.40	3.12	1.28
27	0.80	3.91 (0.01) + 4.08 (0.03) + 4.25 (0.06) + 4.42 (0.10) + 4.59 (0.80) = 4.53	3.24	1.29
28	0.60	3.91 (0.01) + 4.08 (0.03) + 4.25 (0.06) + 4.42 (0.10) + 4.59 (0.20) + 4.76 (0.60) = 4.64	3.36	1.28

Inventory Costs Versus Ordering Strategy

Figure 13–14 shows graphically how the relevant costs vary with the size of the order quantity. Inventory carrying costs, $ICQ/2$, increase linearly with increasing Q, while the procurement costs, DA/Q, decrease at a decreasing rate with an increase in Q. The total variable cost, K, is the sum

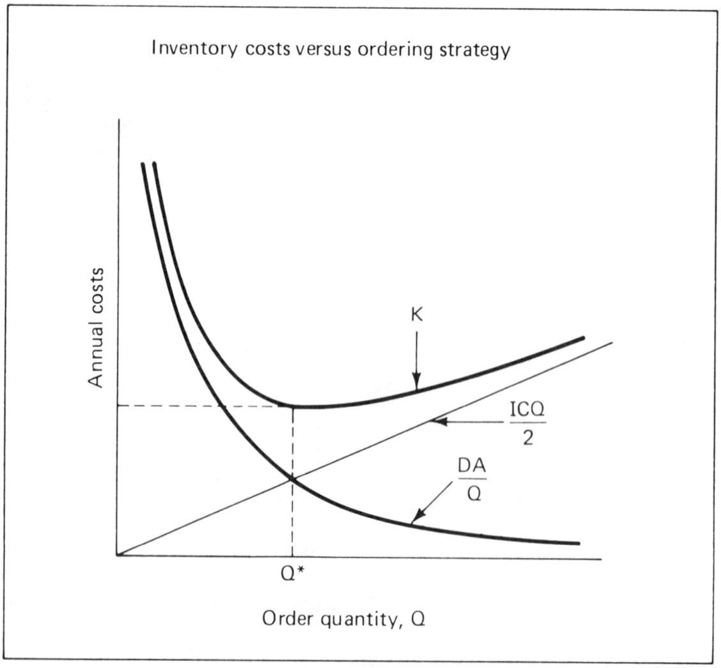

FIGURE 13–4. Inventory Costs Versus Ordering Strategy.

of these two curves. Its curve decreases at first with an increase in Q, and then increases. The low point on this curve is the minimum total cost which corresponds to where Q equals Q star, the economical order quantity.

Inventory Depletion Under Fixed Order Quantity System

Recall that the control of an item in inventory hinges on two fundamental questions: when to order and how much to order. We have just discussed the "how much" question, and derived the basic EOQ model for calculating the economical order quantity for a constant and deterministic demand rate. Now, let us consider the question of when to order. It is usually convenient to answer the question in the form "When the inventory is reduced to a specified level, it is time to reorder." This level of inventory is called the reorder point. In effect, the reorder point recognizes the time lag or lead time between placing the order and receiving it by permitting enough stock in inventory to satisfy the demand during this lead time. In the basic EOQ model, for example, the lead time was assumed to be constant. Therefore, the reorder point was implicitly set at a level equal to the known demand for that period, so that the inventory level would reach zero just as the order is received. Since this type of idealized behavior does not occur in practice, the inventory model must be made more sophisticated to account for variations in replenishment lead time and demand.

We could set the reorder point equal to the expected average demand for the average lead time. But this is usually inadequate for most system requirements because, by definition, actual demand during the lead time would exceed average demand in about half of the lead time periods. Therefore, a buffer or safety stock is added to the expected demand during the lead time in determining the reorder point. The need for safety stock is clearly seen in Figure 13–5 which shows a more realistic pattern of inventory depletion caused by demand varying over time. Note that the order quantity remains fixed.

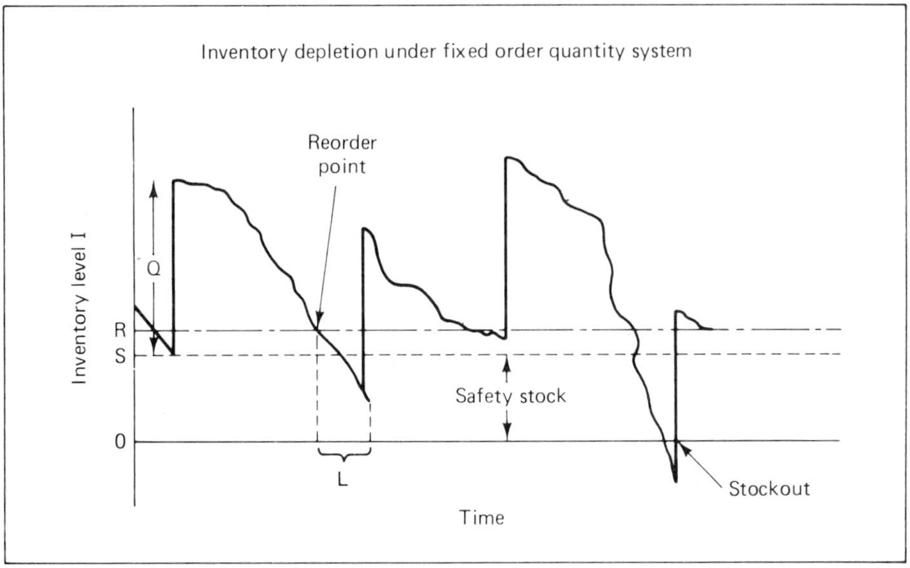

FIGURE 13–5. Inventory Depletion Under Fixed Order Quantity Systems.

Reorder Point and Average Inventory Equations

The reorder point level, *R*, is equal to the sum of the safety stock, *S*, and the average lead time demand, which is the average demand rate, $\bar{D}$, times the average lead time, $\bar{L}$ (Figure 13–6). The average inventory, *I*, is equal to the safety stock plus one half the order quantity, *Q*. We shall call the quantity *Q*/2 the cycle stock. So, the average inventory is simply the sum of the safety stock, which provides protection against stockouts caused by the stochastic behavior of demand and the replenishment process, and the cycle stock, which is one-half of the economical order quantity.

We see from Figure 13–5, which tracks the inventory level over time, that the inventory level falls below and above the safety stock level by the time an order is received. If there were no safety stock, orders that dip into it would have to be backordered. In fact, we can see that at one point even the safety stock was depleted.

$\bar{I}$ = Average inventory

R = Reorder point

S = Safety stock

$\bar{D}$ = Average demand rate

$\bar{L}$ = Average leadtime

Reorder point

$$R = S + \bar{D}\bar{L}$$

Average inventory

$$\bar{I} = S + Q^*/2$$

FIGURE 13–6. Reorder Point and Average Inventory Equations.

Distribution of Weekly Demand for Truck Batteries

By using actual sales and lead time data, it is possible to simulate by means of a computer what would have happened over an extended period of time if an alternative reorder rule had been in effect. The results, in terms of stockouts, average inventory levels, and so forth, can then be compared to actual results. In fact, simulation is frequently used to test and evaluate alternative inventory systems. However, simulation is a tedious and costly technique to use on a routine basis. Fortunately, basic statistical techniques can be applied to measure and predict the results expected from the use of a particular inventory model.

Let us consider a situation in which the lead time is constant. In many inventory situations the elapsed time from placing an order to receiving the material varies so little that it can be considered constant for all practical purposes. Then all we need to know is the distribution of actual demand above the average for the lead time in order to determine the level of safety stock that will provide a specific protection against stockouts or backorders.

Let us assume that Figure 13–7 is the distribution of weekly demand for truck batteries at a large motor pool. It takes exactly one week to get delivery from a factory warehouse, and the distribution summarizes the weekly usage for 100 weeks. Average requirements were 4 batteries a week, which actually occurred in 19 of the 100 weeks. The reorder point, then, would be set so as to include the average usage of 4 batteries plus a buffer stock. We see that demand of more than 8 batteries occurred in two of the 100 weeks. Therefore, by setting the safety stock at 4 batteries (the difference between 8 batteries and the average demand of 4) an out-of-stock condition should occur only about 2

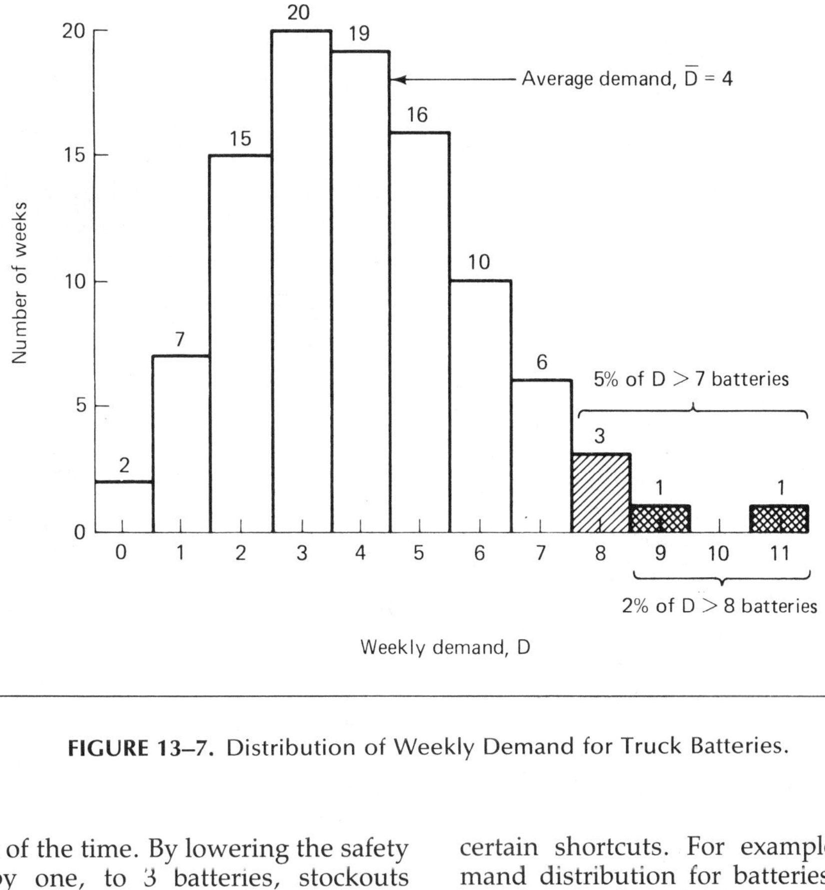

FIGURE 13–7. Distribution of Weekly Demand for Truck Batteries.

percent of the time. By lowering the safety stock by one, to 3 batteries, stockouts would occur whenever weekly demand exceeded 7 batteries, or about 5 percent of the time. Therefore, if the lead time is constant and we know the distribution of demand, we can set the safety stock to provide a specific level of protection against stockouts.

To examine each distribution of historical demand would be a mammoth task. Fortunately, most time patterns of demand can be approximated by well-known statistical distributions. This permits the use of certain shortcuts. For example, this demand distribution for batteries is a close approximation to the Poisson distribution. The Poisson has the convenient characteristic that whenever the average is known, we can describe the complete distribution. You may recall that the standard deviation of the Poisson distribution is equal to the square root of the average. In Figure 13–7, we see that only 2 percent of the values exceeded 8 batteries, which is equal to the average sales (4) plus two times the standard deviation ($2 \times 2 \geqslant 40$).

Alternatively, if the average is known,

the probability of equaling or exceeding a particular value can be read directly from tables of the summed Poisson distribution. Items that have low usage rates tend to display Poisson demand patterns; that is, demands come individually at random. If the testing of representative items indicate that Poisson distributions fit actual demand distribution fairly closely, it is often possible to assume Poisson distributions for a large group of similar items.

Standard Deviation of Demand Rate

For items having larger average demands for the lead time period, say over 20 units, the normal distribution is often a good approximation to actual demand distributions. In addition to calculating the average demand over the lead time period, we also calculate standard deviation (Figure 13–8).

The standard deviation, you will recall, can be calculated by squaring the difference between the actual demand and the average demand for each time period, adding together all of the squared differences, and dividing the sum by the number of periods, n, to get the variance. Then, the standard deviation is just the square root of the variance, which gives us a good measure of distribution of actual lead time demand above the average.

Standard deviation:

$$S_D = \sum_{t=10}^{N} \frac{(D_t - \bar{D})^2}{n}$$

Reorder point:

$$R = \bar{D} + kS_D$$

Average inventory:

$$\bar{I} = kS_D + Q/2$$

FIGURE 13–8. Standard Deviation of Demand Rate.

The safety stock can be set by multiplying the standard deviation by some factor k. The value of k selected depends upon the degree of protection that we require against the occurrence of a stockout. For instance, for k equal to 1.96, we have a 95 percent probability that demand during the lead time will not exceed the inventory on hand; for $k = 1.65$, we have a 90 percent chance of not running out. The reorder point, then, is set equal to the average lead time demand, $\bar{D}$, plus the safety stock, kS_D, and the average inventory is again equal to the sum of the safety stock, ks_D, and cycle stock $Q/2$.

Normal Distribution of Demand

Normal distribution is illustrated in Figure 13–9, where the probability of a stockout in a given order cycle is represented by the shaded area under the tail of the curve. Theoretically, there is always a finite probability of a stockout regardless of how large we make k. And as we approach a 100 percent service level (in other words, no stockouts), the inventory and the costs increase very rapidly.

The calculation of the average demand, the standard deviation, and the safety stock for any item can be performed very rapidly on the computer. In practice, many high-volume items display a normal demand distribution. Tests can be performed on a selected sample from a large group of similar items to test for normality.

FORECASTING

We have discussed several models of inventory systems for recurring demand processes, and we have assumed throughout that the demand processes were stationary and that the average demand was

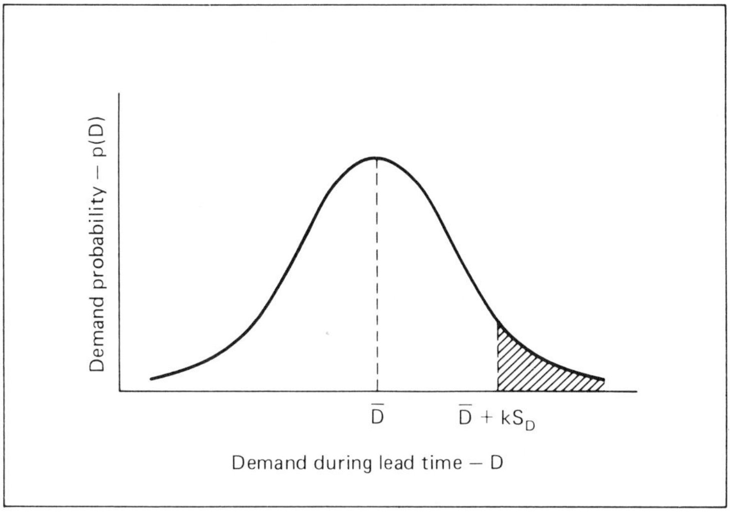

FIGURE 13–9. Normal Distribution of Demand.

known and constant. How do we go about measuring the average demand rate in face of a fluctuating time pattern of demand? And how do we track the forecast demand that is nonstationary; that is, a demand rate that is changing in time? The procedures used for making predictions or forecasts vary widely. A forecasting technique may involve the use of historical data on the item itself; it may involve predictions on electronic technology in the year 2,000, or it may be based on future planned requirements (in the case of repair parts and so forth).

We do not have time here to discuss forecasting techniques in any detail, since different circumstances require varying approaches. We shall, however, briefly examine two methods for estimating average demand rates that have gained wide acceptance for short-term forecasting using historical data: the moving average, and exponential smoothing methods. The moving average method (Figure 13–10) is probably the most commonly used. A moving average is simply the average demand over a fixed number of time intervals.

If we use a base period of B time periods, then the moving average, $\bar{D}$, is the sum of the demands for the past B time periods divided by B. For example, the moving average based on demand for the past 5 weeks, say, is simply 100 units per week. This, then becomes our forecast for next week.

A desirable property of a forecast is that it should track significant changes in the average demand rate, but it should not be too sensitive to random fluctuations in demand. One difficulty in using the moving average method for forecasting is that

$$\bar{D} = \frac{D_n + D_{n-1} + \ldots + D_{n-B+1}}{B}$$

$$100 = \frac{100 + 90 + 105 + 80 + 125}{5}$$

FIGURE 13–10. Moving Average Method.

$$\bar{D} = \bar{D}_{n-1} + (D_n - \bar{D}_{n-1})\ 0 \leq \alpha \leq 1 \qquad (1)$$

$$\boxed{\bar{D}_n = D_n + (1 - \alpha)\, \bar{D}_{n-1}} \qquad (2)$$

$$\bar{D}_n = \alpha D_n + (1 - \alpha)\, (D_{n-1} + (1 - \alpha)^2\, \bar{D}_{n-2}) \qquad (3)$$

$$= \alpha D_n + \alpha(1 - \alpha)\, D_{n-1} + (1 - \alpha)^2\, \bar{D}_{n-2}) \qquad (4)$$

$$= \alpha D_n + \alpha(1 - \alpha)\, D_{n-1} + (1 - \alpha)\, D_{n-2} + \ldots \qquad (5)$$

$$= \alpha \sum_{k=0} (1 - \alpha)^k\, D_{n-k} \qquad (6)$$

FIGURE 13–11. Exponential Smoothing Method.

it is always necessary to have available the demand history for B time periods back. This can take up an unnecessarily large amount of storage in a computer when many items are being handled. The exponential smoothing method (Figure 13–11) of predicting eliminates this problem.

If we denote D_n as the actual demand during the most recent time period n, and $\bar{D}_{n-1}$ as our estimate of average demand made at the end of the previous time period, $n-1$, then our forecast of average demand in the current time period, n, is obtained by adding to our previous estimate of the average demand a fraction of the amount by which demand this period exceeds that estimate. The fraction used is called the smoothing constant, and is conventionally represented by the Greek letter alpha (α).

Rearranging terms, the exponential smoothing formula takes the form of a recursion equation in which the new estimate equals alpha times the actual demand during the current period plus one minus alpha times the old estimate. Since the new estimate, $\bar{D}_n$, includes the old estimate, $\bar{D}_{n-1}$, it is clear that all previous demands are included in obtaining $\bar{D}_n$. By substituting a similar equation for the old estimate, we get this extended expression.

By repeating substitutions, we get a power series in which the new estimate is a sum of the actual demands in past periods, each multiplied by a definite weight which decreases as the past recedes. The weighting of the demand data follows an exponential curve—hence the name exponential smoothing.

In Figure 13–12, we can see how past demand data are weighted informing the new estimate of the average for a smoothing constant of 0.1. The larger the value of alpha, the more weight is assigned to demands in recent periods. For alpha equal to 0.5, for instance, three periods of data account for about 94 percent of the new average.

Finally, it should be mentioned that the simple moving average and exponential smoothing formulas can be modified to adjust for significant trends and seasonal effects evident in the demand pattern.

INCREMENTAL ANALYSIS

With the advent of electronic data processing equipment following World War II, it became feasible to maintain statistics by actual demand for individual items, order by order, by location, and by category of

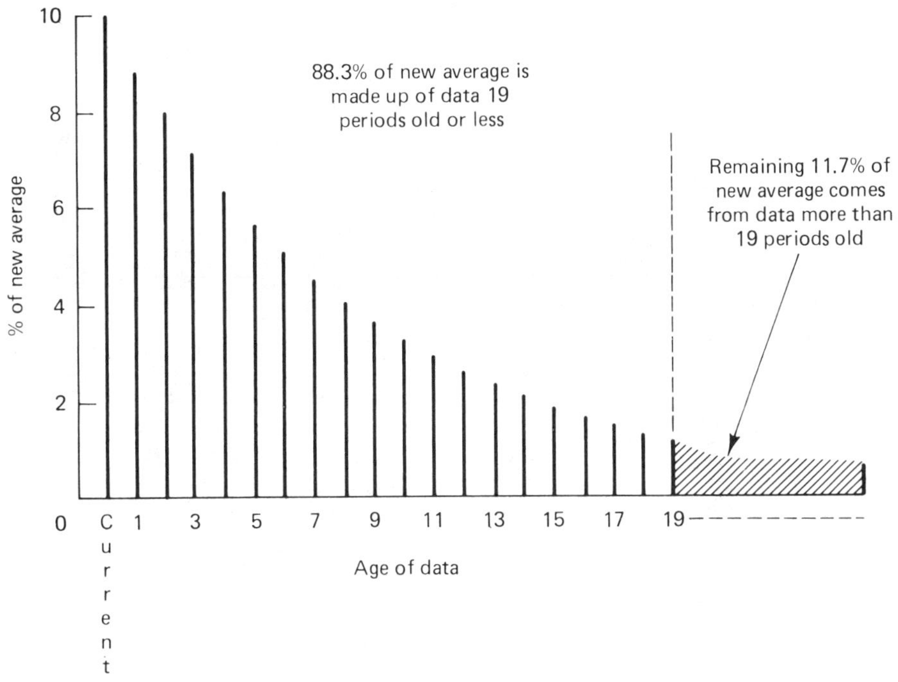

FIGURE 13–12. Weighting of Data with Smoothing Constant = 0.1.

customer for hundreds of thousands of items. At the same time, a considerable amount of operations research has been directed toward determining optimal policies for stock replenishment and production, including the development of stochastic models of demand, taking full advantage of this increase in data handling capability.

So far, we have been considering steady-state inventory situations in which demand is recurring and stock is replenished periodically. Let us now consider a special dynamic situation involving an activity that is provisioned on a one-time basis, and once the action or activity is completed the stock remaining becomes relatively useless. Such situations are called one-time provisionings. Examples would include military actions or expeditions that cannot be resupplied or the provisioning of perishable supplies that can only be stored for a short period of time.

This type of problem is often referred to as the newsboy or Christmas tree problem, since it can be phrased as a problem of how many newspapers a boy should buy on a given day for his corner newsstand, or how many Christmas trees a dealer should purchase for the season. This problem was solved by T. M. Whitin, during World War II, and was one of the first stochastic inventory models developed.

Let us formulate the Christmas tree problem. A Christmas tree vendor can buy as many trees as he likes before the season begins, but he has time for only one delivery. If he purchased too many trees, those not sold at the end of the season are a total loss. If he purchased too few trees, he misses the opportunity for profits where he has customers but no trees. A method called incremental analysis can be used here. The more trees the man buys, the better are his chances of having enough trees on hand to satisfy possible demand;

but this also boosts his chances of having too many trees on hand. The former is analogous to increment gain, the latter to incremental cost.

Suppose the man had purchased a certain number of trees. If he had added one more tree and sold it, he would have more profits. This increase in profits is called incremental gain. If, on the other hand, he could not sell the additional tree, he would have suffered an incremental cost. A comparison of the incremental cost with the incremental gain reveals the net contribution of the additional tree. The essence of incremental analysis is that units are added to the scheme as long as incremental costs are less than incremental gains. When incremental costs are greater than incremental gains, too many units have been added. As long as the incremental costs are less than the incremental gains, there is net contribution to profits. Therefore, it pays to add units to the scheme until the incremental cost, *IC*, equals the incremental gain, *IG*; that is, $IC = IG$. Until this point is reached, profits have increased; after this point, profits would decrease.

Stochastic Inventory Models

When dealing with stochastic models, we compute the expected incremental cost and gain. Otherwise, the approach is the same. In the case of the vendor of Christmas trees, he should continue to add trees to his order as long as the expected cost of each additional tree is less than the expected profit from the tree.

Let us assume that the probability distribution of sales experienced by the man in the past is as shown in Figure 13–13, and that there is no reason to expect it to be different this season. We can now derive a Christmas tree model (Figure 13–14). Let c equal the cost of a tree, m equal the margin of profit on each tree (which is simply the sales price minus the cost), and $P(x)$ equal the probability of being able to sell a given number of trees, x or more.

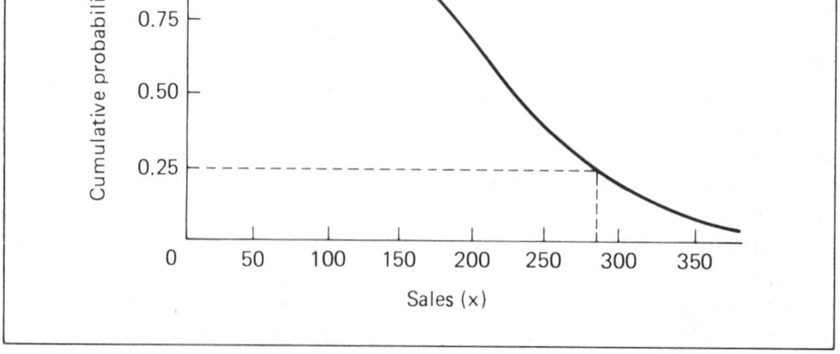

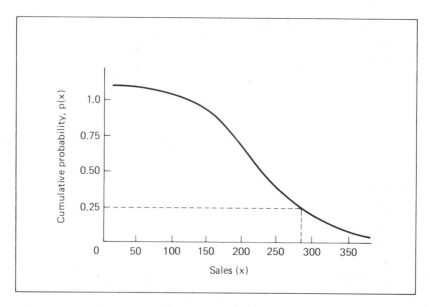

FIGURE 13–13. Weighting of Data with Smoothing Constant = 0.1.

c = Cost of a tree

m = Margin of profit on each tree

P(x) = Probability of being able to sell x or more trees

$$E(IC) = E(IG)$$

$$(1 - P(x)) \quad c = P(x)m$$

$$c - P(x)c = P(x)m$$

$$c = P(x)\ (m + c)$$

$$P(x) = \frac{c}{m + c}$$

FIGURE 13–14. Derivation of Christmas Tree Model.

Then we must find where the expected incremental cost just equals the expected incremental gain or profit.

As each additional tree is purchased, the probability of selling it is $P(x)$, the probability of being able to sell this number x or more trees. The profit margin, if it is sold, is m. The expected value of this incremental gain is just the product of the two, $P(x)$ times m. The probability of not selling the additional tree is $1 - P(x)$; that is, the probability of being able to sell less than x trees. Therefore, the expected value of the incremental or marginal cost is the product of the cost of the tree, c, and $1 - P(x)$. Multiplying and rearranging terms we find the expression for the probability associated with the optimum number of trees to buy is simply $c/(m + c)$, which is just the ratio of the cost to the price of a tree.

Example:

$$c = \$10$$
$$m = \$30$$

$$P(x) = \frac{c}{m + c} = \frac{1}{30 + 10} = 0.25$$

or $\qquad x = 285$ trees

Let's take a simple example. Assume the Christmas tree vendor buys the trees for \$10 and sells them for \$40, or a profit of \$30 a tree. Plugging these values into the probability expression, we get 0.25, which means that the man should buy enough trees so that there is a 25 percent probability of selling the last one. The number of trees corresponding to this probability is approximately 285, the optimum to buy.

INVENTORY ABC ANALYSIS

The ABC analysis[4] is a way of classifying inventory items so that the important ones will be given the most attention. The importance is measured in terms of annual usage value. This value is determined for each inventory item by multiplying the unit cost by the quantity used or forecasted during a year. The ABC system is used to separate items into groups of items that are controlled differently.

Large firms, both manufacturing and distribution organizations, have to inventory and track thousands or more different items. They may be end products, assemblies, subassemblies, component parts, and service parts for products no longer produced. The capital tied up in these items is substantial. The ABC analysis divides inventories into three groupings. The A items are the few items with large-dollar volume. Usually the A items comprise 15 to 20 percent of the total items and account for 70 to 76 percent of the total dollar volume. The B items are the 18 to 22 percent that account for 18 to 22 percent of the investment. While they are less important than A items, they are costly enough

[4]The ABC analysis is known as a Pareto distribution curve, named after the famous Italian economist, Vilfredo Pareto (1848–1923).

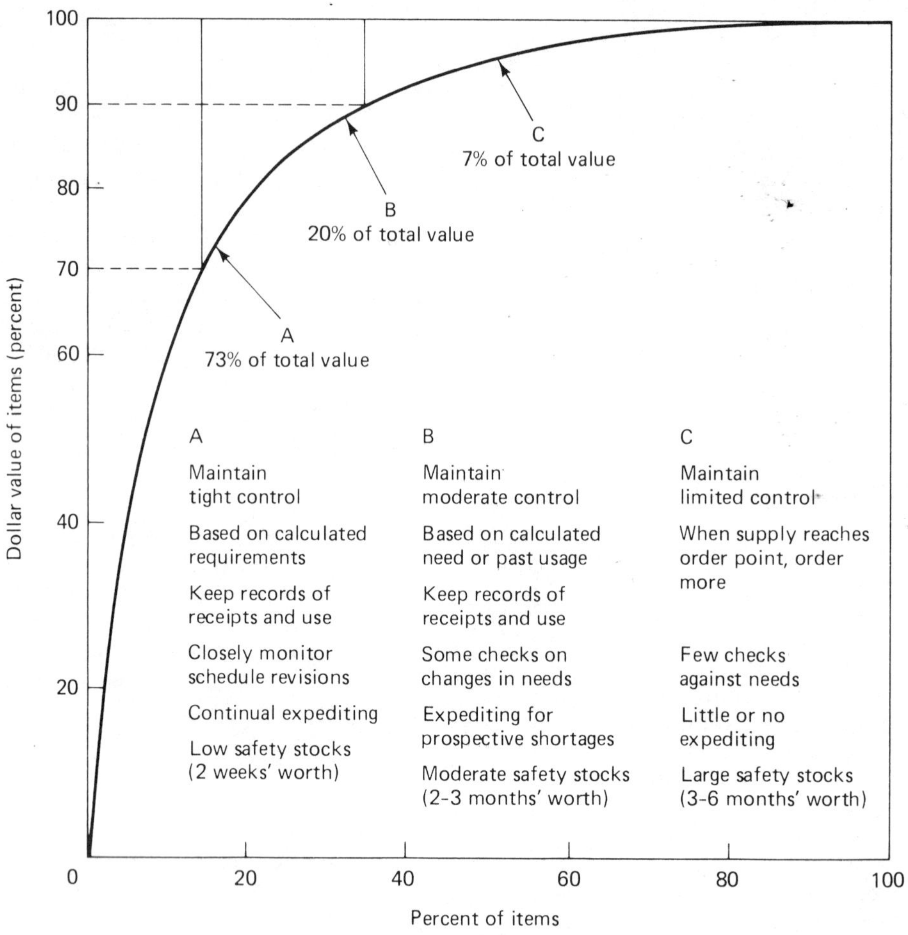

FIGURE 13–15. ABC Inventory Distribution Curve

to keep careful stock records of their use and to monitor them. C items are the large number of items accounting for the small-dollar value. It is not uncommon for around 7 percent of these items to account for around 62 percent of the inventory investment.

Figure 13–15 illustrates the relationship between percentage of value invested in the three inventory groups and percentage of inventory items. The degree of control and review frequency for each group are listed to the lower right in the figure.

Summary

Inventory planning should result in stocking the right amount of each material. Inventories are necessary so that virtually every stock item can be delivered when it is needed. In controlling inventories, it is necessary to establish an operating doctrine, policy decision concerning when to replenish stocks and what quantity to replenish.

Automation and computers play an increasing role in inventory planning. Computers can routinely supply information about what material orders should be placed, automatically print out purchase requisitions and purchase orders, and utilize a list of software packages to supply operating managers with information about inventories. In the past two decades, the emphasis has been on inventory theory, the selection of the order point, and order quantity. This emphasis has come about because of the advent of the computer and the techniques of operations research.

Inventory costs that are relevant in selecting the operating doctrine are the acquisition costs, carrying costs of inventory, cost of the item, and costs associated with being out of stock when units are demanded. Thus, inventory control decisions must consider these cost components and their trade-offs.

The ABC analysis diagram identifies three classes of items requiring tight (A), intermediate (B), and loose (C) control procedures. Symptoms of instability include extreme fluctuations in inventory levels and production rates, along with delays in meeting schedule deadlines and delivery dates.

Most computer manufacturers and many computer consulting firms sell software packages that are designed for inventory control in many types of manufacturing distribution and service organizations. These people bring experience from other implementations and, of course, avoid starting from scratch.

Questions

1. What is the main purpose of maintaining an inventory?
2. What are the five (5) types of inventory models to meet a variety of conditions?
3. What does the basic EPQ model assume? Why is it important to study it at all?
4. How does the EMQ model differ from the EPQ model?
5. Explain the derivation of the simple EOQ model?
6. Using the EPQ model, determine the quantity for the following data:

   D = 10,000 units
   C = \$6
   I = 15%
   S = \$11
7. What are inventory cost factors?
8. Explain the basic differences between the moving average method and the exponential smoothing method of forecasting demand.
9. What is the reorder point and average inventory for the following condition: Safety stock = 200 units; minimum inventory = 100; maximum inventory = 600 units; procurement lead time =

2 months; average demand rate of 240 units per month.

10. What are some of the most commonly used inventory models?
11. Select some product with which you are fairly familiar. Make a list of the parts or materials used in making this item and classify them as:
    a. High value items
    b. Intermediate value items
    c. Low value items
12. Explain the application of Pareto's law to inventory analysis.
13. Visit a service establishment, such as a tire and battery retailer, a discount service merchandise store, or hospital pharmacy. Determine how they maintain their inventory—what records they keep, how they establish their safety stock level, and what procedure they use for ordering stock.

Bibliography

Buffa, Elwood S., and Miller, Jeffrey L. *Production-Inventory Systems: Planning and Control*. Homewood, Ill.: Richard D. Irwin, 1979.

Dudick, T. S., and Cornell, R. *Inventory Control for the Financial Executive*. New York: John Wiley and Sons, 1979.

Fuch, Jerome. *Computerized Investing Control*. Englewood Cliffs, N.J.: Prentice-Hall, 1978.

Greene, James H. *Production and Inventory Control: Systems and Decisions*. Homewood, Ill.: Richard D. Irwin, 1974.

Hadley, G., and Whitin, T. M. *Analysis of Inventory Systems*. Englewood Cliffs, N.J.: Prentice-Hall, 1963.

Johnson, L., and Montgomery, D. *Operations Research in Production Planning Scheduling and Inventory Control*. New York: John Wiley and Sons, 1977.

Koenigsberg, E., and Buchan, J. F. *Scientific Inventory Management*. Englewood Cliffs, N.J.: Prentice-Hall, 1962.

Larson, Stanley E. *Inventory Systems and Controls*. Englewood Cliffs, N.J.: Prentice-Hall, 1976.

Lewis, Colin D. *Scientific Inventory Control*. Boston: Butterworth, 1981.

Love, Stephen F. *Inventory Control*. New York: McGraw-Hill, 1979.

Magee, John F. *Production Planning and Inventory Control*. New York: McGraw-Hill, 1967.

Naddor, E. *Inventory Systems*. New York: John Wiley and Sons, 1966.

Peterson, R., and Silver, E. A. *Decision Systems for Inventory Management and Production Planning*. New York: John Wiley and Sons, 1979.

Plossl, G. W., and Wight, O. W. *Production and Inventory Control*. Englewood Cliffs, N.J.: Prentice-Hall, 1967.

Reinfeld, Nyles V. *Production and Inventory Control*. Reston, Va.: Reston Publishing, 1982.

Smith, Bernard T. *Focus Forecasting: Computer Technique for Inventory Control*. Boston: CBI, 1978.

Starr, M. K., and Miller, D. W. *Inventory Control: Theory and Practice*. Englewood Cliffs, N.J.: Prentice-Hall, 1962.

Tersine, Richard J. *Materials Management and Inventory Systems*. New York: Elsevier, 1976.

———. *Principles of Inventory and Materials Management*. New York: North Holland, 1982.

U. S. Army Ordnance Center and School. *Operations Research Application in Supply*. Pamphlet 901-4. Aberdeen Proving Ground, Md., March 1970.

Wagner, H. M. *Statistical Management of Inventory Systems*. New York: John Wiley and Sons, 1962.

Part VI
Safety Engineering

Chapter 14

Safety Engineering and Management

Occupational Safety and Health Act of 1970

The Williams-Steiger Occupational Safety and Health Act of 1970[1] was enacted by Congress in December 1970 "to assure so far as possible every working man and woman in the United States safe and healthful working conditions and to preserve the nation's human resources." The act was signed by former president Richard M. Nixon in December 1970.

COVERAGE

The provisions of the law apply to every employer who has employees and is engaged in a business affecting commerce. The law applies in all 50 states, the District of Columbia, Puerto Rico, the Virgin Islands, American Samoa, Guam, the Trust Territory of the Pacific Islands, Wake Island, the Outer Continental Shelf Lands, Johnston Island, and the Canal Zone. Federal, state, and local government employees are specifically excluded from coverage, but they may be covered by equally effective requirements. (See Section 19 for programs covering Federal employees and Section 18 (c)(6) for potential coverage of state and local government employees.)

In addition, the act specifically provides that its terms shall not apply to working conditions protected under other federal occupational safety and health laws (such as those under the Federal Coal Mine Health and Safety Act; and under the Atomic Energy Act of 1954, as amended, including state agreements under that act).

DUTIES OF EMPLOYERS AND EMPLOYEES

Each employer under the act has the general duty to furnish each of his employees employment and places of employment, free from recognized hazards causing, or likely to cause, death or serious physical harm; and the employer has the specific duty of complying with safety and health standards promulgated under the act. Each employee has the duty to comply with these safety and health standards, and all rules, regulations, and orders issued pursuant to the act that are applicable to his own actions and conduct. The act took effect on April 28, 1971.

ADMINISTRATION

Administration and enforcement of the act are vested primarily in the secretary of Labor and in The Occupational Safety and Health Review Commission, a quasi-judicial board of three members appointed by the president. Research and related functions are vested in the secretary of Health and Human Services whose functions will, for the most part, be carried out by the

[1]The acronym OSHA can stand for both the Occupational Safety and Health Act and the Occupational Safety and Health Administration. To prevent confusion OSH Act will be used for the Act and OSHA for the Administration or Agency.

National Institute for Occupational Safety and Health.

The secretary of Labor is responsible for both promulgating and enforcing job safety and health standards. Occupational safety and health inspections will be made by inspectors located in offices to be established in many communities throughout the country.

OCCUPATIONAL SAFETY AND HEALTH STANDARDS

In general, job safety and health standards consist of rules for avoidance of hazards that have been proven by research and experience to be harmful to personal safety and health. They constitute an extensive compilation of wisdom that sometimes applies to all employees. An example of this would be fire protection standards. A great many standards, however, apply only to workers while engaged in specific types of work—such as handling compressed gases.

Two of the many thousands of occupational safety and health standards are listed here by way of example:

1. Aisles and passageways shall be kept clear and in good repair, with no obstruction across or in aisles that could create a hazard.

2. In any operations such as chipping, caulking, drilling, riveting, grinding, and pouring babbit metal, in which the eye hazard of flying particles, molten metal, or liquid chemical exists, employees shall be protected by suitable face shields or goggles.

It is the obligation of all employers and employees to familiarize themselves with standards that apply to them and to observe them at all times.

The act authorizes the Secretary of Labor until April 28, 1973, to promulgate as occupational safety and health standards any existing federal standards (such as those presently applying to federal contractors under the Walsh-Healey Act) or any national consensus standards (such as those issued by the National Fire Protection Association). He may do this without complying with the rule-making requirements of the Administrative Procedure Act.

In addition, the secretary of Labor may, upon the basis of information submitted to the secretary of Health and Human Services advisory committees and others, revise, modify, or revoke existing standards as well as promulgate new ones. The promulgation of standards under this section of the act must be done under the procedures set forth in the section itself, including various time limitations, and also under the procedures of the Administrative Procedure Act. Any person adversely affected by a standard issued by the secretary may challenge its validity by petitioning the U. S. Court of Appeals within sixty days after its promulgation. Unless otherwise ordered by the Court, filing such a petition does not operate as a stay of standard.

Also where it is found that employees are exposed to grave danger, the act provides for the establishment of emergency temporary standards, effective immediately upon publication in the *Federal Register*. The act also contains provision for standards that may require:

1. That no employee dealing with toxic materials or harmful physical agents will suffer material impairment of health or functional capacity, even if such employee has regular exposure to the hazard dealt with by such standard for the period of his working life.
2. Development and prescription of labels or other appropriate forms of warning

so that employees are made aware of all hazards to which they are exposed.

3. Prescription of suitable protection equipment.
4. Monitoring or measuring employee exposure to hazards at such locations and intervals and in such manner as may be necessary for the protection of employees.
5. Prescription of the type and frequency of medical examinations or other tests for employees exposed to health hazards. At the request of an employee, the examination or test results shall be furnished to his physician.

The secretary, after a hearing on an employer application, is authorized to grant temporary variances from standards to give the employer sufficient time to come into compliance if he can show a need for certain time-extension and had a protective plan of action. Variances may be granted without time limits if the secretary finds that an employer is using safety measures which are as safe as those required in a standard. Affected employees shall be given notice of each such application and an opportunity for hearing.

COMPLAINTS OF VIOLATIONS

Any employees (or representative thereof) who believe that a violation of a job safety or health standard exists which threatens physical harm, or that an imminent danger exists, may request an inspection by sending a signed written notice to the Department of Labor. Such a notice shall set forth with reasonable particularity the grounds for the notice and a copy shall be provided the employer or his agent. The names of the complainants need not, however, be furnished to the employer. If the secretary finds no reasonable grounds for the complaint and a citation is not issued, the secretary is required to notify the complainants in writing of his determinations or final disposition of the matter. Also, the secretary is required to set up procedures for informal review in a case where a citation is not issued.

ENFORCEMENT

In enforcing the standards, Labor Department safety inspectors may enter without delay, and at any reasonable times, any establishment covered by the act to inspect the premises and all pertinent conditions, structures, machines, apparatus, devices, equipment, and materials therein, and to question privately any employer, owner, operator, agent, or employee.[2] The act permits the employer and a representative authorized by his employees to accompany the inspector during the physical inspection of any work place for the purpose of aiding such inspection. The secretary of Labor also has power, in making inspections and investigations under the act, to require the attendance and testimony of witnesses and the production of evidence under oath. The secretary of Health and Human Services is also authorized to make inspections and question employers and employees in order to carry out those functions assigned under the act.

Where an investigation reveals a violation, the employer is issued a written citation describing the specific nature of the violation. All citations shall fix a reasonable time for abatement of the violation, and each citation (or copies thereof) issued by the department must be prominently posted at or near each place where a violation referred to in the citation occurred. Notices, in lieu of citations, may be

---

[2]See U.S. Department of Labor, *OSHA Inspections*, Programs and Policy Series, OSHA 2098, (Washington, June 1975).

issued for de minimis violations that have no direct or immediate relationship to safety or health.

No citation may be issued after the expiration of six months, following the occurrence of any violation.

Notification of Proposed Penalty

Within a reasonable time after issuance of a citation for a job safety or health violation, the Labor Department shall notify the employer by certified mail of the penalty, if any, which is proposed to be assessed. The employer then has fifteen working days within which to notify the department that he wishes to contest the citation or proposed assessment of penalty. If the employer fails to notify the department within such time that he intends to contest the citation or proposed assessment of penalty, the citation and the assessment shall be final, provided no employee files an objection to the time allowed for abatement (see the next section). If the employer notifies the department within such time that he does wish to contest, the secretary of Labor will so advise the Occupational Safety and Health Review Commission and the commission shall afford an opportunity for a hearing. The commission then will issue orders affirming, modifying, or vacating the citation or proposed penalty. Orders of the commission are final thirty days after the issuance. Review of commission orders may be obtained in the U. S. Court of Appeals.

The review comission's rules of procedure shall provide affected employees (or representatives thereof) an opportunity to participate as parties to hearings under Section 10(c).

Time for Abatement of Hazards

A citation issued by the area director, OSHA, shall prescribe a reasonable time for elimination or abatement of the hazard. This time limit may also be contested if notification of such is filed with the department within fifteen days. The time set by the department for correcting a violation shall not begin to run until there is a final order of the review commission, if the review is initiated by the employer in good faith and not solely for delay or avoidance of penalties.

Employees (or representatives of employees) also have the right to object to the period of time fixed in the citation for the abatement of a violation. If, within fifteen days after a citation is issued, an employee files a notice with the department alleging that an unreasonable time was allowed for abatement, review procedures similar to those specified above apply.

Failure to Correct Violation within Allowed Time

Where time for correction of a violation is allowed, but the employer fails to abate within such time, the area director, OSHA, Department of Labor shall notify the employer by certified mail of such failure and of the proposed penalty. Such notice and assessment shall be final unless the employer contests the same by notice to the secretary within fifteen days.

Upon a showing by an employer of a good faith effort to comply with the abatement requirements of a citation, but that abatement has not been completed because of factors beyond his reasonable control, an opportunity for a hearing will be afforded, after which an order affirming or modifying the abatement requirement will be issued.

PENALTIES FOR VIOLATIONS

Willful or repeated violations of the act's requirements by employers may incur monetary penalties of up to $10,000 for each violation. Citations issued for serious violations incur mandatory monetary penalties of up to $1,000 for each violation, while penalties in the same amount may be incurred where nonserious violations are cited. A serious violation exists where there is a substantial probability that death or serious physical harm could result. Any employer who fails to correct a violation for which a citation has been issued within the period prescribed therein may be penalized up to $1,000 each day the violation persists.

A willful violation by an employer that results in the death of any employee is punishable by a fine of up to $10,000 or imprisonment for up to six months. A second conviction doubles these criminal penalties.

Criminal penalties are also included in the act for making false official statements, and for giving unauthorized advance notice of any inspections to be conducted under the act.

RECORDKEEPING REQUIREMENTS

In order to carry out the purposes of the act, employers are required to keep and make available to the labor secretary (and also to the HHS secretary) records on certain employer activities under the act. Employers are also required to maintain accurate records (and periodic reports) of work-related deaths, injuries, and illnesses. Minor injuries requiring only first aid treatment need not be recorded, but a record must be made if it involves medical treatment, loss of consciousness, restriction of work or motion, or transfer to another job.

Employers can also be required to maintain accurate records of employee exposures to potentially toxic materials or harmful physical agents that are required to be monitored or measured under Section 6(b)(7), and to promptly advise any employee of any excessive exposure and of the corrective action being undertaken. The secretary of Labor, in cooperation with the secretary of Health and Human Services is authorized by the law to issue regulations in this area that shall provide employees or their representatives with an opportunity to observe such monitoring or measuring, to have access to the records thereof and to such records as will indicate their own exposure to toxic materials or harmful physical agents.

For recordkeeping purposes, the secretary's regulations may also require employers to conduct their own periodic inspections.

The secretary is directed to issue regulations requiring employers to keep their employees informed of their protections and obligations under the law through posting of notices or other appropriate means. The information that employers may be required to give their employees may also include the provisions of applicable standards.

STATISTICS

The secretary of Labor, in consultation with the secretary of Health and Human Services, is required to develop and maintain an effective program of collection, compilation, and analysis of statistics on work injuries and illnesses. In so doing he may make private grants or contracts and grants to states or political subdivisions thereof. The secretary may also require employers to file such reports of work injuries and illnesses required to be kept under the act as he shall deem necessary.

Existing agreements between the Department of Labor and a state for collection of occupational safety and health statistics are preserved under the act until replaced by other arrangements under grants or contracts made under the act.

GENERAL NOTICE REQUIREMENT

The secretary of Labor is required to publish in the *Federal Register* a statement of his reasons for any action he takes with respect to the promulgation of any standard, the issuance of any rule, order or decision, the granting of any exemption or extension of time, as well as any action he takes to compromise, mitigate, or settle any penalty assessed under the act.

IMMINENT DANGERS

Any conditions or practices in any place of employment that are such that a danger exists which could reasonably be expected to cause death or serious physical harm immediately or before the imminence of such danger can be eliminated through normal enforcement procedures may be restrained by order of a U. S. District Court upon petition of the secretary of Labor.[3] If the secretary arbitrarily or capriciously fails to seek action to abate an imminent danger of such kind, a mandamus action to compel him to act may be brought in the U. S. District Court by any employee who may be injured by reason of such failure. A Labor Department safety inspector who concludes that such imminent-danger conditions or practices exist in any place of employment is obligated to inform the affected employees and employers of the danger and that he is recommending to the secretary of Labor that relief be sought.

PROTECTION AGAINST HARASSMENT

No person shall discharge or in any manner discriminate against any employee because he exercises any right under the act or files a complaint or other proceeding or because he testifies or is about to testify in any proceeding under the act.[4] Any employee who believes that he has been discharged or otherwise discriminated against in violation of this provision may, within thirty days of such illegal action, file a complaint with the secretary of Labor. The secretary is authorized to investigate the matter and to bring action in the U. S. District Court for appropriate relief, including rehiring or reinstatement of the employee to his former job with back pay. The secretary must notify the complainant of his action on the complaint within ninety days of its receipt.

STATE PARTICIPATION

The act encourages the states to assume the fullest responsibility for the administration and enforcement of their occupational safety and health laws by providing grants to the states for the purposes listed later in this chapter. A specific disclaimer of federal preemption is included in order to permit any state agency or court to assert jurisdiction under state law over any occupational safety or health issue with respect to which no federal standard is in effect under this law.

In addition, any state may assume responsibility for the development and enforcement of occupational safety and health standards relating to any job safety and health issue covered by a standard promulgated under Section 6 of the Occupational Safety and Health Act, if such state submits an approved plan for so doing to the secretary of Labor. The secret-

[3] See U.S. Department of Labor, *Protection for Workers in Imminent Danger*, Policy and Program Series, OSHA 2205 (Washington, April 1975).

[4] See U.S. Department of Labor, *Worker's Rights Under OSHA*, Programs and Policy Series, OSHA 2253, (Washington, November 1973).

ary shall approve such a plan under the following conditions:[5]

1. An agency, or agencies, of the state must be designated or created to carry out the plan.
2. The state standards (and enforcement thereof) must be at least as effective as the counterpart federal standards in providing safe and healthful employment.
3. There must be effective provisions for rights of entry and inspection of work place, including a prohibition on advance notice of inspections.
4. Enforcement capacity must be demonstrated.
5. Adequate funds for administration and enforcement must be assured.
6. Effective and comprehensive job safety, and health programs for all public employees within the state will be established to the extent by the particular state's law.
7. The state, and employers within the state, will make such reports as may be required by the secretary of Labor.

Following approval of a state plan for the development and enforcement of state standards, the secretary of Labor may continue to exercise his enforcement authority with respect to comparable federal occupational safety and health standards until he determines on the basis of actual operations that the criteria set forth above are being applied. Once he makes such determination (but he cannot do so during the first three years after the plan's approval), the federal standards and the secretary's enforcement of them become inapplicable with respect to issues covered under the plan.

[5]See U.S. Department of Labor, *How OSHA Monitors State Plans*, Programs and Policy Series, OSHA 2221 (Washington, January 1975).

However, the secretary is required to make a continuing evaluation of the manner in which each state plan is being carried out and to withdraw his approval thereof whenever there is a failure to comply substantially with any provision thereof. Such a plan shall cease to be in effect upon receipt of notice by the state of the secretary's withdrawal of approval.

The secretary of Labor is authorized, after consultation with the secretary of Health and Human Services to make grants to states for experimental and demonstration projects consistent with the objectives of the act, for administering and enforcing approved programs, for assisting them in identifying their needs, or in developing their plans, in establishing systems for collection of information concerning the nature and frequency of occupational injuries and diseases, for developing and administering programs dealing with occupational safety and health laws consistent with the objectives of the act.

If the secretary of Labor rejects a state plan for development and enforcement of state standards, he shall afford the state submitting the plan due notice and opportunity for hearing before so doing. The subsequent withdrawal of an approved state plan or the rejection of a state's plan is subject to review in the U. S. Court of Appeals.

The law also permits the secretary of Labor to enter into an agreement with any state under which the state will be permitted to continue to enforce its own occupational safety and health standards until approval of its plan for development and enforcement of occupational safety and health standards or until December 29, 1972, whichever comes first.

EDUCATION AND TRAINING PROGRAMS

The act provides for programs to be conducted by the secretary of Labor, in consultation with the Department of Health and

Human Services, for the education and training of employers and employees in the recognition, avoidance, and prevention of unsafe and unhealthful working conditions, and in the effective means for preventing occupational injuries and illness. The act also makes provision for educational and training programs to provide adequate supply of qualified personnel to carry out the law's purposes and for informational programs on the importance and proper use of adequate safety and health equipment to be conducted primarily by the Department of Health and Human Services, but also to some extent by the secretary of Labor.

NATIONAL INSTITUTE FOR OCCUPATIONAL SAFETY AND HEALTH

The act established within former HEW, now HHS, the National Institute for Occupational Safety and Health primarily for the purpose of carrying out the research and educational functions assigned to the HHS Secretary under the act.

In addition to these functions, the institute is authorized to develop and establish recommended occupational safety and health standards; to conduct research and experimental programs determined by the institute's director to be necessary for developing criteria for new and improved job safety and health standards; and to make recommendations to the secretaries of Labor and HHS concerning new and improved standards.

Among the HEW functions which may be carried out by the institute is the one that calls for prescribing regulations requiring employers to measure, record, and make reports on the exposure of employees to potentially toxic substances or harmful physical agents which might endanger their safety and health. Employers required to do so may receive full financial or other assistance for the purpose of defraying any additional expense so incurred. Also authorized are programs for medical examinations and tests as may be necessary to determine, for the purposes of research, the incidence of occupational illness and the susceptibility of employees to such illnesses. These examinations may also be at government expense. Another HHS function will be the annual publication of a list of all known toxic substances and the concentrations at which toxicity is known to occur. There will also be published industrywide studies on chronic or low-level exposure to a broad variety of industrial materials, processes, and stresses on the potential for illness, disease, or loss of functional capacity in aging adults, and also authorized is the making of determinations by HHS, at the written request of any employer or authorized representatives of employees, as to whether any substance normally found in the place of employment has potentially toxic effects. Such determinations shall be submitted to both the employer and the affected employees as soon as possible.

Information obtained by the departments of Health and Human Services and of Labor under research provisions of the act is to be disseminated to employers and employees and organizations thereof.

WORKER'S COMPENSATION

The act does not in any manner affect any workmen's compensation law or enlarge or diminish or affect in any other manner the common law or statutory rights, duties, or liabilities of employers and employees under any law with respect to injuries, diseases, or death of employees arising out of, or in the course of, employment. Provision is made in the law, however, for a fifteen-member National Commission on State Workmen's Compensation Laws to evaluate state workmen's compensation laws in order to determine if such laws provide an adequate, prompt, and equitable system of compensation for injury or death arising out of or in the course of employment.

ASSISTANCE FROM SMALL BUSINESS ADMINISTRATION

The law includes amendments to the Small Business Act that provides for financial assistance to small firms for alterations in its equipment, facilities, or methods of operation to comply with standards established by the Department of Labor or by any state pursuant to the act, if the Small Business Administration determines that such a firm is likely to suffer substantial economic injury without such assistance.[6]

OTHER PROVISIONS

Advisory Committees. The act creates a twelve-member National Advisory Committee to be appointed by the secretary of Labor (including 4 designees of the secretary of HHS) to advise, consult, and make recommendations on matters relating to the administration of the act, and permits the establishment of ad hoc advisory committees to assist the secretary in his standard-setting functions.

Nonobstruction Requirement. Any information obtained by any agency under the act shall be obtained with a minimum burden upon employers, especially those operating small businesses. Unnecessary duplication of efforts in obtaining information shall be reduced to the maximum extent feasible.

Occupational Safety and Health Review Commission. The act established a new independent federal agency, called the Occupational Safety and Health Review Commission. This commission is a quasi-judicial body whose functions are: (1) to hear and review cases of alleged violations brought before it by the secretary of Labor, and, where warranted, (2) to issue corrective orders, and (3) to assess civil penalties. The commission is to be composed of three members, appointed by the President (with the approval of the Senate) to serve 6-year staggered terms. The members will be chosen from among persons who are qualified by reason of training, education, or experience to perform their duties. One of the members shall be appointed by the President to serve as Chairman.

Labor Department Legal Representation. The Solicitor of Labor is authorized to appear for and represent the secretary in any civil litigation brought under the act subject to the direction and control of the attorney general.

Trade Secrets. Any trade secrets revealed to Labor Department personnel during the course of their duties under the act shall be considered confidential for the purpose of 18 USC 1905.

National Defense Tolerances. The secretary of Labor may allow reasonable variations, tolerances, and exemptions from any and all of the act's provisions, if he finds these necessary to avoid serious impairment of the national defense.

Federal Protection for Labor Department Inspectors. The act broadens the provisions of Title 18 of the United States Code, which make it a federal criminal offense to

---

[6]See U.S. Department of Labor, *SBA Loans for OSHA Compliance*, Program and Policy Series, OSHA 2005 (Washington, January 1975).

assault, kill, or otherwise interfere with certain law enforcement officials in the course of their assignments, by extending this protection to all employees of the Department of Labor assigned to perform investigative, inspection, or law enforcement functions.

Annual Reports. Comprehensive annual reports on the act must be prepared and submitted to the president for transmittal to the Congress by both the secretary of Labor and the secretary of Health and Human Services. Reports are also required from the secretary of Labor on the grants program, from the director of the National Institute for Occupational Safety and Health on the operations of that institute, and from the secretary of Labor on occupational safety and health programs for federal employees.

New Assistant Secretary of Labor. The law adds an additional assistant secretary in the Department of Labor to head the new Occupational Safety and Health organization within the department.

Appropriations Authority. Congress has authorized such funds to be appropriated to administer and enforce this law as Congress shall from time to time deem necessary.

ADDITIONAL INFORMATION

Additional information concerning this law may be obtained by contacting the nearest Regional Office, Occupational Safety and Health Administration, U.S. Department of Labor, with appropriate jurisdiction, or you may contact the Office of Information Services, Occupational Safety and Health Administration, U. S. Department of Labor, Washington, D. C. 20210.

Safety Management[7]

INTRODUCTION

Effective and efficient utilization of manpower, material, and money by industry is more essential now than at any other time in the history of the United States. Loss of manpower, material, and money through accident is intolerable. The national interest demands that industry be maintained at a peak of effectiveness but the economy demands that this peak be maintained at the optimum in dollar value. The tremendous economic inroads caused by accidental loss have certainly reduced that effectiveness in optimum value.

Accident prevention is the only effective method of accident reduction. In past years this concept has sometimes been conducted under the term *safety*. Equipment may be operated, programs conducted, and work performed under the safest criteria possible, and in the safest environment possible to create. In order to prevent man from having accidents, any worthwhile program must be predicated on one salient premise: accidents can be prevented and accident prevention is the only possible method for reducing accident experience.

SAFETY VS. ACCIDENT PREVENTION

Safety is defined as "freedom from danger" and principally deals with environment.

[7]By permission of the Department of the Army, U.S. Army Ordnance Center and School, Aberdeen Proving Ground, MD. the following sections have been taken in part and updated from "Safety Management for the Supervisor," subcourse AG 41, pamphlets M41–1, 2, 4–7, September 1972.

Accident prevention embraces safety. In addition, it includes the conditioning of man to the safe use of environment without introducing human error, which might result in a sequence of events leading to an accident. There can be no accident prevention program without safety, but accidents can occur in a safe environment without accident prevention.

In order to prevent accidents in a safe environment, the individual must be educated to the fact that it is necessary for him to operate in the safe environment and that his life may depend on it. Next, he must be trained through exposure to the environment to tolerate and operate safely within it.

Many psychologists agree that man is not psychologically safe. He cannot tolerate tedium; he requires excitement and diversion. However, he can be educated and trained to operate safely even in a hazardous area. To completely prevent accidents we must provide the psychological factors of motivation and to some degree emotional release.

Most safety research has been in the area of hardware improvement and its development and evaluation. This type of research is typified by seat belts, industrial safety equipment, crash force attenuation devices, and the like. This effort is not intended to be minimized in importance; however, the simple truth is that we are simply concerned with the after-the-fact accident environment; minimization of injury or danger after an accident occurs is the end result. Little or no research effort has been directed toward prevention of the actual accident occurence.

In summary, to prevent accidents or create an accident prevention program, we must establish a safe environment, educate and train the individual to operate within it, and provide motivation and to some degree diversion or emotional release. Provision in each of these areas can only be made by management.

SAFETY AND ACCIDENT PREVENTION SUPERVISION

It is extremely important that all personnel understand safety rules and regulations, and the necessity for them. Blind obedience is not sufficient. No supervisor can keep his eyes on all of his men all of the time. If people understand why they are to do a specific task in a specific way and are given the reasons why that way is the best and safest way, they will be better prepared to perform their work in a safe fashion even though the supervisor is not looking over their shoulders.

A group that works with, rather than for, its supervisor will be more productive and efficient in performance. A supervisor is delegated authority; if the employees under his authority are not certain of his fairness, if they think he will exercise his authority over them in unpredictable ways, they will compete with each other to keep the supervisor's favor. This can lead to hostility among the group members, and hostility will destroy the cooperativeness needed for effective safe group performance. Past research has shown that accident rates are higher among personnel whose supervisors rate poorly in leadership ability.

Three qualities are essential for effective safety supervision—consistency, fairness, and stability. If members of the group think the supervisor does not care for them as persons, and if he treats them according to whim, they lose their feeling of security and self-respect. If this occurs, they will not work at maximum efficiency and will be more susceptible to accidents.

Two factors that are highly related to accidents are: (1) unfamiliarity with the task (that is, the person is engaging in a task with which he has had little or no prior training and experience); and (2) isolation (that is, the person is alone when he is performing the task). Generally, good supervision will prevent these circumstances from arising. When, because of work requirements or for some other reason, these circumstances cannot be avoided, supervisors must establish safeguards to reduce the inherent action potential to a minimum.

Safety is one facet of production and can be compared to maintaining a high quality of work, an appropriate quantity of work, and the elimination of waste. The supervisor is charged with maintaining standards of production and seeing to it that the work is accomplished as safely as possible.

The supervisor is the man in the best position to know what his men are doing, how well they are doing it, and what their gripes and fears are. Supervisors must accept responsibility for accidents occurring in areas under their authority. When an accident occurs because of defective equipment, improperly used equipment, or failure to follow instructions, the supervisor has not completely fulfilled his responsibilities. It is important to remember that responsibility is different from blame. Responsibility must be officially delegated, and therefore signifies authority. The supervisor is the man who directs the men under his command. He tells them what to do, and when, where, and how to do it; consequently, he must accept responsibility for the results. This does not mean that the supervisor should diagnose the circumstances surrounding the accident to determine if he has been doing something wrong or ineffectively.

As a leader, the supervisor should constantly be on the alert to improve the relations with his men, thus ensuring successful accomplishment of the work. This applies as much to accident prevention as anything else. The ability to lead is as important in effective accident prevention as it is in other areas of supervision.

PREPARING FOR EFFECTIVE SAFETY SUPERVISION

The supervisor who accepts seriously his full responsibility for safety will have to develop plans to implement and carry out these responsibilities. He will need to learn the work habits and individual quirks of his personnel, since individual work habits and personality differences affect the ability to work safely. (For example, a person who is emotionally unstable and impatient should not be placed on a job which requires a great deal of precision work.)

The supervisor must establish procedures to ensure that each person under his control receives adequate job training, including safety instruction. The supervisor must check on the condition of all equipment and work space under his jurisdiction, and must develop a schedule for periodic inspection to maintain equipment and grounds in safe condition. He must provide constant supervision to be sure that personnel perform their work as instructed and that they do not develop unsafe practices and habits.

The supervisor needs to establish close contact with his men so that he knows each of them as individuals, and so they know him and have confidence in him. He needs to show approval of the safe performance of his personnel.

With specific reference to safe performance, the supervisor needs to investigate every accident which occurs in his jurisdiction, whether or not personal injury or property damage is involved. He needs to search for and find the underlying reasons for these accidents, to devise remedial actions to prevent future occurrences of these accidents, and to evaluate the remedial actions over a period of time to determine if they are effective in preventing accidents. He needs to determine what types of accidents are his most serious problem by studying the accident records. Most of the procedures indicated above are essential to effective supervision, regardless of the area of supervision. With respect to safety, the supervisor need only broaden his understanding of good supervision to include the specific procedures involved in accident prevention.

There are really very few different kinds of supervisory problems. The procedures for solving these problems are the same, whether the issues are accident problems or other kinds of supervisory problems. Development of a solution to a supervisory problem requires implementation of the following procedures.

1. Isolate and identify the problem.
2. Determine the reason for the problem.
3. Select an appropriate remedy.
4. Apply the remedy.
5. Evaluate the effectiveness of the remedy.

These problems can be classified as follows:

1. *Work problems:* such as, errors in performance, insufficent volume of work, poor quality, improper methods, breakage and spoilage.
2. *Procedural problems:* such as, violation of rules and regulations, failure to maintain environment and equipment in proper condition, abuse of privileges, and others.
3. *Behavioral problems:* such as, insubordination, improper assumption of authority, disloyalty, creating disturbances, ridicule or criticism of the organization, and miscellaneous personal problems (for example, domestic or money problems).

Some of the major reasons for these supervisory problems are:

1. Inadequate skill to perform the job.
2. Inadequate instructions or misinformation.
3. Lack of conviction that the procedures for doing the job are the best (which could be due to supervisory failure to give the reasons why the job should be done a certain way).
4. Standard procedures too awkward or difficult, or time-consuming.
5. Personal characteristics of the worker not suited to the job.
6. Environment inadequate (improper ventilation, lighting, and so on).

The supervisory problems cited above, and the reasons for their existence, are as applicable to the accident problem as to other kinds of supervisory functions. Any kind of supervisory problem may ultimately end in an accident, if something is not done to correct it. Work errors, poor quality of work, violations of rules, insubordination, improper environmental conditions—all of these problems can result in accidents. By being sensitive to such problems, the good supervisor can detect them as soon as they arise, determine the cause, and correct the situation before an accident happens.

Summary

This section has pointed out the relationship of accident prevention to the overall supervisory and management functions. Accident prevention is no more or less than good, effective supervision. The personal qualities and knowledge required for effective safety supervision are those needed for effective supervision of any kind. In addition, adequate safety supervision requries a knowledge of the accident problem, causes of accidents, and methods of investigating and correcting accident situations, and of motivating personnel to perform safely. These specific aspects of accident prevention are discussed in the remainder of the chapter. This information forms the nucleus of knowledge needed for a good supervisor to also become a good safety supervisor.

Accident Prevention Fundamentals and Safety Motivation

INTRODUCTION

It's true, accidents are preventable, but many persons, either through ignorance or misunderstanding, believe accidents are the inevitable results of unchangeable circumstances or fate. This belief is not only false, but illogical; it fails to consider the essential law of cause and effect—the basic ingredients of all accidents. Accidents do not happen without cause; and the identification, isolation, and control of these causes are the basic principles of all accident prevention techniques. Even natural elements can be controlled to some extent. It is only in the realm of nature involving such phenomena as lightning, storms, or floods that accidents are extremely difficult to prevent. Even the effects of these can be minimized (for example, securing property when strong winds are expected). These accidents due to nature, estimated at only two percent of all accidents, are arbitrarily classifed as acts of God. An analysis of these so-called acts of God more often than not would reveal that at some point in the sequence of events an act occurred, or an act that should have occurred was omitted, which then made the accident preventable.

DEFINING "ACCIDENT"

In dealing with any problem, a first step is to define it—which events or occurrences properly belong in the problem category, and which do not? In its simplest form an accident is an interruption to an intended course of action resulting in injury to a person or damage to equipment or property.

ACCIDENT CAUSATION

The most important single concept in accident prevention is that most accidents do not occur by chance; they are caused by unsafe acts and conditions, or a combination thereof. Another important concept is that accidents are complex—an accident usually has a combination of causes, rather than a single cause.

The chain of events leading to an accident can be visually presented through use of a domino sequence, as illustrated in Figure 14–1. If one domino in the row is pushed, the rest will fall in succession. But, if the key domino, unsafe act or condition, is removed, the accident domino will not fall. In fact, if any one domino preceding the accident domino is removed, the accident will not occur. This illustrates the fact that if a person had not been fatigued, he might not have committed an unsafe act or he might have been more alert and become aware of an unsafe condition, which he could then have corrected. Why was the person performing this task while he was fatigued? These unknown causes (the domino with the

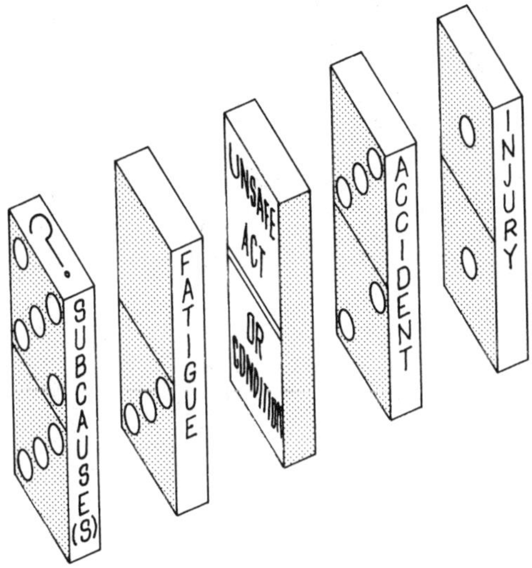

FIGURE 14–1. Accident Chain of Events.

question mark) are the crucial factors. Was the person ignorant of the fact that fatigue could make him more susceptible to having an accident (lack of education and training)? Did he just not care (poor attitude toward safety)? Or was he ordered to do the job anyway (poor supervision)? The domino sequence points out that most accidents have multiple causes. Accidents must be thoroughly investigated to unearth these causes, and this is ordinarily a difficult ask.

In classifying accidents, we have to consider three elements: the individual, the agent (the object, substance, or person immediately causing the injury or property damage), and the environment. Any of these elements, or a combination of them, can be primarily responsible for causing the accident. These are considered separately later in this chapter.

SOURCE RELATIONSHIPS

The source of an accident is the activity out of which the accident arises. Such terms as handling materials, lifting, pushing, and so on, are commonly applied to accident causes, but they actually refer to activities rather than causes. Handling materials is an activity out of which accidents come, but the cause of each accident is a hazardous condition or something that some person does or fails to do in connection with the activity in question. An injury is the result of an accident that was caused by an unsafe act or an unsafe condition. A burn is an injury (result) caused by excessive exposure (unsafe act or condition) to a source of heat. The relative importance of the injury source may vary considerably between operations within the same activity. A warehousing operation using hand methods will show more handling injuries than one using mechanical handling equipment.

DETERMINING ACCIDENT CAUSES

Of all major accident factors, three are of utmost importance in determining the cause of an accident. In most cases, all are involved. They are: unsafe mechanical or physical conditions, unsafe acts, and unsafe personal factors. Several detailed factors often are present in an accidential injury. They occur in a given sequence to produce the final result. Preceding the injury there is an occurrence; for example, an object or a person falls or makes contact with a machine. Preceding the occurrence that produces the injury, there is, in every case, either the unsafe act of a person removing or disconnecting a safety device, for example, or an unsafe physical or mechanical condition (poorly constructed structure, restricted visibility, nonavailability of protective clothing and equipment, and so on) or both. Even before these factors there are possibly other reasons for the unsafe acts or the hazardous conditions, such as poor supervision, which in itself is an unsafe personal factor. The basic idea of prevention is to discover the causative factors and remove them or, if they cannot be removed, control them, thus breaking the sequence and preventing the injury.

CONTROLS

In organizations where spheres of responsibility are clearly assigned, activities are well coordinated, supervision is good, and policies are well defined, corrective measures usually are applied as a part of normal day-to-day operating procedures. But if operations are not so well organized, securing adequate corrective action may prove to be the most difficult part of the supervisor's duty. Corrective action must be prompt and thorough: otherwise vital points will be lost. Only responsible persons should be permitted to apply corrective action and then only with the aid of factual information and data supplied through the echelons of supervision. Principles and methods of corrective action include the following:

1. *Engineering.* Environmental causes of accidents or unsafe conditions can be eliminated through the application of engineering principles. When an operation is mechanically and physically safe, it is unnecessary to be as concerned about the uncertain behavior (unsafe acts) of people. Machines are less apt to fail than are men. To prevent unsafe conditions, equipment and facilities must be designed, constructed, and maintained according to the best principles of safe engineering practices. It may be necessary to make mechanical revisions or modifications to eliminate existing unsafe conditions, or special devices may have to be developed to correct specific unsafe conditions, and in some cases, to prevent unsafe acts. In general, safety engineering involves controlling the working environment to the extent that only a minimum of physical hazards remain. Designs of machine guards, automobile brakes, traffic controls, pressure relief valves, and handrails are varied examples of safety engineering at work.
2. *Education and training.* Just as safety engineering is the most effective way of preventing environmental accident causes (unsafe conditions), safety education is the most effective tool in the prevention of human causes (unsafe acts). Through adequate instruction, personnel gain useful knowledge and develop safe attitudes. Safety consciousness developed in personnel through education will be supplemented and broadened by specific additional instruction in safe working habits, practices, and skills. Training is a particularly important accident prevention control; it gives each man a personal safety tool by developing in him habits of safe practice and operation.
3. *Enforcement.* Usually accidents can be prevented through adequate safety engineering and education. However, there are some people who are a hazard to themselves and others because of their failure to comply with accepted safety standards. For these persons,

strict enforcement of safety practices, backed by prompt corrective action, is necessary. No organized accident prevention effort can be successful without effective enforcement, because accidents are frequently the direct result of violations of safety principles. This is particularly true of vehicle accidents, many of which are caused by unsafe acts constituting traffic law violations. Managers, safety engineers, and supervisors are responsible for enforcing safety standards and regulations. They must issue accident prevention directives that will serve as guides for their personnel. When these directives are not issued and enforced, responsible personnel are tacitly condoning conduct that leads to preventable accidents. Many supervisors are reluctant to impose punishment on personnel involved in accidents. The punishment is not for having the accident; but when warranted, it is normally a violation of an order or procedure that was effected to prevent just such an accident. It is unlikely that the act resulting in the accident was the first violation of the preventative measure.

4. *Management and supervisory support.* Engineering, education and training, and enforcement controls cannot be completely effective without active management support of the entire safety program. Accident prevention is a function of management. Although the department manager has overall responsibility, he will depend largely on his first-line supervisors to uncover unsafe acts and conditions.
5. *Application.* To be completely effective, accident prevention controls cannot be applied randomly. All engineering, education and training, supervision, and enforcement measures must be based on factual evidence and directed toward the solution of specific problems. Only in this way can controls be adequately applied. All facts relating to unsafe acts, conditions, and accidents will be collected and studied to determine which controls will prove most valuable and how they can be applied best.

ROLE OF THE SUPERVISOR

Detailing the fundamentals of accident prevention would not be complete without indicating they are nothing but inanimate techniques and methods, if there are no personnel to make them work.

No one is in a better position to act as a catalyst for effective accident prevention than the first-line supervisor. He is the middle man who interprets management policy to personnel and sees to it that they implement such policy. He is the man responsible for seeing to it that the tasks assigned to him are carried out effectively and efficiently—from training new personnel to getting the ultimate task accomplished.

No one is in a better position to set a good safety example, and to see to it that all aspects of the safety program are carried out—education, engineering, and enforcement. By his personal actions, he can motivate his men to perform safely in all their activites, both on-and-off duty. The safety with which his men perform is an indication of the effectiveness with which they perform. For virtually every kind of accident cause, supervisory personnel are said to have responsibility for corrective action.

SAFETY MOTIVATION

General

It was noted at the outset that one method of accident prevention is to make the environment safe, that is, to introduce factors that make such an environment the desired one for the individual. Such factors could be defined by the word *motivation*. Motivation is a recognized factor in human relationships in industry and the governments.

Supremely important in accident prevention is the desire of individuals not to have accidents and to operate in a safe manner. Personal motivation is probably the most important single area that safety personnel must develop in management, supervisors, and individuals. Some practices of management, as will be demonstrated later, seem to operate to motivate personnel against safety.

The critical need in accident prevention is to get people to perform safely. How can we design safety into human beings? People will do things they are motivated to do. People must be motivated to use the safety knowledge they have acquired. This motivation must be applied constantly. In industry, the supervisor is in the best position to motivate and, therefore, he must know how it works and how to apply it.

What Is Motivation?

For most of our waking hours we are bombarded with suggestions, exhortations, and appeals to buy things; in fact, the modern methods of "brain-washing" are continued during the sleeping hours as well. The manufacturer who has the best promotional methods is often the one with the highest sales. These sales campaigns are designed to motivate us to buy these products; they appeal to basic human desires and needs.

Motivation is the art of getting people to want to do things your way. It should not be thought of as the elimination of freedom to think for oneself and to make decisions and choices; rather it is a guide for use in thinking for ourselves. All motivation stems from the desire for a satisfying life. In safety we try to motivate for the good of those whom we are trying to motivate. To do this, we must arouse and maintain voluntary action for safety among the personnel we wish to motivate.

To be successful and lasting, motivation should be of the positive variety, without negative control and without the use of fear and anxiety-producing techniques. Proper motivation does not seek to produce negative feelings through the depression of physical, mental, and emotional reactions. A motive is an emotional condition which arouses activity in an individual toward an objective. Motivation is supplying the incentives that will direct the individual toward an objective. It is clear from these statements that we must know what motive we want to appeal to before we can motivate.

The Individual Vs. Safety

Psychologists are in agreement that human beings as a group tend to require excitement (curiosity), and consciously and unconsciously seek it. Mankind emerged from the cave through competition, by the elimination of the weak and the survival of the bold and strong. Almost daily hand-to-hand combat served as an emotional outlet for primitive man. Even in medieval times stronger societies almost invariably moved against weaker societies as soon as crops were in. Combats, either individual or in organized armies, was an accepted way of life and this condition was true up to and including our own Civil War period.

Motivation in this direction was strong throughout an extended period encompassing thousands of years. At first survial was the motivating factor; later, to the victor went the spoils; and more recently, the social order and government reward the physically and mentally weak.

Therefore it is not unreasonable to assume that aggressiveness and combativeness have been bred into humans through thousands of years of practice in that direction. However, after the Civil War and after the Industrial Revolution a new facet of organized man began to emerge.

This emergence is sometimes called the social revolution. In any event, personal combat between individuals became more and more unacceptable socially; and while organized war did not show a decline, the technological development of warfare became such that only a fraction of the individuals caught up in war ever experience direct hand-to-hand combat. In effect, the instilled desire of man to live dangerously was suppressed more and more, and as a result this characteristic has emerged in more indirect manifestations. Today these characteristics may be manifested in hot rod driving, skiing, sky diving, and other hazardous sports. In unrestrained cases, such a manifestation may be indicated in the sharp upsurge of apparently unmotivated crime. This critical characteristic may show up in the safety area as insubordination of workers to safety regulations and show-off performance in hazardous occupations.

Management Acts to Motivate

The administrative principles of management in regard to human motivation are known only by results achieved and are without scientific proof. The current knowledge of social psychology is too narrow to lay down ironclad rules in this area.

Individuals take specific actions when the resulting satisfaction in the action outweighs any discomfort or sacrifice involved in such action. The simple issue of orders and directives does not assure their compliance. Every individual has a limit of acceptance, and instructions or orders beyond those limits will not be accepted or carried out. The limit and degree of acceptance can only be raised through motivation. The following fundamental rules have been observed to shape human behavior and are, therefore, keys to individual motivation.

1. Individual reaction is, in part, determined by individual needs. All persons have specific needs, both physical and emotional; most individuals have a great many needs.
2. Personal behavior and response is, in part, determined by personal beliefs. These beliefs may be right or wrong; but nevertheless they will be the filter through which instruction or orders are received.
3. Reaction and beliefs are both directly influenced by the social organization, either formal or informal, to which the individual belongs. Individual aspirations (needs) are created partly by social custom and attitude of the particular social structure with which the individual identifies himself.

These three fundamental behavioral rules give a basis for a management program to motivate workers. These factors are true in any relationship but are vital to an accident prevention program. Each level of management, from the firm's president down to the lowest echelon of supervisor, must be devoted to creating an environmental situation in which the actions of individuals will provide individual satisfaction to himself and at the same time provide adequate and appropriate safe operation of the mission. This achievement will require the application of incentives, within the acceptable framework above, to an individual operation so that the individual operator will comply with instructions and orders in an effective and safe manner. The following is a list of primary motivations or incentives:

1. Financial gain.
2. Personal security (physical and economic).
3. Social status and social respect.
4. Personal development opportunity.

5. Personal power and influence.
6. Personal participation in job planning.
7. Performing a worthwhile job activity.
8. Treatment, by management, as an individual.
9. Attractive environmental conditions at work.
10. Just and adequate job supervision.
11. Socially acceptable (to the individual) work.

All of these factors must be considered in individual motivation by management at all levels of supervision. In actual practice, each specific job function and each individual will be a different problem; therefore, the following discussion will be in the area of principles rather than in providing answers to specific problems.

Education Vs. Motivation

Most safety and accident prevention effort associated with human behavior has been concentrated in the field of education and training. This approach is a normal one since we have learned that human behavior plays the most important role in accident causation and we know that normally people will engage in unsafe acts. For this reason, most accident prevention programs have been centered on the employee or operator on the assumption that influencing his attitude and behavior will result in his continued safety awareness and safe behavior. To an extent this is true; however, all of the awareness in the world is of little constructive use if motivation is lacking.

Learning proper procedures will reduce error, but only motivation will provide consistent adherence to safe procedures. Such motivation must be planned throughout the operation from the top down.

Discipline and Motivation

Discipline, when effectively employed, can sometimes be used to motivate personnel to perform safely. Discipline is essential to the efficient accomplishment of any mission, as long as it is "positive" rather than negative discipline. Discipline that is based solely on the interests of the person doing the discipline is negative.

Negative discipline instills fear and anxiety in the persons exposed to it. From this develops a resentment of authority and what it stands for, and the ultimate result is shirking of duty whenever this can be done without getting caught; accidents can be a result of this.

Positive discipline can be used to reduce accidents. When personnel are shown that the disciplinary (restrictive) measures are in their best interests, they are inclined to go along with these measures. When personnel know these measures are in their interests, fear and anxiety are lessened and the efficiency of performance is increased.

Attitudes and Motivation

Attitude may be simply defined as a readiness to respond in a given manner. Our attitudes are formed by our experiences and they can be changed by new experiences. All of us have ideas about what is expected of us; these ideas help form our attitudes, and our attitudes help determine how we will act. Each individual is really several different persons:

1. The man he thinks he is.
2. The man his supervisor thinks he is.
3. The man his friends (and family) think he is.

When a man's ideas about himself differ from those of his supervisor and friends, there is bound to be conflict. This conflict results in tension and strain, which can easily lead to accidents. It is up to the supervisor to determine the attitudes of his men toward themselves and toward him, to search out the attitudes held by his men that are unrealistic, and to find incentives that will appeal to the individuals under his command so that inappropriate attitudes can be changed in a positive fashion. Thus, the search for information about men's attitudes is really a search for the proper incentives that will motivate men to perform safely. This is essential to good supervision.

THE SUPERVISOR'S ROLE

Effective safety supervision is no more or less than effective general supervision. Just as the good supervisor makes efforts to know and understand his men and to make their work situation a satisfying one, so also does he attempt to make the work situation a safe one. The supervisor should be constantly alert for indications that safety motivation among his personnel is sustained at an appropriate level. Several conditions should be checked periodically. If the following conditions do not exist, the supervisor knows there is room for improvement in safety motivation:

1. There is an increase in desired learning (increased safety in performance, as indicated by a reduction in accidents.)
2. Individual and group efforts toward safety are persistent.
3. Individuals and the group express interest and satisfaction in trying to meet the goal of improved safety in performance.

Summary

In this section we have discussed the role of motivation in promoting safe performance, the functions of motives, incentives, attitude, and discipline in providing motivation for personnel to perform safely, and the role of the supervisor in providing and maintaining safe motivation at a high level among his personnel. Engineering and enforcement alone cannot bring about increased accident reduction. Over the long haul, education for safety will bring about substantial improvements in safe performance, if the knowledge acquired through safety education and training is supplemented by increased safety motivation to apply to knowledge.

Virtually all of the accidents occurring in industry today are caused by unsafe conditions or unsafe acts, and are preventable. When accidents that do occur are promptly and thoroughly investigated and reported, causative factors will be identified and placed in their proper relationships to each other. In organizations where safety responsibilities are clearly defined and assigned, and where all activities are properly conducted under good supervision, these accident causes can be eliminated or controlled through appropriate education, engineering, enforcement, and supervision.

Safety Councils and Safety Meetings

INTRODUCTION

In safety and accident prevention, a management group approach is as valid as it is in any other management planning or problem area.

Membership, at a minimum, should consist of the plant manager, the plant engineer, medical department representative, safety engineer, personnel director, and other senior staff heads.

Generally, such councils are established at the division level; however, the concept is adaptable to units down to and including plant size.[8] Usually, however, smaller units find the safety meeting concept more appropriate. If a safety council is formed on a unit level, the first-line supervisor plays a key role in its establishment and the maintenance of effectiveness. He is the man in the middle who must interpret management policy to the employees and also see to it that the employees carry out the policy. An effective method of achieving unit safety objectives can be through the use of safety councils.

THE SAFETY COUNCIL: GROUP PARTICIPATION

No one man can be expected to possess the diversified knowledge required to know all safety measures for all jobs, operations, and activities within an organization. This would be equal to requiring one man to know all details of every job in the plant. However, supervisors are, or should be, familiar with all jobs, operations, and personnel under their control. A properly organized safety council will consist of staff management or supervisors from the various operations and activities within the organization and thus will have the required diversified knowledge at its beck and call.

SAFETY COUNCIL FUNCTIONS

The safety council members share their knowledge to assist in conducting the safety program through review of safety problems, development of means to combat these problems, and conversion of these ideas into action for more effective accident prevention. The council can also assist in devising safety policy that can be activated by the plant manager. Safety council members are appointed by the plant manager. The size of the safety council depends on the size of the organization in terms of the number of personnel and the number and variety of jobs, operations, and activities in the unit. The scope of the safety council functions extends to all activities that involve safety of personnel. A priority listing of safety problems for the council to act upon can be developed through analysis of the accident records. The most critical problems should be dealt with first.

FREQUENCY OF SAFETY COUNCIL MEETINGS

The safety council should have regularly scheduled meetings. If meetings are called on a haphazard basis, members may feel that it is not really important. There should be at least one meeting of the safety council every three months and more often if practical. In addition to regularly scheduled meetings, special meetings should be called when critical and urgent safety problems arise. In this regard, the supervisor is in the best position to know when a critical safety problem exists. It is his responsibility to notify the safety manager and suggest that a special meeting of the safety council be called.

For example, the occurrence of an electrical fire might indicate the need to immediately call a meeting of the council to discuss the development of a safety campaign dealing with electrical hazards. The more vivid and recent a memory or recollection is, the more learning will take place by discussing it.

PREPARING FOR THE SAFETY COUNCIL MEETING

A detailed agenda for each council meeting should be prepared well in advance of the date set for the meeting. Sufficient information should be included in the agenda to

[8]See U.S. Department of Labor, *Organizing a Safety Committee*, Safety Management Series, OSHA 2231 (Washington, June 1975).

indicate the various safety problems to be discussed, the extent and nature of the probems, the need for doing something about the problem, and suggested approaches to solving the problem. These facts are the foundation for discussion at the meeting.

Supervisors can assist the safety manager in developing agenda for council meetings by noting accident problems as they arise, and by submitting a listing of such problems to the safety officer. In addition to helping him accomplish his job, this kind of procedure helps the supervisor become more aware of hazards and also helps him in his search for methods of identifying and correcting potential hazardous and error-producing conditions. In some instances, accidents have been the result of the supervisor's lack of familiarity with the immediate operations and hazards of the job, or they can be traced to the lack of a proper attitude on the part of the supervisor in taking preventive action against hazards and unsafe human performance. Taking an active part in preparing items for the safety council agenda will develop in the supervisor a more positive attitude toward accident prevention and will teach him to be more alert toward hazards and unsafe behavior of his personnel. Suggestions concerning safety problems to be discussed at safety council meetings should contain detailed comments: for example, the type of accident or hazard involved in the problem, the specific job(s) and activities in which the accident or hazard arises, the possible causes, and recommendations regarding corrective action.

RESULTS OF SAFETY COUNCIL MEETINGS

If a safety council is to be successful, the conclusions drawn from the meeting must be put into effect. To ensure this, the pertinent points coming out of the council meeting must be recorded. The safety manager may act as secretary for the safety council, or this important responsibility for accurately recording the minutes of the meeting may also be rotated periodically so that all supervisory members of the safety council have an opportunity to be recorder. Such experience can enable supervisors to do a better job of conducting safety meetings with their own personnel.

Since the ideas growing out of the safety council meetings will be used to improve the current safety program, these ideas must be well documented. The results of implementing the council's ideas should also be documented by the council recorder. For example, if the safety council's suggestion to conduct a safety promotional campaign is carried out, the results of the campaign should be documented and presented to the safety council members at the next meeting of the council for further discussion. Such information is necessary to determine how successful the campaign has been, to what degree it achieved its objectives, if it should be terminated or continued, and what changes should be made if it is to be continued.

In recording the minutes of a safety council meeting, a detailed agenda is a great help in contributing to completeness and accuracy. Knowing what to expect, the recorder knows what to listen for and which comments should be recorded. In some instances, a topic of discussion may be argumentative and cannot be resolved, and the chairman of the council may have to have the recorder read back the minutes in order to get the highlights of the discussion; in this case, accurate minutes are essential. Questions that are not resolved during the meeting should be carefully noted in the minutes, so that they can be taken up again at the next meeting. If specific accidents are discussed during the meeting, sufficient information should be recorded to identify the accident, how it happened, how it was caused, and what action was taken to prevent a recurrence. The names of council members who are assigned specific duties should be recorded, in order to avoid confusion at a later date.

Copies of the minutes of the council meeting should be sent to all council members, the plant manager and staff personnel, and all supervisors. This should be done as soon after the council meeting as the minutes can be prepared and reproduced. One method of expediting distribution of the minutes is to use a standard blank form for keeping the minutes. A typical standard form appears in Figure 14–2. The standard form also increases the accuracy of the recorder, after he gains familiarity with the form through using it several times. Another method is to combine the minutes of the last council meeting with the agenda of the next meeting, and send both items to appropriate personnel midway between meetings. This method has two advantages: (1) only one distribution is required; and (2) the reader gets a better picture of the relationship between what was accomplished at the last council meeting and what problems will be discussed at the next meeting.

THE SAFETY MEETING

The safety meeting is essentially an extension of the safety council. The safety council is made up of selected representatives of the various activities within an organization; however, the safety meeting is attended by all personnel within a given activity who are under the jurisdiction of a supervisor. In some instances, an activity might be so large, and involve so many personnel, that it is feasible to hold several safety meetings for various groupings of personnel. If this is done, the men should be grouped by similarity of their jobs, so that the things discussed in a given safety meeting will have maximum applicability to all personnel participating in the meeting. Participation of all members of the group should be stressed. Meetings should be held on a regularly scheduled basis, and special meetings should be called when needed. All areas of accident prevention should be dealt with in the safety meetings, including the off-duty accident problem. The supervisor should prepare well in advance for each safety meeting and should evaluate the results of the meetings. Other aspects involved in conducting safety meetings are discussed in the remainder of this section.

SOURCES OF SAFETY INFORMATION FOR THE SUPERVISOR

General

There are many sources of information available to the supervisor, both of a general supervisory nature and specifically related to safety supervision. Some of the specific materials related to safety, which are of great value to the supervisor, are indicated below. In addition, local sources are noted in Table 14–1.

Case Studies of Accidents

The National Safety Council has produced a series of case studies of accidents that include: (1) descriptions of the accidents; (2) background information for each accident; (3) possible solutions; and (4) a summary for each accident. These can be used by supervisors in safety meetings to stimulate interest in accident investigations and to develop skill among his men in analyzing accident information and deriving recommendations for corrective actions. These case studies can be obtained through:

Name of organization____

Minutes of the __________ safety council meeting held on ____________________

1. Meeting called to order by chairman______________________________
2. Those present were:

3. Minutes of previous meeting were approved as read (amended).

4. The following accidents were discussed and corrective action taken:

Description of accident	Cause	Recommended action

a.

b.

c.

etc.

5. Action taken on the following suggestions:

a.

b.

c.

etc.

6. Measures taken were as follows:

a.

b.

c.

etc.

7. Following items were discussed:

a.

b.

c.

etc.

8. Next safety council meeting to be held at __________ on __________.
9. No further business, meeting adjourned at __________ m.

____

(Secretary's signature)

Note: The outline given above is suggestive only. It should be changed to meet the specific and peculiar needs of a given safety council, as the need arises.

FIGURE 14–2. Outline of Form for Recording Minutes of Safety Council Meetings.

TABLE 14.1
Sources and Kinds of Specific Safety Information

Source	*Kinds of Information*
Safety director	Safety posters and films. Safety codes, standards, and regulations. Advice on safety demonstrations, exhibits, or exercises. Guidance on accident investigating and reporting. Guidance on operating overall unit safety program.
Medical officer	Treatment of injuries (accident record). Sanitation, hygiene, first aid. Admissions records assist in reporting lost time (accident reporting). Preventive medicine and environmental health. Physical qualification of personnel.
Personnel officer	Assignment and transfer of men (selection of suitable jobs for men). Knowledge of physical disabilities involved in job selection. Enforcement and discipline. Supervision of plant guards. Posting of traffic signs, signals, and markings.
Plant engineer	Repair and maintenance of buildings. Supervision of fire prevention activities.

National Safety Council
425 N. Michigan Ave.
Chicago, Illinois 60611

Talk Topics

These are a series of booklets published by the National Safety Council that contain supervisors' guides for safety discussions. Each talk topic contains: (1) information about types of accidents; (2) questions and discussion notes; and (3) demonstration hints. These talk topics can be used by supervisors to emphasize particular types of accidents (those having the highest frequency) and to arouse discussion about possible corrective actions to reduce these accidents.

Business and Industry

Many companies have devised their own supervisors' safety program, and many of them are excellent. These can be obtained by request from the individual company. The interested supervisor should write to the type of business or industry that is similar to his operation (light or heavy industry, electronics, and so on).

Summary

This section has considered the functions of the safety council and safety meetings in the safety program, and the role of the supervisor in these functions. The process of participation by all personnel was emphasized as the foundation for effective safety councils and safety meetings. The need for preplanning for such meetings was indicated, including establishment of an agenda, scheduling meetings, frequency of meetings, recording minutes of meetings, and evaluting the results of recommendations derived from such meetings.

Unit safety councils and safety meetings can be effective in creating and maintaining motivation for safety among unit personnel, if they are conducted properly. Such meetings can serve as a basic tool for the supervisor in his constant fight to reduce accidents. If properly planned and conducted, the safety meeting can be used to good advantage in reviewing accidents, developing and implementing recommendations for corrective actions, determining the effectiveness of corrective measures, and evaluating and improving the overall unit safety program, as well as the specific operations for which the individual supervisor is responsible.

Accident Investigation and Reporting

INTRODUCTION

Accident investigation is important and necessary if future accidents of similar nature are to be prevented. Accident investigation determines accident causes by seeking out the elements and sources from which the accident developed. Corrective measures may then be determined by analyzing the causes, making recommendations for their elimination, and instituting corrective measures. Accident investigation also assists in the development of educational materials by producing information that will guide personnel into developing a safety awareness and knowledge of safe conditions and safe work methods.

Theoretically, every minor accident and near-accident should be investigated thoroughly because each—if circumstances had been slightly different—might have yielded a serious injury. The number of minor injury cases and hazardous occurrences is so great, however, that thorough investigation of all of them would be too time-consuming and expensive. Therefore, the practical procedure is:

1. Immediate and full investigation of all lost-time cases and of such minor injuries as appear to involve serious hazards.
2. Investigations, as thorough as circumstances and conditions justify, of minor-injury cases and near-injury occurrences.
3. Continuing analysis of operations and activities to discover and correct hazardous practices and conditions.

PUNITIVE ASPECTS OF ACCIDENT INVESTIGATION

An accident investigator is not attempting to arrive at a finding of guilty or not guilty. His duty is to discover and report all relevant facts, and he has no obligation to fix blame or recommend punishment. The investigator who loses sight of his main objective and thinks that his job is to fix blame rather than to discover what happened and make appropriate corrective recommendations is not as successful as the investigator who remains impartial and impersonal.

ANTICIPATING ACCIDENTS

Although the prevention of future accidents is one of the basic purposes of accident investigation, it is by no means limited to preventing the recurrence of the particular accident investigated. Rarely do the components of an accident reproduce themselves exactly. When an accident occurs, one of the most important duties of an accident investigator is to consider whether or not the accident could have been foreseen and prevented. Also, he must ascertain what action can be taken to increase the probability that future accidents quite different from that momentarily under consideration, and possibly even unprecedented, will be foreseen and thereby prevented from happening. In conducting an accident investigation, the investigator should be concerned with:

1. Determining the hazards involved.
2. Making recommendations for eliminating the hazards.
3. Determining the unsafe behavior involved.
4. Making recommendations for correcting the unsafe behavior.

PRINCIPLES OF ACCIDENT INVESTIGATION

Accident investigation, like crime detection and medical diagnosis, often entails a microscopic search for unknowns. Every factor, however remote or small, must be discovered, evaluated, and considered in order to determine what actually occurred and why it occurred. The work must be fair, painstaking, and thorough. Often it is a difficult assignment, but its accomplishment will make an important contribution to the success of the mission with a minimum loss of life and material. Successive accidents have occurred from the same cause without the primary cause having been discovered because investigators lacked the zeal, ability, or knowledge to get all the facts.

An outstanding example of such incomplete investigations is the series of motor truck accidents that were written off as having been caused by failure of the air-braking system. Subsequent and more detailed investigation revealed that all the drivers were newly licensed. Further, it disclosed that there was time to resort to the hydraulic brakes, but none of the drivers had utilized them. Thus, it was determined that the real cause of these accidents was in the drivers' training program; it did not include instruction concerning the braking system of this type of vehicle. The drivers did not know that when air pressure was lost they still had hydraulic brakes with which to control the vehicle. Had the investigator searched deeper and determined the real primary cause of that first accident, measures could have been directed to ensure adequate training for the drivers, and thereby the prevention of future accidents of this type.

Certain principles of accident investigation should be followed if maximum results are to be secured:

1. Common sense and clear thinking are prime requisites. An investigator must be able to collect his facts, weigh the value of each, and reach conclusions justified by the evidence.
2. Familiarity with the equipment, operation, or process should at least be sufficient to permit an understanding of the possible hazards in any given situation.
3. An understanding of the type of conditions or situations likely to yield accidents is also necessary.
4. Neither the investigator nor the investigators should be under the control of the individual involved, because few persons can be unbiased and objective about a situation or condition involving their own work. There should be an attitude of cooperation to discover the causative factors and correct them.
5. Each clue should be investigated fully. A conclusion that appears reasonable

will often be changed by exploring a factor of apparently little importance.

6. Since both a physical hazard and an unsafe act are present in the great majority of accidents, both should be investigated fully. Every effort should be made to find a means of eliminating the physical hazard. Similarly, appropriate means of correcting the unsafe practices should be sought.
7. An investigation is never satisfactorily completed unless definite recommendations are made for corrective action.
8. More than one person should investigate major accidents on the principle that two heads are better than one.
9. Promptness is essential. Conditions may change quickly and details are quickly forgotten. Prompt investigation assures personnel that their safety is important to the plant manager.
10. Every accident should be investigated in appropriate degree whether it is serious or not, since chance is often the sole difference between a trivial accident and a serious or even fatal injury.

THE INVESTIGATION

When an accident occurs, the first concern is for the injured person; but when his welfare has been provided for, the investigation should be next. The conditions involved in the operation in question and the circumstances of the accident are the deciding factors. Whatever interference with operations is necessary to adequately investigate accidents will ultimately prove justifiable, since accident-free operation is important to mission accomplishment. Upon notification that an accident has occurred, the investigator conducts his investigation in a manner to ensure maximum results. The type of accident and its results will dictate the extent to which the investigator must search for information; however, it is important that each of the following steps in an investigation be taken:

1. Go to the scene promptly. To obtain facts quickly and accurately, arrive at the scene of the accident as soon as possible. Take appropriate measures to safeguard the accident site and preserve and prevent removal of evidence.
2. Interview the injured. If conditions permit, interview injured persons as soon as possible. Note physical or mental characteristics that may have contributed to the accident. Record extent of injuries noted or reported by medical personnel.
3. Interview witnesses. Get statements from all witnesses. Allow each witness to relate what happened in his own way. Do not discuss the blame—just get the facts. Witnesses should be interviewed separately in order that the statement of one will not be colored by overhearing that of another.
4. Obtain physical evidence. Note unsafe mechanical defects. Measure distances or dimensions related to the accident. Photograph the scene and other important evidence related to the accident.
5. List other evidence. Record other evidence of value. Include, as appropriate, weather conditions, locations of traffic signals and signs, adequacy of lighting, machine conditions, work surfaces, housekeeping, operating instructions, safeguards, and hazards.
6. Record data accurately. To simplify further study and analysis, tabulate information accurately for transfer to standard accident report and summary forms.
7. Initiate corrective action. Recommend hazard elimination, change(s) in standing operating procedures (SOP), or training revision(s) to appropriate authority.

CAUSE FACTORS

As previously discussed, one of the primary reasons for accident investigation is to determine the cause factors involved in the accident. The cause of an accident is a combination of simultaneous and sequential circumstances without any one of which the accident could not have happened. Any circumstance that contributes to an accident may be spoken of properly as a cause, or one of the causes of an accident. This makes it only one circumstance of a combination. For practical purposes, a cause of an accident is any behavior, condition, act, or negligence without which the accident would not have happened. Hence, in seeking causes of an accident, look for several factors working together or teaming up to produce the accident.

MULTIPLE-CAUSE CONCEPT

Since we are concerned with all unsafe conditions and practices involved in each accident, we cannot properly talk about *the* cause of an accident. Such thinking is called the single-cause concept. It is a result of generalizations about accident causes due to inadequate investigation and analysis of accidents. It attributes most accidents to some common cause, such as drinking, speeding, bad roads, and so on, or identifies the cause of a given accident only in terms of a specific violation or unfavorable condition. Such thinking is both unscientific and unprofessional, and it contributes very little to the understanding of how accidents can be prevented.

There are many important causes of accidents, and in any single accident there are usually a number of factors occurring in combination to produce the accident. This is called the multiple-cause concept. When we understand this concept, we will look for all of the factors which were involved. We may find that adverse circumstances, such as bad brakes, poor visibility, or slippery roads, may be present without necessarily contributing to a given accident.

It is not always easy to determine whether an obviously unfavorable circumstance actually contributed to an accident. While intoxication is an important factor in many accidents, there might be times when the driver's intoxication is not a cause of his accident. For example, a sober driver might drive his car into the rear of a car driven by a drunken driver who had quite properly stopped his vehicle at a traffic signal. The drunken driver would be arrested for intoxication, but the accident might have occurred even if he had been cold sober. His drunkenness did not necessarily cause the accident. The simple act of determining a rule violation does not necessarily determine the cause of an accident.

THREE TYPES OF CAUSES

In order to get away from the single-cause concept, we need specific guidance in defining and identifying accident causes. Such guidance will help us to improve the investigation of accidents, ensure better analyses, and set the stage for appropriate and realistic corrective action. For these purposes, causes and contributing factors can be classified into three easily recognizable levels known as direct causes, indirect causes, and contributing causes. Every accident has direct and indirect causes. Some accidents have many of each. These may be described briefly as follows.

Direct Causes

Direct causes are unconventional acts or neglects (doing something or failing to do something specified by law or dictated by safe practices) that contribute to the accidents. Unconventional, for this purpose, includes acts or neglects that are unusual, unexpected, improper, or hazardous. They may also be illegal, but all unconventional behavior is not necessarily illegal, nor is an illegal behavior necessarily a direct cause of an accident. Examples of direct causes are:

1. Operating at a speed that may be too fast or too slow for existing conditions.
2. Movement or position that creates a hazardous situation.
3. Inattention, which in turn prevents successful evasive action under the conditions existing.
4. Faulty evasive action taken to avoid or to mitigate an impending accident after the danger is perceived.

Indirect Causes

Indirect causes are irregular or unusual conditions that explain why the principal element (person or equipment) contributed a direct cause to the accident. Indirect causes are connected to the accident through the direct causes. Examples of indirect causes are:

1. Defective conditions, equipment, materials, or structures. These must have been present prior to the accident.
2. Unusual conditions such as weather, visibility, controls, slipperiness, rough terrain, and the like.
3. Conditions of personnel. These are by far the most common indirect causes that explain direct causes. Some of these are permanent conditions, such as poor eyesight, lack of certain kinds of knowledge, or psychological faults; and others may be temporary, such as intoxication, physical exhaustion, or emotional upset.

Contributing Causes

Every accident also has contributing causes, all of which are acts of negligence on the part of some person or organization that permit the indirect cause to exist. Some examples are inadequate traffic laws, inadequate standards, lack of policy, failure of supervisors to perform their duties, lack of enforcement, faulty design or maintenance, inadequate training, lack of safety training, and so on.

ACCIDENT REPORTING

Reporting

Proper reporting is extremely important. The effectiveness of a comprehensive investigation can be seriously reduced if the report is not accurately and properly completed. Facts that are discovered but not reported will have little effect in accident prevention. Incomplete reporting results in inadequate action and, consequently, inadequate prevention of future accidents. Collectively, accident reports provide information in support of operations planning and many other stages of action that may be obscure to the individual reporting a single accident.

Purpose

There are three main reasons for reporting accidents and incidents: first, to notify top management that a mishap of stated proportion and impact has occurred; second, to record essential information that will indicate trends, identify causes, and provide a basis for formulating future plans; and third, to permit an evaluation of the progress being made in the prevention of accidents. Without accurate and comprehensive reports of all accidents, appropriate remedial efforts cannot be developed and implemented.

The Accident Report

An accident is an unplanned event that does damage to persons or property. The accident report form varies from organization to organization, but it virtually always includes time and date, location, personnel involved, equipment or property damaged; and a narrative giving a word picture explaining the who, what, where, when, why and how of the accident, as well as such items as weather, equipment, unsafe mechanical or physical conditions, unsafe acts and unsafe personnel factors. Figure 14-3 gives an example of an abstract report of a fatal accident.

Summary

Accident investigation is an essential element of any safety program. Unless the causative factors are known and understood in their proper relationship to each other, the success of any action taken to prevent recurrence will be left to chance. All too many times the investigator accepts the first, and often the most apparent, causative factor that comes to his attention. Thus we have the single-cause rather than the more effective multiple-cause concept where all the factors involved are known and considered. The multiple-cause concept improves investigation techniques, insures better analyses, and sets the stage for appropriate and realisitc corrective action.

Job Analysis and Job Hazard Analysis

INTRODUCTION

The essential function of a safety program is the prevention of accidents. If supervisors are successful in this area, there will be no requirement for accident investigation and reporting. Some new tools have become available to safety program management personnel for accident prevention. These are systems analysis, job analysis, and high potential hazard analysis. The first two of these are byproducts of industrial management and the third is a safety management concept. System analysis is a tool that can only be fully utilized at the highest management levels; however, the other two analysis situations can be used at every management level.

SYSTEMS ANALYSIS

During the past fifteen years the aerospace industry has introduced a new science into the safety area. This science is called systems analysis and is a method whereby a new product, from conception, through design, and up to and including manufacture of the product, is examined for potential malfunction and hazard. This examination is made scientifically by trained engineers to determine design defects that will occasion failure or malfunction if the design is not corrected. Through this method, potential troubles and reliability are predicted and problems eliminated before any manufacture is ever done. Much of the evaluation and examination is done by computers; however, concepts of system analysis can be conducted without a

Reports control symbol

Place: Machine shop: Approximately 1430 hours. Causation: 440 volts, AC. Personnel category: Employee from electrical maintenance department.

Details of occurrence:

Just prior to the accident, an electrician was in the process of connecting a manual starter on the magnetic separator. He was seen to handle the wires and jump slightly. He dropped the wires to the concrete floor, walked to the rear of the machine, and swung his right foot forward in the direction of the disconnect switch. He was then seen to return to his first position and grasp the metal conduit and three wires. At this time arcing occurred. He fell backwards to the floor, clearing his body from contact with the wires.

Nature and number of injuries:

Fatal: One. The electrician contacted a 440-volt line and was electrocuted.

Causes:

1. Direct cause: employee contacting energized electrical line.
2. Indirect causes:
   a. Main service disconnect switch was partially blocked.
   b. Used foot instead of hand to throw switch into OFF position.
   c. Failure to use voltage tester to assure circuit was deenergized.

Remarks:

1. Employee had a total of 16 years' experience as an electrician.
2. An improvised work table had been positioned near the switch box by the machine operator, partly blocking the box.
3. Test of the disconnect switch revealed that the lever could be in the OFF position and the line still energized. The disconnect is a threefold breaker and must be pushed to its extreme travel in either direction to permit operation.
4. Artificial respiration was not immediately administered.

Recommendations:

1. Electrical circuits must be disconnected, properly grounded, and proved to be deenergized before work is performed.
2. Electrical circuits must be deenergized and properly tagged and/or blocked.
3. All electrical personnel should be reinstructed to check that all parts of electrical units are deenergized and comply with the requirements of National Electric Code, NBFU Pamphlet No. 70, and local installation safety regulations.
4. Artificial respiration should be started at once after any person has been subjected to electrical shock.

(Where possible, references to local safety regulations should be cited.)

FIGURE 14–3. Example of Abstract Report of Accident

computer. This reliability system, originally devised only for material design, now is used in a similar examination of plant layout, production methods, and management programs such as safety or accident prevention.

A system can be defined as an orderly arrangement of interrelated parts or components that act together, in a specific environment, to reach a desired goal or to perform a planned task. The system used to achieve the goal or task may be simple or complex, but in either case the components of the system are interrelated.

Systems, in complex cases, can be reduced to subsystems. The subsystems can then be evaluated separately, but at some point in the analysis all of the subsystems must be evaluated as a single system in which the breakdown of a component or part will affect the whole.

The components of a system can, and often do, include many different things. A system may include tools, materials, plans, instructions, environment, production line layout, and people. It may even include computer programs. Whatever the components are it must be kept in mind that they are interrelated and that the breakdown of any single one will affect the operation of all of the rest of the components.

SYSTEMS RELIABILITY VS. ACCIDENT PREVENTION

Systems analysis is an inspection to detect failure potential before such a potential is built into the system. This inspection automatically is an accident prevention function and is called, by some aerospace manufacturers, systems safety analysis. This concept has brought about rapid changes in safety management concepts and will bring about more.

The Department of Defense has already recognized this concept, and military specifications of aerospace and aircraft hardware require the application of this technique as a part of the contract. This will probably become true in manufacturing contracts for all kinds of hardware sometime in the near future.

Management should bear in mind that this technique applies to management programs, as well as to hardware manufacture, and profit from its use by applying it in an analysis of their accident prevention and production programs.

TYPES OF SYSTEMS ANALYZED

There are four systems of analysis with variations, and one or more systems may be used in a single analysis. The four systems are: (1) failure mode and effect, (2) fault tree, (3) technique for human error prediction (THERP), and (4) cost effectiveness.

Failure Mode and Effect is a method whereby consideration is given to the potential failure or malfunction of each component in the hardware or system. Potential failure is evaluated in the light of its effect on the remainder of the system and its ultimate performance after failure of any given component. The difficulty, of course, is in the ability of the analyst to identify every potential failure within a given system. After potential failures are identified and analyzed, necessary design changes are made. These design changes may include incorporation of completely new design, incorporation of a fail-safe system, incorporation of an alternate or standby system, or some other change to prevent the failure or to minimize its effect on the remainder of the systems or components.

The fault tree method assumes an undesired failure or breakdown occurring within the system and then attempts to determine what all possible results of such a failure would be. These assumed potential failures are diagrammed in the form of a tree extending to all possible independent events that could result. These are analyzed further to determine all probabilities that could affect the task or end result. These are then isolated or engineered out of the system, as described above. This method requires a computer approach in order to establish all probabilities and therefore is expensive. Some parts of this method can be used effectively in analyzing hazard potential in already existent systems.

THERP, technique for human error prediction, utilizes the method of quantitative evaluation of what contribution human error makes in the reduction of product quality or to an operational system breakdown. This method is combined with both of the systems already discussed since many potential failures are human operator induced.

The cost effectiveness method of systems analysis is very nearly described by its name. In this situation a cost comparison is made between the result of failure vs. the cost of preventing the failure or the cost of failure vs. the increased effectiveness of the system without failure. Cost effectiveness is the method most often used to select one of several systems which may be available to solve a problem.

In all of the cases cited, the principal point is the quantitative measurement of the effects of failures. It should be readily apparent that systems analysis is a potent tool in the accident prevention effort. The manager who is oriented to task performance and the interrelationships of all the components in his operational systems will automatically assess accident potential.

JOB ANALYSIS

An extension, or a part, of systems analysis is job analysis. We stated earlier that a system dealt with, in addition to things, people. Job analysis is the determination of essential factors in a specific kind of work and of worker qualifications necessary for its competent performance. It is a device widely used in industry and in government service, and the system involves an accurate and detailed description of each job in terms of duties performed and the necessary physical, mental, and emotional qualifications of the worker. The system also involves a description of the tools and machines used, of the materials handled or contacted, and a technical description of the overall operation. In combination, these elements develop an efficient and safe way of doing a specific job. Management need not undertake to master the job analysis technique as the production manager uses it. It should, however, be familiar with the procedures and be able to analyze jobs and operations sufficiently to discover the hazards involved. The most efficient way to do a job is the safest way to do it; therefore, job hazard analysis increases efficiency.

For most jobs, a comprehensive and accurate job description has been, or can be, prepared. Included in this description are the necessary physical, mental, or emotional qualifications of the individual; a description of the tools and equipment used, materials handled or contacted; and a technical description of overall operations. From the job description, a list of key steps can be compiled. Then, from this compilation, along with analysis of the operation, potential health and injury hazards can be identified. Every aspect of the job is studied: the tools and machines used, necessary movements of the worker, movement of materials, work flow, and other conditions that might have a bearing on optimum performance. The analysis specialist will also solicit information from those skilled persons who perform the tasks being surveyed, safety personnel, and others who can contribute specific information on the operation. Once potential hazards have been identified, safe practices, apparel, and equipment for

Job description ____________		Job location ____________	
Key job steps	Tools, equipment or material	Potential health or injury hazard	Safe practices, apparel, and equipment

Instructions for making job hazard analysis

1. Under "job description," list the name of the job being performed.

2. Under "job location," list the approximate physical location where the job will be performed.

3. In the column labeled "key job steps," list the steps in sequence of the job.

4. List the proper tools, equipment, or material in the column labeled "tools, equipment, or material." Be sure to list the proper item in line with each successive job step.

5. In the "potential health or injury hazard" column, list the accident or unsafe conditions which can result if the two previous steps are not followed properly (items 3 and 4).

6. In the last column, "safe practices, apparel, and equipment," list the safe practices, apparel, and equipment which are needed to prevent those accidents which may result if the preceding three steps are not followed (items 3, 4, and 5).

7. When this form is properly filled out, the reader should be able to read each key job step, and after it, the specific tool, piece of equipment, or material involved, the specific potential health or injury hazard that could result, and the specific safe practice, apparel, and equipment involved.

FIGURE 14–4. Sample Form for Job Hazard Analysis

minimizing the risks of these hazards will also be identified.

There should be a job hazard analysis for every existing job and one should be compiled for each new job. (See Figure 14–4.) To do the work for which it is designed, no job hazard analysis should ever be considered as final in form or all-inclusive in content, but should be subject to revision, checking, and updating to include additional hazards introduced or those missed in previous checks. Should an accident occur, a necessary question is: "What job hazard implications did the accident have?" Whenever a method is changed, regardless of how minor the change, the job hazard analysis must be subjected to a complete overall scrutiny to identify new hazards which may have been created. Hazards on similar jobs may vary to some degree for different individuals, owing to individual qualifications.

PURPOSES OF JOB HAZARD ANALYSIS IN ACCIDENT PREVENTION

The purposes of job analysis or job breakdown include:

1. Identification of physical hazards.
2. Elimination of hazards and guarding against hazardous motions, positions, or actions that cannot be eliminated.
3. Determination of the qualifications required for the safe performance of the work, such as physical fitness, motor skills, special abilities, and so on.
4. Determination of equipment and tools and appropriate maintenance standards needed for safety.
5. Establishment of training standards requisite for safety, including kinds and amounts of instructional content.

Although the job analysis program is concerned primarily with the work, rather than the worker, its uses relate directly to the personnel who perform the work outlined in the job description. It is a program of personnel administration that aims to identify the work with the worker and to have the work done in the one best way by the best qualified person available.

Job analysis will help standardize and simplify jobs and stabilize administrative work. It is an excellent control device, because once a job has been standardized it is easier to measure the output of personnel in similar positions. It makes it easier to select the right person for the job because the qualities needed are clearly defined. Proper job placement ensures that the work will be done properly. It is also a vital morale factor since satisfaction, which comes from doing the job efficiently, is important to the individual worker.

Job analysis aids in the establishment of job relationships and job groupings (homogeneous assignment). Similar or related work should be similarly classified and performed under similar conditions by similarly qualified personnel. Personnel should be located where their jobs can be performed most effiicently. Such analysis assists in the establishment and maintenance of training programs. It is sometimes necessary to assign a person to a job for which he is not fully qualified. Detailed information concerning the duties, tasks, and other requirements of a job, as shown in the job description, provide a basis for devising an on-the-job training program. Further job analysis will help fix responsibilities, establish controls, and identify the position in the chain of command. It assists in the determination of grades on the basis of skills and knowledge required, complexity of duties and responsibities, and other job characteristics.

IDENTIFYING HAZARDS THROUGH JOB ANALYSIS

A major fault with many programs, as we noted earlier, is an after-the-fact approach to accident prevention. In many instances, corrective measures are developed and implemented only after an accident, or a series of accidents, has pointed out a hazard. In the absence of a job hazard analysis, certain types of physical hazards are likely to be overlooked until an accident occurs. A job safety analysis consists of a minimum of the following steps:

1. Break the job down into its elementary steps.
2. List these steps in their proper order.
3. Examine each step critically for physical and mechanical hazards.

There are four basic components of each job that can be potentially hazardous and must be considered in the analysis:

1. *The job process*—the procedures involved in the job.
2. *The machine*—the equipment and machine tools employed in the job, of which there may be one or more.[9]
3. *The material*—the substances and articles, including the finished product but

[9]See U.S. Department of Labor, *Essentials of Machine Guarding*, Safe Work Practices Series, OSHA 2227 (Washington, July 1975).

other than machine tools, employed in the process.[10]

4. *The man*—a collective term that includes all persons who may be involved in the job, such as the operator, supervisor, safety personnel, and the injured person. The intent of job hazard analysis is to protect the man from accidents caused by faults in the other three components of the job. Consequently, the job analysis is concerned with potential hazards involving the job process, the machine, and the materials used. But job analysis is also concerned with likely hazardous acts of the men performing the job. This type of information can be used as a basis for instructional programs and job training.

JOB PLANNING

Work that is repetitive, such as periodic overhauls of specific equipment, can often be routinized almost as completely as quantity production work. Work that is done infrequently or varies each time that it is done cannot be treated in this manner. Safety in nonrepetitive work rests upon careful planning and layout, provision of adequate equipment, careful instruction of workmen, and close supervision. This type of work, when once properly planned and standardized, needs only periodic evaluations unless the work procedures are changed. However, in nonrepetitive work, where routinization of certain procedures and motions is impossible, stress should be placed on training workers in ways of performing specific operations.

In planning a layout of a job, the different operations involved are described and the requisite personnel skills needed to perform these operations are specified. Work such as oiling machinery, washing windows, cleaning, and painting is seldom carefully planned or adequately supervised, but it involves exposure to a wide variety of hazards. It is not necessary, and it may not always be desirable, to routinize such work in great degree. It is highly important from a safety standpoint to analyze these jobs thoroughly. Proper analysis will determine exactly what hazards are involved and will indicate correct control measures. With this information at hand, the instruction and training can be definitely set forth and provided for, together with maintenance of equipment and tools, and proper safety devices.

Planning Housekeeping Jobs

Good housekeeping is often a stepchild in the sense that it seldom receives as careful attention from management as production activities do. Actually, since the maintenance of a reasonably good standard of housekeeping necessitates the periodic cleaning of everything in the activity and the facility, the safety of men doing this type of work demands careful planning and analysis.

Analysis of this type of work should cover:

1. The completeness of safeguarding gears, shafting, belts, and other moving parts under machine frames and in out-of-the-way places. Injury records show clearly that such high-hazard devices as projecting setscrews, gears, and shaft ends are seldom adequately guarded.
2. Protection against falls, particularly in case of window cleaning and overhead cleaning.
3. Protection against the activities of others. This applies to cleanup work carried on in conjunction with modification of equipment or alterations. Usually, in such cases two or more crews (under separate foremen) are operating,

---

[10]For example see U.S. Department of Labor, *Essentials for Materials Handling*, Safe Work Practices Series, OSHA 2236 (Washington, October 1975).

and unless there is joint preplanning and close cooperation, unforeseen hazardous situations are likely to arise.

Planning Incidental Jobs

Occasional jobs should not be allowed to escape careful planning and analysis. They have the same factors of variety that make nonrepetitive jobs hazardous. No two jobs are exactly alike, so the range of hazards is wide. Occasional jobs should be carefully set down and considered. Adequate methods of safeguarding against possible hazards should be instituted, safe equipment provided, careful and thorough instruction given, and close supervision maintained.

PLACEMENT OF PERSONNEL

One of the principles of personnel management in industry is to place the right man on the right job through efficient classification and careful assignment. In the interest of safety, newly assigned personnel should be detailed to duties only after their technical, physical, and mental abilities have been determined and found to be appropriate to the job. This information is readily available from each person's qualification record.

Personnel Tests

There are personnel tests in use to assist in determining the mental and technical abilities of personnel.

Interviews

The chief purpose of the interview is to give or to receive information and to motivate. The type of information sought or given depends upon the specific purpose of the interview. It may be to evaluate an individual's qualifications, to help him solve his personal problems, or to let him know that he is an important part of his organization.

When a person reports to a new duty assignment or job, he brings with him certain abilities, and mental attitudes. They may be either latent or more or less fully developed. These abilities and attitudes will have definite influence upon the manner in which he performs the duty to which he is assigned, and the manner in which he responds to suggestions for improvement in his work methods.

Once the man has been assigned and detailed to a job, his performance, including practices affecting his own safety and that of others, becomes the responsibility of his supervisor. Seeing the man actually at work and in contact with others, the supervisor is in a good position to evaluate properly the individual's abilities and traits of character. He may gain knowledge of such outside factors as domestic relations, financial troubles, backgrounds, and environment that have a bearing on the individual's frame of mind; he learns by experience the best method of getting each person to respond to his orders and suggestions. The interview and personal observations of newly assigned personnel also furnish information on which to base job assignments and training requirements.

HIGH POTENTIAL HAZARD ANALYSIS

An accurate definition of an accident might well be: "Any unplanned event which interrupts a sequence of planned events." A study by W. H. Heinnich indicates that out of every 330 accidents which occur; 300 result in no injury, 29 result in minor injury, and 1 results in a disabling injury.[11] This could be interpreted to mean that each time an organization experiences three disabling injuries there have already been nearly one thousand warnings that these would occur. These warnings were accidents that resulted in only minor injuries and the nine hundred that may have not been (and were probably not) reported at all. Each of these occurrences may have revealed a high potential hazard which, had it been corrected after the first unreported and noninjury causing accident, would have probably prevented some of all or those that later caused injury or property damage.

An adequate system of reporting these occurrences or incidents can result in the establishment of an evaluation system to establish corrective action. Such a system of evaluation is referred to as a high potential hazard analysis system and is almost a must in any working situation established before systems analysis became available. It is also a valid follow-up for programs that were created through systems analysis. Unfortunately in the past, industrial establishments have been almost totally preoccupied with accidents that result in damage to people or property; and such accident analysis as does exist deals principally with accidents of this type. This is an after-the-fact approach and leaves something to be desired in accident prevention. A system is required in which the circumstances of accidents (often called incidents) that do not result in damage will be reported, and in which circumstances that will result in damage if not prevented can be forecast.

Summary

New methods to aid in accident prevention have been developed as byproducts of management and product analysis systems. These are systems, job, and high potential hazard analyses. Even though somewhat sophisticated in approach, systems analysis offers some methods of evaluation that can be used even at the lowest organizational echelons. Job analysis and hazard analysis are excellent tools and ones that can and must be used, not only at all echelons of supervision, but at the level of the lowest job in the job structure. The supervisor who adapts these systems and uses them to reinforce his accident prevention efforts will be rewarded by having very few accident reports to prepare.

[11]W. Herbert Heinnich, *Industrial Accident Prevention*, 4th ed. (New York: McGraw-Hill, 1959).

Safety Inspections and Fire Prevention

Safety inspections or accident prevention surveys can also be termed preventive maintenance, because their primary purpose is to uncover unsafe acts and unsafe conditions before accidents occur. Safety inspections are a necessary segment of a complete safety program. They are essential for maintaining acceptable standards of safety for physical facilities and working practices. Conditions are constantly changing, materials are moved, salvage and waste materials are accumulated, and many other changes occur daily or even by the hour. If machinery is involved, deterioration occurs as a result of use. In offices and similar places of employment, there are changes in layout, additions of equipment, and wear and tear of such items as floors, stairways, floor covering, and equipment. Whenever possible, minor hazards are corrected on the spot by informal recommendations or suggestions to the responsible supervisor. Unsafe acts and unsafe conditions that are found to be permanent, recurring, peculiar to a specific operation, or widespread throughout the unit or activity are recorded and corrective action is taken as soon as possible. Specifically, safety inspections or accident prevention surveys are designed to:

1. Detect specific unsafe conditions, unsafe practices, unsafe procedures, and out-of-date or nonexistent standing operating procedures (SOP) publications.
2. Highlight the need for safeguards for men and machines and to publish current safety SOP publications.
3. Help sell the safety program to personnel and hear their complaints and recommendations on safety matters.
4. Encourage individuals to inspect their own work areas and work practices and to make personal contributions to the safety effort through recommendations.
5. Allow safety personnel to come in closer contact with other unit personnel and to impress on these other personnel that the safety program is conducted for their personal benefit.

INSPECTION PERSONNEL

Inspection personnel must have knowledge of the hazards that might be involved. A lively appreciation of the responsibility involved is also vital. Good judgment is necessary. In the case of highly specialized and inherently hazardous equipment, such as pressure vessels or chemical hazards, technical knowledge and skill of a high order are necessary. Plant safety directors and technically qualified personnel, such as the plant engineer and industrial engineer, provide this type of service.

Safety inspections may also be made by safety personnel, supervisors, maintenance personnel, teams of qualified personnel from within the organization, and unit safety committee members. Supervisors and maintenance personnel are able to accomplish safety inspections within their units and activities. Supervisors make on-the-spot corrections; and maintenance personnel, under appropriate authority, make immediate modifications and repairs to eliminate unsafe conditions.

TYPES OF SAFETY INSPECTIONS

Selection of the type of safety inspection to be made is based on the requirements of the unit or activity concerned. Modification of the following types of inspections to satisfy a particular requirement should be considered.

Periodic Inspections

Periodic inspections are regularly scheduled, occurring weekly, monthly, or at other appropriate intervals. Schedules are based on the needs of each activity, being conducted at varying intervals depending upon the nature of the operation. This type of schedule is preferable to a single inspection schedule covering the entire unit or activity, regardless of the need, one or two days each month. However, all operations are subject to regular inspection. A schedule chart or similar aid will assist in planning and conducting safety inspections, maintaining schedules, and ensuring comprehensive coverage of the unit or activity on a regular basis.

1. Periodic inspections will be planned in the schedule to make the most effective use of safety personnel and time.
2. Particular attention will be given to the convenience of the activities being inspected to minimize disrupting normal operations.
3. A method of inspection notification should be devised and coordinated with the various activities. Naturally hazardous operations and activities require more frequent inspections than others.

When schedules are devised, this factor should be taken into consideration to gain adequate inspection balance.

4. Mobile or movable equipment assigned to any activity may often be used in other parts of the plant. Regardless of whether or not it is used, this equipment also should be subject to periodic inspection; and plans should be made to have it available for the scheduled unit inspection.

Special Inspections

Special inspections are required for several reasons: installation of new equipment, establishment of new procedures, relocation or revision of operations, and other similar modifications. After an accident, special inspections often are necessary to determine if controls are adequate or if new hazards have developed in an operation. This type of inspection is also made in conjunction with national safety campaigns, at the request of supervisors or other personnel who believe hazards exist, and when normal operating conditions are varied.

Spot Inspections

Unannounced, spot inspections usually are conducted to observe a particular phase of an operation or the use of a special item of equipment. These impromptu visits will uncover hazards of a transitory nature and those not evident during periodic inspections because of efforts made to temporarily eliminate them when inspections are announced.

Continuous Inspections

The overall success of the safety program depends upon continuous inspections by supervisors and others responsible for all activities and operations. These inspections become a never-ending search for unsafe acts and unsafe conditions and eventually result in elimination of costly accidents.

One-call Inspection

This is usually conducted by a safety representative from a higher level of management with the unit safety representative and the safety director. A basic purpose of such an inspection is to motivate personnel to perform safely by demonstrating to them the interest of higher management. Such inspection records also can be used to assess the strengths and weaknesses of safety programs throughout the company or division.

Inspection of Research Facilities

The many and varied research programs conducted by industry, universities and research laboratories often involve known and unknown hazardous materials. Constant emphasis should be placed on safety inspections in research organizations. Figure 14–5 gives a checklist of special factors to consider in inspecting research areas.

INSPECTION CHECKLISTS

It is important that the inspector become thoroughly familiar with the standards of good practices for each phase of hazard control. For example, when an inspector knows what good housekeeping is and how it is achieved and maintained, he can detect the evidence of bad housekeeping almost at a glance when he enters a room or department and can make the recommendations necessary for its improvement. Similarly, if he knows machine guards thoroughly, he can quickly detect inadequacy of the guard on any given machine. Inspection personnel should review the standard requirements for those activities to be inspected prior to each

For safety in:

I	II
Equipment and materials safety	Personnel safety

Guard against:

Explosion; abnormal temperatures; fire; release of toxic materials; effect of mass; effect of surroundings	Ingestion or absorbtion of toxicants; tissue damage

During experimental phases of:

Raw materials transfer; equipment fabrication; reaction kinetics; product characteristics analysis	Observation; operation; handling; measurement; analysis

Provide this information and material:

Strength and performance of materials; shielding provisions; cooling (or warming) agents; fire controlling methods and agents; adequate ventilation	All possible knowledge of toxic limits; body protection by remote separation or protective clothing and covering; pure air through chemical or physical toxicant removal

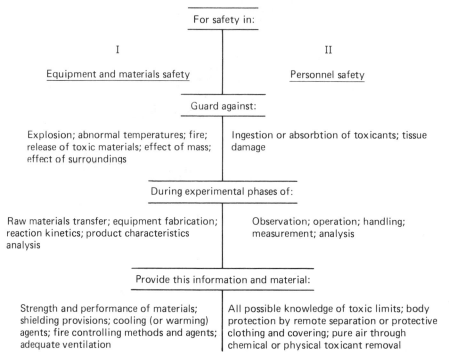

FIGURE 14–5. Checklist for Safety in Research.

inspection. Personnel competent in each operation and activity should accompany the inspecting team and assist in the inspecting to make sure nothing is missed (this is especially true of highly technical and complex operations—it is not possible for inspectors to know everything about all operations; therefore, they should be assisted by personnel who do).

Unless inspections are carefully planned and based on systematic coverage of all activities, they may become nothing more than tours of the unit or plant. This will defeat the purpose of the safety program by failing to produce significant facts which are needed if accidents are to be prevented.

A suitable checklist, prepared and used as an inspection guide for each activity, will prove invaluable to safety personnel and members of inspecting teams. The checklist need not include every item that will be observed in any activity, but rather, should be comprehensive enough to cover the important details of operations and functions that may be hazard producing.

Checklists should be designed to fit the operations of the activity where they will be used, rather than to meet any overall standard of application. A standard checklist on housekeeping and fire prevention can usually be applied to almost all operations. Examples of what to check in a safety inspection are listed below. Appropriate technical manuals, technical bulletins, and so on, contain specific standards; these should be used for detailed and specific items and operating procedures to be inspected. The checklist does not cover all conditions; rather, it is intended as a general guide.

1. *Receiving, shipping, storing.* Equipment, job planning, layout, heights, floor loads, projection of materials, material-handling methods.
2. *Building conditions.* Floors, walls, ceilings, exits, stairs, walkways, ramps, platforms, driveways, aisles, fire doors, fire escapes, code compliance.
3. *Housekeeping.* Waste disposal, tools, objects, materials, leakage and spillage, methods, schedules, work areas, remote areas, windows, ledges, storage.
4. *Electricity.* Equipment, switches, breakers, fuses, switchboards, junctions, special fixtures, circuits, insulation, extensions, tools, motors, grounding code compliance.
5. *Lighting.* Type, intensity, controls, conditions, diffusion, location, glare and shadow control, standards applied.
6. *Heating and ventilation.* Type, effectiveness, temperature, humidity, controls, natural and artificial ventilation and exhausting, code compliance.
7. *Machines.* Points of operation, guards, flywheels, gears, shafts, pulleys, keyways, belts, couplings, sprockets, chains, frames, controls, lighting, tools and equipment, brakes, exhausting, feeding, oiling, adjusting, maintenance, grounding, how attached, workspace, locations, waste disposal.
8. *Personnel.* Training; experience; methods of checking machines before use; methods of cleaning, oiling, adjusting machinery; type of clothing; personal protective equipment; use of guards; tool storage; work practices.
9. *Hand and power tools.* Purchasing standards, inspection, storage, repair, types, maintenance, grounding, use and handling.
10. *Chemicals; petroleum, oils, and lubricants (POL); and radiological materials.* Storage, handling, transportation, amounts used, warning signs, supervision, training, protective clothing and equipment, dispensing, disposal.
11. *Fire prevention.* Extinguishers, alarms, sprinklers, smoking rules, exits personnel assigned, separation of flammable materials and dangerous operations, explosion-proof fixtures, waste disposal.
12. *Maintenance.* Regularity, effectiveness, training of personnel, materials and equipment used, method of locking power source while working on machinery, general methods, repair material storage.
13. *Personal protection.* Type, size, maintenance, repair, storage, assignment of responsibility, purchasing methods, standards observed, rules of use, method of assignment, emergency showers in chemical areas.

CONDUCTING THE SAFETY INSPECTION

The safety inspection should be carefully planned to cover all activities. A priority listing of activities should be prepared. Those activities having the highest frequency of accidents should be inspected more thoroughly and more frequently. The inspection should be planned to make the most effective use of safety personnel and time. Consideration should be given to inspecting an activity so as to cause as little disruption as possible to normal operations. In conducting the inspection, special consideration should be given to:

1. New equipment recently installed.
2. New procedures recently established.
3. Operations recently relocated or revised.

4. Other modifications in operations and equipment.
5. Comments of personnel in regard to safety hazards, poor procedures, and/or recommendations of better and safer ways to perform operations.

INSPECTION RECORDS

Reports and records should be as simple as possible. It is advisable to keep a minimum number of records on the functioning of the inspection service. During an inspection, unsafe conditions or practices are recorded in such a manner as to adequately identify the subject or object to the person responsible for taking corrective measures. This record is also necessary for follow-up action. The maintenance of accurate inspection records is particularly important for analysis purposes; that is, determination of operations and activities that have the highest frequency of unsafe conditions, unsafe acts, and hazardous situations. If you attempt to remember what you have seen, you may forget an important item. Each unit and activity should maintain a record of inspections to include the following information:

1. Date of inspection and name of person or team making the inspection.
2. Hazards uncovered by inspection.
3. Action recommended to correct the hazards.
4. Action accomplished to correct the hazards.

INSPECTION REPORTS

In reporting his findings to the department head or supervisor of the activity being inspected, the safety inspector must ensure that the department head or supervisor understands the safety value of the inspector's recommendations. An inspection is of no value if the control information is not forwarded to the proper authority for action. Recommendations should be practical, constructive, and contain sufficient detail for those in charge to understand exactly what they are intended to accomplish.

SUPERVISORY RESPONSIBILITIES

The supervisor is in the best position to assist in safety inspections. He knows each job under his control, he knows what specific skill are required for each job, he knows the environment conditions surrounding each job, and he knows the men performing in these jobs. Therefore, he can accurately and reliably assess work performance from a safety viewpoint. He can assist in developing safety inspection checklists concerning the particular work for which he is responsible, he can assist in actually conducting the safety inspection, and he can provide valuable insight concerning interpretation of the results of the safety inspection. Through his participation, he should also acquire an appreciation of the purpose and value of safety inspections. This, in turn, will increase his awareness of safety as an integral part of on-the-job performance and as one of his responsibilities.

FIRE PREVENTION

General

The need for fire prevention and protection is indicated by the tremendous fire losses experienced throughout the United States each year. Property losses exceed the billion dollar mark, and around 12,000 persons are killed and many more injured.

The words fire prevention and protection suggest that we are interested in two distinct and different functions in our effort to eliminate fire losses. First, there is prevention by detection of, safeguarding against, and elimination of fire hazards. Second, there is protection by determining the need for, and adequacy of, installed fire protection systems and portable fire-fighting equipment, furnishing essential fire protection services, and inspecting and maintaining all fire protection facilities.

Fire Prevention Principles

Almost all fires are preventable. The faithful application of time-tested and proved methods of prevention and control would eliminate most fires and would limit losses from the remainder. The details involved in the prevention and limitation of fire loss are numerous, but the fundamental principles upon which the details are based are simple. Good housekeeping in operations and activities is essential to effective fire prevention. Accumulations of rubbish, waste, and industrial residue are all sources of fire. Concentration of flammable or explosive gases and vapors are condensed sources of dangerous and destructive fires—fires that are preventable. Although the local fire department, under the supervision of the fire marshal, is responsible for fighting fires and the enforcement of fire regulations, every employee on the grounds and in the factory and offices shares in fire prevention responsibility. Safety personnel have the added responsibility of being continually on the lookout for hazardous conditions that could lead to fires, and for keeping the safety director informed of these findings with recommendations for effective fire control or elimination of fire hazards.

COMMON FIRE HAZARDS

A common hazard is not a minor or unimportant hazard, but one that is common to most operations and activities.

Smoking

Safe smoking is primarily a matter of personal habit and attitude. "No smoking" rules are usually observed in areas where it is obvious that there is a potential loss of life and property by fire. Establishing definite places and times for smoking, well publicized and enforced, will do much to gain individual cooperation. Adequate ash and match receptacles are essential.

Housekeeping

Good housekeeping is perhaps the most important single element in preventing the start and spread of fire. Accumulations of rubbish, waste, and industrial residue must not be allowed:

1. *Trash cans.* Greasy and oily waste, wiping and polishing cloths, and oil mops must be stored in tightly covered metal cans.
2. *Ashcans and refuse receptacles.* The safe handling of ashes, rubbish, and other refuse is a matter of proper storage, periodical removal, and safe disposition.
3. *Old furniture and paper.* Storage of combustible material in out-of-the-way areas should be prohibited. This pertains particularly to dwellings, places of public assembly, and so on. Periodic cleanup campaigns are an effective preventive measure.
4. *Floor oils, polishes, and cleaners.* Floor oils, polishes, cleansing materials, and

the like may be subject to spontaneous ignition and should be stored away from flammable materials. Spontaneous ignition is defined as "the outbreak of fire in combustible materials, such as oily rags or damp hay that occurs without application of direct flame or spark and is usually caused by slow oxidation processes under conditions not permitting escape of heat."

5. *Outdoor housekeeping*. Good housekeeping out of doors is also necessary in preventing fires. The regular removal of rubbish and other unnecessary combustible material such as dry grass, weeds, wood scraps, and so on and the designation of burning areas are effective measures to be taken.

Storage

Fire hazards are created in storage operations when certain materials are stored together by high piling of pallets, locating piles in front of fire doors, blocking of aisles, and so on. The blocking open of fire doors and blocking off of fire protection equipment are other hazards commonly found in storage areas.

Heating

Climatic conditions are an important factor in fire hazards involving heating. Heating units are operated a greater part of the time in northern climates. In southern climates, heating units are used during infrequent periods of cold weather. The infrequent use encourages negligence. Protection of exposed combustible materials and properly installed, serviced, and maintained heating units will eliminate most of the hazards. Unqualified personnel attempting to correct malfunctions or repair stoves and heaters are a major cause of fire. Personnel assigned to service and refuel heating systems must be readily available to service faulty units. Personnel must not be permitted to wear clothing that has been soaked with fuel. It is not uncommon for gasoline-soaked clothing to ignite.

Electrical Fires

Electrical fires are primarily due to arcs, sparks, and overheating. Arcs ignite combustible materials, fuse metal conductors, and produce sparks. Overloaded circuits also deteriorate insulation and thereby ignite combustibles. Dangerous heat is generated in conductors when current is carried in excess of its rated capacity.

Handling Volatile Liquids

Personnel in charge of operations where fuels, solvents, or other volatile liquids are used must be constantly alert to prevent unsafe handling practices. Personnel are not permitted to use fuels such as gasoline to clean clothing, solvents or fuels as cigarette lighter fluid, or open solvent or gasoline containers near electrical repair equipment. The substitution of low flashpoint petroleum solvents in place of approved substances cannot be permitted at any time.

Sparks

Sparks cause many fires. Prevention of fires from sparks coming from locomotives, chimneys, and outside fires is mainly a matter of using noncombustible roof coverings, spark arresters, and care with fires.

SPECIAL FIRE HAZARDS

Chemical Fires

Apparently harmless chemicals may react vigorously, causing fire or explosion, upon contact with such commonplace substances as water, wood, bits of rubbish or metal shavings. Some chemicals, when contacted by other materials, will generate heat, give off flammable gases, or react explosively. Others, through decomposition, may generate heat and ignite spontaneously or support combustion by oxidation. Thus, it becomes necessary for personnel working with various chemicals to be familiar with their fire-causing characteristics to prevent accidental fire or explosion. It is important to remember this fact—chemicals may not be flammable in themselves, but can be fire-causing under certain circumstances.

Flammable Liquids

Strictly speaking, flammable liquids do not burn; it is their vapors, given off during evaporation, that ignite and burn when combined with air. The flashpoint of liquids is the minimum temperature at which the vapors given off by the liquid will ignite and produce flames. Generally, the term *flammable liquid* is applied only to liquid having a flashpoint of less than 140°F, and a vapor pressure of not more than 40 pounds per square inch (absolute) at 100°F, its flashpoint. The flashpoint criterion is a good starting point for considering the safe handling and use of flammable liquids and for setting up effective fire prevention measures. Although flashpoints are the commonly accepted means for determining the relative fire hazards of a liquid, their use without consideration of other physical characteristics of the liquids may be misleading.

Various publications give specific safety standards for handling and storing liquid fuels and other petroleum products. The handling and use of flammable liquids must be carefully controlled to prevent fires and explosions. Prevention measures commonly used include: prevention of evaporation by keeping flammable liquids in closed containers, removal of sources of ignition, adequate ventilation, provision of relief vents, and installation of extinguishing systems where needed.

Flammable Gases

Flammable gases are similar to flammable liquids in many respects. Under pressure or decreased temperature, flammable gases become liquids; flammable liquids will become gases if their pressure is decreased or their temperature raised. In general, flammable gases have physical characteristics similar to the vapors of flammable liquids. However, the flashpoint criterion cannot be used with flammable gases; at normal temperatures, they are in a form which will permit them to mix freely with air. Explosive limits and ranges give some indication of their flammability.

Types. Some of the more commonly used flammable gases are hydrogen, hydrogen sulfide, acetylene, ethane, and propane. Acetylene is a flammable gas usually dissolved under pressure in acetone to make handling safer. Hydrogen and many other gases remain in a gaseous state under normal pressure in cyclinders. Ethane and similar petroleum gases become liquids under moderate pressures and are stored in containers in this form. Although oxygen is not flammable, it will support combustion and should be treated as a flammable gas. Most flammable gases have a characteristic odor; those that do not are odorized so they can be detected in the air before they reach dangerous concentration.

Basic Controls. The first principle of controlling flammable gases is to prevent their escape from containers and subsequent forming of an explosive or flammable gas-air mixture. Because of the compressibility of gases, they are confined under pressure in portable cylinders or other containers which permit large quantities of gases to be stored in concentrated form in relatively small containers.

Handling. Cylinders of flammable gases must be handled carefully to minimize the dangers of fire or explosion. Not only are the gases themselves hazardous, but the pressures exerted on internal surfaces of the cylinders are sufficient to create explosions. Careless handling can result in damage to cylinders and valves and may cause the container to fail, creating dangerous gas leaks. Cylinders are not used for any purpose other than for containing compressed gases.

Storage. Flammable gas cylinders are stored with extreme care to prevent fires or explosions. When stored in the open, the cylinders must be ventilated, away from extreme heat (below 125°F.) and the different types of gases must be separated. Empty cylinders are marked "EMPTY" and stored separately and apart from full containers.

Explosive Dust

Organic materials such as wood and coal along with such metals as magnesium, aluminum, titanium, and so on are flammable under certain conditions. In their solid states, these materials are not generally considered to be flammable, as the term usually denotes a substance which is easily ignited and burns very rapidly. However, substances cannot be disregarded as fire hazards simply because their degree of flammability is low. When these materials are broken down into shavings, fine particles, powders, and dusts, their flammability increases to such an extent that they become explosive. Unless properly regarded as fire hazards and treated as such these materials can become extremely dangerous in dust-producing industrial operations. The best protection against dust explosion is to keep the generation of dust to a minimum and to trap and remove whatever dust is created at its source. All sources of ignition are removed from areas of dust generation to prevent accidental ignition.

Static Electricity

Static electricity is a constant source of danger, particularly when generated near fuels or flammable vapors. It has been responsible for starting many fires that resulted in extensive property damage and personnel injuries. Static electricity is created primarily by the contact and separation of two unlike substances or by almost any sort of motion of persons or material. High static electrical charges are created by persons walking, by moving rubber-tired vehicles, when liquid drops through space, and when petroleum products are pumped through lines and hoses. Although static charges are usually short-lived, they often will produce sufficient heat to ignite flammable gases, vapors, dust, or other low flashpoint materials, particuarly during dry, cool weather.

When the generation of static electricity cannot be prevented, the sparking hazards can be effectively controlled by grounding, bonding, or humidification. Grounding and bonding are particularly important in fueling operations, paint and dope shop work, aircraft and vehicle maintenance, ammunition handling, rock and missile operations, compressed gas use, and many other daily operations.

Static electricity is dangerous, first, because it cannot be seen, and second, because its potential hazards are not commonly known. When supervisory and operating personnel fully understand the dangers associated with static electricity, they will readily recognize the need for implementing immediate and effective control measures. Since static electricity is generated primarily by bringing together and separating two unlike substances, or by motion of almost any kind, the use of effective grounding and bonding measures will greatly reduce the static electrical hazard.

FIRE CLASSIFICATIONS

Fires are grouped into four general classes, each of which can be extinguished by a particular action, agent or piece of equipment. Because all fire extinguishing agents cannot be used on all types of fires, this classification makes it possible to determine and use the agent best suited for fighting a particular type of fire. Therefore, personnel must ascertain before using an extinguishing agent that it is of the type suitable for the fire to be fought and that its use will create no additional hazards. Figure 14–6 contains information about the various types of fire extinguishers, the types of fire for which they are applicable, and the operation principles for their use.

Class A

Fires in this classification will be effectively and safely extinguished by water or solutions containing water. Fires occurring in wood, paper, and rags are typical class A fires. This classification is primarily concerned with the cooling or quenching effect offered by water.

Class B

Fire occurring in flammable liquids, such as gasoline and other fuels, solvents, greases, or similar substances, are termed class B fires. The agents required for extinguishing this type of fire are those that will dilute or eliminate air by exclusion or blanketing, thereby creating a smothering effect.

Class C

Class C fires are those that occur in electrical equipment and facilities. The extinguishing agents used on this class of fire are nonconductors of electricity and work principally on smothering the fire.

Class D

Fires involving combustible metals, for example, magnesium, aluminum, titanium, zirconium, and other oxidized metals, are included. Combustion temperature and energy are high compared to those of hydrocarbon or wood fires.

FIRE APPLIANCES

Hand-operated, portable fire extinguishers are first aid appliances provided for emergency use to extinguish or confine fires to their initial stages. The local fire marshal is responsible for the distribution, inspection, and maintenance of all fire appliances located throughout his political jurisdiction.

Accessibility

Extinguishers are located where they can be reached easily in the event of emergency. The location of each extinguisher is identified by signs or color markings.

Characteristics

Emergency fire extinguishers range in size from small, easily carried types to relatively

Choosing the right type For full information and special exceptions consult the Factory Mutual Approved Equipment manual.	Ordinary combustibles Wood, cloth, paper, rubbish 	Flammable liquids Oil, gasoline, paint, grease 	Electrical equipment Motors, controls, panels, wiring 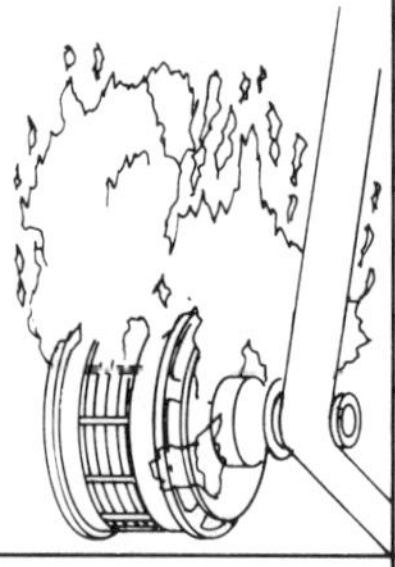	Combustible metals Magnesium, sodium potassium, NaK alloy 
Small hose	OK			
Pump tanks	OK			
Soda-acid	OK			
Water-filled	OK			
Antifreeze	OK			
Carbon dioxide		OK	OK	
Dry-chemical Regular		OK	OK	
Dry-chemical General purpose	OK	OK	OK	
Foam		OK		
Vaporizing liquid			OK	
Special compound				OK

FIGURE 14–6. Know Your Extinguishers. (Reproduced with the permission of Factory Engineering Corp., Norwood, MA.)

large tanks mounted on wheels for convenient movement. The capacities generally range from 1 quart to 60 gallons or more for liquid types, and from 2 to 100 pounds in extinguishers containing CO_2 or dry powder. Extinguisher components such as containers, hoses, nozzles, and valves are designed for use only with the particular extinguishing agent prescribed.

Discharge. The extinguishing agents are discharged from containers by pressure generated in several ways. Some water extinguishers are equipped with hand pumps to provide discharge pressure; carbon dioxide gas extinguishers are set off by pressure created by chemical reactions. On other types of extinguishers, compressed gases such as carbon dioxide or nitrogen

Small hose: A small hose available for quick use indoors fills the same need as one or more portable extinguishers. It has the advantage of an unlimited water supply. It can be equipped to deliver a solid stream or spray, the latter being more effective for some fires.

Pump tanks: A pump tank is essentially a water container with a built-in pump. The pump is operated with one hand and the stream is directed with the other. A second man can keep the tank replenished while the first man works the pump.

Soda-acid: A soda-acid extinguisher contains a water solution of sodium bicarbonate and a bottle of sulfuric acid. The two mix when the extinguisher is inverted. This produces carbon dioxide gas which forces the liquid out. The extinguishing action is essentially that of water.

Water-filled: The stored, pressure-type contains water and compressed air and is operated by depressing a lever. The cartridge type is inverted and bumped on the floor, breaking the seal on a carbon dioxide cartridge. Some types are simply inverted to puncture the cartridge.

Antifreeze: The antifreeze is similar to the water-filled, but contains a water solution with a freezing point below −40°F. It is recommended that only those recharges furnished by the manufacturer and so specified on the nameplate be used in these as in other extinguishers.

Carbon dioxide: A carbon dioxide extinguisher contains liquid carbon dioxide that is released by operating a valve lever or trigger. The liquid changes into a white cloud of "snow" and gas as it issues from the outlet. It is directed on the fire through a funnel-shaped horn.

Dry-chemical, regular: The regular dry-chemical extinguisher contains a sodium-bicarbonate-base powder treated to prevent lumping and to increase effectiveness. One type is under a constant pressure of dry air or nitrogen gas. Another requires puncturing a carbon dioxide cartridge.

Dry-chemical, general purpose: Similar to the regular dry-chemical extinguisher except that the powder is a special type suitable for fires in ordinary combustibles as well as in flammable liquids and electrical equipment. This extinguisher is operated in the same way as the regular type.

Foam: Chemical foam is produced by the reaction of two solutions, one in the extinguisher shell and the other in an inner container. When the extinguisher is inverted, the reaction also produces carbon dioxide which expels the foam in a stream.

Vaporizing liquid: The vaporizing liquid is specially processed by the manufacturer for extinguisher use. One type is operated by pumping. Another has the liquid under constant pressure using air or carbon dioxide; it is operated by pressing a valve.

Special compound: A special powder is available for use on metal fires. It can be applied with a shovel or by a specially designed extinguisher. The extinguisher operates in the same way as a dry-chemical unit and is similar in appearance.

FIGURE 14–6 (Continued)

are used as the pressure sources for forcing the extinguishing agents from the containers. Suitable regulating devices are provided to control the flow.

Range. The range of emergency extinguishing equipment varies, depending on the types of equipment being used. Although some extinguishers have a maximum range of 50 feet, it may not be the most effective range. Even the largest wheeled extinguishers can produce an effective flow for only about 3 to 5 minutes, while small hand extinguishers will empty in a few seconds. In order to make the most effective use of the extinguishing agent in the container, personnel must get as close to the fire as possible and extinguish it quickly. If the extinguisher operator cannot get close to the fire, it is likely that the fire is so intense that the emergency equipment will not be sufficient to extinguish the blaze, regardless of how effectively it is used.

Agents. Fire extinguishing agents produce either a cooling and quenching, or an air dilution or smothering effect, on the fires for which they may be used. Water and water-containing calcium chloride, sodium bicarbonate or potassium carbonate solution, foam, carbon dioxide, carbon tetrachloride solutions, dry chemicals, antifreeze solutions, and ordinary dry compounds such as sand or talc commonly are used as fire extinguishing agents.

Water. Water extinguishes through cooling; through blanketing; through diluting (in the case of liquids readily miscible with water, such as ethyl alcohol); through surface wetting (prevents or retards reaching ignition temperature). It is effective on oil fires only when applied as a very fine spray or heavy mist over the entire surface. If there is a small amount of oil (garage or airplane hangar fires), its use in large volume (fire hose or deluge sprinklers) is effective.

Foam. Various substances can be used to impart an enduring quality to foam produced by the generation of carbon dioxide gas through chemical action in a water solution. The foam cuts off the air through blanketing and has some cooling value as well. Its primary value is in class B fires. It should be applied to cover the entire surface of the liquid. However, vapors being given off will pass through the foam and, if in sufficient concentration, will burn above it.

Carbon tetrachloride. No longer in use because of discharge of harmful gases, and chlorobromoethane, these liquids extinguish through blanketing by rapid volatilization to a heavy vapor that will not support combustion. The liquids have a high electrical resistance and hence are effective for fires in electrical equipment. The fumes are very toxic, and therefore, in closed spaces of limited size, great caution should be exercised. These agents are not too commonly used today.

Carbon dioxide. Carbon dioxide, an inert gas approximately 60 percent heavier than air, extinguishes chiefly by blanketing. It also exerts some cooling effect because of the low temperature of the steam discharged from the cylinder, where the carbon dioxide is held in liquid form by a pressure of 800 to 900 pounds per square inch. It is valuable for class C fires.

Steam. Steam can be used for class B fires in tanks or other enclosed spaces if the volume of steam available is sufficient to reduce the oxygen content below a figure that will support combustion about 14 percent for most oils; about 10 percent if flowing material is to be extinguished.

Dry, powdered materials. Chemical powders that release carbon dioxide at flame temperatures are effective for use in class B and C fires. The composition and degree of fineness of the powder varies with the manufacturer. It consists primarily of sodium bicarbonate with added materials to repel moisture and to make and keep the powder free flowing.

Light water. Light water is a chemical additive developed by the U.S. Navy in conjunction with a private chemical manufacturer. When it is added to water it tends to alter the surface tension characteristics. The chemically treated water tends to float over the fuel or other burn surface and effectively block off all oxygen, thus supressing the fire. It can be used in any area in which foam is used and has the advantage over foam in that when it is disturbed by being walked through or by a hose pulled through it, no flashback results as is often the case in fuel fires.

A second advantage over foam is that it requires smaller quantities to do the same work and suppreses fire more quickly, thus is an ideal agent for airborne fire suppression systems. It is particularly useful in rescue work as a cooling agent to cover rescue crewmen while they penetrate a burn area. A note of caution, however, is that this chemical is highly corrosive to aluminum and electronic components.

FIRE PREVENTION AND PROTECTION PROGRAM

Industrial Plant Fire Marshall

The plant fire marshal is responsible for organizing and implementing the fire prevention and protection program. The objectives of this protection program are to develop plans and facilities, and to orient and train personnel. This program will safeguard life and reduce fire loss to a minimum. The program includes but is not limited to:

1. Furnishing essential fire protection services.
2. Detecting, eliminating, and safeguarding against fire hazards.
3. Inspecting and maintaining all fire protection facilities.
4. Determining the need for, and adequacy of, installed fire protection systems and portable firefighting equipment.

Brigade Chiefs for Large Industries

Brigade chiefs are selected from the principal organization or activity of each area. In assisting the fire marshal, unit fire marshals usually:

1. Inspect buildings, structures, grounds, and fire protection facilities.
2. Submit scheduled reports to the plant fire marshal of findings and correction of deficiencies. Report matters requiring immediate attention, as warranted.
3. Enforce fire regulations.
4. Coordinate emergency plans for evacuation of personnel, control of fire, and salvage of property.
5. Conduct evaluation drills.
6. Ensure that personnel know how to report fires, use extinguishers, and practice prevention measures.

Building Fire Brigade Chiefs

Brigade chiefs are assigned for each important building or activity. They inspect assigned premises at the close of business to detect and eliminate fire hazards. Their activities are coordinated by area fire marshals.

Local Fire Plan

A local fire plan is prepared by each unit, area, and department. The local fire plan sets forth emergency firefighting instructions and designates individuals to carry out the plan. The plan will include, but is not limited to, the following:

1. Emergency firefighting instructions and assigned duties of firefighting squads.
2. A sketch of the floor plan indicating exits and traffic flow for each building.
3. A sketch showing selected assembly area for personnel evacuated from buildings.
4. Instructions for reporting a fire.
5. Letters of appointment of unit and alternate area fire marshals.

FIRE INSPECTIONS

Fire inspections are regularly scheduled, occurring daily, weekly, monthly, or at other appropriate intervals. Schedules are based on the needs of each activity and the requirements set forth in local fire regulations. For example, warehouses, shops, offices, and other buildings are inspected for fire hazards at the close of operations; fire extinguishers are inspected monthly; the area fire marshall will most likely be required to conduct weekly inspections to locate and correct all existing fire hazards. Fire inspections should produce the following:

1. A facility that is safer from fire because of the inspection.
2. An improved attitude toward fire prevention by those in charge of the facility.
3. A written report that can be used for the information and guidance of others to determine progress in prevention measures, and to detect deficiencies that need correcting.

Fire inspection records and report forms are often furnished by the fire marshal. Sometimes a checklist is also furnished. A list of items to be inspected should be prepared for each facility. The following are examples of items that may be included in a checklist:

1. Complete instructions for use of fire extinguishers and for their charging, operation, and maintenance. These instructions should be mastered and followed explicitly. For instance, a high standard of maintenance of all pressure-type extinguishers is necessary to their proper, safe functioning.
2. Fire doors, which might become inoperable through neglect or, chiefly, through obstruction or blocking.
3. Sprinkler heads, which must be kept free from paint, or corrosion. Piled materials, added structures, or added equipment must not interfere with their operations.
4. Fire alarm devices, water control valves, and automatic control devices, which require careful and unfailing inspection.
5. Fire hoses which must be dried, checked as to condition, and returned to proper storage space after each use. Valve leakage must be guarded against, and the hose should be tested at intervals. Linen hose rots quickly if allowed to remain moist.
6. Fire exits must be kept clear, properly marked, and lighted. Stairs or other walkway surfaces must be kept in good condition and nonslippery.
7. Building name or number and fire department telephone number near each telephone. This will facilitate fire reporting in an emergency situation.

Summary

Safety inspections are designed to uncover unsafe acts and unsafe conditions before accidents occur. In addition to those inspections conducted by safety personnel, maintenance teams, safety committees, and so on, each individual should remain on the alert to avoid unsafe acts and unsafe conditions during his every day activities. The type and frequency of safety inspections vary with the activity concerned. Operations, activities, and facilities must be inspected often enough to ensure effective results. Records of those unsafe acts and unsafe conditions are maintained for follow-up action to ensure that all deficiencies are corrected. The role of the supervisor in performing and evaluating the results of safety inspections is emphasized. He is in the best position to know what to inspect and how to use the results of safety inspections as a basis for increasing safe performance among the subordinates.

Fire prevention starts with the basic process of preventing combustibles from reaching ignition temperatures. If the process necessarily involves heating to or above ignition temperatures, air must be excluded. The details involved in the prevention and limitation of fire loss are numerous, but the fundamental principles on which the details are based are simple:

1. *Elimination of hazards.* Prevent the starting of fires by assuring proper construction, arrangement, control of operations, maintenance, good housekeeping, and elimination of unsafe practices.
2. *Prompt discovery and extinguishment.* Except for the relatively few fires initiated by the explosion combustion of dusts, for example, all fires start small. Discovery and extinguishment actions are accomplished by means of automatic sprinklers, automatic fire alarms, standpipes, special protection systems, and maximum portable fire-fighting equipment provided consistent with the fire risk involved and economic use of such equipment.
3. *Limitation of spread.* Provision of suitable barriers and holding to a minimum the volume and value of combustibles present in a given fire area will limit the loss. The fire area is the area within effective fire stops.
4. *Provision for and proper maintenance of adequate exit facilities.* What constitutes adequacy will vary widely with conditions and will include the giving of suitable alarms and the control of the behavior of persons involved to prevent panic or other unsafe acts.

Questions

1. Indicate the aim of the OSH Act and some of the ways by which it may be achieved.
2. Each state had a safety code, so why was it necessary for the U.S. government to enact the OSH Act?
3. What are the functions of the National Institute of Occupational Safety and Health?
4. What is the difference between safety and accident prevention?
5. What two factors are highly related to accidents?
6. Of all major accident factors, three are of utmost importance in determining the cause of the accident. What are they?
7. The whole realm of safety and safety engineering centers largely around people. Comment on this statement.
8. What proportion of accidents do you believe can be blamed on human error, equipment failure, and acts of God?
9. What do you believe to be the percentage of all accidents caused by unsafe acts and the percentage caused by unsafe conditions?

10. What are the functions of a safety council?
11. What are the uses and needs for accident investigation?
12. What are the principles of accident investigations that should be followed?
13. List the typical steps to be followed in an investigation?
14. What are some new tools that have become available to safety engineers for accident prevention? Discuss the use of each.
15. Why are safety inspections worthwhile? Should an inspection checklist be used? If so, why?
16. What are the most common causes of fire?
17. What is the difference between a flammable and a combustible liquid?
18. How are fires classified?
19. What are some common fire extinguishing agents?
20. List four fundamental principles in the prevention and limitation of industrial fire loss.

Bibliography

American Conference of Governmental Industrial Hygienists. *A Manual of Recommended Practice: Industrial Ventilation.* Current ed. Lansing, Mich.: Committee on Industrial Ventilation.

American Industrial Hygiene Association. *Industrial Noise Manual.* Current ed. Akron, Ohio.

Anton, Thomas. *Occupational Safety and Health Management.* New York: McGraw-Hill, 1979.

Association of General Contractors of America. *Manual of Accident Prevention in Construction.* 6th ed. Washington, D.C., 1971.

Bindford, Charles M., et al. *Loss Control in the Occupational Safety and Health Administration.* New York: McGraw-Hill, 1975.

Broadhurst, V. A. *The Health and Safety at Work Act in Practice.* New York: Hayden, 1978.

Cole, R. A. *Industrial Safety Techniques.* New York: John Wiley and Sons, 1975.

De Reamer, Russell. *Modern Safety and Health Technology.* New York: Wiley-Interscience, 1979.

Ellis, Michael D., et al. *Industrial Hygiene.* Englewood Cliffs, N.J.: Prentice-Hall, 1972.

Federal Safety and Health Laws and Standards: Federal Acts and standards pertaining to safety and health, such as the Occupational Safety and Health Act of 1970, and associated standards, the Department of Transportation regulations, and Consumer Product Safety Commission standards, etc.

Grimaldi, John V., and Simonds, Rolbin H. *Safety Management.* 3rd ed. Homewood, Ill.: Richard D. Irwin, 1975.

Hammer, Willie. *Handbook of System and Product Safety.* Englewood Cliffs, N.J.: Prentice-Hall, 1972.

———. *Occupational Safety Management and Engineering.* Englewood Cliffs, N.J.: Prentice-Hall, 1976.

Handley, William, ed. *Industrial Safety Handbook.* 2nd ed. New York: McGraw-Hill, 1977.

Heinnich, W. H. *Industrial Accident Approach: A Safety Management Approach.* New York: McGraw-Hill, 1980.

Herzog, Donald R., and Herzog, Daryl R. "Electrical Problems in Hospitals," *Professional Safety*, 21 (January 1978).

McCormick, E. J. *Human Factors Engineering*. New York: McGraw-Hill, 1976.

National Fire Protection Association. *Fire Protection Handbook*. Current ed. Boston.

National Institute for Occupational Safety and Health. *A Guide to Industrial Respiratory Protection*. 1st ed. Washington, D.C.: U.S. Government Printing Office, 1976.

Olishifski, J. B., and McElroy, F. E. *Fundamentals of Industrial Hygiene*. Chicago: National Safety Council, 1979.

National Safety Council. *Making Safety Work*. New York: McGraw-Hill, 1976.

———. Accident Prevention Manual for Industrial Operations. 7th ed. Chicago, 1974.

———. *Motor Fleet Safety Manual*. Current ed. Chicago.

———. *Supervisors Safety Manual*. 4th ed. Chicago.

Peterson, D. C. *Techniques of Safety Management*. New York: McGraw-Hill, 1971.

Peterson, Jack E. *Industrial Health*. Englewood Cliffs, N.J.: Prentice-Hall, 1972.

Rodgers, William P. *Introduction to System Safety Engineering*. New York: John Wiley and Sons, 1971.

Simonds, R. H., and Grimaldi, J. V. *Safety Management*. Homewood, Ill.: Richard D. Irwin, 1963.

Tarrants, William E., ed. *A Selected Bibliography of Reference Materials in Safety Engineering and Related Fields*. Park Ridge, Ill.: American Society of Safety Engineers, 1977.

Chapter 15

Industrial Hygiene and Environmental Engineering

INTRODUCTION

The previous chapter discussed environment and its safety as a prerequisite in accident prevention. Environment is that which is found in the immediate work place. To provide a safe and healthy place to work requires control of the physical environment and the external conditions that will influence routine operations. Specific concern must be given those elements of the environment that have the potential of causing injury to personnel.

Such environmental control is the responsibility of management and, as such, devolves on all supervisors. Management has most probably furnished an environment that is as free from hazard as is necessary. However, supervisors must be alert to the potential hazards in order to assure that operating personnel utilize the safeguards provided. In other cases, new knowledge has exposed environmental hazards that may have been unknown at the time a certain situation or facility was created. It is the supervisor's responsibility to identify these and bring them to the attention of management.

The importance of a safe environment cannot be overemphasized. Most injuries stem from a combination of two causes—an unsafe physical condition and an unsafe act. Eliminate the unsafe physical condition and one of the contributing causes is eliminated. Unsafe health and physical conditions are most often a product of environment—the general conditions surrounding the work place, the equipment and materials used, or the process employed. Improvement here can help eliminate unsafe health and physical conditions, improve working conditions, and lead to a more efficient operation.

Minimum standards of safety for all health and physical conditions, either by specification or by performance, should be determined and every effort made to meet these standards.

VENTILATION

Ventilation is the process of passing clean air through any space or area for the purpose of diluting or removing undesirable air and its contaminants. The health, efficiency, motivation, and comfort of personnel will be greatly influenced by the quality of ventilation in workshops, offices, and storage areas.

In residential, commercial, and administrative spaces, ventilation is necessary for controlling cooking odors, body odors, tobacco smoke, and other air contaminants, which are produced when people occupy closed areas. Inadequate ventilation of nonindustrial areas seldom produces health hazards; however, many of the most violent complaints of stale air are received from occupants of these spaces. On the other hand, poor ventilation in industrial operations may permit the accumulation of air contaminants that can cause personnel injuries; industrial diseases leading to death; explosions; or fires. Industrial activity may generate dangerous

---

Parts of this chapter have been revised and updated from "Health and Physical Hazards, and Control" by permission from the U.S. Army Ordnance Center and School, Aberdeen Proving Ground, Md., September 1972.

dust, fumes, vapors, and gases from the materials used in operational processes. Heavy concentrations of these industrial byproducts can be extremely hazardous to personnel and property; therefore, it is essential that they be safely removed from the working areas. When other methods of protection have failed to produce a satisfactory environment, ventilation can be used to rid work areas of undesirable atmospheric contaminants.

Many ventilation methods are used to keep atmospheric conditions within safe limits. The particular method selected for an industrial operation will depend on the physical and chemical properties and quantity of hazardous materials present, methods of operation, and other factors.[1] The determination of adequate ventilation is an industrial health problem and is resolved with the help of the sanitary engineer, medical personnel, and industrial hygienist.

COOLING AND HEATING

A primary purpose for heating and cooling air is the comfort of persons occupying the particular area. The fact that the comfort of personnel is directly related to work efficiency is indicated by numerous experiments. Mental work, in particular, is affected by high temperatures and humidities—workers lose interest rapidly in such an environment. In addition to discomfort, unusually high or low temperatures will increase accidents because of the adverse effects on human attitudes and manual dexterity. At temperatures above and below a level where psychological compensation is impossible, serious effects on personnel are experienced. Extremely low temperatures result in chills, colds, frostbite, and even death, while excessive heat causes exhaustion or prostration, which can lead to complications and eventually death. A close check must be maintained by supervisors on industrial working conditions in order to maintain temperature and humidity at proper levels.

ILLUMINATION AND VISION

A person subjected to extremes of illumination—too much or too little—will experience eye fatigue. When eye fatigue occurs, the individual will be affected in various ways—headaches, eye strain, and impairment of vision—thus increasing his accident potential. Adequate illumination of all work areas is necessary if accidents are to be prevented and the vision of individuals protected.

Whether natural or artificial lighting is provided in work and living spaces is usually immaterial if it is good lighting that gives the safe, comfortable and efficient visual performance required for the protection and continued good health of personnel. Four fundamental factors determine the visibility of objects: brightness, contrast, size, and time available for seeing. The proper relationships of these factors will increase the probability that persons will detect potential hazards and either eliminate or avoid them. Conversely, lack of good lighting will contribute to accident potential and inefficiency as well as place unnecessary strain on the eyes of operating personnel.

In some degree, illumination is required for almost every activity; the quantity depends upon the types and amounts of detailed work being done. The quality of light must be maintained at high levels for efficient seeing regardless of the minimum quantity needed for just seeing the task.

Research has indicated that certain colors are more conducive to efficiency and aid in reducing fatigue. Soft blue and green

---

[1]See U.S. Department of Labor, *Handling Hazardous Materials,* Safe Work Practices Series, OSHA 2237 (Washington, September 1975).

colors are preferable to bright, glaring colors in industrial operation as well as administrative offices. Other colors add to the conspicuity of objects for safety identification.

ATMOSPHERIC CONTAMINANTS

Many industrial activities produce atmospheric contaminants harmful to the health of personnel in varying degrees. Dusts of different types, gases, vapors, fumes, and mists are common examples of atmospheric contaminants inherent in everyday industrial activities.

Dusts

Dusts are solid particles of inorganic materials that usually are generated by grinding, drilling, crushing, or sawing, and in the handling of dust-producing materials. Generally, dusts are classified into three types: fibrosis-producing, toxic, or nuisance.

1. Fibrosis-producers are many and result in massive long-range damage to the human body. Some, like asbestos dust, may not result in cancer until 40 years after exposure.
2. Toxic dusts result in more or less instant disability. If there is the smallest doubt, the supervisor should seek the advice of the medical officer or industrial hygienist to determine whether or not a hazard exists.

Gases and Vapors

A gas is a substance that exists as a gas in its normal state at ordinary temperature and pressure. A vapor is the gas given off from a substance that normally exists as a liquid, and in some cases as a solid. Gases and vapors can be divided into four main groups acccording to their physiological effects.

Asphyxiants. Simple asphyxiants are gases and vapors that prevent a person's blood from absorbing adequate oxygen through the lungs; these gases and vapors partly replace the oxygen in the air that is breathed. Methane, other hydrocarbons, hydrogen, nitrous oxide, acetylene, and the inert gases are common simple asphyxiants. Chemical asphyxiants, such as cyanogen compounds and carbon monoxide, prevent blood from absorbing oxygen by filling the blood with excessive amounts of the asphyxiant. Carbon monoxide is a common and frequent hazard to which personnel are exposed.[2] This exposure is greatest in extremely cold weather. The tendency to sit, ride, and sleep in vehicles with the windows tightly closed and the heater and engine running increases exposure to carbon monoxide poisoning, very often a fatal dosage. Aircraft crews are also subjected to this hazard, when carbon monoxide seeps into the closed cockpit because of leaks in the exhaust system. Carbon monoxide is particularly dangerous because it is odorless.

Irritants

Irritant gases and vapors cause inflammation of the respiratory system. Complications such as pneumonia or other pulmonary diseases may result from exposure to such irritating gases and vapors as ammonia, chlorine, sulfur dioxide, hydrogen sulfide, hydrochloric acid, nitrogen oxides, and phosphorous and arsenic trichloride. Not only are the vapors of these gases hazardous as irritants and toxics, but evi-

[2]See U.S. Department of Labor pamphlet, "Carbon Monoxide," Job Health Hazard Series, OSHA 2224 (Washington, June 1975).

dence indicates that, over extended periods of time, they can be cancer producing in some cases.

Anesthetics

Anesthetic gases and vapors have a narcotic or drying-out effect on persons. The central nervous system will be dangerously depressed and respiratory failure may occur, resulting in death. Practically all narcotic gases and vapors belong to the hydrocarbon series: formaldehyde, methyl ether, ethyl ether, gasoline, naphtha, benzine, propyline, dimethyl ketone, methyl acetate, ethyl acetate, carbon tetrachloride, other halogenated hydrocarbons, and related substances.

Poison

Poisonous gases and vapors act directly on the body by injuring or destroying visceral organs, the body's blood-forming system, tissues, or bones, depending on the type of gas or vapor involved. Methyl chloride, methyl bromide, ethyl chloride, vinyl chloride,[3] ethyl bromide, certain alcohol compounds, carbon disulfide aniline, hydrogen sulfide, tetraethyl lead, and nickel carbonyl are all sources of poisonous gases or vapors.

Fumes

Fumes are particles, usually resulting from the condensation of substances that have been heated or burned, produced from chemical or metallurgical processes, molten metal, or by decomposition. The term *fume* is often misused, erroneously including gases or vapors. Fumes have an average particle size of about 0.3 microns. The fume content of the atmosphere is measured in terms of weight, in milligrams, of the fume particles per cubic meter of air. Fumes present health hazards in many ways, depending upon their source; and the fumes produced from metals such as lead,[4] zinc, cadmium, manganese, mercury,[5] and beryllium[6] are particularly harmful and may be fatal to personnel.

Mists

Mists or fogs are suspended droplets of liquid resulting from the condensation of materials from a gaseous to a liquid state, or from the breaking up of a liquid into minute drops. Mists may be droplets of liquids, or a mixture of liquids, and solid particles. Mists are measured in concentrations by weight, in milligrams, per cubic meter of air. Chromic acid and sulfuric acid may produce mists during certain operations that are especially hazardous to humans.

Carcinogens

The OSHA has issued reports on fourteen carcinogens (cancer-causing substances) found in some industries and laboratories. OSHA has promulgated a report on carcinogens under its Job Health Hazard Series.[7]

---

[3]See U.S. Department of Labor pamphlet "Vinyl Chlorate," Job Health Hazard Series, OSHA 2225 (Washington, June 1975).

[4]See U.S. Department of Labor pamphlet, "Lead," Job Health Hazard Series, OSHA 2230 (Washington, June 1975).

[5]See U.S. Department of Labor pamphlet, "Mercury," Job Health Hazard Series, OSHA 2234 (Washington, August 1975.

[6]See U.S. Department of Labor pamphlet, "Beryllium," Job Health Hazard Series, OSHA 2239 (Washington, 1975).

[7]See U.S. Department of Labor report, *Carcinogens*, OSHA 2204 (Washington, January 1975).

SKIN CONTAMINANTS

Many substances and materials used in industrial processes may cause skin irrations, or dermatitis, to personnel. Although most occupational skin afflications are truly dermatitis infections, many of the substances which cause skin irration, such as strong acids, act immediately on the skin to produce an acute effect. Other more diluted substances, such as petroleum fuels, may cause dermatitis only after repeated or prolonged exposures and contact. Certain agents, such as chromic acid, produce characteristic sores which make it easy to determine the cause of the dermatitis. Many other substances have similar skin effects, but it is difficult to isolate the cause of the skin irritations when several of the substances are used in the same operation.

Chemical Agents

The most common dermatitis-producing substances are chemical agents, including many solvents. Through direct action on the skin, these substances and compounds may cause acute or chronic skin injury, depending upon the characteristics of the agents involved in the operation.

Mechanical Agents

The presence of small cuts and scratches will allow tiny particles of wood, metal, steel wool, and other extraneous particles to enter the skin and cause irritation or inflammation. Other mechanically caused dermatitis may result from constant friction or pressure on a particular area of the skin. These are especially prevalent in machine shop operations and supervisors must be alert to prevent such hazards.

Biotic Agents

Various bacteria, fungi, ringworm, and other biological organisms may infect the skin of personnel, causing disease of the skin. Infection is caused when these organisms enter the skin through openings resulting from cuts, burns, and other injuries.

Physical Agents

Exposure of the skin to extreme heat causes burns, while continued heat exposure results in drying and cracking of the skin. Extreme cold freezes the skin causing frostbite, while skin chapping is the result of continued exposure to even moderately cold temperatures. Sources of radiant energy such as X-ray, ultraviolet, and others of this type, cause serious burns to the skin, if exposure is for a long period of time.

Insecticides

Not only are most of the insecticides and rodent poisons irritating to the skin, but they are toxic when inhaled or swallowed. Therefore, effective controls are essential where insecticides and rodenticides are used. Personnel engaged in handling these items must be competent and thoroughly trained as to toxicity of the materials, requirements of operator protection, use precautions, storage precautions, first aid measures, and protective devices and clothing. Many that are breathed in cause damage to humans and are cumulative in the system, building up over a period of years.

PHYSICAL AND BIOLOGICAL HAZARDS

The various physical and biological hazards outlined below are possible sources of injury and disease in many industrial operations.

Abnormal Temperatures and Humidity

Exposure to extreme heat or cold results in disturbances to the human circulatory system. Heat increases the cutaneous circulation of blood while cold constricts the blood vessels and causes diminished circulation. Prolonged exposure to high heat may result in heat exposure, heatstroke, or heat cramps. Very low temperatures may cause frostbite of exposed body parts. Low relative humidity tends to dry mucous membranes in the nose and throat, lowering resistance to infection; excessively high humidity interferes with the evaporation of moisture from the skin. High temperatures and humidity cause an increase in pulse rate, systolic blood pressure, and body temperature; low temperatures and high humidity undermine general vitality, and weaken resistance to respiratory diseases and rheumatic and neuralgic afflictions.

Radiant Energy

Exposure to X rays and radiation from radium and other radioactive substances may produce serious burns and cancer as well as irreparable damage to the blood and blood-forming organs. Ultraviolet rays have a physical action causing intense eye irritation and skin burns. Infrared rays act upon the eyes as heat and may cause permanent injury.

Repeated Motion, Pressure, and Shock

Operations requiring repeated exposure to vibration or shock (use of penumatic tools), may cause bursitis or vasomotor changes. Bones may be injured and muscles seriously affected. As a result, the person may be unable to perform the task through which the injury was incurred because the muscles involved fail to respond.

Infections

Various types of infections are caused from numerous operational exposures. However, prompt medical attention and intelligent control of exposure will materially reduce the possibility of complications.

Dampness

Personnel (washers, tankmen, or vatmen) exposed to excessive dampness caused by continued wetting are susceptible to neuralgia, rheumatism, and respiratory infections.

Defection Illumination

Over a long period of time, defective illumination will cause eye fatigue, errors of refraction, and other sight disorders. This is especially true when poor lighting is found in areas where very fine or detailed work is done.

NOISE HAZARDS

Noise is commonly defined as unwanted sound; also, it is referred to as sound that forces distraction, causes an unpleasant and emotional reaction, or gives a person a distinct feeling of relief upon cessation. Thus, time, place, and psychological reactions, together with the physical characteristics of sound, are contributing factors in noise. Some noises are merely annoying; others have an influence on psychological behavior. Some reduce production and efficiency in activities where speech communication is important, while more intense noises cause injuries and physical damage to the human ear—injuries that can result in permanent deafness. A particular source of noise damage to the ears of aeronautical personnel is the noise of jet and turbine aircraft engines revving up on a flight line. Methods of noise control and the reduction of its associated hazards are problems becoming more acute each year. Industry is giving increased consideration to noise control in conjunction with new developments in equipment design.

Nuisance Noise

When operations require speech communication or spoken orders, unnecessary noise can adversely affect production and efficiency, as well as safety. When noise is intense enough to interfere with normal speech, it becomes hazardous; it increases misunderstanding and requires additional energy to communicate. This accounts for the fact that most office workers prefer quiet, and that intellectual work is done better in quiet surroundings where noise will not interrupt a person's thinking.

Hazardous Noise

At high sound-pressure levels, noise becomes a physiological hazard. Just when noise becomes dangerous to personnel is difficult to evaluate, but the primary hazard is temporary or permanent hearing damage. The effect of noise on a man's hearing depends upon three main factors: intensity, frequency, and duration of exposure. In addition, the susceptibility of an individual to hearing difficulties is superimposed upon these three primary factors and makes specific prediction of dangerous noise levels uncertain. Damage risk evaluations have been devised for determining noise exposure for the average population, but personnel surveillance is necessary if specific individuals are to be protected. Medical, engineering, and safety personnel must evaluate a particular noise situation through both environmental and clincial measurements.

Measuring Noise Loudness

There is a disagreement on how to define hearing impairment. OSHA follows the generally accepted medical criterion that an average hearing level of 25 decibels (dB) at various frequencies marks the beginning of hearing handicaps. This is based on the ability to understand spoken sentences in quiet surroundings. Audible sound to the average human ear ranges from 20–20,000 hertz, or cycles per second of sound waves.

Noise, or the relative loudness of a sound heard by the ear, is measured logarithmically, not arithmetically, in decibels, a unit named after Alexander Graham Bell. Thus, 110 dB is not 10 percent greater than 100 dB, but roughly ten times as loud. A 5-dB change, from 85 to 90 dB, brings almost a threefold increase in noise level. Some common sounds and their noise levels are listed in Table 15–1. Physiological hearing damage begins at exposure to more than 85 dB, the degree depending on the length of exposure and frequency characteristics.

Noise Control Standard

Before the noise standard of 85 dB was proposed in October 1974, OSHA had a standard of 90 dB limit that it adopted in

TABLE 15-1.
Source of Sound and Noise Level

Source of Sound	*Noise Level (dB)*
Jet aircraft, 100 feet away	140
Rock music, amplified	110
Riveter	95
Busy street traffic	80
Quiet radio in home	40
Whisper	25
Rustle of leaves	10

1971 as a standard developed under the Walsh-Healey Public Contracts Acts. But in August 1972 NIOSH sent OSHA a criteria document based on new research into noise hazards. NIOSH, too, pointed out a need for an 85 dB limit, recommending that all newly designed work places be required to meet this limit.[8] Table 15–2 gives the permissible noise exposure for occupational noise allowed by OSHA.

As always, where OSHA health standards are concerned, one of the most controversial parts is the requirement for using engineering controls, instead of personal protective equipment, as the first line of defense against noise. Engineering controls quiet noise at its source through enclosing a machine or redesigning equipment. Administrative control involves management efforts to reduce individual exposures by rotating workers out of the high-noise areas or by shutting down machines for a time. The proposal requires use of feasible engineering and administrative control to bring noise exposures below 90 dB. Even if these controls will not reduce noise below 90 dB limit, they must be used to the extent feasible and supplemented with hearing protection.

TABLE 15-2.
Permissible Noise Exposures for Occupational Noise Allowed by OSHA

Duration Per Day (Hr)	*Sound Level in dB (A)*
8	90
6	92
4	95
3	97
2	100
1.5	102
1	105
0.5	110
0.25 or less	115

[8]See George Clark, "The Noise Control Controversy," in *Job Safety and Health* (Washington: U.S. Department of Labor, OSHA, November 1975), pp. 4–10.

Noise Control

When a noise problem is examined, three factors must be studied to develop corrective measures: the source of noise (type of equipment creating noise); path of sound (areas through which the noise passes); and the receivers, the persons exposed to and affected by the noise through damage to hearing, speech interference, or annoyance. In order to develop a solution to the noise problem, a combination of actions must be accomplished to make the noise acceptable and safe.

Noise Sources. Any vibrating object will radiate sound into the air. The amount of sound depends on the amplitude of vibration of each moving part, the area of each vibrating part, and the time pattern of the vibration.

Paths of Sounds. The attentuation of sound passing through free space is generally considered to result in a decrease of 6 dBs at each doubling of distance from the source. This axiom makes it possible to determine the decibel reading at a noise source when a reading has been taken at any distance. Many factors affect the attenuation of sound in the atmosphere. Wind, temperature, sound reflection, terrain, and structural conditions all have an important bearing on sound dilution. The problem of thinning low frequency sound before it reaches the receiver is usually very costly. A good rule to remember is that the lower the frequency, the greater the mass required to dilute.

Transmission loss is the important factor in the selection of sound-diluting materials. In selecting sound-thinning materials, therefore, it is necessary to measure the sound and identify the frequencies at which the greatest sound-pressure level exists. Selection is based upon the minimum transmission loss necessary.

Receivers. Noise affects individuals in different ways. For example, to the concertgoer, an orchestra makes pleasant listening; while to someone trying to rest, the orchestra may be disturbing, or just plain noisy. Annoyance by sound prompts people to get away from the source as quickly as possible. This results in their doing a job without direct and positive attention or they may react through their other senses. Noise also affects speech communications. The important range for speech commmunication is 600 to 4,800 cycles per second. When the average sound level exceeds 75 decibels, telephone communication becomes difficult or impossible. In addition to disturbing and affecting working conditions, noise in excess of 90 decibels on a continuous basis may cause gradual to rapid loss of hearing (as the intensity increases) among exposed personnel.

Noise-Corrective Measures

If a study of a noise problem reveals that it must be stopped in the interest of safety, appropriate measures are taken to reduce or eliminate the objectionable sounds. Noise may be eliminated at its source by isolating the noise producing operation, by installing soundproof insulation, by using personnel protective devices, or by other means that will effectively reduce the noise hazard. Personnel on duty in unusually noisy activities should wear fitted ear defenders to guard against hearing loss that usually results from continuous exposure to high intensity sound.

RADIOLOGICAL SAFETY

As use of atomic power and nuclear weapons increases, the possibility of personnel coming in contact with the various forms of radioactivity increases. Because of the inherent danger coincidental with the use, handling, safekeeping, and disposal of radioactive materials, atomic power and nuclear weapons are hazards to health unless strict precautionary measures are observed.

Sources of Radiation

Some industrial and nuclear power generating personnel may encounter radiation from many sources on an installation—in reactors, particle accelerators, radioactive isoptes (liquids and solids), diagnostic and therapeutic X-ray machines, X-ray machines used for industrial radiography, radioactive sources used for irradiation of other materials, electronic equipment, and all forms of radioactive wastes. Because radiation sources are found almost anywhere, safety personnel must constantly be alert for possible undetected or unknown sources around the unit or activity.

Types of Radiation

Several types of radiation cause serious injury to personnel who are exposed in excess of recommended levels. The types of radiation most often encountered are

X-rays and gamma rays and alpha and beta particles. Gamma and X-rays, which can travel long distances and penetrate relatively thick materials, present both internal and external hazards to exposed personnel. Unless present in very large quantities, alpha and beta particles present primarily an internal hazard. These particles may be inhaled, ingested, or absorbed into the body where they cause damage to various organs, and ultimately result in disease or death. In order to adequately protect personnel from radiation hazards, it is necessary to guard against contamination of the person's body, clothing, and surrounding equipment and materials.

Monitoring Personnel

Personnel constantly exposed to radiation must be carefully monitored. For positive radiation identification and safety, all personnel who are routinely exposed to radiation must wear film badges. Other approved dosimeters are available. The type of dosimeter used is determined by the nature and intensity of the radiation to which personnel are exposed.

Exposure of Personnel to Microwave Energy

Under uniform states of radiation, where the direction of radiation is fixed or moves in a uniform repetitive manner (such as occurs during scanning by acquisition radar), or remains constant for long periods of time, the body can come into equilibrium with the average microwave power field.

Exposure of personnel to average incident power densities up to 10 milliwatts per square centimeter may be permitted. Use of this value as a permissible exposure limit for humans provides a conservative safety factor and is substantially below the value at which biologically significant heating effects occur. This criterion is not directly applicable to nonuniform, transient conditions, for example, energy fields created by tracking radars.

Education

Proper indoctrination of all personnel exposed to health hazards is absolutely necessary if injuries and illnesses are to be kept as low as possible. Each person must be fully informed of the safe practices involved in his job, the nature of the hazardous substances to which he will be exposed, and the protective measures that have been taken for his personal safety.

Personal Hygiene. Personal cleanliness is most essential where health hazards exist, particularly in operations involving possible skin contamination. Personnel must be informed of the need for personal cleanliness and for changing soiled clothing frequently, and of the possible results from failure to follow good hygienic practices. In order to encourage and facilitate personal cleanliness, suitable washrooms, showers, and locker rooms should be made available to personnel involved in operations that produce health hazards.

Good Housekeeping. Housekeeping must be kept at the highest possible level in areas where health hazards are present. Particular caution will be taken to prevent unnecessary accumulations, spillage, dispersion, evaporation, or generation of hazardous materials. Spills and other uncontrolled contaminations are cleaned up immediately, and suitable receptacles are provided for the disposal of waste products.

Substitution

The most effective means of controlling a health hazard is to substitute a nonhazardous material for a harmful type. Complete substitution will reduce the hazard. When a substitution can be made, it is necessary to ensure that another more serious hazard is not created by the new material, for example, substitution of a nonirritating but highly flammable substance in an engine maintenance operation in place of a nonflammable minor skin irritant.

Isolation

Whenever practical, processes creating health hazards will be isolated as completely as possible. Physical isolation through selected location will eliminate hazards to personnel working nearby. Further isolation of the hazardous substance within the operation may be accomplished by the use of protective shields, barriers, and similar devices. In general, every effort will be made to keep the harmful substances as confined as practical, to minimize and limit the extent of contamination. In some instances, effective isolation is accomplished by using mechanical handling or remote control devices that will prevent operators from contacting any hazardous material. The devices used for handling radioactive materials are good examples of safe remote control equipment.

Process Modifications

Partial or complete hazard elimination may be accomplished by changing or revising a particular process to remove unnecessary handling operations, improve control of dangerous materials, and establish safe working procedures. In most cases, it will be found that the safest procedure is also the most efficient.

Ventilation

Suitable and adequate ventilation is extremely important to protect personnel in operations where harmful dusts, gases, vapors, fumes, and mists may be produced. In many cases, general or ordinary exhaust systems will not satisfactorily remove harzardous polluted air from an operation. For this reason, local, properly designed exhaust systems are provided by qualified personnel when deemed necessary. These systems are extremely desirable because they provide immediate removal of airborne contaminants at the point of generation, preventing their diffusion into the surrounding atmosphere.

1. When new construction is planned, careful consideration must be given to adequate ventilation requirements. This consideration must encompass the planned use of the construction and what burdens the planned use will place on ventilation systems to be incorporated. In these cases building codes should be consulted and their recommendations incorporated into the design criteria. In older construction, considered adequate at the time of construction, ventilation conditions may exist that were in the past either not recognized or were tolerated. These conditions must be found and isolated through the methods indicated above.
2. An example of one of these techniques, substitution, may be the use of a less harmful material such as a nonexplosive, nontoxic solvent in the place of petroleum or carbon tetrachloride solvents that are explosive in one case and toxic in the other. Consideration and study of the particular problem will usually offer a less hazardous solution.

Adequate Cooling and Heating

The greatest productivity and optimum safety of workers is found to be in an ambient temperature of 72°F. Temperatures should be kept under 80°F and never

TABLE 15–3.
Maximum Exposure Table

Body-Freezing Temperatures in Fahrenheit

Less Than 1 Minute Exposure Required to Freeze:	15 Minutes Exposure to Freeze:
Wind 20 mph, temp. 32 below	Wind 10 mph, temp. 16 below
Wind 30 mph, temp. 25 below	Wind 20 mph, temp. 5 below
Wind 40 mph, temp. 20 below	Wind 30 mph, temp. 1 above
	Wind 40 mph, temp. 5 above
Less Than 2 Minutes Exposure Required To Freeze:	25 Minutes Exposure To Freeze:
Wind 10 mph, temp. 37 below	Wind 10 mph, temp. 17 below
Wind 20 mph, temp. 27 below	Wind 20 mph, temp. 5 below
Wind 30 mph, temp. 17 below	Wind 30 mph, temp. 1 above
Wind 40 mph, temp. 15 below	Wind 40 mph, temp. 5 above
5 Minutes Exposure To Freeze:	1 Hour Exposure To Freeze:
Wind 10 mph, temp. 36 below	Wind 10 mph, temp. 1 above
Wind 20 mph, temp. 20 below	Wind 20 mph, temp. 12 above
Wind 30 mph, temp. 12 below	Wind 30 mph, temp. 16 above
Wind 40 mph, temp. 6 below	

exceed 86°F for prolonged exposure. Wet bulb temperatures of 90°F and above necessitate very short exposures and the use of protective devices.

At the other extreme, personnel working on the outside in subfreezing temperatures must be required to wear adequate protective clothing. Table 15–3 illustrates the relatively short periods of time in which the human body or its extremities can freeze. Personnel, such as firemen, linemen, air crewmen, and so on must be extremely careful to dress properly against such cold exposure.

Illumination, Vision, and Color

Adequate lighting and the ability to see certainly are two of the most effective measures available to avoid accidents. It has been estimated that 15 to 25 percent of all industrial accidents have been caused by poor lighting.

Lighting standards for operating vary considerably. The safety engineer will find it convenient to measure the adequacy of lighting in doubtful areas. This measurement may be made through the use of a light meter, which gives a direct reading of the foot-candles of light reaching a work surface. Specific recommended lighting intensities may be found in publications of the American Standards Association and the Illuminating Engineering Society. Some common areas with minimum foot-candles required for lighting are listed in Table 15–4.

It would seem needless to add that to aid in effective vision, glare should be avoided. Light reflected from working surfaces not only blinds workers to hazards on the work area but protracted glare is injurious to the eyes and nervous system. All illumination must be planned in order to keep glare, both direct and reflected, to a minimum. Shadow is also a defect that may cover hazardous locations or interfere with visibility at the work area.

Perception and visibility are improved by the use of suitable colors. It has been found that different colors have strong effects psychologically on human beings. Green and blue tints give a cool effect.

TABLE 15–4.
Recommended Range of Illuminance

Type of Activity or Area	*Foot-Candles (Lux)*
Production manufacturing and repairs	100
Inspection of parts	200
Office areas	70–100
Accounting areas	150
Stairways, halls, washrooms and other service areas	30
Storage rooms, inactive	5
Storage rooms, active	10
Testing, general	50
Testing, fine	200
Wood shops, rough work	30
Wood shops, fine work	100

Ivory and cream are warm colors while white ceilings give maximum brightness.

Personal Protective Equipment

When other means of hazard control fail to provide complete protection to personnel, adequate protective clothing and equipment are worn. These items are carefully selected on the basis of a study of the hazards from which protection is desired and the specifications pertaining to the specific items of procurable clothing and equipment.

Limiting Exposure

When control methods do not prove totally effective, the length of time a person will be exposed to the hazard must be decreased according to allowable concentrations of the hazardous material. In such cases, it is essential that all unnecessary or undue exposure be avoided.

PERSONAL PROTECTIVE EQUIPMENT

Certain activities, particularly those involving specialized industrial operations, present hazards that are difficult to completely eliminate or adequately safeguard. Naturally, the best defense against personnel injuries is to design and operate processes so that complete control is assured where hazards are involved, thus making the hazards potential rather than actual.

When a hazard still exists after all practical engineering revisions have been made, it is essential that personnel be given further protection through the use of personal protective equipment and clothing. The type of protective equipment or clothing needed for a particular operation depends on the nature of the hazards involved. Often, it is necessary for qualified personnel to use detection and measurement devices to determine the nature of the hazards, so that proper protective equipment can be selected.

Personal protective equipment is not considered an adequate substitute for the elimination of unsafe acts and conditions, but rather a supplementary safety measure when required by the seriousness of the hazards involved in an operation. When a hazard exists or is likely to exist despite the use of normal corrective or control measures, safety equipment and clothing are used. When job requirements specify the wearing of protective apparel and devices, this requirement becomes both a part of safety regulations and a condition of employment. In addition, every effort will be made to impress upon workers the value of personal protective clothing and equipment so they will want to wear it for their own protection and welfare. When it has been designated as a requirement, the wearing of protective clothing and equipment in use and in equipment pools or tool cribs are inspected periodically to determine the serviceability of the equipment.

Items in need of repair or replacement are taken out of service or storage and replaced or repaired immediately.

Each physical operation should be analyzed by safety or other technically qualified personnel to predetermine inherent and man-made hazards. Standing operating procedures reflect the results of such operating analysis by including the requirement for protective clothing and equipment (including safety spectacles, prescription or plain) to prevent as much as possible, injury to the head and body, particularly the hands, respiratory system, face, and eyes. Continuous studies will be made leading to the designation of shops or segments thereof as eye hazardous areas. All workmen and other personnel, including visitors, will be required to wear approved eye protection at all times within such areas. Items of protective clothing and equipment will be required and worn where:

1. They are necessary to protect personnel from occupational diseases, trauma, and so on.
2. They are necessary for the safe performance of the task, and protection of other people, government equipment, material, or property.

Face and Eye Protection

Devices to prevent injury to the eyes, or to the face, constitute a major category of personal protective equipment. This equipment is intended to guard against flying particles, dusts, hot metal splashes, splashing chemicals, or injurious light or heat rays. Each eye or face-and-eye protector is designed for a particular hazard. When a choice of protector is given, the kind and degree of hazard and the degree of protection required should govern the selection. When the degree of protection is not an important issue, workers' comfort may be a deciding factor. Table 15–5 may be used as a guide for selection of suitable equipment. Numerous types and styles of eye and face-and-eye protection equipment have been developed to meet the demands for protection against a variety of hazards.

Lenses

Lenses for eye protection constitute the most important part of the protectors. Most types of goggles and spectacles employ glass lenses although plastics may be and are used. Lenses should be made of a good grade of optical glass, and heat-treated to resist impact. Heat-treating toughens the lenses by placing the outer surfaces of the lenses under compression, while the inner part remains under tension. Clear or filter type lenses may be used. Clear lenses are intended to provide protection against flying objects; filter lenses provide protection against glare or injurious radiation in addition to flying objects. Either may be ground for prescription lenses. They should be made to meet specific requirements covering prismatic and refractive power, haze, radiant-energy transmission, and breaking strength. For plastic lenses, requirements for penetration resistance and nonflammability must be met. Table 15–6 is a guide for the selection of the proper shade number of filter lenses for goggles or window plates for helmets used in welding. It is essential that eye protector lenses be cleaned and disinfected before they are issued to another person. Pitted lenses must be replaced.

Ear Protection

When industrial noise is of such intensity that it might be harmful to hearing, good

TABLE 15–5.
Selection of Eye and Face-and-Eye Protective Devices

Hazard involved	*Part To Be Protected*	*Permissible Protective Devices*
Relatively large flying objects	Eyes, face	Goggles (chippers' eyecup, plastic eyeshield, foundrymen's). Spectacles (metal or plastic frame, plastic eyeshield). Face shields.
Dust and small flying particles	Eyes, face	Goggles (chippers' or dust eyecup, plastic eyeshield, foundrymen's). Spectacles (metal or plastic frame, plastic eyeshield). Face shields.
Dust and wind	Eyes	Goggles (dust eyecup, plastic eyeshield). Spectacles (metal or plastic frame, plastic eyeshield).
Molten metal	Eyes, face	Goggles (eyecup, plastic eyeshield, foundrymen's). Spectacles (metal or plastic frame, plastic eyeshield). Face shields.
Gases, fumes, and smoke	Eyes, face	Goggles (flexible fitting, plastic eyeshield).
Liquids	Eyes, face	Goggles (flexible fitting, plastic eyeshield). Face shields.
Reflected light or glare	Eyes	Goggles (plastic eyeshield). Spectacles (metal or plastic frame, plastic eyeshield).
Injurious radiant energy (moderate)	Eyes	Goggles (welders' and cutters' eyecup). Helmets. Hand shields. Face shields (with crown and chin protectors).
Injurious radiant energy (intense)	Eyes, face	Helmets (with metal or plastic frame eye protection). Hand shield (with metal or plastic frame eye protection).

engineering practices dictate that every effort should be made to reduce the noise at its source. This may involve isolation of the noise-producing machine or process, enclosure to baffle the noise, the use of sound absorptive materials to absorb the noise, or perhaps the substitution of a less noisy process. When such a solution is not possible or practicable, the wearing of ear protectors should be required. There are three types of ear protectors—inserts or plugs, muffs, and helmets.

Foot Protection

Personal protective equipment to shield the feet from injury is the accepted method of protection against injuries from heavy falling objects, against crushing from rolling objects, or against lacerations from edged tools. Protective footwear also is used against the hazards of molten metal or electricity. Foot protective devices fall into two main classes—safety shoes and foot guards.

Safety Shoes

Safety-toe Shoes. These are the best known of all safety shoes. In fact, they usually are referred to as safety shoes. They are intended to provide protection to the toes from an impact or crushing force by use of a steel toebox or its equivalent. The toebox is incorporated into the shoe during construction and is an integral part of the

TABLE 15–6.
Guide for Selection Numbers of Filter Lenses for Goggles

Welding Operation	*Suggested Shade Number*
Shielded metal-arc welding:	
1/16-, 3/32-, 1/8-, 5/32-inch electrodes	10
Inert-gas metal-arc welding (nonferrous):	
1/16-, 3/32-, 1/8-, 5/32-inch electrodes	11
Inert-gas metal-arc welding (ferrous):	
1/16-, 3/32-, 1/8-, 5/32-inch electrodes	12
Shielded metal-arc welding:	
3/16-, 7/32-, 1/4-inch electrodes	12
5/16-, 3/8-inch electrodes	14
Atomic hydrogen welding	10–14
Carbon-arc welding	14
Soldering	2
Torch brazing	3 or 4
Light cutting, up to 1 inch	3 or 4
Medium cutting, 1 inch to 6 inches	4 or 5
Heavy cutting, over 6 inches	5 or 6
Gas welding (light), up to 1/8-inch	4 or 5
Gas welding (medium), 1/8-inch to 1/2-inch	5 or 6
Gas welding (heavy), over 1/2-inch	6 or 8

NOTE: In gas welding or oxygen cutting, where the torch produces a high yellow light, it is desirable to use a filter or lens that absorbs the yellow or sodium line in the visible light of the operation.

shoe. These shoes are used wherever there is a hazard from falling or rolling objects, including hand or power truck wheels. They are particularly useful in storage and warehousing operations, and in heavy objects manufacturing; in construction work they offer protection against edged tools (for example, axes and picks). The steel toebox not only protects the toes, but also provides some protection to the instep if the falling object is large enough to hit the instep and the toes. They are made in a variety of styles and for every kind of job, including office work.

Conductive Shoes. This type of shoe is designed to dissipate static electricity accumulating in the body of the wearer and to avoid creating static sparks that might ignite explosive gases or materials. They are effective only when the floors on which the person walks also are conductive and grounded. They should never be worn outdoors because dirt impairs their effectiveness. Conductive shoes are used in hazardous locations (for example, hospital operating rooms, certain operations in the manufacture of explosive or chemicals, or where such materials are processed or used) where explosive concentrations of gases or hazardous liquids or solids might be ignited by a static spark.

Explosives-operations (nonsparking) Shoes. The difference between explosives-operations shoes and conductive shoes is that the heels and soles of nonsparking shoes are not made of conductive rubber. They are used in hazardous locations where the floors are not conductive and grounded (this is necessary for conductive shoes). They also are used in the manufacture of certain explosive compounds or for cleaning tanks that have held gasoline or volatile hydrocarbons.

Electrical-hazard Shoes. These shoes are intended to minimize hazards due to contacts with electrical current, where the path of the current would be from the point of contact to the ground. They are also intended to provide protection to the toes from an impact force. They are used by persons who work on line electrical cicuits or on circuits that may suddenly become alive.

Foundry (molders) Shoes. The use of foundry shoes is intended to provide protection to the feet for operations in which snug ankle fit, closed upper construction, and speed and ease of removal are the functional protective criteria. They are used where there is a hazard from splashing metal, such as pouring molten metals in foundry operations.

Foot Guards

In addition to the basic types of safety shoes, a number of other types of foot guards are in general use.

Metal Foot Guards. Metal foot guards are aluminum alloy or galvanized steel coverings that are attached to the shoes temporarily by means of a heel strap. They protect not only the toes but also the instep against falling or rolling objects.

Foot and Shin Guards. Where there is a hazard to the shin as well as the foot, a combination foot and shin guard is available. The shin guard is made of the same material as the foot guard, is hinged to it, and held in place by straps around the leg. These guards are used where a flying particle hazard exists (breaking up concrete with a jackhammer).

Wooden-soled Sandals. Strap-on sandals, consisting of a wooden sole held in place by straps over the shoes, are used as protection against heat. They also are used where there may be a hazard from acids, caustics, or hot water, or where sharp objects are likely to be encountered under foot.

Gloves and Mittens

Gloves and mittens are intended to provide protection to the fingers, hands, and sometimes the wrists and forearms. Where finger dexterity is necessary, such as picking up small sharp objects or handling certain materials, gloves usually are used; where finger dexterity is not necessary, mittens may be used. Mittens are also made with separate coverings for the thumb, index finger, or other fingers. Gloves and mittens should be worn if there is danger of them being caught in moving machinery. A brief description of the principal types of gloves and mittens follows:

Abrasive and Cut Protection

Literally hundreds of kinds of gloves and mittens are used for general-duty work. Some have band cuffs, others have gauntlet cuffs, still others have elbow-length cuffs. There are those that have reinforced hand pads or finger tips for greater serviceability, others are made of waterproof fabrics, and still others are made of antislip materials for better handling of specific objects. These types of gloves may be classed roughly as light duty or heavy duty. For protection against impact or pinching, gloves may be reinforced with steel fingercaps. Gloves with steel staples for reinforcing are made available as protection against cuts or blows from edge tools.

Flame and Heat Protection. Gloves and mittens are available for protection against flame and heat (furnace operations, welding, foundry work, or other occupations requiring the handling of hot metals or other substances).

Chemical Protection. Gloves for protection against chemicals are made of materials impervious to liquids and fine dusts to protect against irritating, corrosive, or defatting substances. No one type of glove is best for all possible hazards; their selection should be related to a particular acid, solvent, caustic oil, or chemical involved.

Electrical Protection. Rubber gloves are used by utility workers who must work with energized circuits. They are made with long cuffs to protect the hands and wrists from burns and shocks. Rubber gloves should be able to resist 10,000 volts for 3 minutes and should be inspected frequently for physical defects by trapping air inside the glove. They should be tested electrically at intervals to assure that they have not lost their insulating quality. Rubber or plastic gloves, used for protection against liquids, should not be confused with gloves used for electrical protection.

Radiation. Gloves providing protection against X-ray and other radiation are used by medical, industrial, and radiochemical laboratory technicians. They are made of leather or rubber that has been impregnated with lead.

Protector Materials. Materials from which gloves and mittens, hand pads, or sleeves are made are in accordance with the service they are expected to give. Preference may determine what materials are used. Table 15–7 shows some of the materials that are in general use.

TABLE 15–7.
Hazards Associated with Types of Materials

Hazard	*Materials*
Heat	Asbestos or leather aluminized fabric, glass fiber insulation.
Flame	Asbestos, leather, fire-resistant duck, aluminized fabric, glass fiber insulation.
Hot metal splashes, sparks	Asbestos, fire-resistant duck, leather, aluminized fabric.
Electricity	Rubber.
Moisture and water	Rubber, oiled fabric, plastic, coated glass fiber.
Mild acids and alkalis	Rubber, plastic, synthetic fabric, coated glass fiber.
Strong acids and alkalis	Natural rubber, plastic.
Oil and organic solvents	Synthetic rubber, plastic, coated glass fiber.
Flying chips, mild impact	Leather, fabric.
Severe blows, sharp tools	Wire mesh, reinforced leather.
Gamma ray, X ray	Leaded rubber, leaded leather.

Body and Leg Protection

Body and leg protective devices are used for a variety of purposes—for protection against acids and caustic burns, heat and flame, dermatitis, electric shock, impact, and cut hazards. Protectors are worn in various combinations, depending upon the hazards involved. Care must be taken to see that they do not create additional hazards. Loose aprons should not be worn about revolving or reciprocating machinery; the upper garment should always overhang the lower garment when used to protect against dangerous liquids, to prevent the liquid from dribbling inside the clothing; and coats or aprons should be removed before gloves when caustic or corrosive materials have been handled.

HEALTH HAZARD DETECTION DEVICES

Various detection services are commonly used to aid personnel in the detection of hazardous substances, such as flammable gases and vapors in the atmosphere, before they can cause injury or damage to installations or personnel. The following paragraphs describe in detail some of the more frequently used health hazard detection devices.

Combustible Gas Indicators and Alarms

The combustible gas indicator is used to test the atmosphere for concentrations of flammable gases or vapors. This instrument, calibrated for one or more known types of gases, vapors, or mixtures, makes quantitative estimates of the combustible gas present in any given atmosphere. Several different types of indicators are available for use where particular gases and vapors are involved. The indicator is enclosed in a conveniently carried unit. There is an aspirator bulb to draw air into the instrument through a rubber tube, and a meter by which the gas content of the air can be read directly in percentage of the lower explosive limit.

The instrument actually burns the air sample and measures the change in electrical resistance. This is accomplished by the air being drawn over a heated detector filament that is part of a stabilized electrical bridge circuit. Within the unit, the filament is heated by dry cell batteries. As an air sample is taken, the combustible gases or vapors being tested contact the heated surface of the detector filament and, by their burning, raise the normal filament temperature. Consequently, the electrical resistance of the circuit increases in direct proportion to the quantity of the flammable gases or vapors in the sample. This unbalances the bridge circuit and causes a pointer on a calibrated scale to move along the scale face, giving a direct reading of the flammable gas content in a percentage of the lower explosive limit.

Other combustible gas indicators, which use the Wheatstone Bridge principle, are available for use. They measure current flow due to changed resistance caused by the ignition of flammable vapors on the surface of a platinum resistor. The indicators may be calibrated on an original concentration of hexane; therefore, they must be recalibrated when used with other flammable vapors. Small combustible gas indicators are generally used in low concentrations of explosive materials, while larger instruments are available for use in dual ranges.

Combustible gas alarms are used to sample air continuously in any location. These alarms will operate a visual or audible warning signal, or both, if the combustible contents of the atmosphere reach a predetermined point of saturation. The principle of detection used on alarm systems is similar to that of portable indicators. These alarm systems may be used to operate mechanical relays, such as controls that operate ventilating systems at the generation points of combustible gases and vapors.

Carbon Monoxide Indicators

The *hand-operated carbon monoxide indicator* is used to detect the presence and determine the quantity of carbon monoxide present in the atmosphere. This instrument is particularly useful in making surveys of maintenance shops, motor vehicles, aircraft, and industrial operations where carbon monoxide may be produced in small quantities. When internal combustion engines are operated indoors, the area must be carefully monitored for carbon monoxide gas. The instrument is enclosed in a carrying case and carried from the shoulder. This allows its pump crank handle to be operable. The crank operates a small pump which sucks in the air to be tested. A built-in pressure regulator automatically maintains the proper sample flow, indicated on a pressure gauge visible to the operator. A calibrated meter is also provided for the direct reading of the percentage of carbon monoxide present in the air.

A carbon monoxide alarm is available for continuous sampling of the air. It is designed to give an audible and visual signal when the concentration of carbon monoxide reaches a predetermined setting. The alarm may be designed to operate relays controlling ventilation motors, for example, when concentrations reach a danger point, and to stop them when the atmosphere is again at a safe level.

Simple, effective *colorimetric detectors* are available for measuring carbon monoxide concentration in the atmosphere. This gas reacts chemically with substances, such as iodine pentoside or palladium chloride, producing a change in color. A colorimetric chart is provided for comparing the color produced with that on the chart, thus providing an accurate estimate of the carbon monoxide present in the air.

Oxygen Deficiency Indicator

This indicator is a modification of the flame safety lamp used to test atmosphere suspected of being deficient of oxygen. Normally, it will be used to test suspected atmospheres from an external source. Self-contained oxygen-supplying or airline types of respirators are worn when entering areas suspected of being oxygen deficient.

Special Sampling, Detection, and Measuring Devices

These devices usually require specially trained personnel to operate them. They are available for sampling specific or nonspecific atmospheric contaminants.

Midget Impinger. The standard size and midget impingers used for collecting dust, chromic acid, lead, or other metal oxides are examples of special sampling devices. An impinger consists of a collection flask connected to a hand- or motor-driven pump. Air containing the contaminant is pumped into the flask at a known rate and for a prescribed period of time. The content of the flask is then forwarded to the appropriate laboratory for analysis.

Electrostatic Dust and Fume Sampler. This instrument is used for taking quantitative samplings of dust, fumes, and mists, particularly in operations where lead, zinc, cadmium, manganese, and chromium are heated. The particles are drawn into a cylinder where they can be used for determination by weight, count, or chemical analysis in the laboratory. Depositing in the cylinder is caused by an arrangement for preionization of the particles and electrostatic precipitation on the wall of the collecting cylinder.

Chlorinated Hydrocarbons Sampling. Air can be sampled in areas when chlorinated hydrocarbons are used. The air sample is drawn into an electric furnace where chlorinated organic vapors are decomposed and the resulting hydrogen chloride is absorbed in an alkaline solution. Final determination of the concentration present in the atmosphere is made by laboratory analysis.

Electronic Mercury Vapor Detector. The principle of this detector is based on the fact that ultraviolet light scatters when it passes through a mercury-containing atmosphere. The detector is made with a phototube at one end of a chamber and the source of ultraviolet light at the other. A certain current output of the photocell indicates that the air is free of mercury. A decrease in the current output, with all other conditions remaining constant, indicates that mercury vapor is present and is intercepting and scattering the light. This current decrease is a measure of the mercury vapor present.

Radiac Equipment. Since radiation cannot be detected by any of the human senses, we must depend upon instruments to warn us of the presence of radioactivity. The radiac (radioactivity detection, indication, and computation) instruments detect the interaction of radiation with some type of matter. Although most radiac instruments are designed to count pulses (voltage drop), those designed to detect beta and gamma radiation are calibrated in roentgens per hours or milliroentgens per hour. Thus, an average dose is attributed to each pulse.

Sling Psychrometer. Sling psychrometers are used in health studies where the relative humidity has a direct or indirect bearing on the overall problem. They are useful in determining humidity control factors in areas where static electricity creates fire or explosion hazards.

Noise Measurement Devices. Sound-level meters and frequency analyzers are used to study the quantity and quality of any major noise source that may present hazards to personnel. Frequency analyzers measure the intensity of sound in the octave bands of the audible spectrum.

Light Meters. Light meters, based on the standard international candle unit of measure, are used to measure illumination levels of activities where adequate lighting is necessary to prevent accidents, to make work conditions less hazardous to personnel, and to assure adequate illumination.

Summary

Control of the health and physical environment is the responsibility of management, and the organization and administration of every safety program must be predicated on the fact that management has provided, as near as possible, an environment that is free from health and physical hazards. Safe, healthful working conditions are essential to accident-free organization operations. This is particularly true of industrial activities where satisfactory conditions contribute materially to increased worker efficiency and safety. All health and physical hazards are subject to appropriate and effective control measures in order to minimize the dangers of disease and injury to personnel.

Supervisors must ensure that adequate programs exist in education of personnel to job hazards; substitution of nonhazardous material for harmful material; isolation of hazardous operations; modifications; adequate ventilation and illumination; personnel protective equipment; limiting exposure time to hazards, and medical examinations. These are specific control measures that have been developed to lessen health and physical hazards to which individuals are exposed.

Supervisors must be alert that personal protective clothing and equipment, particularly respirators, can never be relied on in lieu of a practicable means of eliminating a hazard. However, in a wide variety of work activities, personal protective clothing and equipment of some kind is necessary. A great variety of well-designed and well-made equipment is commercially available. In every instance, the hazard and exposure must be carefully appraised and the correct protective clothing and equipment provided. Full cooperation in wearing the items of clothing and equipment is essential. The best way to obtain this cooperation is to get active participation in all steps of the program. Particular attention should be given to the promotion of knowledge and understanding of the hazards involved and of the proper control measures required. Only knowledgeable supervisors can obtain this cooperation by demonstrating they are aware of and concerned about potential hazards.

Questions

1. An understanding of the fundamentals of industrial hygiene and environmental conditions is only important to occupational health and safety professionals. Comment.
2. What part of the OSHA standards define OSHA requirements for ventilation systems? Note: You will need to seek this information from the 29 CFR Part 1910 General Industry Safety and Health Standards.
3. What are the four fundamental factors that determine the visibility of objects?
4. List five kinds of atmospheric contaminants that are present in everyday industrial activities.
5. Gases and vapors can be divided into four various groups, based on their physiological effects. What are they?
6. What are carcinogens?
7. What are some common materials used in industrial processes that cause skin irritation and/or infection?
8. What is the difference between sound and noise?
9. Distinguish between engineering control and administrative control of noise according to OSHA health standards.
10. When examining a noise problem, what three factors must be studied to develop corrective action?
11. Occupational noise level exposure regulations are set forth in Title 29 CFR 1910.95 of the OSHAct. What is the current permissible noise exposure level for an eight-hour work day?
12. What are some of the ways to reduce noise levels to which workers may be exposed?

13. List some of the typical personal protection equipment that is used in the metalworking industries.

14. List and describe some of the most frequently used health hazard detection devices.

Bibliography

Beaulieu, Harry J., and Buckan, Roy M. *Quantitative Industrial Hygiene.* New York: Garland, 1981.

Bockrath, Joseph T. *Concepts of Environmental Law for Managers, Scientists and Engineers.* New York: McGraw-Hill, 1977.

Chanlett, Emil, T. *Environmental Protection.* 2nd ed. New York: McGraw-Hill, 1979.

Cunniff, P. F. *Environmental Noise Pollution.* New York: John Wiley and Sons, 1977.

Cralley, Lester, et al. *Industrial Hygiene and Toxicology: Theory and Rationale of Industrial Practice.* Vol. 3. New York: John Wiley and Sons, 1979.

Doelle, Leslie L. *Environmental Acoustics.* New York: McGraw-Hill, 1972.

Eckenfleder, W. W., Jr. *Industrial Water Pollution Center.* New York: McGraw-Hill, 1966.

Egan, M. D. *Concepts in Architectural Acoustics.* New York: McGraw-Hill, 1972.

Flynn, John E., and Segil, Arthur W. *Coordinated Environmental Systems.* New York: Van Nostrand Rheinhold, 1970.

General Electric Co. *Industrial Lighting: Rules of Thumb.* Cleveland, Ohio: Lighting Institute, Rev. June 1971.

———. *Industrial Lighting.* TP-108R, Lamp Products Division. Cleveland, Ohio, March 1977.

———. *Light and Color.* TP-119, Lighting Business Group. Cleveland, Ohio, February 1978.

Hart, A. W. *Industrial Hygiene.* Englewood Cliffs, N.J.: Prentice-Hall, 1976.

Koren, Herman. *Handbook of Environmental Health and Safety: Principles and Practices.* 2 pts. Elmsford, N.Y.: Pergamon Press, 1980.

Lund, H. F. *Industrial Pollution Control Handbook.* New York: McGraw-Hill, 1970.

Magrab, E. B. *Environmental Noise Control.* New York: John Wiley and Sons, 1979.

Marsh, W. A. *Environmental Analysis: For Land Use and Site Planning.* New York: McGraw Hill, 1977.

Mass, R. B. "Industrial Noise and Hearing Conservation." In *Handbook of Clinical Audiology.* Edited by J. Katz. Baltimore: William and Williams, 1978.

McKinney, James D. *The Chemistry of Environmental Agents as Potential Human Hazards.* Woburn, Mass.: Ann Arbor Science, 1981.

Miller, Marshall L. ed. *Occupational Health and Safety Regulations.* Rockville, Md. Govt. Inst., 1980.

Newton, David F. *Elements of Environmental Health.* Columbus, Ohio: Merrell, 1974.

Patty, F. A. *Industrial Hygiene and Toxicology.* 2nd ed. New York: John Wiley and Sons, 1963.

Rossana, A. T. *Air Pollution: Guidebook for Management.* New York: McGraw-Hill, 1969.

Sawyer, C. N., and McCarthy, P. L. *Chemistry for Environmental Engineering.* 3rd ed. New York: McGraw-Hill, 1978.

Trevethick, R. A. *Environmental & Industrial Health Hazards: A Practice Guide*. 2d ed. Philadelphia, Pa.: International Ideas, 1976.

U.S. Department of Labor. *Industrial Hygiene Field Operation Manual*. CPL2-2.20, OSHA. Washington, D.C., 2 April 1979.

White, F. A. *Our Acoustic Environment*. New York: John Wiley and Sons, 1975.

Woodson, Wesley E. *Human Engineering Guide for Equipment Designers*. 2nd ed. Los Angeles: University of California Press, 1970.

Part VII

Human Factors

Chapter 16

Human Factors in Management

The Hawthorne Studies[1]

From 1924 to 1933, the Western Electric Company conducted at its Hawthorne Works a research program or series of experiments on the factors in the work situation that affects the morale and productive efficiency of workers. The first of these, the so-called Illumination Experiments, were studied in cooperation with the National Research Council of the National Academy of Sciences. In the remainder of the studies, the company was aided and guided by the suggestions of Professor Elton Mayo and several of his associates from Harvard University. Because of the large part that Harvard played in the project, it is often referred to as the Hawthorne-Harvard experiments or studies.

The following description of the experiments is drawn from the official report, *Management and the Worker*, by F. J. Roethlisberger of Harvard and the late W. J. Dickson of Western Electric (Harvard University Press, Cambridge, Mass., 1940). The other primary source of information is *The Industrial Worker*, by T. N. Whitehead (two volumes, Harvard University Press, Cambridge, Mass., 1938), dealing with the Relay Assembly Test Room. Other discussions of the subject by persons having direct or indirect connections with the studies are to be found in *The Human Problems of an Industrial Civilization* by Elton Mayo (2nd ed., Harvard University Press, Cambridge, Mass., 1946), *Leadership in a Free Society* by T. N. Whitehead (Harvard University Press, Cambridge, Mass., 1938), and *Fatigue of Workers*, a report by George C. Homans, secretary of the Committee on Work in Industry of the National Research Council. A portion of this report is reprinted in *Human Factors in Management*, edited by S. D. Hoslett, Greenwood Press, Westport, Connecticut, 1951.

[1]Taken from *The Hawthorne Studies 1924/1974*, by permission of the Public Relations Department, Western Electric, Hawthorne Station, Chicago, Ill., 1982.

ILLUMINATION EXPERIMENTS (1924–1927)

In 1924, the Hawthorne Works of Western Electric, in cooperation with the National Research Council of the National Academy of Sciences, embarked on an experiment to determine the "relation of quality and quantity of illumination to efficiency in industry." Figure 16–1 is an aerial photograph of the Hawthorne Works, Western Electric, Chicago, Illinois, circa 1929.

Three formal experiments were conducted with various groups of workers. In these experiments the intensity of illumination was increased and decreased and the effect on output was observed. The effect was puzzling. Output bobbed up and down in some groups or increased continually in others, or increased and stayed level in still others. But in no case was the increase or decrease in proportion to the increase or decrease in illumination. Where a parallel control group was set up for comparison with the test group undergoing changes in lighting, the production of the control group increased about the same as that of the test group.

On the basis that they had not had sufficient control of the illumination in

FIGURE 16–1. Aerial Photograph of Hawthorne Works, Chicago, Circa 1929.

some of the areas where they had been testing, the investigators set up two groups to work by artificial light only. They kept one group, for control, at a steady level of 10 foot-candles. In the test group they decreased the light one foot-candle at a time. The efficiency of *both* groups increased slowly but steadily, until the test group was down to 3 foot-candles, at which point they complained that they couldn't see what they were doing, and production decreased.

The formal investigation having proved so inconclusive, one of the investigators tried some informal experimentation. He put two coil winders in a locker room and reduced the light until it was about equal to that of a moonlight night. The girls maintained their efficiency throughout, and in fact said they became less tired than when working under bright lights.

On the theory that the workers were perhaps responding to something other than their physical environment, the investigators tried another experiment with a coil-winding group. This time they asked the girls how they felt about the changes in illumination. When they increased the light, the girls said they liked it, could work better under the bright light. Then they *pretended* to increase the light, and the girls said they liked it even better. When they decreased the light, and then told the girls, the latter commented unfavorably. Then they only *pretended* to decrease the light, and the girls said the dimmer light was not so pleasant to work under. Throughout this experiment, production did not change materially.

CONCLUSIONS ON THE ILLUMINATION EXPERIMENTS

To the Western Electric people involved, it appeared that:

1. Light was only one factor (and apparently minor) among many which affect employee output.
2. The attempt to measure the effect of the light factor had failed because:

a. The other factors had not been controlled.
b. Studies in regular shop departments or large groups involved so many factors that it was hopeless to expect to isolate any one of them.

At this point, the National Research Council withdrew from the studies, but Western Electric continued them, and soon thereafter had the collaboration of people from Harvard University.

RELAY ASSEMBLY TEST ROOM (1927–1932)

Inasmuch as it had appeared that some of the odd effects of the illuminating experiments resulted from the way workers felt about what they were doing (that is, speeded up because they thought increased production was expected, or slowed down because they were suspicious of the investigator's motives), the investigators tried to set up a situation in which the employees' attitudes would remain constant and unaffected, and other variables might be eliminated.

The factors that were expected to decrease the variables were:

1. Small group
2. Separate room
3. Limited effect of changes in personnel, type of work and introduction of inexperienced operators.
4. Mutual confidence to be established between investigators and operators.

Selection of Relay Assembly Job

The job of assembly relays was selected for this test because:

1. It was a repetitive job.
2. All employees were engaged in the same operation. (This was made even more uniform by reducing the number of relay types assembled in the test room.)
3. A complete operation could be performed in a short time—no more than a minute. This would provide a large body of statistical data.
4. No machine work was involved.

Selection of Operators

Operators for the test room were selected on the following basis:

1. All were experienced operators so that there would be no effect of learning on the results.
2. Operators who were willing and cooperative. (The investigators wanted normal and genuine reactions—no restricting of output as a result of suspicious attitude, no spurting because of overanxiety to cooperate.)
3. Two experienced operators—good friends—were asked to choose the remainder of the group.
4. The group consisted of five assemblers, and one layout operator to assign work and obtain parts.

Test Room Observer

An observer was stationed in the test room throughout the experiments. His job was to keep accurate records of all that happened, to create and maintain a friendly atmosphere, and to exercise a partial supervisory function. (The foreman remained responsible for rate revision, promotion, and so on.)

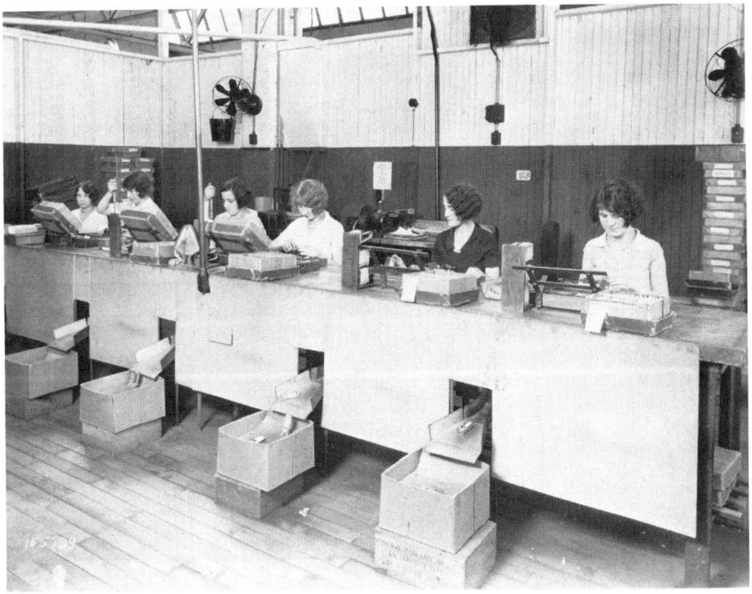

FIGURE 16–2. One View of Relay Assembly Test Room and Six Female Operators.

Test Room Setup

The test room was small, containing one workbench, benches for the recording apparatus, a desk for the observer, clothes lockers, and space for storing parts.

The workbench contained holes and chutes at the right of each girl's workplace, into which she would drop each completed relay. Otherwise the equipment was the same as in the regular department. Figures 16–2 and 16–3 give two views of the relay assembly test room and the six female operators, circa 1927.

Recording of Output

1. *Units.* The number of relay types to be assembled in the test room had been reduced so that the only difference would be in the number of parts to be assembled. It was now necessary to develop a unit of measurement that would enable the investigators to have comparable output figures regardless of the type assembled. It was decided to take the E-901 relay as the unit of measurement; conversion factors based on the piece rates were established for the other types assembled, so that all output figures could be shown in terms of E-901 relays.
2. *Recorder.* An old printing telegraph was set up to punch a hole in a tape for each completed relay. Figure 16–4 depicts the device for production records of the relay assembly test. The tape had five rows of holes, one for each operator. The tape moved at a speed of ¼″ per minute. One hole was punched for each complete relay. When the relay was dropped down the chute, it hit a flapper gate. One day's output was recorded on 120″ of tape.
3. *Numerical register.* A numerical register was included in the circuit for each row

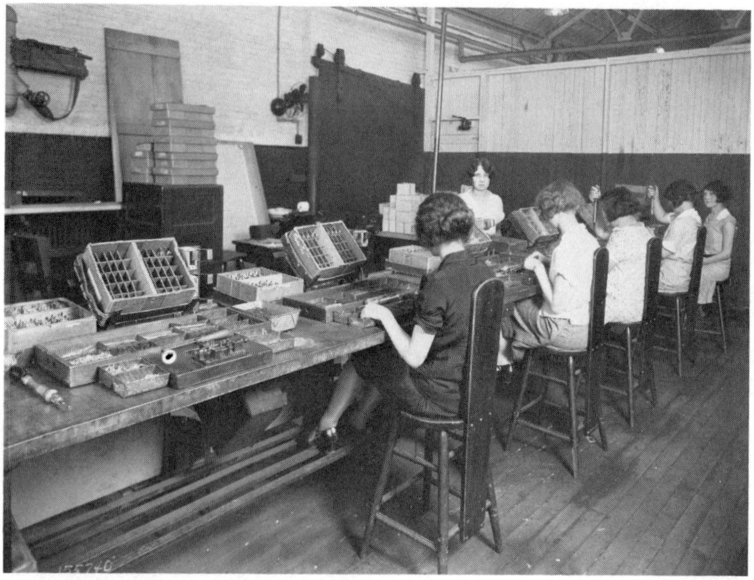

FIGURE 16–3. View of Relay Assembly Test Room and Six Female Operators.

FIGURE 16–4. Device for Production Records of the Relay Assembly Test.

of tape. The registers were read each half hour by the test room observer. Daily totals were checked against the operators' performance records.

4. *Operator's performance record.* The layout operator maintained the operator's performance record. The regular departmental record was used for payroll and other purposes. This showed the type of relay assembled, number completed each day, time required for 50 relays, time out for repairs, and so on. This provided a record independent of the recording device or log chart.

Other Records

1. *The log sheet.* The observer kept a log sheet that was a daily chronological record of each operator's activities, type of relay worked on, time she started on it, intervals of nonproductive time, and so on.
2. *Daily History Record.* The observer kept a record of everything that happened, the changes introduced, and remarks made by the investigators. The kinds of questions the investigators were asking themselves at various stages of the experiment were recorded here.

Physical Examinations of Operators

The operators were examined in the company hospital before the experiments began, and thereafter at intervals of about six weeks. It would be desirable to know whether increased output, if it occurred, would be accomplished at the expense of the operator's health. Or, if rest periods did not increase output, would they serve to improve the operators' health? The investigators recognized the difficulty of measuring health on any quantitive basis; however, it was expected that marked changes, particularly if detrimental, could be recognized.

Division of the Studies into Periods

The entire course of the studies was not mapped out in advance, but developed as the studies progressed. In the beginning the investigators were interested in the effect of a shorter working day and week. Periods I-III were introductory, to get the girls used to the test room. Periods IV-VII (24 weeks) were devoted to rest period studies. Periods VII-XIII (75 weeks) were experiments with shorter working days and weeks, interspersed with check periods of normal working hours. Figure 16–5 shows a graph of production levels vs. test factors in the relay assembly test.

Period I (2 weeks) During Period I the girls remained in the regular department. Their output under normal conditions was recorded; and they had their first physical examinations, which showed that they were all normal and in generally good health.

Period II (5 weeks). During Period II the girls were getting used to working by themselves in the test room, and the investigators were working out plans for keeping records of all that happened during the tests.

Period III (8 weeks). At the beginning of Period III, the six test room girls became a separate wage incentive payment group. In the regular department they had been

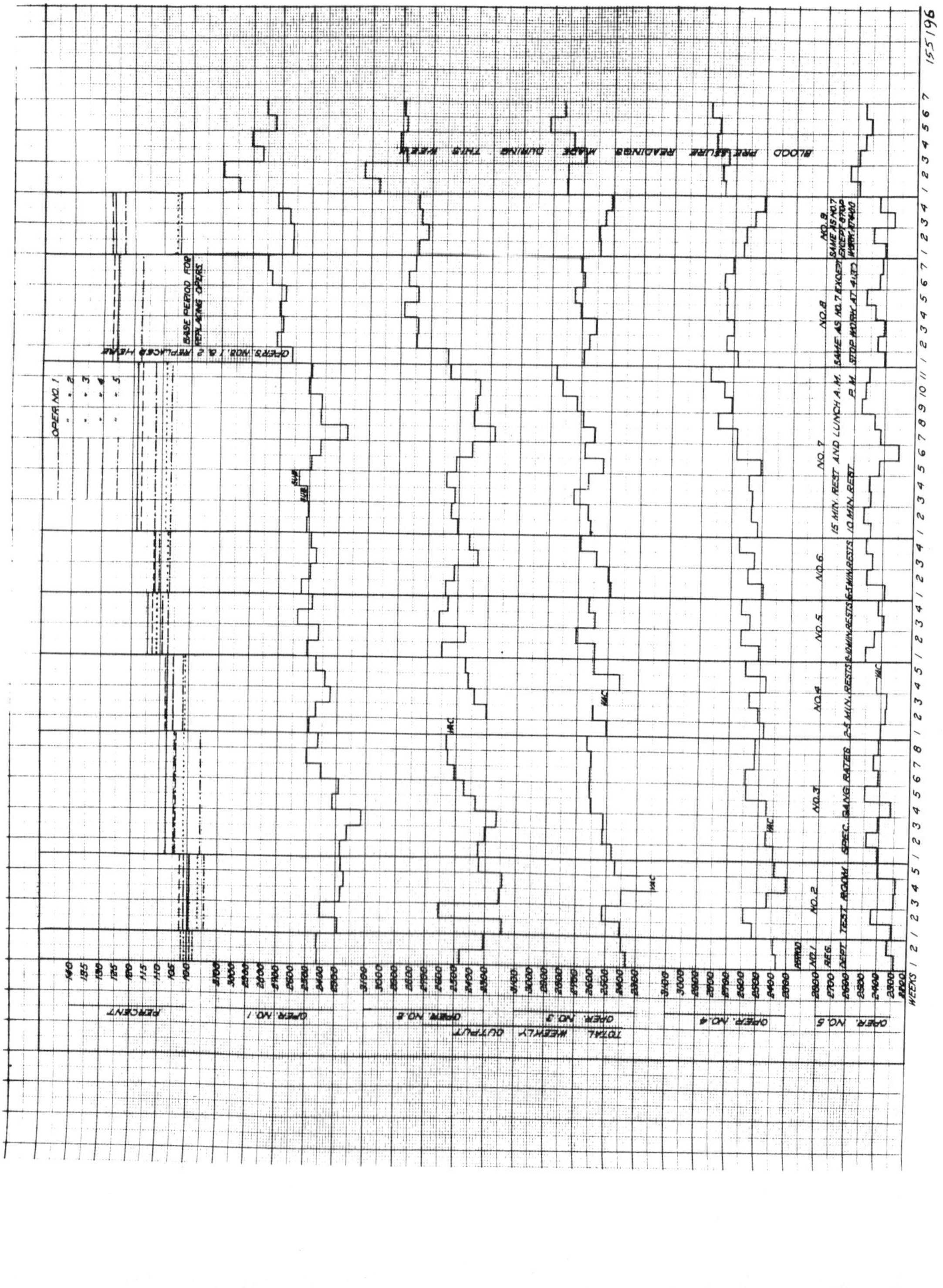

Figure 16-5. A Graph of the Production Levels Versus Test Factors in Relay Assembly Test.

part of a large group, which would be comparatively little affected by one person's effort. In the small group, their earnings would be much more directly affected by their output.

Period IV (5 weeks) At the beginning of Period IV the girls were called to the superintendent's office to talk over plans for two five-minute rest periods during the day. They voted to have the rests at 10:00 o'clock in the morning and 2:00 o'clock in the afternoon, which times were very close to what the records showed to be their lowest output points.

The girls liked the rest periods very much, but still complained of drowsiness in the early afternoon. They thought longer rest periods would be better, but were afraid they would not be able to "make their rate" (a reference to the "bogey" on which their performance was measured in the department, but which was not used in the test room). During this period there was evidence that some of the girls were developing a rather free and easy relationship with the test room observers. After five weeks of two five-minute rest periods showed a slight increase in output, it was decided to try two ten-minute rest periods. The girls were again consulted and were in favor, apparently having lost their fear of not making the bogey.

Period V (4 weeks). Accordingly, for the four weeks of Period V the girls had a ten-minute rest period at 10:00 o'clock in the morning and 2:00 o'clock in the afternoon. Immediately there was a definite rise in output, both in the hourly average and the total. The first day's earnings were 80.6 percent, and the girls and investigators alike were highly interested and enthusiastic. The observers thought the girls were speeding up to compensate for the shortened working time, but the girls themselves had varied opinions, though they all agreed that they liked the longer rest periods.

During this period an incident occurred that illustrates the girls' attitude toward authority and also the method of supervision in the test room. The investigators thought that the girls' increased earnings would be very dramatically demonstrated if they paid the girls each week the percentage earned in the regular department, but paid the girls, once a month, the difference between their earnings and the department earnings as a rather large bonus. Two of the girls immediately objected, indicating they thought it was an attempt to confuse them, so that they could not figure their own earnings. There had been some previous comments to the effect that "we earn 80 percent, but we'll only get 60 percent" and "we'll never get all that money." Accordingly, the investigators dropped the idea, and the girls were greatly relieved.

The incident indicates that the girls had a latent suspicion of authority, a fear that in some way they would be cheated of their higher earnings. It indicates, too, that they felt free to comment about changes in procedure to the test room authorities, and that the test room authorities paid attention to their comments. In this case, the observers discarded a plan that they thought should have seemed perfectly logical to the girls, and reestablished the procedure the girls preferred.

The observers were addressing themselves to the girls' fears rather than to the logics of the situation. This was typical of the supervisory technique employed in the test room.

Period VI (4 weeks). It was decided to try six five-minute rest periods. The girls we- again consulted. They were opposed t- short periods, but agreed to try the-four weeks they followed this schedule. They consistently expressed their disapproval both by critical remarks and by excessive laughing and talking and returning late from rest periods. Output during this period, however, did not particularly reflect this feeling. Two girls increased their output slightly as compared to the previous period; two decreased slightly, and one showed no change.

Period VII (11 weeks). During this period the girls had a 15-minute rest in the morning, during which a lunch was provided by the company restaurant, and a 10-minute break in the afternoon. The lunches were varied, but generally consisted of a sandwich, beverage, and fruit or pudding.

The investigators had had some feeling that the girls' sleepiness in the early afternoon resulted from having had too large a lunch because they had had too little breakfast. However, it did not appear that they ate appreciably smaller lunches during this period; nor was the early afternoon slump in output at all affected.

The girls were enthusiastic about the rest periods and the lunch "on the company." Two of them further increased their hourly output and one maintained the same average as for the previous period. Two girls, however, produced less and in this period they demonstrated an uncooperative and hostile attitude of which there had been occasional evidence in the earlier periods. It was decided, therefore, to transfer these two operators back to the department and to replace them with others who would like to join the test group and had output records comparable with those of the girls who were leaving.

Period VIII (7 weeks). With Period VIII there began a series of experiments with a shorter working day and week. The 15- and 10-minute rest periods continued except in Period XII.

In Period VIII, with new operators taking the place of those who had developed hostile attitudes, the girls were offered the choice of starting ½ hour later than usual or stopping ½ hour earlier. The girls chose the latter, and were very happy about it except for one girl who was breaking up with her boy friend and didn't like the long evenings at home. Despite the fact that working time was now 10 percent less than standard, the total production increased, and hourly output increased sharply.

This continued for 7 weeks, and the investigators, who had been planning to go back to the original working conditions of 48 hours and no rest periods, decided instead to try a further reduction in hours, to see where the total weekly output would begin to fall off.

Period IX (4 weeks). During Period IX, the girls again chose to stop early—one hour earlier than usual. Although encouraged to work at a natural pace, the girls seemed to feel the need to hurry. Operator 2 began to admonish the other girls to stop talking and to work faster. A contest for leadership developed between her and Operators 3 and 4, who had formerly been the fastest operators and had exercised some leadership.

Although the girls increased their hourly output, the cut in working time proved to be too drastic, and weekly production was somewhat lowered, reducing the girls' earnings. The schedule was, therefore, continued for only four weeks.

Period X (6 weeks). The investigators decided now to go back to standard working hours after an extended period of shorter hours. However, it was felt that the rest periods should be retained for a while.

The girls at first felt very tired working longer hours. In the first weeks, comments on tiredness were very frequent, but diminished as time went on. Hourly production decreased slightly, but weekly production reached a new high for all the operators.

Thinking about this high production, which did not seem to show the effect of fatigue resulting from longer hours of work, the investigators wondered if perhaps the frequent physical examinations had caused the girls to be more conscious of health and to improve their health practices. So they made up a questionnaire, asking the girls about changes in their diet, hours of sleep and so on. No particular change was evident in the answers, but the girls suggested that their increased output was caused by "greater freedom," "absence of bosses," "opportunity to set one's own pace and to earn what one makes without being held back by a big group."

A second questionnaire concentrating on conditions in the test room brought out very similar answers with respect to the relaxed supervision, "more freedom," the "smaller group," "the way we are treated." Only one girl mentioned their increased earnings as an important factor. The comments on "less supervision" are on the surface rather paradoxical, since the test room observer acted as their supervisor and was present all day.

During this period there was an increasing amount of social activity among the girls, both inside and outside the plant. They began to have parties at home and sometimes went to the theatre together. This seemed also to affect their relationships at work. A friendly spirit, a willingness to help each other, and other signs of solidarity appeared. When one operator had to be absent, two others assigned themselves the job of keeping up the group earnings while she was away. Conversation and joking became more general, while private conversations diminished. The joking and banter was extended to include the test room investigators and other authorities with whom they had contact.

Period XI (9 weeks). The obvious next step would have been to cut out the rest periods, reverting to standard working conditions. But it was the end of June, and the investigators had promised the girls an experiment with a five-day week during the summer. The five-day schedule was maintained for 9 weeks, two of which were vacation weeks for the whole group.

The girls liked this arrangement very much and their hourly output increased slightly. Weekly output, however, fell off to about the level of Period IX, when they were quitting an hour early. (This, of course, was still far above their output at the beginning of the experiments.) Since they received their base rate for the Saturday mornings they did not work, there was no appreciable loss of earnings.

Period XII (12 weeks). In Period XII the girls reverted to standard conditions, 48 hours per week and no rest periods. The operators were much opposed to the change, though they understood that it was temporary and that there would be other experimental conditions after it. They felt tired, became very hungry and seemed generally restless. Eventually, they developed their own ways of adjusting to the conditions. They had something to eat at about 9:30 in the morning and after lunch it became customary to slack off work, talk and joke, at times quite boisterously.

Attempts of the test room observer to stop the excessive talking were not very effective, and it was interesting to note that the girls did not worry about his threats, since they did not think of him as a "boss." At one point he observed that they were limiting their output, in order to make sure that rest periods would be reinstated. When the observer told them that regardless of output the rest periods would be included in the next period, this practice stopped. During this period hourly output dropped somewhat for all but one of the girls. Operator 3, in particular, showed a marked decrease, apparently, because she was having trouble at home.

After 12 weeks under standard conditions, the rest periods were reinstated in Period XIII.

Period XIII (7 months). During Period XIII the girls worked standard hours except for the 15- and 10-minute rest periods. The girls supplied their own morning lunch, except that the company provided hot tea.

The operators welcomed the return of the rest periods. Morale reached its highest peak. They took pride in their work, tried to beat their former output records, and helped each other to maintain the group earnings. There was no attempt to speed up all along the line; when some girls felt like working fast, others slowed down a little. It was a cooperative aim toward a common goal rather than competition between individuals. Operator 2 had acquired an unofficial position of leadership and exerted pressure on slower girls. This sometimes resulted in friction, but eventually the girls achieved a kind of equilibrium so that some could speed up and others slow down without antagonism.

Period XIII lasted for seven months, during which both hourly output and total output exceeded all previous records.

Summary of Periods I–XIII in the Relay Assembly Test Room

In the two and one-half years of experimentation a number of changes in working conditions had been tried. What were their effects in terms of output, and the girls' health and mental attitude?

1. Except for Periods X, XI, and XII, the output rose steadily for all but operators 1A and 2A. In Period XIII Operator 4 reached an increase of about 40 percent over the base period.
2. In periods VII, X and XIII identical conditions existed—48 hours per week, a 15-minute rest in the morning, with lunch, and a 10-minute rest in the afternoon. But hourly output was higher in Period X than in Period VII, and in Period XIII it was considerably higher.
3. Periods X, XI and XII varied widely in conditions of work, from a 5-day week with rest periods to a 5½-day week without rest periods. Yet there was comparatively little change in output.
4. In only one case did the hourly rate behave as one might have expected. In Period XII, it did go down when the girls resumed the 48-hour schedule, with no rest periods. Even so, the output was considerably higher than it was under the same conditions in Period III.

It appears that there is no simple correlation between working conditions and hourly output.

Now let's look at the total output per week. What happened when rest periods were introduced?

1. It is evident that weekly output did not decline; it increased. There was a decline in Period VII, but this resulted partly from the Christmas and New Year's holidays.
2. The increase in hourly rate compensated for the time lost in shorter working hours in every period except IX and XI, where working time was reduced by 15.3 percent and 13.2 percent respectively.

3. In Period XII weekly output reached a new high level for every operator in spite of the fact that hourly rate of output decreased in this period.

To sum up, output had increased steadily for nearly 2½ years in spite of numerous changes in hours of work. Morale in the test room had steadily improved. The girls had averaged only 3½ attendance irregularities a year (sickness and personal absences plus times late) compared with 15 a year before coming into the test room. Meanwhile, 33 girls in the regular department had averaged 3½ times as many sickness absences, nearly 3 times as many personal absences, and about 3 times as many failures to register as the girls in the test room.

The investigators formulated four hypotheses to explain the greatly improved performance of the operators in the test room:

1. Relief from fatigue—the rest periods
2. Relief from monotony

Detailed study of the half-hourly output records and other data, compared with the literature on fatigue and monotony, led to the conclusion that relief from fatigue was not the answer, and that the evidence as to relief from monotony was inconclusive.

3. Increased wage incentive—the fact that in a small payment group their earnings more closely reflected the amount of their output.
4. Change in method of supervision—the more informal relationship with the test room supervisors diminished the girls' suspicion of management, and allowed them more freedom in their relationships with each other.

To test the possibility that the change to a small wage incentive group was responsible for the improved performance, the investigators decided to try two more experiments—one in which the *only* change in the operators' work would be a change to a small payment group; and one in which the test room situation would be duplicated without a change in wage incentives.

Second Relay Assembly Group

Another group of five relay assemblers was formed into a separate payment group within the regular department. Almost immediately their production increased by 12 percent and remained at that level for nine weeks, when the group was discontinued because of the complaints of the girls in the regular department. This would seem to indicate that the small wage incentive group did have some effect. However, there were two important points to note: First, the output in this group increased immediately but then leveled off; second, the increase amounted to only 12 percent compared with the test group's 30 percent. A complicating factor, also, was that the second relay assembly group were consciously trying to show they were as fast as the test group.

Mica Splitting Test Room

The second experiment on the effect of wage incentives was to set up the mica splitting test room, in which changes in working conditions could be introduced without a change in wage incentives. This was accomplished by segregating in a special room a group of five operators who were on individual piece rates. The first change was the introduction of rest periods, which resulted in a moderate but steady rise in output. The next change was the elimination of overtime work. Production continued to increase for a while, then began to decline slowly but steadily. The third change was a further reduction to a 40-hour week.

Output dropped to a lower level, where it remained steady until the Depression caused such a reduction in work that the test had to be discontinued. The reaction of the girls to the test room situation was as favorable as in the relay assembly test room. Their reaction to rest periods and shorter working hours resulted in an increase in production, though there was a wide variation among the girls and only two of them had increases at all comparable with the increases of all the relay assemblers. There were good reasons for the decreasing production in the later periods, since there was a good deal of worry about the mica splitting job being transferred to the company's plant in Kearny, New Jersey, and finally about the increasing effects of the Depression.

However, even where conditions were similar, the average increase in production was only 15 percent as compared to 30 percent in the relay assembly test room. (And the second relay assembly group, theoretically influenced by wage incentives only, increased production only 12 percent.)

On the original premises of the experiments, one might conclude that the 30 percent increase in the relay assembly test room, minus the 15 percent increase in the mica splitting test room, would show 15 percent as the increase accounted for by the change in wage incentives. However, this conclusion depends on so many things that might or might not be true, that it cannot be taken too seriously.

The two conclusions that the investigators did feel justified in drawing were these:

1. The steady increase in the relay assembly test room was not due to the change in wage incentive only.
2. The effect of this change in wage incentive was so much tied up with the effects of so many other factors that it was impossible to tell how much influence it had.

The underlying premises of both the illumination and the test room experiments had been that a change in working conditions would result in a change in production. Let's represent this idea with a simple diagram:

C—R change produces result

A "good" change produces a good result (i.e., an increase in production); a "bad" change produces a bad result (that is, a decrease in production).

When the illumination failed to substantiate this premise, it was assumed that extraneous factors had interfered, primarily the feelings and attitudes of the operators. Therefore the test room setup was devised with the idea of keeping the operators' attitudes constant while making other changes; there, presumably, the only reactions would be automatic physical reations—the operators would work faster or slower.

But in their attempts to keep constant the attitudes of the girls in the test room, the investigators made many changes in the treatment of the girls, which made their situation very untypical of workers in general. In the very attempt to prevent change, they introduced change.

More and more the investigators came to realize that the significant information they were acquiring had to do with the way people thought and felt—their attitudes. At this stage they began to think of the effect of change somewhat in the manner of the diagram in Figure 16–6.

That is, that change does not lead to a direct and automatic result; change affects the employee's attitude, which in turn affects the result.

So the chief result of the two years of the relay assembly test room had been to demonstrate the importance of employee attitudes and preoccupations. All attempts to eliminate such considerations had been

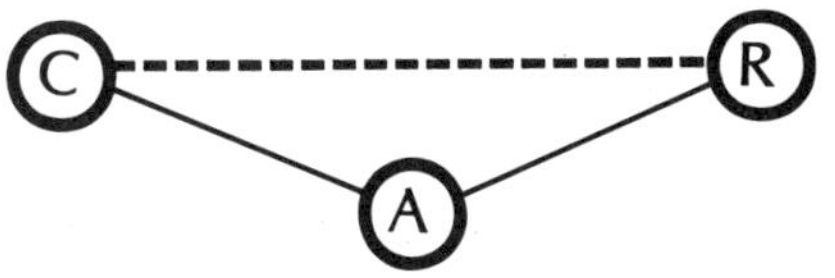

FIGURE 16–6. Change of Attitude to Result Relationship.

unsuccessful. The importance of employee attitudes had been evident in the "apprehension of authority" that had been common to all the operators, although in different degrees, and could be aroused by the slightest provocation. It had been evident in the effects of the experimentally introduced changes in working conditions, which had operated as changes in the meaning of the situation or the operations, rather than as changes in physical circumstances. It had shown itself in the output variations of certain operators, which could be related to their personal preoccupations, and which continued as long as the preoccupations existed.

What practical consequences did these results have for management?

Management regarded these experiments as an attempt to compile a sound body of knowledge upon which to base executive policy and action. And although it was recognized that such research is a long-term proposition, management was ready to make use of any findings that seemed to have been sufficiently tested.

The most important of such findings was that of the usefulness of rest periods. Although the effects of rest periods had not been exactly measured, all the evidence pointed to their desirability. Beginning in 1928, therefore, rest periods were gradually introduced throughout the plant wherever repetitive work was going on, and wherever the results were studied, production at least did not decrease.

The most important result of the research was management's improved understanding of many of its problems. For example, management had formerly tended to make many assumptions as to what would happen if changes were made, for instance, in wage incentives or hours of work.

They now began to question these assumptions and to see that such factors as hours of work and wage incentives are only part of a total situation and that their effects cannot be predicted apart from that total situation.

What impressed management most, however, were the stores of latent energy and productive cooperation that could be obtained from its working force under the right conditions. Among the factors making for these conditions, the attitudes of the employees stood out as being of predominant importance.

INTERVIEWING PROGRAM (1928–1930)

The logical next step was to find out about the attitudes of employees in general about their jobs, their supervision, their working conditions, and so on.

This tied in with a current problem that had arisen in the training of supervisors. A series of supervisory conferences on morale had bogged down for lack of factual information. There were conflicting opinions on the factors involved in cooperation between employees and supervisors. There was no generally acceptable body of information about how employees felt about their jobs and their supervisors. The simple suggestion was made that the way to find out how employees felt was to ask them. Information gained could be used in two ways: complaints on physical conditions would be referred to the organization responsible; comments on supervision would be used in supervisory training conferences.

In 1928 the interviewing program began, first with 1,600 people in the inspection branch. By the end of 1930, 21,000 employees had been interviewed. As the interviews progressed, the interviewers' methods changed. At first they asked about the employee's likes and dislikes, about his working conditions, his job and his supervision. If the employee did not talk freely, the interviewer asked specific questions about these things. The interviewers began to notice, however, that it was difficult to hold employees to the subjects. The employees tended to go off on other subjects, which seemed to be so much on their minds that they kept going back to them in spite of the interviewers' efforts to get back to the assigned subjects.

This experience was so widespread that it began to appear very significant, and the decision was made to change the interviewing method completely.

In the future, the interviewer would state the purpose of the interview, which was still the same. But from that point on he was merely to listen to what the employee said, without interrupting or changing the subject, as long as the employee continued to talk spontaneously. He would follow the employee's ideas with interest, taking only enough notes to enable him to recall what the employee had said. His report would be, as nearly as possible, a verbatim account of what the employee had said.

The verbatim accounts were then studied by a group of analysts who broke the comments down to specific complaints and classified them (washrooms, lighting, ventilation, and so on). When a number of complaints about a certain subject (dirty washrooms, for instance) had been collected, they would be forwarded to the organization responsible (responsible for cleaning the washrooms, for example).

Benefits of the Interviewing Program

What was accomplished by the interviewing program?

First, a number of unsatisfactory working conditions were improved. Often enough, the conditions had been known before, and there were some plans to correct them. However, the fact that so many employees complained of them undoubtedly speeded up the corrective action.

Second, the interviews provided material for a supervisory training program, in which supervisors read sample interviews, from which all identifying information had been removed, and discussed them in conference. The conference had some effect in making supervisors conscious of the feelings employees had toward their treatment by supervisors.

These benefits had been more or less assumed before the interviews began. There were, however, some additional, unexpected benefits. One unexpected benefit was that the very fact that the interviews were going on made supervisors more conscious of their own behavior, more careful in their dealings with employees. A certain amount of automatic improvement in supervision took place. Also unexpected was the enthusiasm of the employees. Over and over they stated how much better they felt now that they had "got something off their chest." In addition, there was a considerable feeling of gratification that management was paying some attention to them, was interested in what they thought.

The interviewers learned a great deal from the interviews obtained from this new method, and what they learned tied in with a difficulty the analysts were having in classifying the complaints in the interviews. You will recall that there was a group whose job was to break down the interviews into individual complaints, which could be classified so that all complaints on the same subject could be counted and investigated. However, the analysts very often found it impossible to understand what the complaints were about, when they were taken out of the context of the complete interview. To the interviewers, too, it was becoming apparent that many of the complaints could not be taken at their face value.

For example, an interviewer talked with Joe Brown, who complained about conditions in the shop, the drafts, smoke, and fumes. As he continued to talk, his conversation was almost entirely about health, diet, disease, about how deceiving a healthy appearance may be. (Brown was very healthy looking.) Then he talked about his brother, who had recently died of pneumonia. He compared himself to his brother. "Here I am healthy, just like my brother; yet tomorrow I may be gone." Brown's complaints about drafts, smoke, and fumes took on quite a different meaning in the context of the whole interview; the complaints were really an indication of his preoccupations about his health.

Another employee complained that his piece rates were too low. As he continued to talk, he related that his wife was in the hospital, and that he was worried about his doctor bills. In effect, the complaint about piece rate is an expression of his concern about his ability to pay his bills.

Another employee complained of his boss being a bully. If the boss gave him an order, he felt the boss was abusing his authority. If the boss said nothing to him, he felt he was being slighted and ignored. As the talk turned to his past experiences, he talked about his father, an overbearing, domineering man whose authority could not be questioned. Gradually the interviewer could see that the employee's dissatisfaction was rooted somewhere in his attitude toward authority, developed during early childhood. He tended to hate anyone in a position of authority in the same way he hated his father.

The investigators began to realize that, to understand what was involved in an employee's complaint, it was only necessary to understand the background of the employee and his personal situation. The complaint in itself might be primarily a symptom of a personal situation that needed to be explored.

As a result of this insight, the interviewers for a while tended to concentrate on the personal situation of employees, particularly on their early home background, applying the concepts of the psychopathologists. As a result, a number of very interesting case studies were developed. This, however, turned out to be rather a dead end. Very few Hawthorne employees were extreme causes of psychoneurosis, for whom this delving into early family life would have a therapeutic value; and, indeed, the interviewers were not professionally equipped for this type of therapy.

In their interest in personal situations of the employees who complained, and in the unusual cases that had been discovered, the investigators had tended to ignore some of the uniform threads that had run through the interviews. When they started to interview supervisors, however, certain characteristics were so uniform that they forced themselves to the attention of the investigators, and turned their attention to the social relationships among people in the working group.

The interviewing of supervisors was done by two representatives of the Harvard Business School. What particularly struck the interviewers was the mass of comments about social distinctions, in differences between supervisory ranks, between office and shop, length of service, men and women, and so on.

Distinctions Between Different Supervisory Ranks

Social distance was not the same between any two consecutive levels. The most marked cleavage was between foreman and general foreman (department chief and division chief were the corresponding office titles).

Distinctions Between Office and Shop

1. Status in the company was not determined by rank alone; it also depended on the type of work. Certain jobs carried more social prestige than others. On the whole, an office worker had a higher social status than a shop worker.
2. This distinction carried through the first few ranks of supervision. A shop group chief or section chief had little or no more prestige than a nonsupervisory in the office.

Distinctions of Seniority or Sex

1. All other things being equal, two group chiefs in the same shop were not considered equal in status unless they had the same length of service and are of the same sex.
2. Occupations performed by men had a higher social status than those performed by women.
3. Employees with long service had a higher status than employees with short service.

None of these distinctions was particularly essential to the manufacture of telephones; they arose because the company was not only a manufacturer of telephones but a human organization in which people were trying to satisfy their hopes and desires.

And, of course, certain characteristics of their working environment reflected these distinctions. The private office of the assistant superintendent certainly set him off from lower ranks of supervision. There were variations in the accommodations of shop and office supervisors (the latter, for instance, had private lockers and were supplied with towels). There were distinctions in pay treatment and payment for absences between shop and office people.

While workers and supervisors of various ranks and conditions felt these differences in social distance, there were many cross-currents of common feeling binding them together. The lowest worker and highest executive may feel the same about length of service. Supervisor and subordinate in the shop may feel the same way about office workers.

Some of these distinctions did not have the same meaning at each level. The distinction between office and shop status, for instance, did not seem to be felt very much by assistant superintendents.

The supervisors' comments about company policies in promotion, rate of pay, about other levels of supervision, and about relations with employees emphasized very strongly the supervisors' feelings about social status in the working situation and pointed up the social significance of the factors affecting them. This tended to illuminate the interviews with nonsupervisory employees, in which much information could be found to indicate the importance of social relationship in all levels of employees.

An overall concept of employee satisfaction or dissatisfaction (whether supervisor or nonsupervisor) is illustrated in Figure 16–7. The diagram illustrates that the worker—whether supervisor or individual—has a certain status determined by his place in the social organization of the company. The effect of changes in working conditions, hours, rates of pay, and so on, may be predicted according to their effect on the various factors that determine this status. The extent to which the employee finds satisfaction in his work depends on how his status corresponds with the social demands he makes of his work, which in turn depends not so much on his relation to the company as his relation to society in general. All these factors are interrelated—changes in any are likely to change all the others, to the extent that the employee feels the change.

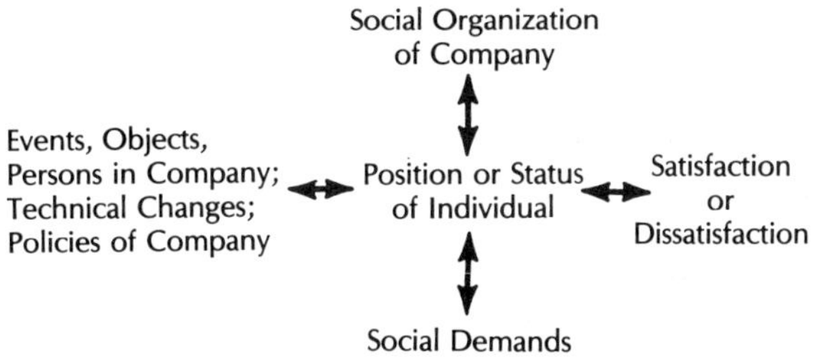

FIGURE 16–7. Social Relationships on the Job.

The effect of all this on the investigators was to turn them to a study of social relationships on the job. They thought they should observe directly the behavior of employees on the job with specific attention to the kinds of things reported in the interviewing program. They were interested in how some of the feelings and attitudes mentioned in the interviews affected work activities, in the actions of groups in maintaining group standards, in the effect of group standards on working efficiency, and the like. The project they established was known as the Bank Wiring Observation Room.

BANK WIRING OBSERVATION ROOM (1931–1932)

The purposes of the project were:

1. To develop a method of studying group behavior that would supplement interviewing with actual observations of behavior in the working group.
2. To obtain more exact information about social groups within the company by making an intensive study of one group under normal shop conditions.

In the group to be chosen there would be no changes in the work situation except that the group would be in a separate room. An observer would be stationed in the room to record production and make notes on all the activities, but he would never give orders or instructions, never make critical comments, never appear too eager to get into the group's conversations or to be too interested in their behavior.

There was also an interviewer who talked to the men off the job. His function was to gain insight into the men's attitudes, thoughts, and feelings. The interviewer rarely appeared in the observation room, since it was thought that the men might talk more freely to someone not familiar with their activities on the job.

The group selected for this experiment consisted of 9 wiremen, 3 solderers, and 2 inspectors working on banks of equipment used in step-by-step central office equipment. The job consisted of setting up the banks side-by-side on frames, wiring the corresponding terminals from bank to bank, soldering the connections, and inspecting, with a test set, for short circuits or breaks in the wire. One solderman soldered the work of three wiremen; the inspection work was shared by two inspectors.

Output Behavior in the Bank Wiring Observation Room

The most obvious fact about the output of the bank wiring room was that each worker was restricting his output, and that none of them was reporting his output correctly to the group chief for his individual record. The total for the week would check with the total week's production, but the daily reports would indicate a steady, level output regardless of the work done.

Beliefs Related to Output Behavior

Interviews with 32 operators (including those in the observation room and others in the regular department) showed that their idea of a day's output had little to do with the criteria set up by the wage incentive engineers. Only two of them stated correctly that they were expected to make the "bogey," which was 914 connections per hour, 7,312 for an 8-hour day. Twenty men said that the wiring of two equipments (6,000 or 6,600 connections on selectors or connectors respectively) was the expected day's work. Some of them said this represented 100 percent efficiency.

It was clear that the official bogey had little to do with their production. They had a standard of their own (6,000 connections a day) set well below the bogey, and well below what they could have done.

The standard was set at this point because of certain beliefs and fears. They were afraid that if they did increase their output appreciably, something would happen. The rate would be cut, the bogey would be raised, someone might be laid off, the slower men might get bawled out. Practically none of them believed that if they increased their output their earnings would increase and nothing else would happen.

(As it happened, they had recently gone from a 48-hour week to a 44-hour week. At the time of the change, their supervisor had assured them that if they maintained the same output they would receive the same pay in spite of the decrease in hours. This actually occurred, and none of the men could understand it, in spite of repeated explanations.)

Just as they believed their output should not go above a certain level, they believed it should not fall too far short of that level. Consequently, their output curves, based on their own reports, were very nearly level.

They kept track of their output very closely without ever writing anything down. One day the interviewer asked a wireman what time it was. The wireman added up the number of levels he had wired and told him the time within 2 minutes.

Although almost all agreed on what constituted a fair day's work, and all maintained a level output record, they did not all turn out the same amount of work. Four of them were close to their standard, four fell far short, and one consistently exceeded it.

Why did this happen? The reasons were pretty well bound up with the social relations of the workers—so these will be described next.

Relations with Supervisors

The workers' relations with the group chief centered on certain main activities.

Daywork Claims. The operators often found it necessary to make excessive day-work claims in order to justify their reporting low output for the day. The group chief knew that many of the claims were unjustified, but signed off just the same, rarely questioning them.

Job Trading. Soldermen and wiremen frequently traded jobs. The group chief presumably had the duty of forbidding this, because it was expected that each man could work faster if he remained on one job. The group chief made little attempt to stop the job trading.

Discipline. The group chief was responsible for preventing horseplay and excessive talking and joking, and for enforcing company rules. In practice, he overlooked disobedience of some of the rules because he agreed with the operators that they were unimportant. He considered that his main job was to get an acceptable day's work out of the workers, and in this he succeeded.

The group chief was very highly regarded by the workers, because he had in effect aligned himself with them and accepted their code of conduct. He conformed to the workers' feelings of how a group chief should act. This group chief, toward the end of the study, was demoted as a result of the general reduction in force, and his place was taken by a group chief who tried to exercise stricter discipline. This resulted in no change in the workers' activities; they simply concealed from him many things that they frankly expressed to the first group chief. They obeyed the stricter group chief no better than they had the more lenient one.

The operators' attitude toward the section chief was much the same as toward the group chief. They recognized a somewhat greater authority, but did not always obey him and frequently argued with him.

The operators exhibited quite different attitudes toward the assistant foreman and foreman. They never disobeyed or argued, and were restrained in their behavior when he was present. The foreman and assistant foreman operated strictly in accordance with the logic of management; they insisted on the rules of the game as specified by management. As far as they knew, the game was being played according to these rules. The output records indicated that this was so. The operators behaved correctly when they were present, and their subordinate supervisors did not inform them otherwise.

Function of Control in the Observation Room

If the function of supervisory control was (1) to transmit orders downward and (2) to transmit upward information about what was happening down the line, it is obvious that neither was happening in the expected fashion. The operators were not acting as management expected, and knowledge of this was not passing upward to higher management. The reason for this was that the operators did not respond in the expected way to the incentives provided for them. If they had worked in accordance with the logics of the wage incentive plan, there would have been no job trading, excessive daywork or restriction of output. Instead the employees were making demands of the group chiefs which he could not deny without becoming disliked. So he and the section chief in effect became part of the group they supervised. Having taken that position, they felt it necessary to conceal from the foreman everything which was contrary to the logic of management. The departmental performance records were therefore distorted, and the foreman was ignorant of much that was going on.

Relations Between Employees

The five occupational groups were found to have varied status in the eyes of the employees. From highest to lowest they were:

Inspectors
Connector wiremen
Selector wiremen
Soldermen
Truckers

The inspectors, who reported to a separate branch, had the highest status. They were somewhat better educated than the other employees, and were paid on an hourly basis (not incentive). They never traded jobs or went for lunches. They wore ties at work, and wore jackets when they came for interviews, as compared with the wiremen and solderers, who came in shirt-sleeves or sweaters.

Wiremen working on connectors had somewhat higher status than those working on selectors. There was no difference in the skill involved, but it happened that new men usually started on the selectors, which were at the back of the room and moved "up" to connectors as vacancies occurred. Sometimes there was an increase in hourly rate, but it was considered a promotion even when no increase was involved.

The position of wireman was considered somewhat superior to that of solderman. Beginners usually started as solderman and moved up to wiring, usually with an increase in hourly rate. The social superiority of wiremen was demonstrated in the fact that job trading was always requested by the wiremen and the soldermen almost always traded without protest. It was always a solderman who went out to get lunches for the group.

Both the wiremen and soldermen demonstrated their superiority to the trucker who served the observation room. They made fun of him, poked his arm when he was stamping numbers on the equipment, tickled his ribs while he was lifting equipment onto the truck. There was no personal feeling involved; they acted this way with any trucker who came into the room.

The Informal Group in Social Activities

During the lulls in activity the men matched coins, played cards, had baseball pools and chipped in to buy candy. In these activities two groups were formed—the first 5 wiremen, Solderman 1 and Inspector 1 who worked at the front of the room, formed one group. The other four wiremen and solderman 4 formed another group at the back of the room. One solderman and one inspector did not participate at all. The two groups were almost completely exclusive of each other; all the gambling games occurred in one group, and all the "binging" (hitting another person on the upper arm with the fist), in the other. Both groups chipped in to buy candy at the club store, but they bought different kinds and neither shared with the other.

Participation in Job Trading

Participation in job trading emphasized the superior status of the connector wiremen. The selector wiremen traded jobs only with their own soldermen, while the connector wiremen traded jobs to some extent with all three soldermen; they apparently felt free to do this, but the selector wiremen did not.

Participation in Helping

All the men helped each other from time to time, although this was frowned upon by management. This activity was not confined within work groups; it seemed to draw the whole group together rather than separate it into parts.

Friendships and Antagonisms

A chart of the work and play activities and the indications of friendship and antagonism that appeared in the group gives a picture of the existence of two chief groups in the organization (Figure 16–8). A group toward the front of the room, which we may call Clique A, consisted of an inspector, three wiremen, and one solderman.

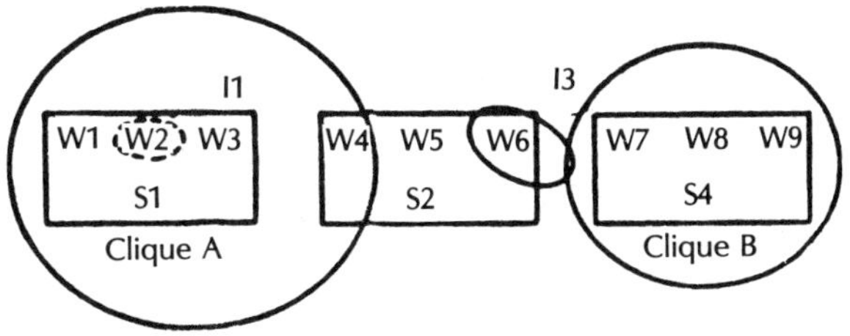

FIGURE 16–8. Chart of Friendships and Antagonisms in the Bank Wiring Observation Room.

The diagram indicates membership in the cliques. W2 is a special case, since he participated in games with Clique A, but that was all. He did not talk much with the others and seemed to be somewhat insecure in the group. Wireman 6 participated in some activities of Clique B, but was not entirely accepted. I3, W5, and S2 were not included in either clique.

A number of suggestions have been made as to why these cliques developed as they did. None is completely satisfactory, but certain characteristics are reasonably clear. One is that Clique A was considered superior to Clique B. Their output was higher, they talked about more serious subjects, got involved in less horseplay. Some of the prestige even carried over to Solderman 1, who had a somewhat higher status than the other soldermen as a result of his association with the group in front.

The Individual's Behavior and His Position in the Group

It appears that the individual's behavior with respect to an informal code of conduct influenced his acceptance in the group. For example, Inspector 1 was welcome in Group A because he did not assume higher status. He often told the wiremen about defects, and even repaired them himself, instead of reporting them. He participated in their activities as an equal, not a superior.

Solderman 1 was accepted because he subordinated himself to the wiremen, as a solderman should. Wireman 2 was not a full-fledged member because he ignored the group's standards of output, consistently turning out and reporting more output than they believed proper.

Wireman 5 was excluded from both groups because he had a tendency to criticize other workers in the presence of bosses.

Wireman 6 belonged with Group A with respect to his output (higher than Group B but not above the group standard) but he horsed around too much to suit Group A, and he had a tendency to try to assert leadership over the entire group, which they did not accept.

The entire group of men had certain ideas or sentiments as to the way a worker should conduct himself. They were:

1. You should not turn out too much work; if you do, you are a "rate-buster."
2. You should not turn out too little work; if you do, you are a "chiseler."
3. You should not tell a superior anything to the detriment of a fellow worker; if you do, you are a "squealer."
4. You should not try to maintain social distance or act important; if you are an inspector, for example, you should not act like one.

The individual's position in the group was largely, though not entirely, determined by the extent to which his behavior was in line with those sentiments.

The members of Clique A, the people who held the most favored position in the room, followed these rules of behavior in all respects. Members of Clique B followed rules 1, 3, and 4. They slipped somewhat with respect to rule 2; their output was rather low. They made up for this by a greater insistence on the other rules. Squealing, for instance, was particularly abhorrent to them, because more of their actions were wrong from the standpoint of management, and they hated any show of superiority because they apparently felt that they were in a subordinate position to Group A.

The Group's Methods of Control

The methods used by the group to bring pressure on the individual and control his conduct was neither gentle nor subtle. They included sarcasm, name-calling, "binging," and ridicule. They ostracized persons whose behavior was against their interests.

They protected themselves against interference by bringing into line those outsiders—such as supervisors and inspectors—who were in a position to interfere in their affairs. When one inspector got out of line, they caused him to be transferred. They would finish a large number of equipments at once, then charge daywork because they had to wait for him to inspect the equipments. They dropped solder and screws in his test set so that it short-circuited. Pretending to help him, they would pull the plugs on his test set out just far enough so that it wouldn't work. They goaded him until he finally blew up and made exaggerated statements about the group's behavior to his supervisors. The Bank Wiring section chief and foreman supported their people, and the inspector was transferred.

The group protected themselves against management by keeping their output records level and uniform. In this way they felt that they were protecting themselves against changes.

Why the Group Felt a Need to Protect Itself

To understand why this group felt a need to protect itself, it was necessary to understand the position of the group in the company structure. Three major groups had an important effect on the worker and his job: management, supervisors, and technologists—or perhaps supervisors and technical specialists as the visible representatives of abstract management. The technical specialists—engineers, cost accountants, rate settlers—are employed by management, in part at least, to improve processes and methods. They tend to be experimentally minded. They look at the worker with a critical eye, thinking of ways in which his job can be improved.

To the worker, however, his job, the way he does it, and his relations with other workers, are not objective matters. They are full of social significance. Changes in them affect his status, and may upset his feelings of self-importance.

Frequently plans to improve efficiency do not take the worker's feelings into account. The worker is frequently called upon to adjust himself to changes about which he has not been consulted; and from his position at the bottom level of the organization, he cannot be expected to feel the same way about the changes as do those who are planning them. Many of these changes tend to subordinate the worker still further in the company's social structure.

This attitude was reflected in the response of the group to supervision. Most of the problems of the supervisors were in getting the workers to conform to the rules of the technical organization. The worker's conduct was considered right or wrong insofar as it followed those rules; the supervisor was judged according to his success in enforcing those rules. These rules were considered to be economically advantageous to the worker; but to the worker they were merely annoying—they seemed to be merely ways of showing authority over him.

For example, the rule about not helping each other to wire was intended to promote efficiency and therefore increase the earnings of the worker. To the wiremen it was just an arbitrary rule. They liked to help each other. It was a way of expressing their solidarity, their group spirit, and they felt sure that it did not slow them down—it gave them a lift.

To sum up, in the bank wiring observation room there had grown up an informal organization that controlled the behavior of its members for the sake of protecting itself against technical and supervisory interference. The group was banded together to resist change or threat of change. The members felt the need of resistance because of their position in the company structure and their relation with other groups in the company.

SIGNIFICANCE OF THE HAWTHORNE EXPERIMENTS FOR THE SUPERVISOR

Now, we've been talking about some events that took place at Hawthorne between 1927 and 1932. If you read *Management and the Worker*, however, where in many cases you will find verbatim reports of what workers said, you will find that people felt and thought and talked about the same as they do now.

What is the significance of all this for the supervisor today?

The Individual

First, the interviewing program demonstrated very clearly that complaints cannot always be taken at face value. Complaints are often symptoms of underlying problems or preoccupations that employees cannot recognize without help or cannot state except to a person who, they feel, will understand. What can the supervisor do about this? He can listen more and talk less. He can try to understand. He can try to behave in such a way that employees will want to talk to him.

Second, a point clearly demonstrated in the illumination experiments in the relay assembly test room and the bank wiring room is that an individual's behavior can rarely be predicted in terms of a simple cause-and-effect relationship. Rather, the individual's response is usually determined by a complex system of related factors—as illustrated in Figure 16–9—which must be considered as a whole before predicting behavior.

The Company Social Structure

The interviewing program, particularly the interviews with supervisors, brought out the significance of the social relationships throughout the company, and the importance to the employee of the symbols of prestige and status connected with his job. Employees, for instance, were much more concerned with wage differentials as symbols of status than with absolute amounts of wages. There were other obvious symtols of prestige—double pedestal desks, different types of calendar pads, name in the telephone directory, and so on. Symbols of status are of great importance to the individual, and activity that threatens to change them will usually provoke a defensive response.

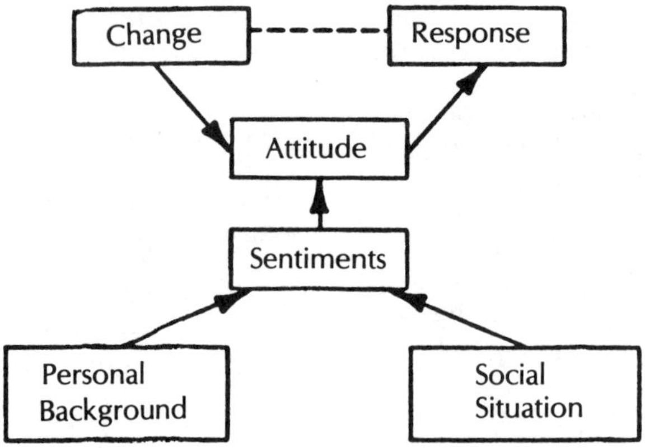

FIGURE 16–9. Interrelated Factors in Human Behavior.

The Informal Group

The bank wiring observation room demonstrated the workings of an informal group, the various levels of membership in the group, the unofficial code under which it operated, and its methods of enforcing that code. Its reason for existence was shown to be the resistance to change. On the other hand, one group in the relay assembly test room demonstrated that under certain conditions a group will not be affected adversely by change. The differences in attitudes between these groups are full of significance for those who are interested in the effects of supervisory action and attitudes.

Influence on Change in Individual and Group Behavior

People get adjusted to things as they are, or at least to a kind of balance or equilibrium such that the minor variations that constantly occur are accepted and compensated for. When changes are made that upset this equilibrium, we have an employee relations problem. Changes put into effect without regard for the sentiments and beliefs of individuals and groups are frequently interpreted as lowering the individual or group in the company structure.

Therefore, to make changes with the least possible violation of the sentiments of the group requires that the supervisor understand what those sentiments are and what they are based on. He must understand the position of the people in the informal organization and must know what symbols in the working environment are significant to those positions. To achieve that understanding, the supervisor must listen to his employees; he must behave in such a way that his employees will trust him and speak more frankly to him; and he must be alert in his observation of the working relationships that develop around him.

The Hawthorne Works Today

At the corner of Cicero Avenue and Cermak Road, the area straddling the Chicago-Cicero, Illinois line, is the 141-acre Hawthorne Works of the Western Electric Company owned by American Telephone and

Telegraph Co. In the years after its opening in 1903 it dominated the U.S. communications business, producing all of the telephones used in the United States. For a time, Hawthorne produced washing machines, vacuum cleaners, and toasters, before concentrating on telecommunication equipment.

By late 1982, the corner tower and a portion of the old multistory building were all that was left of the original core of the Hawthorne Works. The rest of the old building, 1.4 million square feet, was demolished. Over the years, the old multistory building has been joined by other lower buildings on the site.

For much of the century, the Hawthorne Works employed around 40,000 people, and was one of the largest factories in the country. After dipping as low as 7,000 workers during the Depression, employment at the plant soared to an all-time high of 48,000 workers during World War II. By 1970, however, only 23,364 people worked at the plant; a year later, employment was down to 17,567. At the end of 1981, employment was 5,748 people. Figure 16–10 is a graph of employment covering the period 1970 through 1981.

What has happened to Hawthorne over the last few years is not unlike what has occurred at many other old-line manufacturing facilities. Technology, to a large extent, has passed the old factories by, making their product obsolete and their production methods outmoded. Such plants have lost millions of dollars of business and have been forced to lay off thousands of people. In the case of Hawthorne, as in so many others, the main villain is the silicon chip.

Twenty years ago, when you picked up your telephone and began to dial, you triggered a complex series of electromechanical devices at a telephone switching stations miles away. These machines switched signals from line to line, thereby completing your call. That switching equipment filled rooms. Now that same switching can be accomplished by tiny silicon chips on circuit boards a fraction of the size of the old switching equipment.

Hawthorne used to manufacture the electromechanical switching apparatus, employing thousands of skilled workers to assemble and wire the devices, but when its parent AT&T began changing over to electronic switching systems, the require-

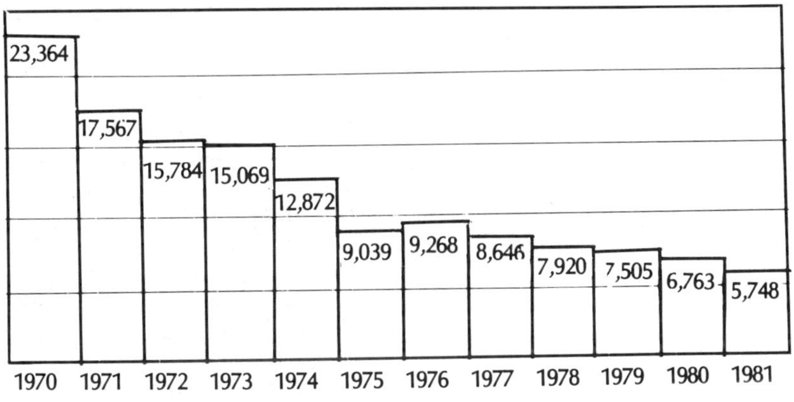

FIGURE 16–10. Employment at Western Electric's Hawthorne Works.

ment for Hawthorne's products began to dwindle. Over the last few years, Western Electric centralized its remaining electromechanical manufacturing operations at other plants at the expense of Hawthorne. Other Hawthorne operations were moved to modern, more efficient plants in the Chicago suburbs.

Hawthorne didn't capture much of the electronics business. It has been concentrated in the plants that pioneered it, or put near research facilities, so that new technology can be quickly implemented. Hawthorne has also been hurt by its age; its buildings have, in some cases, not proved suitable for making advanced electronic equipment because of design and climate problems.

Three principal businesses remain at Hawthorne today: the manufacture of the fiber-clad copper cable that AT&T uses to string the nation's phone system together; the making of wound-film capacitors that are among the building blocks of electrical devices; and, in a bow to high technology, the production and assembly of some of the same circuit boards that replaced the plant's traditional products. These operations require far fewer workers than Hawthorne previously employed.

While Hawthorne officials believe that the three lines of business remaining at the plant are viable, they worry about the advancing state of the art in communications technology. By the end of the century, fiber optics cable may eliminate the need for the copper clad cable made at Hawthorne; and a wound-film capacitor may give way to a new type called barrier-layer capacitor. Both could spell the end, or at least major changes, for still more of Hawthorne's operations.

Summary

The Hawthorne studies originally focused on the effects of environment on worker output, but led to a discovery of the importance of worker attitude and morale on output. The studies were dramatic in revealing some of the things that bring job satisfaction to industrial workers, resulting in increased productivity, improvement in quality, and lower absenteeism.

The original investigation was undertaken to determine the effect of varying the intensity of illumination on the production of workers in the factory. The results showed that regardless of whether the lighting was brighter, dimmer, or constant, production increased. This led to a new and more carefully designed study to investigate rest periods and the length of the working day. Other phases of the five-year study related to motivation and work.

The history of industrial engineering and industrial psychology is beyond the scope of this chapter on human factors. Suffice it to note that these disciplines share an interest in human performance, causes of inefficiency, and methods of improving performance.

The human factors in management approach has had a relatively small effect on the design of organization structures, but it does influence reward schemes, supervision, personnel control approaches, communication approaches, and management style. The human factors in management approach has emphasized participative management, more information sharing, and more sensitive management styles.

Questions

1. What research study began the human relations movement in American industry?
2. What were the conclusions from the illumination experiments conducted in 1924–1927 at the Hawthorne Works of Western Electric Company in Cicero, Illinois?
3. The basic studies by Elton Mayo and his group at the Hawthorne Works took place over a five-year period (1927–1932) and covered three phases. What were the three phases?
4. What did the study of the relay assembly test room involve?
5. What was accomplished from the interviewing program (1929–1930)?
6. What were the purposes of the bank wiring observation room? What was learned from this experiment?
7. What is the significance of the Hawthorne experiments for the supervisor today?
8. What did industrial psychologists learn about work groups from the Hawthorne Works studies?
9. What impact, if any, does technology have on work organizations?
10. How has technology affected the products, the factory, and employment, at the Hawthorne Works of the Western Electric Company?

Bibliography

Cass, Eugene L., and Zimmer, Frederick G., eds. *Man and Work in Society*. New York: Van Nostrand Reinhold, 1975.

Hoslett, Schuyler D. *Human Factors in Management*. Westport, Conn.: Greenwood Press, 1951.

Landsberger, Henry A. *Hawthorne Revised*. Ithaca, N.Y.: Cornell University, 1958.

Mayo, Elton L. *The Human Problems of an Industrial Civilization*. New York: Viking Press, 1960.

Roethlisberger, F. J., and Dickson, W. J. *Management and the Worker*. Cambridge, Mass.: Harvard University Press, 1940.

Whitehead, T. N. *Leadership in a Free Society*. Cambridge, Mass.: Harvard University Press, 1937.

———. *The Industrial Worker*. Cambridge, Mass.: Harvard University Press, 1938.

Wren, Daniel A. *The Evolution of Management Thought*. New York: Ronald Press, 1972.

Chapter 17

Consideration of Human Factors in Industrial Engineering

INTRODUCTION

If you set out to build a better mousetrap, you not only have to know a lot about traps but also a lot about mice. The relationship between the mouse and the trap constitutes a system. A person qualified to undertake such a task might be considered a mouse factors engineer. In the same sense, an individual who attempts to develop relationships between men and machines, and is an expert on man-machine systems, is a human factors engineer. The intent of this chapter is not to make the reader such an expert. It is, however, intended to establish an appreciation for what such an expert can do in the development and evaluation of man-machine systems.

Let's assume that while you are reading this chapter you are seated in a chair. Is it comfortable for long periods of time? Are the lighting conditions of the proper wattage and presented at a correct angle for optimal reading? Is the environment surrounding you at a comfortable temperature and is the noise level acceptable such that you are not distracted? These and other questions are the type asked by the human factors engineer whenever a human being and an environment interact. Thus, human factors engineering is the application of behavioral principles to make man and his environment more compatible. Throughout this chapter we will develop the importance of this expertise in a number of given examples, and hope to demonstrate that the steps between conception and development of the system should include consideration of human factors.

This chapter was written by P. E. Freedman, Department of Psychology, University of Illinois at Chicago, Illinois.

HUMAN FACTORS

To apply human factors we must ask the relevant questions with respect to a system and then, we hope, provide the right answers. Let us take for our example an eating system. By this we mean the system by which a human being consumes food via the utensils that would be necessary. It should be noted that the use of a knife, fork, and spoon, by Western standards, might be the simplistic answer to such a system, but there are alternatives. In some countries no machines are used and eating is done with the hand, while in others two sticks, called chopsticks, are used as the eating utensils. Therefore, let us take a naive approach to the system and review the questions or factors that we might want to take into consideration. Size of utensils may be a serious factor: that includes a part that is utilized by the hand as well as the part that is inserted into the mouth. There should also be a consideration of the shape of those parts as well as any angulation in relationship to hand-mouth elements. One must also consider the weight of the instruments and the way they are balanced. If they are to pierce any part of the food, the relative sharpness becomes a consideration. Since they involve both olfaction and taste, the taste and odor of the materials used to construct the eating utensils must be a factor as well as their ability to be cleaned. Since they come in contact with the tongue or lips, the texture becomes an important variable. And as they are involved in a gustatory activity, color and ornamentation also may be considered relevant variables. We may even find that variables such as comfort in handling, number of utensils needed, storage, and maintenance are important factors. If all of these questions arise with respect to eating utensils, how many factors arise with respect to a space capsule?

The ideal human factors engineer would have the skills of a psychologist, computer analyst, statistician, mathematician, anthropologist, anthropometrist, medical and physical specialist, business and economics expert, sociologist, engineer, and physicist. Figure 17–1 illustrates this complexity. While it is obvious that no one person embodies all of these areas of expertise, the practicing human factors engineer often consults with these various people. In addition, very often the answer to a specific question asked by a human factors engineer doesn't already exist; therefore part of his job is that of an experimental psychologist. He must run the critical experiments and find the answer for himself.

Now that we have introduced the term *system*, let's explain it. A system, minimally, is one man or woman plus one machine that work together to achieve a goal. Thus one woman yielding one hammer to knock in a nail constitutes a man-machine system. (At this point one might argue that in our modern age one should talk about person-machine systems; however this remains an awkward phrase for the field.)

Perhaps at the other extreme, the thousands of people, plus the astronauts, plus all the ground stations where there are computers and tracking devices and communications systems, and the spacecraft itself with all of its elaborate feedback systems and propellants also constitute a man-machine system.

A system has four basic functions:

1. Sensing
2. Information storage
3. Information processing and decision-making
4. Responding

How important the man is in each of these functions and how important the machine is depend upon the nature of the system. In some cases, man will do most if not all of a particular function. In other cases, the machine will play that role. Although the nature of the system will dictate the role of the man, many of the possible dimensions are illustrated in Figure 17–2. We only have space to discuss some of these.

With respect to sensing or information reception, man has at least eleven sensory devices to respond to the environment: vision; hearing; taste; olfaction; sensitivity to pain, touch, heat, cold; a kinesthetic sense that tells us where our limbs are; equilibrium; and sensitivity to particular chemicals. The sensing function of the machine becomes important when the stimulus input is beyond the limits of human capability. Thus, if the amount of light is subthreshold or if the amount of stimulation is beyond the spectrum of human reception, as are radar waves, or if the level of stimulation is so extreme that it could be dangerous to man, the role of the machine will become very important. In addition, a machine aids man in sensing when the input load exceeds the capacity of the human being.

With respect to information storage, if the information is voluminous or complex, its encoding and storage by man is limited. Man can also become confused over input, has capacity limitations, and of course,

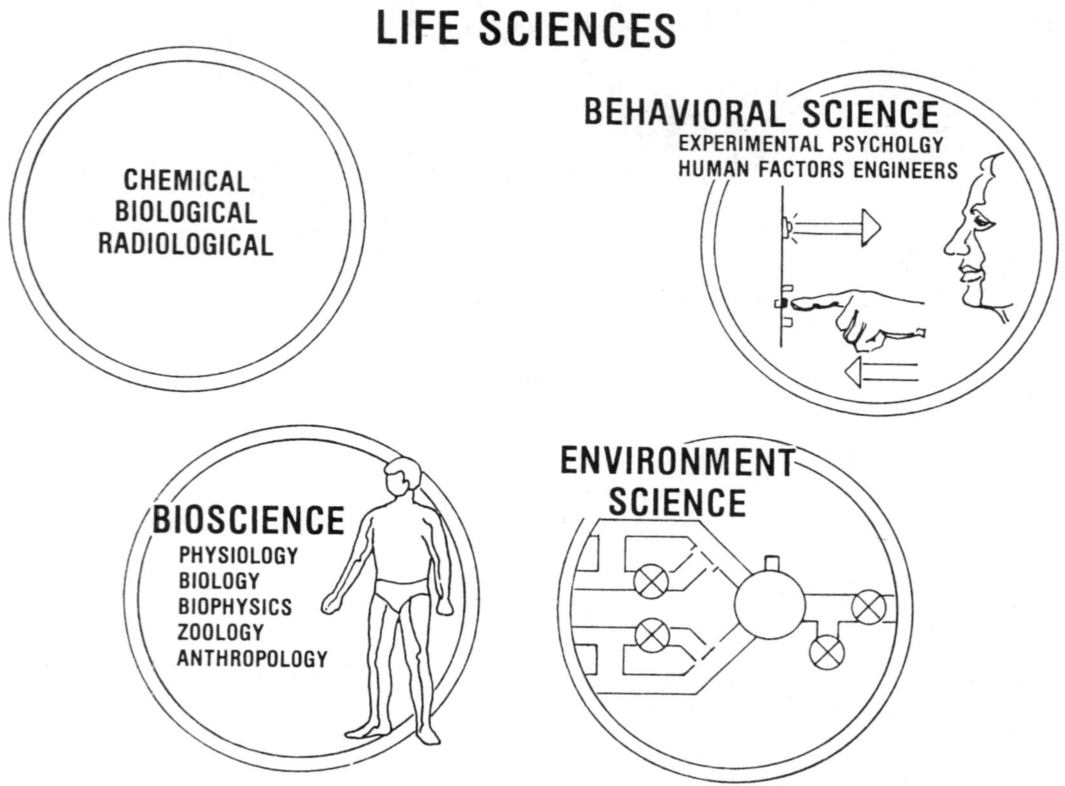

Source: Dr. Daryl R. Herzog, Psychiatric Medical Group of Orange County, Inc., LaHabra, CA, 1983

FIGURE 17–1. A Representation of Some of the Areas of Expertise Represented in Human Factors Considerations.

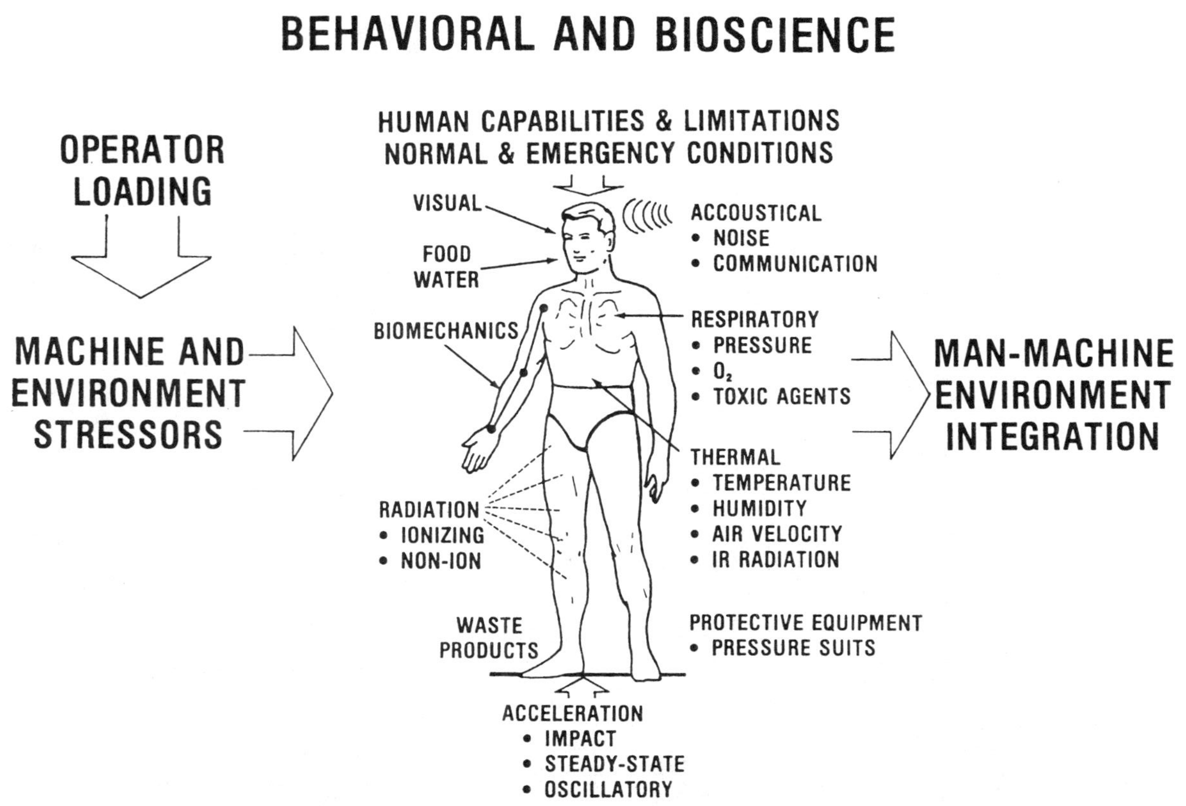

Source: Dr. Daryl Herzog, Psychiatric Medical Group of Orange County, Inc., LaHabra, CA, 1983

FIGURE 17–2. Aspects of Concern for the Man in the Man-machine Interaction.

forgets. The machine, whether it be a filing system, or—what is more common today—a computer, has almost infinite capacity for information storage. Of course, if a machine is to be used for storage, then this function must also include a retrieval process.

With respect to information processing and decisionmaking, both man and machines are capable of these processes. With respect to the machine, which we may best represent by a computer, the decision can take the form of an if-then statement. When the *ifs*, qualifiers, are large but finite, the computer is probably a better decision-making device. For example, in the space aeronautics field, whether or not the spaceship should take off depends on an extremely large number of factors such as fuel considerations, weather, all systems functioning, and so forth. One man, or even many men would have difficulty processing all of those pieces of information to make a decision as to whether a flight should take off. However, man enters the picture when the number of *if* statements are not finitely stateable. For example, add to our aerospace problem the knowledge that one of the astronauts has diarrhea, a facet that may not be included in the computer input system. Whereas the computer may say *go*, the man at the head of the system may say *no go* and override the computer.

And finally, whether man or machines function best in responding or acting again depends on several factors. Man has several disadvantages here. He is limited in strength, rate of responding, and tolerance of repetitive motions. All of those functions are not limitations on machines. Indeed, we are fast becoming a robotic world in which man's basic input is design of the robot and an occasional monitoring, while the machine is left to do almost all of the work.

FEEDBACK

Systems can also be classified in terms of the type and amount of feedback involved. Feedback is essentially some report to the individual of the consequences of an action or response in the system. In monitoring the system for information, we have to determine if the system is working correctly, and if it is not, must allow whatever correction is possible. The closed loop system is most typical of man-machine interactions where man is principally an observer. Often this is referred to as a tracking operation. Thus, from driving a nail to driving a car, the operator knows the state of the system. Whenever possible, an open loop system should be avoided. This is represented, perhaps as well as anything, by the tendency by the military to use guided missiles rather than dumb and blind projectiles.

EVALUATION CRITERIA

The role of the human factors engineer is important in the creation of a new system or the evaluation of an already existing system. In either case, certain criteria are involved in the evaluation of the proposed or existing system. Some of these criteria are objective. For example, whether we are talking about a ball bearing or a spaceship as the product of the system, are the standards sufficient to meet performance criteria in terms of accomplishing the mission? Will the ball bearing stand up to the pressures involved in operating the machinery in which it is inserted? Will the spaceship allow sufficient protection, speed, accuracy, support, and so on, for the mission to be accomplished? Next, there are subjective criteria in evaluation. Questions here involve the use of human judgment, human comfort, human usage, and human acceptability. Even if the objective standards are met, the problems with subjective criteria in evaluation may lead to a breakdown in the system. Very efficient telephone-answering machines have been developed to accept messages from callers when the occupant is out. However, if the request for a message is in such a format as to cause the caller to reject the idea of talking to a machine, the function of the system breaks down. Some have tried to solve this subjective problem by leaving humorous directions for the caller.

Finally, evaluation of any system must include cost criteria. Costs, of course, involve the money necessary to develop and to modify the system to meet higher evaluation criteria. However, also involved are the costs of maintenance and replacement and human costs such as fatigue, accidents and death, ethics, and morale. A case in point relates to the air controllers' behavior in the early 1980s. The system was reasonably efficient, and within limits the subjective criteria were met insofar as the human beings could function effectively with the machines within certain time periods of work, but the long-term effects led to a rejection of the way the system was functioning and resulted in a nationwide strike.

A final consideration with respect to cost criteria involves the system's efficiency, which refers to the output divided by the input. This is an energy criteria and can never be greater than one. However, everything else being equal, the more efficient the system, the more desirable it is.

Finally, in the evaluation of an existing system or in the creation of a new system, the system's reliability becomes an extremely important factor. Some systems have components in series. A must occur, and then B, then C. If there is a breakdown in B, C will never occur. Essentially, this component is the weakest link in the chain and determines whether the system will function appropriately. The reliability of the system is equal to the product of the reliability of all of its components when the items are in series. It should be noted that, as the numbers of elements in a system with serial components increase, the reliability of the system decreases.

If the system function is critical, components should be provided in parallel. This means that two or more elements in the system are capable of performing the same function. For example, there are two sets of brakes on most modern cars. A front set and a rear set. If one set should fail, it would still be possible to bring the car to a halt. The backup system provided for astronauts in space flight is another example of components in parallel. With items in parallel the reliability of the system would be calculated by the formula,

$$R \text{ system} = [(1 - (1 - r^m)]^n$$

where m is equal to the number of units in parallel per function, n is equal to the number of functions, and r is the component's reliability. As the number of elements in parallel increases, the reliability of the system increases, and the reliability of the system is greater than the reliability of the single component. Needless to say, all of the factors that decrease critical performance of a machine (for example, wear, corrosion, breakdown) and man (for example, fatigue, disease, age, debilities) contribute to lowering the reliability of a system.

Given the nature of the system, the human factors engineer functions basically in one or two capacities. He is brought in to improve an already existing system, or he is brought in on the development of a new system. In the first capacity, the human factors engineer would analyze the present performance of the system and identify any weak points. He would then introduce changes utilizing the current state of the art or would experiment and conceivably improve the system. Finally, he would reanalyze the system in its revised format.

DEVELOPING A NEW SYSTEM

Obviously, the development of a new system is much more complex. We start with an ill-defined purpose, goal, or mission that the new system is to accomplish, and with the conditions under which this purpose is to be accomplished. Secondly, we transfer whatever knowledge is available from already existing similar systems that have a similar purpose. If the system is being designed to produce a product, certain criteria such as rate of production, quality, minimum standards, durability, precision, cost, and reliability must be considered. If the goal of the system is to perform a mission, the considerations must include accomplishment of the primary task or tasks, accomplishment of secondary tasks, efficiency, reliability, precision, time, cost, and safety. Whatever the nature of the system, its mission will be limited by cost considerations, time considerations, and the limits of human and machine capabilities.

The development of a system begins with the identification of the system's elements:

1. *Equipment.* Primary equipment, checkout or test equipment, and repair maintenance tools would be examples of necessary equipment.
2. *Personnel.* This would include operators, maintenance men, systems directors, support and backup personnel.
3. *Procedures.* To include individual and group operations; preventative, emergency, and trouble shooting procedures; and command control subsystems.

Secondary or support elements would include:

1. *Technical data.* Including operating instructions, technical manuals, procedural checklists, and blueprints.
2. *Communications.* To include transmitting/receiving equipment, communications procedures, and communications personnel.
3. *Logistics.* Including stores and spare parts, logistics channels, associated paperwork (and red tape).
4. *Organization.* Including command structure and communication organizational channels.

Special consideration of human factors must be made for horizontal (simultaneous) versus vertical (consecutive) system events. For example, in the operation of an automobile, the first event, it is hoped, is fastening the seat belt. Then a series of both horizontal and vertical events will begin to occur:

1. Turn key	Apply gas	
2. Release hand brake	Apply footbrake	
3. Apply gas	Steer	Shift
4. Apply brake	Steer	

Types of systems will differ in the stages of development that they go through. However, as a general rule, the earlier the evaluation of human factors enters into the development of a system, the cheaper and better the final system will be. Where practical, the human factors engineer should be consulted at each stage of development. Failure to do this may result in the type of tank that the army developed, which was an efficient fighting machine, but the steps to enter the tank were too small to accommodate the average army boot. Too often, the developers of a system take human factors for granted or treat them as a common sense factor, and consequently fail to see the importance of the human factors consultant in the development process. Very often this is an expensive omission.

When the system does call for human factors decisions, two processes come into play. The first is experience. This involves both common sense based on a certain sensitivity to human factors considerations and a knowledge of prior research on human factors.

HUMAN FACTORS RESEARCH

When experience is not adequate to provide the information needed for human factors decisions, one must turn to research. Simply stated, research is the systematized accumulation of information under controlled conditions. Its advantage is that it increases the probability of accurate and applicable answers to important questions. Its disadvantage is that it is expensive in terms of time and money. Behavioral related research may be one of two types. In its purest form, laboratory research may be best to address particular questions. This brings the problem into the relatively sophisticated and controlled conditions of the behavioral laboratory. However, laboratory research is valuable only if its results can be properly generalized to the system in question. If the sterility of the laboratory promotes conditions that produce different behavior than one would find in an in vivo system, laboratory research would not be applicable. When this is the case, one can turn to field observation techniques. By doing field observation research—that is, setting up conditions within the system, and observing the effects of particular variables—one sacrifices the exact control and measurement that one has in a laboratory. But if the sacrifice of control leads to discoveries that are more applicable to a given system, the sacrifice is worthwhile. One must be careful in field observation research that the experimenter-observer does not become a variable in the study. In other words, if the people who are the subjects for some variable procedure introduced into the system behave differently because they know they are being observed, then this procedure will be faulty. Care must be taken in field observation work to preclude the experimenter from being an extraneous variable in the experimenting procedure.

Whichever technique is judged the most applicable, certain conditions for experimental designs must be taken into account. The first is the specification of the independent variable. The independent variable is the event to be varied under the control of the experimenter. Examples of independent variables are amount of light for efficient control, number of different displays that a single individual can monitor, amount of time that individual can operate efficiently in a continuing system, or amount of time involved in training individuals to operate in a system.

The second decision for research design involves the dependent variable or variables. This generally is the behavior that results from changes in the independent variable. For example, one could introduce three different intensities of light in a particular situation and try to determine which one produces the most efficient behavior. Even the term efficient would have to be specifically stipulated. One may mean accuracy independent of time, or time involved to achieve a criterion of accuracy, or some combination of both accuracy and time. It is critical for the human factors engineer in coordination with system developers to decide what criterion is critical for the operation of the system. This will determine the definition of the dependent variable.

The third consideration for experimental design is specification of a control condition or control group. If the system is already in operation, the control condition is the operation of the system as it is currently constituted. The experimental condition would be the operation of the system when any change is introduced.

Finally, all other possible significant variables should be held as constant as possible, or completely counterbalanced so that they do not systematically covary with the independent variable. For example, even the day of the week that a variable is introduced could be significant. Suppose one introduced a lighting variable into an automobile factory on a Wednesday and compared it with productivity on a Monday or a Friday. One would find that productivity on Wednesdays is indeed different than on either a Monday or a Friday, not necessarily because of the lighting conditions but more probably because of a morale factor. Obviously, to control for this extraneous variable, one would compare production under one lighting condition with production under another lighting condition on the same day of the week.

After an experiment has been set up and run, the decision as to whether any one particular level of a variable in a system is superior to another rests with statistics. A difference of any size can happen by chance alone. The application of statistics tells us what the probability is that our difference did occur by chance. Behavioral experiments generally use .05 level of probability as the critical level; that means if a particular difference could have occurred by chance 5 times in a hundred or less, the independent variable will be accepted as the most probable cause of the difference. If, however, the difference is above the .05 level, let us say the .10 level, such that it could occur by chance alone 10 times in a hundred, the decision to accept the independent variable as the cause of the difference is much weaker and it may even be not acceptable. The cutoff level of probability for decisionmaking should not be held rigid. The decision as to whether to accept and therefore institute a new procedure or level of a variable should rest, at least in part, with the cost of such a decision.

An important consideration when one uses experimental technology to answer questions in human factors is subject selection. In experiments one must use subjects whose behavior can reasonably be generalized to the target population in the system. The ideal subject pool would be the population that is already involved in the system or that would be expected to become involved in the system. Such a pool may not always be available. If, for example, one was doing research on the use of a special weapons technology to be operated by privates in the armed forces, one would ideally use privates selected from the armed forces. However, if the research had been contracted to individuals in university settings, the most logical targets to save time and money would be university students. Let us further assume that these researchers are faculty on the staff of Harvard University. Although one could find comparable behaviors among Harvard students and army privates, one could also find many reasons for not having confidence in generalizing between the two populations.

In order to review the considerations one must make in setting up a good experiment, let us take as an example the selection of the best warning signal one might use in order to gain people's attention. First, one can rely on common sense and prior experience to determine, to some degree, the nature of the stimuli that one would use for such a purpose. Auditory stimuli with intensity sufficient to attract attention but not so intense as to cause alarm or fear would be logical candidates for a warning stimulus. Therefore one would select candidates from a range of types of stimuli of different frequencies and composition in order to determine which of these is the best to attract attention. For convenience, let's limit ourselves to four auditory stimuli, each of five-second duration. We will use a high-pitched tone (8,000 hertz), a low pitched tone (500 hertz), a beeping sound (3,000 hertz), and a fourth constant tone (3,000 hertz). The next decision would lie with the selection of a population. Since the experimental question is conceived of as applying to a general audience, one would look for subjects of convenience rather than special target populations. We might select a college class. Obviously, during the hour the class should be engaged in some activity other than constantly monitoring the time shown on television screens. Therefore we might conduct this experiment while a lecture is being delivered. Our data would be the number of times a particular signal was detected vis á vis the other signals, and also the latency between the onset of the signal and the time that was recorded by the students who attended to it. The application of statistics would tell us whether significant differences existed between attention to one signal versus another.

HUMAN SENSORY SYSTEMS

Now that we have a rough idea of the skills and tools that the human factors engineer needs to do his job, we can look at specific variables that are important in the man-machine interaction. This interaction is largely a matter of communication between the man and the machine. Man, utilizing his motor capacities, communicates changes for the system through controls to the machine. The machine, in turn, puts out information displays, which, through the sensory capacities of man, are communicated to the controlling individual. Starting with the sensory capacities of man, let us take two of the most commonly used sensory systems in a man-machine interaction: vision and hearing. We will use the automobile as an extended example, not because it is a particularly complicated system, but because it is one that is known by all of us. It is also a system that has evolved over the years and has been subject to extensive criticism.

The automobile and its driver constitute a closed loop system. When the machine indicates that certain behaviors would be appropriate, the person who is operating the vehicle is aware of the necessary behaviors.

Vision, obviously, is the most important sense in the driving of an automobile. Without vision, it is impossible to drive. One is often amused at the truck that traditionally appears in one city or another with the letters on it exclaiming "blind man driving." That blind man, however, is "venitian." I have seen blind people do almost everything else, including skiing with a guide, but I have never seen a blind man drive.

Before we get into the critical role of vision in this system, let us consider man's sensory capacities in general with respect to their ability to detect a signal. Man's senses are subject to two types of thresholds, both of which are of concern to the human factors engineer. The first is the absolute threshold. Research has shown that there are wavelengths of light and frequencies of sound to which the human cannot respond. For example, there are micromillimeters of light longer than red and shorter than violet that the human eye cannot detect. There are frequencies of tone below 20 hertz and above 20,000 hertz to which man is not sensitive. Signals beyond these limits would not be of use in a man-machine system. In addition to absolute thresholds, we must also be concerned with relative thresholds. This refers to the amount of change in a given stimulus necessary for that change to be detected. The selection of red and green for stop and go in traffic lights was well conceived from the standpoint that these two color stimuli are easily differentiated. However, when the initial decision on traffic lights was made and universalized, people did not take into account that some individuals are indeed red-green color blind. That is to say, the relative thresholds in determining the difference between red and green is nonexistent. It would have been better to have selected a color differential such as red and blue to accommodate these individuals. With respect to relative thresholds, man can be asked to be a nominal judge, an ordinal judge, an interval judge, and a ratio judge. The simplest and usually most accurate judgment is the nominal judgment. This is simply a matter of asking the organism whether A is different from B. The parking brake light on the automobile dashboard is an example of a nominal system. It lights up when the brake is depressed and it is off when the brake is off. The gas gauge in some cars requires ordinal judgments from the operator. Such judgments are generally not accurate nor are they linear; the needle pointing to the left indicates that there is less gas available in the tank than when the needle is pointing to the right of center. Exactly how much is not really known. Ordinal judgments require the decision as to whether A is greater than B. If we ask the additional question, Is the difference between A and B the same or greater than the difference between C and D? we are asking for interval judgments. We make interval decisions when we attempt to parallel-park a car, estimating the distance we need when backing into the space in relation to the length of our car and its turning radius. Finally, the judgment that is most complex and entails all of the previous judgments is the ratio judgment. This implies that the scale of judgment we are using has an absolute zero and the relationship of the numbers is proportionate. The speedometer of your car, if it is accurate, will present such a judgment system. There is an absolute zero of no speed, and when we are going 60 miles an hour in a 30-mile-per-hour zone, we know we are going twice the speed limit.

Given these types of judgments on all sensory systems, let us return to our example of the visual system as it is used in the automobile. First and foremost, visual information is necessary for the steering of the automobile. While most automobiles have provided adequate visual perception of the world outside of the automobile from the front end, several concessions to design have put rear vision at a disadvantage. Consequently, blind spots in rear-view vision may put driving decisions in jeopardy. Vision also comes into play with respect to the instrument system of the automobile. Three aspects of vision are critical: acuity, brightness, and color (a combination of hue and saturation). Acuity refers to the ability of our retinal receptors (rods and cones) to detect details. The cones function in bright light and are color sensitive. The rods function in dim lumination and are achromatic. Cones are centered in the back of the middle of the eyeball, whereas rods are more peripheral. Finally, because of their neurological connections, the cones are much better able to detect details than are the rods.

When this knowledge is applied to a display package for our automobile, certain decisions must be made along human factors lines. Although certain pieces of visual information are coming in at all times, some information is more important than others. The primary display is the road. This should include not only the front view but also the rear view and side views of the road. The placement of rear-view and sideview mirrors is critical to compensate for any blind spots. The next important visual instrument would be the speedometer. It should be placed where it could be constantly monitored without distracting vision from the road. Its numbers must be large enough to meet minimal visual acuity and one might use a differential color to indicate critical speeds such as 55 and 30. For night driving, it should be reasonably bright. The gas gauge, although it is important, does not have to be constantly monitored and therefore can be put in a slightly peripheral position. Other visual displays that carry information about oil level, parking brake, battery, and so on can also be relegated to peripheral locations and can utilize light indicators to warn of malfunction. Red has traditionally been used as the color of these types of lights since red has been associated with danger.

Audition is also a sense that provides valuable feedback in any human factor system. Sound, as a sensory input, has the advantage over visual stimuli insofar as orientation towards the input is not required. You must be looking in the direction of a visual stimulus to have it affect your behavior. Auditory input will be received regardless of direction of attention. Three distinct audio inputs that now characerize most automobiles are the horn, the clicking of directional signals, and the warning buzzer telling the driver that he has not fastened his seat beats. As an aside, the latter stimulus, the seat belt buzzer, provides an example of how well-intentioned human engineering may go awry. Initially, when the seat belt was required for safety purposes, a buzzer was included that buzzed continually if the seat belt was not used. The purpose of this was to prompt the driver to use the seat belt and therefore terminate the signal. In contrast with the anticipated behavior, most people had the annoying buzzer disconnected. New cars now use a short initial buzzing just to remind the driver.

Other considerations for auditory stimuli include selections of range and intensity. The human ear is most sensitive to tones between 1,000 and 3,000 hertz. And, while loud and sudden noises certainly attract immediate attention, they may also arouse startle responses and disorient the individual when the situation calls for a controlled response.

We have thus far emphasized only two of the many senses that man has to interact with machines, but others are just as important to man-machines systems. Kinesthesis, for example, is all too often taken for granted. That we know the position of our limbs without having to utilize other senses is very important to the operation of any system. Indeed, the mere act of walking would be impaired significantly if we were lacking in this sense.

INFORMATION PROCESSING

Having discussed the sensory channels of system input, we can now turn to the nature of the information that is detected by the sensors. Ideally, the amount of information that the individual receives could be measured in bits. Bits of information are easily conceived when one talks about digital computers or number of numbers. However, the quantification of information in the human system is often not digital but rather analogic. One can ask, for example, how many bits of information have been received by you in the process of reading this paragraph. It would not be clear that everyone would agree as to the number of individual items or units of information. In the design of a system, the designer will select a source of information to be transmitted to the human observer. The source will rely on some channel of communication and will involve an input. The input is the amount of stimulus information flowing through the channel. The output of the information is measured by the amount of information received from a channel. The output cannot exceed the input, but very often the output is less than the input, and consequently, there is a loss of information in the transmission. This loss of information between input and output in the transmission is labeled equivocation. Any distortion in the output during transmission is referred to as noise.

Without question, machines can communicate with machines much more rapidly and with much more accuracy than machines can communicate with man. Therefore, when selecting a channel for information transmission to humans, the designer should be fully conscious of the optimal dimensions for such communication. For example, vision is the best modality and within that modality the best single dimension is hue or color. If one is concerned with the best temporal-spatial single dimension, the position of a pointer on a dial is the best way to communicate. Generally speaking, the capacity of the channel in any one dimension is seven plus or minus two pieces of information. It is not surprising that telephone numbers are seven digits. This is certainly not to say that man cannot handle more information than seven units. But going well beyond seven units of information requires more repetitive presentations and longer periods of study for storage.

Another important factor in communication in man-machine systems is stress. Stress refers to the motivational pressure put on the human being by the system. Moderate amounts of stress are optimal insofar as the stress keeps the individual alert and attentive to information being communicated within the system. Extremely low levels of stress lead to low motivational levels to receive information, whereas high levels of stress add too much noise to a system for communication to be accurate.

One technique for increasing communication in the system is the use of multiple inputs. Multiple inputs refer to the use of either multiple channels or multiple modalities of information input. For example, a triple input system in our example of a design of an automobile would be the sounding of a buzzer when the seat belt is not used coupled with the flashing of the red light on which the words *seat belt* are printed. Multiple inputs are important for efficient communication if they indicate the same event. If however, multiple inputs are coexistent that indicate diverse events, there is a competition for attention and inefficiency may be introduced into the system. For example, when driving a car in dense traffic at high speeds, one is less apt to notice that one has not turned off the directional signal.

Another technique for transmission of information involves coding, which is the process of representing information symbolically. A red light is a coded signal for warning or stop. A green light is a symbol or code for go. One must be careful that the individual who is the recipient of a coded message has properly learned the meaning of the code. For example, on written driving tests in the state of Illinois, the candidate is asked to identify the meaning of road signs by their shape and color. Such coding enables people who are unfamiliar with the language of a state or country in which one is driving to identify the message indicated by the sign. Beside overcoming language barriers, coding makes possible the communication of a large amount of information in a very short transmission because of previous learning.

The use of speech in communication is extremely important. Speech is coded information. Its intelligibility depends upon the learning experience of the individual recipient. An American with no Oriental language training can sit and listen to a tape recording of Chinese and get no information transmission from it. However, speech, and its written representation, are the major channels for communication within a given culture. Television, radio, movies, tapes, computers, and so on, are all examples of machines talking to people. The obvious variables involved in efficiency in such types of communication include rate of input, loudness or clarity, repetition, and duration of information statements. Significantly, the range of frequency spectrum for speech, which is from 300 to 6,000 hertz, embodies the frequencies to which man's hearing is most sensitive (1,000 to 3,000 hertz).

A critical element of speech communication is intelligibility. Intelligibility is a function of the above-mentioned variables but also includes a very important concept of signal-to-noise ratio. If you are having a discussion at a very noisy cocktail party, in order to communicate with another individual, you must raise the decibel level of your speaking voice considerably above the level of noise at the party. Obviously, as noise level goes up and signal level is held constant, the degree of intelligiblity decreases. Finally, an extremely important factor in speech communication is motivation. If a machine or another individual is attempting to communicate with a human being, the message must contain information that the recipient considers has value to him in responding to the system. If motivation is absent in a message, very little information will be communicated.

Thus far, with respect to speech communication, we have only considered speech from the machine to the man, or from one man to another. We are rapidly approaching an age where speech communication will be used for the man to communicate with the machine. Critical to this dimension of man-machine interaction would be our ability to attune the machine to the nuances of the individual's voice. When this is done, we will virtually be able to tell the system what we want it to do.

INFORMATION DISPLAYS

Having discussed the sensory characteristics of people, we must now consider the display of information. Information display is the machine's attempt to communicate with man. Critical decisions must be made with respect to the way information is communicated from the machine. The first limitation on information display is the amount of information that is essential for presentation. Obviously, the most important information should be most dominant. Although the machine may be made to display information in great detail, the importance of the detail and its consequences should dictate how accurate and complex the information display should be.

The key to a well-developed information display is the use of contrast. Contrast is an attention-getting device. If the function of the display is to provide the human observer with critical information about changes in the system, the device or devices used to indicate that information must contrast with the normal condition of the system. This is why, for example, certain portions of a dial that indicate danger or damage are presented in red. Ordinarily, people don't look at the position of dials with respect to numbers unless they are trained to do so. This is also why a good display should be dynamic rather than static. A static display would be represented by a nonflashing sign. If, when you entered your car, a little sign above the dashboard said "fastern your seatbelts," you might attend to it the first two or three times you drive your car, but after that it would blend into the decor of the car. A more effective clue to remind you to fasten your seat belts is the one currently used—a light plus a buzzer signal.

In addition to deciding on the placement of various indicators in the display mode, one also has to make various decisions about the nature of each display. Suppose the designer of the system wishes to use a meter device to indicate information about the state of the system. Having made that decision, he is faced with a series of decisions specifically related to the type of meter to use. For example, should the angle of displacement for the entire scope of the meter scale be 90°, 180°, or something larger? How refined should the units of demarcation on the meter be, and how large should the marking be? Is there a danger or signal level that is particularly important, and how should it be designated? Should the back of the meter be mirrored to ensure true eye alignment? Does the meter need to be illuminated? Fortunately, the answers to most of these questions are available through prior research and are at the fingertips of the human factors engineer. Some of the questions can be answered by common sense. For example, the answer to the last—should the meter be used in dim illumination—is, of course, it must be illuminated.

Decisions with respect to individual items in a display cannot be made independently of a configuration of an entire display. The center of the display should contain the most important information-conveying items and can be expected to allow the presentation of the most detail. More peripheral items receive less attention and convey less detail. Items that indicate important but rare instances of system problems may be relegated to peripheral visual display but can utilize an auditory attention-getting device to make sure that the operator is aware of any problem and can turn to that indicator to find the nature of the problem. The total configuration of information display would also involve such variables as height, expected distance of viewing, and curved versus flat display. If a single individual is to be the operator or monitor of the system, a somewhat curved display would be advantageous since it would present more information equally distant to the individual. However, if several people are monitoring the system, a flat presentation would be most convenient.

In summary, certain characteristics can be stipulated for effective instrument display. These are:

1. The display can be read quickly in the manner desired.
2. The display can be read as accurately as demanded by the operator's need, and not more accurately than needed.
3. The display is free of factors that produce ambiguity.
4. The information is provided in its most immediately meaningful format and does not require mental translation into other units.
5. Changes in indicators are easily detected.
6. Information is current and time delay is minimized.
7. The failure of an indicator to operate is easily detected.

MOTOR RESPONSE SYSTEMS

In discussing how the machine communicates to man, we have considered how the machine displays information to the human sensorium. When man operates on the system, on the other hand, his responses are communicated to the machine through the machine's control. For our first consideration, we must look at the characteristics of the human motor response system. Four basic parameters must be accounted for in considering the motor capability of man. These are accuracy, speed, amplitude or strength, and endurance. Since these trade off against each other, decisions must often be made regarding which should be given the highest priority. For example, generally the more speed that is required of a movement, the less accuracy is produced. Also, accuracy will suffer if endurance, the ability for the response to be maintained over repetitions or long periods of time, is increased.

One concern of motor processes is the degree of precision required in the response. This includes considerations for the degree of error the system will tolerate and still be effective. A vast literature in the psychological journals is related to motor responses and their parameters. For a consideration of motor responses let us return to our example of the automobile. Driving an automobile requires many responses that could be called upon simultaneously. Consequently, if one is driving at high speeds, the response requirements should be critically considered. In terms of accuracy of responding, the standard automobile allows for a reasonable degree of error. Analogue responding is more demanding in a system than is digital responding. Therefore, as many responses as possible should be put in a digital format. In the automobile, many functions that require responding are on-off digital response requirements. This would include headlights, windshield wipers, defroster, and the like. The more demanding that analogue responding (steering, acceleration, and in some instances radio tuning) is, the greater, and in some cases more continuous, the attention it requires. A good friend of mine who was driving while attempting to tune his radio with a dial tuner ended up in a hospital after having hit a tree.

In many automobiles, both speed and strength requirements are machine aided. In particular, the use of power steering, power brakes, and also button-pressing radio tuning transfer a great deal of the demands from the man to the machine. In some cars, the addition of a constant speed control device relates to a final response consideration, that of endurance. While many features of the automobile allow the operator a great deal of relaxation and comfort in the operation of the vehicle, the trade-off may be a relaxation of attention to the point of danger. When vigilance is relaxed, the response time of the system increases. Response time has three basic components. The first component is the time between the demand for a response and the initiation of that response. The more complex the signal that calls for a response, the slower the initiation of that response because of the information processing required. The second component of response time is the reaction time itself. This relates to the nature of motor requirement that is involved in making the required response. The third component is the system's response time. Given that the human element has made its response, this becomes a question of how long it takes the machine part of the system to complete the task required.

Critical to the selection of a response in any given system is the notion of transfer. Transfer is a concept related to the appropriateness of previously learned responses. If one has learned a response to a prior system, which is now required for a very similar new system, the transfer is highly positive. In other words, prior learning will facilitate responding in the new system. At the other extreme, if prior learning in a similar system required one response, and now the new system requires a quite different response, the transfer will be negative. The prior learning of a competing response to a similar stimulus will now interfere with the formulation of a new response to the new system. Negative transfer can be quite disastrous to the functioning of a system. As a case in point, consider an incident regarding my own behavior in a very simple system called the bicycle. As a youth, I grew up with a standard American bicycle that had foot brakes. After a prolonged period of adult life that did not include a bicycle, I bought a three-speed hand-brake model. A week after having obtained the bicycle I was challenged to a race around the block by a neighborhood youth. In turning a corner, I realized that at the speed I was going I was destined to hit a parked car. I intended to slow down, but in the stress of the moment I proceeded to do what I had always done when I wanted to slow down: press down on the foot brake (which wasn't there). Another example of negative transfer with respect to the automobile is the tendency for people who are in a skid to steer away from the direction of the skid, while the appropriate response is to steer in the direction that one is skidding.

One of the most critical types of motor responses involved in the man-machine interaction is tracking. Tracking is the response by the man in the system, based on feedback, that keeps the machine in pursuit of the goal of the system. In our automobile example, tracking would be represented by our attempt to keep the car on the road in the prescribed lanes by the use of the steering wheel. We are also tracking when we attempt to keep the speedometer needle at 30 mph. Our ability to successfully track depends upon a number of variables, among them a realistic representation of the target-follower relationship, complexity of feedback information, precision of feedback information, background noise that may interfere with our tracking, compatibility between the display and our ability to control the system, and control sensitivity.

In designing a system, one should be sensitive to display-control compatibility. Generally speaking, we turn dials clockwise in order to increase something. That something may be the amount of light or the volume of sound. We would also want our system to respond in the direction of our controlling device whenever possible. For example, we would like our car to turn left when we turn the steering wheel left. These are compatible responses. In contrast, incompatible responses are found when we talk about the operation of a rudder to steer a boat, and the removal of lugs from certain wheels on a car. Underlying the compatibility notion is the principle of transfer that we have discussed already.

DESIGN OF CONTROLS

Using his response to the system, man communicates with the machine by means of controls. Consequently, the selection and design of the controls are a critical part of any man-machine system. Generally, we think of controls being manipulated either by the hands or by the feet. As a general rule of thumb, operations best done with the hands should be relegated to the hands and the same holds true with the feet. When an operation can be handled reasonably well by hands or feet, and the feet are not overtaxed, it is generally better to relegate that function to the feet. However, one should not forget that other parts of the body can be used for control. For example, in some types of pressing operations the knee is used to operate the presser, and doctors who need to run water during surgery have controls that can be turned on with an elbow.

A vast literature based on experimental psychology indicates the advantages and disadvantages of almost every type of control device imaginable. In general, the important considerations are as follows. First, errors may arise in the use of controlled devices if the controls can be confused. When necessary, controls should be carefully labeled as to their function and direction of operations. One of the important characteristics of controls is their demand characteristics. By this we mean the amount of attention the operator must give to the control while he is performing more critical operations. Let us assume we have one lever in our automobile that can turn on the heater, air-conditioner, or defroster. If you are driving down the road and the windshield becomes clouded, you will want to activate the defroster. If the defrost function required some intermediate adjustment of the lever, we might have to take our eyes off the road momentarily in order to find that adjustment. As a consequence, the proper design would be to put the defrost function in the last position of the lever, so that we could throw the lever to the correct position rapidly without looking away from the road. Another source of error in control occurs when the controls are crowded together in an inadequate space. Here we have the problem of either selecting the incorrect control because it is in the vicinity of the control we are after, or inadvertently operating one control while manipulating another one. Errors due to forgetting enter the system when the ordinary sequence of controlled events is altered. If you drive your automobile to work in the daytime, when you reach the work station you generally go through a sequence of control procedures that would include turning off the heater, the radio, and the ignition. If, for some reason, you change your route and go through a tunnel that requires your headlights, it is highly probable that when you get to work you will forget to turn off the lights. We have already mentioned the errors that can crop up because of incompatibility between the operation of the control and the direction of the system. Fortunately, in system designs that are universal, designers generally have adopted standards in compatibility.

Returning to our example of the car, let us consider the location, type, and importance of the various instruments that control the car's functioning. With the exception of a relatively small number of countries throughout the world, the driver sits on the left-hand side of the car. The three most critical controls in the automobile are the steering wheel, the accelerator, and the brake. Decisions regarding the steering wheel are related to its gear ratio in the steering mechanism, its radius, and angle of tilt. With the accelerator and the brake, since they are both pedal operated, our concern is with a traverse from zero to complete depression, and with location. It is comforting to note that at least all automobiles have the accelerator on the right side and the brake on the left. The location of other controls, although used less frequently, are critical. I have owned a car in which the control for the window wiper was positioned so that one had to reach through the steering wheel to operate it. Fortunately, on most cars that control is now easily accessible as part of the directional signal lever. One control that has not been completely standardized is that used to activate a horn. Some cars have the horn button in the center of the wheel, others have it somewhere on the radius of the wheel, some have it around the top of the rin, and others have it along the bottom of the rim of the wheel. A useful exercise might be to think of ways one could design a study to determine the best placement for a horn control.

ANTHROPOMETRY

So far we have talked about the sensory and response capacity for a system developed for the average man. But who or what is the average man? When we build a system, we attempt to design it so as to maximize the functioning capabilities of the operator. Or, if the system is fixed in some way, we must stipulate the characteristics of the operator that can maximally use this system. In either case, we must measure man. The measurement of man is the science of anthropometry. If everyone were the same size, weight, girth, and so on, then there would be no need for anthropometry. Obviously, people vary. But to what extent? Where is the tenth percentile of a person's head size? What percentage of the population has a shoe size greater than size 10, or wider than D?

To make any piece of equipment, clothing, or work space optimally suitable to all possible users would be extremely expensive. Therefore, the next question becomes: What is the optimal size(s) necessary to accommodate the majority of possible users? In many cases, the data on sizes are already available. However, when a new demand for a system arises, research must be undertaken to establish the size that fits the average user. A case in point is the development of a protective ceramic shield that was developed by the army during the Vietnam War to protect the chests of pilots of bubble-shaped helicopters. To test the prototype of the shield, it was necessary to take several sized pilots up as operators of the helicopter to see if they could reach all of the necessary controls. This procedure also points out the importance of testing a sized product in the dynamic situation in which it is to be used, of testing the product with a person who will be using it in the field.

Another important consideration for the human factors engineer is the organization of the work space with its critical components. Are the components of the work space ideally located to produce the most efficient system? To establish the optimal workshop arrangement, it is often best to watch operators within the system at work. The tools of this type of experimental work may include film, eye movement recording, personal observations with time sampling, and subjective analyses utilizing such things as interviews or questionnaires presented to the operators. A critical factor that must always be taken into account when one attempts to evaluate a system, and in this case the workshop arrangement of a system, is that the observations, whether they may be of any of the type previously mentioned, should not interact with the behavior being observed or recorded. Whenever an observer, an attention-attracting device, or an interviewer is present, people within the system may respond differently by virtue of this unique intrusion. A classical case is the Hawthorne study (described in Chapter 16) where it was found that no matter what changes took place in the factory environment, performance improved. This result is attributable to the attention paid to the workers when the observations were done.

For an exercise in consideration of workshop arrangement, let us consider the kitchen. While the concept of a kitchen is universal, the best design of a kitchen will vary with the culture since the type of food preparation will determine the type of kitchen that is optimal. Let's use the American kitchen for our example. Where would one place the various appliances for optimal use? Should the stove or the refrigerator be placed closest to the sink? How much work space is desirable? Where should the eating utensils and the dishes be placed to minimize time and effort? Think of the kitchen with which you are most familiar. How would you redesign it to make it an optimal work environment?

Not only must one be concerned with the placement of critical elements in the work space, but one must attempt to maximize the ambient conditions surrounding the work space. These ambient considerations can generally be classified as illumination, noise, atmospheric conditions, and vibrations. Questions that one might ask in this category would include: Is the amount of light sufficient for the task to be done? Is there glare that interferes with the task? Is the noise level created by the workers, machines, or the external environment detracting and fatigue causing? Are the temperature and humidity levels comfortable for maximal performance?

A final matter for consideration is safety. Depending upon the nature of the task, risks will vary. A checklist of potential safety hazards might include: exposed high voltage wiring, exposed gears or moving machine parts, the presence of poisonous or volatile liquids and gases, fire hazards, and improperly marked existing hazards. One of the most critical factors in on-the-job accidents involves fatigue or lack of attention. One of the best ways to assure a low rate of accident proneness is adequate training.

You may, by this point, be somewhat overwhelmed by the requirements for a thorough human factors analysis of any given man-machine system. Remember, the two critical considerations are: Have I asked all of the relevant questions, and Where can I find the answers?

The response to the first question is that general checklists are available for a variety of systems. If no such checklists are available, one must consider the task of establishing one. This would include gathering of experts related to the given system. It might also involve consultation with a human factors engineer. If the system is complex, it would be advisable to have at hand the human factors engineer. A list of some of the relevant references and journals is included to give you guidance.

Questions

1. Stipulate five human factors questions one might raise in a college classroom system.
2. What considerations are important with respect to assembly-line conveyor-belt response requirements? Discuss this in relation to the four response parameters.
3. Do a response frequency analysis of a cook preparing a meal in a kitchen (real or hypothetical).
4. Design an experiment to determine if work breaks improve performance. Stipulate dependent and independent variations and control conditions.
5. Stipulate how the four basic functions of a system relate to a bank.
6. Design a bedroom, including clothes closet, wake-up system, and so on, for a person who is both deaf and blind. Be imaginative.
7. Do a vertical and horizontal analysis of responses involved in riding a bicycle.
8. List a function in a human factors system for each of eleven sense modalities.
9. Redesign the automobile to be built for the richest men in the world to own and drive.
10. What does a human factors engineer do, and what does he offer the industrial engineer?

Bibliography

JOURNALS

Behavioral Research Methods and Instrumentation

Human Factors

Journal of Applied Psychology

Organizational Behavior and Human Performance

Perceptual and Motor Skills

BOOKS

Chapanis, A. *Man-Machine Engineering.* Monterey, Calif.: Brooks/Cole, 1965.

Croney, J. *Anthropometrics for Designers.* New York: Van Nostrand Reinhold, 1971.

Lenihan, J. *Human Engineering: The Body Re-examined.* New York: G. Braziller, 1975.

McCormick, E. J. *Human Factors Engineering.* 3rd ed. New York: McGraw-Hill, 1970.

———. *Human Factors in Engineering and Design.* New York: McGraw-Hill, 1976.

Meister, D. *Human Factors: Theory and Practice.* New York: Wiley, 1971.

Poulton, E. C. *Tracking Skill and Manual Control.* New York: Academic Press, 1974.

Woodson, W. *Human Factors Design Handbook.* New York: McGraw-Hill, 1981.

Chapter 18

Human Factors and Electrical Safety in a Medical Setting

INTRODUCTION

Electricity has had a tremendous impact on mankind. In the field of health care, numerous advances in diagnosis and treatment have been made as a result of its use. Biomedical electronics and instrumentation form one of the most advancing subareas of the electrical environment in health care. Yet, its ability to do good is also associated with its potential to do injury.

The improper use of electricity introduces the possible hazards of burn, explosion, fire, shock, and power failure, with the possibility of serious injury, disability, or death, and damage to the function of electromedical equipment. The greater utilization of different types of apparatus and the quantity and complexity of electrical and electronic equipment in diagnostic and therapeutic patient support have magnified the safety program. When multiple units are used on the same patient, the safety problem becomes compounded and therefore additional caution must be taken.

THE SAFETY ENVIRONMENT

Certainly, one of the objectives of any progressive medical clinic or hospital is to provide a safe and healthful work place for its personnel and patients. Medical science and environmental conditions in many parts of the world have reduced, and in some instances even eliminated, certain types of diseases. At the same time, the human community still is subject to a state of unhealthy occupational safety.

There is a profound need for the applications of safety engineering to the broad spectrum of biomedical equipment and its uses. Our discussion of this need must, of necessity, be more of the nature of mentioning problems than of presenting the results of completed research. A few examples of conditions relating to safety precautions in a medical setting are summarized in this chapter. The types of electrical injuries are: electrical burns, lacerations, electric shock, and falls caused by electrical shock. There is another type associated with electrical injuries called conjunctivitis, which is an inflammation of the mucous membrane of the eye. It may be painful while it lasts, but the temporary discomfort is not serious.

ELECTRICAL INJURIES

The capacity of an electric current to cause injury when some part of the body is interjacent between two conductors having different electrical potential varies enormously. The hazards from the use of electricity are electric shock, electric tissue damage, fire and explosion, and eye flash.

The first man-made electric shock was recorded in Holland in 1746, when two physicists, George von Kleist and Peter van Masschenbroek, accidently discharged a Leyden jar and the current went through their bodies. The first recorded death from

TABLE 18–1.
National Estimate of Emergency-Department Treated Cases Associated With Electric Wire or Wiring Systems Injuries, 1980

Diagnosis	*Weighted Count*	*Locale by Type*	*Weighted Count*
Electrical burns	3,170	Home	5,461
Lacerations	2,220	Public	675
Electric shock	822	Sports or recreation site	218
Contusions, abrasions	567	Apartment or condominium	181
Strain or sprain	443	Industrial site	162
Foreign body	302	School	136
Puncture	166	Street or highway	118
Fractures, concussions, not stated, other, chemical and thermal burns, dermatitis and conjunctivitis, hematoma	665	Farm	114
		Unknown	1,290
Total cases	8,355		8,355

SOURCE: Correspondence with the U.S. Consumer Product Safety Commission, Hazard Identification and Analysis, National Injury Information Clearing House, Washington, D.C., February 12, 1981.

commercial electric energy occurred in 1879 in Lyons, France, when a stage carpenter was electrocuted by a 250-volt AC dynamo. An early U.S. electrical accident occurred in New York City when a telegraph lineman was electrocuted on October 11, 1889.

According to survey data collected and reported in 1980 by the U.S. Consumer Product Safety Commission, Washington, D.C.,[1] there were 8,355 emergency admissions to hospitals caused from injury associated with electrical wiring or wiring systems. A diagnosis of the injury and its place of occurrence are given in Table 18–1. Note that most frequent injury is electrical burn, accounting for 37.9 percent of all injuries associated with electrical wire or wiring systems. The body parts most frequently injured are the hand, finger, head, and eye. The location where accidents most frequently occur is the home for 65.4 percent; public places account for approximately 8.06 percent.

More germane to this discussion are the frequency data on accidents occurring in public places, such as health care facilities, restaurants, theaters, and so on. Table 18–2 presents the frequency of diagnosis and the body part affected. Electrical burns account for 56 percent of the injuries, and electric shock for 4.7 percent. Males sustained most of the injuries (that is, 86.7 percent of the total cases) and patients ranging in age from 25 to 35 accounted for 53.2 percent of the total cases.

Electricity can cause mild to severe burns and burn-type tissue damage in three distinct ways:

1. Electrical spark or arcs can cause an individual's clothing to ignite.
2. The heat energy generated by an electrical arc occurring relatively close to an individual can cause burn injuries.

[1]U.S. Consumer Product Safety Commission, *Neiss Frequency Report on Product: 0605 Electrical Wire or Wiring Systems for 1980* (Washington, D.C.)

TABLE 18–2.
National Estimate of Emergency-Department Treated Cases Associated With Electric Wire or Wiring Systems Injuries at Public Locations, 1980

Diagnosis	*Treated Cases*	*Body Parts*	*Treated Cases*
Electrical burns	378	Shoulder	225
Laceration	131	Knee	134
Electric shock	32	Hand	121
Strain or sprain	134	Lower leg	104
		25–50% body	32
		All parts of the body	32
		Not accounted for	27
Total cases	675		675

3. Electrical current passing directly through the body can cause burns by the heat generated and tissue changes by the current itself. The exact effects of electrical current on tissue are not fully understood.

In injuries involving direct contact with electricity, the victim must be freed from the source of electric current as quickly as possible. Before contact with the victim, the rescuer should make sure that the current is off. The rescuer should be properly grounded and should use insulated or nonconducting material to rescue the victim.

If the victim is not breathing, mouth-to-mouth resuscitation must be started immediately. Ventricular fibrillation (irregular movement of heart muscles) may cause the heart to stop beating. Cardiac massage should then be used, along with artificial respiration, until the victim can be defibrillated.

Direct contact electrical burns can be very deceiving. The external wounds may appear relatively small, but damage to underlying tissues and blood vessels can be extensive. These victims should be carefully observed for signs of shock caused by hemorrhage or intestinal perforation.

ELECTRICAL SHOCK

The human body acts as a resistance to electric current flow between the points of entry and exit. If this resistance was constant, a gradually larger voltage applied across the two points of contact would cause aproportional increase of current flow through the body. At some value of voltage, the current flow would be great enough to have the effects indicated in Table 18–3. The current values shown in the table are those of an average adult in response to an electric current flow path from hand to foot.

A practical application of analysis involving the single-loop equation, $V = IR$, which relates to safety, is the matter of electrical shock.[2] A short circuit is a current path that bypasses the load (that is, the principal resistance in the circuit). The actual situation is sketched in part (a) of Figure 18–1, and the corresponding circuit diagram is outlined in part (b).

[2]For a good reference see Willie Hammer, *Occupational Safety Management and Engineering*, "Electrical Hazards," Chapter 19 (Englewood Cliffs, N.J.: Prentice-Hall, 1976).

TABLE 18–3.
The Effects of Electrical Shock

60 Hz AC Current 1 Sec. Duration	*Effects on Adult Humans*
1 mA	No sensation when externally applied; though myocardium can induce ventricular fibrillation down to 20 μA.
1 $\leqslant$ 5 mA	Mild surprise, to painful sensation.
,5 $\leqslant$ 10 mA	Painful shock.
10 $\leqslant$ 15 mA	Local muscle contraction. If contacted by hand or arm, may paralyze the area and cause "freezing" or inability to release grip.
15 $\leqslant$ 30 mA	Paralysis of the area or body member in contact and cause "freezing."
30 $\leqslant$ 50 mA	Breathing difficult and may stop, can cause unconsciousness.
50 $\leqslant$ 100 mA	Possible ventricular fibrillation of the heart.
100 $\leqslant$ 200 mA	Certain ventricular fibrillation of heart.
200 $\leqslant$ 400 mA	Severe burns and muscular contractions, heart arrest most likely.
4 $\leqslant$ 5 A	Paralyses the heart. Irreparable damage to body tissues.
> 5 A	Causes burning of tissues.

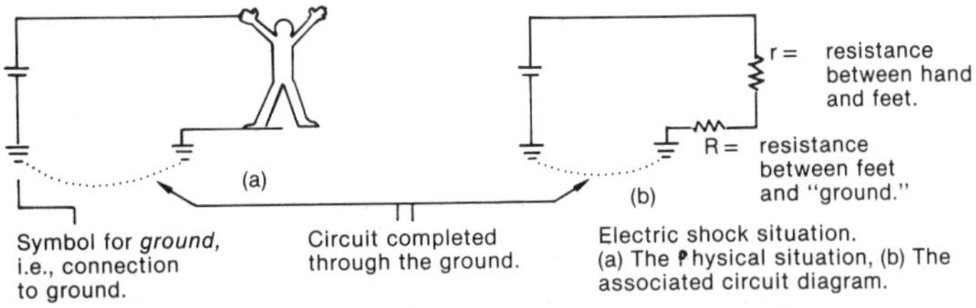

FIGURE 18–1. Analogy of an Electric Circuit and Pesan to an Associated Circuit Diagram.

Without covering the matter of "grounding" now, the reader is asked to accept the fact that if the high-potential side as well as the low-potential side of a source of EMF (electromotive force) are connected to the ground, then the ground can provide a current path to complete a circuit of the single-loop type. Now suppose the person in Figure 18–1 is touching one terminal of an EMF source, then the single-loop equation and our knowledge of the addition of resistance in series permit us to write

$$I = \frac{V}{r + R},$$

where r is the body resistance between the hand touching the voltage terminal and the feet, and R is the resistance between the feet and the ground.[3]

[3]Donald E. Tilley, and Walter Thumm, *Physics for College Students With Applications to Life Science* (Menlo Park, Calif.: Cummins, 1974), p. 327.

The resistance of the body consists of that offered by the skin at the point of contact and the internal resistance. The epidermis is nonvascular and when dry it has a very high resistance, which may reach 100 k Ω per sq. cm. (kilo ohms per square centimeter). The resistance offered by the dermis is low because this layer contains blood vessels, and body fluids are good electrical conductors. The only poor conductors inside the body are the bones. The internal resistance of the body is relatively small. The soles of the feet and the palms of the hand are considerably more resistant than other areas because of the thick layer of epidermis.

The resistance to electric current in tissue varies in order from the greatest to the least, as follows: bone, fat, tissue, skin, muscle, blood, and nerve. The resistance of the skin varies from person to person and from one area of the body to another. it varies with the amount of moisture that it contains, the temperature, and the applied voltage.

After an electric current has penetrated the skin, it passes rapidly through the body along lines of least resistance, that is, through the tissue fluids and along blood vessels, leading to degeneration of the vessel walls and formation of thrombi. The vascular injury usually occurs at some part of the body away from the site of initial injury and accounts for the apparent progressive nature of lesion.

Modern medical diagnostic and therapeutic techniques probing the internal parts of the body and organ transplants have brought to our attention internal shock hazards, which have become an important matter apart from external hazards. For example, when heart catheterization and cardiac pacemakers first became well known, a rush of fatalities occurred, often without an adequate explanation. The cause of death in these early-cases was most likely ventricular fibrillation produced by very minute electric currents, perhaps a thousand times less than the threshold value for fibrilation initiated by currents entering the surface of the body.

GROUNDING

In electrical terminology, a *ground* is a conductor connected to the earth, the absolute potential of which is arbitrarily taken as zero. An important aspect of grounding relates to safety.[4] Consider the case of an X-ray machine. Should some fault develop in the electrical wiring (for example, abrasion of insulation causing an exposed wire), it is possible that the metal case could become connected to the electrical supply. If it comes in contact to the high-potential side of the circuit, then the unsuspecting technician could, by touching the machine, have a high potential difference V set up between different parts of his body, which has an electrical resistance r. If the current I is great enough, he will suffer a possibly dangerous electrical shock. On the other hand, if the X-ray machine is properly grounded, then when the technician touches the machine case with his hand, he receives no passage of electric shock since there exists no potential difference between his hand and other parts of his body which are at ground potential.

Line-operated electrocardiographs (ECG) should be supplied with a three-terminal, powerline plug. The existence of multiple connections beween a subject and a line-operated ECG creates the potential hazard of uncomfortable or even mild electric shock. Protection of the patient and the

[4]Recommended readings are: Carl W. Walter, "Green Grounding Wire Spells Electric Safety in Hospitals," *Hospital Topics* (Chicago: American Hospital Association, Feb. 1972), pp. 25–29, 34; and William S. Watkins, "Grounding: The Most Misunderstood of All Electrical Safety Requirements," *Professional Safety* (January 1978): 25–31.

operator from currents greater than 5 mA must be provided by fuses or circuitry to furnish protection.

Present-day electrical codes require a separate ground wire, even in ordinary housewiring. Almost all hospitals and clinics have been wired to comply with the electrical wiring codes. This is why the three-pronged electric plug is now in common usage. However, in a few older institutions appliances still have electric cords with the two-pronged electric plug.

DANGEROUS ELECTRIC CURRENT AND EFFECTS

The current is the major cause of damage resulting from the flow of electric current through a person. Small currents are relatively harmless. A person can withstand a static shock of several kV (kilovolts) with only minor discomfort. That is what happens when the humidity is low and one touches a metal object after walking across a carpet. The current is very small.

When the current increases, the situation becomes more harmful. One can readily feel the shock from 1 to 3 mA (milliamperes). A 1-mA current is perceptible, and at 5 mA to 10 mA it becomes painful. From 10 mA to 30 mA causes muscle contractions and voluntary muscle control is lost. Beyond this level, one goes through stages of muscular paralysis and respiratory interference. Ventricular fibrillation may be induced by 70 mA currents if the duration is one second or more. Death can occur in the 70 to 200 mA range.

Shocks of 200 mA and more may not cause instant death but rather inflict severe burns and arrest respiration. This strange phenomenon is explained by the fact that low current values above a certain threshold level may cause ventricular fibrillation, while high currents may produce momentary heart standstill, which usually reverts to normal rhythm. Actual current values depend on several variables, such as AC or DC, frequency of the AC, duration of contact, where and how contact is made on the body. The facts determining the effect of a current passing through the body are as follows: the current path, the current magnitude, the direction of the current, and the duration of the current.[5]

The Path of the Current

A current flow through vital organs is the most dangerous. Death from electric current is virually always due to either cardiac or respiratory arrest, and the closer the current path is to the brain or to the critical organs, the greater the danger.

The Magnitude of the Current

It is known that the current, rather than the voltage, is of major significance in physiological damage. Given the common 120-volt AC, it is known that the current will then depend upon the impedance (Z) because $I = V/Z$. The impedance will depend upon the two contact points, as well as the area of the contact and the condition of the skin at the contact points. Also, this impedance will vary with the frequency of the AC, and be different again for applied DC voltages.

Duration of the Current

Obviously, the shorter the contact time the better. Minimum current necessary to produce ventricular fibrillation, which is fatal in man if permitted to continue, is around 70 mA for shock duration of one second or longer. The biological damage due to electric shock follows a relationship like this: damage oc $(I/A)^2T$, where I is the current

[5]Donald R. Herzog, and Daryl R. Herzog, "Electrical Problems in Hospitals," *Professional Safety*, 23 (January 1978): 20–24. Also same authors in "Electrical Safety in Medical Environments," *Medical Electronics* 14.3 (June 1983).

magnitude through the region of contact, A is the area of contact, and T is the duration of contact.

A current path through the heart is the most serious. Using Ohm's law ($R = V/I$), and the AC Ohm's law analogue ($V = IZ$), it is clear that for a given voltage, the current will depend on the body's resistance. This resistance will depend on the contact resistance. The impedance for AC will be different from the resistance for DC. The typical resistance between two points on the body ranges from 1,000 to 20,000Ω (ohms). It is important to realize that these current thresholds were determined for shocks with electrical contact made on the surfaces of the body. These are the current values that were used to establish conventional safety standards in hospitals.

For internal body connections, the situation is different. For example, pacemaker leads placed on the myocardium provide a direct path to the heart for accidental currents. Likewise, diagnostic catheters that may be conductive or filled with conductive fluid, or both, provide a direct path to internal organs. Therefore, it is worth noting that the threshold of fibrillation in such instances may be a thousand times lower than when the electrodes make contact with the body skin, and that currents as low as 0.02 mA have been known to produce fibrillation.

ELECTRICAL HAZARDS IN OPERATING ROOMS

The danger of explosion in operating rooms because of volatile agents used in anesthesia is well known. Although the trend is to employ less explosive anesthetics, ether, because of many of its other desirable characteristics, remains in usage and is likely to continue to be used.

It is true that mobile X-ray units and other electric and electronic gear for use in operating rooms may be quite safe, in that dangers from the electricity involved in their operation have been eliminated by having the units hermetically sealed and flash-proofed for use in explosive atmospheres. However, the dangers arising from the accumulation of static charge still exist. It is quite possible to acquire relatively small charges and yet achieve relatively high potential differences. And static electricity of high voltage on an insulated conductor, such as a metal stretcher with rubber casters, or a mobile X-ray unit on rubber wheels, can discharge through the air if another object, such as a person at different potential, comes near. The spark involved in such a discharge may contain more than enough energy to ignite an explosive anesthetic mixture, even though the spark may be much too small to be seen.

Tests have shown that potential differences of several thousand volts can be generated between the floor and an operating table when a wool blanket is stripped from a rubber mattress. All these effects are worse in places of low relative humidity. The more moist the air, the more readily the accumulated charge leaks off before a high potential difference sufficient to cause a spark may be built up. To aid this charge leakage, it is not uncommon practice to drape a wet towel around the base of an operating table and thereby ensure better electrical contact with the floor. Also, the relative humidity of the operating room is appropriately controlled to minimize the buildup of static electrical charge.

The above statements are not construed as implying that the moisture itself makes the air electrically more conductive. Actually, pure water is more or less an insulator, although not a good one, because it is usually very slightly ionized. However, if the air is relatively moist, condensation on surfaces such as clothing, floors, and equipment of all kinds takes place.

It would be better to wear leather-soled rather than rubber-soled shoes while one is performing duties in a hospital operating room because leather is a better conductor than rubber. Actually, however, since leather tends to be slippery and leather soles cannot be cleaned readily, cotton overshoes, or shoes with special conductive rubber are sometimes worn.

The use of electrosurgical units and other electrical equipment mandates that all electrical outlets and wiring be inspected routinely every month for proper connections, adequate grounding, and safe electrical materials, such as well-insulated cables and unbroken electrical plugs and outlets. Even with the advantage of newer transistorized and integrated circuit electrosurgical units, preventive inspection and maintenance of plugs and cables should be done to prevent short circuits and electrical hazards.

SAFETY PROCEDURE IN THE UROLOGICAL ENDOSCOPIC SUITE

For safety and hygiene, all irrigating fluid should drain into collecting pails rather than floor drains because these drains are unhygienic and therefore a source of contamination. Furthermore, inadequate drainage may permit the irrigating fluid to accumulate on the floor; this may result in increased conductivity around the electrosurgical foot pedal, aggravating a potential electrical leak in the wiring of the electrical cables and resulting in possible electrical shocks to the urologic personnel.[6]

The use of electrosurgical equipment is a potential threat to both patient and clinical personnel in regard to electrical shock that can be not only distressful but hazardous. For this reason, periodic evaluation by biomedical engineering or electrical engineering personnel is mandatory to evaluate all electrical wire systems and equipment.

ELECTRICAL HAZARDS IN PATIENT CARE AREAS

Electrical hazards in medical institutions generally fall into two major categories: electrical shock to the body and electrostatic spark generated in the presence of an explosive atmosphere.[7] The existence of these two categories presents a dilemma: that is, procedures to eliminate the accumulation of static charge (conductive flooring, conductive clothing, and so on) in turn lead to current flow through people using defective electrical appliances. Obviously, fault currents can more readily pass through conductive shoes. But in most cases, such currents are relatively small. Fault or leakage currents are currents taking paths other than those intended. The present electrical codes in the United States permit a leakage current of 1 mA or 0.001 ampere.

Compounding this electrical current hazard is the fact that electrodes applied internally, rather than on the surface of the body, give rise to far more complex safety problems than those associated with externally applied electrodes. A further complication arises from the increasing use of electrical apparatus in medical clinics and hospitals for diagnosis, for treatment, and for patient monitoring.

The patient, often exposed to dangerous electrical stimulation because of his disease or medication, is generally grounded. Bedside plumbing, motorized beds, lamps, and electrical devices for signaling and for entertainment are so commonplace that their possible hazard may often be ignored. Nevertheless, these conveniences usually provide unavoidable access to "ground."

---

[6]Alice Morel, and Gilbert J. Wise, *Urological Endoscopic Procedures,* 2d ed. (St. Louis, Mo.: C.V. Mosby, 1979), p. 27.

[7]Tilley and Thumm, *Physics for College Students,* p. 424.

This grounding may well make part of the patient the path of leakage currents that would otherwise flow elsewhere. It is also possible that defective wiring actually permits contact with electric power at above ground potential.

A normally harmless leakage current in a lamp can become dangerous if the patient has implanted electrodes. Take the case of a patient who reaches over to turn on his bedlamp, which is a two-wire lamp that has a leakage current of 1 mA and thus still passes present safety requirements. If the patient is connected to a monitor, this 1-mA current could pass through the patient's arm, then through his trunk to the grounded monitor, with a portion of the current going through the patient's heart. Figure 18–2 depicts a patient connected to a grounded physiological monitor and switching on a table lamp that has a leakage current. Possible route of leakage current to ground is shown by a dotted line. If a grounded electrode were attached to his heart, all of the 1 mA might flow through his heart, causing either heart standstill or perhaps ventricular fibrillation. The existence of this leakage path would go undetected, unless perhaps a doctor or a nurse, accidentally touching both lamp and monitor, also noticed a shock. Fortunately, as a rule, when a patient is monitored, an alarm sounds if his heart starts fibrillating or standstill is noted, so that resuscitation may be effected at once.

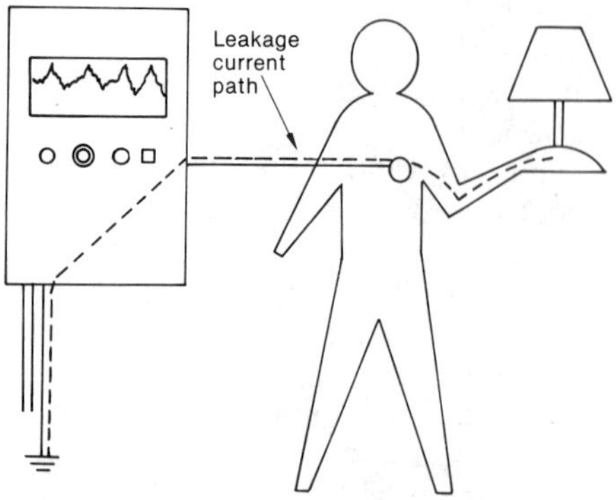

FIGURE 18–2. Patient Connected to a Grounded Physiological Monitor and Switching on a Table Lamp.

A most important consideration in this field of electrical hazards is the interplay of any given electrical appliance with other electrical equipment being used. Compatibility of any piece of electrical apparatus with any other equipment being used on the patient is imperative.

EQUIPMENT INTERACTION HAZARDS

To most people, including medical personnel, it seems safe if there is no conductive connection between a voltage source and a user. This is simply not true since most electrical apparatus operates on AC. An obvious example, if AC is used, is that leakage currents may arise owing to inductive coupling in a transformer or, as is more common, capacitive coupling. The capacitor represents an open circuit for DC, but in DC anything that qualifies as a capacitor—that is, two conductors separated by a nonconductor—will permit AC passage.

Consider the case depicted in Figure 18–3, of a twenty-six-year-old male who underwent heart catheterization because of a congenital pulmonary ailment.[8] Equipment used included an electrocardiogram monitor and a motorized injection apparatus for cineangiography (X-ray movie making of flow in blood vessels). The injection syringe was primed with Hypaque (a saline solution not allowing the passage of X rays to provide the necessary contrast between the blood and other body tissue). When the saline-filled cathe-

[8]*Op. cit.*, p. 425.

ter was coupled to the syringe, that is, to the injection apparatus, the ECG display showed 60 Hz (hertz = 60 cps) interference. Disconnecting the catheter restored the ECG trace, which then indicated the heart was in fibrillation. The chest was opened, cardiac massage performed, and the heart then electrically defibrillated. Fortunately, the patient recovered and underwent uneventful surgery six weeks later.

What was done wrong? Apparently the three-prong power plug of the motorized injector apparatus had been replaced with a two-prong plug with no means for a ground. A 79-V leakage potential then existed between the casing of the injector and ground. At the moment of connection of the catheter, with the aid of the conductive properties of the saline solution, there was a current from the injector apparatus through the patient's heart down through the right-leg ECG lead to the ground.

Consider the case of an electrical hazard to a male patient. The patient was in an ICU (intensive care unit), connected by internal electrodes to an ECG monitor and the intracardiac blood pressure was being monitored by a conductive catheter inserted into his heart. The blood pressure measuring transducer and related electronic monitoring device was grounded through a different outlet and, therefore, at a different point in the hospital wiring system. The ECG was grounded at the main distribution some distance away, and it was there that a ground wire from the blood pressure monitor was connected.

The patient was therefore connected between two grounds that were the same, provided there were no leakage current flows in either ground wire. But a hospital worker plugged an electric floor polisher into an outlet near the ECG outlet. This resulted in a leakage current of one ampere through a 100 ft 12-gauge copper grounded wire having a resistance of an estimated 160 mΩ (milliohms). This caused a potential difference of 160 mV between the ground of the ECG monitor probe and the ground of the blood pressure monitor probe. If we make a reasonable assumption that the impedance of the heart between the two probes was 3,200Ω, then the patient's heart was subjected to a current of 0.05 mA. Fortunately, the current was low enough not to cause a heart standstill. Figure 18–4 shows the arrangement.[9]

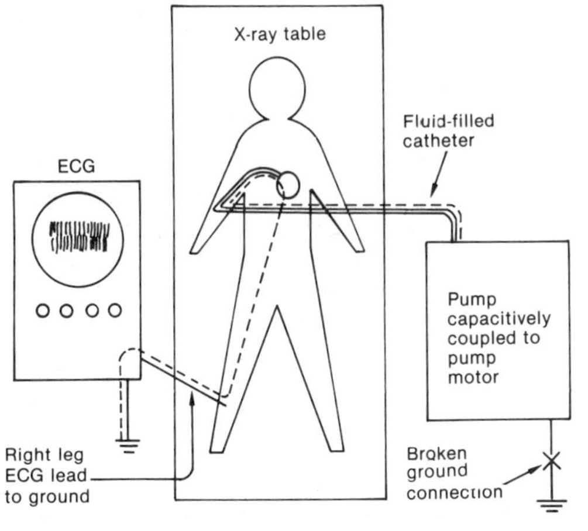

FIGURE 18–3. Components of Patient Diagnostic Equipment and No Means for Grounding.

MEDICAL DIATHERMY EQUIPMENT

Medical diathermy equipment is apparatus that utilizes a radio frequency generator. The operation of medical diathermy equipment may thus constitute a serious source of interference to authorized radio communications services, unless appropriate steps are taken to prevent such interference. The most common frequency employed is 2,450 mHz (megahertz). The

[9] *Op. cit.*, p. 426.

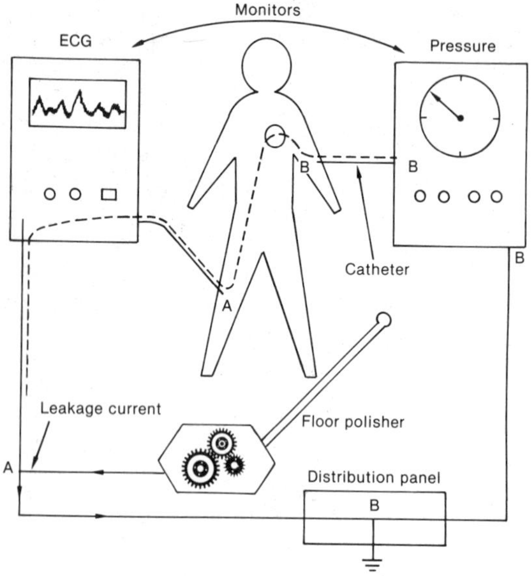

FIGURE 18–4. Components of Patient Diagnostic Equipment and an Outside Apparatus causing Detrimental Interaction.

power is usually around 125 watts, as compared to megawatts (10^6 watts) used in communications networks.

If a part of the body is placed between two microwave electrodes or antennae, considerable thermal energy can be generated at subcutaneous levels. The clinical procedure for producing such body heating is called diathermy. In general, medical microwave diathermy is indicated in any condition in which heating of subcutaneous and muscular tissues to a relatively greater depth than possible by the direct application of heat would be beneficial; for example, the localized heating of inflammatory regions, such as in certain types of arthritis.

The problem of dosage in microwave diathermy has not been adequately solved. The total energy applied to the body surface can be determined, but not the actual amount of energy effectively absorbed in the underlying tissue. Studies are proceeding in this field because of interest in more effective treatment and because of the possible dangers inherent in microwave exposure. Some studies have revealed that temperatures of 40°C (104°F) or higher can be consistently obtained in human muscles in some 20 minutes of exposure.

POTENTIAL HAZARDS AND SAFETY CONSIDERATIONS

A potential risk problem for hospitals is the thermal degradation of polyvinyl chloride (PVC). PVC is a synthetic, plastic, polymer wire insulating material that releases hydrogen chloride (HCl) gas when it is thermally degraded. Inhalation of HCl, either as a gas or in combination with water vapor, is irritating to all mucous membranes. Thermal degradation of 25 ft. of PVC wire yields 1.4 mg HC1/L, which is 70 times greater than the recommended maximum concentration.[10]

Investigation into and analysis of accidents in hospitals have shown that the hazards are usually associated with the simultaneous use of two or more instruments. Recognizing this, several groups have written safety standards that limit the allowable potential difference between any two conductors, and they must be tested using all combinations of two conductors. A simple scanning circuit using programmable operational amplifiers (PRAMS) and MOS digital circuitry makes the series of safety checks quickly and efficiently. The design includes both the ability to detect dangerous conditions and a digital annun-

[10]J.F. Eder, "Polyvinyl Chloride—Its Risk Potential in the Hospital," *Journal of Clinic Engineering* H.3 (July–September 1979): 265–68.

ciator to indicate which of the many leads being checked simultaneously is at fault. The scanning rate is rapid enough to allow the detection of dangerous transients. Preliminary results indicate that this battery-operated device, which is portable, is useful in providing an electrically safe environment for patients.[11]

Routine testing of medical instrumentation for purposes of increased reliability and safety is becoming a part of standard practice in hospitals. Many test procedures are standardized and large classes of similar equipment are often involved; a need exists for automatic testing. Automatic testing can result in increased standardization, saving of time, and reduction of tedium associated with repetitive work.[12]

The Federal Communications Commission (FCC) ruled in early 1981 that manufacturers of machinery or devices that interfere with the normal operation of other equipment be subject to heavy damages. The FCC acted after a barrage of complaints that electrical and electronic pollution is more than just a nuisance. It can interfere with life-support equipment in hospitals or cause electrically controlled brakes on trucks and buses to fail. Manufacturers must now give serious consideration to shielding and filtering their machinery or apparatus for the market. Anti-electrical pollution devices will be needed for computers and associated peripheral equipment, electronic scientific and industrial instruments. The FCC adopted regulations in 1980 to limit the voltage of computer games after complaints that it was interfering with radios of emergency service and police cars.

In another example, the cardiac pacemaker implanted in the human body requires a highly effective shield. The implanted cardiac pacemakers must be protected from interference by microwave ovens and from some dental drills.

Written policies and procedures should be established for the methods and frequency of testing and verification of performance of all electrical and electronic patient care equipment, and should be based upon established safety requirements, performance criteria and manufacturers' claims. This applies to both fixed and mobile equipment, with particular emphasis on life-support equipment, such as defibrillators, infant incubators and warmers, physiological monitoring systems, as well as devices with a high hazard potential, for example, electrosurgical equipment.[13]

Physicians and biomedical scientists have had only a peripheral interest in electrical safety. Although electrical safety in medical clinics and hospitals is receiving increased attention in the literature of biomedical engineers and safety engineers, it has not been given much consideration in the curricula of medical colleges, nursing schools, or health service training institutions. One remedy for this problem is to combine the knowledge of engineers and safety professionals, along with medical instruction developers to design a systematic curriculum for an institutional module in hospital electrical safety.

[11] J.W. Steadman, "Dangerous Electricity Annunciator and Detector," *Instrument Society of America Transactions* 14.2 (1975): 118–21.

[12] For a description of such a system, see J.D. Henderson, and C.C. Bowman, "An Automatic Medical Equipment Test System," *Journal of Clinical Engineering* 3.3 (July–September 1978): 245–50.

[13] Joint Commission on Accreditation of Hospitals, *Accreditation Manual for Hospitals* (Chicago, February 1978), p. 23.

Summary

The general purpose of this chapter has been to mention and discuss a few examples of potential electrical hazards in medical clinics and hospitals in order to create an awareness of the important factors related to electrical safety in medical environments.

These usual types of electrical injuries are electrical burns, lacerations, electric shock, and falls caused by electrical shock. Contact burns are the main result of electric current passing through the body. Burns caused by low or medium voltage DC, vary in severity, as do thermal burns. High-current, high-voltage burns from DC or AC circuits are dangerous. The burns can normally be seen at the point of current entry and current departure from the body. The internal tissue along the path of the current most likely will also be damaged.

Electric shock is usually painful, but it is not necessarily associated with actual damage to the tissue of the body. Nevertheless, as a direct result of a moderately severe shock, a person may grip and be unable to release a conductor. Electric shock may cause cessation of respiration (asphyxia). Current passing through the body may temporarily paralyze either the nerves or the area of the brain that controls breathing. Death may occur by direct interference with the action of the heart so that the heart does not pump the blood through the circulatory system. Once ventricular fibrillation occurs in a person, the heart will not spontaneously recover from fibrillation without external assistance.

Electric shock intensity and effect depend on current path, frequency, and duration. The microshock problems that normally confront the patient with an implanted device or a catheter inserted within the tissue present a serious risk.

Electrical hazard locations are often where beds are clustered about in patient-care areas and in intensive-care units in which patients are cared for collectively. Here, there is often assemblage of electrical biomedical apparatus. Continuity of power, protection against both macroshock and microshock, elimination of arcing and sparking, limitation of ground-fault current, and equalization of leakage current are requisite.

Most electrical equipment is designed to operate with maximum efficiency and safety only when used for the purposes and under the conditions for which it was designed to function. In general, perfect insulation, isolation, current limitation, and grounding are the main prerequisites for achieving electrical safety.

Many electrical accidents are caused by human mistake or ignorance. Where there is potential hazard, very careful work planning is necessary. In a medical clinic or hospital, electrical safety can be improved through employee training and investigation of accidents or failures. Clear and effective employee instructions can improve safety. All employees, from physician-surgeon to medical technicians, should be instructed in the proper use and care of electrical medical equipment. Maintenance and repair tasks must be done by competent biomedical engineering technicians.

Questions

1. Give three distinct ways that electricity can cause mild to severe burns and burn-type tissue damage.
2. Which is more important to human safety, the amount of current or the voltage? Does the other have any importance?
3. Distinguish between system grounding and equipment grounding.
4. What are the variables that determine the effects of an electric current passing through a human body?
5. List several ways to avoid or reduce problems with static electricity.
6. What is ventricular fibrillation? What range of current could cause ventricular fibrillation? Is ventricular fibrillation more likely to occur with alternating or direct current? Will a person with ventricular fibrillation recover without medical assistance?
7. List the hazards to heart catherization patients from the catheter and other nearby electrical apparatus? How would you ensure the patient's safety?
8. List the hazards to a patient in an intensive care unit who is connected to a bedside monitor and central station? How would you ensure safety of the patient? List the precautions you would take and the special equipment you would use.
9. What protection do fuses and circuit breakers provide that grounding cannot provide?
10. List four hazards involved in the use of electricity.

Bibliography

Stanley, Paul E., Ed. *Handbook of Hospital Safety*. Boca Raton, Fla.: CRC Press, 1981.

Stoner, David L., et al. *Engineering a Safe Hospital Environment*. New York: John Wiley and Sons, 1982.

Weiss, Marvin D. *Biomedical Instrumentation*. Philadelphia: Chilton Book Co., 1973.

Index